PROFESSIONAL
APPLICATION LIFECYCLE MANAGEMENT
WITH VISUAL STUDIO® 2010

W9-AAY-754

Continues

PROFESSIONAL

Application Lifecycle Management with Visual Studio® 2010

PROFESSIONAL

Application Lifecycle Management with Visual Studio® 2010

Mickey Gousset
Brian Keller
Ajoy Krishnamoorthy
Martin Woodward

WILEY

Wiley Publishing, Inc.

Professional Application Lifecycle Management with Visual Studio® 2010

Published by
Wiley Publishing, Inc.
10475 Crosspoint Boulevard
Indianapolis, IN 46256
www.wiley.com

Published simultaneously in Canada

ISBN: 978-0-470-48426-5

Manufactured in the United States of America

10 9 8 7 6 5 4 3 2 1

For general information on our other products and services please contact our Customer Care Department within the United States at (877) 762-2974, outside the United States at (317) 572-3993 or fax (317) 572-4002.

Wiley also publishes its books in a variety of electronic formats. Some content that appears in print may not be available in electronic books.

Library of Congress Control Number: 2010921244

This book is dedicated to my wife, Amye Gousset. Once again, I scratched the itch to write, and once again, she provided me all the love and support I needed to make it happen. Amye, I love you more and more each day.

— MICKEY GOUSSET

This book is dedicated to my parents, Ray and Sue Ellen Keller, who laid the foundation for me to embark upon a lifetime of learning and a love of technology. As a kid, they let me hijack the family computer to teach myself how to program, and as a young adult, they gave me the inspiration to explore my passions, and the freedom to learn from my failures. Mom and Dad, I love you.

— BRIAN KELLER

I dedicate this book to my best friend and my wife, Vidhya, and our wonderful children, Atul and Aditi. Thank you for everything.

— AJOY KRISHNAMOORTHY

To Catherine, William, and Jamie.

— MARTIN WOODWARD

ABOUT THE AUTHORS

 MICKEY GOUSSET is a Senior Technical Developer for Infront Consulting Group, a consulting company focused on the Microsoft System Center family of products. He has been a Microsoft Team System MVP five years running, a certified professional in Team Foundation Server and SCOM 2007, and co-author (along with Jean-Luc David and Erik Gunvaldson) of the book *Professional Team Foundation Server* (Indianapolis: Wiley, 2006). Gousset runs "Team System Rocks!" (http://www.teamsystemrocks.com), a community site devoted to Visual Studio Team System and Visual Studio 2010, where he also blogs about Visual Studio and Team Foundation Server. He is also a co-host of the popular Team Foundation Server podcast, "Radio TFS" (http://www.radiotfs.com). He has spoken on Visual Studio and Team Foundation Server topics at various user groups, code camps, and conferences, including Microsoft Tech Ed Developer — North America 2008 and 2009. When not writing or working with computers, Mickey enjoys a range of hobbies, from playing on Xbox Live ("Gamer Tag: HereBDragons") to participating in local community theater. Nothing beats his favorite pastime though — sitting on his couch with his lovely wife Amye, and their two Chihuahuas, Lucy and Linus.

 BRIAN KELLER is a Senior Technical Evangelist for Microsoft, specializing in Visual Studio and application lifecycle management. Keller has been with Microsoft since 2002, and has presented at conferences all over the world, including TechEd, Professional Developers Conference (PDC), and MIX. Keller is also a regular personality on MSDN's Channel 9 Web site, and is co-host of the popular show, "This Week on Channel 9." Outside of work, he can usually be found enjoying the great outdoors while either rock climbing, backpacking, skiing, or surfing.

 AJOY KRISHNAMOORTHY is a Senior Product Manager in the Microsoft Patterns and Practices group. In this role, he focuses on planning the areas of investments and business strategy for Patterns and Practices. Prior to this role, Krishnamoorthy worked as a Senior Product Manager for Microsoft Visual Studio Team System. He has more than ten years of consulting experience, playing variety of roles, including developer, architect, and technical project manager. Krishnamoorthy has written articles for online and printed magazines, and co-authored several books on ASP.NET. You can check out his blog at http://blogs.msdn.com/ajoyk. Krishnamoorthy has an MBA from Ohio State University. Any spare time is spent with his family, playing board/card games with friends, watching sports (especially when the Ohio State Buckeyes are playing), and learning to play "Tabla."

 MARTIN WOODWARD is currently the Program Manager for the Microsoft Visual Studio Team Foundation Server Cross-Platform Tools Team. Before joining Microsoft, Woodward was voted Team System MVP of the Year, and has spoken about Team Foundation Server at events internationally. Not only does Woodward bring a unique insight into the inner workings of the product he has experienced from more than a half-decade of real-world use at companies big and small, he is also always happy to share. When not working or speaking, Woodward can be found at his blog, http://www.woodwardweb.com.

CREDITS

ACKNOWLEDGMENTS

FIRST OFF, I WANT TO THANK AJOY, BRIAN, AND MARTIN for taking this journey with me. You have been incredible people to work with, and have truly made this a great experience. I'd like to thank everyone at Wiley and Wrox, specifically Bob Elliot and Kevin Shafer, our editors. This book could not have happened without their help and constant attention to detail. We also had some amazing people doing technical edits on this book, including Clark Sell, Peter Provost, Siddharth Bhatia, Mario Rodriguez, Justin Marks, David Williamson, and I'm sure many other names that I've overlooked. To everyone who has helped to make this book the great product that it is, I thank you. Finally, a big thank you to my family for your understanding, love, and support during the late nights and long weekends when I disappeared into my office to write.

— MICKEY GOUSSET

THE EFFORTS OF SO MANY PEOPLE went into the realization of this book that it's hard to know where to begin. Perhaps most fundamentally is the work of the engineering team within Microsoft's developer division, who have an insatiable drive for shipping great software that helps other software development teams around the world realize their full potential. Visual Studio 2010 is an incredibly exciting release, and is the inspiration for this book. David Williamson was the primary technical reviewer for the chapters I contributed, and his thoughtful suggestions contributed greatly to the quality of this book. I also received help from Anutthara Bharadwaj, Daryush Laqab, Ed Glas, Euan Garden, Gautam Goenka, Habib Heydarian, Katrina Lyon-Smith, Mark Mydland, Michael Rigler, Tanuj Vohra, Ted Malone, Vinod Malhotra, and scores of others over the last year and a half. Finally, I would like to thank our publisher and my co-authors, who I am proud to share this accomplishment with.

—BRIAN KELLER

I OWE A BIG THANKS TO MY good friend Jean-Luc David for his persistence in getting me to work on this book. I was fortunate to have the chance to work with a talented team of fellow authors. Mickey, Brian and Martin, thank you, and I truly enjoyed working with you on this book.

Several members of the Visual Studio team offered their help, and I am thankful for that. I owe a lot of gratitude to Aaron Bjork, Siddharth Bhatia, John Socha-Leialoha, Sunder Raman, David Brokaw, Gokula Thilagar, Habib Heydarian, Justin Marks, and Brad Sullivan. They were all busy shipping a product, but never hesitated to help me when I reached them with questions, or needed more information and access to pre-release bits. Thanks to every one of you for your timely help.

I want to thank my manager John deVadoss and my colleagues at Patterns and Practices for their great support and encouragement throughout the course of this writing project.

Finally, I can't thank my family enough for allowing me to spend countless hours during evenings and weekends on this book. Vidhya, Atul, and Aditi, none of this would have been possible without your encouragement, support, and understanding. I have missed several rounds of board games, trips to the play area, bed-time routines, and more. I promise you that I will do the best to make up for the lost time. Thank you for everything.

— AJOY KRISHNAMOORTHY

I WOULD LIKE TO ACKNOWLEDGE THE HELP, advice, and assistance from the people both inside and outside the Visual Studio team at Microsoft. Special thanks go to Aaron Hallberg, Brian Randell, Buck Hodges, Clark Sell, Jim Lamb, Julie MacAller, Mario Rodriguez, Matthew Mitrik, and William Bartholomew, without whom my contributions to this book would not have been possible. Thanks also to Rob Caron, Jeff Beehler, Brian Harry, Doug Neumann, Eric Sink, and Corey Steffen for encouraging my involvement in the Visual Studio community over the past five years.

I would like to thank my co-authors for bringing me into this project, and for helping me fulfill a lifetime ambition of writing a book. I would also like to thank my dad, Roy Woodward, and my much missed mum, Val Woodward. They got me started down this whole computing path by getting me a Vic-20 at the age of 6, and got me a typewriter at the age of 8. With that sort of start, you'd think I'd have written a computer book at the age of 10, but instead I re-wrote "Ghostbusters" and co-authored a novel about a pink sofa. Well Mum — I got there in the end.

Last but not least, I would also like to thank my wife, Catherine, for her encouragement and support, and for helping me find the time to write this book in our already busy lives. She has heard the phrase, "I'm nearly done, just finishing this last bit up," more times than anyone deserves, yet, bizarrely, has still not figured out that she is way out of my league.

— MARTIN WOODWARD

CONTENTS

INTRODUCTION

IN JUNE 1999, MICROSOFT STARTED TO RE-EVALUATE HOW Visual Studio was being used as part of the software development process. Microsoft was continuing to serve the needs of an individual programmer through the highly productive "code-focused rapid-application-development" features of Visual Studio, but wasn't doing much to help programmers work together as a *team*. And what about software architects — how should they be working with the programming team? And testers? Project managers?

Many teams had begun to set up their own solutions using a mixture of third-party, in-house, and vendor-provided tools to address such challenges as version control, bug tracking, and team communications. But this mishmash of tools can be tricky to set up and maintain, and even more difficult to integrate. Microsoft sought to address this challenge by providing an *integrated* set of tools designed to address the needs of the entire software development team. Thus, Visual Studio Team System was born, and was first released with the Visual Studio 2005 product line.

Team System was built from a foundation of tools and technologies that Microsoft had been using internally for many years to build some of the most complex software projects ever undertaken. Team System appealed not only to programmers, but to all members of the development team — architects, application developers, database developers, testers, and project managers. Team System was built to address the entire software development lifecycle, more broadly known as *application lifecycle management*.

Three years later, Visual Studio 2008 Team System evolved from the previous version to include even more tools and functionality for all members of the project team to use.

THE NAME CHANGE

Observant readers will notice that nowhere in the title of this book do the words "Team System" appear. And, other than in the brief history you just finished reading, you won't see the words "Team System" listed anywhere else in this book. So, what happened to "Team System"?

Microsoft did some research and found that by creating two Visual Studio brand names, customers felt confused over the differences between the products. "Visual Studio" had been positioned as the basic tool for developers to use, while "Visual Studio Team System" was positioned as a set of tools for software development teams. However, almost all professional developers work on teams, and, hence, the term "Team System" was somewhat meaningless. So, the decision was made to drop the "Team System" name, and consolidate everything around a united Visual Studio brand family.

There are other somewhat subtle reasons for this change as well. However, the long and short of it is that, in the 2010 product lineup, the "Team System" brand no longer exists, but the products and technologies are still there (and better than ever).

VISUAL STUDIO 2010 PRODUCT LINEUP

Table I-1 outlines the new product lineup for Visual Studio 2010.

TABLE I-1: Visual Studio 2010 Product Lineup

PRODUCT NAME	DESCRIPTION
Microsoft Visual Studio 2010 Ultimate with MSDN	The comprehensive suite of application lifecycle management tools for software teams to help ensure quality results from design to deployment.
Microsoft Visual Studio 2010 Premium with MSDN	A complete toolset to help developers deliver scalable, high-quality applications.
Microsoft Visual Studio 2010 Professional with MSDN	The essential tool for basic development tasks to assist developers in implementing their ideas easily.
Microsoft Visual Studio Test Professional 2010 with MSDN	The primary tool for manual and generalist testers who need to define and manage test cases, execute test runs, and file bugs. The Test Professional product includes Microsoft Test Manager, which is introduced in Chapter 14.
Microsoft Visual Studio Team Foundation Server 2010	The server component for team development, version control, work item tracking, build automation, and reporting.
Microsoft Visual Studio Lab Management 2010	The tools to support virtual labs, and enable better developer and tester collaboration when paired with other Visual Studio tools.

Visual Studio 2010 Premium contains all the functionality of Visual Studio 2010 Professional, and Visual Studio 2010 Ultimate contains all the functionality of Visual Studio 2010 Premium. Visual Studio 2010 Ultimate also includes all of the functionality available in Visual Studio Test Professional 2010.

Table I-2 provides a detailed look at the functionality contained within each Visual Studio 2010 edition:

TABLE I-2: Visual Studio 2010 Editions

VISUAL STUDIO EDITION	FUNCTIONALITY
Microsoft Visual Studio 2010 Ultimate	IntelliTrace
	Unified Modeling Language (UML)
	Architecture Explorer
	Logical class designer
	Test case management
	Manual testing
	Test record and playback
	Layer diagrams
	Web performance testing
	Load testing
Microsoft Visual Studio 2010 Premium	Coded user interface (UI) testing
	Performance profiling
	Code coverage
	Database change management
	Database unit testing
	Test impact analysis
	Static code analysis
	Code metrics
	Database deployment
	Test data generation
Microsoft Visual Studio 2010 Professional	Silverlight development
	Web development
	Windows Presentation Foundation (WPF) development

continues

TABLE I-2 *(continued)*

VISUAL STUDIO EDITION	FUNCTIONALITY
	Multi-core development
	Cloud development
	Windows Forms development
	Office development
	Customizable IDE

This book focuses on the functionality contained in Visual Studio 2010 Premium and Visual Studio 2010 Ultimate.

MODERN SOFTWARE DEVELOPMENT CHALLENGES

Software developers share common challenges, regardless of the size of their teams. Businesses require a high degree of accountability — software must be developed in the least amount of time, with no room for failure.

Some of these challenges include the following:

➤ *Integration problems* — Most tools commonly used by software development teams come from third-party vendors. Integrating with those tools can pose a major challenge — in many cases, it requires duplicating or copying data into multiple systems. Each application has a learning curve, and transmitting information from one application to another (incompatible) application can be frustrating and time-consuming.

➤ *Geographically distributed teams* — Many development and management tools don't scale for geographically distributed teams. Getting accurate reporting can be difficult, and there is often poor support for communication and collaborative tools. As a result, requirements and specifications can be mapped incorrectly, causing delays and introducing errors. Global teams require solid design, process, and software configuration management all integrated into one package. There aren't many software packages that can deliver all these features, and those that do exist tend to be incredibly expensive.

➤ *Segmentation of roles* — Specialization can be a huge problem on a team. Experts can assume that other departments are aware of information that doesn't end up in the status reports, but may greatly affect the project as a whole. Interdepartmental communication is a huge and prevalent challenge.

➤ *Bad reporting* — This is an offshoot of the segmentation problem. In most cases, reports must be generated manually by each team, which results in a lack of productivity. There aren't any effective tools that can aggregate all the data from multiple sources. As a result, the project lead lacks the essential data to make effective decisions.

➤ *Lack of process guidance* — Ad hoc programming styles simply don't scale. If you introduce an off-cycle change to the code, it can cascade into a serious problem requiring hours and days of work. Today's software has a high level of dependencies. Unfortunately, most tools don't incorporate or enforce process guidance. This can result in an impedance mismatch between tools and process.

➤ *Testing as a second-class citizen* — Shorter cycles and lack of testing can introduce code defects late in the process. Manual testers are almost completely unaddressed by software development tools vendors. Consequently, poor collaboration between developers and testers often results in wasted back-and-forth effort and software defects.

➤ *Communication problems* — Most companies use a variety of communication methods (such as email, instant messaging, memos, and sticky notes) to send information to team members. You can easily lose a piece of paper, or delete an important email message, if you are not careful. There aren't many centralized systems for managing team communications. Frequent and time-consuming status meetings are required to keep the team on track, and many manual processes are introduced (such as sending email, as well as cutting and pasting reports). Fundamentally, the problem is that there is no communication between the tools and the project leads.

Companies introduce methodologies and practices to simplify and organize the software design process, but these methodologies must be balanced. The goal is to make the process predictable, because in a predictable environment, methodologies keep projects on track. Conversely, methodologies add tasks to the process (such as generating reports). If your developers spend too much time doing these tasks, they'll be less productive, and your company won't be able to react competitively.

ENTER VISUAL STUDIO 2010

Application lifecycle management is the concept of managing your software development project throughout all phases of its life. Building upon Visual Studio 2005 Team System and Visual Studio 2008 Team System, the application lifecycle management capabilities of Visual Studio 2010 were designed to mitigate or eliminate many of these challenges.

There are three founding principles behind the application lifecycle management capabilities of Visual Studio 2010: *productivity*, *integration*, and *extensibility*.

Productivity is increased in the following ways:

➤ *Collaboration* — Team Foundation Server centralizes all team collaboration. Bugs, requirements, tasks, test cases, source code, and builds are all managed via Team Foundation Server 2010. All reporting is also centralized, which makes it easy for project leads to track the overall progress of the project, regardless of where the metrics are coming from.

➤ *Manage complexity* — Software development projects are more complex than ever, and getting more complex year by year. Team Foundation Server helps to manage this complexity by centrally tracking your entire software development process, ensuring that the entire team can see the state and workflow of the project at any given time. Additionally, tools such as the architecture tools provided in Visual Studio 2010 Ultimate can help reduce the complexity of applications by providing designs that can be used to visually reverse-engineer existing code bases.

Integration is improved in the following ways:

➤ *Integrated tools* — These facilitate communication between departments. More importantly, they remove information gaps. With the Visual Studio 2010 family of products, integration isn't an afterthought — it's a core design consideration for the toolset.

➤ *Visibility* — Visual Studio 2010 and Team Foundation Server increase the visibility of a project. Project leads can easily view metrics related to the project, and can proactively address problems by identifying patterns and trends.

Extensibility is provided in the following ways:

➤ *Team Foundation Core Services API.* — Most of the platform is exposed to the developer, providing many opportunities for extensibility and the creation of custom tools that integrate with Team Foundation Server.

➤ *IDE* — The Visual Studio 2010 IDE itself is extensible, allowing third parties and end users to add everything from additional tool capabilities to even new language compilers to the development environment.

APPLICATION LIFECYCLE MANAGEMENT

To best demonstrate how Visual Studio 2010 can help in the process of application lifecycle management, let's run through a typical scenario with a fictional software development company called eMockSoft. eMockSoft has recently signed a partnership with a distributor to release its catalog of products. The distributor has requested a secure Web service to transmit inventory and pricing information to internal and external partner organizations.

Let's look at the scenario as it applies to application lifecycle management and the Visual Studio 2010 tools.

Requirements

The project manager meets with the sponsor to obtain requirements for the project. The requirements will inform the development team about what the project sponsor expects the software to deliver. The project manager can use a tool of choice (such as Visual Studio, Excel, or Microsoft Project) to store these requirements in Team Foundation Server. The project sponsor can validate and track these requirements using a SharePoint-based team project portal generated by Team Foundation Server. The team project portal surfaces reports and other artifacts stored in Team Foundation Server to a Web-based SharePoint site.

The infrastructure architect can now begin the system design.

System Design and Modeling

Based on the client specifications, the infrastructure architect can use the new UML tools in Visual Studio 2010 to define the external Web service. Meanwhile, the project manager can track the progress of the designs, including the diagrams that were generated. Based on the specifications, the project manager can then break work down into tasks (also stored in Team Foundation Server) to be assigned to developers on the team.

Code Generation

The developer receives work assignments and reviews the UML diagrams that were designed by the architect. The developer checks the specifications — this application requires a secure Web service using Web Services Enhancements (WSE) 3.0. The developer writes the necessary code, and does some preliminary testing, using static code analysis and unit testing tools built into Visual Studio 2010. Throughout the day, the developer checks the code and tests into Team Foundation Server 2010.

Testing

The tester checks the progress of the development team by monitoring the nightly builds and automated tests. Using Visual Studio Lab Management 2010, each nightly build triggers the automatic creation of a virtual machine that is ready each morning for the tester to begin testing with. The tester uses Visual Studio Test Professional 2010 to author, manage, and execute a suite of manual test cases each day to surface potential bugs for the development team. The tester files a bug in Team Foundation Server that is assigned to the developer to fix.

All bug reports are stored in Team Foundation Server, and provide team members and project sponsors with full visibility into the progress of the project.

Putting It into Context

This is a just simple example that examines just a few of the ways in which Visual Studio 2010 can assist with application lifecycle management. Throughout this book, you will discover other examples that can help your team become a more cohesive unit and ship better software.

WHO IS THIS BOOK FOR?

This book primarily targets teams of professionals in the field of commercial or enterprise software development — in other words, intermediate to advanced users. You are likely to find the book useful if you are any of the following:

➤ A developer, tester, or architect who wants to learn how the Visual Studio 2010 family of products can help you perform your job

➤ A project manager who must manage a software development project

This book is not designed for the absolute beginner. The focus is on practical application of the tools, code samples, and hands-on scenarios. The book's organization makes it easy to use as both a step-by-step guide and a reference for modeling, designing, testing, and coordinating enterprise solutions at every level.

Visual Studio 2010 is designed for software teams of all sizes. So, whether you have a team of 5 or 2,000 members, this book includes useful information for you related to Visual Studio 2010 and application lifecycle management. Unlike most Wrox books, this book targets all roles in the software development organization — architects, developers, testers, project leads, and management — not just developers.

WHAT DOES THIS BOOK COVER?

This book includes a complete overview of the application lifecycle management capabilities of Visual Studio 2010. The book is divided into five main parts, based around the different roles on the software development team:

- ➤ Part I: Architect
- ➤ Part II: Developer
- ➤ Part III: Tester
- ➤ Part IV: Team Foundation Server
- ➤ Part V: Project/Process Management

Part I: Architect

This section of the book examines the tools available in Visual Studio 2010 related to the architect role. After a brief introduction to architecture concepts, the discussion dives into all the new UML tools available, including use case diagrams, activity diagrams, sequence diagrams, class diagrams, and component diagrams. You then learn about the Architecture Explorer and how it can be used to understand the architecture of your application. Finally, this section wraps up with a discussion of layer diagrams.

Part II: Developer

This section of the book covers all the topics of most interest to a developer who is creating an application with Visual Studio 2010. Unit testing, refactoring, static code analysis, and code coverage are all covered in detail. The capability to handle development, testing, and deployment of database applications is also covered, as are advanced application debugging techniques using the new IntelliTrace functionality.

Part III: Tester

Visual Studio 2010 has numerous tools available for testers to use, and this section covers all of them. The examination starts out with a look at Web performance and load testing. After that, the new manual testing functionality is discussed, as well as the capability to automate user interface tests. This section concludes with a look the new lab management capabilities of Visual Studio 2010, which allow you to make use of virtual machines to automatically spin up test environments that can be used to execute tests.

Part IV: Team Foundation Server

This section is all about the capabilities that Team Foundation Server provides. It discusses the new architecture of Team Foundation Server 2010, and then delves into the version control system and some best practices surrounding branching and merging using Team Foundation Server. Finally, there is an in-depth look at some of the new changes to the automated build process, Team Foundation Build.

Part V: Project/Process Management

The final section of the book deals with the Project and Process Management functionality of Visual Studio 2010 and Team Foundation Server. The new process templates that ship with the product are examined, along with the new backlog and capacity planning features. The reports that ship with Team Foundation Server also are examined. Finally, some of the more common process template customizations are shown.

CONVENTIONS

To help you get the most from the text and keep track of what's happening, we've used a number of conventions throughout the book.

> *Boxes like this one hold important, not-to-be forgotten information that is directly relevant to the surrounding text.*

> *Notes, tips, hints, and tricks are offset and placed in italics like this.*

> **SIDEBAR**
>
> Asides to the current discussion are offset like this.

As for styles in the text:

➤ We *highlight* new terms and important words when we introduce them.

➤ We show keyboard strokes like this: Ctrl+A.

➤ We show filenames, URLs, and code within the text like so: `persistence.properties`.

➤ We present code in two different ways:

```
We use a monofont type with no highlighting for most code examples.
We use boldface to emphasize code that is of particularly importance in the
present context.
```

SOURCE CODE

As you work through the examples in this book, you may choose either to type in all the code manually, or to use the source code files that accompany the book. All the source code used in this book is available for download at www.wrox.com. Once at the site, simply locate the book's title (either by using the Search box, or by using one of the title lists) and click the Download Code link on the book's detail page to obtain all the source code for the book.

> *Because many books have similar titles, you may find it easiest to search by ISBN; this book's ISBN is 978-0-470-48426-5.*

Once you download the code, just decompress it with your favorite compression tool. Alternately, you can go to the main Wrox code download page at www.wrox.com/dynamic/books/download .aspx to see the code available for this book and all other Wrox books.

ERRATA

We make every effort to ensure that there are no errors in the text or in the code. However, no one is perfect, and mistakes do occur. If you find an error in one of our books, such as a spelling mistake or a faulty piece of code, we would be very grateful for your feedback. By sending in errata, you may save another reader hours of frustration, and you will be helping us provide even higher quality information.

To find the errata page for this book, go to www.wrox.com and locate the title using the Search box or one of the title lists. Then, on the book details page, click the Book Errata link. On this page, you can view all errata that has been submitted for this book and posted by Wrox editors. A complete book list, including links to each book's errata, is also available at www.wrox.com/misc-pages/ booklist.shtml.

A complete book list including links to errata is also available at www.wrox.com/misc-pages/booklist.shtml.

If you don't spot "your" error on the Book Errata page, go to www.wrox.com/contact/techsupport.shtml and complete the form there to alert us about the error you have found. We'll check the information and, if appropriate, post a message to the book's errata page and fix the problem in subsequent editions of the book.

P2P.WROX.COM

For author and peer discussion, join the P2P forums at http://p2p.wrox.com. The forums are a Web-based system for you to post messages relating to Wrox books and related technologies, and to interact with other readers and technology users. The forums offer a subscription feature to email you topics of interest of your choosing when new posts are made to the forums. Wrox authors, editors, other industry experts, and your fellow readers are present on these forums.

At http://p2p.wrox.com, you will find several different forums that will help you not only as you read the book, but also as you develop your own applications. To join the forums, just follow these steps:

1. Go to http://p2p.wrox.com and click the Register link.

2. Read the terms of use and click Agree.

3. Complete the required information to join, as well as any optional information you wish to provide, and click Submit.

4. You will receive an email message with information describing how to verify you account and complete the joining process.

You can read messages in the forums without joining P2P, but in order to post your own messages, you must join.

Once you join, you can post new messages and respond to messages other users post. You can read messages at any time on the Web. If you would like to have new messages from a particular forum emailed to you, click the "Subscribe to this Forum" icon by the forum name in the forum listing.

For more information about how to use the Wrox P2P, be sure to read the P2P FAQs for answers to questions about how the forum software works, as well as many common questions specific to P2P and Wrox books. To read the FAQs, click the FAQ link on any P2P page.

PART I
Architect

1

Introduction to Software Architecture

WHAT'S IN THIS CHAPTER?

➤ Why designing visually is important

➤ Microsoft's approach to a modeling strategy

➤ Modeling tools in Visual Studio 2010 Ultimate

In this introductory chapter, you'll learn about the main themes — domain-specific languages (DSLs), model-driven development (MDD), and the Unified Modeling Language (UML) — and how they apply to the Visual Studio 2010 Ultimate. As part of this discussion, you'll learn what Microsoft has to say on those subjects, as well as some impartial views from the authors.

This chapter examines the evolution of distributed computing architectures — from simple object-oriented development, through component and distributed-component design, to the service-oriented architectures (SOAs) — that represent the current state of the art.

This chapter wraps up with a brief glimpse at the new architecture tools in Visual Studio 2010. New modeling tools, as well as support for the most common Unified Modeling Language diagrams, have been added to Visual Studio 2010, making the architecture tools first-class citizens in the product.

Let's begin by first establishing the case for even undertaking visual modeling — or visual design — in the first place.

DESIGNING VISUALLY

Two elementary questions immediately come to mind. Why design at all, rather than just code? Why design visually?

To answer the first question, consider the common analogy of building complex physical structures, such as bridges. Crossing a small stream requires only a plank of wood — no architect, no workers, and no plans. Building a bridge across a wide river requires a lot more — a set of plans drawn up by an architect so that you can order the right materials, planning the work, communicating the details of the complex structure to the builders, and getting a safety certificate from the local authority. It's the same with software. You can write a small program by diving straight into code, but building a complex software system will require some forethought. You must plan it, communicate it, and document it to gain approval.

Therefore, the four aims of visual design are as follows:

➤ To help you visualize a system you want

➤ To enable you to specify the structure or behavior of a system

➤ To provide you with a template that guides you in constructing a system

➤ To document the decisions you have made

Traditionally, design processes like the *Rational Unified Process* have treated design and programming as separate disciplines, at least in terms of tools support. You use a visual modeling tool for design, and a separate integrated development environment (IDE) for coding. This makes sense if you treat software development like bridge building, and assume that the cost of fixing problems during implementation is much higher than the cost of fixing those problems during design.

For bridges, that is undoubtedly true. But in the realm of software development, is it really more costly to change a line of code than it is to change a design diagram? Moreover, just as bridge designers might want to prototype aspects of their design using real materials, so might software designers want to prototype certain aspects of their design in real code.

For these reasons, the trend has been toward tools that enable visual design and coding within the same environment, with easy switching between the two representations, thus treating design and coding as essentially two views of the same activity. The precedent was set originally in the Java space by tools such as Together-J and, more recently, in the .NET space by IBM-Rational XDE, and this approach has been embraced fully by the Visual Studio 2010 Ultimate.

Now, let's tackle the second question. If the pictorial design view and the code view are alternative but equivalent, representations, then why design visually at all? The answer to that question is simple: A picture paints a thousand words. To test that theory, just look at the figures in this chapter and imagine what the same information would look like in code. Then imagine trying to explain the information to someone else using nothing but a code listing.

MICROSOFT'S MODELING STRATEGY

As mentioned, Microsoft's Visual Studio 2010 modeling strategy is based on a couple of ideas:

➤ Domain-specific languages (DSLs)

➤ Model-driven development (MDD)

These topics together comprise Microsoft's new vision for how to add value to the software development process through visual modeling.

First, let's set the scene. The Object Management Group (OMG) has a licensed brand called *Model-Driven Architecture (MDA)*. MDA is an approach to MDD based on constructing platform-independent UML models (PIMs) supplemented with one or more platform-specific models (PSMs). Microsoft also has an approach to MDD, based not on the generic UML but rather on a set of tightly focused DSLs. This approach to MDD is part of a Microsoft initiative called *software factories*, which, in turn, is part of a wider Dynamic Systems Initiative.

> *If you would like a more in-depth exploration of software factories, check out the book,* Software Factories: Assembling Applications with Patterns, Works, Models and Tools, *written by Keith Short, Jack Greenfield, Steve Cook, and Stuart Kent (Indianapolis: Wiley, 2004).*

Understanding Model-Driven Development

As a software designer, you may be familiar with the "code-generation" features provided by UML tools such as Rational Rose and IBM-Rational XDE. These tools typically do not generate "code" at all but merely "skeleton code" for the classes you devise. So, all you get is one or more source files containing classes populated with the attributes and operation signatures that you specified in the model.

> *The words "attribute" and "operation" are UML terminology. In the .NET world, these are often referred to as "field" and "method," respectively.*

As stated in Microsoft's modeling strategy, this leads to a problem:

> *"If the models they supported were used to generate code, they typically got out of sync once the developers added other code around the generated code. Even products that did a good job of 'round tripping' the generated code eventually overwhelmed developers with the complexity of solving this problem. Often, these problems were exacerbated, because CASE tools tried to operate at too high a level of abstraction relative to the implementation platform beneath. This forced them to generate large amounts of code, making it even harder to solve the problems caused by mixing handwritten and generated code."*

The methods that are generated for each class by UML code-generation tools typically have complete signatures but empty bodies. This seems reasonable enough, because, after all, the tool is not psychic. How would it know how you intend to implement those methods? Well, actually, it could know.

UML practitioners spend hours constructing dynamic models such as statecharts and sequence diagrams that show how objects react (to method invocations) and interact (invoke methods on other objects). Yet, that information, which could be incorporated into the empty method bodies, is lost completely during code generation.

> *Note that not all tools lose this kind of information during code generation, but most of the popular ones do. In addition, in some cases, UML tools do generate code within method bodies — for example, when you apply patterns using IBM-Rational XDE — but, in general, the point is valid.*

Why do UML tools generally not take account of the full set of models during code generation? In part, it's because software designers do not provide information on the other models with sufficient precision to be as useful as auto-generated method bodies. The main reason for that is because the notation (UML) and tools simply do not allow for the required level of precision.

What does this have to do with MDD? Well, MDD is all about getting maximum value out of the modeling effort, by taking as much information as possible from the various models right through to implementation. As Microsoft puts it:

> *"Our vision is to change the way developers perceive the value of modeling. To shift their perception that modeling is a marginally useful activity that precedes real development; to recognition that modeling is an important mainstream development task . . ."*

Although the example of UML dynamic modeling information finding its way into implemented method bodies was useful in setting the scene, don't assume that MDD is only (or necessarily) about dynamic modeling. If you've ever constructed a UML deployment model and then tried to do something useful with it — such as generate a deployment script or evaluate your deployment against the proposed logical infrastructure — you will have seen how wasted that effort has been, other than to generate some documentation.

So, what's the bottom line? Because models are regarded as first-class development artifacts, developers write less conventional code, and development is, therefore, more productive and agile. In addition, it fosters a perception among all participants — developers, designers, analysts, architects, and operations staff — that modeling actually *adds value* to their efforts.

Understanding Domain-Specific Languages

UML fails to provide the kind of high-fidelity domain-specific modeling capabilities required by automated development. In other words, if you want to automate the mundane aspects of software development, then a one-size-fits-all generic visual modeling notation will not suffice. What you need is one or more DSLs (or notations) highly tuned for the task at hand — whether that task is the definition of Web services, the modeling of a hosting environment, or traditional object design.

A DSL is a modeling language that meets certain criteria. For example, a modeling language for developing Web services should contain concepts such as Web methods and protocols. The modeling language should also use meaningful names for concepts, such as fields and methods (for C#), rather than attributes and operations. The names should be drawn from the natural vocabulary of the domain.

The DSL idea is not new, and you may already be using a DSL for database manipulation (it's called SQL) or XML schema definition (it's called XSD).

Visual Studio 2010 Ultimate embraces this idea by providing the capability to create DSLs for specific tasks. DSLs enable visual models to be used not only for creating design documentation, but also for capturing information in a precise form that can be processed easily, raising the prospect of compiling models into code.

The only DSL that Visual Studio 2010 Ultimate provides "out of the box" is the UML support. Users have the capability to create their own DSLs using the DSL toolkit.

In that context, "your own problem domain" need not be technology-focused (such as how to model Web services or deployment infrastructures) but may instead be business-focused. You could devise a DSL highly tuned for describing banking systems or industrial processes.

FROM OBJECTS TO SERVICES

The design features provided by Visual Studio 2010 Ultimate have been influenced not only by Microsoft's vision for MDD but also by a technological evolution from object-based architectures, through (distributed) component-based architectures, to the SOAs, that represent the current best practice in distributed system design.

Understanding Objects and Compile-Time Reuse

When object-oriented programming (OOP) became popular in the mid-1990s, it was perceived as a panacea. In theory, by combining state (data) and behavior (functions) in a single code unit, you would have a perfectly reusable element — a cog to be used in a variety of machines.

The benefit was clear. There would be no more searching through thousands of lines of code to find every snippet that manipulated a date — remember the Y2K problem? By encapsulating all date-manipulation functionality in a single Date class, you would be able to solve such problems at a stroke.

Object orientation turned out not to be a panacea after all, for many reasons, including (but not limited to) bad project management (too-high expectations), poor programming (writing procedural code dressed up with objects), and inherent weaknesses in the approach (such as tight coupling between objects).

For the purposes of this discussion, let's concentrate on one problem in particular, which is the style of reuse that objects encouraged — what you might call *copy-and-paste reuse*.

Consider the following copy-and-paste reuse scenario. You discover that your colleague has coded an object — call it Book — that supports exactly the functionality you need in your application. You copy the entire source code for that object and paste it into your application.

Yes, it has saved you some time in the short term, but now look a little farther into the future.

Suppose the Book class holds fields for Title and ISBN, but in your application, you now need to record the author. You add a new field into your copy of the Book source code, and name that field Author.

In the meantime, your colleague has established the same need in his application, so he, too, modifies the Book source code (his copy) and has the foresight to record the author's name using two fields: AuthorSurname and AuthorFirstname.

Now, the single, reusable Book object exists in two variants, both of which are available for a third colleague to reuse. To make matters worse, those two variants are actually incompatible and cannot easily be merged, thanks to the differing representations of the author name.

Once you've compiled your application, you end up with a single executable file (.exe) from which the Book class is indivisible, so you can't change the behavior of the Book class — or substitute it for your colleague's variant — without recompiling the entire application (if you still have the source code, that is!).

As another example (which will be continued through the next sections), imagine you're writing a technical report within your company. You see one of the key topics written up in someone else's report, which has been sent to you by email. You copy that person's text into your document, change it a little, and now your company has two slightly different descriptions of the same topic in two separate reports.

Understanding Components and Deploy-Time Reuse

At this point, you might be shouting that individual classes could be compiled separately and then linked together into an application. Without the complete source code for the application, you could recode and replace an individual class without a full recompilation; just link in the new version.

Even better, how about compiling closely related (tightly coupled) classes into a single unit with only a few of those classes exposed to the outside world through well-defined interfaces? Now the entire sub-unit — let's call it a *component* — may be replaced with a newer version with which the application may be relinked and redeployed.

Better still, imagine that the individual components need not be linked together prior to deployment, but may be linked on-the-fly when the application is run. Then there is no need to redeploy the entire application; just apply the component updates. In technological terms, this describes DLLs (for those with a Microsoft background) or JAR files (for the Java folks). And, in .NET terms, this describes assemblies.

Continuing with the nonprogramming analogy, consider hyperlinking your technical report to the appropriate section of your colleague's report, and then distributing the two documents together, rather than copying your colleague's text into your document.

Understanding Distributed Components and Run-Time Reuse

Continuing with this line of thought, imagine that the components need not be redeployed on client devices at all. They are somehow just available on servers, to be invoked remotely when needed at run-time.

In the nonprogramming example, consider not having to distribute your colleague's report along with your own. In your own report, you would simply hyperlink to the relevant section in your colleague's document, which would be stored — and would remain — on an intranet server accessible to all recipients.

One benefit of this kind of remote linking is that the remote component may be adapted without having to be redeployed to numerous clients. Clients would automatically see the new improved version, and clients constrained by memory, processing power, or bandwidth need not host the components locally at all.

This leads to a distributed component architecture, which, in technology terms, means Distributed Common Object Model (DCOM), Common Object Request Broker Architecture (CORBA), or Enterprise Java Beans (EJB). All of these technologies support the idea of a component (or object) bus via which remote operations may be discovered and invoked. In Figure 1-1, the component bus is indicated by the grayed-out vertical bar.

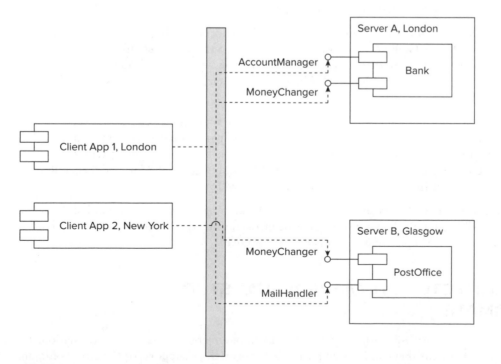

FIGURE 1-1

Of course, as remote components are modified, you must ensure that none of the modifications affect the abilities of clients to use those components, which is why you must make a distinction between interfaces and implementations:

➤ *Interface* — A component interface defines the contract between that component and the clients that use it. This contract must never be broken, which, in practice, means that existing operations may not have parameters added or taken away, though it may sometimes be permissible to add new operations. The semantics (or behavior) of the operation should remain unchanged.

➤ *Implementation* — A component implementation may be changed at will in terms of the use of an underlying database, the algorithms used (for example, for sorting), and maybe even the programming language in which the component is written, as long as the behavior is unaffected as far as the client is concerned.

This distinction between interface and implementation raises some very interesting possibilities. For example, a single component implementation (for example, Bank) may support several interfaces (for example, AccountManager and MoneyChanger), whereas the MoneyChanger interface may also be supported by another implementation (for example, PostOffice).

Moreover, the underlying implementations may be provided by various competing organizations. For example, you could choose your bank account to be managed by the Bank of BigCity or the National Enterprise Bank, so long as both supported the AccountManager interface.

Distributed Services and the Service-Oriented Architecture

What's wrong with the distributed components approach?

To start with, the same underlying concepts have been implemented using at least three different technologies: the OMG's CORBA, Microsoft's DCOM, and Sun Microsystems' EJB. Though comparable in theory, these approaches require different programming skills in practice and do not easily interoperate without additional bridging software such as DCOM/CORBA bridges and RMI-over-IIOP.

Furthermore, distributed component technologies encourage stateful intercourse between components by attempting to extend the full object-oriented paradigm across process and machine boundaries, thereby triggering a new set of challenges (such as how to manage distributed transactions across objects), requiring yet more complex technology in the form of the CORBA Transaction Service, or the Microsoft Transaction Server (MTS).

To a certain extent, an SOA alleviates these problems by keeping it simple — by making the services stateless, if possible, and by allowing services to be invoked using the widely adopted, standard over-the-wire protocol Simple Object Access Protocol (SOAP).

NEW ARCHITECTURE TOOLS IN VISUAL STUDIO 2010 ULTIMATE

The architecture tools in Visual Studio 2010 Ultimate have undergone a large transformation. There are several new diagrams that can be used for modeling, as well as support for the most common UML diagrams. All of these new diagram options can be used to help you more fully understand the software system that is being built. These tools allow you to create models at different levels of detail, depending on your need.

This section provides a very brief overview of each of the new modeling diagrams. The chapters that follow in the book provide an in-depth look into each diagram type.

As mentioned previously, Visual Studio 2010 fully supports UML now, specifically UML 2.1.2. Only five UML diagrams are supported out-of-the-box:

➤ Use case diagrams

➤ Activity diagrams

➤ Sequence diagrams

➤ Component diagrams

➤ Class diagrams

However, future releases of the product will add support for more UML diagrams.

There are other tools and diagrams, not related to UML, included with Visual Studio 2010 Ultimate. The Architecture Explorer can be used to understand the architecture of existing code, or of managed assemblies. Dependency graphs are used to provide a graphical view of the information from Architecture Explorer. Layer diagrams can be used to describe the logical architecture of your system and can even be used during the build process to enforce architecture considerations on the code base.

Use Case Diagrams

A *use case diagram* is a summary of who uses your application and what they can do with it. It describes the relationships among requirements, users, and the major components of the system.

Use case diagrams show the relationships between users (actors) and use cases within a system or application. They provide an overall view of how a system is used and the various roles and actions that take place within the system. Figure 1-2 shows an example of a use case diagram.

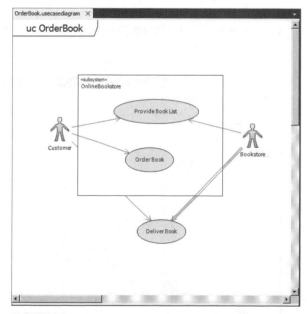

Activity Diagrams

Use case diagrams can be broken down into *activity diagrams*. An activity diagram shows the software process as the flow of work through a series of actions. Figure 1-3 shows an example of an activity diagram.

FIGURE 1-2

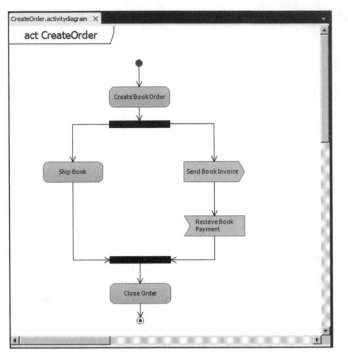

FIGURE 1-3

Sequence Diagrams

Sequence diagrams display interactions between different objects. This interaction usually takes place as a series of messages between the different objects. Figure 1-4 shows an example of a sequence diagram.

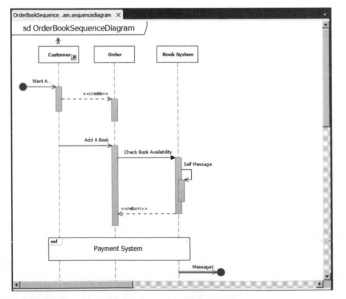

FIGURE 1-4

Component Diagrams

Component diagrams help visualize the high-level structure of the software system. Figure 1-5 shows an example of a component diagram.

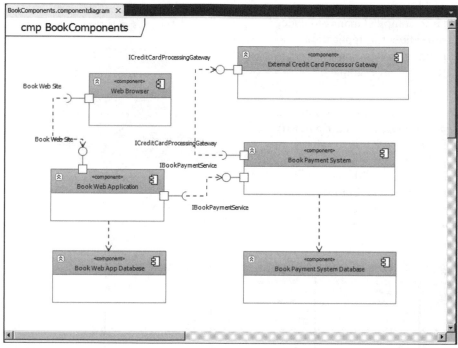

FIGURE 1-5

Class Diagrams

Class diagrams describe the objects in the application system. They do this without referencing any particular implementation of the system itself. Figure 1-6 shows an example of a class diagram.

Layer Diagrams

Layer diagrams are used to describe the logical architecture of your system. A layer diagram organizes the objects in your code into different groups (or layers) that describe the different tasks those objects perform. Figure 1-7 shows an example of a layer diagram.

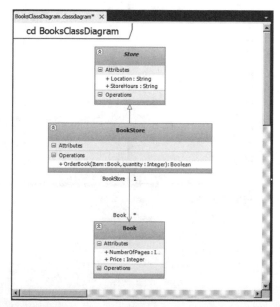

FIGURE 1-6

Architecture Explorer

The new *Architecture Explorer* tool provided by Visual Studio 2010 helps in understanding the existing architecture of a code base. This tool allows you to drill down into an existing code base, or even into compiled managed code, to help you understand how the application works, without having to open a single code file. Figure 1-8 shows an example of Architecture Explorer.

The Architecture Explorer can also lead into the world of *dependency graphs*, which are a new type of view in Visual Studio 2010 Ultimate that makes it easy to understand code that is new or unfamiliar. Dependency graphs make use of the Directed Graph Markup Language (DGML) to show the relationships between different areas of code in an easy-to-understand, graphical fashion.

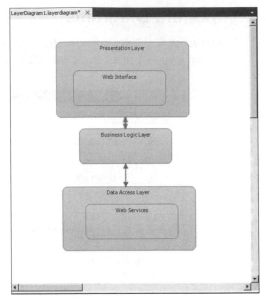

FIGURE 1-7

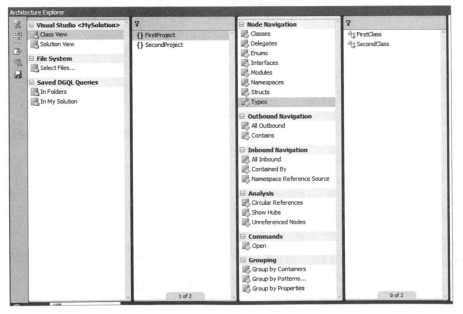

FIGURE 1-8

> *The Architecture Explorer is not the only way to create dependency graphs. Chapter 4 also shows other ways that dependency graphs can be created.*

SUMMARY

This chapter began by establishing the case for even doing design — specifically visual design — in the first place. The discussion highlighted the two main pillars that support that vision — namely, MDD and DSLs.

Because the underlying technologies have also evolved over time, thereby influencing the kinds of design you'll produce, this chapter also traced that evolution of concepts from the original object-oriented paradigm, through components and distributed-components, to the SOAs that represent the current wisdom.

This chapter concluded with a brief look at some of the new UML diagrams that are available in Visual Studio 2010, as well as the new Architecture Explorer tool.

Chapter 2 looks at how these UML diagrams are used and implemented in Visual Studio 2010 Ultimate. These diagrams are extremely useful from a modeling perspective, especially for communicating what the project is trying to accomplish, and how the different systems will interact.

2

Top-down Design with Use Case Diagrams, Activity Diagrams, and Sequence Diagrams

WHAT'S IN THIS CHAPTER?

➤ How to create and use use case diagrams

➤ How to create and use activity diagrams

➤ How to create and use sequence diagrams

Chapter 1 introduced you to architecture and modeling in the software space, and hinted at all the new architectural goodness available in Visual Studio 2010 Ultimate. This chapter dives deeper into three aspects of that, by looking at use case, activity, and sequence diagrams.

One of the strengths with modeling tools is that they enable you to design how the architecture of the application should be. Part of that is defining common terms around the problem domain, and then ensuring that everyone on the team understands those concepts. Using the use case, activity, and sequence diagrams, you can model your application, while ensuring that everyone on the team understands exactly what is being built.

This chapter is divided into three main sections:

➤ Use Case Diagrams

➤ Activity Diagrams

➤ Sequence Diagrams

Each section begins by examining a completed diagram and explaining the different components of it. Next, the discussion looks at all the objects that are available when building a particular diagram. And, finally, you will see a step-by-step walkthrough of how to build the diagram shown at the beginning of the section.

USE CASE DIAGRAMS

A *use case diagram* provides a graphical overview of the functionality of a system. It shows who is using the system and what they can do with it.

A use case diagram does not show details of use cases themselves, but instead provides a summary view of use cases, actors, and systems. Details (such as the order in which steps must be performed to accomplish the use case) can be described in other diagrams and documents, and then linked to the related use case. Use cases (and, by extension, use case diagrams) deal only with the functional requirements of a system. The architecture and any internal details are described elsewhere.

Understanding a Use Case Diagram

The best way to understand any diagram is to look at an example and take it apart. Figure 2-1 shows an example of a basic use case diagram of a customer interacting with an online bookstore system.

In Figure 2-1, you can see that a customer can view a list of books offered by the online bookstore. The customer can also order books from the online bookstore. The bookstore can also update the list of available books. Once a customer has ordered some books, the bookstore will deliver those books to the customer.

In this diagram, the objects labeled `Customer` and `Bookstore` are called *actors*. An actor represents a user, organization, or external system that can interact with your application. By default, the `Actor` object is represented by the person icon shown in Figure 2-1. However, this icon can be replaced with a different image by modifying the `Image Path` property of the object.

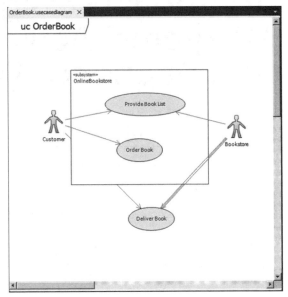

FIGURE 2-1

The oval-shaped objects labeled `Provide Book List`, `Order Book`, and `Deliver Book` are called *use cases*. A use case represents the actions that can be performed by one or more actors.

The lines drawn between the actors and the use cases are called *associations*. An association indicates that an actor can take part in a particular use case. For example, the `Customer` actor can view a list of books at the online bookstore.

The square box named `OnlineBookstore` is called a *subsystem*. A subsystem is the application, or part of the application, being worked on. In a particular use case diagram, a subsystem can represent the entire application, or possibly just a single class of the application. Any use cases that the subsystem supports are drawn inside the subsystem. In Figure 2-1, the `Provide Book List` and `Order Book` use cases are part of the `OnlineBookstore` application, so they are drawn inside the subsystem. The `Deliver Book` use case is outside the scope of the application, so it is drawn external to the subsystem.

Although Figure 2-1 is a very simple use case diagram, it is still very informative. You can also have more complex use case diagrams, with multiple subsystems, actors, and use cases. A best practice would be to start off describing the system with a few major use case diagrams. Each of those diagrams should define a major goal of the system. Once those goals have been defined, use some of the other objects from the use case diagram toolbox to define the system in more detail.

Let's break the `Order Book` use case down in more detail. Figure 2-2 shows a use case diagram that does this by using the `Include` relationship.

The `Include` relationship shows that a use case uses all the behavior of the included use case. To differentiate it from a regular association, the `Include` relationship is represented as a dotted line with an arrow on the end (per the UML 2.1.2 specification). The arrow should always point to the more detailed use case. The `Include` relationship is also labeled with the keyword <<include>>. Each of the included use cases is a step that the actor may have to take in order to complete the main use case. In this example, in order for the customer to order a book at the online bookstore, the customer must choose a book and then pay for the book.

A use case diagram does not specify in what order the particular use cases should happen, or when a particular use case is necessary. To make that information clear, attach an `Artifact` object to the general use case. Do this by dropping an `Artifact` object onto the use case diagram, and then dragging a `Dependency` relationship between the `Artifact` element and the general use case, as shown in Figure 2-3.

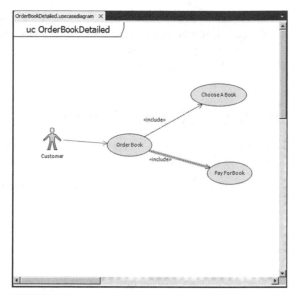

FIGURE 2-2

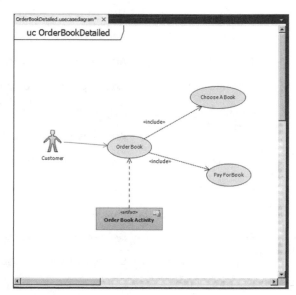

FIGURE 2-3

An `Artifact` element allows you to attach a separate document to the use case (for example, a text file that describes the steps to take). Later in this chapter, you'll learn how you can attach an activity diagram to this artifact and use case.

Use Case Diagram Toolbox

Figure 2-4 shows the different elements and associations available for use case diagrams.

Table 2-1 describes the different elements and associations.

FIGURE 2-4

TABLE 2-1: Use Case Diagram Toolbox Objects

NAME	DESCRIPTION
Pointer	Turns the mouse back into a regular mouse pointer
Actor	Adds a person or external system that initiates or participates in a use case
Use Case	Adds an interaction between the system and a use case
Comment	Adds a comment for more details
Subsystem	Represents a part of the system
Artifact	Adds a reference to a diagram or document
Association	Links an actor with a use case
Dependency	Defines how a use case requires another use case
Include	Defines how a use case reuses another use case
Extend	Defines how a use case occurs only with another use case occurs
Generalization	Defines how a use case is a specialized version of a more general use case
Comment Link	Connects a comment to a diagram element

Creating a Use Case Diagram

Let's look at the process of creating the use case diagram shown in Figure 2-1. To get started, create a new modeling project by selecting File ➪ New ➪ Project to open the New Project window. Select the Modeling Project template, give the project a name and location, and click OK. A new modeling project will open in Solution Explorer. Right-click on the project in Solution Explorer, and, from the context menu, select Add ⇨ New Item.

Select the Use Case Diagram template and name it `OrderBook.usecasediagram`. Click the Add button to create this diagram. A blank use case diagram named `OrderBook.usecasediagram` will be created in the modeling project and opened in Visual Studio.

First, from the toolbox, drag a subsystem boundary onto the use case diagram. This subsystem can be used to represent either an entire system or its major components. In the Properties window, change the `Name` property for the subsystem to be `OnlineBookstore`.

Next, add the actors to the use case diagram. Remember, the actors represent classes of users, organizations, and external systems that interact with the system being built. Drop two `Actor` objects onto the use case diagram, one on either side of the `OnlineBookstore` subsystem. In the Properties window, name the left actor `Customer` and the right actor `Bookstore`. The use case diagram should appear similar to Figure 2-5.

FIGURE 2-5

> To add multiple objects of the same type from the toolbox, double-click on the toolbox object. Then, click multiple times on the diagram to add the objects. When finished, press the Esc key to return the cursor to its regular functionality.

Once the actors are in place, drop the appropriate use cases onto the diagram. The use cases represent the activities that actors can perform. Drop two use cases inside the `Online Bookstore` subsystem, and rename them `Provide Book List` and `Order Book`. Add one use case outside the subsystem and name it `Deliver Book`.

Finally, to finish this simple use case, use the `Association` object to show how each actor is related to each use case. Double-click the `Association` object in the toolbox to select it. Click and hold on the `Customer` actor, and drag a line to the `Provide Book List` use case. An association is created between the actor and the use case. Do the same to the `Order Book` and `Deliver Book` use cases. Create associations the same way between the `Bookstore` actor and the `Provide Book List` and `Deliver Book` use cases.

When finished, the use case diagram should appear similar to Figure 2-1.

ACTIVITY DIAGRAMS

An *activity diagram* is used to show a business or software process as a work flow through a series of actions. These actions could be performed by any number of objects, including people, software, or computers. Activity diagrams can be used to model the logic captured in a particular use case, or to model detailed business logic. One easy way to think of activity diagrams would be to think of them as a flow chart.

An activity diagram always has a starting node, a series of activities, and a final node, indicating the end of the activity.

Understanding an Activity Diagram

To get started, let's look at an example of an activity diagram. Figure 2-6 shows the sequence of activities for ordering a book from an online bookstore.

In Figure 2-6, a customer first chooses a book to order. After a book is chosen, the customer must make a decision whether to order more books, or confirm the order. Once the customer is finished selecting books, the customer confirms the book order, and then pays for the book.

The black dot at the upper left of the diagram is called the *initial node*. Every activity diagram must have this element. This indicates the starting point for the activity.

The rounded-corner rectangles on the diagram are actions. This diagram contains three actions: `Choose A Book`, `Confirm Order`, and `Pay For Book`. Actions represent a step in the activity, where either a user or the system performs an action.

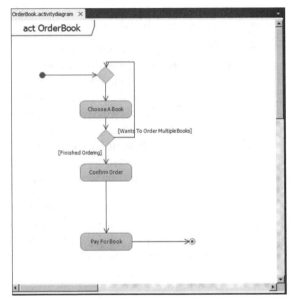

FIGURE 2-6

The top diamond-shaped element is a *merge node*. This node is used to merge multiple branches, usually split by a decision node (described shortly). A merge node has two or more inputs and one output.

The middle diamond-shaped element is a *decision node*. This node is used to create branching flows in the activity. In Figure 2-6, after a book is chosen, the customer has a choice of confirming the order, or selecting more books. A decision node should have only one input, and two or more outputs.

The Connector element is used to show the flow between the different elements on the activity diagram.

Concurrent Flow in an Activity Diagram

Activity diagrams can also be used to describe a sequence of actions that execute at the same time. This sequence of actions is known as a *concurrent flow*. Figure 2-7 shows an example of a concurrent flow activity diagram related to ordering a book on line.

At the start of this activity diagram, an order is created. After an order is created, two different branch processes are started. The black bar that the Create Book Order action leads into is called a *fork node*, and is used to divide a single flow into concurrent flows. In this case, one flow leads to the Ship Book action. The other leads to the Send Book Invoice element.

The Send Book Invoice element is not a regular action element. It is a Send Signal Action element. This indicates an action that sends a message to another activity for something to happen. The Receive Book Payment is an Accept Event Action element. It is an action that waits for a message before the flow can continue. In the case of Figure 2-7, a book invoice will be sent, potentially to a payment system. The flow in the activity diagram waits until a response is received back, indicating that the book has been paid for. Both the Ship Book and the Receive Book Payment actions are then merged back into a single process using a *join node*. The activity ends with the closing of the order.

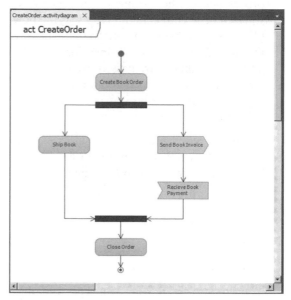

FIGURE 2-7

 The fork node and/or join node can be set to a vertical orientation if desired.

Data Flows in an Activity Diagram

Data flowing into and out of an activity can be represented in two different ways. The first way is using an *object node*. This is usually the simplest method to describe the data flowing between activities. Think of an object node as a variable in a program. It stores a value (or multiple values) passed from one action to the next.

Most activity diagram control flows carry some sort of data, as shown in Figure 2-8. A customer enters shipping information, and that data is passed on so the books can be shipped.

In Figure 2-8, the round-cornered rectangles represent actions in the diagram, where actual processing or other business logic occurs. The square-cornered rectangles represent the flow of objects or data from one action to the next. In Figure 2-8, the customer name, shipping address, and phone number are passed from the action where the customer enters that information to the action where the books are shipped to the customer.

The object node has a property called `Type`, where the type of the object can be set. By default, there are four primitive types to choose from:

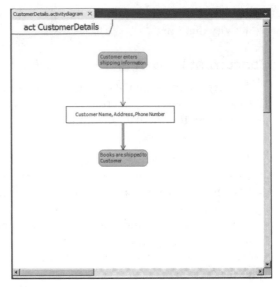

FIGURE 2-8

- ➤ `Boolean`
- ➤ `Integer`
- ➤ `String`
- ➤ `Unlimited Natural`

You can also create your own types and objects, such as an `Address` class. This allows you to create the types you need, and set the object node to the appropriate type.

The second way to represent data flowing into and out of an activity is by using *input and output pins*, as shown in Figure 2-9.

In Figure 2-9, the top activity contains an output pin. The output pin represents data that an action produces — in this case, the order detail information. The bottom activity contains an input pin. The input pin represents the data that an activity consumes — in this case, the customer name, address, and phone number for shipping the order.

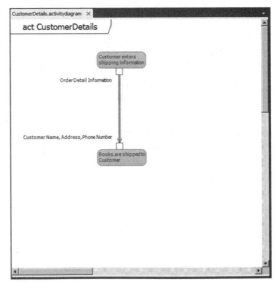

FIGURE 2-9

> When using input and output pins, be sure to give them a name that indicates the role of the objects they produce or accept (for example, a parameter name).

As with the object node, the input and output pins have a `Type` property that can be set to the appropriate object type.

Activity Diagram Toolbox

Figure 2-10 shows the different elements and associations available for activity diagrams.

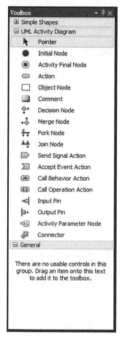

FIGURE 2-10

Table 2-2 describes the different elements and associations.

TABLE 2-2: Activity Diagram Toolbox Objects

NAME	DESCRIPTION
Pointer	Turns the mouse back into a regular mouse pointer
Initial Node	Adds the start of the activity
Activity Final Node	Adds an end to the activity
Action	Adds a single step that occurs in the activity
Object Node	Represents an object that participates in the activity

continues

TABLE 2-2 *(continued)*

NAME	DESCRIPTION
Comment	Adds a comment for more details
Decision Node	Divides a single incoming flow into a choice between alternate outgoing flows
Merge Node	Combines incoming alternate flows into a single outgoing flow
Fork Node	Divides a single incoming flow into concurrent outgoing flows
Join Node	Combines incoming concurrent flows into a single outgoing flow
Send Signal Action	Adds an action that sends a signal
Accept Event Action	Adds an action that waits for a signal or event
Call Behavior Action	Adds an action that calls another activity
Call Operation Action	Adds an action that calls an operation
Input Pin	Represents data that an action requires
Output Pin	Represents data that an action produces
Activity Parameter Node	Represents data that an activity requires or produces
Connector	Adds a connection or flow between elements on the diagram

Creating an Activity Diagram

Let's look at the process of creating the activity diagram shown in Figure 2-6. Using the same modeling project created earlier in the section, "Creating a Use Case Diagram," right-click on the project in Solution Explorer, and, from the context menu, select Add ➪ New Item.

Select the Activity Diagram template and name it OrderBook.activitydiagram. Click the Add button to create this diagram. A blank activity diagram named OrderBook.activitydiagram will be created in the modeling project and opened in Visual Studio.

From the toolbox, drag an Initial Node element onto the diagram. This indicates the starting point for this activity. Next, drag three Action elements onto the diagram. Using the properties of the elements, name these items Choose A Book, Confirm Order, and Pay For Book.

From the toolbox, drag a Merge Node above the Choose A Book action. Drag and drop a Decision Node between the Choose A Book and Confirm Order actions. Finally, drag an Activity Final node to the right of the Pay For Book action. The diagram should resemble Figure 2-11.

Next, you must add the connectors to show the flow of activity through this activity diagram. Double-click the Connector element to select it. On the activity diagram, drag a line between the Initial Node element and the Merge Node. Continue connecting the other elements on the diagram as follows:

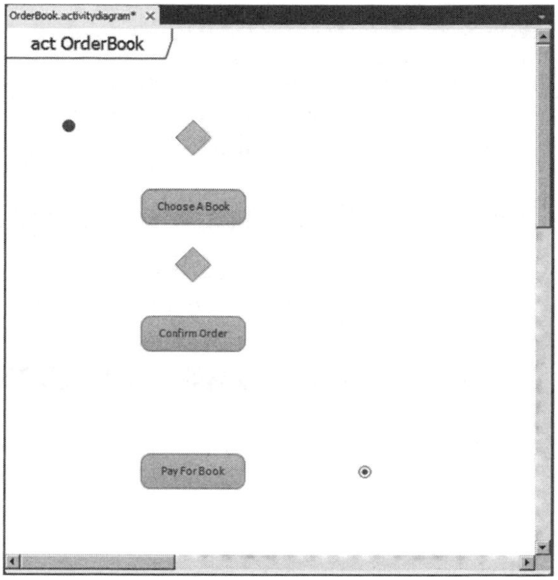

1. Connect the Merge Node to the Choose A Book action.

2. Connect the Choose A Book action with the Decision Node.

3. Connect the Decision Node with the Confirm Order action.

4. Connect the Decision Node with the Merge Node.

5. Connect the Confirm Order action with the Pay For Book action.

6. Connect the Pay For Book action with the Activity Final Node.

FIGURE 2-11

Finally, modify the Guard property of the connector elements, leaving the decision node to specify the reasons for the different pathways. On the connector to the Confirm Order action, add the guard Finished Ordering. On the connector to the Merge Node, add the guard Wants To Order Multiple Books.

When finished, the diagram should appear similar to Figure 2.6.

Adding an Activity Diagram to a Use Case Diagram

Earlier in this chapter when examining use case diagrams, you added an artifact element to the diagram (see Figure 2-3). One available option with artifact elements is the capability to associate them with an activity diagram (and, as an extension, any physical document).

To do this, select the Artifact element on the use case diagram. In the properties window for the element, select the Hyperlink property. This will open the Open File dialog box, allowing you to select a diagram, document, or other file to associate with the Artifact element on the use case diagram.

> To ensure that the file path remains valid on a team member's computer, only select files contained in the Visual Studio solution. Also, be aware that referencing Visual Studio UML diagrams outside the current project will not work properly.

SEQUENCE DIAGRAMS

A *sequence diagram* is used to show the sequence of interactions between classes, components, subsystems, or actors. A sequence diagram is read from top to bottom, indicating the flow of time through the system. From left to right, the diagram itself shows the flow of control from one element to the next.

Understanding Sequence Diagrams

To get started, let's look at an example of an activity diagram. Figure 2-12 shows the sequence of flow for ordering a book from the online bookstore.

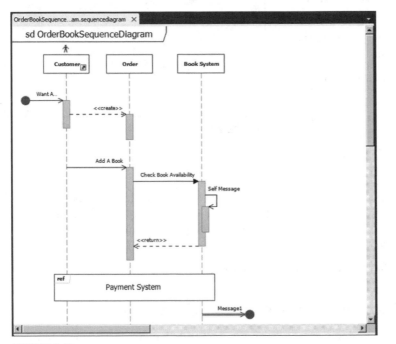

FIGURE 2-12

In Figure 2-12, a customer first has the desire to purchase a book. At that point, the customer adds a book to a shopping cart. The order system checks the availability of the book and performs some internal processing. The availability of the book is returned to the ordering system. The payment system is represented by a separate sequence diagram, so a reference placeholder is inserted into this diagram. Finally, a message is sent to an unknown (or unspecified) system at the end of the process.

The three vertical lines on the diagram (Customer, Order, and Book System) are called *lifelines*. These vertical lines represent participants in the described interaction. Time progresses down the lifeline, from top to bottom. Notice the Customer lifeline has a symbol representing a person above it. This symbol is called an *actor*, and indicates that this lifeline represents a participant external to the system being developed. This symbol can appear above any lifeline by setting the Actor property to True. An actor lifeline can also be created by dragging an actor from the UML Model Explorer onto the sequence diagram.

The box at the top of a lifeline has rounded corners to indicate that it has been generated from program code, and is shown as a regular rectangle if it has been drawn by hand.

The initial message that starts with a black dot in the upper left of the diagram is known as a *found message*. It indicates an asynchronous message from an unknown or unspecified participant into this sequence diagram.

The grey vertical shaded rectangles on each lifeline are called *execution occurrences*. These represent a period when the participant is executing an operation. Execution usually begins when the participant receives a message. From within an execution block, other messages can be sent to other participants, or even to itself.

To get started in this process, the customer creates an order. This is done using a *create message*. This message creates a participant. If a participant is being created, this should be the first message it receives.

Next, the customer adds a book to the shopping cart. This is represented using an *asynchronous message*. An asynchronous message is shown as a solid arrow leading from one lifeline to another, with no return arrow. An asynchronous message is one that does not require a response before the sender can continue. It shows only the call from the sender. It can be used to represent communication between separate threads or the creation of a new thread.

The Order lifeline must check to see if the book is available. This is done using a *synchronous message*. A synchronous message looks similar to an asynchronous message, except that it includes a dotted line and arrow, indicating a return at the end of the message. With a synchronous message, the sender must wait for a response before the workflow can continue. The sequence diagram shows both the call and the return. Synchronous messages are normally used to represent ordinary function calls in a program.

While in an execution occurrence, a participant may need to send messages to itself to accomplish a task. These messages are called *self messages*, and are shown as an asynchronous call starting and ending from the same lifeline.

A sequence diagram can also send messages to unknown or unspecified participants. This type of message is called a *lost message*. In Figure 2-12, this message is represented as an asynchronous call leaving the Book System lifeline, and ending in a black dot.

Notice the box labeled Payment System. The Payment System itself is defined in another sequence diagram. However, the payment system is relevant to this particular sequence diagram as well. Instead of replicating the information in the Payment System sequence diagram, a reference is placed to it instead. This reference is called an *interaction use*. It is used to enclose a sequence of messages that are defined in another diagram.

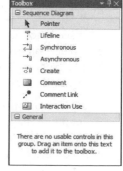

FIGURE 2-13

Sequence Diagram Toolbox

Figure 2-13 shows a screenshot of the different elements available for sequence diagrams.

Table 2-3 describes the different elements and associations.

TABLE 2-3: Sequence Diagram Toolbox Objects

NAME	DESCRIPTION
Pointer	Turns the mouse back into a regular mouse pointer
Lifeline	Adds a participant (such as a class or object) to an interaction sequence
Synchronous	Adds a message that calls an operation and expects a response
Asynchronous	Adds a message that calls an operation but does not expect a response
Create	Adds a message that calls an operation that creates an instance of the target
Comment	Adds a comment for more details
Comment Link	Connects a comment to a diagram element
Interaction Use	Adds an interaction use to create a reusable sequence or to reference another sequence

Creating a Sequence Diagram

Let's look at the process of creating the activity diagram shown in Figure 2-12. Using the same modeling project you have been using throughout this chapter, right-click on the project in Solution Explorer, and, from the context menu, select Add ➪ New Item.

Select the Sequence Diagram template and name it `OrderBookSequenceDiagram` `.sequencediagram`. Click the Add button to create this diagram. A blank sequence diagram named `OrderBookSequenceDiagram.sequencediagram` will be created in the modeling project and opened in Visual Studio.

From the toolbox, drag a `Lifeline` element onto the diagram. This element will indicate the customer who is ordering the book. Using the Properties window, change the `Type` property to be `Customer` and set the `Actor` property equal to `True`. Drag two more `Lifeline` elements onto the diagram, and set the `Type` properties to `Order` and `Book System`, respectively.

This sequence diagram is started with a message from an unknown source. This is represented with an asynchronous message. Select the `Asynchronous` element in the toolbox, then draw a line from a blank space on the diagram to the `Customer` lifeline. This will create the starting point into the sequence diagram, indicated by a black dot. Change the `Name` property to `Want A Book`.

Next, a create message must be sent to create a participant. If a participant receives a create message, it should be the first message it receives. Click the `Create` element in the toolbox. On the `Customer` lifeline, click the grey execution box area, and drag a line to the `Order` lifeline. A dotted line will be created between the two lifelines, and a grey execution box will appear on the `Order` lifeline.

To start the ordering process, the customer must add an item that he or she wants to buy. This will be represented using an `Asynchronous` message call. An `Asynchronous` element represents an interaction where the sender can continue immediately without waiting for the receiver. In the toolbox, select the `Asynchronous` element. Click on the `Customer` lifeline and drag a line to the `Order` lifeline. A solid line will be created between the `Customer` and `Order` lifelines. Change the name of the element to `Add A Book`.

Once a book is added, the book availability must be determined. This is done using a `Synchronous` message call. A `Synchronous` element represents an interaction where the sender waits for the receiver to return a response. In the toolbox, select the `Synchronous` element. Click the `Order` lifeline and drag a line to the `Book System` lifeline. A solid arrow will be created between the `Order` and `Book` lifelines. In addition, a dotted arrow will be created from the `Book System` lifeline to the `Order` lifeline. This indicates control is to be returned to the sender — in this case, the `Order` lifeline. Change the name of the element to Check Book Availability.

A participant can also send a message to itself — for example, if it were triggering internal methods for doing work. Select the `Asynchronous` element from the toolbox. On the `Book System` lifeline, click the `Check Book Availability` execution block. Drag a line farther down in the same block and release. This creates a solid arrow from the `Check Book Availability` execution block back onto the same execution block.

There is a complete payment system sequence that is not represented on this particular sequence diagram, but instead is shown on a separate diagram. To represent the contents of that separate diagram, use the `Interaction Use` element. Click the `Interaction Use` element in the toolbox. Drag a box across the different lifelines that are included in this reference. Change the name of the element to `Payment System`.

Finally, you can represent a message to an unknown or unspecified participant. This is known as a *lost message*. Select the `Asynchronous` element from the toolbox. At the bottom of the `Book System` lifeline, drag a line from the lifeline to a blank area on the diagram. An arrow will be created from the lifeline to a created black dot, indicating this message goes to an unknown participant.

SUMMARY

This chapter examined the capabilities of use case diagrams, activity diagrams, and sequence diagrams. You looked at an example use case diagram, and learned about its different components. You also learned how to create a use case diagram. Next, you learned about activity diagrams, where, in addition to examining an example of how to build a diagram, you also learned how to link an activity diagram back to a use case diagram. This chapter concluded by discussing sequence diagrams, their components, and how to create them.

Chapter 3 provides an in-depth look at two more important diagrams. Component diagrams are used to show the different parts of a design of a software system, while class diagrams are used to show the classes within an application and the relationship between those classes.

3

Top-down Design with Component and Class Diagrams

WHAT'S IN THIS CHAPTER?

➤ How to create and use component diagrams

➤ How to show the internal parts of a component diagram

➤ How to create and use a class diagram

Chapter 2 discussed use case, activity, and sequence diagrams, and how they can be used to understand the problem space, as well as to begin mapping out how the application should be built and what the application is trying to accomplish. Once you have that information under your belt, the next step is to start trying to visualize (from a high level) the structure of the system, and then drill down into the classes and other objects that will be used by the application. This is where component diagrams and class diagrams come in.

This chapter begins by introducing component diagrams. It will break down an existing component diagram to provide a good understanding of all the parts that are available. It will look at all the elements from the component diagram toolbox, as well as describe all the different properties available to all the elements. The component diagram discussion will wrap up with step-by-step instructions on how to create a component diagram, as well as how to use a component diagram to model the internal workings of higher-level components.

After that, it is all about UML class diagrams (formerly known as logical class diagrams). As with component diagrams, this chapter examines some existing class diagrams, and covers the different toolbox elements and properties of those elements. The chapter concludes with a discussion of the step-by-step creation of a basic class diagram.

The terms "class diagram," "logical class diagram," and "UML class diagram" will be used interchangeably throughout this chapter, but are meant to refer to the same diagram type.

COMPONENT DIAGRAMS

As you learned in Chapter 2, the sequence diagram allows you to model and visualize the messages of a system. With the *component diagram*, you can visualize the components of the system that implement the system functionality, as well as other puzzle pieces of the system (such as Web services, user interfaces, COM components, and so on). A component diagram will depict the relationships between various components of your application or system.

A component diagram shows the parts of a design for a software system. These components could be executables, DLLs, or even entire systems. At this level, you aren't necessarily trying to decide exactly how things are being built. Rather, you are just trying to break down the architecture into something more manageable and understandable. A component diagram can be used to visualize the high-level structure of the system, and the service behavior that those components both provide and consume.

Think of a *component* as a modular unit that is replaceable. You don't know how the internals of the component work. Instead, you know what interfaces a component provides or consumes. Components on a component diagram have *interfaces*, either required interfaces or provided interfaces. An interface can be anything, from a Web site to a Web service. A *required interface* indicates functionality that a component expects to consume. A *provided interface* indicates functionality that a component provides for other components to consume. Each required interface on a component diagram should be linked to a provided interface.

Creating component diagrams has a couple of nice benefits. It can help the development team understand an existing design and see potential ways to improve it. More importantly, thinking of the system as a collection of components with well-defined interfaces improves the separation between components, which can make the design easier to change as the requirements change.

Understanding a Component Diagram

The best way to understand any diagram is to look at an example and take it apart. Figure 3-1 shows an example of a basic component diagram of the online bookstore system.

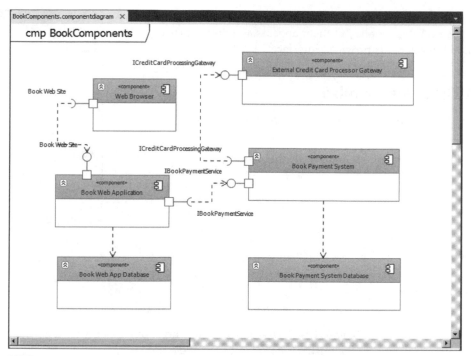

FIGURE 3-1

In Figure 3-1, the square objects labeled Web Browser and Book Web Application are called *components*. As mentioned previously, a component is a reusable piece of system functionality. A component provides and consumes behavior through interfaces, and can use other components. Another way to think about a component is that it is a kind of class.

> *Click the chevron symbol on a component element to show just the component header, and hide other component information.*

As mentioned, components expose interfaces that are either a functionality that a component provides for other components (a provider interface), or functionality that a component needs from other components (a required interface). Required interfaces are represented by an open circle called a *hook*. The Web Browser component exposes a required interface named Book Web Site. Provided interfaces are represented by a closed circle called a *lollipop*. The Book Payment System component exposes a provided interface named IBookPaymentService.

Required interfaces and provided interfaces are linked together using a `Dependency` element. A `Dependency` element appears as a dotted arrow linking a required interface to a provided interface.

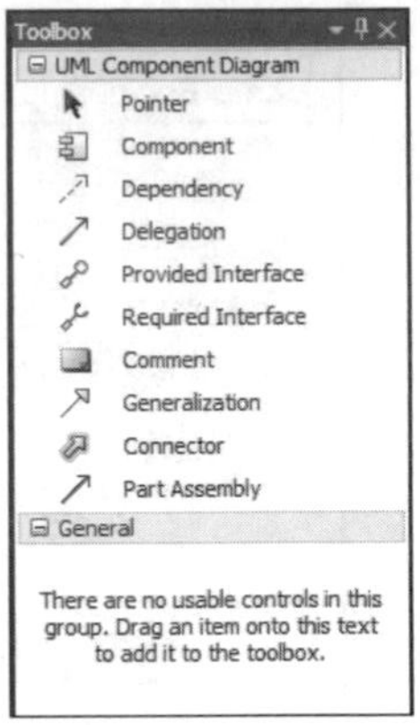

Component Diagram Toolbox

Figure 3-2 shows the different elements and associations available for component diagrams.

Table 3-1 describes the different elements and associations.

FIGURE 3-2

TABLE 3-1: Component Diagram Toolbox Objects

NAME	DESCRIPTION
Pointer	Turns the mouse back into a regular mouse pointer.
Dependency	Defines how an element depends on another element. Begin the relationship from the dependent element.
Component	Adds a component that defines a reusable unit of system functionality.
Delegation	Designates behavior between a port on an outer component and an interface on an inner component.
Provided Interface	Adds an interface that a component provides to other components.
Required Interface	Adds an interface that a component requires from other components.
Comment	Adds a comment for more details.
Generalization	Defines how a component derives from another component. Begin the relationship from the derived component.
Connector	This connection tool creates a default relationship between shapes, based on the types of shapes being connected.
Part Assembly	This tool specifies a connection between parts in a component. It connects a required interface on one part to a provided interface on another part.

Component Diagram Element Properties

Each element on a component diagram has properties that can be manipulated using the Properties window in Visual Studio 2010. To see the properties of an element, right-click on the element in the diagram and select Properties. The properties will appear in the Properties window.

Table 3-2 describes the different properties available to component diagram elements.

TABLE 3-2: Component Diagram Element Properties

PROPERTY	DEFAULT	ELEMENT	DESCRIPTION
Name	A default name	All	Identifies the element.
Qualified Name	Package::Name	All	Uniquely identifies the element. Prefixed with the qualified name of the package that contains it.
Work Items	0	All	The number of work items associated with this element.
Description	(none)	All	General notes about the element can be added here.
Is Indirectly Instantiated	True	Component	The component exists only as a design artifact. At run-time, only its parts exist.
Is Abstract	False	Component	The component definition can be used only as a generalization from which other components can be specialized.
Is Leaf	False	Interface	This interface cannot be specialized.
TemplateBinding	(none)	Interface	The template type that this type instantiates. Expand the parameter to see the bindings of the template parameters.
TemplateParameters	(none)	Interface	Lists the type's parameters. Used if this is a template type. To see the properties of individual parameters, click [...].

TABLE 3-2 *(continued)*

PROPERTY	DEFAULT	ELEMENT	DESCRIPTION
Visibility	Public	Component, Part, Port, Interface	Public — Globally visible.
			Package — Visible within the package.
			Private — Visible within the owning component.
			Protected — Visible to components derived from the owner.
Type	Type on creation	Part	The type of a part is a component or class.
Multiplicity	1	Part	Indicates how many instances of the specified type form part of the parent component.
			1 — Exactly one.
			0..1 — One or none.
			* — A collection of any number.
			n..m — A collection of from n to m instances.
LinkedPackage	Model	Diagram	The default namespace for elements added to this diagram.

Creating a Component Diagram

Let's look at the process of creating the component diagram shown in Figure 3-1. Using the same modeling project from Chapter 2, right-click on the project in Solution Explorer, and, from the context menu, select Add ⇨ New Item.

Select the Component Diagram template and name it BookComponents.componentdiagram. Click the Add button to create this diagram. A blank component diagram named BookComponents.componentdiagram will be created in the modeling project and opened in Visual Studio 2010. At this point, you are ready to add components onto the diagram.

There are two options for adding components to the diagram. Using the toolbox, click the Component element, then click a blank area of the diagram. An empty Component element will appear on the diagram. This is useful for creating new components.

Existing components from other diagrams in the same modeling project can also be added to the diagram. Either open the existing diagram, or open the UML Model Explorer window (by selecting View ⇨ Other Windows ⇨ UML Model Explorer). Right-click on the component to add to the component diagram, and then select Copy. Right-click on a blank area of the component diagram and select Paste Reference to create a copy of the component on the new diagram.

> *You can also just drag the component from the Model Explorer onto the diagram.*

From the Toolbox window, click the `Component` element and click a blank area on the diagram to create a new `Component` element. Select the component and change its name to `Web Browser`. Following this same method, add the following components to the component diagram:

➤ `Book Web Application`

➤ `Book Web App Database`

➤ `External Credit Card Processor Gateway`

➤ `Book Payment System`

➤ `Book Payment System Database`

Once these components have been added, the component diagram should resemble Figure 3-3.

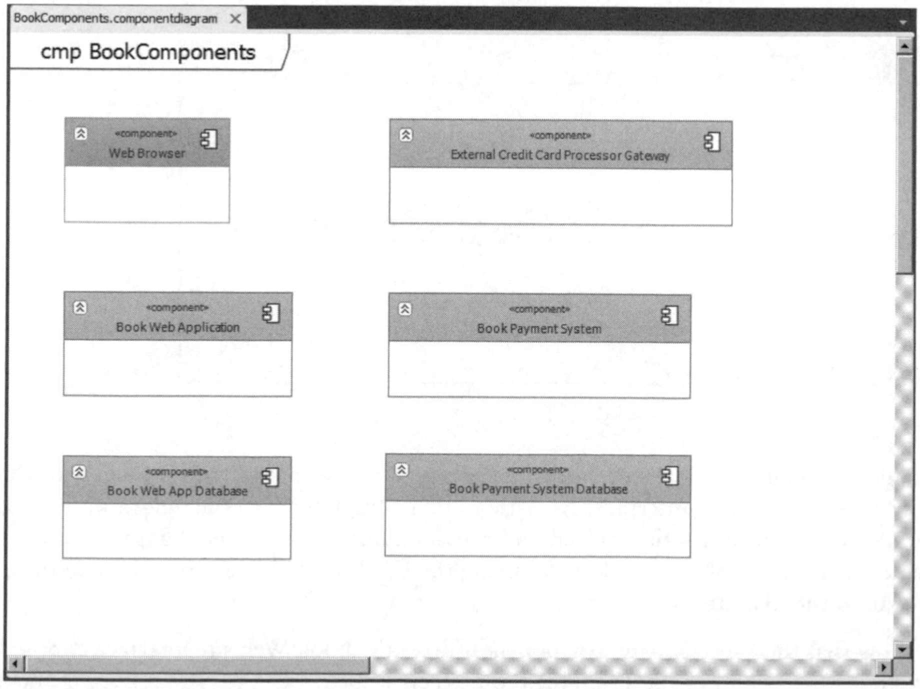

FIGURE 3-3

Now that all the components have been added to the diagram, the next step is to show all the provider relationships for components with interfaces that expose service behavior. From the Toolbox window, click the `Provided Interface` element, and then click on the `Book Web Application` component. The provided interface symbol (or lollipop) will attach itself to the `Book Web Application` component, with a default name of `Interface1`. This component is going to represent the Web site used for ordering books. Select the `Provided Interface` element, and, in the Properties window, rename it to `Book Web Site`.

Add another `Provided Interface` element to the `Book Payment System` component, and name it `IBookPaymentService`. This element will expose a Web service for interacting with the payment system. Finally, add a `Provided Interface` element to the `External Credit Card Processor Gateway` component and name it `ICreditCardProcessingGateway`. This element will expose a Web service for interacting with the external credit card processor. The component diagram should now resemble Figure 3-4.

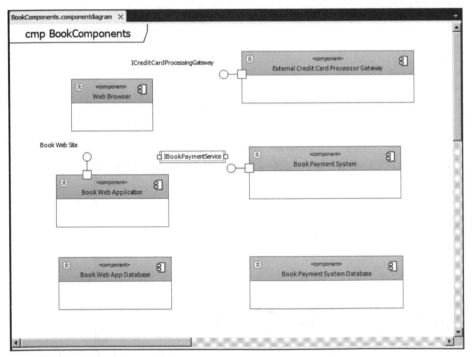

FIGURE 3-4

Next, you must add the required interfaces. Remember, required interfaces represent behavior that a component consumes through an interface. As with adding components to the diagram, there are two options for adding interfaces (both required and provided interfaces) to the diagram. You can add a new interface from the Toolbox window, or, using the UML Model Explorer, you can drag an existing interface onto the diagram.

First, you must show that the `Web Browser` component utilizes the book Web site interface exposed by the `Book Web Application` component. From the toolbox, click the `Required Interface` element, then click the `Web Browser` component on the diagram. Rename the interface to `Book Web Site`.

The interface elements can be easily repositioned on a component by dragging them to the appropriate location.

Next, let's add a required interface to the `Book Web Application` by using the UML Model Explorer. If the UML Model Explorer window is not visible, open it by going to View ⇨ Other Windows ⇨ UML Model Explorer in Visual Studio.

The UML Model Explorer shows all the elements that have been added to the central model. In the UML Model Explorer, click and drag the `IBookPaymentService` interface to the `Book Web Application` component. This creates another instance of the `IBookPaymentService` provided interface. However, you need this interface to be a required interface. To change the interface type, select the `IBookPaymentService` provided interface on the `Book Web Application` component. Click the smart tag that appears above the element and select "Convert to Required Interface." The interface type will change from provided to required.

You can also select the smart tag for a required interface and change it into a provided interface.

Finally, select the `Required Interface` element in the Toolbox window and click the `Book Payment System` component to create a required interface on that component. Rename the interface to be `ICreditCardProcessingGateway`. The component diagram should now resemble Figure 3-5.

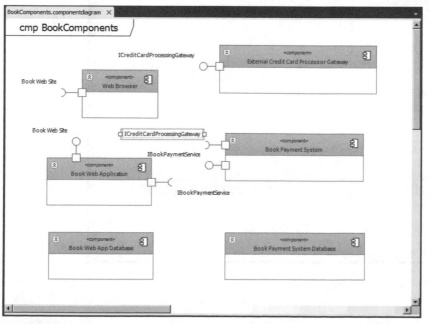

FIGURE 3-5

With the components defined and the provided and required interfaces known, the next step is to show which provided interfaces satisfy which required interfaces. This is done using the `Dependency` element. A `Dependency` element always connects a required interface (or hook) to a provided interface (or lollipop).

In the Toolbox window, select the `Dependency` element. On the component diagram, select the `Book Web Site` required interface on the `Web Browser` component, then select the `Book Web Site` provided interface on the `Book Web Application` component. A dotted arrow will be created from the required interface to the provided interface, indicating that the provided interface satisfies the required interface. On the component diagram, select the dependency dotted arrow that was just created. In the Properties window, change the name to be `HTTP`. This will provide a visual indicator on the component diagram that this is an HTTP connection between the two components.

In the Toolbox window, select the `Dependency` element again. On the component diagram, select the `IBookPaymentService` required interface on the `Book Web Application` component. Then select the `IBookPaymentService` provided interface on the `Book Payment System` component. Finally, select the `Dependency` element from the toolbox, and connect the `ICreditCardProcessingGateway` required interface on the `Book Payment System` component to the `ICreditCardProcessingGateway` provided interface on the `External Credit Card Processor Gateway`. The component diagram should now resemble Figure 3-6.

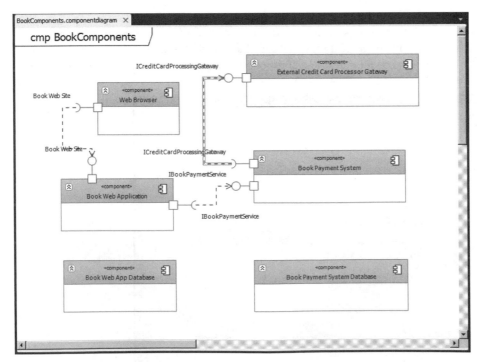

FIGURE 3-6

The final step in creating this component diagram is to show the dependency relationship between the components and the databases that they use.

To create the dependency relationship between the `Book Web Application` and the `Book Web App Database` components, select the `Dependency` element from the Toolbox window, click the `Book Web Application` component, and then click the `Book Web App Database` component. A dotted arrow will be drawn between the two, indicating the dependency of the Web application on the database. Do the same thing between the `Book Payment System` component and the `Book Payment System Database` component. The component diagram is now complete, as shown in Figure 3-7.

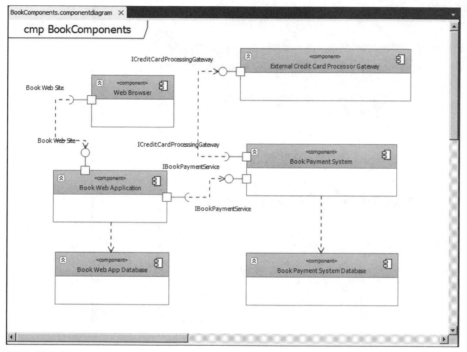

FIGURE 3-7

Showing Internal Component Parts

To show how a larger component is comprised of smaller components, a component can also be placed inside other components on a component diagram. This section shows you how to create a component model of a Web service for the example book Web site. This Web service component is comprised of both a customer application server and a back-end order-processing server.

Using the same modeling project from earlier in this chapter, right-click on the project in Solution Explorer, and, from the context menu, select Add ⇨ New Item.

Select the Component Diagram template and name it `BookWebService.componentdiagram`. Click the Add button to create this diagram. A blank component diagram named `BookWebService.componentdiagram` will be created in the modeling project and opened in Visual Studio.

From the Toolbox window, click the `Component` element and click a blank area on the diagram to create a new component element. Select the component and change its name to be `Book Web Service`. Select another `Component` element from the Toolbox window and click inside the `Book Web Service` component to create the new component inside the `Book Web Service` component. Name this component `CustomerApplicationServer`. Add a second component inside the `Book Web Service` component and name it `OrderProcessingServer`. The component diagram should now resemble Figure 3-8.

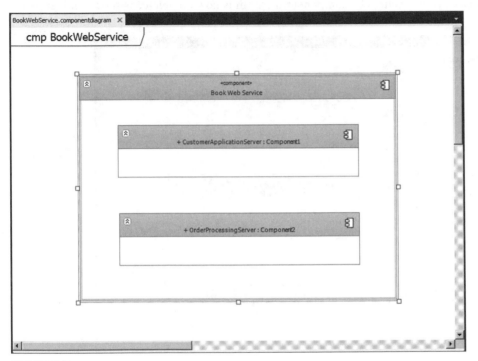

FIGURE 3-8

A component placed inside another component is called a *part*. A part is considered an attribute to its parent component, in the same way an attribute belongs to an ordinary class. A part has its own type, which is usually also a component. The label of a part has the same form as an attribute:
`+PartName : TypeName`

Inside the parent component, each part can have provided and required interfaces that are defined for its type. If you added existing components using the UML Model Explorer, any defined provided or required interfaces for that component will automatically be instantiated.

Add two required interfaces to the `CustomerApplicationServer` named `OrderBook` and `PaymentAuthorization`. Add a provided interface named `Sales`. To the `OrderProcessingServer`, add a provided interface named `OrderBook`. The component diagram should now resemble Figure 3-9.

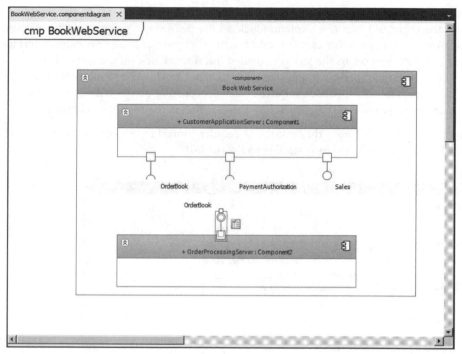

FIGURE 3-9

A nested component diagram can also show that an interface of the parent component is actually provided or required by one of its parts. This is done using a `Port` element. A `Port` element is placed on the parent component boundary, and the place the parent of the component's interface on the port. Finally, you connect the port to an interface of an internal part, using the `Delegation` element.

The example Web service has two external interfaces — a Web site provided interface, and a `PaymentAuthorization` required interface. Those interfaces are actually handled by the `CustomerApplicationServer` part. To handle this on the diagram, you must add ports to the `Book Web Service` component, add the external interfaces, and then connect the internal interfaces to the appropriate ports.

From the toolbox, select the `Port` element, then click on the `Book Web Service` component to create a port, which appears as a square box on the component. Change the name of the port element to be `WebsitePort`. Add a second port to the `Book Web Service` component and name it `PaymentAuthorizationPort`.

Once both ports are added, it's time to create the external interfaces for the `Book Web Service` component. From the toolbox, select the `Provided Interface` element, and then click the `WebsitePort` element on the diagram. A provided interface element will be added to the diagram, connected to `WebsitePort`. Change the name of the provided interface to `Website`. Add a required interface element, attached to the `PaymentAuthorizationPort` element, and change its name to `Payment Authorization`.

To finish out this component diagram, you must connect the internal components to the created ports. This is done using the Delegation element. Click on the Delegation element in the Toolbox window, then click on the WebsitePort element, and finally, click on the Sales provided interface. A solid arrow will connect the port to the Sales provided interface. Click on the Delegation element in the Toolbox window, then click on the PaymentAuthorizationPort element, and finally, click on the PaymentAuthorization required interface. A solid arrow will connect the PaymentAuthorization required interface with the PaymentAuthorizationPort element.

Add a Part Assembly element between the OrderBook required interface and OrderBook provided interface. The finished diagram should look similar to Figure 3-10.

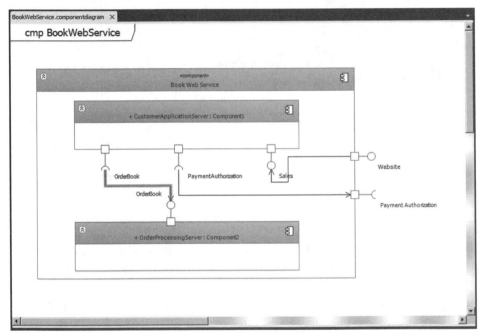

FIGURE 3-10

CLASS DIAGRAMS

Class diagrams depict the classes within an application or system and the relationship that exists between them. Different symbols represent the varying relationships that may exist (such as inheritance or association). This information is described independent of any reference to a particular implementation of the class. The purpose of the class diagram is to focus on the logical aspects of the classes, instead of how they are implemented.

 This chapter discusses UML class diagrams, or logical class diagrams. There is another type of class diagram, called a .NET class diagram, used to visualize program code. That is not discussed in this chapter.

In a class diagram, a *type* is a class, interface, or enumeration. Class and interface objects can have attributes defined. An *attribute* is a value that can be attached to an instance of a class or an interface. Classes and interfaces can also have operations defined. An *operation* is a method or function that can be performed by an instance of a class or interface.

On a class diagram, you can draw associations between any pairs of types. An *association* indicates that the system being developed stores links between the instances of the associated types. An association is a diagrammatic method of showing an attribute or pair of attributes. For example, if you have a class `BookStore` that has an attribute of type `Book`, you can state that definition by drawing an association between `Bookstore` and `Book`.

Using the Model Explorer, you can locate interfaces you have defined on the component diagram and drag those directly onto the class diagram to create them.

Understanding a Class Diagram

Let's look at a couple of examples of class diagrams to understand the different pieces. Figure 3-11 shows an example of the three standard kinds of types available for a class diagram:

➤ Classes are used to represent data or object types. `BookOrder` represents a class.

➤ `Color` represents an enumeration. An enumeration is used to represent a type that has a limited number of literal values.

➤ `Ordering` represents an interface. Interfaces are used when you must differentiate between a pure interface versus a concrete class with internal implementations.

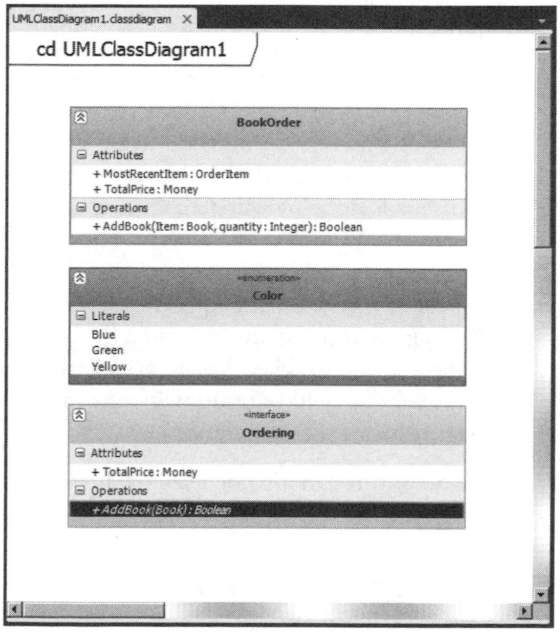

FIGURE 3-11

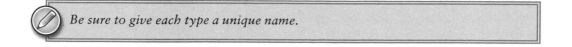

Be sure to give each type a unique name.

Classes and interfaces contain both attributes and operations. An attribute is simply a named value that every instance of the type can have. An operation is a method or function that instances of the type can perform. The `BookOrder` class has two attributes (`TotalPrice` and `MostRecentItem`), and one operation (`AddBook`). As you can see from the diagram, attributes are listed under the `Attributes` section, while operations are listed under the `Operations` section. These sections can be collapsed by clicking the plus sign to the left of each section.

Enumerations contain a list of values called *literals*. When using an enumeration, be sure to give each literal value a separate name. Literal values can also be assigned a numeric number as well, by setting the `Value` field in the Properties window.

Figure 3-12 shows another example of a class diagram. In this example, you see two classes, `BookStore` and `Book`. You want to show how these classes are related or linked to each other. This is done by using an `Association` element. The `Association` element appears as

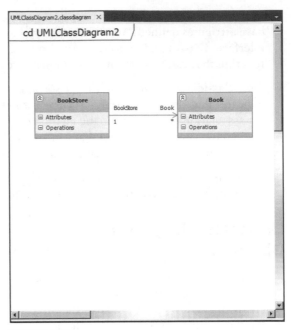

FIGURE 3-12

a line connecting the two classes. An `Association` element is used to represent any kind of linkage between two elements, regardless of how the linkage is actually implemented in the code itself. Figure 3-12 shows that the `BookStore` class has an association with the `Book` class, in that a `BookStore` may have multiple books in it (indicated by the asterisk on the right side of the association).

Class diagrams can also be used to show inheritance, dependency, and package information as well.

Class Diagram Toolbox

Figure 3-13 shows the different elements and associations available for class diagrams.

Table 3-3 describes the different elements and associations.

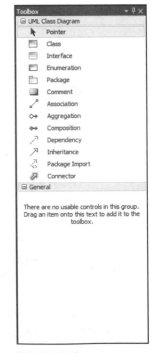

FIGURE 3-13

TABLE 3-3: Class Diagram Toolbox Objects

NAME	DESCRIPTION
Pointer	Turns the mouse back into a regular mouse pointer.
Class	Adds a type that defines a class.
Interface	Adds an interface to specify the attributes and operations that classes require to realize this interface.
Enumeration	Adds a type that defines a list of specific values.
Package	Adds a package to organize types according to their namespaces.
Comment	Adds a comment for more details.
Association	Defines how an element interacts with another element. Begin the relationship from the referencing type.
Aggregation	Specifies that the source type refers to parts of the target type. The parts can be shared with another owner.
Composition	Specifies that the source type has parts of the target type. The parts cannot be shared with another owner.
Dependency	Defines how a type depends on another type. Begin the relationship from the dependent type.
Inheritance	Defines how a type inherits or realizes the members of another type.
Package Import	Defines how a package imports types defined in another package. Begin the relationship from the package that uses another package.
Connector	This connection tool creates a default relationship between shapes, based on the types of shape being connected.

Class Diagram Type Properties

Each type on a class diagram has properties that can be manipulated using the Properties window in Visual Studio. To see the properties of a type, right-click on the type in the diagram and then select Properties. The properties will appear in the Properties window.

Table 3-4 describes the different properties available to class diagram types.

TABLE 3-4: Class Diagram Type Properties

PROPERTY	DEFAULT	APPEARS IN	DESCRIPTION
Name	A default name	All elements	Identifies the element.
Qualified Name	Containing Package::Type Name	All elements	Identifies the element uniquely. Prefixed with the qualified name of the package that contains it.
IsAbstract	False	Class	If True, the class cannot be instantiated, and is intended for use as a base class.
IsLeaf	False	Class, Interface	If True, the type is not intended to have derived types.
Visibility	Public	Class, Interface, Enumeration	Public — Globally visible.
			Private — This type is visible within the package that owns it.
			Package — Visible within the package.
Work Items	0	All elements	The number of work items associated with this element.
Description	(blank)	All elements	You can make general notes about the item here.
TemplateBinding	(none)	Class, Interface, Enumeration	The template type that this type instantiates. Expand the parameter to see the bindings of the template parameters.
TemplateParameters	(none)	Class, Interface, Enumeration	Lists the type's parameters. Used if this is a template type. To see the properties of individual parameters, click [. . .].

Class Diagram Attribute Properties

In a class diagram, you can add attributes to classes and interfaces. As mentioned previously, an attribute defines values that can be attached to instances of a class or interface.

Each attribute on a class or interface has properties that can be manipulated using the Properties window in Visual Studio. To see the properties of an attribute, right-click on the type in the diagram and then select Properties. The properties will appear in the Properties window.

Table 3-5 describes the different properties available to class diagram attributes.

TABLE 3-5: Class Diagram Attribute Properties

PROPERTY	DEFAULT	DESCRIPTION
Is Static	False	If True, a single value for this attribute is shared between all instances of this type. Also, the name of the attribute is underlined where it appears on the diagram.
Name	(a new name)	Should be unique within the type.
Type	(none)	A primitive type (such as Integer), or a type that is defined in the model.
Visibility	Public	+ Public — Visible globally.
		- Private — Not visible outside the owning type.
		# Protected — Visible to types derived from the owner.
		~ Package — Visible to other types within the same package.
Work Items	0	Count of associated work items. Read-only.
Is Leaf	False	If True, it is not intended to allow redefinition of this attribute in derived types.
Is Derived	False	If True, this attribute is calculated from other attributes.
Description	(empty)	For general notes, or for defining constraints on the values of the attribute.
Multiplicity	1	1 — This attribute has a single value of the specified type.
		0..1 — This attribute can have a value of null.
		* — This attribute's value is a collection of values.
		1..* — This attribute's value is a collection that contains at least one value.

continues

TABLE 3-5 *(continued)*

PROPERTY	DEFAULT	DESCRIPTION
		n..m — This attributes value is a collection that is contained between the n and m values.
Is Ordered	False	If True, the collection forms a sequential list. This is for Multiplicity of more than 1.
Is Unique	False	If True, there are no duplicate values in the collection. This is for Multiplicity of more than 1.

Class Diagram Operations Properties

In a class diagram, you can add operations to classes and interfaces. Remember, an operation is a method or function that can be performed by an instance of a class or interface.

Each operation on a class or interface has properties that can be manipulated using the Properties window in Visual Studio. To see the properties of an operation, right-click on the operation in the diagram and then select Properties. The properties will appear in the Properties window.

Table 3-6 describes the different properties available to class diagram operations.

TABLE 3-6: Class Diagram Operations Properties

PROPERTY	DEFAULT	DESCRIPTION
Name	(a new name)	Should be unique within the containing type.
Parameters	(none)	A list that has the form name:Type, name:Type, [...]. The types can be primitive types, or types that are defined in the model. Click [...] to edit the list.
Return Type	(none)	(none), or a primitive type, or a type that is defined in the model.
Visibility	Public	+ Public — Visible globally.
		- Private — Not visible outside the owning type.
		# Protected — Visible to types derived from the owner.
		~ Package — Visible to other types within the same package.
Signature	+Name()	Summarizes the visibility, name, parameters, and return type of the operation. Change these properties by editing the signature on the diagram, or editing the individual properties.

PROPERTY	DEFAULT	DESCRIPTION
Work Items	0	Count of associated work items. Read-only.
Concurrency	Sequential	Sequential — The operation is (or will be) designed without concurrency control. Calling this operation concurrently might result in failure.
		Guarded — The operation will automatically block until other instances of it have completed.
		Concurrent — The operation is designed so that multiple calls to it can execute concurrently.
Is Static	False	If True, this operation is shared between all instances of this type, and the name of the operation will appear underlined on the diagram.
Is Abstract	False	If True, no code is associated with this operation. Therefore, the owning class is abstract.
Is Leaf	False	The designer intends that this operation cannot be overridden in derived classes.
Is Query	False	If True, no significant changes to the state of the system are made by this operation.
Multiplicity	1	1 — A single value of the specified type.
		0..1 — Can be null.
		* — A collection of values of the specified type.
		1..* — A collection containing at least one value.
		n..m — A collection that is contained between the n and m values.
Is Ordered	False	If True, the collection forms a sequential list. For Multiplicity more than 1.
Is Unique	False	If True, there are no duplicate values in the collection. For Multiplicity more than 1.

Class Diagram Association Properties

In a class diagram, you can draw associations between any pair of types. Remember, a type is a class, interface, or enumeration.

Each association on a class or interface has properties that can be manipulated using the Properties window in Visual Studio. To see the properties of an association, right-click on the association in the diagram and then select Properties. The properties will appear in the Properties window.

Table 3-7 describes the different properties available to class diagram associations.

TABLE 3-7: Class Diagram Association Properties

PROPERTY	DESCRIPTION
Name	Identifies the association. Also appears on the diagram near the mid-point of the association.
Qualified Name	Identifies the association uniquely. Prefixed with the qualified name of the package that contains the association's first role.
Work Items	The number of work items linked to this association.
First Role, Second Role	Each end of the association is called a *role*. Each role describes the properties of the equivalent attribute on the class at the opposite end of the association.

Table 3-8 describes the different properties available to the `First Role` and `Second Role`.

TABLE 3-8: Class Diagram Role Properties

PROPERTY	DEFAULT	DESCRIPTION
Role Name	Name of the type at this role	The name of the role. Appears near the end of the association on the diagram.
Aggregation	None	None — Represents a general relationship between instances of the classes.
		Composite — The object at this role consists of or owns the object at the opposite role.
		Shared — Object at this role owns the object at the other role, but may share ownership.
		The exact interpretation is open to local convention.
Is Derived	False	If True, the object at this end of the link is calculated from other attributes and associations.
Is Derived Union	False	If True, the role is the union of a set of roles in derived types.
Is Navigable	True	The association can be read in this direction. Given an instance of the opposite role, the software that you are describing can efficiently determine the associated instance of this role. If one role is navigable and the other is not, an arrow appears on the association in the navigable direction.

PROPERTY	DEFAULT	DESCRIPTION
Is Read Only	False	If True, an instance of the association cannot be changed after it is created. The link is always to the same object.
Multiplicity	1	1 — This end of the association always links to one object.
		0..1 — Either this end of the association links to one object, or there is no link.
		* — Every object at the other end of the association is linked to a collection of objects at this end, and the collection may be empty.
		1..* — Every object at the other end of the association is linked to at least one object at this end.
		n..m — Each object at the other end has a collection between n and m links to objects at this end.
Is Ordered	False	If True, the returned collection forms a sequential list. For Multiplicity more than 1.
Is Unique	False	If True, there are no duplicate values in the returned collection. For Multiplicity more than 1.
Visibility	Public	Public — Visible globally.
		Private — Not visible outside the owning type.
		Protected — Visible to types derived from the owner.
		Package — Visible to other types within the same package.

Creating a Class Diagram

Let's look at how to create a class diagram. Using the same modeling project from before, right-click on the project in Solution Explorer, and, from the context menu, select Add ⇨ New Item.

Select the UML Class Diagram template and name it BooksClassDiagram.classdiagram. Click the Add button to create this diagram. A blank UML class diagram named BooksClassDiagram will be created in the modeling project and opened in Visual Studio.

In the Toolbox tab, click the Class element and then click a blank space on the UML class diagram. This will create a class object on the diagram. In the properties for the class, change the name to be `Store`. This is going to be a generic store class that the book store object will inherit from. Set the `Is Abstract` property of the `Store` class to `True`, to indicate it is an abstract class.

> Notice how, when setting the class to be abstract, the font of the title changes to italics.

The `Store` class has a couple of generic attributes that apply to all stores, such as location and store hours. Right-click on the `Store` class and select Add ➪ Attribute to create a new attribute. Name the attribute `Location`. Select the `Location` attribute, and, in the Properties window, set the `Type` property to be `String`. Add a second attribute named `StoreHours` and set its type to be `String` as well. The class diagram should appear similar to Figure 3-14.

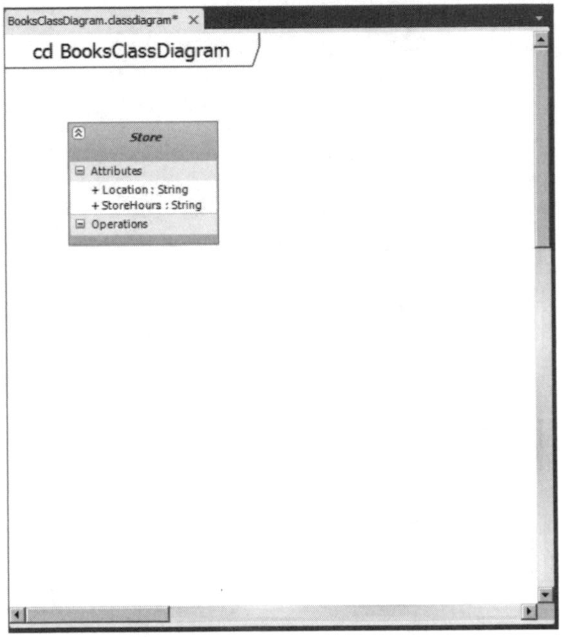

Next, you must create the book store class. The book store class will inherit from the `Store` class created earlier. Using the Toolbox window, add another `Class` object to the diagram, and name it `BookStore`. Select the `Inheritance` element in the Toolbox window. Click on the `BookStore` class, then on the `Store` class. A solid arrow will appear pointing from the `BookStore` class to the `Store` class, indicating that the `BookStore` inherits from the `Store`.

FIGURE 3-14

The inherited operations and attributes are not typically shown on specialized types, which is why the `Store` class attributes are not displayed on the `BookStore` class. However, you can use the smart tag on the inheritance arrow to add inherited operations to the specialized class. Simply click the smart tag and select Override Operations. Then, select which operations to show on the specialized class.

Let's add an operation for ordering books to the `BookStore` class. Right-click on the class and select Add ➪ Operation. Name the operation `OrderBook`. You must set the parameters and the return type for this operation. Select the `OrderBook` operation and go to the Properties window. In the Properties window, set the `Return Type` to be `Boolean`. Click the ellipses in the `Parameters` field to open the Parameter Collection Editor window.

In the Parameter Collection Editor window, click the Add button to create a new parameter. Set the name of the parameter to be `Item`, and the type to be `Book`. Click the Add button again to create a second parameter named `Quantity` with a type of `Integer`. Click the OK button to close the Parameter Collection Editor window. The class diagram should resemble Figure 3-15.

Finally, let's create a class for the books. Add another class object to the class diagram and rename it Book. Add two attributes to the Book class: Price of type Integer, and NumberOfPages of type Integer. Create an association between the BookStore and the Book classes. Select the Association element from the Toolbox window, click on the BookStore class and then click on the Book class. This creates a connecting line between the two classes, as shown in Figure 3-16.

FIGURE 3-15

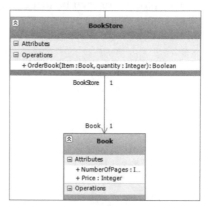

FIGURE 3-16

A BookStore can have multiple books in it, so you must modify the Multiplicity property for the Book class. Select the Association linking the BookStore and Book classes. In the Properties window, click the plus sign next to the Second Role property to expand it. Change the Multiplicity value to be *, indicating the BookStore can contain multiple books.

Figure 3-17 shows the final result of the class diagram.

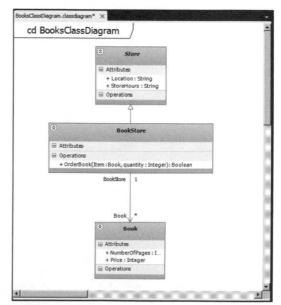

FIGURE 3-17

SUMMARY

This chapter examined component and class diagrams. You learned about what component diagrams can be used for, and the different elements available to component diagrams. You also learned about the different properties available to component diagram objects. A step-by-step walkthrough showed you how to create a component diagram. After that, you learned about class diagrams and how they can be used. You learned about the different elements that are available for class diagrams, and about all the different properties for class diagrams. The chapter concluded by looking at how to create a class diagram.

Chapter 4 discusses how the Architecture Explorer can be used to drill down into the existing project, which helps to understand the different aspects of the project. The information in the Architecture Explorer can then be turned into a graphical view by creating a dependency graph.

4

Analyzing Applications Using Architecture Explorer

WHAT'S IN THIS CHAPTER?

➤   Exploring the Architecture Explorer

➤   Using the Architecture Explorer to understand existing code

➤   Visualizing existing code using dependency graphs

Every software developer has been in the following situation at some point and time. You have just started a new job with a new company, expecting to come in and write some brand new, fancy application. You are up to speed on some of the latest coding technologies, methodologies, and languages. You arrive for work ready to sit down and use everything you know to crank out some brand new code to help the company succeed.

And then it happens. There is a legacy system that was built several years ago that must be updated. And you are the lucky developer who has been assigned to make that update. Never mind that you have no idea or concept of how the application works, the inner workings of the calls between different objects, or how it interacts with other third-party add-ins.

Before Visual Studio 2010 Ultimate, the only solution to this problem was to get your hands dirty in the code. You would have to open up the code files and start tracing (as best you could) how the logic flows between the different classes and components that make up the application. Maybe you would even try (as best you could) to diagram out the logic flow on a piece of scratch paper.

Visual Studio 2010 Ultimate changes all that with the introduction of the Architecture Explorer tool. Using Architecture Explorer, you can quickly learn more about your current application by visualizing the organization and relationships among the various parts. By using Architecture Explorer in conjunction with dependency graphs, a developer is able to analyze an existing system and quickly understand it. These tools also allow the developer to find areas in the application that should be improved or modified.

This chapter examines both Architecture Explorer and dependency graphs. The chapter begins with a discussion about the Architecture Explorer tool, what it is, and how it was designed to be used. From there, you will learn about using Architecture Explorer and how it can be used to drill down into your existing application.

After that, you will learn how to take the information from Architecture Explorer and make it graphical by turning it into a dependency diagram. Dependency diagrams are a nice way to graphically view your code, as well as code contained in other managed DLLs (such as the .NET Framework).

UNDERSTANDING THE CODE BASE

Though the example used through this chapter is rather simplistic, it works well to introduce the different capabilities of Architecture Explorer and dependency diagrams. So, let's take a look at the code base you will be using throughout this chapter, so that later sections will make more sense.

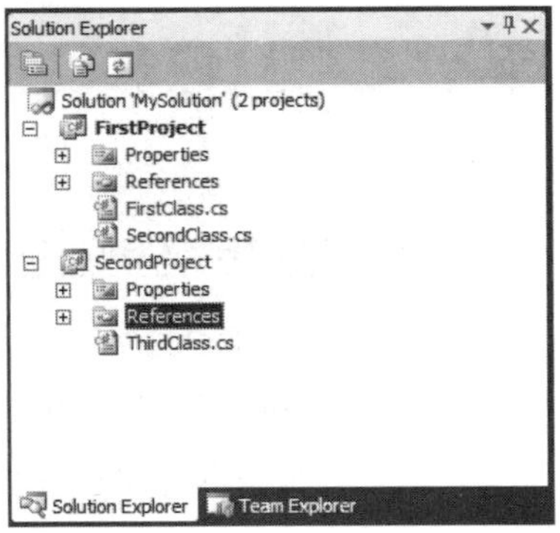

Figure 4-1 shows the projects and code files that make up the sample solution.

This solution is made up of two project files:

FIGURE 4-1

➤ `FirstProject` — This project contains two class files, `FirstClass.cs` and `SecondClass.cs`. The `FirstClass.cs` class file contains two methods, `Method1` and `Method2`. The `SecondClass.cs` class file contains one method, `Method3`.

➤ `SecondProject` — This project contains one class file, `ThirdClass.cs`. The `ThirdClass.cs` class file contains three methods: `Method4`, `Method5`, and `Method6`.

Getting confused yet? Let's add to it a little more:

➤ `Method1` calls `Method3` and `Method2`

➤ `Method2` calls `Method1`

➤ `Method3` doesn't call any other methods

➤ `Method4` calls `Method1`

➤ `Method5` calls `Method3`

➤ `Method6` doesn't call any other methods

Whew! All of that sounds just a little bit confusing, and this is only a contrived solution with two projects and three classes. Imagine what it would seem like with a real software solution with hundreds of projects and thousands of classes and methods. As you are about to learn, though, Architecture Explorer and dependency graphs are going to help with the understanding of any project, both small and large.

ARCHITECTURE EXPLORER BASICS

In Visual Studio 2010 Ultimate, Architecture Explorer is used to drill down into your existing code, allowing you to select the code you want to visualize using a dependency graph. Architecture Explorer can be used to browse existing source code open in Visual Studio 2010 Ultimate, as well as compiled managed code located in .dll or .exe files. Architecture Explorer can be extended by third parties, providing the capability to browse other domains of code or other items. Once you have drilled down into your code and selected the items you are interested in, you can turn that information into a dependency graph.

Understanding the Architecture Explorer Window

Architecture Explorer is only available in the Visual Studio 2010 Ultimate. To open Architecture Explorer, open Visual Studio 2010 Ultimate. From the main menu of Visual Studio, select View ⇨ Architecture Explorer. Alternately, from the main menu of Visual Studio, you can select Architecture ⇨ Windows ⇨ Architecture Explorer.

> 🖉 *The shortcut keys for opening Architecture Explorer are Ctrl+\ and Ctrl+R.*

Figure 4-2 shows an initial view of Architecture Explorer.

FIGURE 4-2

Architecture Explorer represents structures as *nodes*, and relationships as *links*. As you browse through your code base using Architecture Explorer, nodes will be displayed in successive columns to the right. The first column in Figure 4-2 shows the initial domains and views that are available for browsing. Selecting a domain or view will cause a new node to appear to the right, with the results of that selection.

> *You can browse all the way to the level of statements for Visual C# and Visual Basic projects. For other languages, you can browse to the procedure level.*

When you select a node in a column, the next column will show node information that is logically related to the selection made in the initial column. For example, selecting a class in a column will show the members of that class in the following column. You have the capability to select multiple nodes in multiple columns and then display that information as a dependency graph.

Architecture Explorer Options

As you can see in Figure 4-2, there are five options (represented as icons) available on the left side of the Architecture Explorer window.

The first option provides the capability to create a new dependency graph document from all the nodes currently selected in Architecture Explorer. To include only the nodes in the current column, you can press and hold the Ctrl key before clicking this option.

The second option enables you to add the selected nodes from Architecture Explorer to an existing dependency graph that is currently visible in Visual Studio. As with the first option, to include only the nodes that are in the current column, you can press and hold the Ctrl key before clicking this option.

The third option enables you to export the information from Architecture Explorer into a .dgml file. A Directed Graph Markup Language (DGML) file is the XML schema used to define a dependency graph. Selecting this option will export all the information open in all the columns into a .dgml file that can be viewed at a later date.

The fourth option resets Architecture Explorer to its initial state, cleaning up the window and allowing you to start from the beginning.

As you drill down into the architecture of your application using Architecture Explorer, behind the scenes, Visual Studio is keeping track of what you do by creating a query using a new language called the Directed Graph Query Language (DGQL). There will be times when you want to return Architecture Explorer to a certain state, drilled down to a certain level. This is accomplished by using the fifth option on the toolbar, which allows you to save the state of Architecture Explorer as a query that can be re-run at a later time.

Navigating Through Architecture Explorer

To begin navigating through Architecture Explorer, select one of the rows in the first column. You have several options.

Under the column heading, Visual Studio, you can choose to view the information in your solution either by classes or through a solution view, which allows you to view the different files in your solution. If you don't want to drill down through all the files in a solution, you can click the Select Files option and open just the files you are interested in.

Optionally, you can open and run a saved DGQL query. You can choose to open a query that has been saved in the current solution, or a query that has been saved to a shared folder. Opening the query will run the query, and set Architecture Explorer to the appropriate state.

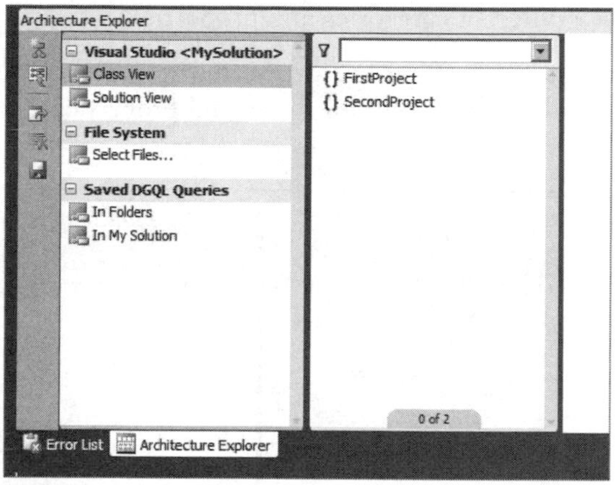

For this example, let's navigate through the code using the Class View options. In Architecture Explorer, select Class View under Visual Studio <My Solution>. This opens a new column to the right of the selected column, displaying a list of all the different namespaces in the solution, as shown in Figure 4-3.

In Figure 4-3, you see that the two namespaces currently in the solution (`FirstProject` and `SecondProject`) are displayed on the right of the screen.

Obviously, for a large project, you could have many namespaces, which could result in a large scrolling list in this column. The list box at the top of the column enables you to filter the information in this column. For example, if you only wanted to see namespaces that began with the "Second," you could type **Second** in the list box, press Enter, and the contents of the column would be filtered, as shown in Figure 4-4.

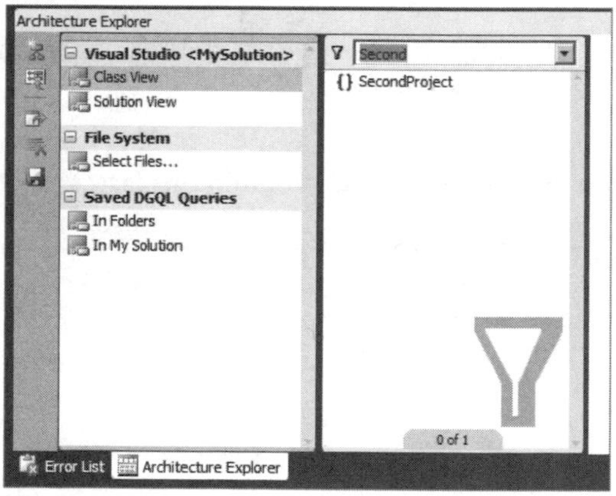

Notice the differences between Figure 4-3 and Figure 4-4. Figure 4-3 displays all the namespaces in the solution. Figure 4-4 displays only the namespaces that match the filter expression. Also, notice the filter icon that is added in the lower right of the column, giving a visual indication that the column is currently being filtered.

FIGURE 4-3

FIGURE 4-4

When you type in a filter, a substring search is performed. For example, if you enter **c** for the filter statement, it will match on both `FirstProject` and `SecondProject`.

To clear the filtering on a column, simply delete the filter statement and press Enter. This will remove the filter and display the entire contents of the column.

From the namespace column, you can navigate into the different classes contained in a particular namespace. Selecting the `FirstProject` namespace opens a new column to the right, containing the classes contained in the `FirstProject` namespace — in this case, `FirstClass` and `SecondClass`. As mentioned previously, you have the capability to filter on this column by entering your filter criteria into the list box at the top of the column. You also have the capability to filter based on different categories and properties.

Click the filter button located to the left of the filter list box at the top of the column. This displays all the possible categories and properties that can be filtered on, as shown in Figure 4-5.

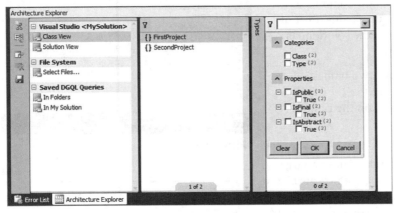

FIGURE 4-5

For this particular column on classes, you have the following filter options:

➤ Class

➤ Type

➤ IsPublic

➤ IsFinal

➤ IsAbstract

➤ IsInternal

You have the option of selecting one or multiple filter options, allowing you to drill down into the information contained in the column in a variety of ways.

Exploring Options for Namespaces

In addition to the filtering options mentioned previously, you have another option for controlling what is displayed in a column. Notice in Figure 4-5, just to the left of the column containing the classes, there is a collapsed column with the name Types. Clicking on that collapsed column will expand it, as shown in Figure 4-6.

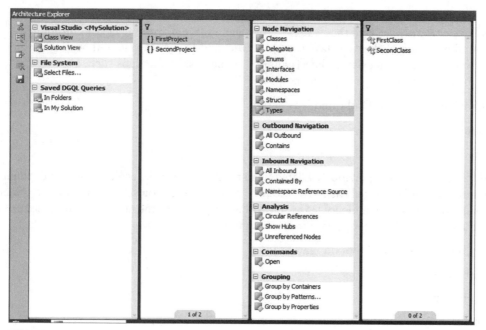

FIGURE 4-6

This column provides a variety of options for determining what is initially displayed in the column. The first section is the Node Navigation section. By default, the Types node is selected, which shows all the different available types — in this case, FirstClass and SecondClass. You have the capability to select the following nodes for display:

- Classes
- Delegates
- Enums
- Interfaces
- Modules
- Namespaces
- Structs
- Types

You can select multiple nodes by holding down the Ctrl key while you select the nodes. Each time you select a node, the column to the right will recalculate with the new data to display.

You have the capability to organize the link types into two categories: outbound and inbound. These categories describe the direction of the link in relation to the currently selected node.

An *outbound link* points from the currently selected node to the next related node. For example, say that you have currently selected the FirstProject namespace. If you select All Outbound under Outbound Navigation, the two classes, FirstClass and SecondClass, will be displayed. FirstClass and SecondClass exist in the FirstProject namespace, and, as such, are the next related nodes beneath the FirstProject namespace.

You have following options for Outbound Navigation:

➤   All Outbound

➤   Contains

An *inbound link* points from a previously related node to the currently selected node. For example, say that you have currently selected the FirstProject namespace. If you select All InBound under Inbound Navigation, the solution file MySolution will be displayed in the next column. MySolution exists above the FirstProject namespace from a hierarchical perspective.

The following options exist for Inbound Navigation:

➤   All Inbound

➤   Contained by

➤   Namespace Reference Source

You also have the capability to perform Analysis and Grouping options. Using the Analysis options, you can look for circular references, or *hubs* (for example, classes) that are not being called or used. The Grouping options also allow you to group by container or properties or by using a pattern specified in a DGML file.

The following options exist for Analysis:

➤   Circular References

➤   Show Hubs

➤   Unreferenced Nodes

The following options exist for Grouping:

➤   Group by Containers

➤   Group by Patterns

➤   Group by Properties

Exploring Options for Classes

Previously, you learned about some of the Node Navigation options from a namespace perspective. Let's continue the example by selecting the FirstClass class in Architecture Explorer to see what Node Navigation options are from a class perspective. Figure 4-7 shows Architecture Explorer after the FirstClass class has been selected.

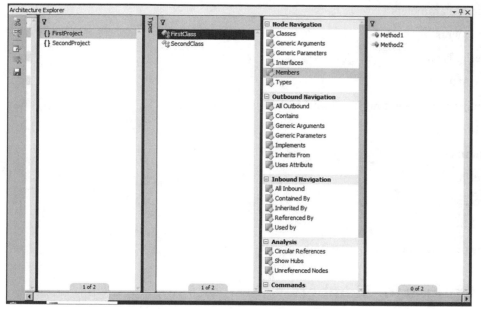

FIGURE 4-7

By default, Node Navigation defaults to Members. As you can see in Figure 4-7, `FirstClass` has only two members, two methods named `Method1` and `Method2`. As you might expect, the filtering options at the top of the column work the same as they have in previous columns. However, now that you are working on a class level as opposed to a namespace level, you have different navigation options.

From the Node Navigation options, you can view any of the following information about the selected class:

- ➤ Classes
- ➤ Generic Arguments
- ➤ Generic Parameters
- ➤ Interfaces
- ➤ Members
- ➤ Types

Outbound Navigation has several more options available to it, as you would expect. Classes can inherit from other classes, implement interfaces, and have attributes. The following are the Outbound Navigation options:

- ➤ All Outbound
- ➤ Contains
- ➤ Generic Arguments

➤ Generic Parameters

➤ Implements

➤ Inherits From

➤ Uses Attribute

Inbound Navigation also has more options, including the following:

➤ All Inbound

➤ Contained By

➤ Inherited By

➤ Referenced By

➤ Used By

The Analysis patterns and Grouping options are the same as before.

Exploring Options for Members

In this example, let's drill down one more level by looking at some of the Node Navigation options available at a member level. In Architecture Explorer, let's select the `Method1` method, as shown in Figure 4-8.

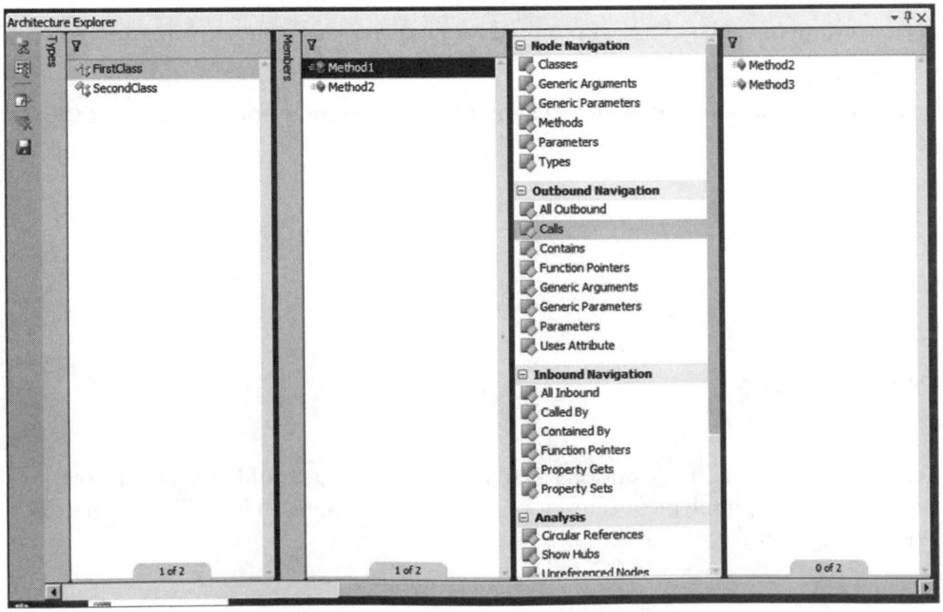

FIGURE 4-8

As you would expect, the Node Navigation options have changed again. By default, when you select a method, the resulting column in Architecture Explorer shows all the outbound calls that method makes (that is, all the methods that the selected method uses).

From a Node Navigation perspective, you can view any of the following information about the selected method:

➤ Classes

➤ Generic Arguments

➤ Generic Parameters

➤ Methods

➤ Parameters

➤ Types

Outbound Navigation has several more options available to it, as you would expect. The following are the Outbound Navigation options:

➤ All Outbound

➤ Calls

➤ Contains

➤ Function Pointers

➤ Generic Arguments

➤ Generic Parameters

➤ Parameters

➤ Uses Attribute

Inbound Navigation also has more options, including the following:

➤ All Inbound

➤ Called By

➤ Contained By

➤ Function Pointers

➤ Property Gets

➤ Property Sets

The Analysis patterns and Grouping options are the same as before.

Architecture Explorer Queries

As you continue to drill down into your code, Architecture Explorer will continue to expand to the right. As you can imagine, this could lead to a rather convoluted path through Architecture

Explorer. Obviously, once you have found the information you are concerned with, it would be nice to be able to instantly return to that information, rather than have to drill all the way back down once more.

Architecture Explorer allows you to do this by saving your path through it as a DGQL query. To do this, in Architecture Explorer, click the "Save Query to Favorites" button. You will be prompted to save your query, which contains all the information you have selected and navigated through using Architecture Explorer.

By default, the query will be saved to `My Documents\Visual Studio 2010\ ArchitectureExplorer\Queries`. You can also save queries directly into your solution as well.

> *By saving your queries with your solution, they can be placed into Team Foundation Version Control with the rest of your solution. This allows you to version-control your queries, as well as make the queries available to anyone who is using your solution file.*

Figure 4-9 shows how you can access your queries using Architecture Explorer.

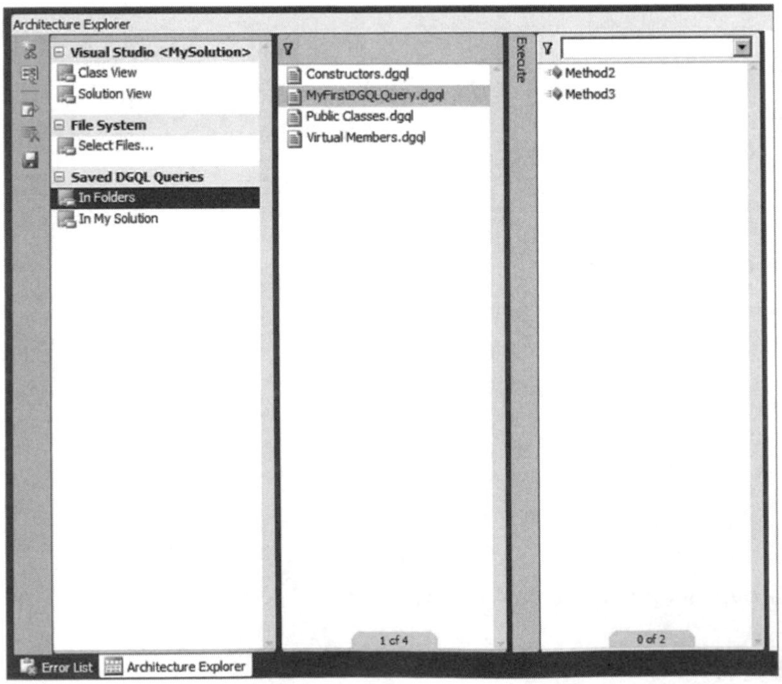

FIGURE 4-9

In the first column, under Saved DGQL queries, you can select either the In Folders or the In My Solution option. The In Folders option looks in the `My Documents\Visual Studio 2010\ArchitectureExplorer\Queries` for DGQL queries, while the In My Solution option looks in your solution for any referenced queries.

DEPENDENCY GRAPHS

They say a picture is worth a thousand words, and dependency graphs prove that saying. Architecture Explorer is invaluable for its capability to drill down into the code base. But it can also present so much information that it can be a bit overwhelming as well. Given its capability to continuously scroll to the right, you could become confused after doing an intense, deep drill-down. Wouldn't it be nice to be able to visualize the information from Architecture Explorer? Dependency graphs allow you to do just that.

A dependency graph can be used to explore the relationships and organization of an existing code base. These graphs make it easy to understand code that is new or unfamiliar to you. The relationships on the graph make it readily apparent how different areas of code relate to one another, and can show you how a change to one area of code could cause potential issues for other areas of the code. As you will see, you have multiple ways to view your dependency graph information.

> *A dependency graph will show only those dependencies in code that have gone through a successful build. Any code that did not build successfully will not appear on the dependency graph.*

> *Dependency graphs are also referred to as* directed graphs. *The two terms are used interchangeably.*

Creating the First Dependency Graph

You actually have several different options for creating a dependency graph. Since the first half of this chapter has dealt with Architecture Explorer, let's will continue that thread, and show how you can create dependency graphs from Architecture Explorer. Later, you will learn how you can create dependency graphs without using Architecture Explorer to get a quick overview of your source code or compiled code.

Previously, using Architecture Explorer, you learned how to drill down into your source code. You saw how to select the `FirstProject` namespace, the `FirstClass` class, and the `Method1` method. From here, let's select `Method2` and `Method3` in Architecture Explorer.

To display this information as a dependency graph, simply click the "Create A New Graph Document" button on the Architecture Explorer window. This will take all the information selected in Architecture Explorer and display it as a dependency graph, as shown in Figure 4-10.

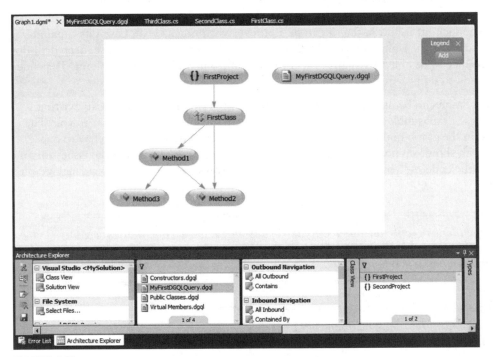

FIGURE 4-10

As you can see, this graph provides an easy-to-understand graphical overview of the information contained in Architecture Explorer. You can see that the `FirstProject` namespace contains the `FirstClass` class. The `FirstClass` class contains two methods, `Method1` and `Method2`. And `Method1` makes references to both `Method2` and `Method3`.

But the dependency graph can do much more than just show the layout of method calls. By hovering the mouse over a node in the graph, you can view detailed information about that node. Figure 4-11 shows the information that is displayed for `Method1` when the mouse is hovered over the `Method1` node.

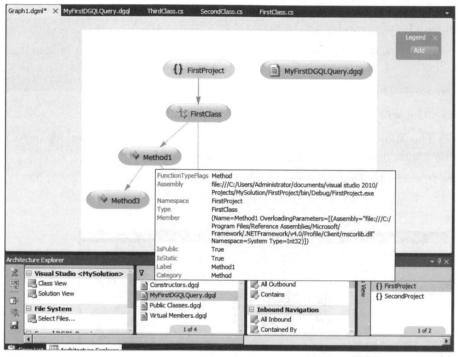

FIGURE 4-11

This information shows the type of function this is (in this case, a method). It shows the assembly where this method resides, along with namespace and type information. It also shows helpful information such as whether the method is static, and if it is a public or private method. All this information can help you understand your code base better, without having to open a code file.

However, if you want to view the code file for a particular node, that is easy to do from the dependency graph. You simply right-click on the node and select View Content from the context menu. This will open the code file associated with the selected node.

You can easily add more nodes to an existing dependency graph. Let's say you create an initial dependency graph using Architecture Explorer. Now, let's say that you want to add more nodes to the graph to make it more detailed. Select the nodes you want to add in Architecture Explorer, and then click the "Add Selected Nodes to Existing Graph" button on the left-hand side of the Architecture Explorer window. This adds the selected nodes to the existing graph.

Creating a Dependency Graph without Architecture Explorer

You also have the capability to create a dependency graph without even opening Architecture Explorer. This can be very handy when you want to analyze the entire code base of your code, without having to worry about drilling down through particular elements using Architecture Explorer. For example, you can drag and drop a .NET assembly onto a blank diagram and it will automatically decompose the assembly for you.

From the main menu of Visual Studio 2010, select Architecture ⇨ Generate Dependency Graph. This provides you with four options for generating your dependency graph:

➤ *By Assembly* — This will add a node to the graph for each assembly element in your solution.

➤ *By Namespace* — This will add a node for each namespace in your solution.

➤ *By Class* — This will add a node for each class in your solution.

➤ *Custom* — This allows you to select from a variety of options for what to include in your dependency graph, including assembly, namespace, and class.

Figure 4-12 shows an example of a dependency graph generated using the By Assembly option.

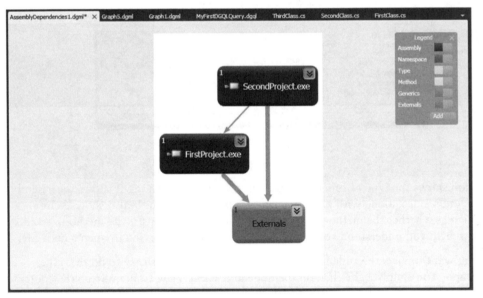

FIGURE 4-12

Each project will generate its own assemblies, which, in the example project, would be `FirstProject.exe` and `SecondProject.exe`. In addition, there is a reference to an `Externals` assembly, which includes the references and calls into the .NET Framework. Though the black-and-white picture may not show it well, the legend is color-coded to help you easily understand the different aspects of your dependency graph.

Navigating Through Your Dependency Graph

You may be thinking that the information shown in Figure 4-12 is nice, but it is not that helpful. It sure would be nice if you could drill down into the dependency graph, in a manner similar to how you drill down into information in Architecture Explorer. Well, guess what? You can!

By clicking the chevrons located at the top-right of a node, you can expand the node to view the detailed information in that node, as shown in Figure 4-13.

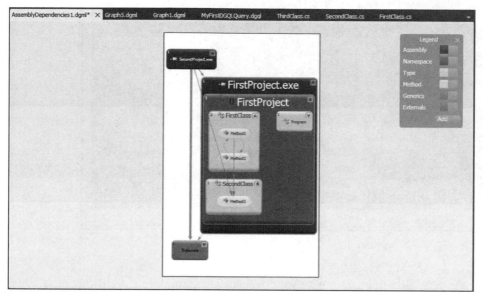

FIGURE 4-13

`FirstProject.exe` is comprised of the `FirstProject` namespace. The namespace contains three classes: `FirstClass`, `SecondClass`, and `Program`. `FirstClass` contains two methods, `Method1` and `Method2`. `SecondClass` contains one method, `Method3`.

The dependency graph shows the interactions between the different methods. It also shows that the `SecondProject.exe` assembly makes calls to `Method3` in the `SecondClass` class. To view exactly which object is making this call, you can expand the information for that assembly on the dependency graph.

> *The information displayed in Figure 4-13 is the same information displayed in Figure 4-10, just in a different format. A dependency graph can be formatted using a variety of different options.*

The next question you might have is whether you can drill down into that external node. The answer is, yes! Using a dependency graph, you can drill down into external assemblies (such as the .NET Framework). This is an incredibly powerful tool. You now have the capability to delve into the .NET Framework and map how all the objects and methods interact with each other, allowing you to come to a much better and deeper understanding of how the .NET Framework works. Figure 4-14 shows an example of this.

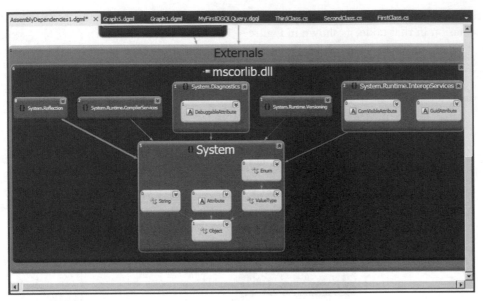

FIGURE 4-14

You also have the capability to interact with your dependency graph by right-clicking on the graph, and selecting from a variety of context menu options. You will recognize many of the options from Architecture Explorer. The exact options will depend on what is selected on the dependency graph.

You can select a specific node on a graph and then choose the Selection menu option from the context menu. This enables you to do the following:

➤ Select all incoming links to the selected node

➤ Select all outgoing links from the selected node

➤ Select both incoming and outgoing links from the selected node

➤ Select all connected nodes to the selected node

➤ Select all children of the selected node

You have the capability to add groups and categories to the graph, enabling you to organize the graph in a more readable fashion.

Let's refer back to Figure 4-10 to show another nice feature of dependency graphs, which is the capability to apply different analyzers to the information on the graph. You saw these analyzers before when working with Architecture Explorer, but they make even more sense when seen in conjunction with the dependency graph.

Let's say you were to right-click on the graph shown in Figure 4-10, select Analyzer, and then select Circular References. This analyzer looks for circular references, or infinite loops, in your graph. When those references are found, it highlights them (in red) on the dependency graph, instantly bringing them to your attention, as shown in Figure 4-15.

FIGURE 4-15

A second analyzer that is available is the Show Hubs analyzer. This analyzer shows which hubs are in the top 25 percent of high-connected nodes. This is a quick-and-easy way to see which hubs are involved with a majority of the work in the application.

A third analyzer that is available is the Unreferences Nodes analyzer. This analyzer highlights any nodes that are not referenced by any other nodes. They are orphans. This is a good way to find areas of the code that are not being used, either because of oversight, or because they are no longer needed.

Dependency Graph Legend

In the upper-right corner of each dependency graph is the *legend* (see Figure 4-10). The legend can be used to help you understand all the different components that make up the dependency graph. One nice feature of the legend is that it is completely customizable, allowing you to control the shapes and colors that are used on the graph, thus enabling you to customize the graph to your needs.

For the dependency graph shown in Figure 4-10, if you were to click the Add button on the legend, you would have the following four options that could be added to the graph:

- ➤ Node Property
- ➤ Node Category
- ➤ Link Property
- ➤ Link Category

Each of these options has sub-options underneath it that can be added to the legend. For Node Property, the options are the following:

- ➤ IsAbstract
- ➤ IsFinal
- ➤ IsPublic
- ➤ IsStatic
- ➤ FunctionTypeFlags
- ➤ Hub
- ➤ StronglyConnected

For Node Category, the options are the following:

- ➤ Class
- ➤ Method
- ➤ Namespace
- ➤ Solution
- ➤ Source File

For Link Property, the option is the following:

➤   Circular Link

And, finally, for Link Category, the options are the following:

➤   Calls

➤   Contains

Once a new item has been added to the legend, its appearance can be customized. You can click on the icon in the legend and select from the following four customization options:

➤   *Background* — This lets you select a color for the background of the node.

➤   *Stroke* — This selects the color that outlines the node.

➤   *Foreground* — This sets the text color in the node.

➤   *Icons* — This allows you to select from a wide variety of icons to add into the node itself.

Figure 4-16 shows an example of a dependency graph that has been "spruced up" using these options.

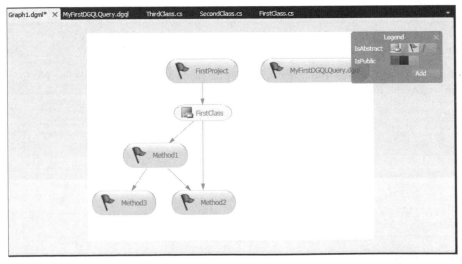

FIGURE 4-16

Dependency Graph Toolbar

Figure 4-17 shows the dependency graph toolbar.

FIGURE 4-17

This toolbar can be used to modify the look and feel of a dependency graph. At the far left of the toolbar are the zoom controls. As you can imagine, a dependency graph can grow to be quite large. These tools allow you to zoom into and out of areas of the graph that you are interested in. The drop-down list box can be used to fit the graph to the page, or to select pre-specified zoom options.

The next five toolbar icons are used to specify the directional flow of the dependency graph. These options include (reading from left to right) left-to-right, right-to-left, top-to-bottom, and bottom-to-top. By default, the third option (a top-to-bottom flow) is used. Simply click the appropriate button on the toolbar, and the dependency graph will re-orient itself. The fifth option is the Force Directed Layout view. This view shows the nodes as clusters or hubs. In this view, the graph is arranged with the most-dependent nodes near the center, and the least-dependent nodes at the outer edges of the clusters of hubs.

The next four buttons allow any regular dependency graph to be turned into a matrix view. Select the Dependency Matrix View toolbar button to create a matrix view. Figure 4-18 shows an example of the Dependency Matrix View. This takes the information from the dependency graph and turns it into a matrix, where the intersecting portions of the matrix indicated interactions between the different nodes. The next two buttons are sort buttons (the buttons marked AZ), which can be used to change the sort order of the rows and columns in the dependency matrix. The final button of that group is the Show Reflexive View button, which shows a different take on the dependency matrix.

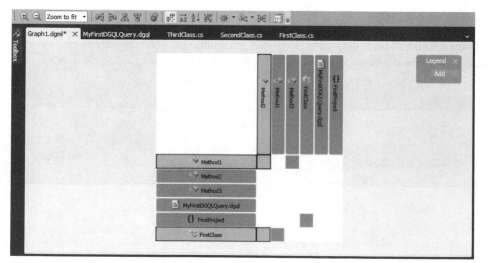

FIGURE 4-18

The next button on the toolbar provides the capability to control when cross-group links are shown. By default, cross-group links are shown only on selected nodes. Using this button, that can be changed to show all cross-group links on the graph, or to hide all cross-group links on the graph.

The next two buttons are extremely useful when dealing with large diagrams. The Neighborhood Browse Mode button allows you to show only those nodes that are a specific number of links away from a selected node. To turn on this mode, click this button, then select from the drop-down list the level of nodes you want to view. This allows you to take a large diagram and view it in more discrete chunks.

Next to the Neighborhood Browse Mode button is the Butterfly mode button. This button turns the graph into a butterfly tree view by hiding links that do not live on a path through the selected nodes.

Be careful, because circular links do not appear while in this mode. As well, dependencies that are more than one level away from the selected node will not necessarily appear in order. As with the Neighborhood Browse Mode, the Butterfly Mode is a good way of dealing with large diagrams, breaking them down to make them easier to understand.

SUMMARY

This chapter examined both Architecture Explorer and dependency graphs. The chapter started off discussing Architecture Explorer, why you would want to use it, and how to use it. From there, you walked through an example of using Architecture Explorer, while learning about many of its features.

The discussion then moved on to dependency graphs. You learned how dependency graphs can be created with information from Architecture Explorer, as well as directly from solutions or compiled assemblies. You also learned about dependency graphs in depth and how to use all the options available.

Chapter 5 is the final chapter on the architecture tools available in Visual Studio 2010 Ultimate. Chapter 5 looks at layer diagrams, how they are built, and how they are useful in dividing your code base into understandable sections, as well as how they can be used as a validation tool during the build process.

5

Using Layer Diagrams

WHAT'S IN THIS CHAPTER?

➤ Understanding a layer diagram

➤ Creating layer diagrams

➤ Defining dependencies on a layer diagram

➤ Validation using a layer diagram

In the past several chapters, you have learned about some of the different modeling diagrams available in the Visual Studio 2010 Ultimate. This chapter examines the final diagram — the layer diagram.

Layer diagrams are used to describe the structure of an application at a high level. These diagrams can also be used to verify that the developed code conforms to the high-level design laid out in the layer diagram. One nice feature about layer diagrams is the capability to validate application design architecture against the code base, ensuring that the code and architecture continue to match during the development process.

In a way similar to a traditional architecture diagram, a layer diagram shows the major components of the architecture design. Dependencies between the components are also laid out on the diagram. A diagram consists of one or more nodes, referred to as *layers*. A layer can be used to represent any sort of logical group — for example, a namespace or a class file. When you define dependencies on a layer diagram, you can specify them on the diagram because of the architecture design, or you can automatically discover them based on the dependencies already built into the code. Layer diagrams can also be incorporated into the automated build process, allowing you to verify that code changes match to architectural constraints.

This chapter examines layer diagrams in detail. You will first learn how a layer diagram is created. Next, you will learn how layers are added to a diagram, both by using the toolbox and by building layers from an existing code base. You will see how the Layer Explorer can be used to provide a detailed look at what artifacts are contained within a layer. This chapter wraps up by looking a layer validation, and how to include layer validation in the build process.

CREATING A LAYER DIAGRAM

To use a layer diagram, you must add a new one to the solution with which you are currently working. Creating a new blank layer diagram requires the use of either an existing modeling project, or the creation of a new modeling project in the current solution. Because layer diagrams are simply another type of diagram in Visual Studio, they must have a modeling project to be stored in.

To create a new blank layer diagram in the solution, select Architecture from the Visual Studio main menu, and then select New Diagram. This opens the Add New Diagram window, as shown in Figure 5-1.

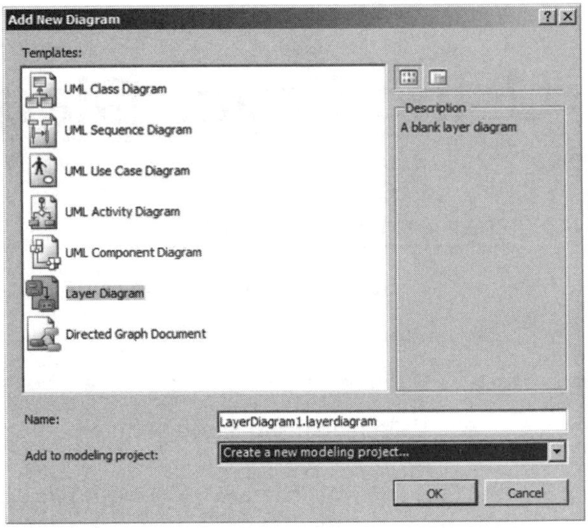

In the Add New Diagram window,
select the Layer Diagram. In the Name field, enter the name of your layer diagram. All layer diagrams end in .layerdiagram, to indicate a diagram is a layer diagram.

FIGURE 5-1

If the solution contains an existing modeling project, it can be selected in the "Add to modeling project" drop-down box. If the current solution does not contain a modeling project, then select "Create a new modeling project" in the drop-down list box, and the Add New Diagram window will prompt you to create a new modeling project.

Once you have selected the layer diagram model type, given a name to the model, and selected the appropriate option from the modeling project drop-down list box, click the OK button. If a new modeling project is being created, the Create New Modeling Project window will open, as shown in Figure 5-2.

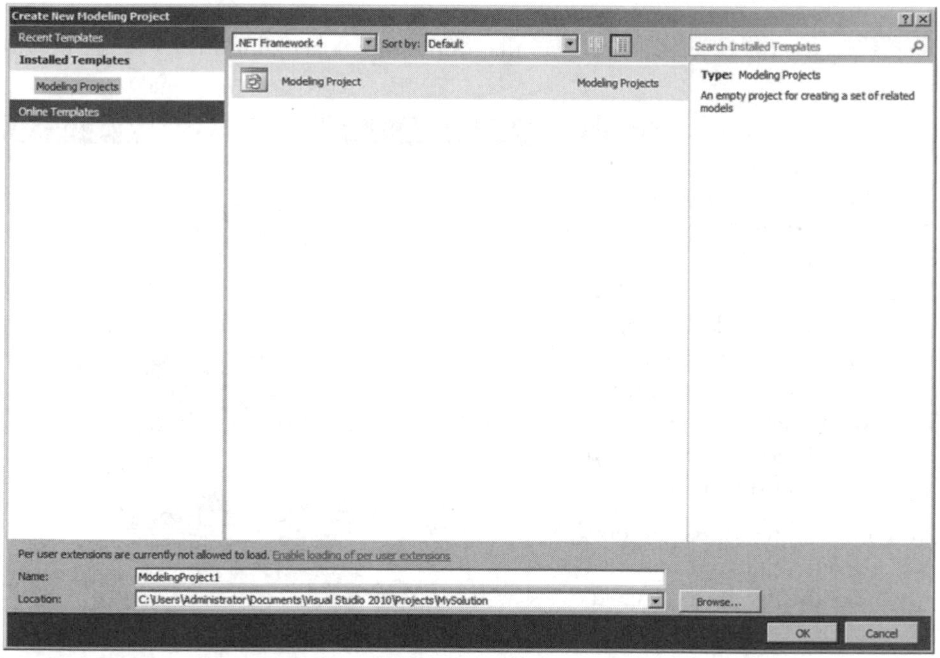

FIGURE 5-2

Obviously, Modeling Project is the only option available for creating a new modeling project, though the .NET Framework support for the modeling project can be controlled by selecting the appropriate version for the framework at the top of the window. Enter a name for the modeling project and the location to store the project and then click OK. The modeling project will be created, a new blank layer diagram will be created inside the modeling project, and the new blank layer diagram will be opened in a tab in Visual Studio.

> *Although a layer diagram is located in a modeling project, it can link to any artifact in the current Visual Studio solution.*

DEFINING LAYERS ON A LAYER DIAGRAM

The next step is to define the different layers on the layer diagram. Each layer on a layer diagram appears as a rectangle. Different layers can be nested inside each other, which is called *grouping*. The different layers in a layer diagram are used to define logical groups of artifacts, including methods, classes, and namespaces.

Layers can be defined on the layer diagram by dragging objects from the layer diagram toolbox, dragging objects from Solution Explorer, or dragging objects from the Architecture Explorer.

There are multiple ways to add layers to the layer diagram. The easiest way is to use the layer diagram toolbox. Let's use the objects in the layer diagram toolbox to define a layer diagram with three sections.

Drag a layer object from the toolbox onto the blank diagram. A rectangle will appear on the diagram with the default name Layer 1. Double-click the layer and change the name to UI Layer. Next, drag another layer object from the toolbox, and place it directly below the UI Layer object. Double-click this object and rename it Business Logic Layer. Finally, drag a third layer object onto the diagram below the other two and rename it Data Access Layer. Figure 5-3 shows what the layer diagram should look like at this point.

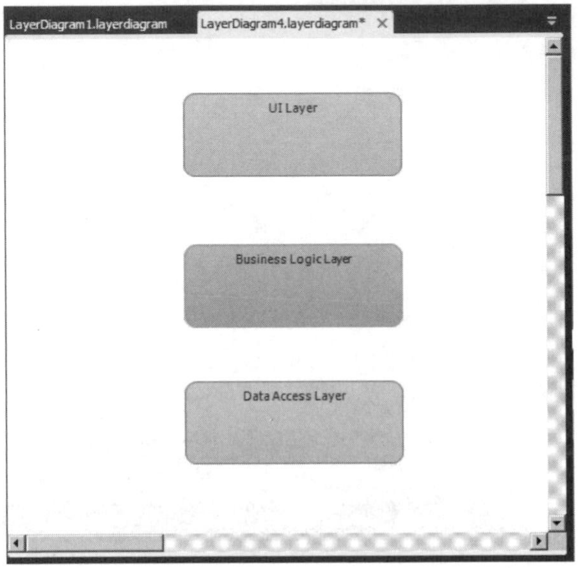

At this point, you have created three "unlinked" layers. The layers are referred to as "unlinked" because currently no code files are associated with these layers. This is useful to help represent different parts of an application that have not yet been developed. You will continue to build off this layer diagram later in this chapter. But, for now, let's continue to look at the different ways layers can be added to a layer diagram.

FIGURE 5-3

Creating a Layer for a Single Artifact

As mentioned previously, a layer represents a logical grouping of artifacts. There may be times when a single artifact (such as a project, or even a single code file) must be represented as its own layer. This is easy to do with a layer diagram. In fact, you can use any of the following sources to add layers to a layer diagram:

➤ *Solution Explorer* — From within Solution Explorer, you can drag and drop any file or project contained in the Solution Explorer onto the layer diagram surface. A new layer will be created with the name of that file or project, and will contain a link to the file or project.

➤ *Architecture Explorer* — Using the Architecture Explorer, you can drill down to the information you are interested in (such as namespaces), and drag and drop those namespaces onto the surface. Those namespaces will appear as a layer on the diagram, again with that layer linked to the information that was dropped onto the diagram.

➤ *Dependency Graphs* — You also have the capability to drop dependency graph information directly onto a layer diagram to create layers.

Adding Multiple Objects to a Layer Diagram

When you drag and drop multiple items to a layer diagram at the same time, the default action is to create a single layer on the diagram, with all the objects contained within that layer. To create a layer for each artifact that is dropped as a group, simply hold down the Shift key while dropping the artifacts onto the layer diagram. A layer for each artifact will appear on the diagram, and each layer will be linked to its appropriate artifact.

To add an artifact to an existing layer, simply drop the artifact onto an existing layer on the layer diagram. A link will be established between the layer and the artifact.

As a general rule, you should always place artifacts in the same layer if they have some sort of close interdependence. Artifacts that can be easily updated separately (or, for example, are used in separate applications) should be in different layers.

The Layer Explorer

To understand how links are added to a layer diagram and how to view the linked information between a particular layer on a layer diagram and its linked artifacts, let's continue to build off the layer diagram from Figure 5-3.

From Solution Explorer, right-click on `FirstClass.cs`, and drag and drop it onto the UI Layer of the layer diagram. Visually, the only thing that changes on the diagram is that the number "1" appears in the top-left corner of UI Layer. This number indicates the number of artifacts that have been linked to this particular layer. Now, drag the `SecondClass.cs` object from the Solution Explorer onto the Business Logic layer. You should see the number "1" appear on that layer. Finally, drag the `ThirdClass.cs` object from the Solution Explorer to the Data Access Layer. The layer diagram should now resemble Figure 5-4.

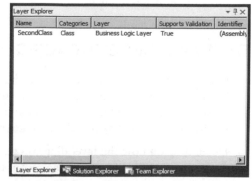

FIGURE 5-4

In Figure 5-4, you see three layers, with each layer containing one artifact. But how do you go about viewing which artifacts are contained within which layers? That is where the Layer Explorer comes in.

The Layer Explorer is used to view artifacts that are linked to a particular layer, and to move artifacts between layers. To open the Layer Explorer, right-click on a layer in the layer diagram and select View Links. By default, the Layer Explorer will open on the right-hand side of Visual Studio, usually as a tab in the same window as the Solution Explorer, as shown in Figure 5-5.

FIGURE 5-5

The Layer Explorer will display all the artifacts that are linked to a particular layer. As shown in Figure 5-5, the Layer Explorer contains a series of columns that display different properties about the linked artifacts:

➤   The Name column displays the name of the linked artifact.

➤   The Categories column displays information about the type of artifact. This could be class, namespace, or project file, just to name a few.

➤   The Layer column displays the layer that the artifact belongs to.

➤   The Supports Validation column indicates whether the linked artifact participates in the layer-validation process. If this column is set to False, the linked artifact does not participate. If this column is set to True, the linked artifact does participate, and the layer-validation process can verify that the project conforms to dependencies to or from this element.

➤   The Identifier column is used to provide a reference to the linked column.

To display all the artifacts on a layer diagram, click anywhere on the layer diagram. This will de-select any layers that have been selected, which, in turn, will display all the artifacts linked to different layers in the Layer Explorer.

To delete an artifact from the layer diagram, select the artifact in the Layer Explorer, right-click on the artifact, and select Delete. This will delete the artifact from both the Layer Explorer and the layer diagram.

To move an artifact from one layer to another, you have a couple of options. In the Layer Explorer, you can right-click on the artifact in question and select Cut. Then, in the layer diagram, right-click on the appropriate layer and select Paste. You can also simply drag the artifact from the Layer Explorer onto a layer on the layer diagram. The artifact will be removed from its initial layer and added to the new layer.

An artifact can be a member of multiple layers. One way to add an artifact to multiple layers is to drag the object onto the multiple layers from Solution Explorer. A second option is to right-click on the artifact in the Layer Explorer, select Copy, then right-click on the layer in the layer diagram and select Paste. In either event, a second instance of the artifact will appear in the Layer Explorer, but linked to a different layer.

DEFINING DEPENDENCIES

Once the layers have been defined in the layer diagram, the next step is to identify the dependencies between the different layers. A dependency between two layers exists whenever an artifact that exists in one layer references or uses an artifact that exists in another layer. For example, a class in the Business Logic Layer calls or makes reference to a class in the Data Access Layer.

Depending on how the layer diagram was built, you may want to have the dependencies discovered for you automatically, or you may want to define them by hand. More than likely, you will use a combination of the two options.

If the layer diagram was created by dragging existing code artifacts onto the diagram (such as files from a project in Solution Explorer or Architecture Explorer), then the dependencies between the different layers those objects exist in can be found automatically. If you right-click on the layer diagram surface and select Generate Dependencies, Visual Studio will analyze the artifacts that exist in each layer, identify all the dependencies between the different artifacts, and then represent those dependencies on the layer diagram as a series of arrows connecting one layer to another.

A dependency can be a *uni-directional* dependency, meaning that Layer1 is dependent on objects in Layer2, but Layer2 is not dependent on any objects in Layer1. Dependencies can also be *bi-directional*, meaning that, just as there are objects in Layer1 that depend on Layer2, there are objects in Layer2 that depend on Layer1.

Dependencies on a layer diagram can also be defined by hand. This is helpful especially when the layer diagram is being created as part of the design phase. In that phase, you don't know the specific code artifacts that you will be creating. But you do know the different high-level areas of your application, and you want to define how they will interact, or depend on each other.

Let's use the layer diagram from Figure 5-4 and add some dependencies between the different layers. In the layer diagram, you have three different layers: the UI Layer, the Business Logic Layer, and the Data Access Layer.

The UI Layer is dependent on artifacts in the Business Logic Layer. Without the Business Logic Layer, there is no information for the UI Layer to display. This dependency is represented by using a Dependency object from the layer diagram area of the Visual Studio toolbox. Click the Dependency object in the layer diagram area of the Visual Studio toolbox. Then, on the layer diagram, click the UI Layer followed by the Business Logic Layer. A dependency arrow will connect the two layers, stretching from the UI Layer to the Business Logic Layer, as shown in Figure 5-6.

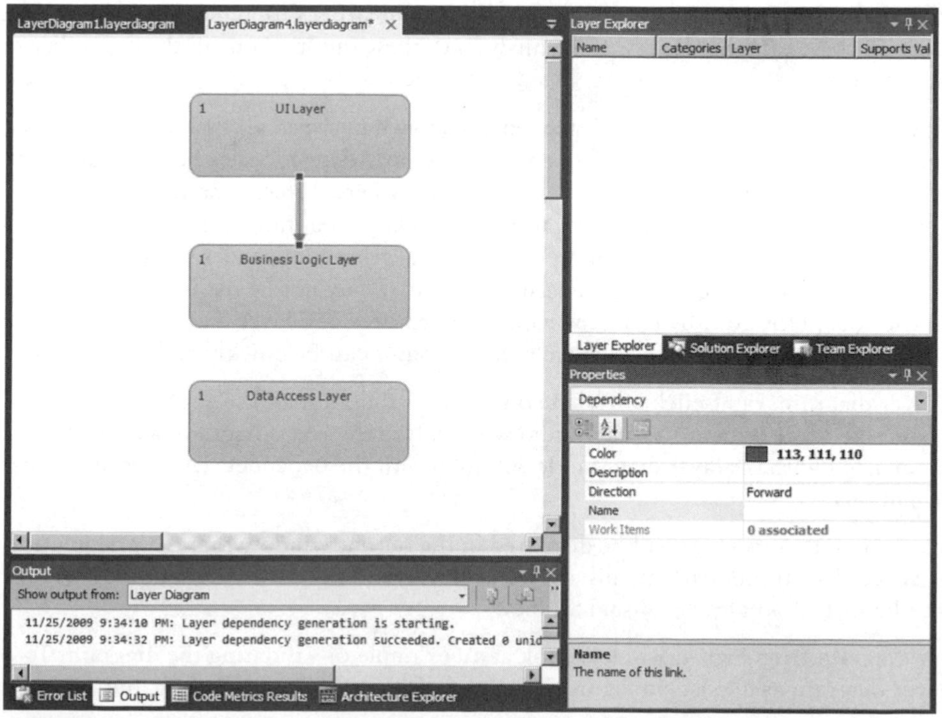

FIGURE 5-6

A dependency object has properties, just like any other object in Visual Studio. The property window at the bottom-right of Figure 5-6 displays the properties available. A name and description of the dependency can be defined. The direction of the dependency arrow can also be controlled here. If the direction needs to be reversed, select Backward in the Direction property. The dependency can also be turned into a bi-directional dependency by selecting "Bi-directional" in the Direction property.

You also have a dependency between the Business Logic Layer and the Data Access Layer. The Business Logic Layer cannot perform its functions, or provide information to the UI Layer, without information from the Data Access Layer. Using the same method described previously, you can create a dependency between the two layers by selecting the Dependency object and connecting the Business Logic Layer and the Data Access Layer.

Dependencies cannot be generated for certain types of artifacts in a layer diagram. For example, if a text file is added to a layer in a layer diagram, there will be no dependencies generated either to or from that particular layer around that text file. To determine if an artifact is going to generate dependencies, select the layer that contains the artifact, and open the Layer Explorer by right-clicking on the layer and selecting View Links. In the Layer Explorer, if the value in the Supports Validation column is set to `False`, then the artifact will not generate any dependencies for that layer.

VALIDATING THE LAYER DIAGRAM

At this point, you may be saying to yourself, "Okay, layer diagrams are great and all, but what is the actual benefit to me? Why do I want to go to all this effort of creating different layers and linking my code artifacts to these different layers?" The answers to these questions lie in the capability to validate the architecture.

Validation allows you to verify that all the dependencies defined between all the different layers are being respected. This provides the capability to enforce rules and dependencies between different layers. For example, you may have segregated your code base where different namespaces are not supposed to interact. You can define that segregation using a layer diagram and dependencies, and then add your code artifacts to their appropriate layers. If a developer miscodes something (such as accessing a namespace he or she is not supposed to access), it may not be readily apparent by just looking at the code. However, by using the validation features of a layer diagram, an error will immediately be thrown, pinpointing the problem area, so that it can be quickly and easily resolved.

To validate a layer diagram, right-click anywhere on the layer diagram and select Validate Architecture from the context menu. Visual Studio will analyze the layer diagram, as well as all the artifacts associated with the layer diagram. It will follow all the dependencies to ensure that there are no violations.

If no problems are found, a message will be displayed in the output window that the architecture validation has succeeded. If problems are discovered in the layer diagram validation, they will be displayed in the Error List window in Visual Studio.

Using the layer diagram from Figure 5-6, let's look at an example of validating the diagram. To validate the layer diagram as it exists in Figure 5-6, right-click on the layer diagram and select

Validate Architecture. Visual Studio will go through the validation process, including compiling the code, and then verify any dependencies that may exist on the diagram. Figure 5-7 shows the results from the Output window in Visual Studio.

In this example, the architecture validation was successful, because the artifacts in the UI Layer depend on artifacts in the Business Logic layer. No errors were found.

Now, let's make one small change to the same layer diagram to invalidate it. Let's reverse the direction of the dependency between the UI Layer and the Business Logic Layer. Instead of the UI Layer depending on the Business Logic Layer, the Business Logic Layer is going to depend on the UI Layer.

To do this, select the dependency arrow that connects the two layers. In the Properties window, change the direction property from Forward to Backward. This will reverse the dependency and have it point from the Business Logic Layer to the UI Layer.

Now, let's right-click on the layer diagram and select Validate Architecture. Visual Studio will run through the same validation process, but this time an error will be thrown, as shown in Figure 5-8.

The error indicates that a dependency on the layer diagram has not been satisfied. In the layer diagram shown in Figure 5-8, the UI Layer contains the class named `FirstClass`, and the Business Logic Layer contains the class named `SecondClass`. `FirstClass` has a dependency on `SecondClass`, so, therefore, the UI Layer has a dependency on the Business Logic Layer. However, as can be seen from the diagram in Figure 5-8, that is not what is defined. Instead, the Business Logic Layer is defined to have a dependency on the UI Layer.

Because the dependencies listed in the diagram do not match the actual dependencies in the code, an error is thrown when the diagram

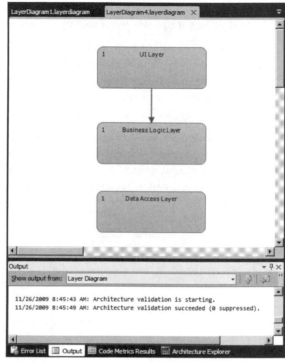

FIGURE 5-7

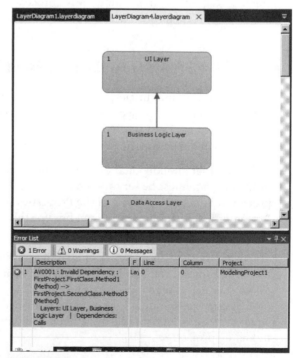

FIGURE 5-8

is validated. At this point, the error would need to be resolved before moving forward. There are several different options for resolving the error.

The first option would be to change the dependency information on the layer diagram — in this case, reversing the direction again of the dependency arrow. A second option would be to modify the links of the different layer diagrams. For example, move FirstClass and SecondClass to be in the same layer. And, a third option would be to modify the code base to remove the dependency in the code, and satisfy the dependency defined in the layer diagram.

If for some reason you don't want to change the code base, or modify the dependency information in the layer diagram, you can suppress the validation error. Right-click on the error message in the Error List window, select Manage Validation Errors, and then select Suppress Errors. This will suppress this error message and prevent this specific error from being thrown again the next time the layer diagram is validated.

 If you right-click on the error message, and select Go To, *you can easily navigate to the code that is causing the dependency violation.*

More than likely, the first time that validation is run against a layer diagram there will be conflicts. At that point, the code base will need to be updated until the conflicts no longer exist. As new code is developed and existing code is refactored, there may be the occasion to add new artifacts to the layer diagram. This may or may not be necessary, depending on how the initial layer diagram was created. Regardless, this is an iterative process, so be patient, and be sure to make the correct design decisions as related to what you want to build.

LAYER DIAGRAMS AND THE BUILD PROCESS

Layer diagrams (and, in fact, almost any diagram contained within a modeling project) can be used to help validate your project or solution during the build process. In this context, "build process" means pressing F5 in Visual Studio to compile and run your code locally, as well as to incorporate your modeling diagrams as part of an automated build using Team Foundation Build.

To ensure that an individual diagram is included in the build process, the Build Action property of the diagram must be set to Validate. To do this, select the appropriate diagram in the modeling project in Solution Explorer. In the Properties window for that diagram you will see the Build Action property. In the drop-down box for this property, select Validate to ensure that this diagram is validated as part of the build process.

To ensure that the architecture of all diagrams included in the modeling project is validated during the build process, the Validate Architecture property of the modeling project must be set to True. To do this, select the modeling project in Solution Explorer. In the Properties window for the modeling project, you will see a property named Validate Architecture. Set this property equal to True to enforce (during a build) validation of all the diagrams contained within the modeling project.

Finally, to ensure that any code changes made by anyone on the team conform to the architecture defined on the layer diagram, layer validation can be added to the automated build process. This way, any time a build is run on the solution, all team member contributions are taken into consideration, and any differences or exceptions to the architecture will be reported as a build error on the build report.

To automate layer diagram validation during the build process, add the following to the `TFSBuild.proj` file or to the build process template that is used:

```
<ValidateArchitectureOnBuild>true</ValidateArchitectureOnBuild>
```

Alternatively, in the build script, you can run MSBuild using the following property:

```
msbuild /p:ValidateArchitectureOnBuild=true
```

SUMMARY

Layer diagrams provide a nice architectural way of structuring out the design of the application, and confirming that the code being developed matches the original architectural design.

This chapter looked at how to create layer diagrams, and how to add layers to the diagram. You saw how to create blank layers, how to create layers on the diagram, and how those layers can be validated against the code base to ensure no design or architecture decisions have been violated.

This ends this section of the book on the architecture tools in Visual Studio 2010 Ultimate. Chapter 6 starts the next section of the book, which is focused on the different tools available to developers to help write better code. In Chapter 6, you will learn about some of the new features in Visual Studio 2010 of most interest to developers.

PART II
Developer

6

Introduction to Software Development

WHAT'S IN THIS CHAPTER?

➤ New Visual Studio 2010 features of most interest to developers

➤ Overview of test impact analysis

➤ Code analysis improvements

➤ Profiler enhancements

➤ Tools for database development and extensibility to support multiple database vendors

➤ Advanced debugging with IntelliTrace

➤ Code editor improvements

➤ Improvements to the "test-first" experience

Visual Studio has traditionally been the application to support development on the Microsoft platform with the tools to create and compile applications. However, over the course of many years, organizations often develop large and complex code bases. The code is typically edited by a number of developers as the application moves through the lifecycle, and the application also changes to meet the changing business requirements.

Soon, simply having the tools at your disposal to create applications is no longer enough. You need tools to help you to analyze existing code bases, and to help you to identify hot spots that might be causing you problems. You need tools to help identify the code with known maintainability or security issues. You need something that will help you make sense of this mass of code that you have inherited, and have confidence that not only does the application still work after making your changes, but that it is more efficient, and the quality of the code is improving as your team matures. This is where Visual Studio 2010 comes in.

Visual Studio 2010 is also very useful in new "green field" development, on the rare occasions that you are starting a project from scratch. The same tools that help you work with large code bases can be used from day one to ensure that all new code created maintains the same standards you envisaged during that project kick-off meeting. As the code base grows, and more developers come onto the project, you can ensure that you are not spending time prematurely optimizing code, but rather easily identifying new performance bottlenecks as they occur.

Visual Studio 2010 provides developers of both managed and unmanaged code with an enhanced set of advanced tools for identifying inefficient, insecure, or poorly written code. You can specify coding best practices, and ensure that those are checked with every build, as well as ensuring that the code is fully unit tested every time.

With Visual Studio 2010, Microsoft also acknowledges that development isn't just about code running on the client or on the Web server. An important factor of the development process occurs in the database. With Visual Studio 2010, you are able to do the same kind of change management and unit testing with your database schema as you can with source code. You may also gain a better understanding of your existing database schemas, and you have the capability to migrate any changes to those schemas in a repeatable, reversible, scripted manner.

The next few chapters will introduce the additional functionality provided by Visual Studio 2010 for the developer.

Initially, the discussions in the following chapters will focus on improving the quality and maintainability of your code through the unit testing capabilities included in Visual Studio. The discussions then examine potential issues in your code base using the code analysis and code metrics tools in both managed and unmanaged components. Then, you will learn about profiling and analyzing how your code is performing to determine which areas need the most attention. You will also learn about the advanced tools available to support database development, testing, and deployment in the team environment. Finally, you will become familiar with the advanced debugging tools.

WHAT'S NEW FOR DEVELOPERS IN VISUAL STUDIO 2010

Visual Studio 2010 introduces a number of new and important features. Obviously, the whole of Team Foundation Server is vitally important in the daily work of a developer (as is discussed Chapter 17), but there are a number of new tools and features also worth mentioning, including the following:

- Test impact analysis
- Improved code analysis
- Profiler enhancements
- Database extensibility
- Improved "test first" development experience
- Advanced debugging

TEST IMPACT ANALYSIS

Once you have established a set of programmatic unit tests for your code, the library of tests can become very large. Visual Studio 2010 checks which unit tests have been affected by a change to your managed source code and highlights this subset of the total test suite as recommended tests in the Test View window. When you have re-run your unit tests, it will highlight which ones have been verified as working. Chapter 7 provides more information on unit testing and test impact analysis.

IMPROVED CODE ANALYSIS

Earlier versions of Visual Studio shipped with code analysis functionality to allow developers to analyze source code to check for common issues and security flaws. In Visual Studio 2010, custom Code Analysis Rules Sets have been added that make it much easier to determine on which rules your development team should concentrate. Chapter 8 focuses on this.

PROFILER ENHANCEMENTS

The overall user interface (UI) experience of the profiler functionality in Visual Studio has been significantly improved, making it much easier to quickly understand the large amount of data captured in the code profiling functionality, and zoom into areas of concern. In addition, client-side JavaScript performance may be profiled, as well as the interactions between tiers in a typical n-tier system. Support for multi-threaded applications is much improved, including finding issues such as thread blocking. The code profiling experience is also now available when running inside a virtual machine. Chapter 9 provides more information on the profiler.

DATABASE EXTENSIBILITY

The database development functionality is now much more extensible. This allows for third-party developers to develop a Database Schema Provider to enable offline design, development, testing, and change management of database systems other than SQL Server. Quest Software provides Oracle support, IBM has demonstrated DB2 support, and Microsoft has indicated that it is working with other partners as well. Chapter 10 provides more information on database development, testing, and deployment.

> *For information on additional Database Schema Providers, see*
> `http://msdn.microsoft.com/en-us/teamsystem/dd408380.aspx`.

ADVANCED DEBUGGING WITH INTELLITRACE

Examined in depth in Chapter 11, the new advanced debugging features of Visual Studio 2010 play a similar role to that of a black box in an airplane. The debugger keeps track of a number of interesting events during the execution of your managed code program, thus allowing you at a later time to play back the execution and see what happened at those points. You can also load and debug a trace debugging log file attached to a bug logged by someone testing the application to inspect what happened in the run up to the crash.

IMPROVED "TEST-FIRST" DEVELOPMENT EXPERIENCE

While a pretty basic function of any Integrated Development Environment, the improvements in the code editor are worth mentioning in any recap of new features. The code editor has been re-implemented in Windows Presentation Foundation (WPF) and uses the Managed Extensibility Framework (MEF) for extensibility. Along the way, the experience when writing in a test-first style is much improved. It is now much easier to generate method stubs based on a call in a unit test that has not yet been implemented in the target class. Not only that, but the code navigation experience has received significant attention, making it much easier to navigate around your large code base than in previous releases of Visual Studio.

SUMMARY

This chapter provided a quick look at the areas of Visual Studio 2010 that will be of most interest to developers, and provided a preview of what to look forward to in this next section of the book.

Chapter 7 focuses in detail on the unit testing, why you should care about it as a developer, and what tools Visual Studio provides to not only help you unit test your code, but also to learn which code is being tested, and what tests were impacted by any changes made to your code.

7

Unit Testing with the Unit Test Framework

WHAT'S IN THIS CHAPTER?

➤ Common concepts and benefits of unit testing

➤ Creating your first unit test using the Visual Studio unit testing framework

➤ Executing, managing, and viewing the results of unit tests

➤ Data-driven unit tests

➤ Testing non-public members from tests

➤ Generating test stubs from code

➤ Enabling code coverage and test impact analysis

Programmatic unit testing involves writing code to verify a system at a lower and more granular level than with other types of testing. It is used *by* programmers *for* programmers, and is quickly becoming standard practice at many organizations. All editions of Visual Studio 2010 (apart from the free Express editions) include unit testing features that are fully integrated with the IDE and with other features (such as reporting and source control). Developers no longer need to rely on third-party utilities (such as NUnit) to perform their unit testing, although they still have the option to use them.

This chapter describes the concepts behind unit testing, why it is important, and how to create effective unit test suites. You learn about the syntax of writing unit tests, and you will learn how to work with Visual Studio's integrated features for executing and analyzing those tests. The discussion then goes into more detail about the classes available to you when writing your unit tests, including the core `Assert` class and many important attributes. You will also see how easy it is to create data-driven unit tests, whereby a unit test is executed once per record in a data source, and has full access to that bound data.

Also described in this chapter are the features Visual Studio offers for easily accessing non-public members from your unit tests. In addition, you will learn how Visual Studio enables the generation of unit tests from existing code, as well as the generation of member structures when writing unit tests.

In this chapter, you will learn how Visual Studio can help measure the effectiveness of your tests. *Code coverage* is the concept of observing which lines of code are used during the execution of unit tests. You can easily identify regions of your code that are not being executed and create tests to verify that code. This will improve your capability to find problems before the users of your system do. And, you will learn about the test impact analysis feature, which allows you to quickly and easily see what tests must be run for particular changes to the code base. Code coverage and test impact analysis are only available in the Visual Studio 2010 Premium and Ultimate editions.

UNIT TESTING CONCEPTS

You've likely encountered a number of traditional forms of testing. Your quality assurance staff may run automated or manual tests to validate behavior and appearance. Load tests may be run to establish that performance metrics are acceptable. Your product group might run user acceptance tests to validate that systems do what the customers expect. Unit testing takes another view. Unit tests are written to ensure that code performs as the *programmer* expects.

Unit tests are generally focused at a lower level than other testing, establishing that underlying features work as expected. For example, an acceptance test might walk a user through an entire purchase. A unit test might verify that a `ShoppingCart` class correctly defends against adding an item with a negative quantity.

Unit testing is an example of *white box testing*, where knowledge of internal structures is used to identify the best ways to test the system. This is a complementary approach to *black box testing*, where the focus is not on implementation details but rather on overall functionality compared to specifications. You should leverage both approaches to effectively test your applications.

Unit testing as a concept has been around for decades. However, in recent times, the process of performing unit tests by writing code to execute those tests has become popular. This form of programmatic unit testing is now what many people refer to as a "unit test" — and sometimes use the term "unit test" to cover all forms of testing conducted using the programmatic unit testing frameworks, even if those tests are actually not tests of the unit of code, but are actually full integration tests.

Benefits of Unit Testing

A common reaction to unit testing is to resist the approach because the tests seemingly make more work for a developer. However, unit testing offers many benefits that may not be obvious at first.

The act of writing tests often uncovers design or implementation problems. The unit tests serve as the first users of your system, and will frequently identify design issues or functionality that is lacking. The act of thinking about tests causes the developer to question the requirements of the application, and, therefore, seek clarification from the business very early in the lifecycle of the software development project. This makes things easy and inexpensive to rectify as the clarification is received.

Once a unit test is written, it serves as a form of living documentation for the use of the target system. Other developers can look to an assembly's unit tests to see example calls into various classes and members. An important benefit of unit tests for framework APIs is that the tests introduce a dependency at compile time, making it trivial to determine if any code changes have impacted the contract represented by the API.

Perhaps one of the most important benefits is that a well-written test suite provides the original developer with the freedom to pass the system off to other developers for maintenance and further enhancement knowing that their intentions of how the code would be used are fully covered by tests. Should those developers introduce a bug in the original functionality, there is a strong likelihood that those unit tests will detect that failure and help diagnose the issue. In addition, because there is a full set of unit tests making up the regression tests, it is a simple task for the maintenance team to introduce a new test that demonstrates the bug first, and then confirm that it is correctly fixed by the code modification. Meanwhile, the original developer can focus on current tasks.

It takes the typical developer time and practice to become comfortable with unit testing. Once a developer has saved enough time by using unit tests, he or she will latch on to them as an indispensable part of the development process.

Unit testing does require more explicit coding, but this cost will be recovered, and typically exceeded, when you spend much less time debugging your application. In addition, some of this cost is typically already hidden in the form of test console- or Windows-based applications that a developer might have previously used as a test harness. Unlike these informal testing applications, which are frequently discarded after initial verification, unit tests become a permanent part of the project, run each time a change is made to help ensure that the system still functions as expected. Tests are stored in source control as part of the same solution with the code they verify and are maintained along with the code under test, making it easier to keep them synchronized.

> *Unit tests are an essential element of regression testing.* Regression testing
> *involves retesting a piece of software after new features have been added to*
> *make sure errors or bugs are not introduced. Regression testing also provides an*
> *essential quality check when you introduce bug fixes in your product.*

It is difficult to overstate the importance of comprehensive unit test suites. They enable a developer to hand off a system to other developers with confidence that any changes they make should not introduce undetected side effects. However, because unit testing only provides one view of a system's behavior, no amount of unit testing should ever replace integration, acceptance, and load testing.

Writing Effective Unit Tests

Because unit tests are themselves code, you are generally unlimited in the approaches you can take when writing them. However, you should follow some general guidelines:

➤ Always separate your unit test assemblies from the code you are testing. This separation enables you to deploy your application code without unit tests, which serve no purpose in a production environment.

➤ Avoid altering the code you are testing solely to allow easier unit testing. A common mistake is to open accessibility to class members to allow unit tests direct access. This compromises design, reduces encapsulation, and broadens interaction surfaces. You will see later in this chapter that Visual Studio offers features to help address this issue. However, be open minded that often what makes code easy to test in isolation makes that code more maintainable.

➤ Each test should verify a small slice of functionality. Do not write long sequential unit tests that verify a large number of items. While creating focused tests will result in more tests, the overall suite of tests will be easier to maintain. In addition, identifying the cause of a problem is much easier when you can quickly look at a small failed unit test, immediately understand what it was testing, and know where to search for the bug.

➤ All tests should be autonomous and isolated. Avoid creating tests that rely on other tests to be run beforehand. Tests should be executable in any combination and in any order. To verify that your tests are correct, try changing their execution order and running them in isolation.

➤ Test both expected behavior (normal workflows) and error conditions (exceptions and invalid operations). This often means that you will have multiple unit tests for the same method, but remember that developers will always find ways to call your objects that you did not intend. Expect the unexpected, code defensively, and test to ensure that your code reacts appropriately.

The final proof of your unit testing's effectiveness will be when it saves you more time during development and maintenance than you spent creating the tests. Experience has shown that you will realize this savings many times over.

Third-Party Tools

Unit testing is not a new concept. Before Visual Studio introduced integrated unit testing, developers needed to rely on third-party frameworks. The de facto standard for .NET unit testing has been an Open Source package called *NUnit*. NUnit has its original roots as a .NET port of the Java-based JUnit unit testing framework. JUnit is itself a member of the extended xUnit family.

There are many similarities between NUnit and the unit testing framework in Visual Studio. The structure and syntax of tests and the execution architecture are conveniently similar. If you have existing suites of NUnit-based tests, it is generally easy to convert them for use with Visual Studio.

Visual Studio's implementation of unit testing is not merely a port of NUnit. Microsoft has added a number of features that are unavailable with the version of NUnit available as of this writing. Among these are IDE integration, code generation, new attributes, enhancements to the `Assert` class, and built-in support for testing nonpublic members.

VISUAL STUDIO UNIT TESTING

Unit testing is a feature available in all but the free Express editions of Visual Studio. This section describes how to create, execute, and manage unit tests.

Unit tests are themselves normal code, identified as unit tests through the use of attributes. Like NUnit 2.0 and later, Visual Studio uses .NET reflection to inspect assemblies to find unit tests.

> *Reflection is a mechanism by which details about .NET objects can be discovered at execution time. The* System.Reflection *assembly contains members that help you identify classes, properties, and methods of any .NET assembly. Reflection even enables you to call methods and access properties of classes. This includes access to private members, a practice that can be useful in unit testing, as you will see later in this chapter.*

You will also use attributes to identify other structures used in your tests and to indicate desired behaviors.

Creating Your First Unit Test

This section takes a slower approach to creating a unit test than you will in your normal work. This will give you a chance to examine details you could miss using only the built-in features that make unit testing easier. Later in this chapter, you'll look at the faster approaches.

In order to have something to test, create a new C# Class Library project named ExtendedMath. Rename the default Class1.cs to Functions.cs. You'll add code to compute the Fibonacci for a given number. The Fibonacci Sequence, as you may recall, is a series of numbers where each term is the sum of the prior two terms. The first six terms, starting with an input factor of 1, are {1, 1, 2, 3, 5, 8}.

Open Functions.cs and insert the following code:

```
namespace ExtendedMath
{
    public static class Functions
    {
        public static int Fibonacci(int factor)
        {
            if (factor < 2)
                return (factor);
            int x = Fibonacci(--factor);
            int y = Fibonacci(--factor);

            return x + y;
        }
    }
}
```

You are now ready to create unit tests to verify the Fibonacci implementation. Unit tests are recognized as tests only if they are contained in separate projects called *test projects*. Test projects can contain any of the test types supported in Visual Studio. Add a test project named ExtendedMathTesting to your solution by adding a new project and selecting the Test

Project template. If the test project includes any sample tests for you (such as `UnitTest1.cs` or `ManualTest1.mht`), you can safely delete them. Because you will be calling objects in your `ExtendedMath` project, make a reference to that class library project from the test project. You may notice that a reference to the `Microsoft.VisualStudio.QualityTools.UnitTestFramework.dll` assembly has already been made for you. This assembly contains many helpful classes for creating units tests. You'll use many of these throughout this chapter.

As you'll see later in this chapter, Visual Studio supports the generation of basic unit test outlines, but in this section, you'll create them manually to make it easier to understand the core concepts.

Once you have created a new test project, add a new class file (not a unit test; that file type will be covered later) called `FunctionsTest.cs`. You will use this class to contain the unit tests for the `Functions` class. You'll be using unit testing objects from the `ExtendedMath` project and the `UnitTestFramework` assembly mentioned earlier, so add `using` statements at the top so that the class members do not need to be fully qualified:

```
using ExtendedMath;
using Microsoft.VisualStudio.TestTools.UnitTesting;
```

Identifying Unit Test Classes

To enable Visual Studio to identify a class as potentially containing unit tests, you must assign the `TestClass` attribute. If you forget to add the `TestClass` attribute, the unit tests methods in your class will not be recognized.

To indicate that the `FunctionsTest` class will contain unit tests, add the `TestClass` attribute to its declaration:

```
namespace ExtendedMath
{

    [TestClass]
    public class FunctionsTest
    {
    }
}
```

Unit tests are required to be hosted within public classes, so don't forget to include the `public` descriptor for the class. Note also that parentheses after an attribute are optional if you are not passing parameters to the attribute. For example, `[TestClass()]` and `[TestClass]` are equivalent.

Identifying Unit Tests

Having identified the class as a container of unit tests, you're ready to add your first unit test. A unit test method must be public, nonstatic, accept no parameters, and have no return value. To differentiate unit test methods from ordinary methods, they must be decorated with the `TestMethod` attribute.

Add the following code inside the `FunctionsTest` class:

```
[TestMethod]
public void FibonacciTest()
{
}
```

Unit Test Success and Failure

You have the shell of a unit test, but how do you test? A unit test indicates failure to Visual Studio by throwing an exception. Any test that does not throw an exception is considered to have passed, except in the case of `ExpectedException` attribute, which will be described later.

The unit testing framework defines the `Assert` object. This object exposes many members, which are central to creating unit tests. You'll learn more about `Assert` later in the chapter.

Add the following code to the `FibonacciTest`:

```
[TestMethod]
public void FibonacciTest()
{

  const int FACTOR = 8;
  const int EXPECTED = 21;

  int actual = ExtendedMath.Functions.Fibonacci(FACTOR);

  Assert.AreEqual(EXPECTED, actual);
}
```

This uses the `Assert.AreEqual` method to compare two values, the value you expect and the value generated by calling the `Fibonacci` method. If they do not match, an exception will be thrown, causing the test to fail.

When you run tests, you will see the Test Results window. Success is indicated with a green checkmark and failure with a red X. A special result, inconclusive (described later in this chapter), is represented by a question mark.

To see a failing test, change the EXPECTED constant from 21 to 22 and rerun the test. The Test Results window will show the test as failed. The Error Message column provides details about the failure reason. In this case, the Error Message would show the following:

```
Assert.AreEqual failed. Expected:<22>, Actual:<21>
```

This indicates that either the expected value is wrong, or the implementation of the Fibonacci algorithm is wrong. Fortunately, because unit tests verify a small amount of code, the job of finding the source of bugs is made easier.

REMEMBER THE THREE A'S

When writing a unit test method, it is useful to remember the "Three-A's" pattern for your method — Arrange, Act, Assert. First, you arrange your test by setting up the variables, then you invoke the code under test, and finally assert that the invoked code has passed the expectations. Use paragraphs of code (with empty lines between) for each of the A's.

Using this patterns makes is easy to look at test code written by others, and to determine exactly what is being done. In addition, it encourages you to only test one thing per test method.

Managing and Running Unit Tests

Once you have created a unit test and rebuilt your project, Visual Studio will automatically inspect your projects for unit tests. You can use the Test List Editor and Test View windows to work with your tests, as well as run tests directly from your code.

The easiest way to open these windows is by enabling the Test Tools toolbar and clicking either the Test View or Test List Editor buttons. They are also available by selecting Test ➪ Windows.

Test View

Test View provides a compact view of your tests. It enables you to quickly select and run your tests. You can group tests by name, project, type, class name, and other criteria. Figure 7-1 shows the Test View window.

Double-click on any test to navigate to that test's code. To run one or more tests, select them and click the Run Selection button (the first button in the toolbar).

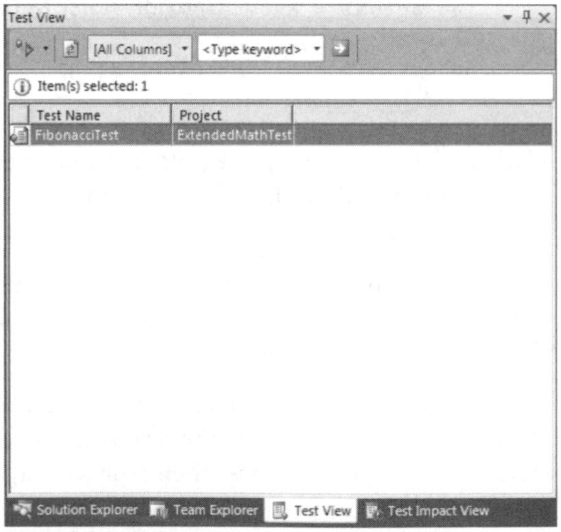

Test List Editor

The Test List Editor offers all of the features of the Test View window, but provides more options for organization and display of your tests. Figure 7-2 shows the Test List Editor.

FIGURE 7-1

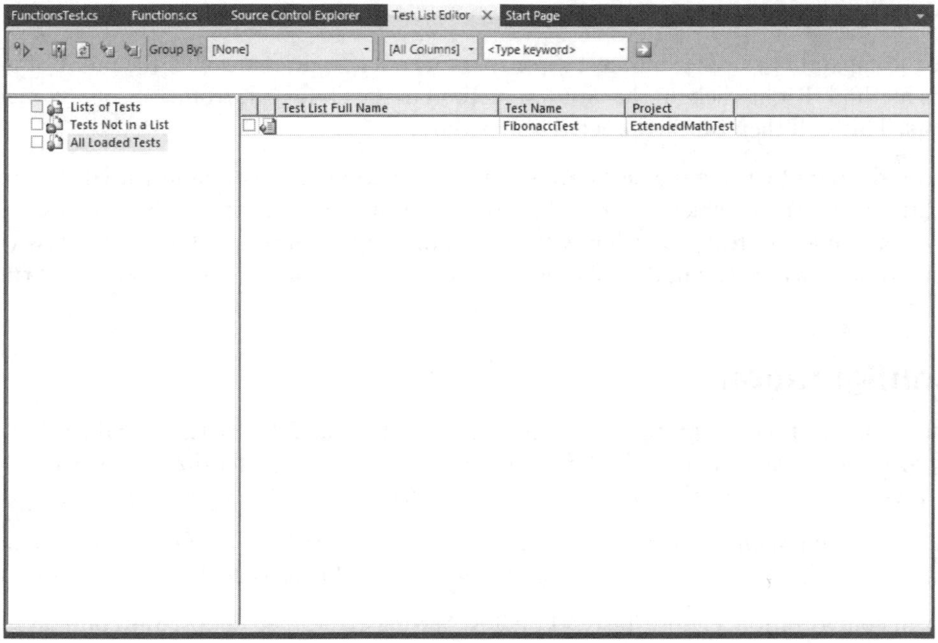

FIGURE 7-2

By default, all tests are listed, but you can organize tests into lists. In Test List Editor, right-click on the Lists of Tests node on the tree on the left-hand side. Select New Test List and the Create New Test List dialog will appear, as shown in Figure 7-3. You can also create a new test list by choosing Test ➪ Create New Test List.

Give the list a name and optionally a description. You can also place this list within another list.

Once you have created a list, you can drag tests from the Test Manager list onto it. The list enables you to easily select all related tests for execution by checking the box next to the list name.

FIGURE 7-3

You can also group by test properties. First, click the All Loaded Tests node to ensure that all tests are listed. Then, in the Group By drop-down list, scroll to and select Class Name. You will then see your tests in collapsible groups by class name.

If you have many tests, you will find the filtering option useful. With filters, you can limit the list of tests to only those that match text you enter. Next to the Group By list is a Filter Column drop-down and a text box. Enter the text you wish to match in the text box; you can optionally select a column you would like to match against. For example, if you wish to show only tests from a certain class, enter that class name then select Class Name in the Filter Column list. When you click the Apply Filter button, only tests from that class will be displayed. If the Filter Column is set to [All Columns], tests will display if any of their fields contain the text you enter.

Running Tests Directly from Code

You also have the capability to run a unit test directly from code. To do that, open the unit test and navigate to the method. Right-click on the unit test method in the code and, from the context menu, select Run Tests. This will then run the selected test method.

You can also run the tests by using the keyboard shortcuts. The two most commonly used shortcuts are probably Ctrl+R or Ctrl+T (which will run the tests in the current context in debug mode). Therefore, if you are in a unit test method, it will just run that test in the class. The whole class will then run if you are somewhere else in the solution (such as in the code under test). Then it will run all tests.

Test Run Configuration

Whenever you run a set of tests, a group of settings apply to that run. Those settings (called the *test run configuration*) are stored in an XML file with a `.testsettings` extension. A test run configuration is created automatically for every new test project, named `local.testsettings`.

The settings include items such as the naming structure of your results files, configuration of remote test execution, enabling of code coverage, and specifying additional files to deploy during your tests.

To edit a test run configuration, choose Test ⇨ Edit Test Settings, and then choose the configuration you wish to modify. You can also double-click the configuration file in Solution Explorer. Figure 7-4 shows the Test Settings interface.

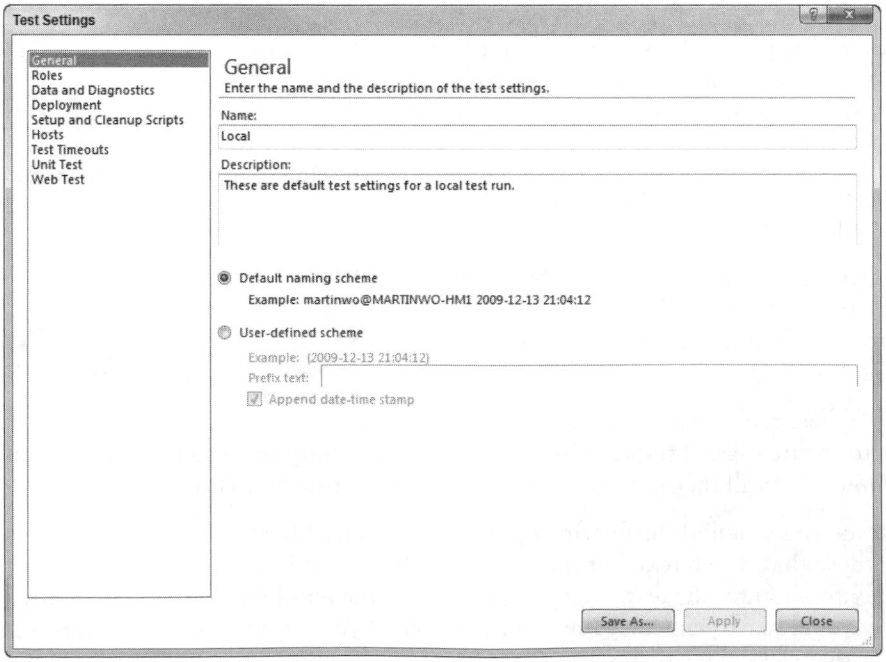

FIGURE 7-4

You may have more than one test run configuration, perhaps to support different execution environments or code coverage settings, but you must select a single configuration as "active" when you run your tests. To set another configuration as active, choose Test ➪ Select Active Test Settings and then choose the correct configuration.

The default configuration settings will generally be fine for your initial unit testing. As you begin to require additional unit testing features, you may need to adjust these settings. For example, later in this chapter, you will learn how to monitor code coverage with Visual Studio. In that discussion, you will learn how to use the test run configuration to enable that feature.

Test Results

Once you have selected and run one or more unit tests, you will see the Test Results window. This window displays the status of your test execution, as shown in Figure 7-5.

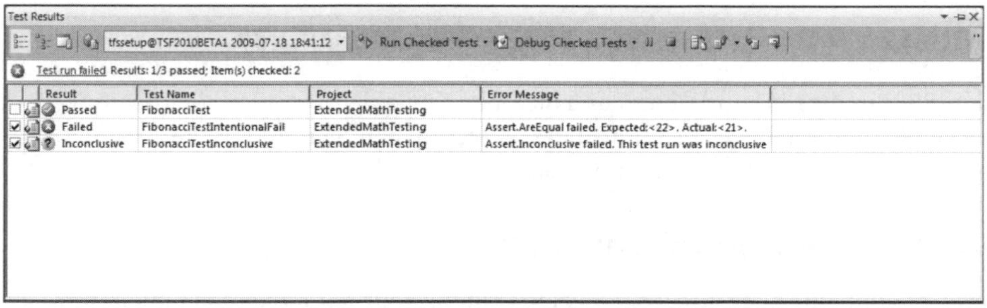

FIGURE 7-5

You can see that one of the tests has failed, one has passed, and one was inconclusive. The error message for any nonpassing test is displayed. You can double-click on any test result to see details for that test. You can also right-click on a test result and choose Open Test to navigate to the unit test code.

Notice that the nonpassing tests are checked. This convenient feature enables you to make some changes and then quickly rerun just those tests that have not passed.

Debugging Unit Tests

Because unit tests are simply methods with special attributes applied to them, they can be debugged just like other code.

Breakpoints can be set anywhere in your code, not just in your unit tests. For example, the `FibonacciTest` calls into the `ExtendedMath.Fibonacci` method. You could set a breakpoint in either method and have execution paused when that line of code is reached.

However, setting program execution will not pause at your breakpoints unless you run your unit test in debugging mode. The Test View, Test Results, and Test List Editor windows all feature a drop-down arrow next to the Run button. For example, in Test List Editor, click on the arrow next to the Run Checked Tests button. You will see a new option, Debug Checked Tests. If you choose this, the selected unit tests will be run in debug mode, pausing execution at any enabled breakpoints and giving you a chance to evaluate and debug your unit test or implementation code as necessary.

> *If you have enabled code coverage for your application, you will see a message indicating that you cannot debug while code coverage is enabled. Click OK and you will continue debugging as normal, but code coverage results will not be available. Code coverage is examined in detail later in this chapter.*

Keep in mind that the Run/Debug buttons are "sticky." The last selected mode will continue to be used when the button is clicked until another mode is chosen from the drop-down list.

PROGRAMMING WITH THE UNIT TEST FRAMEWORK

This section describes in detail the attributes and methods available to you for creating unit tests. All of the classes and attributes mentioned in this section can be found in the `Microsoft.VisualStudio.TestTools.UnitTesting` namespace.

Initialization and Cleanup of Unit Tests

Often, you'll need to configure a resource that is shared among your tests. Examples might be a database connection, a log file, or a shared object in a known default state. You might also need ways to clean up from the actions of your tests, such as closing a shared stream or rolling back a transaction.

The unit test framework offers attributes to identify such methods. They are grouped into three levels: Test, Class, and Assembly. The levels determine the scope and timing of execution for the methods they decorate. Table 7-1 describes these attributes.

TABLE 7-1

ATTRIBUTES	FREQUENCY AND SCOPE
`TestInitialize, TestCleanup`	Executed before (`Initialize`) or after (`Cleanup`) any of the class's unit tests are run
`ClassInitialize, ClassCleanup`	Executed a single time before or after any of the tests in the current class are run
`AssemblyInitialize, AssemblyCleanup`	Executed a single time before or after any number of tests in any of the assembly's classes are run

Having methods with these attributes is optional, but do not define more than one of each attribute in the same context. Also, keep in mind that you cannot guarantee the order in which your unit tests will be run, and that should govern what functionality you place in each of these methods.

TestInitialize and TestCleanup Attributes

Use the TestInitialize attribute to create a method that will be executed one time before every unit test method in the current class. Similarly, TestCleanup marks a method that will always run immediately after each test. Like unit tests, methods with these attributes must be public, nonstatic, accept no parameters, and have no return values.

Following is an example test for a simplistic shopping cart class. It contains two tests and defines the TestInitialize and TestCleanup methods.

```csharp
using Microsoft.VisualStudio.TestTools.UnitTesting;

[TestClass]
public class ShoppingCartTest
{
    private ShoppingCart cart;


    [TestInitialize]
    public void TestInitialize()
    {
        cart = new SomeClass();
        cart.Add(new Item("Test");)
    }


    [TestCleanup]
    public void TestCleanup()
    {
        // Not required - here for illustration
        cart.Dispose();
    }

    [TestMethod]
    public void TestCountAfterAdd()
    {
        int expected = cart.Count + 1;
        cart.Add(new Item("New Item");)
        Assert.AreEqual(expected, cart.Count);
    }

    [TestMethod]
    public void TestCountAfterRemove()
    {
        int expected = cart.Count - 1;
        cart.Remove(0);
        Assert.AreEqual(expected, cart.Count);
    }
}
```

When you run both tests, TestInitialize and TestCleanup are both executed twice. TestInitialize is run immediately before each unit test and TestCleanup immediately after.

ClassInitialize and ClassCleanup Attributes

The ClassInitialize and ClassCleanup attributes are used very similarly to TestInitialize and TestCleanup. The difference is that these methods are guaranteed to run once and only once no matter how many unit tests are executed from the current class. Unlike TestInitialize and TestCleanup, these methods are marked static and accept a TestContext instance as a parameter.

The importance of the TestContext instance is described later in this chapter.

The following code demonstrates how you might manage a shared logging target using class-level initialization and cleanup with a logging file:

```
    private System.IO.File logFile;


[ClassInitialize]
    public static void ClassInitialize(TestContext context)
    {        // Code to open the logFile object      }


[ClassCleanup]
    public static void ClassCleanup(TestContext context)
    {        // Code to close the logFile object      }
```

You could now reference the logFile object from any of your unit tests in this class, knowing that it will automatically be opened before any unit test is executed and closed after the final test in the class has completed.

> *This approach to logging is simply for illustration. You'll see later how the* TestContext *object passed into these methods enables you to more effectively log details from your unit tests.*

The following code shows the flow of execution if you run both tests again:

```
ClassInitialize
    TestInitialize
        TestCountAfterAdd
    TestCleanup
    TestInitialize
        TestCountAfterRemove
    TestCleanup
ClassCleanup
```

AssemblyInitialize and AssemblyCleanup Attributes

Where you might use ClassInitialize and ClassCleanup to control operations at a class level, use the AssemblyInitialize and AssemblyCleanup attributes for an entire assembly. For example, a method decorated with AssemblyInitialize will be executed once before any test in that current assembly, not just those in the current class. As with the class-level initialize and cleanup methods, these must be static and accept a `TestContext` parameter.

```
[AssemblyInitialize]
    public static void AssemblyInitialize(TestContext context)
    {       // Assembly-wide initialization code      }


[AssemblyCleanup]
    public static void AssemblyCleanup(TestContext context)
    {        // Assembly-wide cleanup code        }
```

Consider using `AssemblyInitialize` and `AssemblyCleanup` in cases where you have common operations spanning multiple classes. Instead of having many per-class initialize and cleanup methods, you can refactor these to single assembly-level methods.

Using the Assert Methods

The most common way to determine success in unit tests is to compare an expected result against an actual result. The `Assert` class features many methods that enable you to make these comparisons quickly.

Assert.AreEqual and Assert.AreNotEqual

Of the various `Assert` methods, you will likely find the most use for `AreEqual` and `AreNotEqual`. As their names imply, you are comparing an expected value to a supplied value. If the operands are not value-equivalent (or are equivalent for `AreNotEqual`), then the current test will fail.

A third, optional argument can be supplied: a string that will be displayed along with your unit test results, which you can use to describe the failure. Additionally, you can supply parameters to be replaced in the string, just as the `String.Format` method supports. The string message should be used to explain why failing that `Assert` is an error. If you have multiple `Assert`s in a single test method, then it is very useful to provide a failure message string on every `Assert` so that you can very quickly identify which `Assert` failed.

```
[TestMethod]
public void IsPrimeTest()
{
    const int FACTOR = 5;
    const bool EXPECTED = true;

    bool actual = CustomMath.IsPrime(FACTOR);


    Assert.AreEqual(EXPECTED, actual, "The number {0} should have been computed as
                    prime, but was not.", FACTOR);
}
```

Assert.AreEqual and AreNotEqual have many parameter overloads, accepting types such as string, double, int, float, object, and generic types. Take the time to review the overloads in the Object Browser.

When using these methods with two string arguments, one of the overrides allows you to optionally supply a third argument. This is a Boolean, called ignoreCase, that indicates whether the comparison should be case-insensitive. The default comparison is case-sensitive.

Working with floating-point numbers involves a degree of imprecision. You can supply an argument that defines a delta by which two numbers can differ yet still pass a test — for example, if you're computing square roots and decide that a "drift" of plus or minus 0.0001 is acceptable:

```
[TestMethod]
public void SquareRootTeset()
{
    const double EXPECTED = 3.1622;

  const double DELTA = 0.0001;
    double actual = CustomMath.SquareRoot(10);


    Assert.AreEqual(EXPECTED, actual, DELTA, "Root not within acceptable range");
}
```

> When asserting that two instances of a complex type are equal, you are actually testing the behavior of the Equals() operator on that class. This is important to bear in mind if you are ever overriding the Equals operator in your own classes.

Assert.AreSame and Assert.AreNotSame

AreSame and AreNotSame function in much the same manner as AreEqual and AreNotEqual. The important difference is that these methods compare the *references* of the supplied arguments. For example, if two arguments point to the same object instance, then AreSame will pass. Even when the arguments are exactly equivalent in terms of their state, AreSame will fail if they are not, in fact, the same object. This is the same concept that differentiates object.Equals from object.ReferenceEquals.

A common use for these methods is to ensure that properties return expected instances, or that collections handle references correctly. The following example adds an item to a collection and ensures that what you get back from the collection's indexer is a reference to the same item instance:

```
[TestMethod]
public void CollectionTest()
{
    CustomCollection cc = new CustomCollection();
    Item original = new Item("Expected");
    cc.Add(original);
```

```
    Item actual = cc[0];


    Assert.AreSame(original, actual);
}
```

Assert.IsTrue and Assert.IsFalse

As you can probably guess, IsTrue and IsFalse are used simply to ensure that the supplied expression is true or false as expected. Returning to the IsPrimeNumberTest example, you can restate it as follows:

```
[TestMethod]
public void IsPrimeTest()
{
    const int FACTOR = 5;


    Assert.IsTrue(CustomMath.IsPrime(FACTOR), "The number {0} should have been
            computed as prime, but was not.", FACTOR);
}
```

Assert.IsNull and Assert.IsNotNull

Similar to IsTrue and IsFalse, these methods verify that a given object type is either null or not null. Revising the collection example, this ensures that the item returned by the indexer is not null:

```
[TestMethod]
public void CollectionTest()
{
    CustomCollection cc = new CustomCollection();
    cc.Add(new Item("Added"));
    Item item = cc[0];


    Assert.IsNotNull(item);
}
```

Assert.IsInstanceOfType and Assert.IsNotInstanceOfType

IsInstanceOfType simply ensures that a given object is an instance of an expected type. For example, suppose you have a collection that accepts entries of any type. You'd like to ensure that an entry you're retrieving is of the expected type, as shown here:

```
[TestMethod]
public void CollectionTest()
{
    UntypedCollection untyped = new UntypedCollection();
    untyped.Add(new Item("Added"));
    untyped.Add(new Person("Rachel"));
```

```
        untyped.Add(new Item("Another"));

        object entry = untyped[1];


    Assert.IsInstanceOfType(entry, typeof(Person));
    }
```

As you can no doubt guess, `IsNotInstanceOfType` will test to ensure that an object is not the specified type.

Assert.Fail and Assert.Inconclusive

Use `Assert.Fail` to immediately fail a test. For example, you may have a conditional case that should never occur. If it does, call `Assert.Fail` and an `AssertFailedException` will be thrown, causing the test to abort with failure. You may find `Assert.Fail` useful when defining your own custom `Assert` methods.

`Assert.Inconclusive` enables you to indicate that the test result cannot be verified as a pass or fail. This is typically a temporary measure until a unit test (or the related implementation) has been completed. As described in the section, "Code Generation," later in this chapter, `Assert.Inconclusive` is used to indicate that more work is needed to complete a unit test.

> *There is no* `Assert.Succeed` *because success is indicated by completion of a unit test method without a thrown exception. Use a return statement if you wish to cause this result from some point in your test.* `Assert.Fail` *and* `Assert.Inconclusive` *both support a string argument and optional arguments, which will be inserted into the string in the same manner as* `String.Format`*. Use this string to supply a detailed message back to the Test Results window, describing the reasons for the nonpassing result.*

Using the CollectionAssert class

The `Microsoft.VisualStudio.TestTools.UnitTesting` namespace includes a class, `CollectionAssert`, that contains useful methods for testing the contents and behavior of collection types.

Table 7-2 describes the methods supported by `CollectionAssert`.

TABLE 7-2

METHOD	DESCRIPTION
AllItemsAreInstancesOfType	Ensures that all elements are of an expected type
AllItemsAreNotNull	Ensures that no items in the collection are `null`
AllItemsAreUnique	Searches a collection, failing if a duplicate member is found

METHOD	DESCRIPTION
AreEqual	Ensures that two collections have reference-equivalent members
AreNotEqual	Ensures that two collections do not have reference-equivalent members
AreEquivalent	Ensures that two collections have value-equivalent members
AreNotEquivalent	Ensures that two collections do not have value-equivalent members
Contains	Searches a collection, failing if the given object is not found
DoesNotContain	Searches a collection, failing if a given object is found
IsNotSubsetOf	Ensures that the first collection has members not found in the second
IsSubsetOf	Ensures that all elements in the first collection are found in the second

The following example uses some of these methods to verify various behaviors of a collection type, CustomCollection. When this example is run, none of the assertions fail, and the test results in success. Note that proper unit testing would spread these checks across multiple smaller tests.

```
[TestMethod]
public void CollectionTests()
{
    CustomCollection list1 = new CustomCollection();
    list1.Add("alpha");
    list1.Add("beta");
    list1.Add("delta");
    list1.Add("delta");


    CollectionAssert.AllItemsAreInstancesOfType(list1, typeof(string));
    CollectionAssert.AllItemsAreNotNull(list1);

    CustomCollection list2 = (CustomCollection)list1.Clone();


    CollectionAssert.AreEqual(list1, list2);
    CollectionAssert.AreEquivalent(list1, list2);

    CustomCollection list3 = new CustomCollection();
    list3.Add("beta");
    list3.Add("delta");
```

```
    CollectionAssert.AreNotEquivalent(list3, list1);
    CollectionAssert.IsSubsetOf(list3, list1);
    CollectionAssert.DoesNotContain(list3, "alpha");
    CollectionAssert.AllItemsAreUnique(list3);
}
```

The final assertion, `AllItemsAreUnique(list3)`, would have failed if tested against `list1` because that collection has two entries of the string `"delta"`.

Using the StringAssert class

Similar to `CollectionAssert`, the `StringAssert` class contains methods that enable you to easily make assertions based on common text operations. Table 7-3 describes the methods supported by `StringAssert`.

TABLE 7-3

METHOD	DESCRIPTION
Contains	Searches a string for a substring and fails if not found
DoesNotMatch	Applies a regular expression to a string and fails if any matches are found
EndsWith	Fails if the string does not end with a given substring
Matches	Applies a regular expression to a string and fails if no matches are found
StartsWith	Fails if the string does not begin with a given substring

Following are some simple examples of these methods. Each of these assertions will pass.

```
[TestMethod]
public void TextTests()
{
    StringAssert.Contains("This is the searched text", "searched");

    StringAssert.EndsWith("String which ends with searched", "ends with searched");

    StringAssert.Matches("Search this string for whitespace",
                new System.Text.RegularExpressions.Regex(@"\s+"));

    StringAssert.DoesNotMatch("Doesnotcontainwhitespace",
                new System.Text.RegularExpressions.Regex(@"\s+"));

    StringAssert.StartsWith("Starts with correct text", "Starts with");
}
```

`Matches` and `DoesNotMatch` accept a string and an instance of `System.Text.RegularExpressions.Regex`. In the preceding example, a simple regular expression that looks for at least one whitespace character was used. `Matches` finds whitespace and the `DoesNotMatch` does not find whitespace, so both pass.

Expecting Exceptions

Normally, a unit test that throws an exception is considered to have failed. However, you'll often wish to verify that a class behaves correctly by throwing an exception. For example, you might provide invalid arguments to a method to verify that it properly throws an exception.

The ExpectedException attribute indicates that a test will succeed only if the indicated exception is thrown. Not throwing an exception or throwing an exception of a different type will result in test failure.

The following unit test expects that an ObjectDisposedException will be thrown:

```
[TestMethod]

[ExpectedException(typeof(ObjectDisposedException))]
public void ReadAfterDispose()
{
    CustomFileReader cfr = new CustomFileReader("target.txt");
    cfr.Dispose();
    string contents = cfr.Read();  // Should throw ObjectDisposedException
}
```

The ExpectedException attribute supports a second, optional string argument. The Message property of the thrown exception must match this string or the test will fail. This enables you to differentiate between two different instances of the same exception type.

For example, suppose you are calling a method that throws a FileNotFoundException for several different files. To ensure that it cannot find one specific file in your testing scenario, supply the message you expect as the second argument to ExpectedException. If the exception thrown is not FileNotFoundException and its Message property does not match that text, the test will fail.

Defining Custom Unit Test Properties

You may define custom properties for your unit tests. For example, you may wish to specify the author of each test and be able to view that property from the Test List Editor.

Use the TestProperty attribute to decorate a unit test, supplying the name of the property and a value:

```
[TestMethod]

[TestProperty("Author", "Deborah")]
public void ExampleTest()
{
    // Test logic
}
```

Now, when you view the properties of that test, you will see a new entry, `Author`, with the value `Deborah`. If you change that value from the Properties window, the attribute in your code will automatically be updated.

TestContext Class

Unit tests normally have a reference to a `TestContext` instance. This object provides run-time features that might be useful to tests, such as details of the test itself, the various directories in use, and several methods to supplement the details stored with the test's results. `TestContext` is also very important for data-driven unit tests, as you will see later.

Several methods are especially useful to all unit tests. The first, `WriteLine`, enables you to insert text into the results of your unit test. This can be useful for supplying additional information about the test, such as parameters, environment details, and other debugging data that would normally be excluded from test results. By default, information from the test run is stored in a *test results file*, an XML file with a `.trx` extension. These files can be found in the `TestResults` subdirectory of your project. The default name for the files is based on the user, machine, and date of the test run, but this can be modified via the test run configuration settings.

Here is a simple example of a unit test that accesses the `TestContext` to send a string containing the test's name to the results:

```
[TestClass]
public class TestClass
{
    private TestContext testContextInstance;

    public TestContext TestContext
    {
        get { return testContextInstance; }
        set { testContextInstance = value; }
    }

    [TestMethod]
    public void TestMethod1()
    {
        TestContext.WriteLine("This is test {0}", TestContext.TestName);
    }
}
```

The `AddResultFile` method enables you to add a file, at run-time, to the results of the test run. The file you specify will be copied to the results directory alongside other results content. For example, this may be useful if your unit test is validating an object that creates or alters a file, and you would like that file to be included with the results for analysis.

Finally, the `BeginTimer` and `EndTimer` methods enable you to create one or more named timers within your unit tests. The results of these timers are stored in the test run's results.

Creating Data-Driven Unit Tests

An excellent way to verify the correct behavior of code is to execute it using realistic data. Visual Studio provides features to automatically bind data from a data source as input to unit tests. The unit test is run once for each data row.

A unit test is made data-driven by assigning attributes for connecting to and reading from a data source. The easiest way to do this is to modify an existing unit test's properties in the Test List Editor window. Begin with a normal unit test outline, and then open the Test List Editor. Select the unit test and view its properties.

First, establish the connection to the data source by setting the Data Connection String property. You may either enter it manually or click the button labeled with ellipses ("...") to use dialogs. You have three options for data sources. You can link to an ODBC data source, such as a database or Excel spreadsheet. You can also use a comma-delimited file or an XML file as a datasource. The DeploymentItem attribute may be used with a test method to specify the source file containing the test data.

As mentioned previously, the unit test will be called once per row in the data source. You can set how rows are fed into the unit test via the Data Access Method property. Sequential will feed the rows in exactly the order returned from the data source, whereas Random will select random rows. Rows are provided to the unit test until all rows have been used once.

Setting these properties will automatically decorate the selected unit test with the appropriate attributes. You do not need to use the Properties window to create data-driven tests. For example, you may wish to copy attributes from an existing data-driven test to quickly create another.

To access the data from within the unit test, use the DataRow property of the TestContext. For example, if you bound to a table with customer data, you could read the current customer's ID from the CustomerID column with the following:

```
long customerID = TestContext.DataRow["CustomerID"];
```

Besides a column name, the DataRow property also accepts a column offset. If CustomerID were the first column in the table, you could supply a zero as the argument with the same result.

Because the unit test is run once per row in the data source, you want to be able to tell which rows caused certain results. Fortunately, this detail is already tracked for you. In the Test Results window, right-click on the test result and choose View Test Results Details. You will see a list of pass/fail results for each record in the database, enabling you to easily see which rows caused your test to fail.

Visual Studio makes it very easy to write comprehensive tests against actual data. However, keep in mind that it is not enough to test only valid data, such as your real customer data. You will also want to have unit tests that verify your code's behavior when invalid data is supplied.

DEVELOPING THE TEST-DRIVEN WAY WITH RED-GREEN-REFACTOR

Now that you understand what a unit test is and how to write one, you might consider the next time you have to implement some functionality to write the tests first. By doing this, you start to question how your code should work very early in the development lifecycle. In addition, by thinking about what your code *needs* to do rather than *how* it should do it, you can focus on writing the minimal amount of code necessary to meet the requirements, rather than getting bogged down in premature optimizations of the code.

Test-first development is probably best known as the test-driven development (TDD) software development technique popularized by Kent Beck in his book *Test-Driven Development: By Example* (Boston, Addison-Wesley Professional, 2002) and by Jim Newkirk and Alexei A. Vorontsov in *Test-Driven Development in Microsoft .NET* (Redmond, WA: Microsoft Press, 2004). Both books are required reading if you are interested in learning more about the benefits of test-first approaches and how to adopt them with your team.

ACCESSING NONPUBLIC MEMBERS FROM TESTS

What if you want to test a class member that is not public? For example, suppose you're writing a private function that is never publicly accessed and is only used internally by other members. You'd like to test this method, but your test code does not have access to private members (or to internal members if the code is in a separate assembly).

There are four main approaches for addressing this issue:

➤ Make the private members you need to test public.

➤ Make the private members you need to test internal, and add the test assembly to the internalsVisibleTo attribute on the original assembly.

➤ Ensure that the private members are reachable through a public member and test via those public members.

➤ Use .NET reflection in the tests to load and directly invoke the nonpublic members.

With Visual Studio, this final approach is abstracted for you. The following two sections describe how Visual Studio helps to automate this previously manual task.

Testing private members is a controversial subject. Some people prefer to test only via public members to allow for easier refactoring. Others argue that an API should never be modified just for the sake of easier testing. If you agree with the former opinion, you can safely skip the remainder of this section.

Using PrivateObject to Access Nonpublic Instance Members

Suppose you'd like to test the private field and method of the following class:

```
public class Example
{
    public Example() {}

    private string password = "letmein";

    private bool VerifyPassword(string password)
    {
        return (String.Compare(this.password, password, false) == 0);
    }
}
```

Because the field and method are marked `private`, a unit test will not have the capability to directly access them. How can you ensure that `VerifyPassword` is working correctly?

Visual Studio introduces the `PrivateObject` class, which is a wrapper around reflection code that enables you to access nonpublic members in a fairly straightforward manner.

Table 7-4 summarizes the methods supported by `PrivateObject`.

TABLE 7-4

METHOD	DESCRIPTION
GetArrayElement	Returns the selected item from a private array member. Supports multidimensional arrays with additional arguments.
GetField	Returns the value of the target field.
GetFieldOrProperty	Returns the value of the target field or property.
GetProperty	Returns the value of the target property.
Invoke	Invokes the target method, optionally passing parameters.
SetArrayElement	Assigns the given value to the indicated element of a private array. Supports multidimensional arrays with additional arguments.
SetField	Assigns the supplied object to the target field.
SetFieldOrProperty	Assigns the supplied object to the target field or property.
SetProperty	Assigns the supplied object to the target property.

To use it, you first create an instance of the `PrivateObject` class, passing a `Type` object for the class you wish to work with:

```
using System;
using Microsoft.VisualStudio.TestTools.UnitTesting;

namespace Explorations
{
    [TestClass]
    public class ExampleTest
    {
        private PrivateObject privateObject;
        const string PASSWORD = "letmein";

        [TestInitialize]
        public void TestInitialize()
        {

            privateObject = new PrivateObject(typeof(Example));
        }
    }
}
```

Now you can create your tests. Use the `GetField` method of the `PrivateObject` instance to access nonpublic fields, supplying the name of the desired variable. Similarly, use `Invoke` to call methods, supplying the method name as the first argument, followed by any parameters to that method:

```
using System;
using Microsoft.VisualStudio.TestTools.UnitTesting;

namespace Explorations
{
    [TestClass]
    public class ExampleTest
    {
        private PrivateObject privateObject;
        const string PASSWORD = "letmein";

        [TestInitialize]
        public void TestInitialize()
        {
            privateObject = new PrivateObject(typeof(Example));
        }


    [TestMethod]
    public void ComparePrivatePassword()
    {
        string password = (string)privateObject.GetField("password");
        Assert.AreEqual(PASSWORD, password);
    }
    [TestMethod]
    public void TestPrivateVerifyPassword()
```

```
        {
            bool accepted = (bool)privateObject.Invoke("VerifyPassword", PASSWORD);
            Assert.IsTrue(accepted);
        }
    }
}
```

Because `PrivateObject` uses reflection, you must cast the results of these calls from the generic `Object` type back to the correct underlying type.

Using PrivateType to Access Nonpublic Static Members

`PrivateObject` is used to access instance-based members of a class. If you must access static nonpublic members, you use the `PrivateType` class, which has a very similar interface and is a wrapper of reflection code.

Table 7-5 summarizes the methods exposed by `PrivateType`.

TABLE 7-5

METHOD	DESCRIPTION
GetStaticArrayElement	Returns the selected item from a private static array member. Supports multidimensional arrays with additional arguments.
GetStaticField	Returns the value of the target static field.
GetStaticProperty	Returns the value of the target static property.
InvokeStatic	Invokes the target static method, optionally passing parameters.
SetStaticArrayElement	Assigns the given value to the indicated element of a private static array. Supports multidimensional arrays with additional arguments.
SetStaticField	Assigns the supplied object to the target static field.
SetStaticProperty	Assigns the supplied object to the target static property.

The usage is very similar to `PrivateObject`. Create an instance of the `PrivateType`, indicating which type you wish to work with, and then use the methods to access members as with `PrivateObject`. Suppose you added a private static count of password failures with a wrapping private property called `FailureCount`. The following code could read and test that property:

```
[TestMethod]
public void TestPrivateStaticFailureCount()
{
    PrivateType example = new PrivateType(typeof(Example));
    int failureCount = (int)example.GetStaticProperty("FailureCount");
    Assert.AreEqual(failureCount, 0);
}
```

Again, you create an instance of `PrivateType`, passing the type reference for the class you wish to access. Then you use that instance, invoking `GetStaticProperty` to retrieve the value you wish to test. Finally, you ensure that the value is zero as expected.

> *Use caution when testing static data. Because static data is shared and is not automatically reset between your tests, sometimes the order of your tests will affect their results. In other words, if you test that a value is initialized to zero in one test, and then set it to a test value in another test, if the order of those tests is reversed, the zero test will fail. Remember that you must be able to run your tests in any order and in any combination.*

CODE GENERATION

Remember the work you did earlier in this chapter to create your first unit test? You created the first unit tests manually to help convey basic concepts, but Visual Studio has support for automatically generating code. You may generate unit tests from your implementation code or generate limited implementation code when writing your tests.

Generating Tests from Code

If you have ever needed to add unit testing to an existing project that had none, it was likely a frustrating experience. Fortunately, Visual Studio has introduced the capability to generate outlines of unit tests based on selected implementation code.

Let's begin with the `Functions` class you used earlier in this chapter. Open `Functions.cs` and ensure it contains the following code:

```
using System;

namespace ExtendedMath
{
    public sealed class Functions
    {
        private Functions() {}

        public static int Fibonacci(int factor)
        {
            if (factor < 2)
                return (factor);
            int x = Fibonacci(--factor);
            int y = Fibonacci(--factor);

            return x + y;
        }
    }
}
```

If you have been following the examples in this chapter, delete your existing `FunctionsTest.cs` file. Now, you can right-click in your code and choose Create Unit Tests, or click the Create Tests button from the Test Views toolbar. The Create Unit Tests dialog will appear, as shown in Figure 7-6.

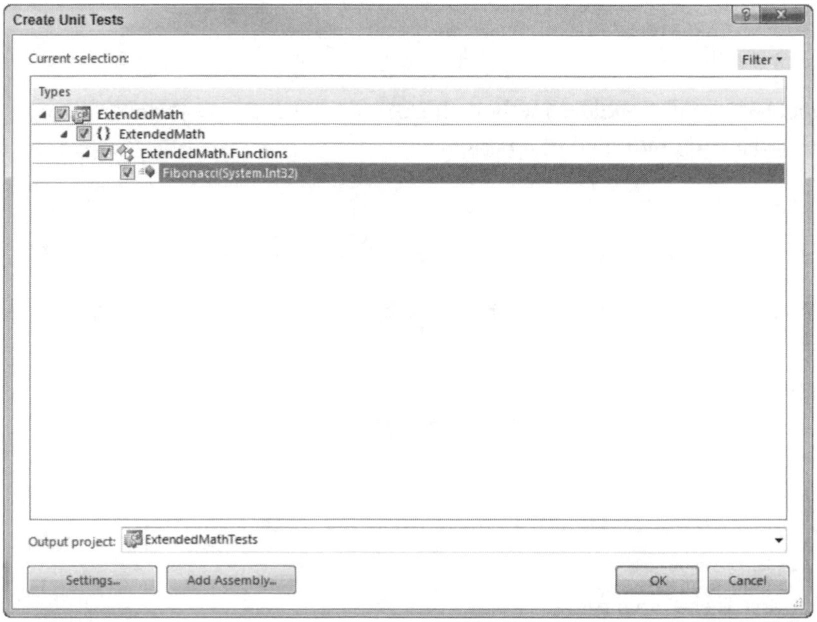

FIGURE 7-6

> *Right-clicking in code is context-sensitive, and the dialog will default appropriately based on where you clicked. For example, if you click from your class definition, all of that class's members will be selected for generation by default. Clicking on a method will default with only that method selected.*

Select the members for which you would like to generate unit tests and then click OK.

Visual Studio will create a new class file, `FunctionsTest.cs`, if it does not already exist. Inside, you will find a class, `FunctionsTest`, marked with `[TestClass]` attribute.

At the top of the class is a `TestContext` field initialized to `null`, with a `TestContext` property to enable you to access context from your tests:

```
private TestContext testContextInstance;

public TestContext TestContext
{
```

```
        get
        {
            return testContextInstance;
        }
        set
        {
            testContextInstance = value;
        }
    }
```

Next, you will find commented-out placeholder methods for ClassInitialize, ClassCleanup, TestInitialize, and TestCleanup, wrapped in a region:

```
#region Additional test attributes
//
//You can use the following additional attributes as you write your tests:
//
//Use ClassInitialize to run code before running the
//first test in the class
//
//[ClassInitialize()]
//public static void MyClassInitialize(TestContext testContext)
//{
//}
//
//Use ClassCleanup to run code after all tests in a class have run
//
//[ClassCleanup()]
//public static void MyClassCleanup()
//{
//}
//
//Use TestInitialize to run code before running each test
//
//[TestInitialize()]
//public void MyTestInitialize()
//{
//}
//
//Use TestCleanup to run code after each test has run
//
//[TestCleanup()]
//public void MyTestCleanup()
//{
//}
//
#endregion
```

Finally, you will see the actual generated unit test:

```
/// <summary>
```

```
///A test for Fibonacci
///</summary>
[TestMethod()]
public void FibonacciTest()
{
    int factor = 0; // TODO: Initialize to an appropriate value
    int expected = 0; // TODO: Initialize to an appropriate value
    int actual;
    actual = Functions.Fibonacci(factor);
    Assert.AreEqual(expected, actual);
    Assert.Inconclusive("Verify the correctness of this test method.");
}
```

The generated code defines a basic structure that depends on the signature of the member being tested. In this example, it recognized that `Fibonacci` accepts an integer and returns an integer, including an `Assert.AreEqual` for you. The TODO indicates that `factor` and `expected` are only default values, and you must adjust them to ensure correct test values.

> *Keep in mind that generated code will often benefit from careful refactoring, and your generated unit tests will be no exception. For example, look for ways to consolidate common tasks into shared functions.*

Optionally, but by default, generated tests end with calls to `Assert.Inconclusive` to indicate that the unit test needs further inspection to determine its correctness. See the section "Using the Assert Methods," earlier in this chapter, for more information.

CODE COVERAGE

The unit testing features in Visual Studio have full support for code coverage. Code coverage automatically inserts tracking logic (a process called *instrumentation*) to monitor which lines of code are executed during the execution of your tests. The most important result of this is the identification of regions of your code that you have not reached with your tests.

Often, you may have branching or exception-handling logic that isn't executed in common situations. It is critical to use code coverage to identify these areas because your users certainly will. Add unit tests to cause those areas of code to be executed, and you'll be able to sleep soundly at night.

> *Code coverage is a useful tool, but it should not be relied upon as an exclusive indicator of unit test effectiveness. It cannot tell you the manner in which code was executed, possibly missing errors that would result with different data or timing. A suite of unit tests based on a variety of different inputs and execution orders will help to ensure that your code is correct, complete, and resilient. Use code coverage to help identify code your tests are missing, not to tell you when your tests are complete.*

A tenet of effective unit testing is that the removal of any line of code should cause at least one unit test to fail. This is, of course, an ideal but is worth keeping in mind as you develop your systems.

Enabling Code Coverage

Code coverage is activated via a setting in the Test Settings. Open the configuration for editing by choosing Test ⇨ Edit Test Settings and selecting the configuration. Once you have the Configuration Settings dialog active, select "Data and Diagnostics" and check the box next to Code Coverage.

Click the Configure button to open the Code Coverage Detail window. Select the assemblies you wish to instrument from the Code Coverage Configuration list. If you don't see an assembly you'd like to instrument, you can click Add Assembly to manually add it. Figure 7-7 shows the Code Coverage Configuration page.

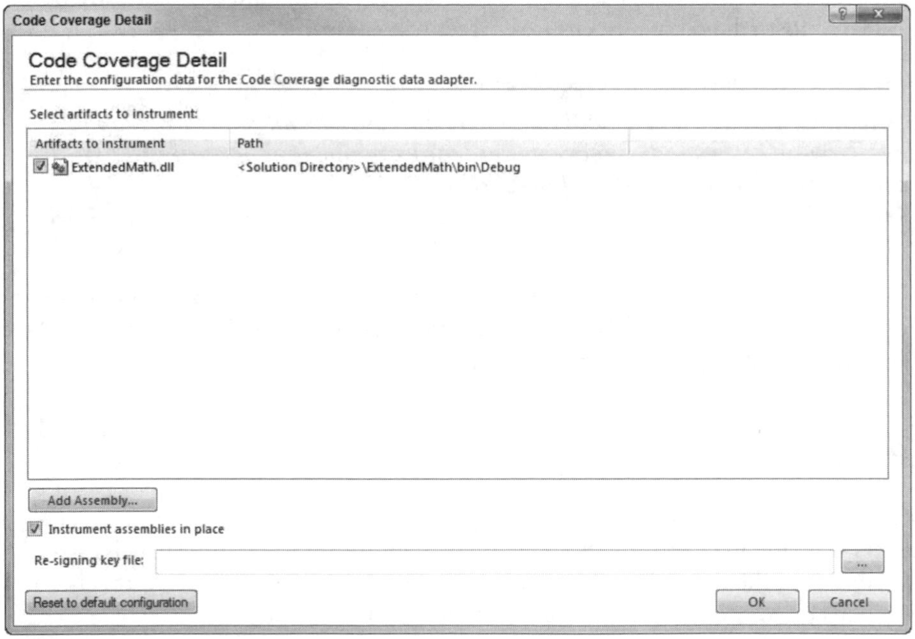

FIGURE 7-7

The instrumentation process modifies your original assemblies, invalidating original signatures. If you are working with signed assemblies, use the Re-signing key file field to specify a key file with which to sign the instrumented assembly.

Viewing Code Coverage Results

Once you have enabled coverage and selected the assemblies to instrument, run your unit tests as normal. You will then be able to see results of the coverage in the Code Coverage Results window. This window will show counts of lines and percentages of code covered and uncovered. You may expand the view by clicking the plus signs to see details at the assembly, class, and member levels.

Executable lines of code will be highlighted in red if they have not been run by your tests and in blue if they were. Code that is purely structural or documentation will not be highlighted. Figure 7-8 illustrates the results of a code coverage test.

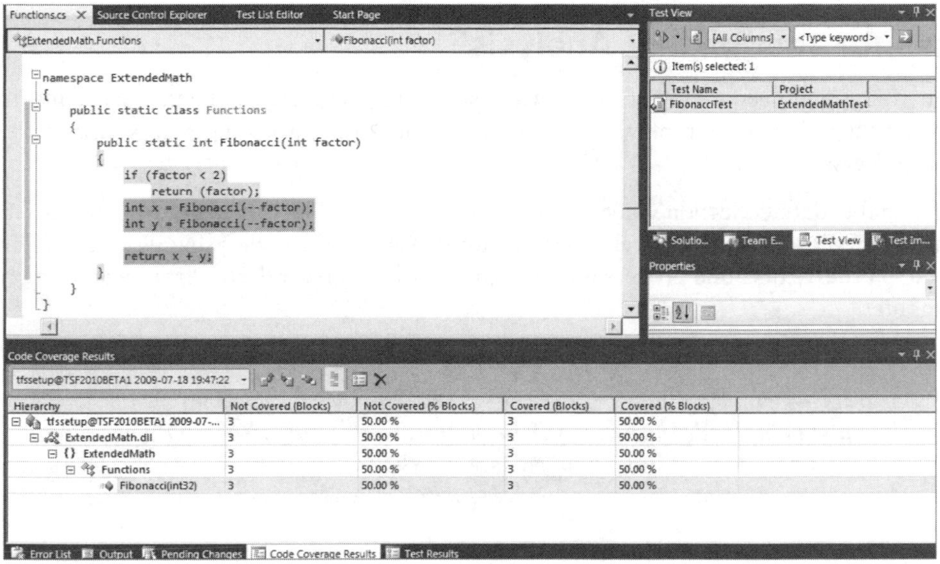

FIGURE 7-8

In this example, you have achieved 50 percent code coverage of the `Fibonacci` method. By viewing the method, you can see by the color-coding that half the method has been tested.

Again, keep in mind that 100 percent code coverage does not mean you have finished writing your unit tests. Proper testing may involve multiple executions of the same code using different data. Code coverage is one measure of effectiveness but certainly not the only one. Plan your testing cases up front, and then use code coverage to alert you to scenarios you forgot to test.

TEST IMPACT ANALYSIS

Having unit tests that run and verify your code is working correctly is a must-have in the modern development world. Depending on the size and complexity of your code, you may have hundreds or even thousands of unit tests. And, as you are making changes to your code, you should run your tests to ensure that you have not introduced any new errors into the system. However, as you can imagine, running the entire suite of unit tests every time you make a code change can take a considerable amount of time. Wouldn't it be nice to know exactly which tests you need to run to test the code changes you just made?

Well, now you have that capability. Visual Studio 2010 introduces a new feature designed to do just that: test impact analysis. With test impact analysis, as you make code changes, you can view which tests are impacted by the code change — not just unit tests, but even manual tests that have been previously executed against a build with the appropriate data collectors enabled. This allows you to quickly and easily run just the tests needed to verify the code changes. You also have the capability to view tests that are related to a particular method before you start making changes, so you can see ahead of time what tests may be affected. This allows you to ask the question, "If I change this method, what tests would need to be run to verify it?"

Prerequisites for Test Impact Analysis

There are some things you need to do before you can use test impact analysis. First and foremost, you must be using the unit testing framework within Visual Studio, and storing your source code in Team Foundation Version Control.

Next, you must enable data collection when you run your unit tests. This allows Visual Studio 2010 Team Foundation Server to collect data related to the unit tests and the code being tested. This data can be collected via the Team Build process automatically, or it can be collected from tests run on your local computer.

> *If the unit tests are run locally or via the Microsoft Team Manager product, the test results must be uploaded into Team Foundation Server and associated with a team build in order for test impact analysis to work*

To enable data collection for your test project, follow these steps:

1. In Visual Studio, open the solution containing the test project for which you want to enable data collection.
2. In Solution Explorer, double-click the `Local.testsettings` file to open the Test Settings window.
3. In the Test Settings window, select Data and Diagnostics.
4. In the list, check the Test Impact check box.
5. Click the Apply button, then click the Close button to close the Test Settings window.

You can also enable data collection as part of the Team Build process. To do that, you must enable data collection in the build definition of your build. For more information, see Chapter 21. Basically, you would follow these steps:

1. Using Team Explorer, create a new build definition, or modify an existing build definition.
2. Click Process in the navigation bar of the build definition.
3. Scroll to the Testing Category in the Build process parameters list.
4. Set the Analyze Test Impacts property to True.
5. For Test Container TestSettings File, specify a `.testsettings` file that you have already enabled data collection on.
6. Save your changes to the build definition.

Identifying Relationships Between Code and Tests

There are two ways to make use of the test impact analysis feature in Visual Studio 2010. You can view (and optionally run) the tests that have been impacted by your code changes. You can also select a code method, and see all the tests that would be impacted by making changes to that method.

View Tests That Have Been Impacted

To view the tests that have been impacted by code changes, follow these steps:

1. In Visual Studio, select Test ➪ Windows ➪ Test Impact View to open the Test Impact View window.

2. In the Test Impact View Window toolbar, click Show Impacted tests.

The Test Impact View window will display all the tests that have been impacted by the code changes, as shown in Figure 7-9. You can choose to highlight one or more tests, and click Run Selection to run the tests. If no tests have been affected, the window will display the phrase, "No tests are impacted."

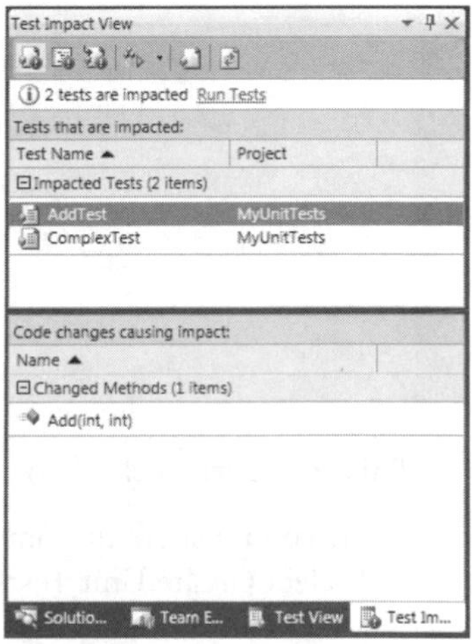

View Tests for a Particular Method

To view all the tests that could be impacted by changing a particular method, follow these steps:

1. In Visual Studio, select Test ➪ Windows ➪ Test Impact View to open the Test Impact View window.

2. In the Test Impact View window, click Show Calling Tests.

3. In the Visual Studio code editor, right-click the method for which you want to list tests, and select Show Calling Tests.

The Test Impact View window will display all the tests that call the selected method, as shown in Figure 7-10. You can choose to highlight one or more tests, and click Run Selection to run the tests.

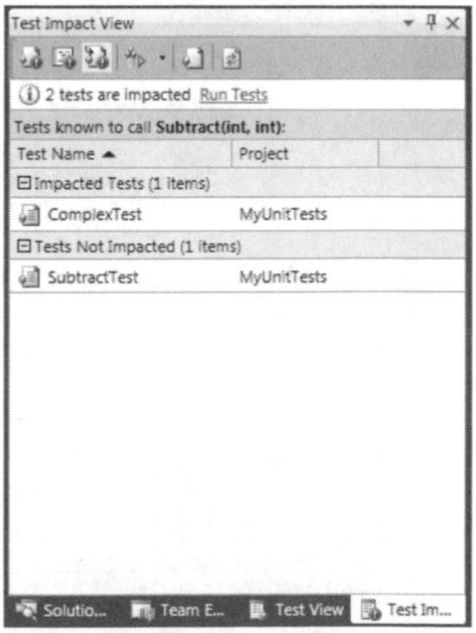

Test Impact Analysis Example

The best way to show the effectiveness of test impact analysis is through an example. In the following example code, you create a very simple calculator class library with three methods:

➤ `Add` — Adds two numbers together

➤ `Subtract` — Subtracts two numbers

➤ `Complex` — Uses both the `Add` and `Subtract` methods to perform a more complex operation

```
using System;
using System.Collections.Generic;
```

FIGURE 7-9

FIGURE 7-10

```
using System.Linq;
using System.Text;

namespace Calculator
{
    class MyCalculator
    {
        public int Add(int p1, int p2)
        {
            return (p1 + p2);
        }

        public int Subtract(int p1, int p2)
        {
            return (p1 - p2);
        }

        public int Complex(int p1, int p2, int p3)
        {
            int value = 0;

            value = Subtract(Add(p1, p2), p3);

            return (value);
        }
    }
}
```

This code is then checked into version control in Team Foundation Server 2010.

Next, you must create some unit tests to test your methods. Right-click on `class MyCalculator` and select Create Unit Tests to open the Create Unit Tests window, as shown in Figure 7-11.

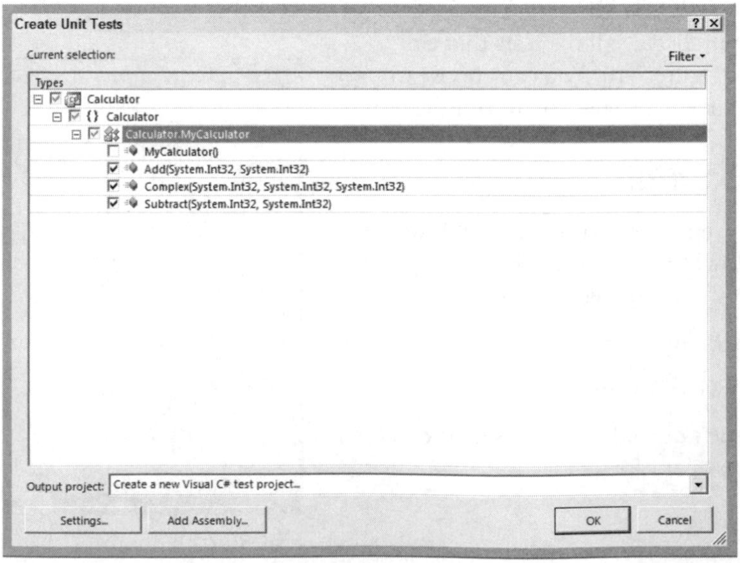

FIGURE 7-11

Select the `Add`, `Subtract`, and `Complex` methods. Click the OK button to close the wizard. Enter **MyUnitTests** as the name of the test project and click Create. A new test project named `MyUnitTests` is created. Inside this test project is a class file named `MyCalculatorTests.cs`. Inside this file are three test methods that have been stubbed out: `AddTest`, `SubtractTest`, and `ComplexTest`.

The test methods require some modifications to be valid tests. Modify the `AddTest` method to look like this:

```
[TestMethod()]
      public void AddTest()
      {
          MyCalculator target = new MyCalculator();

          int p1 = 4;
          int p2 = 5;
          int expected = 9;

          int actual = target.Add(p1, p2);

          Assert.AreEqual(expected, actual);

      }
```

Modify the `SubtractTest` method to look like this:

```
[TestMethod()]
      public void SubtractTest()
      {
          MyCalculator target = new MyCalculator();

          int p1 = 10;
          int p2 = 6;
          int expected = 4;

          int actual = target.Subtract(p1, p2);

          Assert.AreEqual(expected, actual);

      }
```

Finally, modify the `ComplexText` method to look like this:

```
[TestMethod()]
      public void ComplexTest()
      {
          MyCalculator target = new MyCalculator();

          int p1 = 3;
          int p2 = 4;
          int p3 = 2;
```

```
        int expected = 5;

        int actual = target.Complex(p1, p2, p3);

        Assert.AreEqual(expected, actual);
    }
```

Run the unit tests to ensure that they are valid, then check all changes into Team Foundation Server.

Now that you have your unit tests created and checked into version control, you must enable data collection on the test project. In Solution Explorer, double-click `Local.testsettings`. This opens the Test Settings window. Select Data and Diagnostics in the left-hand side of the window. Check the box next Test Impact. Click the Apply button, and then the Close button to close the Test Settings window.

Data collection is now enabled, but before test impact analysis can be utilized, you must upload the test results into Team Foundation Server, and, to do that, you must have a build to upload them against. (See Chapter 21 for more information on creating a new build definition.) Once you have created a build definition, run the unit tests created previously. In the Test Results window, click the Publish button (the first button in the section, before the Group By drop down) to open the Publish Test Results window. Select a build with which to associate the test results, and click OK to close the Publish Test Results window. Once the publishing of the test results is complete, you are now ready to make use of the test impact analysis functionality.

Let's make a code change to the `Add` method. Modify the `Add` method to be the following:

```
public int Add(int p1, int p2)
    {
        int value = 0;

        value = p1 + p2;

        return (value);
    }
```

To see what tests have been impacted, open the Test Impact View window, as shown in Figure 7-12.

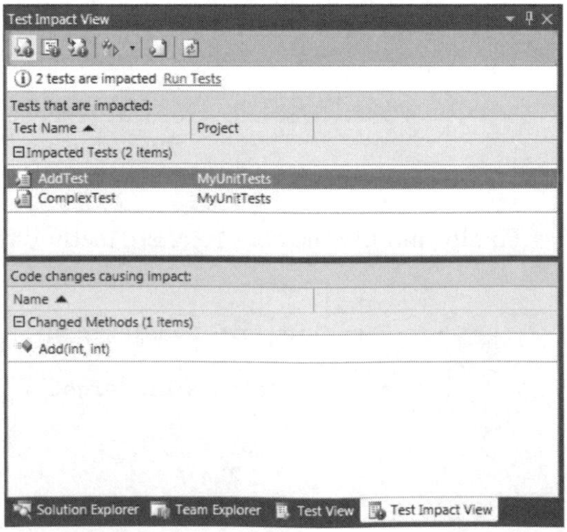

With the Show Impacted Test button selected, you can see there are two tests that will need to be run: `AddTest` and `ComplexTest`. By selecting a specific impacted test, you can see what methods are causing the impact (in this case, the changes to the `Add` method). Notice the Run Test link at the top of the window. Clicking this link will automatically run all impacted tests for you, providing a quick and easy way to run those tests.

FIGURE 7-12

SUMMARY

Microsoft has brought the advantages of unit testing to the developer by fully integrating features with the Visual Studio development environment. If you're new to unit testing, this chapter has provided an overview of what unit testing is, and how to create effective unit tests. This chapter examined the creation and management of unit tests, and detailed the methods and attributes available in the unit test framework. You should be familiar with attributes for identifying your tests, as well as many of the options that the `Assert` class offers for testing behavior of code.

You've learned how to generate code with Visual Studio, either by generating tests from code or code from tests. As you saw, it is also very easy to bind unit tests to a data source to create data-driven tests. This chapter also showed that Visual Studio offers a simple way to access private members for testing, addressing a need that previously required manual workarounds.

You learned how to use code coverage to help identify where your unit tests may have missed some scenarios. And, finally, you learned about test impact analysis, and how it can be used to identify what tests to run after code changes have been made.

If you have been using other frameworks for your unit testing to date, you'll enjoy not having to leave the IDE to work with your tests, as well as the familiar options and syntax that Visual Studio offers.

You should become familiar with the benefits of unit testing, keeping in mind that unit tests are not a replacement for other forms of testing, but a very strong supplement.

Obviously, testing is an important aspect to prove that your code is ready to be deployed into production. However, just because the code passes all the unit tests doesn't mean that it is necessarily ready to ship.

Chapter 8 examines the code analysis tools in Visual Studio that help you quickly look for common mistakes, security issues, or even violations of standards. You also learn about how to use Code Metrics to help you identify parts of the systems that may prove difficult to maintain.

8

Managed Code Analysis and Code Metrics

WHAT'S IN THIS CHAPTER?

➤ Understanding why code analysis is important

➤ Enabling and running code analysis in Visual Studio 2010

➤ Correcting code analysis rule violations

➤ Creating a custom code analysis rule

➤ Understanding code metrics and how to use them

This chapter describes the code analysis and code metric features included with Visual Studio 2010 Premium and Visual Studio 2010 Ultimate. These tools can quickly and easily inspect your code to find common mistakes, make suggestions for improvements, and even indicate violations of standards.

The discussion begins by examining the origins of the Static Code Analysis tool. You'll learn about Microsoft's .NET "Design Guidelines for Class Library Developers" and how it is related to the tools.

Then you will learn a bit about the tool itself and how to take advantage of its full integration with Visual Studio 2010. This includes enabling static code analysis review for your projects, selecting rules to apply, and working with the results of the analysis. Static code analysis is also available for database projects, but that particular use of static code analysis will not be covered in this chapter. For more information on using static code analysis with database projects, see Chapter 10.

However, using the IDE is not always an option, and sometimes you need additional flexibility. The Static Code Analysis tool is available to you from the command line. You will learn how to use the command line for code analysis and how to include code analysis with your automated builds.

The Static Code Analysis rules that ship with Visual Studio will probably not be sufficient for the specific standards and practices of your own projects. To address this, you will learn how you can create and integrate new custom rules. You will learn about the mechanics of rules and the new Introspection engine. You will then create an example rule using introspection and call it from the Visual Studio IDE.

This chapter wraps up with a look at Code Metrics, a tool in Visual Studio that can provide insight into how well-written your code is. Each code metric is examined in detail, and you learn how to understand what code metrics are trying to tell you.

THE NEED FOR ANALYSIS TOOLS

Ensuring that developers follow best practices and write consistent code is a major challenge in today's software development projects. The act of documenting standards and practices is often skipped or overlooked. However, even in projects for which standards have been established, getting developers to read and follow those practices is another major challenge.

One of the best resources available for .NET developers is Microsoft's .NET Framework "Design Guidelines for Class Library Developers" (Design Guidelines). These guidelines document Microsoft's (formerly) internal practices for developing class libraries, and are freely available at `http://msdn.microsoft.com/library/en-us/cpgenref/html/ cpconnetframeworkdesignguidelines.asp`.

The guidelines cover a wide range of subjects, including naming conventions, usage guidelines, and performance and security considerations. When put into practice, they help ensure that your approach will be consistent with that of other developers. In addition, they have evolved over a number of years to reflect a considerable amount of knowledge, best practices, and lessons learned.

As useful as the design guidelines are, the reality of software creation is that many developers will not be familiar with their contents. Most times, this is not a fault of the developer, but rather the process that the developer must follow. For some companies, design guidelines are not as important as simply getting the project finished, regardless of the long-term benefit that following those guidelines will have. The desire to automate the process of evaluating code for compliance with these guidelines led to the creation of *FxCop*.

USING MANAGED CODE ANALYSIS

FxCop is a tool used to analyze managed code against a library of rules. You can create rules for almost any purpose — naming conventions, security, attribute usage, and so on. FxCop contains nearly 200 rules, based on the .NET Framework Design Guidelines described earlier.

FxCop has been available from Microsoft on the `GotDotNet.com` site for several years. Before that, it had been used internally at Microsoft for analysis of its own frameworks to help ensure predictable and consistent interfaces. Previous versions of FxCop have been standalone applications, separated from the Visual Studio IDE.

With Visual Studio Team System 2005, FxCop was rebranded as the Managed Code Analysis tool, and fully integrated with the IDE, enabling analysis to be performed with a simple build of your application. The FxCop heritage of Managed Code Analysis is generally hidden when you're using the IDE. But, as you'll see, the FxCop name still appears when creating new rules and using command-line options.

An example project will be presented throughout this chapter. To begin the project, create a new C# Class Library project and name it `SampleLibrary`. Rename the `Class1.cs` file to `PayCalculator.cs`, and insert the following code, which, as you'll soon see, fails to meet several code analysis guidelines:

Available for download on Wrox.com

```csharp
using System;

namespace SampleLibrary
{
    public class PayCalculator
    {
        public enum Pay_Level
        {
            EntryLevel = 20,
            Normal = 35,
            Senior = 50
        }

        public static int MaximumHours;
        public const double BONUS = 0.10;

        static PayCalculator()
        {
            MaximumHours = 100;
        }

        public static double ComputePayment(int hours, Pay_Level level)
        {
            if (hours > MaximumHours)
            {
                throw new ArgumentOutOfRangeException("Employee works too much");
            }

            return ((int)level * hours);
        }
    }
}
```

filename 484265_ch08_code01.zip

While this code will compile and run as expected, you can make several improvements to it, and the Code Analysis tool will help you find them. These improvements will help make your code easier to understand, and possibly catch potential run-time errors (such as buffer overflows).

Built-in Managed Code Analysis Rules

As mentioned earlier, Visual Studio ships with nearly 200 rules for Managed Code Analysis, each of which helps to enforce the practices documented in the .NET Framework Design Guidelines, as well as other practices recommended by Microsoft. This section briefly describes each of the 11 rule groups to help you understand when you might apply them to your projects.

Table 8-1 describes the groups of rules included with Visual Studio 2010.

TABLE 8-1: Groups of Rules

RULE GROUP (NUMBER OF RULES)	DESCRIPTION
Design (62)	Typically focused on the interfaces and structure of code, this group enforces proper implementation of common concepts such as classes, events, collections, namespaces, and parameters. These rules revolve around the Microsoft .NET Framework Design Guidelines (`http://msdn.microsoft .com/en-us/library/czefa0ke(VS.71).aspx`).
Globalization (11)	This group includes practices to support the internationalization of code. This can include avoiding strings of literal text, correct use of `CultureInfo`, and formatting.
Interoperability (17)	This group is focused on the correct use of COM Interop. Included are rules for proper use of `PInvoke`, the `ComVisible` attribute, and marshalling.
Maintainability (6)	These are rules to help make your code easier to maintain. This group identifies potential problems such as complexity and overuse of inheritance.
Mobility (2)	These are rules to help detect code that will not run effectively in mobile or disconnected environments.
Naming (24)	This group enforces naming standards as described in the Design Guidelines. Using these rules verifies that names of items such as assemblies, classes, members, and variables conform to standards. Some rules will even help to detect misspellings in your assigned names.
Performance (17)	These rules help to detect places in your code that may be optimized for performance. They detect a wide variety of wasteful or extraneous code.
Portability (3)	These are rules to find code that might not be easily portable between operating environments.

RULE GROUP (NUMBER OF RULES)	DESCRIPTION
Reliability (6)	The rules in this group will help to detect problems with your code that may lead to intermittent failures, including failure to dispose of objects, improper use of the garbage collector, bad threading use, and more. These rules can be extremely useful, because intermittent errors are frequently the most difficult to identify and correct.
Security (26)	These rules help to identify insufficient or incorrect security practices. Rules exist to find missing attributes, improper use of permissions, and opportunities for SQL injection attacks.
Usage (42)	These rules cover a broad spectrum of recommended practices. Whereas the design group rules typically involve API structure, these rules govern the methodologies of code. Practices include proper exception management, handling of arithmetic overflow, serialization, and inheritance.

Of course, the rules that ship with Visual Studio are only a starting point. Microsoft and others will certainly make additional rules available, and you can add your own custom rules and rule groups as well. You'll learn how to create custom Managed Code Analysis rules later in this chapter.

Code Analysis Rule Sets

Visual Studio 2010 has introduced a new concept revolving around code analysis called *code analysis rule sets*. In previous editions, you had to spend time looking through all the code analysis rules and deciding which rules to use and which ones not to use. With Visual Studio 2010, code analysis rules can now be grouped into rule sets, making it easy for everyone to get started using code analysis. The code analysis rules that ship by default are already grouped into specified rule sets, but you have the capability to create your own custom rule sets as needed.

Table 8-2 shows the rule sets included with Visual Studio 2010.

TABLE 8-2: Rule Sets

RULE SET	DESCRIPTION
Microsoft All Rules	This rule set contains all code analysis rules.
Microsoft Basic Correctness Rules	This rule set focuses on logic errors and common mistakes made when using the .NET framework APIs.
Microsoft Basic Design Guideline Rules	This rule set focuses on enforcing best practices to make code easy to understand and use.
Microsoft Extended Correctness Rules	This rule set expands on the basic correctness rules to maximize the reported logic and framework usage errors.

continues

TABLE 8-2 *(continued)*

RULE SET	DESCRIPTION
Microsoft Extended Design Guideline Rules	This rule set expands on the basic design guideline rules to maximize the number of reported usability and maintainability issues.
Microsoft Globalization Rules	This rule set focuses on problems that may occur if your application has not been properly localized.
Microsoft Minimum Recommended Rules	This rule set focuses on the most critical problems in your code, including security holes and application crashes. This is the default rule set applied to newly created projects.
Microsoft Security Rules	This rule set contains all Microsoft security rules.

To create a new rule set, in Visual Studio, select File ➪ New File, and then select Rule Set File under the General tab. Using this new rule set, you can use the Add or Remove child rule set buttons to add existing rule sets to your custom rule set.

Enabling Managed Code Analysis

By default, code analysis is disabled for projects in Visual Studio. To enable analysis, open your project's Properties window and select Code Analysis from the left-hand side tabs. You will see a drop-down of the different rule sets available for use with code analysis. You will no longer see a collapsed list of rules as with previous versions, but instead you will see the new menu showing the selected rule set, as shown in Figure 8-1.

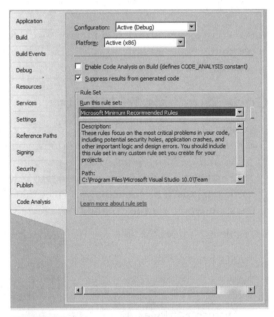

FIGURE 8-1

 To enable and configure Code Analysis for ASP.NET applications, from the main menu in Visual Studio, select Website ➪ Code Analysis Configuration. Code Analysis may also be enabled (but not configured) from the Build page of the ASP.NET project's Property Pages.

To enable code analysis upon build, check the box labeled "Enable Code Analysis on Build." Select the desired rule set in the drop-down list box, or choose multiple rule sets. Save your settings via Save Selected Items on the File menu, or by pressing Ctrl+S.

To view the rules contained in an individual rule set, select the rule set in the drop-down list box, then click the Open button. This opens the individual rules that comprise that rule set. Rules or entire groups of rules can be disabled by unchecking their boxes.

In addition, each rule in a rule set can be set to one of the following:

➤ *Warning (the default)* — Warnings serve as an advisory that something may need to be corrected, but they will not prevent the project's build from succeeding.

➤ *Error* — You may want to set certain rules or groups of rules to Error if they are critically important, thus preventing a build when those rules are violated.

➤ *Inherit* — Inherit means this rule will use the same indicator that the group it is contained in uses.

➤ *None* — This means no setting.

Use the drop-down in the Action column to choose among Warning, Error, None, or Inherit. As with enabling rules, this can be done for specific rules or for entire groups of rules.

Figure 8-2 illustrates how to enable and disable specific rules and how each can be set to Warning or Error as necessary.

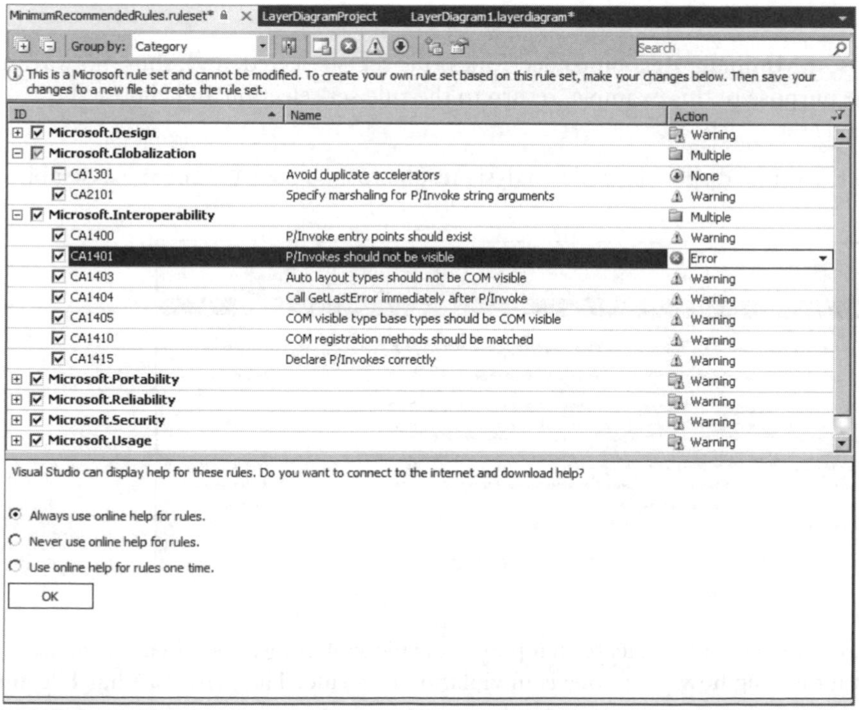

FIGURE 8-2

Finally, you can specify different sets of code analysis properties for each configuration. By default, settings apply to the Active build configuration, but you can be more specific. For example, you may wish to treat certain critical rules as Errors in your Release builds, but as Warnings in Debug. You might instead decide to disable code analysis entirely for your Release builds. Simply choose a build type from the Configuration drop-down menu, and then review your settings. To make changes affecting all build configurations, select the All Configurations option, and then modify and save your settings.

Executing Static Code Analysis

Once you have enabled code analysis and configured the rules to reflect your development standards, code analysis will be performed each time you build your project. Go ahead and build your sample project now.

> *You can also execute code analysis on your project by choosing Build ⇨ Run Code Analysis on [Project Name] or by right-clicking the desired project within Solution Explorer and selecting Run Code Analysis.*

The output window will include details about your build, including results from calling code analysis. After the build, the Error List window may appear, displaying a number of warnings and possibly some errors. The Error List does not automatically open if there are only warnings. If you do not see the Error List, choose View ⇨ Error List.

By default, the Microsoft Minimum Recommended Rules rule set is selected, and, thus, no warnings are generated. For the purpose of this example, return to the rule set selection and choose the Microsoft All Rules rule set.

Figure 8-3 shows the Error List displaying code analysis results for the SampleLibrary assembly.

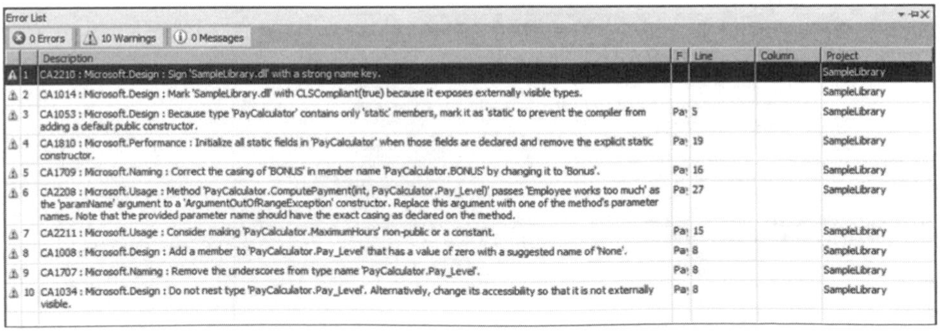

FIGURE 8-3

Analysis of the SampleLibrary code indicates ten potential rule violations. Each item in the list has a full description indicating how your code is in violation of a rule. The Error List has File and Line columns that indicate (when appropriate) specific source files and code related to each warning.

Some warnings do not relate to specific code, but perhaps to a lack of an attribute or security setting. In such cases, there will be no value in the File column. Others may refer directly to problem code, perhaps naming violations or performance issues. You can double-click on the warning, and the code editor will switch to the related code.

Each time you run code analysis, the results are stored in an XML file. This file is named `<Project Name>.CodeAnalysisLog.xml`, and is located in your project's build output directory (that is, `\bin\Debug` or `\bin\Release`). For the `SampleLibrary` project, the file will be `SampleLibrary.dll.CodeAnalysisLog.xml`.

If you open the file from within the IDE, you will see the raw, unformatted XML. However, the XML has an associated XSL template that formats the data into HTML, similar to what is shown in Figure 8-4.

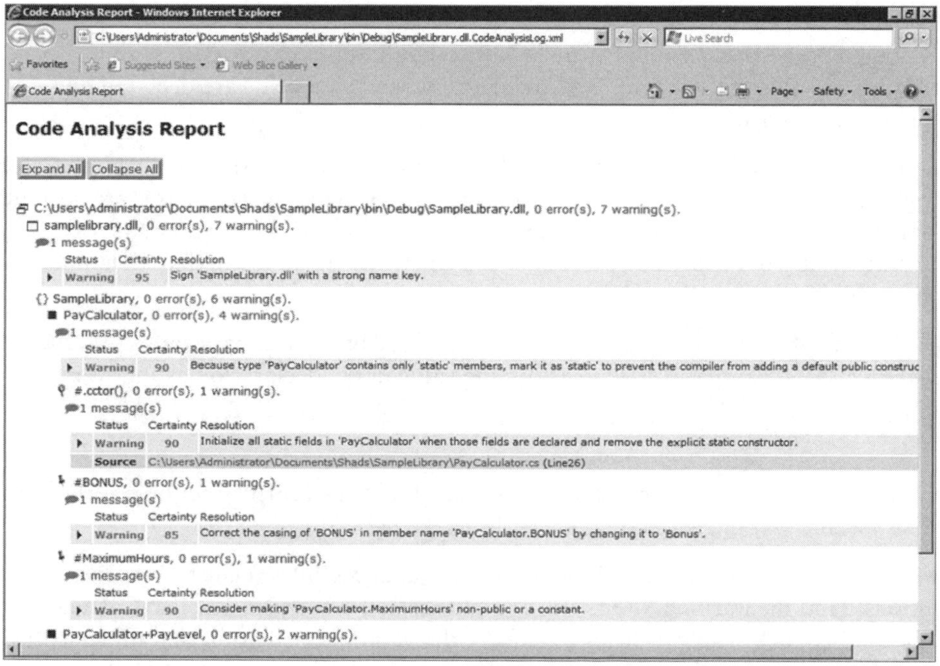

FIGURE 8-4

To see this view, open the XML file with Internet Explorer. To customize rendering, you can supply your own XSL templates. If you choose to do this, you should make a copy of the included template and modify the copy to suit your needs. The base template is found in your Visual Studio installation directory as `\Team Tools\Static Analysis Tools\FxCop\Xml\CodeAnalysisReport.xsl`.

Working with Rule Violations

Several issues should be addressed in the sample `PayCalculator` class. For each warning or error, you must determine whether the rule actually applies to your project or a specific section of code.

If it does, you must modify the project to address the issue; otherwise, you may choose to ignore the rule. This section describes how to act on identified issues, and how to ignore, or suppress, a given rule.

Although, as part of this discussion, you will immediately go into the code and make corrections as necessary, your organization or project may require the use of work items to track any changes. Or perhaps you don't have time to immediately address an identified problem but would like to use a work item as a reminder.

Fortunately, you can easily create work items directly from Code Analysis rule violations. Simply right-click on the warning or error and choose Create Work Item from the menu. Choose the correct team project, and you will be shown the New Work Item dialog. Make any necessary changes and save your new work item.

Correcting Problems

Looking through the Error List shown in Figure 8-3, you should see item CA1810, with a description of "Initialize all static fields in 'PayCalculator' when those fields are declared and remove the explicit static constructor."

Right-click on this warning and choose Show Error Help. This will display the documentation for the rule that triggered this warning, including suggestions for resolving the issue. You are currently assigning the value of `100` to `MaximumHours` inside the static constructor of `PayCalculator`. The rule's Help text states that your code may perform more efficiently if you make that assignment when the variable is defined.

To address this issue, double-click on this warning and you'll be brought to the static constructor of the `PayCalculator` class. Change the code to assign the value in the declaration as follows:

```
public static int MaximumHours = 100;
```

Next, delete the static `PayCalculator` constructor entirely. Build the project and look at the Error List window. The specific warning should no longer be in the list.

There is another easy problem to correct. Many of the code analysis rules relate to standard naming conventions. Find the warning "Remove the underscores from type name 'PayCalculator .Pay_Level'" and double-click. The rule helps to enforce the naming convention that underscores should not be used in type names. Use the built-in refactoring support to rename it. Right-click on the `Pay_Level` enumeration and choose Refactor ⇨ Rename. Change the name to `PayLevel`, click OK, and then Apply.

Mark the `PayCaclulator` class definition static as follows:

```
public static class PayCalculator
```

Rules can also help ensure that you're using the Framework correctly. You can see from the following warning that the rule has detected that you might not be creating the `ArgumentOutOfRangeException` correctly; "Method 'PayCalculator.ComputePayment(int, PayCalculator.Pay_Level)' passes 'Employee works too much' as the 'paramName' argument to a 'ArgumentOutOfRangeException' constructor. Replace this argument with one of the method's parameter names. Note that the provided parameter name should have the exact casing as declared on the method." To fix this, change the line that throws the exception to the following:

```
if (hours > MaximumHours)
{

  throw new ArgumentOutOfRangeException("hours", "Employee works too much");
}
```

One of the remaining warnings, "Mark 'SampleLibrary.dll' with CLSCompliantAttribute(true) because it exposes externally visible types," is a fairly common suggestion. Consider addressing this when creating a reusable library assembly that might be consumed by code of more than one .NET language. Common Language Specification (CLS) compliance specifies that your assembly must meet the common structure and syntax supported by all .NET languages as defined in the CLS. Keep in mind that there may be times when CLS compliance is not possible, such as when exposing unsigned types.

To address this warning, open `AssemblyInfo.cs` and add the following line:

```
[assembly: System.CLSCompliant(true)]
```

The `assembly:` notation is used because the attribute applies to the entire assembly, and not to a specific class or member. Other assembly-level attributes can be found in the `AssemblyInfo.cs` file.

Now, build the project. The violations you corrected should no longer generate messages in the Error List. The remaining five warnings will be addressed shortly.

Suppressing Messages

Visual Studio 2010 ships with many rules, and not all of them are appropriate for every project. There is a chance that some rules will trigger warnings that simply don't apply to certain parts of your project. To prevent these irrelevant messages from recurring, right-click on the rule violation and choose Suppress Message(s).

When you suppress a message, Visual Studio automatically adds an attribute to your code to indicate that a rule should not apply. The `SuppressMessage` attribute can be applied to a code construct, such as a field, method, or class, and to an entire assembly.

> *Suppressing a message is not the same as disabling a rule. Suppression prevents the specific violation of a rule from recurring, but other violations of the same rule will still be identified. You should disable a rule only if you're certain it could never be meaningfully applied to any part of your project.*

Let's continue with the `SampleLibrary` example and use message suppression to clean up more of the code analysis violation messages.

The warnings for CA1709 states, "Correct the casing of 'BONUS' in member name PayCalculator .BONUS." Assume that your organization has different naming conventions for constants, and you know that this rule will not apply to this BONUS constant. Right-click on the message and choose Suppress Message ➪ In Source. The message will be crossed out in the Error List, and the PayCalculator class will be modified to include the following attribute immediately before the declaration of BONUS:

```
[System.Diagnostics.CodeAnalysis.SuppressMessage(
    "Microsoft.Naming",
    "CA1709: IdentifiersShouldBeCasedCorrectly",    MessageId = "BONUS")]
```

The next time Code Analysis is run, the engine will recognize this attribute. Moreover, even when the CA1709 rule is violated at this point, no message will be created. Messages for any other violations of this rule elsewhere in the code will still be reported as normal.

> *In many cases (especially in ASP.NET applications), Visual Studio will automatically generate helper or wrapper code. Previous versions of FxCop had difficulty working with such generated code and often flagged many warnings — for example, naming convention violations, which would have to be investigated and generally excluded. Fortunately, the .NET Framework 2.0 provided a new attribute,* GeneratedCodeAttribute, *that the Managed Code Analysis tool uses to identify code that it does not need to analyze.*

Two more messages don't apply to the project. "Consider making 'PaymentCalculator .MaximumHours' non-public or a constant" reminds you that external users of the class could change its value. This is the behavior you want, so right-click on the message and choose Suppress Message ➪ In Source. The message "Add a member to 'PaymentCalculator.PayLevel' that has a value of zero with a suggested name of 'None'" also does not apply, as all employees are required to have an employee level. Suppress this message in source as well.

As you can see, suppressing messages can quickly add a number of attributes to your code. If you find that you always suppress a given message, it is probably better to exclude the rule altogether; then your code will not require the additional SuppressMessage attributes. However, as noted previously, use caution when doing this, because you could unintentionally be missing valid violations that should be addressed.

The warning "Sign 'SampleLibrary.dll' with a strong name key" applies to the overall assembly. If you know that you'll never use this assembly in the Global Assembly Cache (GAC), and will have no other need for strong names, you can suppress this message. Right-click the warning and select Suppress Message ➪ In Project Suppression File. Do this for all the remaining warnings. However, because there is no specific code to which the SuppressMessage attribute can be applied, a new file, GlobalSuppressions.cs, will be added to the project with the following code:

```
[assembly: System.Diagnostics.CodeAnalysis.SuppressMessage(
    "Microsoft.Design",
    "CA2210:AssembliesShouldHaveValidStrongNames")]
```

There is one warning left: "CA 1034: Microsoft.Design: Do not nest type 'PayCalculator.Pay_level'. Alternatively, change its accessibility so that it is not externally visible." Suppress this warning message, build the project, and you should now see an empty Error List. This indicates all enabled Code Analysis rules have either been passed or suppressed.

> *The effect of assembly-level suppression is basically the same as if you had excluded the rule altogether. The advantage of the attribute-based approach is that it is easy to see which rules have been suppressed project-wide by viewing the* GlobalSuppressions.cs *file. In addition, you could add comments to that file to indicate the reason for suppressing the rule to other developers. Excluding a rule by not selecting it in the Code Analysis section of the project's properties has the same effect but does not offer a way to document why certain exclusions were made.*

USING THE COMMAND-LINE ANALYSIS TOOL

Like the versions of FxCop that preceded Visual Studio 2010, a command-line interface is available for static code analysis. This tool, called FxCopCmd.exe, can be found in your Visual Studio 2010 installation directory under Team Tools\Static Analysis Tools\FxCop.

FxCopCmd can perform any of the code analysis functions that are available to you in the Visual Studio IDE. In fact, the IDE uses FxCopCmd under the covers to execute analysis and generate reports.

FxCopCmd Options

Table 8-3 shows some of the options that FxCopCmd.exe supports.

TABLE 8-3: FxCopCmd Options

OPTION	DESCRIPTION
/f[ile]: <directory/file>	Assembly file(s) or directory(ies) to analyze. If a directory is used without a filename, Code Analysis will try to analyze all files in that directory with .dll or .exe extensions. You can specify this option more than once. It is required, unless you specify a project file with the /project option.
/r[ule]:<directory/file>	A rule assembly file or a directory to browse for rule assemblies. If a directory without a filename is supplied, Code Analysis will look for rules in any files with a .dll extension. You can specify this option more than once.

continues

TABLE 8-3 *(continued)*

OPTION	DESCRIPTION
`/r[ule]id:<[+|-]`	Enables or disables a specific rule, supplying its `Category` and `Category#CheckId>` CheckId values — for example, `/rid: +!Microsoft .Usage#CA2225`.
`/ruleset:<<+|-|=>file>`	Specifies the rule set to be used for the analysis.
`/rulesetdirectory:<directory>`	Specifies a directory to search for rule set files specified by the `/ruleset` switch.
`/o[ut]:<file>`	Names a file in which the results of the analysis will be stored in XML form. Required, unless the `/console` option is used.
`/p[roject]:<file>`	Loads a project file that contains the settings for FxCopCmd to use (discussed shortly). Required if you do not use both the `/file` and `/rules` options.
`/t[ypes]:<type list>`	Used to constrain analysis to only the specified type(s). Supply a list of comma-delimited type names. Wildcards can be used to specify multiple types. (Optional)
`/i[mport]:<directory/file>`	Loads analysis reports or project files to exclude items from the current test that appear as excluded in the imported file. You may specify a file or a directory. If a directory is specified, Code Analysis will attempt to load all files with an .xml extension. (Optional)
`/s[ummary]`	Displays a summary after analysis. (Optional)
`/v[erbose]`	Gives more detailed status output. (Optional)
`/q[uiet]`	Suppresses output of status details. (Optional)
`/u[pdate]`	Saves the results of the current analysis to the specified project file. Ignored if you do not supply the `/project` option. (Optional)
`/c[onsole]`	Uses the console to display the analysis results. This is required unless you have specified the `/out` option.
`/c[onsole]xsl:<file>`	Applies an XSL file to transform XML output before displaying.
`/plat[form]:<directory>`	Location of platform assemblies. (Optional)

OPTION	DESCRIPTION
`/d[irectory]: <directory>`	Location to search for assembly dependencies. (Optional)
`/help (or) /?`	Help about command-line options.
`/fo[rceoutput]`	Write output XML and project files, even in the case where no violations occurred.
`/dic[tionary]:<file>`	Use a custom dictionary file.
`/ignoreinvalidtargets [Short form: /iit]`	Silently ignore invalid target files.
`/asp[net]`	Analyze only ASP.NET generated binaries, and honor global suppressions in `App_Code.dll` for all assemblies under analysis.
`/searchgac [Short form: /gac]`	Search Global Assembly Cache for missing references.
`/successfile [Short form: /sf]`	Create `.lastcodeanalysissucceeded` file in output report directory if no build-breaking messages occur during analysis.
`/timeout:<seconds> [Short form: /to:<seconds>]`	Overrride timeout for analysis deadlock detection. Analysis will be aborted when analysis of a single item by a single rule exceeds the specified amount of time. Specify a value of 0 to disable deadlock detection.
`/savemessagestoreport:<Active|Excluded|Absent (default: Active)> [Short form: /smr:<Active|Excluded|Absent (default: Active)>]`	Save messages of specified kind to output report.
`/ignoregeneratedcode [Short form: /igc]`	Suppress analysis results against generated code.
`/overriderulevisibilities [Short form: /orv]`	Run all overridable rules against all targets.
`/failonmissingrules [Short form: /fmr]`	Treat missing rules or rule sets as an error, and halt execution.
`/cul[ture]`	Culture for spelling rules.
`/outxsl:<file> [Short form: /oxsl:<file>]`	Reference the specified XSL in the XML report file; use `/outxsl:none` to generate an XML report with no XSL style sheet.
`/applyoutxsl [Short form: /axsl]`	Apply the XSL style sheet to the output.

Notice that most of the commands have long and short forms available. For example, /summary and /s are equivalent. Arguments support the use of wildcards (*) to specify multiple items. Arguments with spaces in them must be surrounded with double quotes.

For example, to conduct analysis of a single assembly CustomLibrary.dll, use the following command:

```
FxCopCmd /f:SampleLibrary.dll /o:"FxCop Results.xml" /s
```

The /f (or /file) argument indicates which assembly to analyze, and the /o (or /output) option indicates that analysis output should be stored as XML in FxCop Results.xml. Finally, the /s (or /summary) option will display a short summary of the results of the analysis.

FxCopCmd Project Files

FxCopCmd's command-line options offer a good deal of flexibility, but to fine-tune your analysis, you should consider using a *project file*. A project file enables you to set options such as targets and rule assemblies, exclusions, and output preferences. You can then simply use the /project option to tell FxCopCmd to use those settings, instead of supplying a detailed list of arguments.

You should create a default FxCopCmd project file that you can copy and customize for each project. Create a new file named EmptyCodeAnalysisProject.fxcop and enter the following:

```
<?xml version="1.0" encoding="UTF-8"?>
<FxCopProject Version="1.36" Name="Temporary FxCop Project">
      <ProjectOptions>
      </ProjectOptions>
      <Targets>
      <Target Name="$(TargetFile)" Analyze="True" AnalyzeAllChildren="True" />
      </Targets>
      <RuleFiles>
      </RuleFiles>
      <FxCopReport Version="1.36" LastAnalysis="2004-04-20 22:08:53Z">
      </FxCopReport>
</FxCopProject>
```

Copy this to a new file and add your project's settings. The rules and files specified in your project file serve as the basis for FxCopCmd execution. Additional rules and target files can be specified on the command line with the /rules and /file options.

For example, here is a simple project file that specifies a target assembly, SampleLibrary.dll, and includes one rule assembly, the default Code Analysis naming conventions assembly:

```
<?xml version="1.0" encoding="UTF-8"?>
<FxCopProject Version="1.36" Name="Sample Library Code Analysis Project">
      <ProjectOptions>
      </ProjectOptions>
      <Targets>

            <Target Name="C:\SampleLibrary\bin\Debug\SampleLibrary.dll"
                  Analyze="True"
```

```
        AnalyzeAllChildren="True" />
    </Targets>
    <RuleFiles>

        <RuleFile Name="$(FxCopDir)\Rules\NamingRules.dll" Enabled="True"
        AllRulesEnabled="True" />
    </RuleFiles>
    <FxCopReport Version="1.36" LastAnalysis="2004-04-20 22:08:53Z">
    </FxCopReport>
</FxCopProject>
```

Save this to a file named `SampleLibrary.fxcop`. To execute Code Analysis for `SampleLibrary` using this project file, use the following command:

```
FxCopCmd /p:SampleLibrary.fxcop /o:"FxCop Results.xml" /s
```

Build Process Code Analysis Integration

You have now seen how to use FxCopCmd from the command line to analyze your code and report potential defects. However, with the full integration of code analysis with the Visual Studio IDE, why would you need to use FxCopCmd?

A common use of FxCopCmd is to enable automated code analysis from a build process. You can do this with Team Build, Visual Studio 2010's MSBuild, or one of many other build automation packages available (such as NAnt).

By integrating Code Analysis with your builds, you can ensure that your entire team's work is being evaluated against a consistent set of rules. You will quickly discover when a developer has added nonstandard code. Developers will quickly learn those rules and practices, because they don't want to be the person responsible for "breaking the build."

CREATING CODE ANALYSIS RULES

Visual Studio 2010 includes many code analysis rules, but no matter how comprehensive the rules from Microsoft are, they can never fully cover the specific requirements of your own projects. Perhaps you have specific naming conventions, or a standard way to load database connection strings. In many cases, you can create a custom code analysis rule to help diagnose the issue and help developers take corrective action.

Reflection and Introspection

Many static analysis tools use simple source-code inspection to identify issues. However, with FxCop, Microsoft decided to leverage the inherent functionality of .NET itself as the basis for creating rules. A very useful feature of .NET is called *reflection*. Using reflection, you can programmatically inspect other assemblies, classes, and members. You can even invoke methods or access fields, public or private, given appropriate security settings. Reflection is done without establishing a link to the target assembly at compilation time, a practice known as *late binding*.

Initial versions of FxCop relied on reflection as the basis for rules. However, a newer option is available, called *introspection*. Similar to reflection, introspection can inspect a target assembly to discover its types, and details about those types. It can also invoke members of those types. Introspection does this in a much faster manner than reflection, and supports multi-threaded operations. Furthermore, introspection does not lock the files under analysis, a problem suffered by previous versions of FxCop that needed to use reflection.

Given the clear advantages of introspection over reflection, Microsoft has leveraged introspection with the rules that are shipped with Visual Studio 2010. Let's use introspection for a custom rule.

Creating a New Rule

Creating a new rule can be challenging, so let's walk through the creation of one. Let's continue working with the SampleLibrary created earlier in this chapter. You'll recall that, when you ran code analysis on the SampleLibrary, a number of potential issues were flagged. There is actually another problem with the code that is not detected by the set of rules included with Visual Studio 2010.

In this section, you'll create a fairly simple rule to help correct a potentially serious issue. Exposing constant values from an assembly is a normal and expected practice, but with .NET, there is a surprising side effect.

When a second assembly references a source assembly that exposes a constant value, the value of that constant is actually stored directly in the intermediate language (IL) of the referencing assembly. This means that, even when you change and recompile the original assembly, the value is not changed in the referencing assembly. This can lead to extremely difficult-to-diagnose problems, and will require you to recompile all referencing assemblies, even though those assemblies have not changed.

To address this, let's create a new rule, AvoidExposingPublicConstants, which searches a target assembly for publicly visible constant values. Begin by creating a new C# Class Library project named CustomCodeAnalysisRules.

Code Analysis loads designated assemblies and searches them for rule classes. Code Analysis rules implement a core interface called IRule. Rules that use introspection also implement IIntrospectionRule. However, these and other related interfaces and classes are wrapped by the BaseIntrospectionRule class.

Let's use this class as the basis for your own rules. To use this base class, let's add a reference in the CustomCodeAnalysisRules project to the FxCopSdk.dll and Microsoft.Cci.dll assemblies found in the \Team Tools\Static Analysis Tools\FxCop directory.

Creating a Base Rule

As mentioned earlier, most of the included code analysis rules inherit (typically indirectly) from a base class called BaseIntrospectionRule. While each custom rule could inherit directly from this class, it's easier to create a common base class that inherits from BaseIntrospectionRule. This is because the constructor to BaseIntrospectionRule requires three arguments. The first argument is the name of the rule, and the second is the name of the XML file containing rule data. The final argument is a reference to the rule assembly type.

If you created a rule assembly with multiple rules, each rule would have to supply those three arguments each time. However, with a new base class, you can abstract away the last two arguments and keep your rule code streamlined.

Create a new file called `BaseStaticAnalysisRule.cs` and add the following code:

```
using System;
using Microsoft.FxCop.Sdk;

namespace CustomCodeAnalysisRules
{
    public abstract class BaseStaticAnalysisRule : BaseIntrospectionRule
    {
        protected BaseStaticAnalysisRule(string name) :
            base(name,
                "CustomCodeAnalysisRules.Rules",
                typeof(BaseStaticAnalysisRule).Assembly ) { }
    }
}
```

Because the values of the second and third parameter to the `BaseIntrospectionRule` constructor will be the same for all rules in your assembly, you use this simple class as a wrapper in which those values can be set. The second argument, `CustomCodeAnalysisRules.Rules`, needs further explanation and is described in detail later in this chapter in the section "Creating Rules.xml."

Implementing the Rule

Now that you have a base class to use for all of your custom rules, you can create a rule. A rule has two main components:

➤ *Rule implementation code* — This is the code that analyzes the target assembly and determines whether the standard or guideline it is trying to enforce has been violated.

➤ *Rule descriptive XML* — Having the implementation code is not enough. An embedded XML fragment is required in order to help Managed Code Analysis display the rule, and provide details such as descriptions and resolutions to the user.

Before you can create the rule's implementation, you must have an approach for evaluating and inspecting a target assembly. While there are many ways you could write code to do this, Microsoft has made the job much easier by including the `Microsoft.Cci` assembly with Visual Studio 2010. Let's take a look at what this assembly is and how to use it.

Using the Microsoft.Cci Assembly

The `Microsoft.Cci` assembly (or Common Compiler Infrastructure) originated from Microsoft Research and contains classes that provide features for language-based tools, such as compilers. This assembly is especially helpful for code analysis because it offers many classes that map directly to common programming constructs (such as classes, fields, members, and methods). You'll use these classes to inspect target assemblies to identify the places where your rule applies.

> *You may be familiar with the* System.CodeDom *namespace. It is very useful for creating intermediate representations of programming constructs, and then using a language provider to generate code in a desired language, such as VB.NET. Conversely,* Microsoft.Cci *offers additional features for reading and inspecting existing code, exactly the task you face when creating a code analysis rule.*

Table 8-4 lists the major classes offered by Microsoft.Cci, organized by programming concept.

TABLE 8-4: Microsoft.Cci Classes

PROGRAMMING CONCEPT	RELATED MICROSOFT.CCI CLASSES
Assembly	CompilationUnit
Namespace	Namespace
Types	Class, Struct, Interface
Type Member	Member
Member	Method, Field, Property, Event, EnumNode
Method	Method, InstanceInitializer, StaticInitializer
Statement	Block, AssignmentStatement, If, For, ForEach, DoWhile, While, Continue, ExpressionStatement, VariableDeclaration, Return, Switch, Lock
Expression	Variable, AssignmentExpression, UnaryExpression, BinaryExpression, NaryExpression, Literal, Parameter, Local
Exception-Related	ExceptionHandler, Throw, Try, Catch, Finally
Instructions and Operations	Instruction, OpCode

The members of the Microsoft.Cci namespace are organized in a hierarchical structure, with related classes organized under a parent type.

For example, the Member class is the parent for the types of things you'd expect to have as class members, Method, Property, Field, Event, and others. If you have a Method instance, you can use its members to obtain references to the items it contains. For example, the Instructions property returns an InstructionList that you can use to loop through the operations of the method. Similarly, the Method class also has a Parameters field, returning a ParameterList instance that can be used to inspect each parameter of the method.

The IIntrospectionRule Interface

As mentioned earlier, one of the abstractions the base class makes is the implementation of the `IIntrospectionRule` interface. This interface provides the opportunity to specify the conditions under which you want your rule to be invoked. `IIntrospectionRule` contains the following members:

```
ProblemCollection Check(Member member);
ProblemCollection Check(Module module);
ProblemCollection Check(Parameter parameter);
ProblemCollection Check(Resource resource);
ProblemCollection Check(TypeNode type);
ProblemCollection Check(string namespaceName, TypeNodeList types);
```

These overloads of the `Check` method provide the capability to indicate that your rule should be called when a specific kind of programming construct is currently the focus of the code analysis engine. You do not need to implement all of the `Check` methods in your custom rules, only the ones that expose the constructs you need.

In this chapter's example, you are looking for constants in an assembly, so you must observe the various members of each class, looking for those that are constants and exposed publicly. Therefore, you must use the `Check(Member member)` overload. This method will be called each time the analysis engine finds any type member, be it a constant, method, field, property, or other member type.

Writing the Rule Implementation Code

You now have a base class for your rule, and an understanding of the `Microsoft.Cci` namespace and `IIntrospectionRule` methods that will help you write the implementation. Create a new class file, `AvoidExposingPublicConstants.cs`.

First, add `using` statements for the namespaces you'll use:

```
using System;
using Microsoft.FxCop;
using Microsoft.FxCop.Sdk;
```

Now, create the class, inheriting from the `BaseStaticAnalysisRule` you created earlier:

```
namespace CustomCodeAnalysisRules
{
    public class AvoidExposingPublicConstants : BaseStaticAnalysisRule
    {
        public AvoidExposingPublicConstants() :
                base("AvoidExposingPublicConstants") {}

        public override ProblemCollection Check(Member member)
        {
            Field f = member as Field;
            if (f == null)
            {
                // Not a field
                return null;
            }
```

```
            if (member.DeclaringType is Microsoft.FxCop.Sdk.EnumNode)
            {
                // Inside an enumeration
                return null;
            }

            if (member.IsVisibleOutsideAssembly && f.IsLiteral)
            {
                // Is publicly visible and is a constant
                Problems.Add(new Problem(GetResolution(member.Name.Name)));
            }

            return Problems;
        }

        public override TargetVisibilities TargetVisibility
        {
            get { return TargetVisibilities.ExternallyVisible; }
        }
    }
}
```

The constructor must only supply the name of the rule to the base class constructor, which will forward the name of your XML data store and the assembly type reference automatically to the `BaseIntrospectionRule`.

As determined earlier, you must implement the `Check(Member member)` overload from the `IIntrospectionRule` and search each member for constants. The first thing you do is attempt to convert the `Member` to a `Field` instance. If this fails, you know the member was not a field, and you can move on to the next member. If it is a `Field`, you check the `Member` to determine whether it was declared inside of an enumeration. You're not interested in enumerations, so you return `null` in this case.

Finally, you verify that the member is publicly visible with the `IsVisibleOutsideAssembly` property, and that it is a constant (or literal) value with the `IsLiteral` property. If these expressions are true, you have a publicly visible constant, and your rule has been violated.

When a rule has been violated, you must create a new `Problem` instance and add it to your rule's `ProblemsCollection` collection, provided by the `BaseIntrospectionRule` class. The argument to a `Problem` constructor is a `Resolution` instance. The `BaseIntrospectionRule` class offers a `GetResolution` helper method that loads the resource data from the embedded XML data for the current rule. Arguments to `GetResolution` are automatically inserted into any placeholders such as {0} and {1} in the rule's resolution text, in the same manner as `String.Format`.

The new `Problem` is added to the `ProblemsCollection` collection, and the `ProblemsCollection` collection is returned, indicating to the Code Analysis tool that a new violation has been added.

The final item in the rule implementation is the `TargetVisibility` property. This property is used by the Code Analysis tool to determine when items should be fed into the rule's `Check` method(s). The `TargetVisibilities` enumeration has values such as `All`, `ExternallyVisible`, `NotExternallyVisible`, `AnonymousMethods`, `None`, `Obsolete`, and `Overridable` that can be combined to indicate when the rule should be tested. In this case, you only care about publicly visible members, so you return `TargetVisibilities.ExternallyVisible`.

Creating Rules.xml

With the implementation written, you must now create an XML node that describes the rule and provides text to help the user understand and address rule violations. The outer `Rules` node specifies the name of the group of rules — for example, `Performance Rules`. It contains one or more `Rule` nodes, each describing a single rule.

Add a new XML file to the project. Name the file `Rules.xml` and enter the following:

```xml
<?xml version="1.0" encoding="utf-8" ?>
<Rules FriendlyName="Custom Code Analysis Rules">
  <Rule TypeName="AvoidExposingPublicConstants" Category="Wrox.Custom"
   CheckId="CS0001">
    <Name>Avoid exposing public constants</Name>
    <Description>The values of public constants are compiled into any referencing
assemblies.  Should that value change, it is not sufficient to recompile
    the source
assembly because that value will also be stored in those referencing assemblies.
Avoid public constants for this reason.</Description>
    <Resolution>Change public constant '{0}' to a readonly variable, or mark it as
     private or internal.</Resolution>
    <MessageLevel Certainty="99">Warning</MessageLevel>
    <FixCategories>NonBreaking</FixCategories>
    <url>/Custom/AvoidExposingPublicConstants.html</url>
    <Email>yourname@yourcompany.com</Email>
    <Owner>Contact Person's Name</Owner>
  </Rule>
</Rules>
```

> ⊗ You must embed the XML into the rule assembly, or the Code Analysis tool will not be able to load the XML, and your rule will fail. Set this by right-clicking on the XML field and choosing Properties. Under the Advanced section, find the Build Action property and select Embedded Resource. When you build the assembly, the XML will be included in the meta-data.

The `Rule` node has a `TypeName` attribute (which should match the name of the rule class), a `Category` (which is used when displaying violations), and a `CheckId` (which uniquely identifies that rule — for example, in `SuppressMessage` attributes). `Name` is a short, but friendly, version of the rule name. `Description` contains the full description of what the rule is detecting.

`Resolution` is the full text shown to users to help them correct the violation. It may contain placeholders, such as `{0}`, which will automatically be replaced with values from the implementation code, as discussed earlier in this chapter. This is extremely useful to help users quickly identify where problems exist.

`Resolution` also supports an optional `Name` attribute that enables you to specify multiple resolutions for the same rule, which can be selected at analysis time by your rule. To do so, instead of using the `GetResolution` method, use `GetNamedResolution`, supplying the name you wish to match.

`MessageLevel` provides a `Certainty` that the rule is applicable, with values from 0 to 99. A 99 indicates there is little doubt the rule has been violated and should be addressed. A lower value means violations of the rule are difficult to detect with great certainty. Use this value to indicate to the user how likely it is that a specific member or assembly has violated the rule.

The element value of the `MessageLevel` can be any of the `Microsoft.VisualStudio` `.CodeAnalysis.Extensibility` enumeration values, including `Information`, `Warning`, `CriticalWarning`, `Error`, or `CriticalError`. Use these to indicate the relative severity of violating a rule. You can see this and the `MessageLevel` value in practice when you open the XML report from a Code Analysis run, as shown in Figure 8-4.

`FixCategories` indicates whether the changes needed to correct a rule violation should generally be considered breaking or nonbreaking. Values come from the `Microsoft.VisualStudio` `.CodeAnalysis.Extensibility` enumeration and can be `Breaking`, `NonBreaking`, or `DependsOnFix` (which ties back to the concept of multiple named resolutions).

For example, let's say you have a custom rule that has two named resolutions, each used for different rule-violation scenarios. One resolution is easy to implement, and you consider it nonbreaking. But the other is complex to correct, requiring a breaking change.

The `Url` is the path to an optional file that will show full details of the rule to the user, beyond what is given in the IDE. `Email` is the optional address of a contact person for help on the rule. `Owner` is the optionally provided name of a contact person for the rule.

Deploying a Rule

You now have a complete rule assembly with embedded XML containing the supporting data for the contained rule(s). The easiest way to get Visual Studio 2010 to use the contained rules is to move the assembly into the `\Team Tools\Static Code Analysis\FxCop\Rules` subdirectory of your Visual Studio installation directory. This will cause the IDE to recognize the rule assembly and read the contained rules so that you can select them for inclusion. The rule is added to the `Microsoft.AllRules` rule set by default.

A useful way to debug new rules is to create a single solution containing both the custom rule project and a sample target project with code that violates the rule. Open the Properties window for the rule assembly project and choose the Build Events tab. Add a post-build event command line to copy the rule assembly from the source project to the `\Team Tools\Static Code Analysis\` `FxCop\Rules` directory.

 Note that on Windows Vista and Windows 7 machines, you will need administrative access to copy the rule.

A problem with this approach is that if you open the Code Analysis properties window in either project, the custom rule assembly will be loaded and locked by the IDE. When this happens, you must close and reopen Visual Studio. However, this approach will generally make your rule debugging process much easier.

Learning from Existing Rules

You've now seen how to create your own rules and integrate them into the Code Analysis tool of Visual Studio 2010. You will certainly find many uses for additional rules, but before you begin creating them, you should invest some time learning from examples.

The recommended approach for those wishing to implement custom rules is to look at how the rules included with Visual Studio 2010 were written. While you don't have direct access to the source code for these rules, there is a tool that can help. Reflector, written by Lutz Roeder and now maintained by RedGate (`www.red-gate.com/products/reflector`), uses the power of .NET's reflection services to peer inside any assembly and generate an approximation of the source code. The target assembly can be any assembly, including those from Microsoft.

After obtaining Reflector, find the existing rules files in your Visual Studio 2010 installation directory under `Team Tools\Static Analysis Tools\FxCop\Rules`. Using Reflector, open one of the rule assemblies, such as `PerformanceRules.dll`. You can then navigate to the `Microsoft .Tools.FxCop.Rules.Performance` namespace, where you will see all of the rules in the Performance category.

Opening each rule will show you the details you've learned about earlier in this chapter. The rules inherit from base helper classes, just as you saw with `AvoidExposingPublicConstants` and `BaseStaticAnalysisRule`. Opening the Resources node for any rule assembly enables you to view the XML data that was embedded in the assembly. Opening members such as the `Check` methods will show you code that, while not exactly original, will give you enough detail to determine how you might accomplish the same tasks in your own rules.

CODE METRICS

The Code Metrics tool is a set of software metrics that provide insight into the code that is being developed. Code Metrics provides a quick-and-easy way to determine the complexity of the code, and to isolate code areas that may be difficult to maintain in the future. Code metric information is calculated at the method level, and then rolled up all the way to the assembly level. Visual Studio 2010 calculates five different code metrics:

➤ *Cyclomatic Complexity* — This measures the structural complexity of the code. It is created by calculating the number of different code paths through the code, including `if` statements, looping, and so on. A high number for Cyclomatic Complexity indicates that the code may be too complex, and should be refactored.

➤ *Depth of Inheritance* — This indicates the number of class definitions that extend to the root of the class hierarchy. While inheritance in itself is not bad, having a lengthy inheritance level can make the code difficult to understand and troubleshoot. As with Cyclomatic Complexity, you want to have a low number for Depth of Inheritance.

➤ *Class Coupling* — This indicates the total number of dependencies that a class has on other classes. This calculation does not include primitive or built-in types. A high level of Class

Coupling indicates that changes in other classes could affect a specific class. You want a low number for Class Coupling.

➤ *Lines of Code* — This indicates the number of executable lines of code in a method. This is an approximate count, based off the IL code, and only includes executable lines of code. Comments, braces, and white space are excluded. For Lines of Code, a low value is good, and a high value is bad.

➤ *The Maintainability Index* — This is a combination of several metrics, including Cyclomatic Complexity, average Lines of Code, as well as computational complexity. This metric is calculated using the following formula:

$$MAX(0,(171-5.2*\ln(\text{Halstead Volume})-0.23*(\text{Cyclomatic Complexity})$$
$$-16.2*\ln(\text{Lines of Code}))*100/171)$$

The Maintainability Index is a value between 1 and 100. Unlike the previous four metrics, for Maintainability Index, the higher the value, the easier the code will be to maintain. Table 8-5 shows the Maintainability Index ranges and what they indicate.

TABLE 8-5: Maintainability Index Ranges

COLOR	LEVEL	RANGE
Green	High Maintainability	Between 20 and 100
Yellow	Moderate Maintainability	Between 10 and 20
Red	Low Maintainability	Between 0 and 9

To run Code Metrics against your code, simply right-click the specific solution or project within Visual Studio, and select Calculate Code Metrics. The Code Metrics Results window will display with the results, as shown in Figure 8-5.

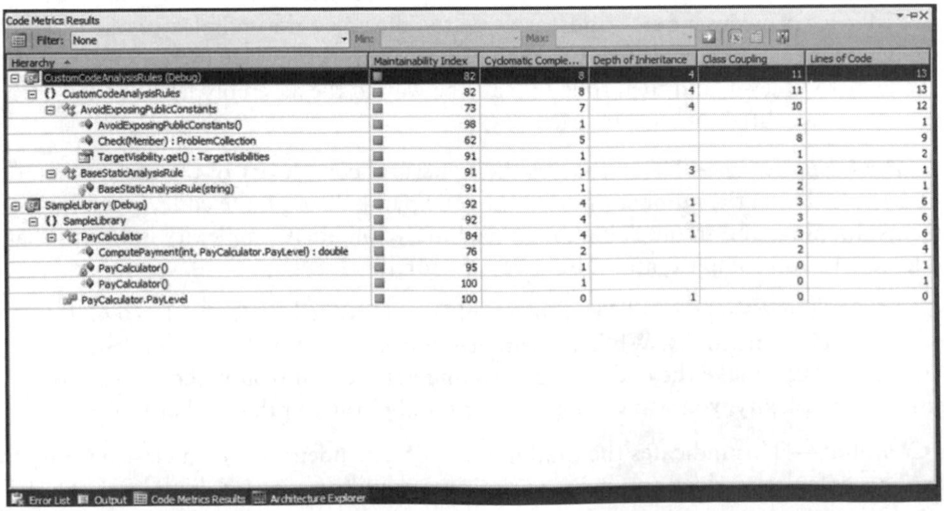

FIGURE 8-5

SUMMARY

This chapter demonstrated the need for static analysis tools and introduced you to the .NET Framework "Design Guidelines for Class Library Developers." These guidelines are a very important resource that Microsoft has made freely available, and the basis for Visual Studio 2010's included Code Analysis rules.

In this chapter, you learned about the Managed Code Analysis tool, including how it now integrates with Visual Studio 2010 and enables rule analysis to be performed with a simple build. You learned how to configure and execute analysis, and how to work with the resulting rule violation messages.

To support projects using a repeatable build process, or those that need additional flexibility, you learned how to use the command-line Managed Code Analysis tool, and how to create FxCopCmd project files to store settings.

You walked through the process of creating your own rule, and integrating it with your analysis process. You created the simple `AvoidExposingPublicConstants` rule as an example of how to use the new introspection engine to create new Managed Code Analysis rules in Visual Studio 2010.

Finally, you were introduced to Code Metrics. The five different code metric values were explained, and you saw how easy it was to run and view the results of the code metrics calculation.

Chapter 9 looks at the code profiling capabilities of Visual Studio 2010, and how they can be used to find and fix performance problems in your code.

 YOU CAN DOWNLOAD THE CODE FOUND IN THIS BOOK. VISIT WROX.COM AND SEARCH FOR ISBN 9780470484265

9

Profiling and Performance

WHAT'S IN THIS CHAPTER?

➤ Understanding the profiling features in Visual Studio 2010

➤ Understanding available profiling types

➤ Using Performance Explorer to configure profiling sessions

➤ Profiling reports and available views

➤ Profiling JavaScript

One of the more difficult tasks in software development is determining why an application performs slowly or inefficiently. Before Visual Studio 2010, developers were forced to turn to external tools to effectively analyze performance. Fortunately, Visual Studio 2010 Ultimate Edition includes profiling tools that are fully integrated with both the IDE and other Visual Studio 2010 features.

This chapter introduces Visual Studio 2010's profiling tools. Note that the profiling features discussed in this chapter are available in Visual Studio 2010 Premium Edition or higher.

You'll learn how to use the profiler to identify problems such as inefficient code, over-allocation of memory, and bottlenecks. You will learn about the two main profiling options — sampling and instrumentation — including how to use each, and when each should be applied. In Visual Studio 2010, there are now two sampling options: one for CPU sampling, and the other for memory allocation sampling. This chapter examines both of these. This chapter also briefly reviews the new profiling method, introduced in Visual Studio 2010, to see thread contentions using concurrency profiling.

After learning how to run profiling analyzers, you will learn how to use the detailed reporting features that enable you to view performance metrics in a number of ways, including results by function, caller/callee inspection, call tree details, and other views.

Not all scenarios can be supported when using the Visual Studio 2010 IDE. For times when you need additional flexibility, you will learn about the command-line options for profiling applications. This will enable you to integrate profiling with your build process and to use some advanced profiling options.

INTRODUCTION TO PERFORMANCE ANALYSIS

Profiling is the process of observing and recording metrics about the behavior of an application. Profilers are tools used to help identify application performance issues. Issues typically stem from code that performs slowly or inefficiently, or code that causes excessive use of system memory. A profiler helps you to more easily identify these issues so that they can be corrected.

Sometimes, an application may be functionally correct and seem complete, but users quickly begin to complain that it seems "slow." Or, perhaps you're only receiving complaints from one customer, who finds a particular feature takes "forever" to complete. Fortunately, Visual Studio 2010 profiling tools can help in these situations.

A common use of profiling is to identify *hotspots*, sections of code that execute frequently, or for a long duration, as an application runs. Identifying hotspots enables you to turn your attention to the code that will provide the largest benefit from optimization. For example, halving the execution time of a critical method that runs 20 percent of the time can improve your application's overall performance by 10 percent.

Types of Profilers

Most profiling tools fall into one (or both) of two types: *sampling* and *instrumentation*.

A sampling profiler takes periodic snapshots (called *samples*) of a running application, recording the status of the application at each interval, including which line of code is executing. Sampling profilers typically do not modify the code of the system under test, favoring an outside-in perspective.

Think of a sampling profiler as being like a sonar system. It periodically sends out sound waves to detect information, collecting data about how the sound refracts. From that data, the system displays the locations of detected objects.

The other type, an instrumentation profiler, takes a more invasive approach. Before running analysis, the profiler adds *tracing markers* (sometimes called *probes*) at the start and end of each function. This process is called *instrumenting* an application. Instrumentation can be performed in source code or, in the case of Visual Studio, by directly modifying an existing assembly. When the profiler is run, those probes are activated as the program execution flows in and out of instrumented functions. The profiler records data about the application and which probes were hit during execution, generating a comprehensive summary of what the program did.

Think of an instrumentation profiler as the traffic data recorders you sometimes see while driving. The tubes lie across the road and record whenever a vehicle passes over. By collecting the results from a variety of locations over time, an approximation of traffic flow can be inferred.

A key difference between sampling and instrumentation is that sampling profilers will observe your applications while running any code, including calls to external libraries (such as the .NET Framework). Instrumentation profilers gather data only for the code that you have specifically instrumented.

Visual Studio Profiling

Visual Studio 2010 offers powerful profiling tools that you can use to analyze and improve your applications. The profiling tools offer both sampling and instrumented approaches. Like many Visual Studio features, profiling is fully integrated with the Visual Studio IDE and other Visual Studio features, such as work item tracking, the build system, version control check-in policies, and more.

> *The profiling tools in Visual Studio can be used with both managed and unmanaged applications, but the object allocation tracking features only work when profiling managed code.*

The profiling tools in Visual Studio are based upon two tools that have been used for years internally at Microsoft. The sampling system is based on the Call Attributed Provider (CAP) tool, and the instrumentation system is based on the Low-Overhead Profiler (LOP) tool. Of course, Microsoft did not simply repackage existing internal tools and call it a day. They invested considerable development effort to add new capabilities and to fully integrate them with other Visual Studio features.

USING THE PROFILER

The Visual Studio developers have done a good job making the profiler easy to use. You follow four basic steps to profile your application:

1. Create a performance session, selecting a profiling method (CPU sampling, instrumentation, memory sampling, or concurrency) and its target(s).

2. Use the Performance Explorer to view and set the session's properties.

3. Launch the session, executing the application and profiler.

4. Review the collected data as presented in performance reports.

Each step is described in the following sections.

Creating a Sample Application

Before describing how to profile an application, let's create a sample application that you can use to work through the content of this chapter. Of course, this is only for demonstration, and you can certainly use your own existing applications instead.

Create a new C# Console Application and name it `DemoConsole`. This application will demonstrate some differences between using a simple class and a structure.

First, add a new class file called `WidgetClass.cs` with the following class definition:

```
namespace DemoConsole
{
    public class WidgetClass
    {
        private string _name;
        private int _id;

        public int ID
        {
            get { return _id; }
            set { _id = value; }
        }

        public string Name
        {
            get { return _name; }
            set { _name = value; }
        }

        public WidgetClass(int id, string name)
        {
            _id = id;
            _name = name;
        }
    }
}
```

Now, let's slightly modify that class to make it a value type. Make a copy of the `WidgetClass.cs` file named `WidgetValueType.cs` and open it. To make `WidgetClass` into a structure, change the word `class` to `struct`. Now, rename the two places you see `WidgetClass` to `WidgetValueType` and save the file.

You should have a `Program.cs` already created for you by Visual Studio. Open that file and add the following two lines in the `Main` method:

```
ProcessClasses(2000000);
ProcessValueTypes(2000000);
```

Add the following code to this file as well:

```
public static void ProcessClasses(int count)
{
    ArrayList widgets = new ArrayList();
    for (int i = 0; i < count; i++)
        widgets.Add(new WidgetClass(i, "Test"));

    string[] names = new string[count];
    for (int i = 0; i < count; i++)
        names[i] = ((WidgetClass)widgets[i]).Name;
}
```

```
public static void ProcessValueTypes(int count)
{
    ArrayList widgets = new ArrayList();
    for (int i = 0; i < count; i++)
        widgets.Add(new WidgetValueType(i, "Test"));

    string[] names = new string[count];
    for (int i = 0; i < count; i++)
        names[i] = ((WidgetValueType)widgets[i]).Name;
}
}
}
```

You now have a simple application that performs many identical operations on a class and a similar structure. First, it creates an `ArrayList` and adds 2 million copies of both `WidgetClass` and `WidgetValueType`. It then reads through the `ArrayList`, reading the `Name` property of each copy, and storing that name in a string array. You'll see how the seemingly minor differences between the class and structure affect the speed of the application, the amount of memory used, and its effect on the .NET garbage collection process.

Creating a Performance Session

To begin profiling an application, you must first create a performance session. This is normally done using the Performance Wizard, which walks you through the most common settings. You may also create a blank performance session or base a new performance session on a unit test result. Each of these methods is described in the following sections.

Using the Performance Wizard

The easiest way to create a new performance session is to use the Performance Wizard. In Visual Studio 2010, there is a new menu item called Analyze. That is where you will find the Performance Wizard and other profiler menu items. Select Analyze ⇨ Launch Performance Wizard. A three-step wizard will guide you through the creation of your session.

The first step, shown in Figure 9-1, is to select the profiling method.

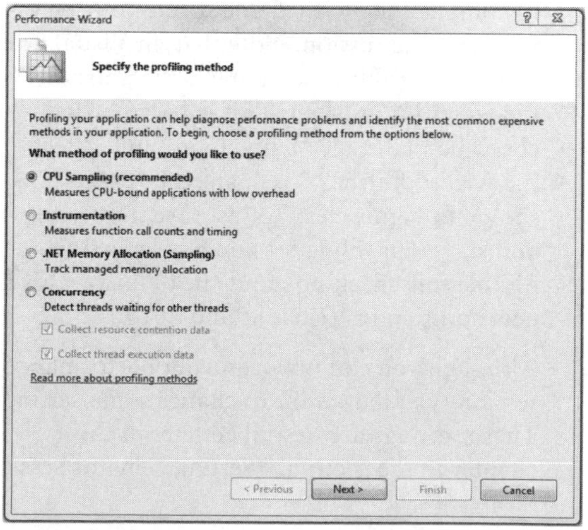

Those of you familiar with this screen from Team System 2008 will notice the new profiling options. As mentioned earlier, Visual Studio 2010 has the following four profiling options:

FIGURE 9-1

➤ CPU Sampling

➤ Instrumentation

➤   .NET Memory Allocation (Sampling)

➤   Concurrency

CPU Sampling is the recommended method to get started, and is chosen by default, as you see in Figure 9-1.

The second step, shown in Figure 9-2, is to select the application you will profile. In this case, you will profile the recently created `DemoConsole` application. You should see the `DemoConsole` application listed under "One or more available projects." If there are multiple applications listed there, you can select more than one to profile.

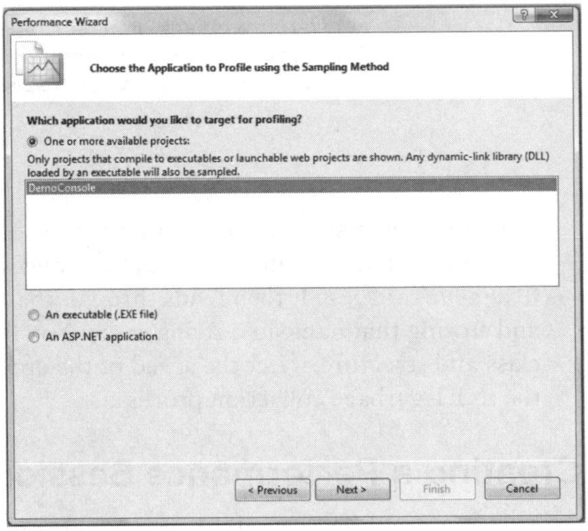

As you see in Figure 9-2, with Visual Studio 2010 you can also profile an executable (or `.exe` file) or an ASP.NET application. If you choose to profile an executable, then you must provide the path for the executable with any command-line arguments and the start-up directory. If you choose to profile an ASP.NET application, you must supply the URL for the Web application. Select the `DemoConsole` application as the target for profiling.

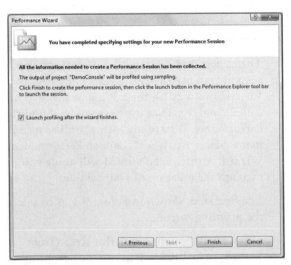

FIGURE 9-2

The final step in the wizard summarizes the selection in Step 1 and Step 2. Click Finish to complete the wizard and create your new performance session. Note that, in Visual Studio 2010, the profiling session is set to start after the wizard is finished. This is because the check box labeled, "Launch profiling after the wizard finishes," is enabled by default, as shown in Figure 9-3. To just save the settings and start a profiling session at a later time, disable this check box and click Finish. This is a new addition in Visual Studio 2010.

Although you can now run your performance session, you may want to change some settings. These settings are described later in this chapter in the section, "Setting General Session Properties."

FIGURE 9-3

Adding a Blank Performance Session

There may be times (for example, when you're profiling a Windows Service) when manually specifying all of the properties of your session would be useful or necessary. In those cases, you can skip the Performance Wizard and manually create a performance session.

Create a blank performance session by selecting Analyze ⇨ Profiler ⇨ New Performance Session. You will see a new performance session, named "Performance1," in the Performance Explorer window. This window is described in detail later in this chapter in the section "Using the Performance Explorer."

After creating the blank performance session, you must manually specify the profiling mode, target(s), and settings for the session. As mentioned previously, performance session settings are described later in this chapter in the section "Setting General Session Properties."

Creating a Performance Session from a Unit Test

The third option for creating a new performance session is from a unit test. Refer to Chapter 13 for a full description of the unit testing features in Visual Studio 2010.

There may be times when you have a test that verifies the processing speed (perhaps relative to another method or a timer) of a target method. Perhaps a test is failing because of system memory issues. In such cases, you might want to use the profiler to determine what code is causing problems.

To create a profiling session from a unit test, first run the unit test. Then, in the Test Results window, right-click on the test and choose Create Performance Session from the context menu, as shown in Figure 9-4.

Visual Studio 2010 then creates a new performance session with the selected unit test automatically assigned as the session's target. When you run this performance session, the unit test will be executed as normal, but the profiler will be activated and collect metrics on its performance.

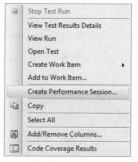

FIGURE 9-4

Using the Performance Explorer

Once you have created your performance session, you can view it using the Performance Explorer. The Performance Explorer, shown in Figure 9-5, is used to configure and execute performance sessions and to view the results from the performance sessions.

The Performance Explorer features two folders for each session: `Targets` and `Reports`. `Targets` specifies which application(s) will be profiled when the session is launched. `Reports` lists the results from each of the current session's runs. These reports are described in detail later in this chapter.

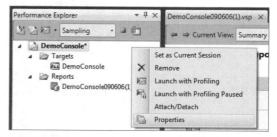

FIGURE 9-5

Performance Explorer also supports multiple sessions. For example, you might have one session configured for sampling, and another for instrumentation. You should rename them from the default "Performance*X*" names for easier identification.

If you accidentally close a session in Performance Explorer, you can reopen it by using the Open option of the File menu. You will likely find the session file (ending with `.psess`) in your solution's folder.

Setting General Session Properties

Whether you used the Performance Wizard to create your session or added a blank one, you may want to review and modify the session's settings. Right-click on the session name (for example, `DemoConsole`) and choose Properties (refer to Figure 9-5). You will see the Property Pages dialog for the session. It features several sections, described next.

> *This discussion focuses on the property pages that are applicable to all types of profiling sessions. These include the General, Launch, Tier Interactions, CPU Counters, Windows Events, and Windows Counters pages. The other pages each apply only to a particular type of profiling. The Sampling page is described later in this chapter in the section "Configuring a Sampling Session," and the Binaries, Instrumentation, and Advanced pages are described in the section "Configuring an Instrumentation Session," later in this chapter.*

General Property Page

Figure 9-6 shows the General page of the Property Pages dialog.

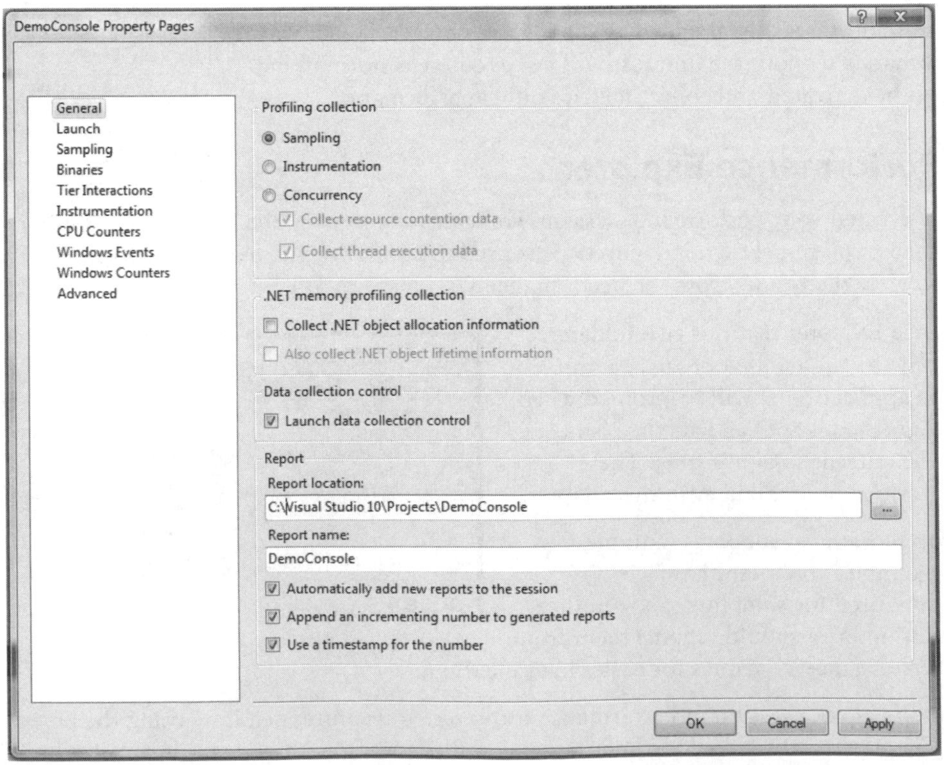

FIGURE 9-6

The "Profiling collection" panel of this dialog reflects your chosen profiling type (that is, Sampling, Instrumentation, or Concurrency).

The ".NET memory profiling collection" panel enables the tracking of managed types. When the first option, "Collect .NET object allocation information," is enabled, the profiling system will collect details about the managed types that are created during the application's execution. The profiler will track the number of instances, the amount of memory used by those instances, and which members created the instances. If the first option is selected, then you can choose to include the second option, "Also collect .NET object lifetime information." If selected, additional details about the amount of time each managed type instance remains in memory will be collected. This will enable you to view further impacts of your application, such as its effect on the .NET garbage collector.

The options in the ".NET memory profiling collection" panel are off by default. Turning them on adds substantial overhead, and will cause both the profiling and report-generation processes to take additional time to complete. When the first option is selected, the Allocation view of the session's report is available for review. The second option enables display of the Objects Lifetime view. These reports are described later in this chapter in the section "Reading and Interpreting Session Reports."

In the "Data collection control" panel, you can toggle the launch of data collection control while the profiling is launched. If you have checked the "Launch data control collection" checkbox, then, during the profiling session, you will see the "Data Collection Control" window, as shown in Figure 9-7.

Using this window, you can specify marks that could become handy while analyzing the report after the profiling session is completed. You will do that by choosing the "Marks" view while viewing the report.

Finally, you can use the Report panel to set the name and location for the reports that are generated after each profiling session. By default, a timestamp is used after the report name so that you can easily see the date of the session run. Another default appends a number after each

FIGURE 9-7

subsequent run of that session on a given day. (You can see the effect of these settings in Figure 9-17 later in this chapter, where multiple report sessions were run on the same day.)

For example, the settings in Figure 9-6 will run a sampling profile without managed type allocation profiling, and the data collection control will be launched. If run on January 1, 2010, it will produce a report named `DemoConsole100101.vsp`. Another run on the same day would produce a report named `DemoConsole100101(1).vsp`.

Launch Property Page

While the sample application has only one binary to execute and analyze, your projects may have multiple targets. In those cases, use the Launch property page to specify which targets should be executed when the profiling session is started or "launched." You can set the order in which targets will be executed using the "move up" and "move down" arrow buttons.

Targets are described later in this chapter in the section "Configuring Session Targets."

Tier Interaction Proprety Page

Tier Interaction profiling is a new capability introduced in Visual Studio 2010. This method captures additional information about the execution times of functions that interact with the database.

Multi-tier architecture is commonly used in many applications, with tiers for presentation, business, and database. With Tier Interaction profiling, you can now get a sense of the interaction between the application tier and the data tier, including how many calls were made and the time of execution.

As of this writing, Tier Interaction profiling only supports the capturing of execution times for synchronous calls using ADO.NET. It does not support native or asynchronous calls.

To start collecting tier interaction data, select the "Enable tier interaction profiling" checkbox, as shown in Figure 9-8.

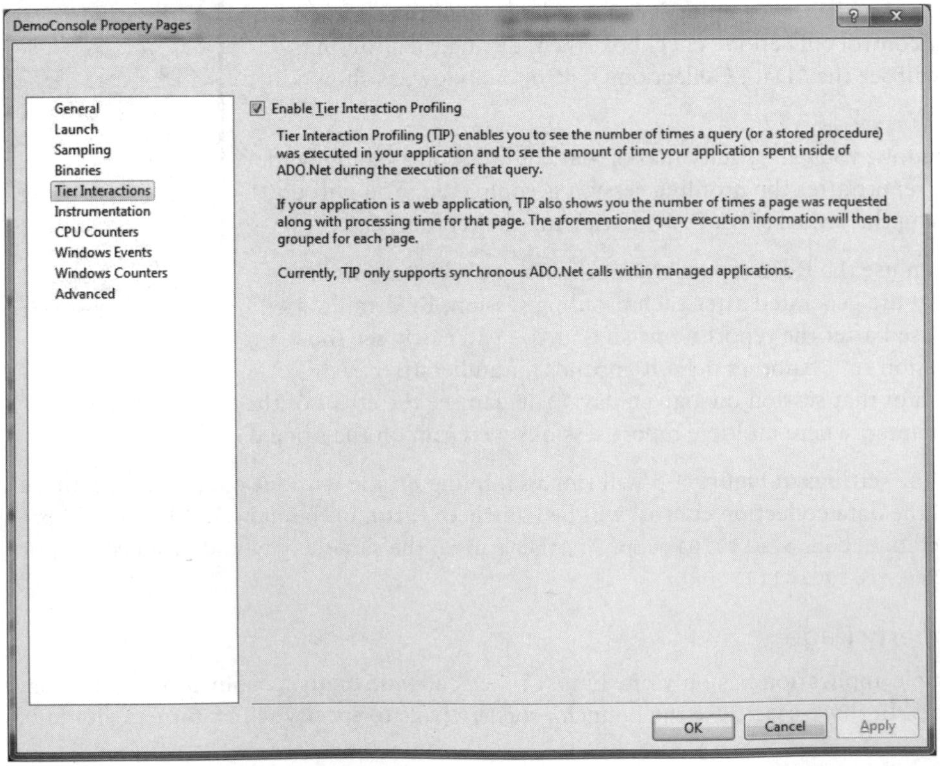

FIGURE 9-8

After you run the profiling with this selection turned on, you will be presented with the profiling report. Select the Tier Interactions view from the current view drop-down, shown in Figure 9-9. This example shows the results of running the profiling on the "TheBeerHouse" sample application. You can download this application from http://thebeerhouse.codeplex.com/.

Current View: Tier Interactions						
Name	Database	Count	Total Elapsed Time	Min Elapsed Time	Max Elapsed Time	Avg Elapsed Time
◢ /TBH_Web/default.aspx		3 Requests	9,655.35	197.19	9,175.25	3,218.45
◢ Database Connections						
\\.\pipe\9C6954F0-BF30-4E	C:\TEMP\BEERHOUSE\TBH	24 Queries	143.71			
◢ /TBH_Web/ShoppingCart.aspx		5 Requests	572.66	65.60	256.02	114.53
◢ Database Connections						
\\.\pipe\9C6954F0-BF30-4E	C:\TEMP\BEERHOUSE\TBH	22 Queries	136.20			
▷ /TBH_Web/GetArticlesRss.aspx		16 Requests	548.41	0.62	430.53	34.28
◢ /TBH_Web/ShowProduct.aspx		2 Requests	134.04	42.80	91.24	67.02
◢ Database Connections						
\\.\pipe\9C6954F0-BF30-4E	C:\TEMP\BEERHOUSE\TBH	9 Queries	39.43			
▷ /TBH_Web/ArchivedPolls.aspx		1 Request	113.64	113.64	113.64	113.64
▷ /TBH_Web/GetProductsRss.aspx		16 Requests	107.72	0.65	50.91	6.73
▷ /TBH_Web/GetThreadsRss.aspx		16 Requests	74.19	0.63	44.77	4.64
/TBH_Web/images/go.gif		1 Request	44.42	44.42	44.42	44.42
/TBH_Web/Images/Store/glass4		1 Request	10.26	10.26	10.26	10.26
/TBH_Web/images/stars50.gif		1 Request	3.73	3.73	3.73	3.73

Database connection details:

Command Text	Query Calls	Total Elapsed Time	Min Elapsed Time	Max Elapsed Time	Avg Elapsed Time
🔍 dbo.aspnet_Profile_GetProperties	5	80.00	1.39	27.10	16.00
🔍 dbo.aspnet_PersonalizationAllUsers_GetPageSettings	5	17.75	1.06	8.14	3.55
🔍 dbo.aspnet_Membership_GetUserByName	1	17.02	17.02	17.02	17.02
🔍 dbo.aspnet_Profile_SetProperties	5	13.50	1.54	4.86	2.70
🔍 dbo.aspnet_PersonalizationPerUser_GetPageSettings	5	4.53	0.12	3.87	0.91
🔍 tbh_Store_GetShippingMethods	1	3.40	3.40	3.40	3.40

FIGURE 9-9

This view shows the different ASPX pages that are called, and the number of times they were called. For example, the "default.aspx" page was requested three times, and the "ShoppingCart.aspx" page was requested five times.

In addition, this view also shows the associated database connections, and how many queries were called with each of the Web pages. For example, the "ShoppingCart.aspx" page made 22 queries. You will get this detail by expanding the "ShoppingCart.aspx" line.

The bottom window shows the details of the queries that were called, and the number of times each of these queries was called. This view also includes information on the timing of these queries. You can quickly see that the information captured about the interaction between the application tier and data tier can come in handy in debugging performance and bottleneck issues associated with the interaction between these two tiers.

CPU Counters Property Page

The CPU Counters property page (shown in Figure 9-10) is used to enable the collecting of CPU-related performance counters as your profiling sessions run. Enable the counters by checking the Collect CPU Counters checkbox. Then, select the counters you wish to track from the "Available counters" list, and click the right-pointing arrow button to add them to the "Selected counters" list.

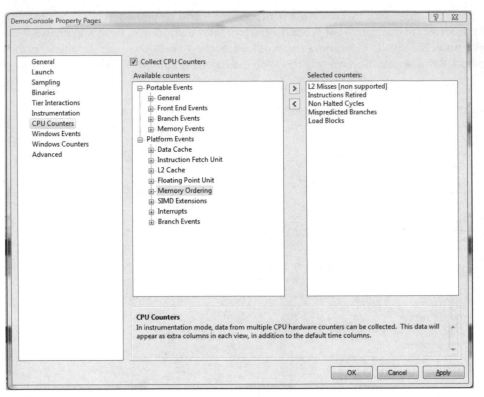

FIGURE 9-10

Windows Events Property Page

The Windows Events property page enables you to collect additional trace information from a variety of event providers. This can include items from Windows itself, such as disk and file I/O, as well as the .NET CLR. If you're profiling an ASP.NET application, for example, you can collect information from IIS and ASP.NET.

Windows Counters Property Page

The Windows Counters property page (shown in Figure 9-11) is used to enable the collection of Windows counters. These are performance counters that can be collected at regular intervals. Enable the counters by checking the Collect Windows Counters box. Then, select the Counter Category you wish to choose from. Select the counters from the list, and click the right-pointing arrow button to add them to the list on the right.

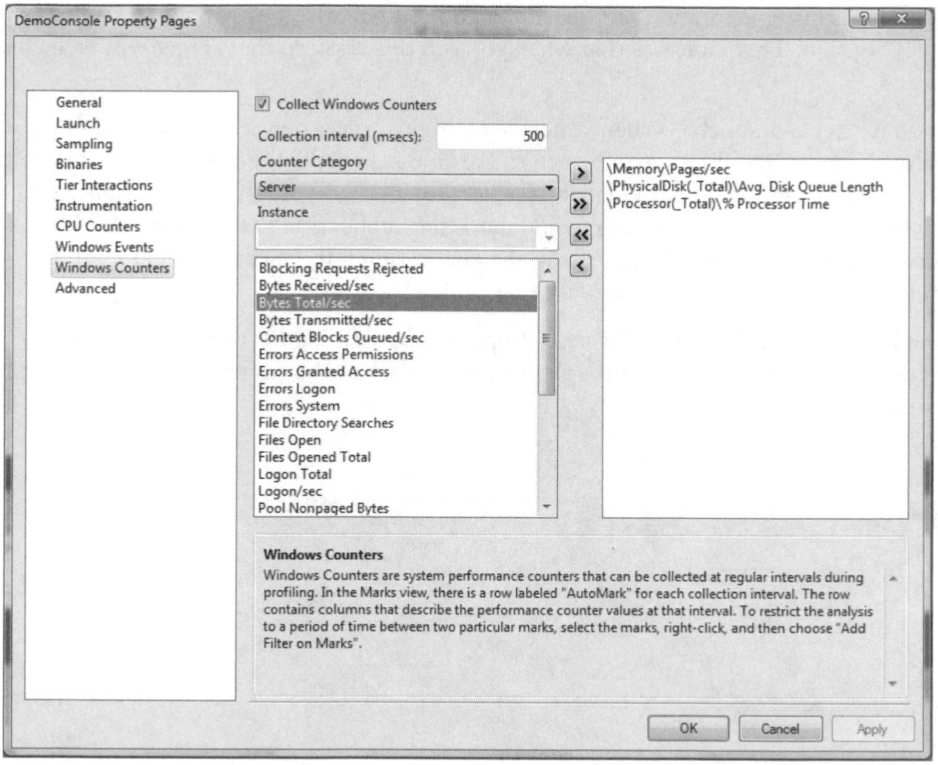

FIGURE 9-11

Configuring Session Targets

If you used the Performance Wizard to create your session, you will already have a target specified. You can modify your session's targets with the Performance Explorer. Simply right-click on the `Targets` folder and choose Add Target Binary. Or, if you have a valid candidate project in your current solution, choose Add Target Project. You can also add an ASP.NET Web site target by selecting Add Existing Web Site.

Each session target can be configured independently. Right-click on any target and you will see a context menu like the one shown in Figure 9-12.

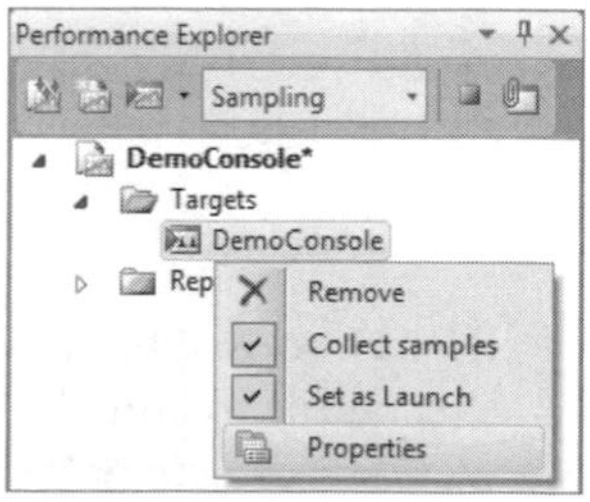

FIGURE 9-12

> *The properties of a target are different from those of the overall session, so be careful to right-click on a target, not the performance session's root node.*

If the session's mode is instrumentation, an Instrument option will also be available instead of the "Collect samples" option. This indicates that when you run this session, that target will be included and observed.

The other option is "Set as Launch." When you have multiple targets in a session, you should indicate which of the targets will be started when the session is launched. For example, you could have several assembly targets, each with launch disabled (unchecked), but one application .exe that uses those assemblies. In that case, you would mark the application's target with the "Set as Launch" property. When this session is launched, the application will be run, and data will be collected from the application and the other target assemblies.

If you select the Properties option, you will see a Property Pages dialog for the selected target (shown in Figure 9-13). Remember that these properties only affect the currently selected target, not the overall session.

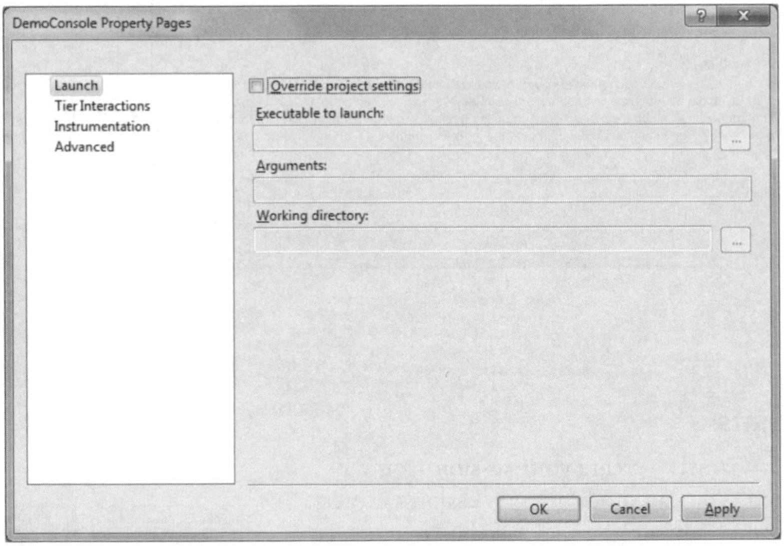

FIGURE 9-13

If you choose Override Project Settings, you can manually specify the path and name of an executable to launch. You can provide additional arguments to the executable and specify the working directory for that executable as well.

> *If the selected target is an ASP.NET application, this page will instead contain a "Url to launch" field.*

The Tier Interactions property page will show up here if you have chosen the tier interaction for the performance session.

The Instrumentation property page (shown in Figure 9-14) has options to run executables or script before and/or after the instrumentation process occurs for the current target. You may exclude the specified executable from instrumentation as well.

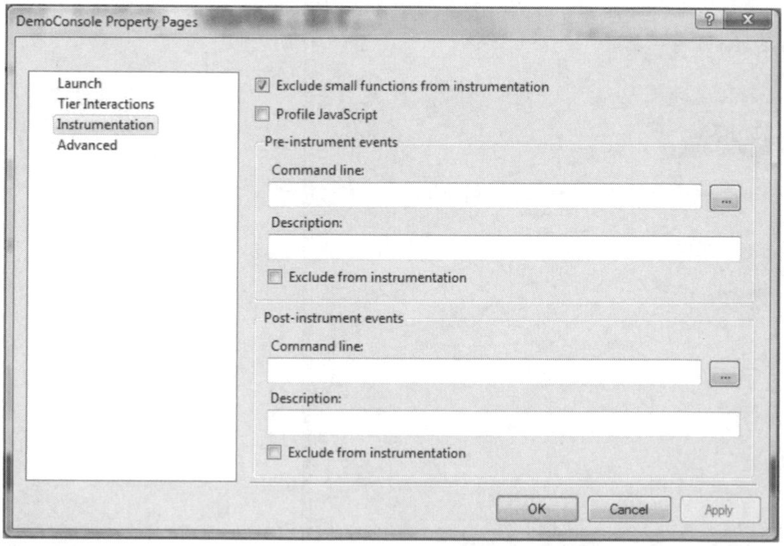

FIGURE 9-14

> *Because the instrumentation of an assembly changes it, when you instrument signed assemblies it will break them because the assembly will no longer match the signature originally generated. To work with signed assemblies, you must add a post-instrument event, which calls to the strong-naming tool, sn.exe. In the "Command-line" field, call sn.exe, supplying the assembly to sign and the key file to use for signing. You must also check the "Exclude from Instrumentation" option. Adding this step will sign those assemblies again, allowing them to be used as expected.*

The Advanced property page is identical to the one under the General project settings. It is used to supply further command-line options to VSInstr.exe, the utility used by Visual Studio to instrument assemblies when running an instrumentation profiling session.

The Advanced property page is where you will specify the .NET Framework run-time to profile, as shown in Figure 9-15. As you see in the figure, the machine being used for demonstration purposes here has .NET 2.0 and .NET 4.0 Beta installed; hence, those two options can be seen in the drop-down.

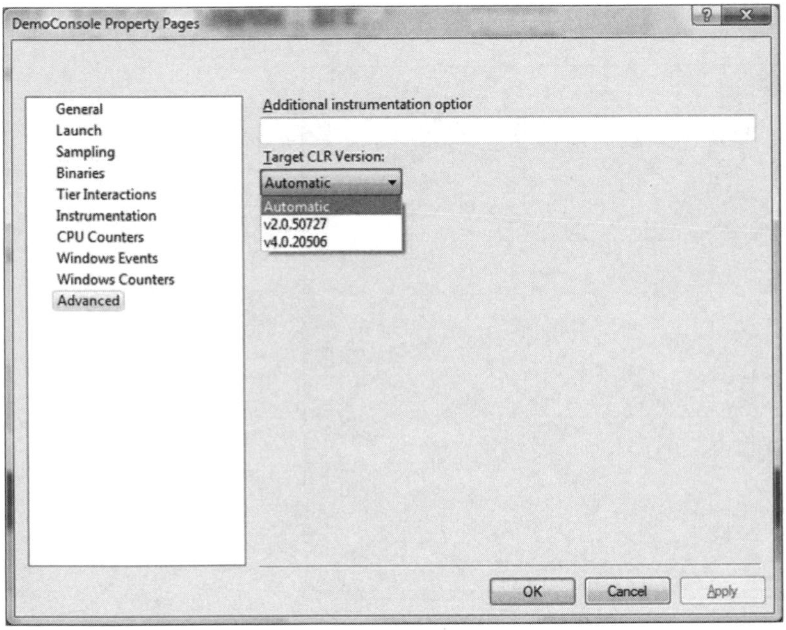

FIGURE 9-15

Configuring a Sampling Session

Sampling is a very lightweight method of investigating an application's performance characteristics. Sampling causes the profiler to periodically interrupt the execution of the target application, noting which code is executing and taking a snapshot of the call stack. When sampling completes, the report will include data such as function call counts. You can use this information to determine which functions might be bottlenecks or critical paths for your application, and then create an instrumentation session targeting those areas.

Because you are taking periodic snapshots of your application, the resulting view might be inaccurate if the duration of your sampling session is too short. For development purposes, you could set the sampling frequency very high, enabling you to obtain an acceptable view in a shorter time. However, if you are sampling against an application running in a production environment, you might wish to minimize the sampling frequency to reduce the impact of profiling on the performance of your system. Of course, doing so will require a longer profiling session run to obtain accurate results.

By default, a sampling session will interrupt the target application every 10 million clock cycles. If you open the session property pages and click the Sampling page, as shown in Figure 9-16, you may select other options as well.

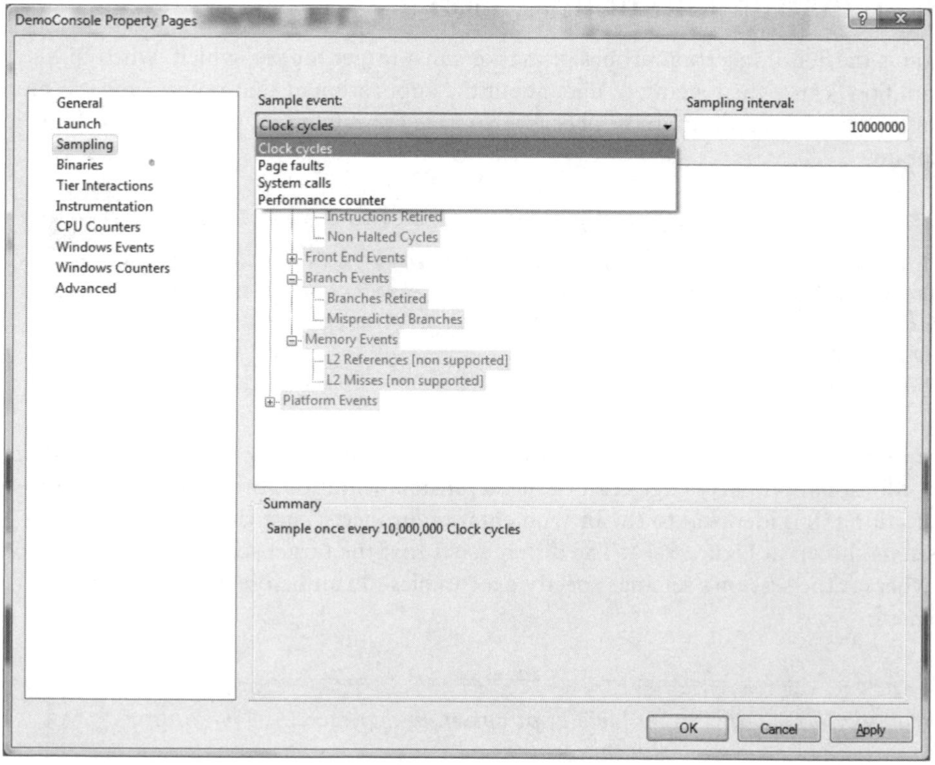

FIGURE 9-16

You can use the "Sampling interval" field to adjust the number of clock cycles between snapshots. Again, you may want a higher value (resulting in less frequent sampling) when profiling an application running in production, or a lower value for more frequent snapshots in a development environment. The exact value you should use will vary, depending on your specific hardware and the performance of the application you are profiling.

If you have an application that is memory-intensive, you may try a session based on page faults. This causes sampling to occur when memory pressure triggers a page fault. From this, you will be able to get a good idea of what code is causing those memory allocations.

You can also sample based on system calls. In these cases, samples will be taken after the specified number of system calls (as opposed to normal user-mode calls) has been made. You may also sample based on a specific CPU performance counter (such as misdirected branches or cache misses).

> *These alternative sampling methods are used to identify very specific conditions; sampling based on clock cycles is what you need most of the time.*

Configuring an Instrumentation Session

Instrumentation is the act of inserting probes or markers in a target binary, which, when hit during normal program flow, cause the logging of data about the application at that point. This is a more invasive way of profiling an application, but because you are not relying on periodic snapshots, it is also more accurate.

> *Instrumentation can quickly generate a large amount of data, so you should begin by sampling an application to find potential problem areas, or hotspots. Then, based on those results, instrument specific areas of code that require further analysis.*

When you're configuring an instrumentation session (refer to Figure 9-1 for the profiling method options), three additional property pages can be of use: Instrumentation, Binaries, and Advanced. The Instrumentation tab is identical to the Instrumentation property page that is available on a per-target basis, as shown in Figure 9-14. The difference is that the target settings are specific to a single target, whereas the session's settings specify executables to run before/after *all* targets have been instrumented.

> *You probably notice the Profile JavaScript option in Figure 9-14. That option will be examined a little later in this chapter.*

The Binaries property page is used to manage the location of your instrumented binaries. By checking "Relocate instrumented binaries" and specifying a folder, Visual Studio will take the original target binaries, instrument them, and place them in the specified folder.

For instrumentation profiling runs, Visual Studio automatically calls the VSInstr.exe utility to instrument your binaries. Use the Advanced property page to supply additional options and arguments (such as /VERBOSE) to that utility.

Configuring a .NET Memory Allocation Session

.NET memory allocation profiling method interrupts the processor for every allocation of managed objects. The profiler will collect details about the managed types that are created during the application's execution. (See Figure 9-1 for the profiling method options.) The profiler will track the number of instances, the amount of memory used by those instances, and which members created the instances.

When you check the "Also collect .NET object lifetime information" option in the General properties page (Figure 9-6), additional details about the amount of time each managed type instance remains in memory will be collected. This will enable you to view further impacts of your application, such as its effect on the .NET garbage collector.

Configuring a Concurrency Profiling Session

Concurrency profiling is a method introduced in Visual Studio 2010. Using this method, you can collect the following two types of concurrency data:

- ➤ *Resource contention* — This captures information every time a function in the application is waiting for a resource because of a synchronous event.

- ➤ *Thread execution* — This captures information on thread contention, processor utilization, execution delays, and other system events.

Executing a Performance Session

Once you have configured your performance session and assigned targets, you can execute (or launch) that session. In the Performance Explorer window (Figure 9-5), right-click on a specific session, and choose "Launch with profiling."

> *Before you launch your performance session, ensure that your project and any dependent assemblies have been generated in Release Configuration mode. Profiling a Debug build will not be as accurate, because such builds are not optimized for performance and will have additional overhead.*

Because Performance Explorer can hold more than one session, you will designate one of those sessions as the current session. By default, the first session is marked as current. This enables you to click the green launch button at the top of the Performance Explorer window to invoke that current session.

You may also run a performance session from the command line. For details, see the section "Command-Line Profiling Utilities," later in this chapter.

When a session is launched, you can monitor its status via the output window. You will see the output from each of the utilities invoked for you. If the target application is interactive, you can use the application as normal. When the application completes, the profiler will shut down and generate a report.

When profiling an ASP.NET application, an instance of Internet Explorer is launched, with a target URL as specified in the target's "Url to launch" setting. Use the application as normal through this browser instance, and Visual Studio will monitor the application's performance. Once the Internet Explorer window is closed, Visual Studio will stop collecting data and generate the profiling report.

> *You are not required to use the browser for interaction with the ASP.NET application. If you have other forms of testing for that application (such as the Web and load tests described in Chapter 13), simply minimize the Internet Explorer window and execute those tests. When you're finished, return to the browser window and close it. The profiling report will then be generated and will include usage data resulting from those Web and load tests.*

Managing Session Reports

When a session run is complete, a new session report will be added to the `Reports` folder for the executed session. The section "Setting General Session Properties," earlier in this chapter (as well as Figure 9-6), provides more details about how to modify the report name, location, and other additional properties in the General property page description.

As shown in Figure 9-17, the `Reports` folder holds all of the reports for the executions of that session.

Double-click on a report file to generate and view the report. Or, you can right-click on a report and select "Open" to view the report within Visual Studio (as shown in Figure 9-17).

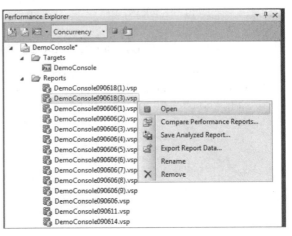

FIGURE 9-17

In Visual Studio 2010, you can also compare two performance reports. With this capability, you can compare the results from a profiling session against a base line. This will help, for example, in tracking the results from profiling sessions from one build to the next. To compare reports, right-click on a report name and select "Compare Performance Reports . . ." (as shown in Figure 9-17).

This will open up a dialog to select the baseline report and the comparison report, as shown in Figure 9-18.

Choose the baseline file and the comparison file, and click OK. This will generate an analysis that shows the delta between the two reports, and an indicator showing the directional move of the data between these two reports (Figure 9-19). This gives you a clear sense of how the application profile is changing between two runs.

FIGURE 9-18

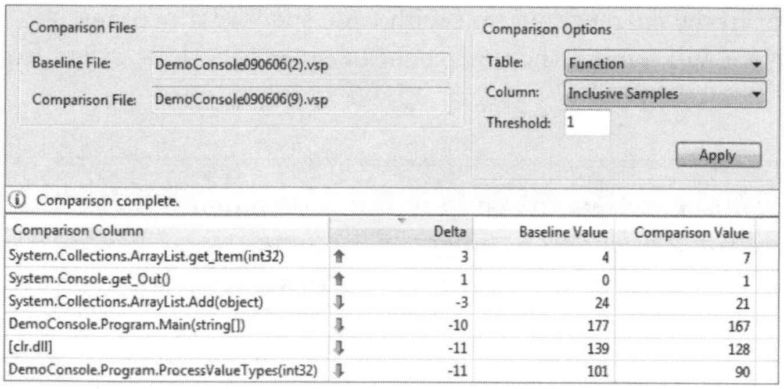

FIGURE 9-19

Another useful option to consider when you right-click on a report is "Export Report Data. . .". When you select this option, it will display the Export Report dialog box shown in Figure 9-20. You can then select one or more sections of the report to send a target file in XML or comma-delimited format. This can be useful if you have another tool that parses this data, or for transforming via XSL into a custom report view.

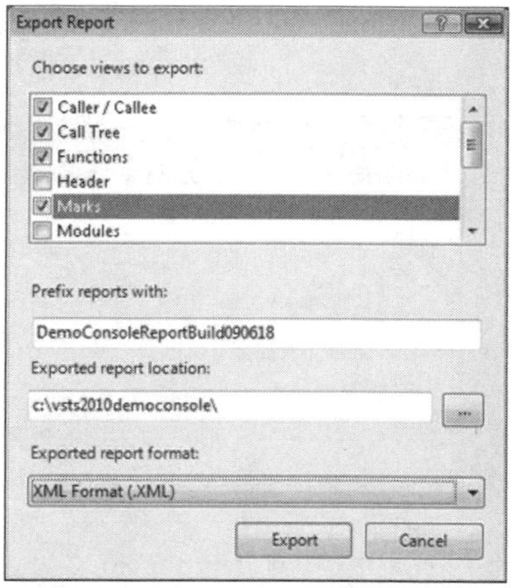

Reading and Interpreting Session Reports

A performance session report is composed of a number of different views. These views offer different ways to inspect the large amount of data collected during the profiling process. The data in many views are interrelated, and you will see that entries in one view can lead to further detail in another view. Note that some views will have content only if you have enabled optional settings before running the session.

FIGURE 9-20

The amount and kinds of data collected and displayed by a performance session report can be difficult to understand and interpret at first. The following sections examine each section of a report, describing its meaning and how to interpret the results.

In any of the tabular report views, you can select which columns appear (and their order) by right-clicking in the report and selecting Choose Columns. Select the columns you wish to see, and how you want to order them, by using the move buttons.

Report Information and Views

The specific information displayed by each view will depend on the settings used to generate the performance session. Sampling and instrumentation will produce different contents for most views, and including .NET memory profiling options will affect the display as well. Before exploring the individual views that make up a report, it is important to understand some key terms.

Elapsed time includes all of the time spent between the beginning and end of a given function. *Application time* is an estimate of the actual time spent executing your code, subtracting system events. Should your application be interrupted by another during a profiling session, elapsed time will include the time spent executing that other application, but application time will exclude it.

Inclusive time combines the time spent in the current function with time spent in any other functions that it may call. *Exclusive time* will remove the time spent in other functions called from the current function.

> *If you forget these definitions, hover your mouse pointer over the column headers and a tool tip will give you a brief description of the column.*

Summary View

When you view a report, Summary view is displayed by default. There are two types of summary reports, depending on whether you ran a sampling or instrumented profile. Figure 9-21 shows a Summary view from a sampling profile of the `DemoConsole` application.

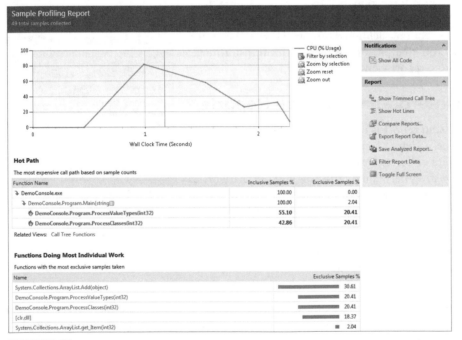

FIGURE 9-21

The Summary view in Visual Studio 2010 has three data sections (on the left of the screen), one Notifications section (in the top right of the screen), and a Report section (in the lower-right portion of the screen), as shown in Figure 9-21.

The first data section you see in the Summary view is the chart at the top showing the percentage of CPU usage. This chart provides a quick visual cue into any spikes you have in CPU usage. You can select a section of the chart (for example, a spike in the chart), and then you can either zoom in by selecting the "Zoom by Selection" link to the right of the chart, or you can filter the data by selecting the "Filter by Selection" link, also to the right of the chart.

The second section in the Summary view is the Hot Path. This shows the most expensive call paths. (They are highlighted with a flame icon next to the function name.) It's not a surprise that the call to "ProcessClasses" and to "ProcessValueTypes" were the expensive calls in this trivial example.

The third data section shows a list of "Functions Doing Most Individual Work." A large number of exclusive samples here indicate that a large amount of time was spent on that particular function.

> *Notice that several of the functions aren't function names, but names of DLLs —
> for example, [clr.dll]. This occurs when debugging samples are not available
> for a function sampled. This frequently happens when running sampling profiles,
> and occasionally with instrumented profiles. The section, "Common Profiling
> Issues," later in the chapter describes this issue and how to correct it.*

For the DemoConsole application, this view isn't showing a lot of interesting data. At this point, you would normally investigate the other views. For example, you can click on one of the methods in the Hot Path to take you to the function details page, but because the DemoConsole application is trivial, sampling to find hotspots will not be as useful as the information you can gather using instrumentation. Let's change the profiling type to instrumentation and see what information is revealed.

At the top of the Performance Explorer window (Figure 9-17), change the drop-down field on the toolbar to Instrumentation. Click the Launch button (it's the third one with the green arrow) on the same toolbar to execute the profiling session, this time using instrumentation. Note that instrumentation profiling will take longer to run. When profiling and report generation are complete, you will see a Summary view similar to that shown in Figure 9-22.

Instrumentation Profiling Report
5763.69 milliseconds of total elapsed time

— CPU (% Usage)
Filter by selection
Zoom by selection
Zoom reset
Zoom out

Report
Show Trimmed Call Tree
Compare Reports...
Export Report Data...
Save Analyzed Report...
Filter Report Data
Toggle Full Screen

Wall Clock Time (Seconds)

Hot Path

The most expensive call path based on execution times

Name	Inclusive %	Exclusive %
DemoConsole.exe	100.00	0.00
DemoConsole.Program.Main(string[])	100.00	0.03
DemoConsole.Program.ProcessValueTypes(int32)	51.71	29.61
DemoConsole.Program.ProcessClasses(int32)	48.26	26.36

Related Views: Call Tree Functions

Functions With Most Individual Work

Functions with the highest exclusive application times

Name	Exclusive Time %
DemoConsole.Program.ProcessValueTypes(int32)	29.61
DemoConsole.Program.ProcessClasses(int32)	26.36
System.Collections.ArrayList.Add(object)	24.12
System.Collections.ArrayList.get_Item(int32)	19.87
DemoConsole.Program.Main(string[])	0.03

FIGURE 9-22

The Summary view of an instrumented session has three sections similar to the Summary view of a sampling session.

You can also get to the Call Tree view (which will be examined shortly) or Functions view using the shortcut link provided below the Hot Path information.

The Summary view has an alternate layout that is used when the ".NET memory profiling collection" options are enabled on the General page of the session properties. Figure 9-23 shows this view.

FIGURE 9-23

Notice that the three main sections in this view are different. The first section, Functions Allocating Most Memory, shows the functions in terms of bytes allocated. The second section, Types With Most Memory Allocated, shows the types by bytes allocated, without regard to the functions involved. Finally, Types With Most Instances shows the types in terms of number of instances, without regard to the size of those instances.

Also note the Notifications section and the Report section to the right of the CPU usage chart. If you click on the View Guidance link in the Notifications section, you will be shown any available errors or warnings. In this case, as shown in Figure 9-24, there is one warning. You'll learn what this means later in this chapter under the section, "Objects Lifetime View."

FIGURE 9-24

Using the Summary view, you can quickly get a sense of the most highly used functions and types within your application. In the following discussions, you'll see how to use the other views to dive into further detail.

Functions View and Functions Details View

Let's switch to the "Functions" view. You do that by selecting "Functions" from the "Current View" drop-down at the top of the report. In this view, you can begin to see some interesting results.

The Functions view shown in Figure 9-25 lists all functions sampled or instrumented during the session. For instrumentation, this will be functions in targets that were instrumented and called during the session. For sampling, this will include any other members/assemblies accessed by the application.

Function Name	Elapsed Inclusive T...	Elapsed Exclusive ...	Application Inclusi...	Application Exclusi...	Elapsed Inclusive T...	Elapsed Exclusive ...	Application Inclusi...	Application Exclusi...	Number of Calls
DemoConsole.Program.Main(string[])	5,763.69	1.90	1,877.50	0.00	100.00	0.03	100.00	0.00	
DemoConsole.Program.ProcessClasses(int32)	2,781.34	1,519.33	654.30	361.05	48.26	26.36	34.85	19.23	1
DemoConsole.Program.ProcessValueTypes(int32)	2,980.46	1,706.83	1,223.20	656.32	51.71	29.61	65.15	34.96	1
System.Collections.ArrayList..ctor()	0.02	0.02	0.00	0.00	0.00	0.00	0.00	0.00	2
System.Collections.ArrayList.Add(object)	1,390.11	1,390.11	405.91	405.91	24.12	24.12	21.62	21.62	4,000,000
System.Collections.ArrayList.get_Item(int32)	1,145.51	1,145.51	454.22	454.22	19.87	19.87	24.19	24.19	4,000,000

FIGURE 9-25

Note that `ArrayList.Add` and `ArrayList.get_Item` were each called 4 million times. This makes sense, because `ProcessValueTypes` and `ProcessClasses` (which use that method) were each called 2 million times. However, if you look at the Hot Path information in the Summary views, there is a noticeable difference in the amount of time spent in `ProcessingValueTypes` over `ProcessClasses`. Remember that the code for each is basically the same — the only difference is that one works with structures, and the other with classes. You can use the other views to investigate further.

From the Functions view, right-click on any function, and you will be able to go to that function's source, see it in module view, see the function details, or see the function in Caller/Callee view (discussed in detail shortly). You can double-click on any function to switch to the Functions Details view. You can also select one or more functions, right-click, and choose Copy to add the function name and associated data to the clipboard for use in other documents.

As with most of the views, you can click on a column heading to sort by that column. This is especially useful for the four "Time" columns shown in Figure 9-25. Right-clicking in the Functions view and selecting "Show in Modules view" will show the functions grouped under their containing binary.

In this view, you can see the performance differences between functions, which could help you to focus in on an issue.

Double-clicking on a function from the "Function View" loads up the "Function Details" view. Figure 9-26 shows the section of this view that is a clickable map with the calling function, the called functions, and the associated values.

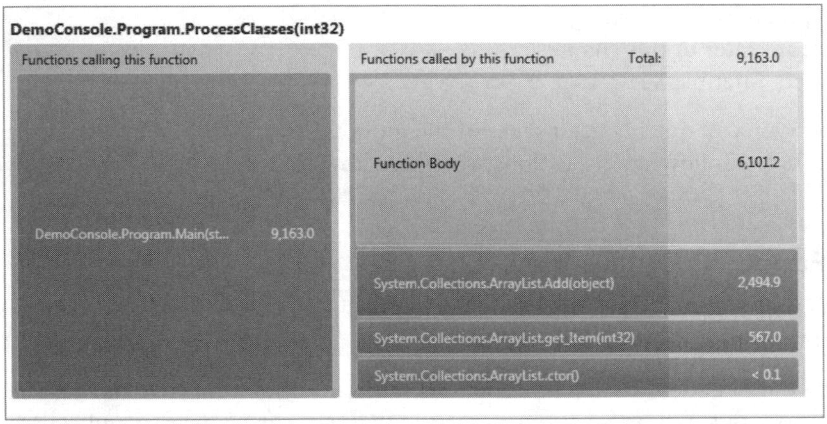

FIGURE 9-26

The "Caller/Callee" view presents this data in a tabular fashion.

Caller/Callee View

As shown in Figure 9-27, the Caller/Callee view displays a particular function in the middle, with the function(s) that call into it in the section above it, and any functions that it calls in the bottom section.

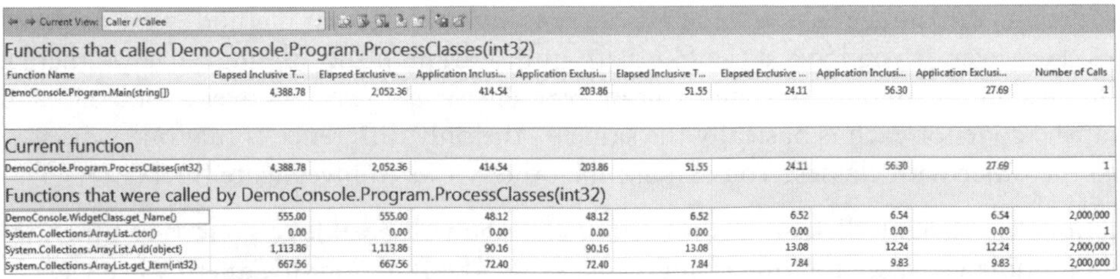

FIGURE 9-27

This is particularly useful for pinpointing the execution flow of your application, helping to identify hotspots. In Figure 9-27, the `ProcessClasses` method is in focus and shows that the only caller is the `Main` method. You can also see that `ProcessClasses` directly calls four functions. The sum of times in the caller list will match the time shown for the set function. For example, select the `ArrayList.get_Item` accessor by double-clicking or right-clicking it, and choose Set Function. The resulting window will then display a table similar to what is shown in Figure 9-28.

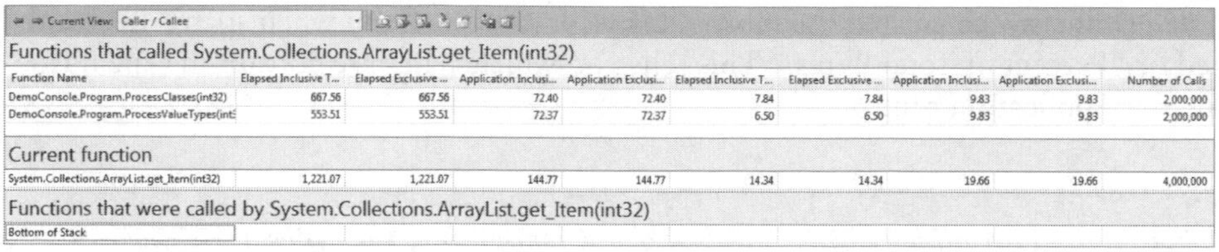

FIGURE 9-28

You saw `ArrayList.get_Item` in the main Functions view, but couldn't tell how much of that time resulted from calls by `ProcessValueTypes` or `ProcessClasses`. Caller/Callee view enables you to see this detail.

Notice that there are two callers for this function, and that the sum of their time equals the time of the function itself. In this table, you can see how much time that the `ArrayList.get_Item` method actually took to process the 2 million requests from `ProcessValueTypes` versus those from `ProcessClasses`. This allows you to analyze the processing time differences, and, if it is substantially different, to drill down on the differences to find out what could be causing the performance difference.

Call Tree View

The Call Tree view shows a hierarchical view of the calls executed by your application. The concept is somewhat similar to the Caller/Callee view, but in this view, a given function may appear twice if it is called by independent functions. If that same method were viewed in Caller/Callee view, it would appear once, with both parent functions listed at the top.

By default, the view will have a root (the function at the top of the list) of the entry point of the instrumented application. To quickly expand the details for any node, right-click and choose Expand All. Any function with dependent calls can be set as the new root for the view by right-clicking and choosing Set Root. This will modify the view to show that function at the top, followed by any functions that were called directly or indirectly by that function. To revert the view to the default, right-click and choose Reset Root.

Another handy option in the context menu is "Expand Hot Path." This will expand the tree to show the hot paths with the flame icon. This is a very helpful shortcut to jump right into the functions that are potential bottlenecks.

Allocation View

If you configured your session for managed allocation profiling by choosing "Collect .NET object allocation information" on the General property page for your session (Figure 9-6), you will have access to the Allocation view. This view displays the managed types that were created during the execution of the profiled application.

You can quickly see how many instances, the total bytes of memory used by those instances, and the percentage of overall bytes consumed by the instances of each managed type.

Expand any type to see the functions that caused the instantiations of that type. You will see the breakdown of instances by function as well, so, if more than one function created instances of that type, you can determine which created the most. This view is most useful when sorted by Total Bytes Allocated or "Percent of Total Bytes." This tells you which types are consuming the most memory when your application runs.

> *An instrumented profiling session will track and report only the types allocated directly by the instrumented code. A sampling session may show other types of objects. This is because samples can be taken at any time, even while processing system functions (such as security). Try comparing the allocations from sampling and instrumentation sessions for the same project. You will likely notice more object types in the sampling session.*

As with the other report views, you can also right-click on any function to switch to an alternative view, such as source code, Functions view, or Caller/Callee view.

Objects Lifetime View

The Objects Lifetime view is available only if you have selected the "Also collect .NET object lifetime information" option of the General properties for your session (Figure 9-6). This option is only available if you have also selected the "Collect .NET object allocation information" option.

> *The information in this view becomes more accurate the longer the application is run. If you are concerned about the results you see, increase the duration of your session run to help ensure that the trend is accurate.*

Several of the columns are identical to those in the Allocation view table, including Instances, Total Bytes Allocated, and "Percent of Total Bytes." However, in this view, you can't break down the types to show which functions created them. The value in this view lies in the details about how long the managed type instances existed and their effect on garbage collection.

The columns in this view include the number of instances of each type that were collected during specific generations of the garbage collector. With COM, objects were immediately destroyed, and memory freed, when the count of references to that instance became zero. However, .NET relies on a process called *garbage collection* to periodically inspect all object instances to determine whether the memory they consume can be released.

Objects are placed into groups, called *generations*, according to how long each instance has remained referenced. Generation zero contains new instances, generation one instances are older, and generation two contains the oldest instances. New objects are more likely to be temporary or shorter in scope than objects that have survived previous collections. So, having objects organized into generations enables .NET to more efficiently find objects to release when additional memory is needed.

The view includes Instances Alive At End and Instances. The latter is the total count of instances of that type over the life of the profiling session. The former indicates how many instances of that type were still in memory when the profiling session terminated. This might be because the references to those instances were held by other objects. It may also occur if the instances were released right before the session ended, before the garbage collector acted to remove them. Having values in this column does not necessarily indicate a problem; it is simply another data item to consider as you evaluate your system.

Having a large number of generation-zero instances collected is normal, fewer in generation one, and the fewest in generation two. Anything else indicates there might be an opportunity to optimize the scope of some variables. For example, a class field that is only used from one of that class's methods could be changed to a variable inside that method. This would reduce the scope of that variable to live only while that method is executing.

Like the data shown in the other report views, you should use the data in this view not as definitive indicators of problems, but as pointers to places where improvements might be realized. Also, keep in mind that, with small or quickly executing programs, allocation tracking might not have enough data to provide truly meaningful results.

COMMAND-LINE PROFILING UTILITIES

Visual Studio abstracts the process of calling several utilities to conduct profiling. You can use these utilities directly if you need more control, or if you need to integrate your profiling with an automated batch process (such as your nightly build). The general flow is as follows:

1. Configure the target (if necessary) and environment.
2. Start the data logging engine.
3. Run the target application.
4. When the application has completed, stop the logging data engine.
5. Generate the session report.

These utilities can be found in your Visual Studio installation directory under `\Team Tools\ Performance Tools`. For help with any of the utilities, supply a `/?` argument after the utility name.

Table 9-1 lists the performance utilities that are available as of this writing:

TABLE 9-1: Performance tools

UTILITY NAME	DESCRIPTION
Vsinstr.exe	Used to instrument a binary
Vsperfcmd.exe	Used to launch a profiling session
Vsperfmon.exe	Starts the monitor for the profiling sessions
Vsperfreport.exe	Used to generate a report once a profiling session is completed
VsperfCLREnv.exe	Used to set environment variables required to profile a .NET application

> *Refer to MSDN documentation at* `http://msdn.microsoft.com/en-us/`
> `library/bb385768(VS.100).aspx` *for more information on the command-line*
> *profiling tools.*

Virtual Machines

Before Visual Studio 2010, if you were running your application from within a virtual machine (such as with Virtual PC, VMWare, or Virtual Server), you were not be able to profile that application. (Profiling relies upon a number of performance counters that are very close to the system hardware.) But, such is no longer the case. With Visual Studio 2010, you can now profile applications that are running within a virtual environment.

Profiling JavaScript

In Visual Studio 2010, you can now profile JavaScript. With this option, you can now collect performance data for JavaScript code. To do that, you will start by setting up an instrumentation session. Then, in the Instrumentation property page, select the Profile JavaScript option, as shown in Figure 9-29.

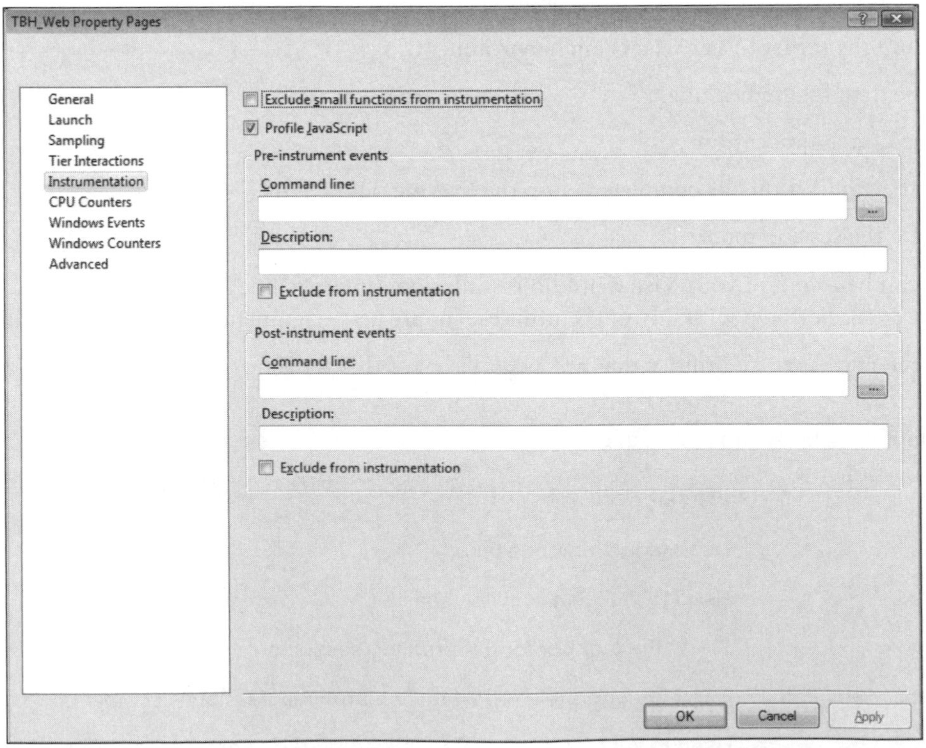

FIGURE 9-29

When you run this profiling session, the profiler will include performance information on JavaScript functions, along with function calls in the application. This example again uses the "Beer House" application. (You can find this application source code at http://thebeerhouse.codeplex.com.)

Figure 9-30 shows the Function Details view with the called functions and the elapsed times. It also shows the associated JavaScript code in the bottom pane, and that helps in identifying any potential issues with the script. This feature will be very helpful to assess the performance of JavaScript functions and identify any issues with the scripts.

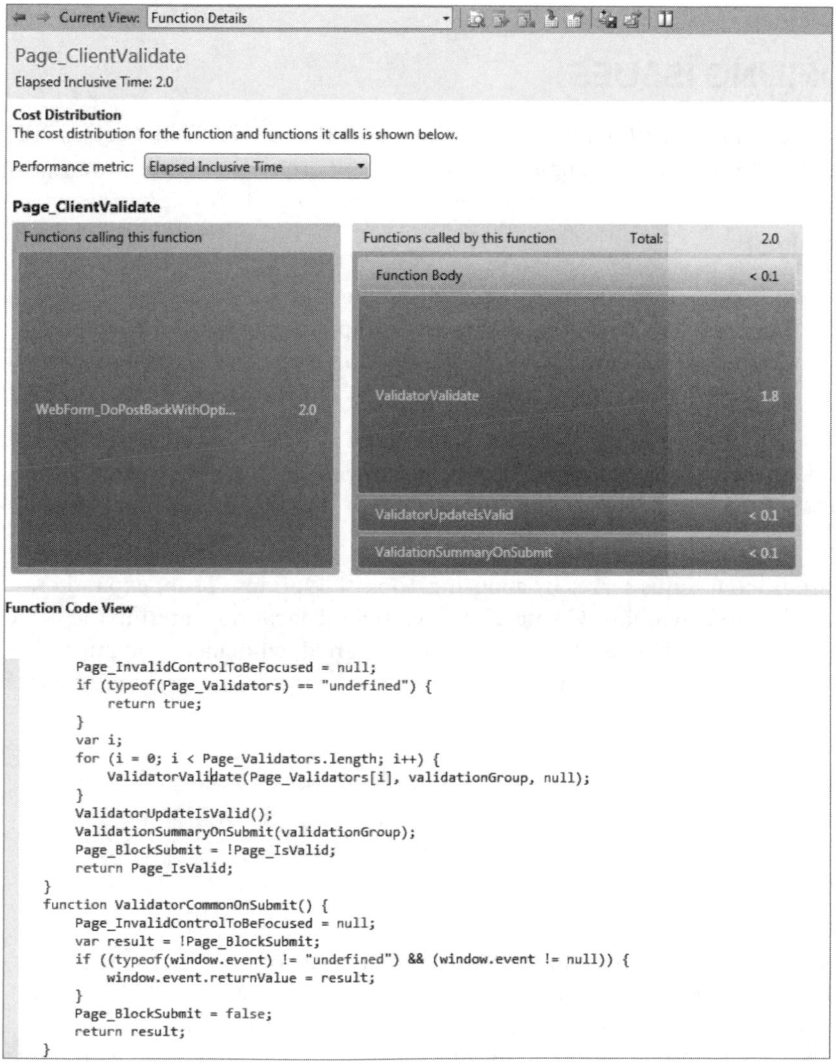

FIGURE 9-30

Just My Code

When you run a sampling session, the report includes profiling data from all the code in the project. In most cases, you are only interested in the performance information of your code. For example, you don't need to have the performance data of .NET Framework libraries, and, even if you have it, there is not a lot you can do with that data. In the Summary view of the profiling report, you can now toggle between viewing data for all code, or just the application code. The setting for that is in the Notifications section in the Summary view, as shown in Figure 9-31.

Notifications ^
🔲 Show Just My Code

FIGURE 9-31

COMMON PROFILING ISSUES

Profiling is a complex topic, and not without a few pitfalls to catch the unwary. This section documents a number of common issues you might encounter as you profile your applications.

Debugging Symbols

When you review your profiling reports, you may notice that some function calls resolve to unhelpful entries such as [ntdll.dll]. This occurs because the application has used code for which it cannot find debugging symbols. So, instead of the function name, you get the name of the containing binary.

Debugging symbols, files with the .pdb extension (for "program database"), include the details that debuggers and profilers use to discover information about executing code. Microsoft Symbol Server enables you to use a Web connection to dynamically obtain symbol files for binaries as needed.

You can direct Visual Studio to use this server by choosing Tools ⇨ Options. Then, expand the Debugging section and choose Symbols. Create a new symbol file location, entering the value **http://msdl.microsoft.com/download/symbols**. Because symbols are downloaded, you must also choose a local directory to serve as a storage area. Now, close and reopen a report; the new symbols will be used to resolve function names.

> *The first time you render a report with symbols set to download from Microsoft Symbol Server, it will take significantly longer to complete.*

If, perhaps because of security restrictions, your profiling system does not have Internet access, you can download and install the symbol packages for Windows from the Windows Hardware Developer Center. As of this writing, this is www.microsoft.com/whdc/devtools/debugging/symbols.mspx. Select the package appropriate for your processor and operating system, and install the symbols.

Instrumentation and Code Coverage

When running an instrumentation profile, be certain that you are not profiling a target for which you have previously enabled *code coverage*. Code coverage, described in Chapter 7, uses another form of instrumentation that observes which lines of code are accessed as tests are executed. Unfortunately, this instrumentation can interfere with the instrumentation required by the profiler.

If your solution has a test project and you have previously used code coverage, open your Test Run Configuration under Test ➪ Edit Test Run Configurations, and select the Code Coverage page. Ensure that the binaries you are profiling do not have code coverage enabled. If they do, uncheck them and rebuild your solution. You should then be able to use instrumentation profiling without conflict.

SUMMARY

In this chapter, you learned about the value of using profiling to identify problem areas in your code. Visual Studio 2010 has extended the capabilities for profiling.

This chapter examined the differences between sampling and instrumentation, when each should be applied, and how to configure the profiler to execute each type. You learned about the different profiling methods. You saw the Performance Explorer in action, and learned how to create and configure performance sessions and their targets.

You then learned how to invoke a profiling session, and how to work with the reports that are generated after each run. You looked at each of the available report types, including Summary, Function, Call Tree, and Caller/Callee.

While Visual Studio 2010 offers a great deal of flexibility in your profiling, you may find you must specify further options or profile applications from a batch application or build system. You learned about the available command-line tools available. Profiling is a great tool that you can use to ensure the quality of your application.

In Chapter 11, you will learn about a great new capability introduced in Visual Studio 2010 called "IntelliTrace," and Chapter 10 introduces you to other nifty debugging capabilities (including data tips and breakpoints). You will see the capabilities of Visual Studio 2010 to track and manage changes to database schemas using source control, generate test data, create database unit tests, utilize static analysis for database code, and more.

10

Database Development, Testing, and Deployment

WHAT'S IN THIS CHAPTER?

➤ The need to bring database development lifecycle management alongside application lifecycle management

➤ Using Visual Studio 2010 to work with databases in an "offline" manner

➤ Making changes to your database schema

➤ Testing a database schema, including the automatic generation of pseudo-random test data

➤ Deploying updates to your database schema

Until now, this book has dealt with tools and techniques that can be used to help you build and test software *applications*. But *databases* are a critical component utilized by many (if not most) software applications. And yet, they are traditionally underserved by tools that can facilitate development, testing, and deployment. Database developers are usually left to cobble together disconnected tools for developing and deploying database changes. Furthermore, database developers often follow a process that is disconnected from the process followed by the application development team, resulting in an error-prone and labor-intensive system of collaboration. With Visual Studio 2010, you can finally bring the process of managing changes to your database into the same toolset and process framework used by the other members of your software development team.

In this chapter, you will see how Visual Studio allows you to track and manage changes to database schemas using source control, generate test data, create database unit tests, utilize static analysis for database code, and automatically create deployment scripts based on the changes modeled in your development environment. You will see how Visual Studio can remove the traditional boundaries that exist between database development teams and application development teams, enabling better coordination and, ultimately, allowing you to produce higher-quality software.

> *The features covered in this chapter will work with Microsoft SQL Server 2005 and SQL Server 2008 databases, and Microsoft is working with third parties to create add-ins that will extend this support to other databases as well. As of this writing, Microsoft has announced partnerships to deliver support for both Oracle and IBM DB2, with support for additional databases expected in the future.*

THE CHALLENGES OF DATABASE CHANGE MANAGEMENT

Database developers face unique challenges not generally faced by their application developer counterparts. Such challenges include (but are not limited to) the following:

➤ It can be difficult to create development and test environments that accurately mimic the schema of production databases. Even when a development or test database is created from an exact snapshot of the production database, these environments can quickly drift out of sync.

➤ Because of privacy or compliance concerns, organizations must often restrict access to the data contained within a production database. Lack of realistic data can prevent a team from being able to accurately test a database, causing bugs to surface later only after changes have been applied to a production database.

➤ Bugs experienced in a production database can be exponentially more expensive to diagnose and repair than the same bugs caught during the development or testing phases, and may result in costly interruptions to business functions (for example, lost or incorrect customer orders, corrupt records, or even a breach of sensitive data).

➤ At the risk of oversimplifying application deployment, deploying an update to an application usually just involves replacing the older version with a newer version of that application. When a user launches the application again, he or she will load the newer version of that application. But managing updates to a database can be much more complex. A database is a *stateful engine* containing existing data that must be preserved, as well as relationships and constraints that must be maintained. Usually, an experienced database administrator must handcraft scripts for applying updates while also ensuring that operations are performed in a proper order. This is both a costly and error-prone process. Errors during this process can result in extended periods of downtime, and may introduce additional bugs.

➤ The process of deploying an update to one production database may be different than the process required to make the same changes to another production database. This is caused when production databases drift out of sync, and is especially true for software vendors who must distribute upgrades to their customers who are running their own copies of production databases. Those production databases may be running different versions of a database schema, may contain custom fixes or modifications, and could even be running on different database engines (for example, SQL Server 2005 versus SQL Server 2008). The variety of possible production database configurations can require very complex deployment scripts with conditional branching logic. This, in turn, introduces another opportunity for deployments to fail, or for bugs to creep into the system.

The remainder of this chapter examines the approach offered by Visual Studio 2010 for solving these (and other) problems associated with database development.

OFFLINE SCHEMA DEVELOPMENT

The approach used by Visual Studio 2010 for database change management has been described by Microsoft as *offline schema development*. Offline schema development allows you to work on changes to your database schema without maintaining a connection to the production database. In many organizations, access to a production database is only granted to database administrators, not the development teams. Being able to develop and test offline in an environment resembling that of the production environment is crucial. It's also highly advisable to develop and test in isolation from the production environment so as to minimize the risk of untested or unauthorized changes from being deployed into production.

As changes are made in the development environment, Visual Studio can help you test those changes in the development environment and/or in a dedicated test environment. Visual Studio can also generate pseudo-realistic data for conducting your tests, all without requiring access to actual production data. It is only when changes have been sufficiently tested and are deemed ready for deployment that a connection is then re-established to the production database. Visual Studio then generates the necessary scripts required to upgrade the production database to match what has been modeled in the development environment.

Following are the four main steps that make up this *database development lifecycle*:

1. Taking the schema offline
2. Iterative development
3. Schema testing
4. Build and deploy

These four phases of the database development lifecycle are explored conceptually in the following discussions. You should notice that these stages match the stages of an application development lifecycle quite nicely, and can even be performed in conjunction with changes made to your application.

Taking the Schema Offline

The first step toward enabling database change management with Visual Studio is to create a new project that will store the offline representation of your database schema. As discussed earlier, the term *offline* is used to describe the notion of building and testing changes to your database in isolation from the production database. The mechanics of creating a project and importing your database schema are detailed later in this chapter in the section "Creating a Database Project."

The process of taking a database schema offline is a task that will usually be performed by a database administrator. This process could also be performed by a database developer, provided that he or she has sufficient permissions to access the production database.

While it is recommended that you store your database project in a version control system such as Visual Studio Team Foundation Server 2010, this is not a requirement.

Figure 10-1 shows the process of taking a database schema offline and storing it in version control.

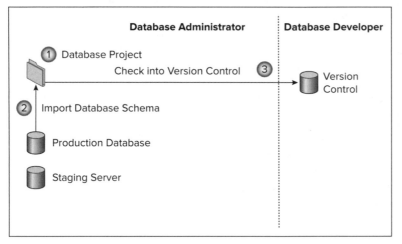

FIGURE 10-1

Iterative Development

With the schema offline, you are now free to work on changes to your database schema. Later in this chapter in the section "Making Schema Changes," you will see that Visual Studio provides several ways of making changes, ranging from hand-editing individual .sql files to making sweeping changes at once by using built-in refactoring tools. If you choose to store your project in a version control system (such as Team Foundation Server), then you can have multiple people working on changes to the database schema, even simultaneously (known as *parallel development*). Changes can be checked-in, checked-out, branched, merged, and compared just like any other file under source control.

Figure 10-2 shows the process of iterative development.

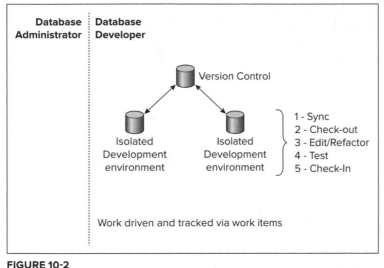

FIGURE 10-2

Schema Testing

As with any software development project, changes that you make to your database schema should be tested prior to being deployed into a production environment. But testing a database can be a bit more complicated than testing a traditional software application. Effectively testing the database schema usually relies on first having a certain amount of data in the database.

If you are lucky, then you may be able to import existing data from an existing production database to aid in your testing efforts. But, for a brand new database, or when making such changes as adding or changing tables, this data may not yet exist in a production database. And, if your database contains sensitive data (for example, customer contact information, health records, or financial data), then it is unlikely that you will be permitted to use production data for your testing purposes.

The solution to this problem lies in Visual Studio's capability to generate data that conforms to your database schema. For a given database schema, Visual Studio can generate an unlimited amount of data that matches the data types and column relationships defined in your schema. This data can be injected into a test database and used as the basis for conducting your tests. You will become familiar with Visual Studio's data generation capabilities later in this chapter in the section "Data Generation."

After you have established a set of data with which to run your tests, Visual Studio can also be used to author and execute database unit tests that exercise your database functions, triggers, and stored procedures. As with other unit tests you might write with Visual Studio (such as those used for testing C# or Visual Basic code), database unit tests can be executed as part of an automated build, which can be used to quickly determine if changes made to a database schema have introduced any bugs.

Figure 10-3 shows the process of building a test database, populating it with test data, and executing database unit tests. Database testing is discussed later in this chapter in the section "Database Testing."

Build and Deploy

After database schema changes have been sufficiently tested, you are now ready to apply those changes to your production environment. Traditionally, at this stage, a database administrator (DBA) might be called upon to hand-code a `.sql` script. But hand-coding scripts can be time-consuming, error-prone, and may require extensive

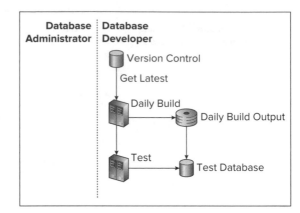

FIGURE 10-3

conditional logic to account for customizations or versioning differences between different instances of production databases. Furthermore, many database changes must be made in a precise order to preserve the integrity of the schema and prevent data loss.

Visual Studio eliminates the need to ever hand-code database deployment scripts again. Visual Studio first compiles your database project into a handful of files known as the *build output*. When you are ready to deploy those changes to a target database, Visual Studio then analyzes the differences between your target database and the changes you have modeled in your database project (as represented in your build output). Based on these differences, Visual Studio then automatically creates a script for you that can be used to upgrade your target database. The process of comparing your build output with your target database and producing an upgrade script is known as the *deployment phase*.

The deployment phase can be run multiple times if you are deploying changes to multiple target databases. The deployment tools can even be run on machines that do not have Visual Studio installed, and Microsoft permits free redistribution of these deployment tools to your customers. (You will learn more about this later in this chapter in the section "Redistributable Deployment Engine.")

Now you no longer need to hand-code multiple upgrade scripts or write conditional logic to account for the different versions of a database your customer might be running. You must simply distribute your project's build output along with the deployment tools, and the proper scripts will automatically be generated based on whatever target database is specified. You may even wish to package this functionality along with the installer for your application, thus ensuring that matching versions of your software application and the corresponding database are deployed in sync.

Figure 10-4 shows the build and deployment processes.

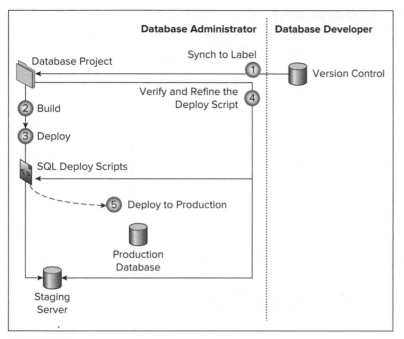

FIGURE 10-4

Now that you have a conceptual understanding of the database deployment lifecycle employed by Visual Studio, it's time to see how this works with a sample project.

CREATING A DATABASE PROJECT

The walkthrough in this chapter uses Microsoft's classic Northwind sample database running on a local instance of SQL Server 2008 Express Edition. Instructions for installing the Northwind sample database and attaching it to a running instance of SQL Server 2008 Express Edition can be found on this book's companion Web site (www.wrox.com). The steps outlined in this chapter should also work with Northwind running on SQL Server 2005, or any of the higher-end (non-Express) editions of SQL Server (such as Standard or Enterprise).

The first step toward enabling database change management with Visual Studio is to create a new project for your database. Close any existing solutions you have open, and then click on File ➪ New ➪ Project. Select Database ➪ SQL Server, as shown in Figure 10-5. Select SQL Server 2008 Wizard, name your project MyDatabaseProject, and click OK.

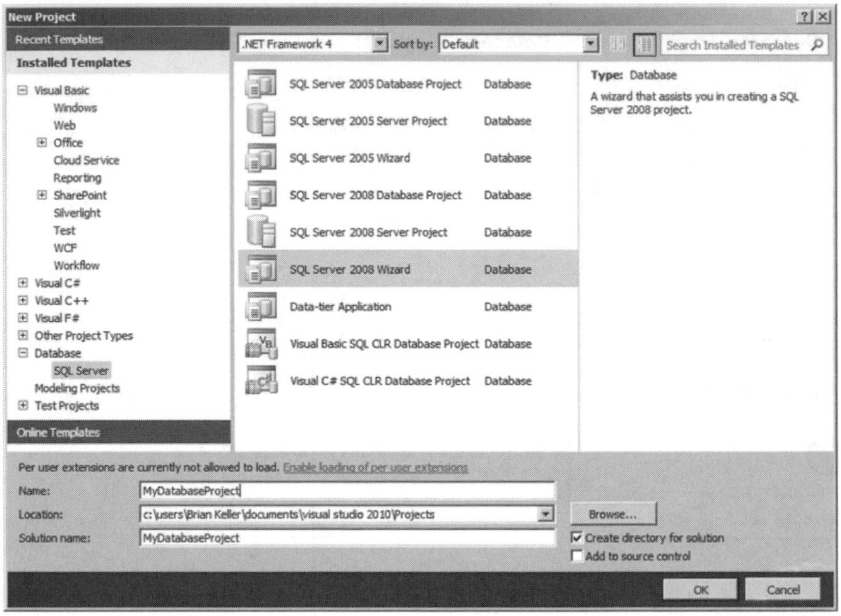

FIGURE 10-5

The New Database Project Wizard appears and will guide you through the process of configuring your database project. Click on Project Properties on the left-hand pane and you will see the page shown in Figure 10-6.

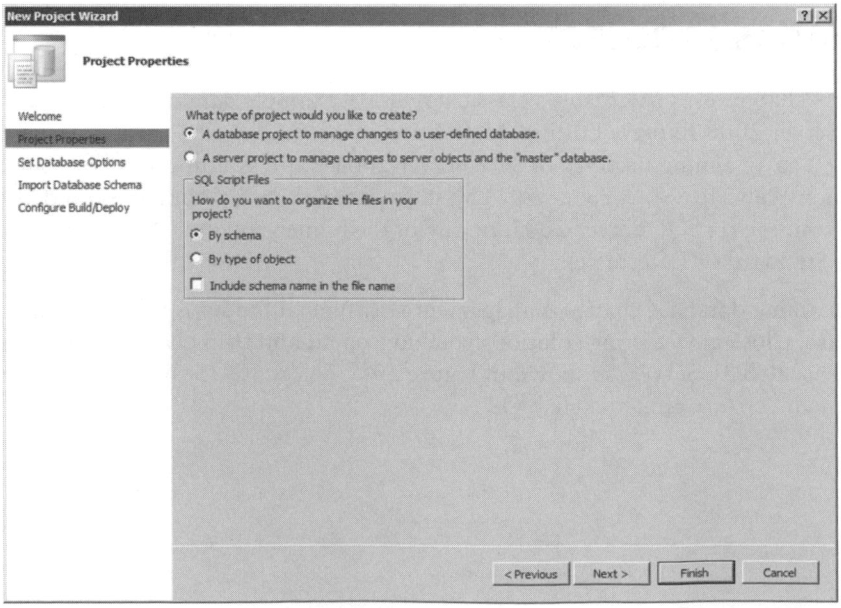

FIGURE 10-6

Visual Studio 2010 supports the capability to manage the changes made to both your user-defined databases (a *database project*) and changes to the configuration of the database server itself (a *server project*). A server project can help you manage and deploy changes to your master database (for example, logon accounts or linked servers) and validate that database server settings are correct at deploy time. In this walkthrough, you will manage changes to a user-defined database, Northwind, so retain the default setting for this option.

The remaining options on this page are mostly a matter of personal preference. They affect the way that your database schema files are named and stored within your database project. Keep the default settings and click Next.

The Set Database Options page will vary based on the version of SQL Server you are working with. Figure 10-7 shows options for SQL Server 2008. For this walkthrough, you can keep the default settings, but you can read more about each option in the SQL Server Books Online documentation for your version of SQL Server. Click Next.

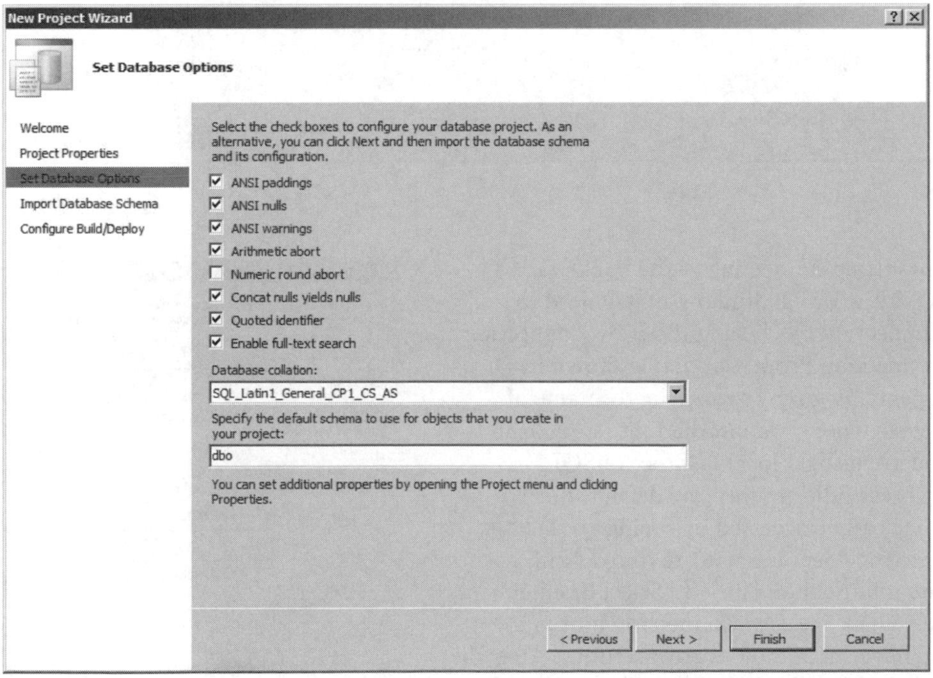

FIGURE 10-7

You should now see the Import Database Schema page shown in Figure 10-8. If you were creating a database from scratch, you could simply skip this page and Visual Studio would create a database project with an empty database schema. But, since you want to use the schema from the existing Northwind database, enable the "Import existing schema" checkbox, which will enable the rest of the options on this page.

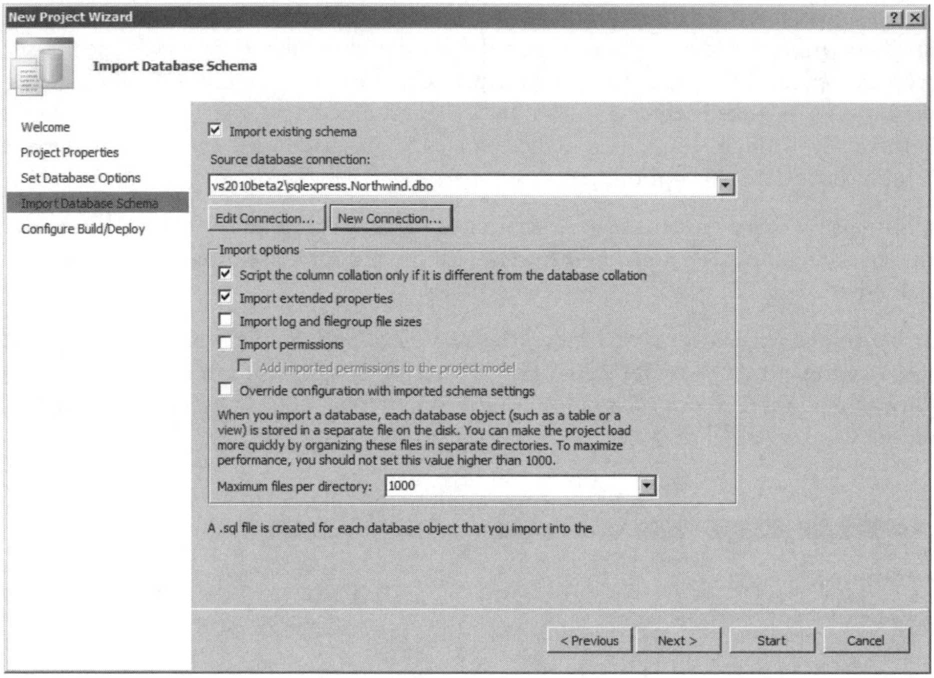

FIGURE 10-8

If this is your first time connecting to the Northwind database from within Visual Studio you will need to define a new connection by clicking the New Connection button. The Connection Properties dialog shown in Figure 10-9 appears. Begin by specifying the name of the database server where you installed the Northwind database. If you are using a local instance of SQL Server 2008 Express Edition, then, by default, this database instance can be accessed by typing **LOCALHOST\ SQLEXPRESS** into the "Server name" textbox. Now, type **Northwind** into the box labeled "Select or enter a database name." Click the Test Connection button to ensure that you have entered the correct settings. After the test passes, click OK to close the test notification window. Click OK again to confirm your connection settings.

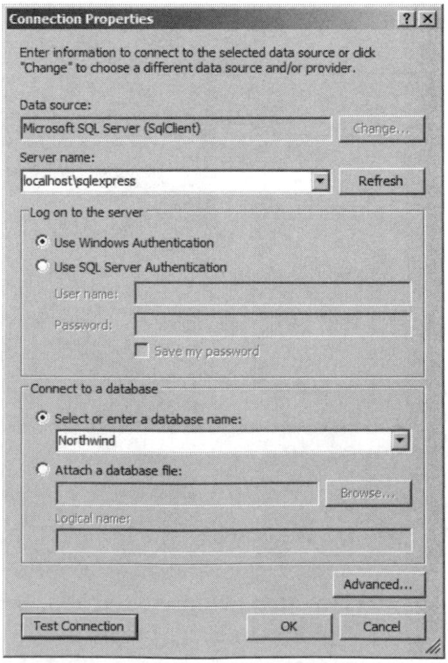

Once your connection to Northwind is configured, select it in the "Source database connections" drop-down list shown in Figure 10-8. Note that Visual Studio will fully qualify your database name (for example, replacing LOCALHOST with your machine's computer name). For this walkthrough, you can keep the defaults on the rest of this page and click Next.

FIGURE 10-9

Database projects in Visual Studio expose a myriad of advanced configuration options, especially during the schema import, build, and deployment phases. Databases themselves can be very complex, and Visual Studio attempts to account for these complexities by providing configuration options for working with practically any database configuration you might encounter.

For right now, try not to get overwhelmed with all of the additional settings you will see. The most important settings will be covered in this chapter, and the rest are detailed in the product's documentation, should you ever need to work with more complex databases.

The final page of the New Project Wizard (Figure 10-10) allows you to configure your project's initial build and deploy settings. You can always change these settings later, so for now, just click Finish.

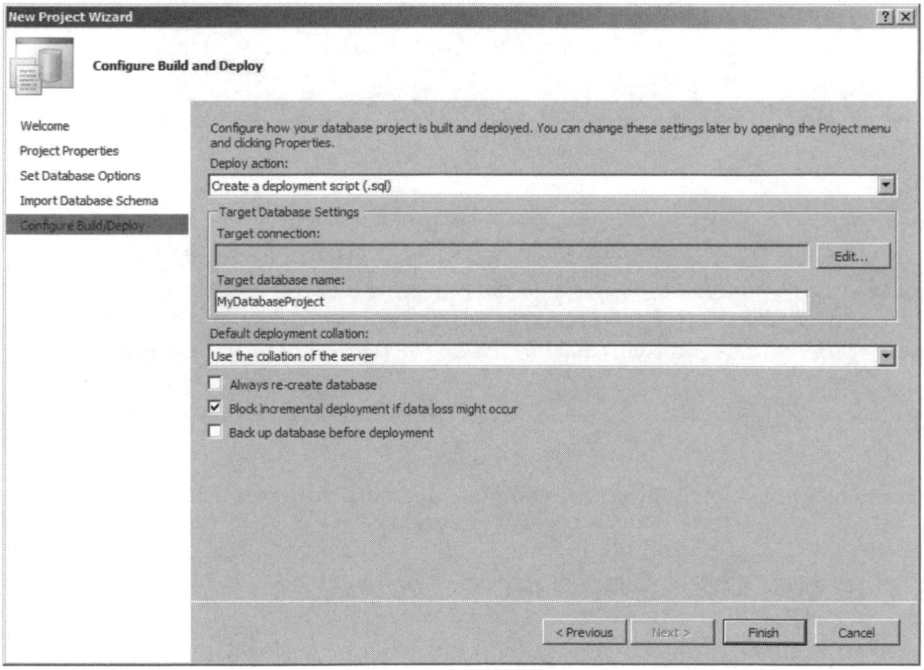

FIGURE 10-10

Visual Studio will now attempt to connect to your target database server (SQL Server 2008 Express Edition) and import the schema from your database (Northwind). When the schema has been successfully imported, you should see a completion summary like that shown in Figure 10-11.

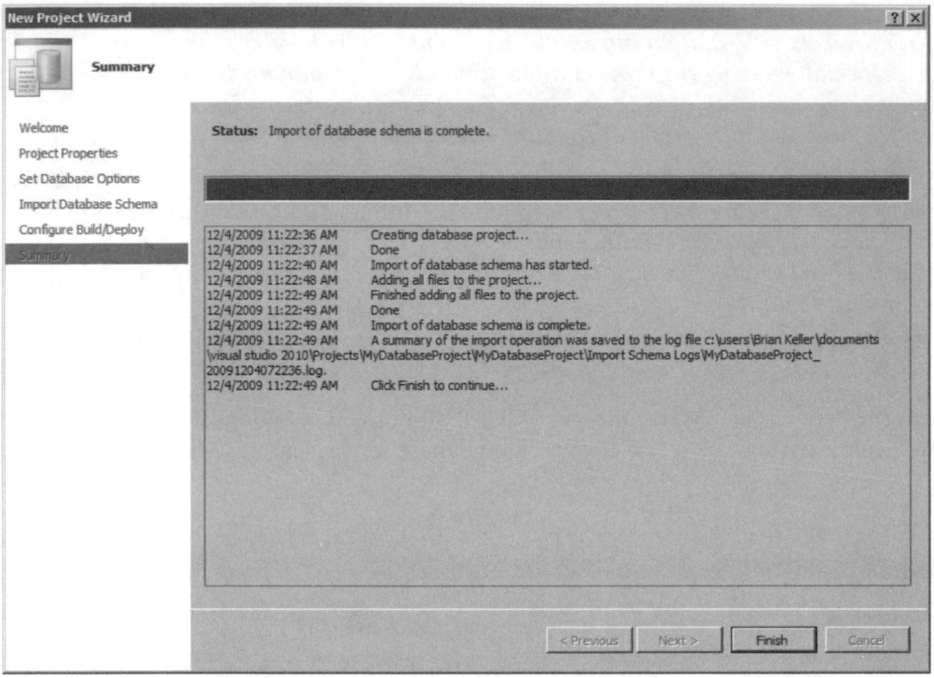

FIGURE 10-11

> *This step can fail if you don't have the requisite permissions for accessing the target database. The full list of required permissions for working with database projects in Visual Studio can be found in the documentation. Some operations will require different sets of permissions based on the version of SQL Server you are using.*

Click Finish again to close the New Project Wizard. Your database project is now ready to use.

EXAMINING THE DATABASE PROJECT

A database project varies slightly from other projects you may have worked with in Visual Studio. In this section, you will become familiar with the structure of a database project, and will learn some ways of visualizing the dependencies within your database schema.

Solution Explorer versus Schema View

As shown in Figure 10-12, you can examine the on-disk layout of your project files from Solution Explorer (View ➪ Solution Explorer).

Accessing files via Solution Explorer is a legitimate way of accessing your database project, but Visual Studio also includes a special Schema View (View ➪ Database Schema View), as shown in Figure 10-13, which can be a more natural way of working with your schema objects. Schema View is based on Visual Studio's in-memory model of your database schema, and can be used to quickly visualize the structure of your schema (such as which columns make up a table, or which parameters are used by a stored procedure).

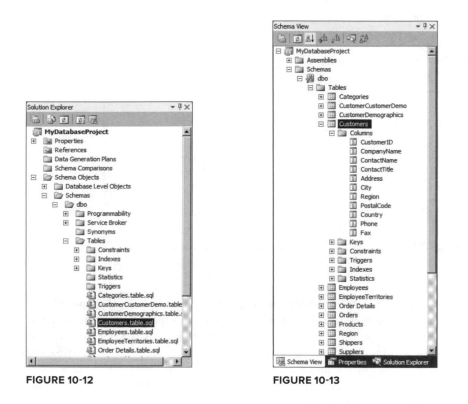

FIGURE 10-12   **FIGURE 10-13**

Schema View should feel very familiar if you are used to managing databases within SQL Server Management Studio. Spend a few minutes now exploring the Schema View by expanding and collapsing some nodes of the object tree.

Schema Dependency Viewer

Schema View can be used to quickly browse all of your schema objects and can help you explore some of the relationships within your database schema. But a faster and more comprehensive way of visualizing relationships between objects is to use the Schema Dependency Viewer.

To access the Schema Dependency Viewer, first select the object within the Schema View for which you want to analyze the dependency relationships. One example might be the Customers table (Schemas ➪ dbo ➪ Tables ➪ Customers). Right-click on Customers and select View Dependencies. The Schema Dependency Viewer opens, as shown in Figure 10-14, and provides a list of all of the schema objects that depend on the Customers table (Referenced By) and all of the schema objects that the Customers table, in turn, depends on (References).

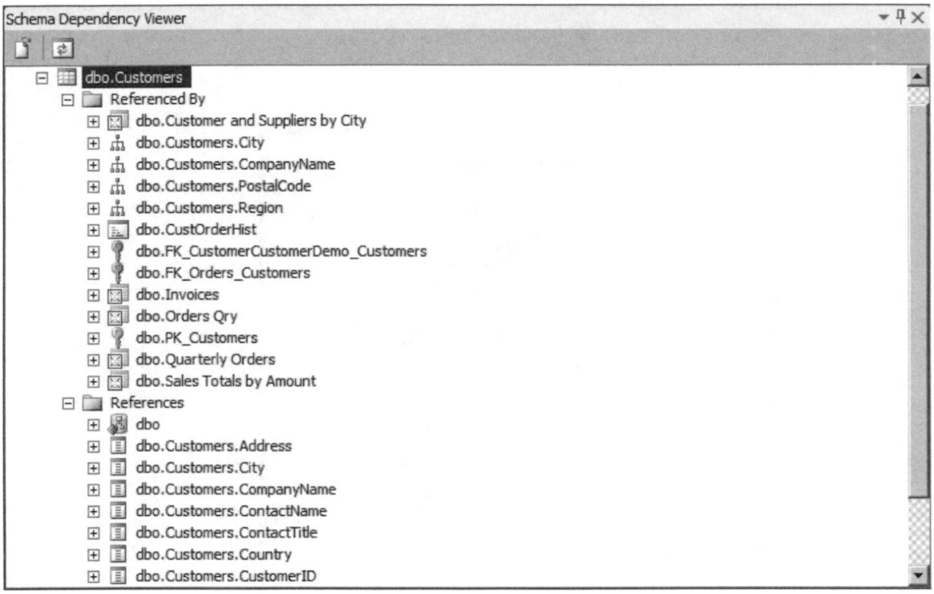

FIGURE 10-14

The Schema Dependency Viewer is helpful for determining the potential impact of proposed changes. For example, you can see that changes to the Customers table may require you to make changes to the "Customer and Suppliers by City" view, since it is referenced as a dependency. Later in this chapter, in the section "Making Schema Changes," you will learn how Visual Studio can help make many changes to dependent objects automatically, but there are still some cases where you must still manually manage changes to related objects. The Schema Dependency Viewer can help you understand where to make necessary changes.

T-SQL File Structure

Now that you have looked at a few ways of exploring the structure and relationships of your schema objects, you should next inspect the contents of the files on disk that make up your schema objects. Return to Schema View, and find the Customers table (Schemas ➪ dbo ➪ Tables ➪ Customers). Double-click on Customers to open a file called Customers.table.sql within the Visual Studio editor. The contents of this file are as follows:

```
CREATE TABLE [dbo].[Customers] (
    [CustomerID]    NCHAR (5)      NOT NULL,
    [CompanyName]   NVARCHAR (40)  NOT NULL,
    [ContactName]   NVARCHAR (30)  NULL,
    [ContactTitle]  NVARCHAR (30)  NULL,
    [Address]       NVARCHAR (60)  NULL,
    [City]          NVARCHAR (15)  NULL,
    [Region]        NVARCHAR (15)  NULL,
    [PostalCode]    NVARCHAR (10)  NULL,
    [Country]       NVARCHAR (15)  NULL,
    [Phone]         NVARCHAR (24)  NULL,
    [Fax]           NVARCHAR (24)  NULL
);
```

If you are familiar with Transact SQL (T-SQL), then you are already familiar with how Visual Studio stores objects in a database project. The above T-SQL script defines a new table, Customers, containing 11 columns with the specified data types.

At this point, you may be wondering why Visual Studio uses T-SQL for defining all objects from scratch. What if you were working with an existing database, as is the case with the Northwind database? If you executed the previous T-SQL script on the Northwind database, it would cause an error. Attempting to create a new table called Customers would fail because of a naming collision, since there is already a table called Customers.

As you will see later in this chapter in the section "Deploying Database Changes," Visual Studio's deployment engine is responsible for interpreting the schema objects in your database project (such as the Customers table) and generating the appropriate T-SQL scripts for applying changes to your target database. The fact that this object is a CREATE script within your database project will be irrelevant when you build and deploy your changes.

The actual deployment script generated in the deployment phase will depend on the pre-existing state of the Customers table in your target database, as compared with the state of this table as modeled in your database project. In the deployment script, this object will either be represented by an ALTER TABLE statement (for example, if you made changes to columns), a DROP TABLE statement (if you deleted this table from your database project), a CREATE TABLE statement (if this table doesn't yet exist in the target database), or would be omitted entirely from your deployment script (if you didn't make any changes to the Customers table).

Microsoft's choice of T-SQL for storing database objects is convenient, since T-SQL is an established and well-documented language for working with SQL Server. Additionally, many third-party and Open Source tools also operate on T-SQL files, and some even advertise compatibility with Visual Studio.

MAKING SCHEMA CHANGES

Now that you have a database project that is an offline representation of your database schema, you are ready to make some changes. One way to make changes to your database schema is by directly manipulating the T-SQL files that make up your database objects.

Editing T-SQL Files Directly

Begin by opening the `Customers` table again. From within Schema View, expand Schemas ➪ dbo ➪ Tables and double-click on Customers. For this example, you will add columns for storing both a customer's work phone number and his or her home phone number. Find the following line:

```
[Phone]       NVARCHAR (24) NULL,
```

Immediately after this line, add a new line:

```
[WorkPhone]   NVARCHAR (24) NULL,
```

In Schema View, expand the Columns node below Customers. You should still only see the original `Phone` column in this list. Now, save the `Customers.tables.sql` file. Saving the file causes Visual Studio to perform a background analysis of your changes and make the appropriate changes to its in-memory model of your database. These changes should now be reflected in Schema View. Expand the Customers ➪ Columns node again, and you should now see that `WorkPhone` is listed in addition to the `Phone` column.

Detecting Schema Syntax Errors

Now you will see how Visual Studio can help protect the integrity of your database schema by analyzing the syntactical correctness of your schema. Change the name of the `Customers` table to `Clients`. Find the following line:

```
CREATE TABLE [dbo].[Customers] (
```

Change this to the following:

```
CREATE TABLE [dbo].[Clients] (
```

Now, trigger another refresh of Visual Studio's in-memory model of your database schema by saving the file. After the analysis of your changes has finished, you will see a long list of errors and warnings in Visual Studio's Error List. (If the Error List is not already open, click View ➪ Error List.) This list of errors and warnings is analogous to the errors and warnings you would receive if you attempted to compile a C# or Visual Basic file that had errors. Figure 10-15 shows a partial list of these errors and warnings.

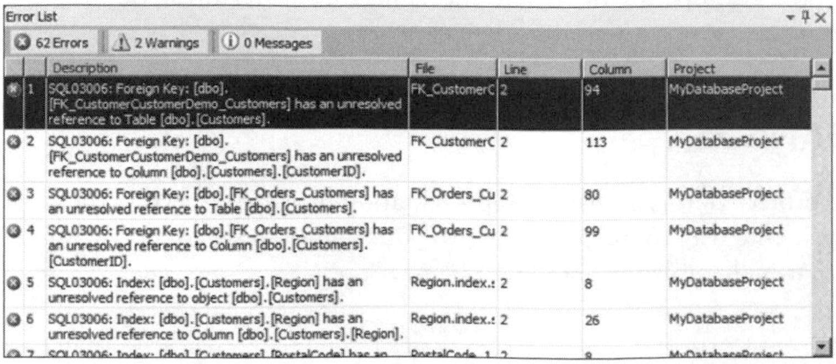

FIGURE 10-15

Visual Studio has detected that the changes you made to the `Customers` table have caused other parts of your schema that depended on the `Customers` table to break. In the previous section, "Schema Dependency Viewer," you saw that there are dependency relationships that existed between the `Customers` table and other objects in your database (for example, indexes, views, and stored procedures). To successfully rename the `Customers` table to `Clients`, you would need to update all of those references as well. This is an example of where Visual Studio's database refactoring capabilities are useful.

Database Refactoring

Visual Studio includes tools for automatically conducting common database refactoring operations. If you are familiar with using Visual Studio to refactor source code files (for example, C# or Visual Basic), then this process will already be familiar to you. Refactoring can save you a great deal of time by automatically finding and updating all relevant sections of your database project with a given change. Automatic refactoring also greatly reduces the chances of introducing bugs caused by human error as compared with manual refactoring.

Undo the last change you made by renaming the `Clients` table back to `Customers`. The first line of your T-SQL file should once again be as follows:

```
CREATE TABLE [dbo].[Customers] (
```

Save this file, which should cause Visual Studio to re-analyze your database project and eliminate all errors and warnings. For the best results, you should always attempt to eliminate any errors and warnings prior to attempting a database refactoring.

Rename Refactoring

One of the most basic types of refactoring operations is that of performing a rename. Consider the impact of renaming a table within your database schema. In addition to updating the actual table definition, you must also update any references to that table (such as indexes, stored procedures, and so on). Even a simple rename can be a laborious exercise, and failing to correctly update every reference can result in a broken schema. Visual Studio can perform these updates for you automatically by using the built-in support for rename refactoring.

Right-click the `Customers` table from within the Schema View and select Refactor ⇨ Rename. The resulting dialog, shown in Figure 10-16, prompts you for a new name for this table. Replace `[Customers]` with `[Clients]` and click OK.

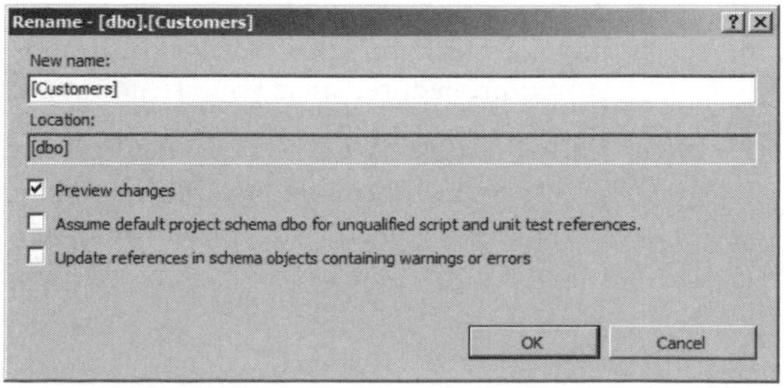

Visual Studio will now attempt to discover all of the objects within your schema that must be updated so that they reference your table by its new name. The Preview Changes

FIGURE 10-16

dialog shown in Figure 10-17 allows you to inspect the changes before they are made. Click on a few schema objects and examine the proposed changes.

When you are finished previewing this list, click the Apply button. Visual Studio will now automatically make all of the previewed changes, save your files, and update the in-memory model of your schema. You should not have any errors or warnings in your Error List, since you have now successfully renamed your table using Visual Studio's refactoring functionality.

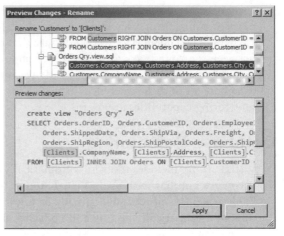

FIGURE 10-17

Other Refactoring Types

Visual Studio also provides support for a handful of other refactoring operations that you should consider using instead of making updates manually. In addition to rename refactoring, Visual Studio offers the following built-in refactoring types:

➤ *Move to Schema* — Used for moving objects between schemas within your database, such as between the dbo schema and the guest schema. Using different schemas can be a way of logically breaking down different areas of your database or implementing granular security.

➤ *Expand Wildcards* — Wildcard expansion can be used to speed up transactions and to create more robust views or stored procedures. For example, consider the following:

```
SELECT * FROM CLIENTS
```

The Expand Wildcards refactoring operation will convert this stored procedure to the following:

```
SELECT [dbo].[Clients].[CustomerID], [dbo].[CLIENTS].[CompanyName],
    (other columns here) FROM CLIENTS
```

Now, even if you add columns to the Clients table, it will not affect the results of this stored procedure, since you are no longer using a wildcard.

➤ *Fully Qualify Name* — Fully qualifying object references within your schema is a best practice for improving readability and eliminating ambiguity. For example, you might have two objects with the same name in different schemas. Fully qualifying these references helps to ensure that you are referring to the right object. For example, consider the following:

```
[CustOrderHist]
```

The Fully Qualify Name refactoring operation will convert this reference to the following:

```
[dbo].[CustOrderHist]
```

Now, even if you have another object called `CustOrderHist` in another schema, there is no ambiguity about which instance you are referring to.

Not all refactoring operations apply to each type of object within your database schema. For example, the Expand Wildcards refactoring type can be used with stored procedures, but wildcards are not valid syntax for a table definition; hence, this refactoring operation won't be available in the refactoring drop-down list for a table.

Preservation of Intent

As you will see later in this chapter in the section "Deploying Database Changes," Visual Studio will automatically create a database deployment script by comparing the differences that exist between your source (your database project) and your deployment target (the physical database you are updating). If an object exists in your source database project, but not in your target database, this will result in a `CREATE` statement in your deployment script. Likewise, if an object does not exist in your source database, but is present in your target database, it will result in a `DROP` statement in your deployment script (although this behavior can be overridden, as you will see later).

In most cases, the behavior just described works as expected, and will result in a successful deployment. However, consider the process of renaming an object using Visual Studio's built-in refactoring tools.

In the earlier example, you renamed the `Customers` table to `Clients`. When Visual Studio conducts a comparison of your source database to that of the pre-existing `Northwind` database during the deployment phase, it will determine that `Customers` no longer exists, and that there is a new table called `Clients`. Without any further information, this would result in a `DROP` of the `Customers` table and a `CREATE` of the `Clients` table. The problem with this approach is that it would result in data loss, since none of the data from the original `Customers` table would be preserved, and you would be left with an empty `Clients` table.

Visual Studio's solution to this problem is to maintain a *refactoring log* that is responsible for providing the deployment engine with the information necessary to distinguish between a `DROP`/`CREATE` and a Rename or a Move to Schema refactoring operation.

Switch to the Solution Explorer and open the file called `MyDatabaseProject.refactorlog`. A snippet of that file is included here:

```
<Operation Name="Rename Refactor" Key="…" ChangeDateTime="…">
<Property Name="ElementName" Value="[dbo].[Customers]" />
<Property Name="ElementType" Value="ISql100Table" />
<Property Name="ParentElementName" Value="[dbo]" />
<Property Name="ParentElementType" Value="ISql90Schema" />
<Property Name="NewName" Value="[Clients]" />
</Operation>
```

This XML snippet will instruct the deployment engine that, instead of dropping the `Customers` table and creating the `Clients` table, what you really want to achieve is a rename of `Customers` to `Clients`. This capability is known as *preservation of intent,* and is a sophisticated way that Visual Studio helps maintain the integrity of existing data within your database.

> *The database refactoring log only gets created (or maintained) if you use Visual Studio's built-in refactoring tools. This is another reason why using automated refactoring is superior to trying to implement equivalent changes by hand-coding the T-SQL project files.*

Generally speaking, you won't have to maintain the database refactoring log by hand. The one exception can occur if you are managing your database project using source control. If you are merging code from different branches or from different contributors, then you must merge changes to the database refactoring log in sync with the corresponding changes in the T-SQL in your database project.

T-SQL Script Templates

Another way that Visual Studio facilitates making changes to your database project is by providing you with a few dozen T-SQL script templates for representing common database constructs. You can access script templates from Schema View by right-clicking on an object, then selecting either Add or Append. Figure 10-18 shows the list of script templates that can be applied to a table object.

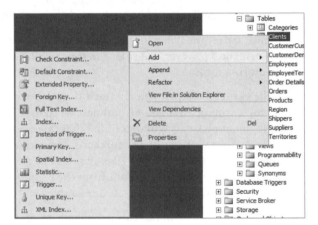

After selecting your desired script template, you will be prompted to name the object. After you name the object, Visual Studio will create the appropriate T-SQL code as a template for you to complete.

FIGURE 10-18

Insert a new check constraint on the `Clients` table named `CK_PostalCodeLength`, which will result in the following T-SQL template:

```
ALTER TABLE [dbo].[Clients]
    ADD CONSTRAINT [CK_PostalCodeLength]
    CHECK  (column_1 > 0)
```

Left unchanged, this check constraint will result in a schema validation error, because `column_1` is meant only as template code and must be replaced by your desired constraint logic.

In the United States, ZIP codes can either be represented as five digits or nine digits (plus a hyphen separator after the fifth digit). The following code will ensure that the length of data in the `PostalCode` column is either five or ten characters:

```
ALTER TABLE [dbo].[Clients]
    ADD CONSTRAINT [CK_PostalCodeLength]
    CHECK ((LEN(PostalCode) = 5) OR (LEN(PostalCode) = 10))
```

Save this file. The Check Constraint script template is a very simple example, but Visual Studio ships with a diverse set of script templates that you can use for accelerating the development of your development schema.

DEPLOYING DATABASE CHANGES

Now that you have made some changes to your database project, it's time to deploy those changes to an actual database. In this section you will begin by deploying your changes to a test database. After you have tested your changes (as described in the later section "Database Testing"), you will deploy your changes to the original `Northwind` database.

From Solution Explorer, right-click the `MyDatabaseProject` project and select Properties. Click the Deploy tab. If this is your first time configuring your database project deployment settings, you must click on Edit, next to the Target Connection textbox. Configure the Connection Properties dialog to connect to the `localhost\SQLEXPRESS` server and type **`TestMyDatabaseProject`** as the database name. Click on OK.

Enter the following settings on the Deploy tab:

➤ *Deploy action* — Create a deployment script (`.sql`)

➤ *Deployment script name* — `TestMyDatabaseProject.sql`

➤ *Target database name* — `TestMyDatabaseProject`

When you are finished, your project deployment settings should resemble Figure 10-19. Save these settings.

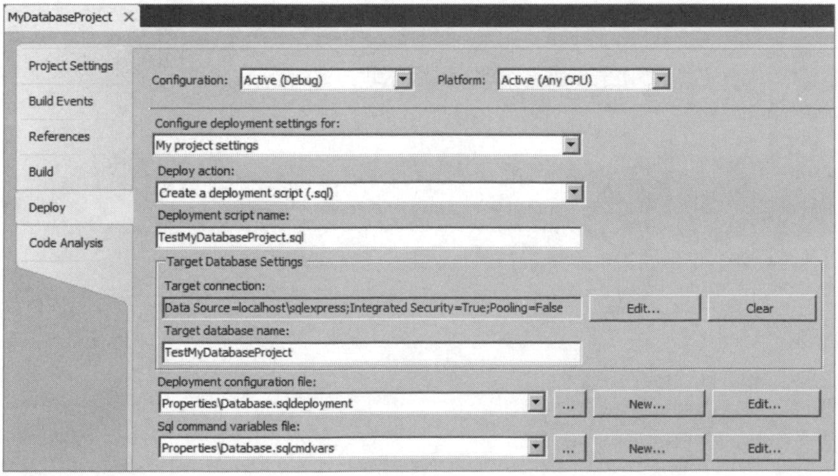

FIGURE 10-19

These settings instruct Visual Studio to create a deployment script (called `TestMyDatabaseProject` `.sql`) capable of deploying the schema modeled in your database project to a database (called `TestMyDatabaseProject`) running on your local instance of SQL Server Express.

You must make one additional change before you can deploy this database. Currently, your database project specifies the name and settings for the MDF and LDF files that make up your original `Northwind` database. Since you are deploying to a test database on the same database server as your original `Northwind` database, you must change your database project to prevent filename conflicts with the existing MDF and LDF files being used by your `Northwind` database.

From Solution Explorer, open Schema Object ➪ Database Level Objects ➪ Storage ➪ Files. Delete both files from this location (`Northwind.sqlfile.sql` and `Northwind_log.sqlfile.sql`). Another solution would have been to parameterize the filenames using the `$(DatabaseName)` variable, which is stored in your project settings (currently `TestMyDatabaseProject`). But for this example, you don't need to retain any configuration settings for these files, so it is safe to delete these objects.

Now, click Build ➪ Deploy Solution. Visual Studio will now compare your source database (your database project) with your target database (`TestMyDatabaseProject`) in order to build the correct deployment script for making your target database schema match that of your source database schema. Once this step has completed, from Solution Explorer, right-click on the MyDatabaseProject project node and select Open Folder in Windows Explorer. Navigate to the sql ➪ debug folder and open the `TestMyDatabaseProject.sql` file. You can open this file in any text editor, such as Visual Studio or SQL Server Management Studio, as shown in Figure 10-20.

```
TestMyDatabaseProject.sql -...)
/*
Deployment script for TestMyDatabaseProject
*/

GO
SET ANSI_NULLS, ANSI_PADDING, ANSI_WARNINGS, ARITHABORT, CONCAT_NULL_YIELDS_NULL, QUOTED_IDENTIFIER ON;

SET NUMERIC_ROUNDABORT OFF;


GO
:setvar Path1 "C:\Northwind\"
:setvar Path2 "C:\Northwind\"
:setvar DatabaseName "TestMyDatabaseProject"
:setvar DefaultDataPath "c:\Program Files\Microsoft SQL Server\MSSQL10.SQLEXPRESS\MSSQL\DATA\"
:setvar DefaultLogPath "c:\Program Files\Microsoft SQL Server\MSSQL10.SQLEXPRESS\MSSQL\DATA\"

GO
USE [master]

GO
:on error exit
GO
IF (DB_ID(N'$(DatabaseName)') IS NOT NULL
    AND DATABASEPROPERTYEX(N'$(DatabaseName)','Status') <> N'ONLINE')
BEGIN
    RAISERROR(N'The state of the target database, %s, is not set to ONLINE. To deploy to this database, its state mu
    RETURN
END

GO
IF (DB_ID(N'$(DatabaseName)') IS NOT NULL)
BEGIN
```

FIGURE 10-20

You (or your database administrator) now have an opportunity to make any desired changes to this `.sql` deployment script prior to executing it against your database. Don't make any changes now, but spend a couple of minutes browsing the T-SQL logic in this script. You will

notice that the majority of the script is composed of CREATE statements. This is because the
TestMyDatabaseProject database did not exist previously, so the database objects must be
created for the first time.

You can execute this script manually (using SQL Server
Management Studio or Visual Studio), or you could
have also instructed Visual Studio to automatically
execute your deployment script for you. Do that now
by returning to the project properties dialog (right-
click on MyDatabaseProject and select Properties) and
opening the Deploy tab. Change the Deploy action
setting to "Create a deployment script (.sql) and deploy
to the database". Save the project properties and click
Build ⇨ Deploy again. Visual Studio will now analyze
your source and target schemas again, create a .sql
deployment script, and execute this script to create the
TestMyDatabaseProject database. If you have SQL
Server Management Studio installed, you can connect to
your local instance of SQL Server Express and verify that
the TestMyDatabaseProject was created successfully, as
shown in Figure 10-21.

FIGURE 10-21

Later in this chapter, in the section "Redistributable Deployment Engine," you will learn how to
use Visual Studio's redistributable database deployment engine to create a deployment package for
your database project. This deployment package can be used on machines without Visual Studio
installed to analyze a target database and create a .sql deployment script specifically for a given
SQL Server instance.

Visual Studio exposes dozens of advanced configuration options for changing the way your project
gets built and deployed. For purposes of this walkthrough (and for most databases you will likely
encounter), you can accept the defaults provided by Visual Studio. However, you should be aware of
these options; spend a few minutes clicking through the database project properties dialogs now to
browse the available options.

For example, from the Deploy tab, click on the Edit button underneath Deployment configuration
file. There are two options on this page worth pointing out:

➤ *Block incremental deployment if data loss might occur* — By default, this setting is
   enabled. With this setting enabled, Visual Studio will avoid making changes to your
   database if it detects that data will be possibly lost to the schema. One example of this
   is if you change the data type for a column to one with less storage or precision (for
   example, from char(100) to char(50), or from bigint to int). If you are making
   such changes and are comfortable with the potential for data loss, then you can disable
   this option.

➤ *Generate DROP statements for objects that are in the target database but that are not in
   the database project* — By default, this setting is disabled. With this setting disabled, Visual
   Studio will refrain from deleting objects that reside in the target database, even if they are

not specified in your project schema. If you are certain that you want to delete objects that are not specified in your schema, then you can enable this option. This can be an effective way of cleaning up obsolete objects from your database, but should only be utilized if you are certain that those objects are not necessary. One example of where you would probably want to leave this option disabled is if you are creating a redistributable deployment package to send to customers of your software package (see the section "Redistributable Deployment Engine," later in this chapter). Then, you may not want to enable this feature in the event that your customers have additional schema objects that may be required for their specific deployment customizations.

These are just two of the many advanced build and deployment options you will find throughout the database project properties. All of these settings are detailed in the product documentation should you need them later on. But you don't have to change any of these settings for the walkthrough in this chapter.

DATA GENERATION

Now that you have successfully deployed your database schema to a test database, you will need some sample data with which to author and execute your tests. If you have access to the data in a production database, then you might be able to import the data from the production database into your testing database. However, since most development teams aren't allowed to work with production data (because of privacy or other regulatory concerns), this may not be an option. Furthermore, as your schema evolves, the data in the production database may not conform to the new schema you are testing.

Another option is to generate sample data by hand, entering data row by row. For all but the simplest databases, however, this can be an extremely time-consuming process, and it requires a thorough knowledge of the underlying schema to create data that conforms to the constraints of your schema.

Visual Studio has built-in data generation capabilities that can simplify this task by rapidly generating data that conforms to your database schema.

Data Generation Plan

To begin creating test data, you will need a *data generation plan*. A data generation plan (represented as a .DGEN file) contains all of the settings necessary for Visual Studio to create data that conforms to your database project's schema.

From within Solution Explorer, right-click the MyDatabaseProject project and select Add ➪ Data Generation Plan. Name your data generation plan TestMyDatabaseProject.dgen and click Add. Your new data generation plan will open with some default settings, as shown in Figure 10-22.

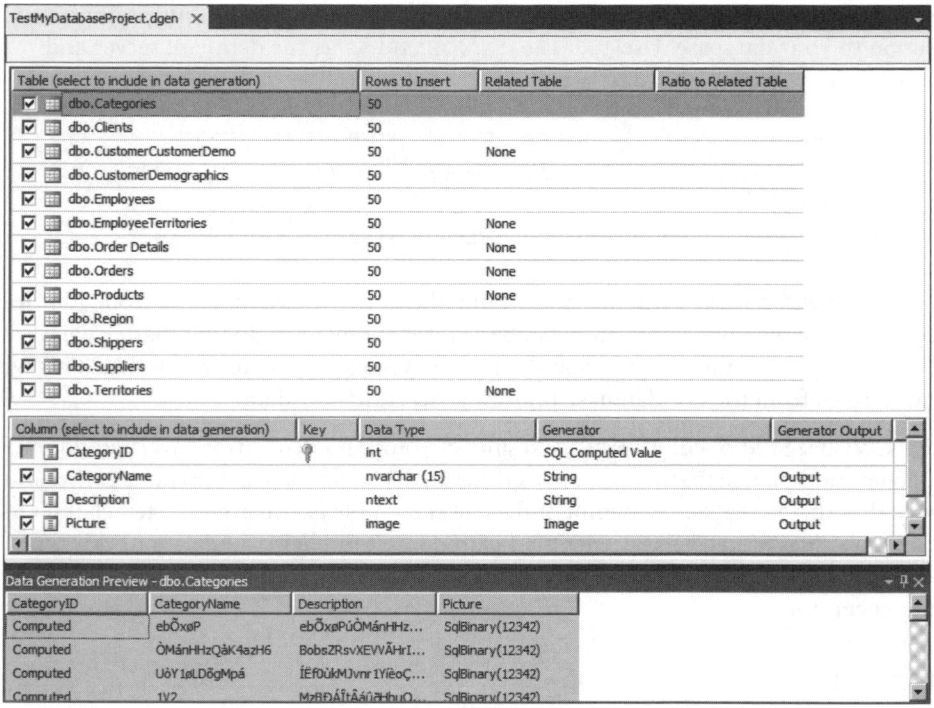

FIGURE 10-22

The uppermost portion of this view lists all of the tables within your schema. Selecting a table will show a list of the columns in that table. You can enable the Data Generation Preview window by clicking Data ➪ Data Generator ➪ Preview Data Generation. The Data Generation Preview shows a sampling of the values that will be inserted into each table/column.

The values for each column are generated using a pseudorandom algorithm based on the data type for each column and other constraints (such as foreign key relationships). Visual Studio uses a seed value as the input for the pseudorandom algorithm. In most cases, you will want to leave the seed value unchanged so that you have predictable data generation results with each data generation execution. But you can change this value on a column-by-column basis by changing the Seed value for each column in the Properties Window. You can also change the Default seed under Tools ➪ Options ➪ Database Tools ➪ Data Generator ➪ General, but this value is only used when you create a new data generation plan. Later in this chapter, in the section "Data Generators," you will learn how to further customize the data that gets generated so that it is more human-readable.

You can also specify the number of rows to insert into each table by changing the "Rows to Insert" value for each table. You can represent this value directly, or as a ratio to another table. For example, you may wish to more realistically simulate your production data by declaring that every client has placed ten orders. Do this now by changing the Related Table value of the Orders table to [dbo].[Clients]. Now change the "Ratio to Related Table" value to 10:1. Note that Orders now has a "Rows to Insert" value of 500, which is ten times that of Clients.

Press F5 to instruct Visual Studio to execute your data generation plan. You will be prompted to define a connection to your database. Use `localhost\SQLEXPRESS` as the database server and `TestMyDatabaseProject` as the target database.

> ✖ *Be careful not to accidentally generate data for the original* `Northwind` *database during this step.*

After clicking OK, you will be asked whether you would like to delete existing data from your test database. Since you are deploying to an empty database at the moment, it doesn't matter what you answer here, but for the rest of this chapter, you should always answer Yes to this dialog. This will delete any existing rows from the test database prior to generating new data.

In a few moments, Visual Studio will display the results of your data generation. You should notice that your data generation plan actually failed. This is because you defined a constraint earlier in this chapter to ensure that the `PostalCode` column of the `Clients` table is either five or ten characters long. Unfortunately, Visual Studio's data generation plan doesn't implicitly understand this type of constraint when it is generating data. But you can easily customize your data generation plan by configuring data generators.

Data Generators

A *data generator* essentially corresponds to an algorithm that Visual Studio will use to create test data. By default, Visual Studio will automatically choose a data generator for each column based on the column's underlying data type. For example, a column data type of `nvarchar` or `nchar` will, by default, be mapped to the String data generator. The String data generator will automatically generate pseudorandom alphanumeric values up to the maximum number of characters specified for the data type. Because the values are pseudorandom, they will not be human-readable, but, depending on your testing purposes, they might be sufficient.

Visual Studio also has several more advanced data generators that can be used to generate more realistic data, if you desire. For example, you may wish to generate human-readable data if you plan on exposing your test data to manual testers or for end-user acceptance testing. You can also use data generators to create data that conforms to certain constraints in your database. You will do this now to create data that conforms to the `PostalCode` column constraint you defined earlier.

Start by selecting the `Clients` table in the top pane of the `TestMyDatabaseProject.dgen` designer. Now, find `PostalCode` in the list of columns in the bottom pane of this designer and change the Generator value to `Regular Expression`. A *regular expression* is a very effective way of describing the structure of string data. Regular expressions are commonly used to describe and validate data formats such as telephone numbers, Social Security Numbers, and email addresses. You can find several tutorials for learning regular expressions online.

Now, view the Properties Window (View ➪ Properties Window) for the `PostalCode` column and change the Expression value to the following:

```
[1-9]{5}(-[1-9]{4})?
```

Press Enter and you should instantly see the effect that using this regular expression will have on your data generation plan. In the Data Generation Preview window, you should now see a mix of 5-digit ZIP codes (for example, 98052) and 5+4-digit ZIP codes (for example, 98052-6399).

This data will conform to your `PostalCode` column constraints, and it is human-readable, using ZIP codes that match the structure of those used in the United States. Press F5 and instruct Visual Studio to generate data for your `TestMyDatabaseProject` database. The data generation should now complete successfully. You can validate your sample data by viewing the `TestMyDatabaseProject` database within SQL Server Management Studio.

Data generators each have their own set of properties that can be used to control the shape of the values they produce. For another example, select the Products ➪ UnitPrice column and inspect the Data Generation Preview window. By default, data is uniformly distributed between the minimum and maximum values for a given data type.

But this isn't very realistic, and might confuse a user who is examining a test database. It might also cause user interfaces (for example, Web pages or smart client applications) being tested along with your database to break because the values are too large. To fix this, from the Properties Window, change the Distribution to `Normal`, Max to `1000`, and Min to `1`. Your preview data should now be normally distributed between 1 and 1000, which is probably much more representative of your actual production data.

You can create very sophisticated data generation plans with Visual Studio by continuing to refine your use of data generators. Another useful data generator is the Data Bound Generator, which can be used to import data from another data source. For example, you might wish to bind the `Country` field of the `Clients` table to a data source that contains an actual list of countries where your clients are located, or the `ProductName` column of your `Products` database to an actual list of products, and so on.

Finally, you can define your own custom data generators for creating even more complex patterns of data. More information on each data generator, as well as data generator extensibility, can be found in the product documentation.

DATABASE TESTING

Now that you have generated some sample data for your database, you are ready to begin testing your schema. Visual Studio provides the capability to author and execute *database unit tests* that can provide validation directly against objects within your database schema.

Functions, Triggers, and Stored Procedures

Visual Studio makes it easy to create unit tests for functions, table-level triggers, and stored procedures. Visual Studio can automatically create T-SQL stubs that exercise these objects. You can then use one of several built-in test conditions for verifying that you received correct results.

Start by opening Schema View and expanding Schemas ➪ dbo ➪ Programmability ➪ Stored Procedures. Right-click on the Ten Most Expensive Products stored procedure, and select Create

Unit Tests. The dialog shown in Figure 10-23 will appear. This dialog allows you to quickly create unit test stubs for any of your stored procedures, functions, or table-level triggers. Select either Visual Basic or Visual C# for your test project type. Give your project a name of `TestNorthwind`. Select "Create new class" and provide a name of `TenMostExpensiveProductsUnitTest`. Click OK.

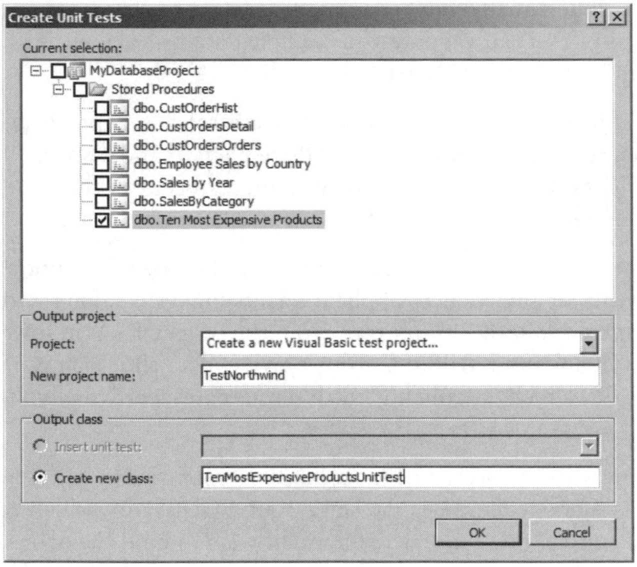

FIGURE 10-23

You will now be prompted to configure your test project, as shown in Figure 10-24. Apply the following settings:

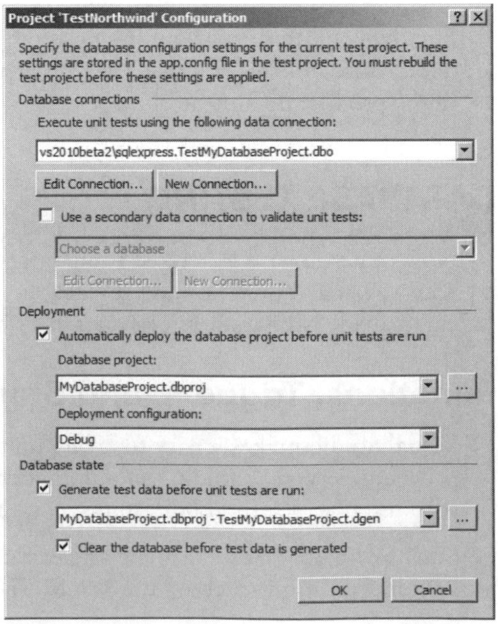

➤ *Execute unit tests using the following data connection* — Select the same connection you used previously for connecting to the `TestMyDatabaseProject` database on your local SQL Server Express instance. Note that for some testing scenarios, you may wish to define a lower-privileged account to verify (for example) that users can't get access to secure data. But for this walkthrough, you can keep the existing connection settings.

➤ *Use a secondary data connection to validate unit tests* — Leave this checkbox unchecked, but note that if you chose to use a lower-privileged account for the

FIGURE 10-24

previous connection, then you may wish to use a higher-privileged account when validating unit test results.

> *Deployment* — Enable this checkbox and select your database project (`MyDatabaseProject.proj`). Select Debug as the Deployment configuration.

> *Generate test data before unit tests are run* — Enable this checkbox and select the data generation plan you created earlier.

> *Clear the database before test data is generated* — Enable this checkbox.

From Solution Explorer, delete the `UnitTest1` file that is included by default with new test projects. This file will either end in a `.vb` or `.cs` extension, depending on the language you selected for your test project.

The unit test stub for testing the Ten Most Expensive Products stored procedure will now appear as shown in Figure 10-25. The top pane, the T-SQL editor, is the logic that calls the stored procedure you are testing. You might choose to customize this unit test stub, such as by providing test values for parameters. This particular stored procedure doesn't have any parameters, so you don't need to modify anything.

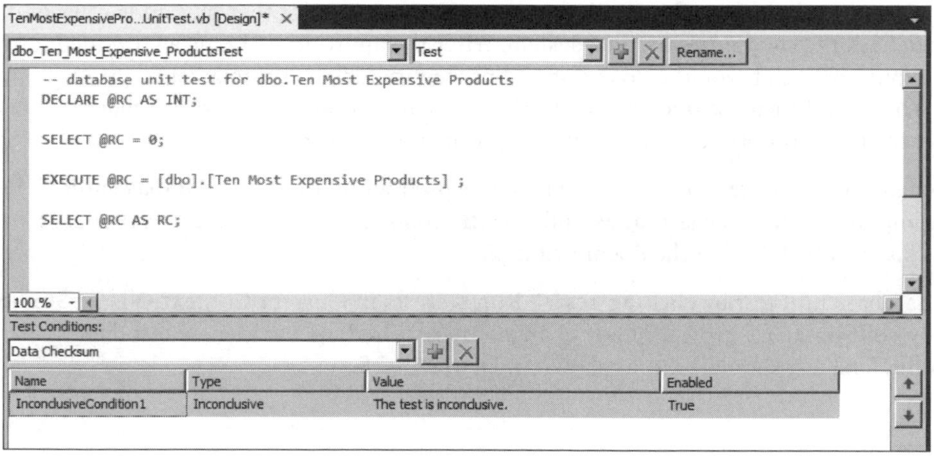

FIGURE 10-25

You can declare pre- and post-test scripts that should be executed before and after any given unit test. Pre-test scripts are usually used to prime a database with test data, such as inserting a row into a table of orders. Post-test scripts are usually used to clean up this test data, or to undo changes made during the execution of the test.

You can insert pre- and post-test scripts by clicking on the drop-down at the top of the screen that says Test and selecting Pre-test or Post-test. You can also define global test initialization and cleanup logic by first selecting (Common Scripts) from the leftmost drop-down and then selecting "Test initialize" or "Test cleanup." These scripts will be executed for each test.

Return to the unit test stub for the Ten Most Expensive Products stored procedure. You will now add validation checks to help ensure that the execution of this stored procedure is successful. In the Test Conditions pane, click on the red X to remove the `InconclusiveCondition1` validation result. This result is included by default to remind you that you haven't yet defined any validation logic for this test.

Now, click the Test Conditions drop-down and select Row Count. Click the green plus sign icon to add this condition to your test conditions. From the Properties Window (View ⇨ Properties Window), set the Row Count to 10. Since this stored procedure is supposed to return the top ten most expensive products, you should expect to receive exactly ten rows in your ResultSet. Anything else should trigger this test to fail.

You can add multiple test conditions to a given unit test. For example, you might want to use the Execution Time test condition to verify that a given stored procedure takes no more than 5 seconds to execute.

You can use the Scalar Value test condition to verify that a given row and column matches a specific value. To use the Scalar Value test condition effectively, you would need to know what the state of your database should be at the time the test is executed.

For example, you might be testing a stored procedure that returns a list of items in a customer's online shopping cart. One way to achieve this is to write a pre-test script that first adds rows of data to a table that defines the shopping carts in a system. After the appropriate items were added to the shopping cart, your test script would invoke a stored procedure for returning a list of the shopping cart contents. You would then use one or more Scalar Value test conditions to verify that the `ResultSet` returns the appropriate data as defined by your pre-test script.

You can also create your own test conditions that can be used with evaluating database unit tests. Information on creating a class that extends the `Microsoft.Data.Schema.UnitTesting` `.Conditions` class can be found in the documentation.

Execute your database unit test by clicking Test ⇨ Run ⇨ Tests in Current Context. Visual Studio will now deploy your database project (if any changes are required), generate new test data, and execute your unit. The test should pass, as shown in Figure 10-26.

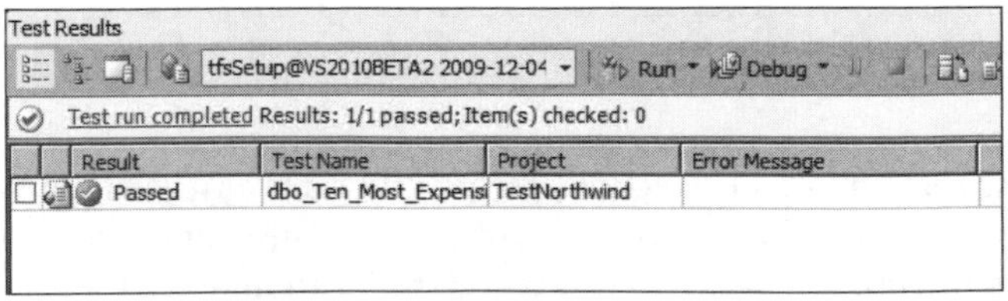

FIGURE 10-26

Writing Advanced Database Unit Tests

The process just outlined works well for testing stored procedures, table-level triggers, and functions. As you have seen in the previous discussion, Visual Studio allows you to author these tests using a familiar database scripting language (T-SQL) and provides a simple properties grid for defining test conditions. But there are times when you may wish to write more complex tests.

Visual Studio allows you to write more advanced tests using the power of the .NET Framework and either C# or Visual Basic. In fact, everything you did earlier using the database unit testing designer was actually utilizing C# or Visual Basic in the background. (The actual language used depends on the language you picked for your test project in Figure 10-23.)

Explore the structure of your existing test project to learn how Visual Studio executes your database unit tests. From within Solution Explorer, right-click on `TenMostExpensiveProductsUnitTest` (the file extension will be either `.cs` or `.vb`), and click View Code. This class contains a method (marked with a `TestMethod()` attribute), which is responsible for executing the test you designed earlier, along with any additional pre- or post-test scripts. These scripts will be executed using ADO.NET.

The actual T-SQL scripts for your test class are stored in a resource file with the same name as your test class. To view the resource file, you may need to first click the Show All Files button at the top of the Solution Explorer pane. Next, expand the node for your database unit test by clicking the plus (+) sign next to the source code file in Solution Explorer. This will expose a file by the same name, but with a `.resx` extension. You can double-click this file (to view it in a grid-based designer), or right-click and choose Open With to select Visual Studio's built-in XML Editor.

Visual Studio will store your connection strings, data generation plan, and other settings in the `app.config` file for your test project. Finally, the file `DatabaseSetup.vb` (or `.cs`) is responsible for deploying your database project and executing your data generation plan based on the settings in the `app.config` file (which you declared using the dialog in Figure 10-24).

Spend a few minutes exploring the structure of these files. You can later customize unit tests you created with the database unit test designer, or create entirely new database unit tests from scratch, simply by writing C# or Visual Basic code and manipulating the appropriate T-SQL scripts. For example, you may choose to data-bind your database unit tests so that they are created dynamically based on data from another source. Or, you may wish to define more complex test conditions than the ones exposed via the database unit test designer (for example, basing the expected results for one test off of the actual results for another). These scenarios and more are possible.

For an excellent article describing Visual Studio's database unit testing framework in greater detail, see `http://msdn.microsoft.com/en-us/magazine/cc164243.aspx`.

Effective Database Testing

Designing an effective plan for testing your database is not too unlike the process of putting together a test plan for other software applications. Your test plan should seek to maximize test coverage while minimizing wasted effort by automating tasks that will be executed repeatedly. Ultimately, a good test plan is one that finds bugs early on in the development process so that they can be fixed before they ever creep into a production environment.

The following sections that describe database testing tenets are not comprehensive, but should give you an idea of things to consider when compiling your database testing plan.

Keep a Clean Database

Database testing often involves the injection of some data (for example, inserting a customer order), the execution of some database logic (for example, calling a trigger, stored procedure, or function) that uses or modifies that data, and analysis of the results of the test to determine whether or not the test was successful. However, if you aren't careful, the results of setting up and executing one test may have unintended consequences on other tests.

One approach for preventing tests from impacting one another is to wrap each test in a transaction. This is done by structuring your test script as follows:

```
begin transaction

   -- Author your test script here

rollback transaction
```

This approach will restore your database state after your test is executed. However, the drawback of this approach is that it won't undo any pre- or post-test scripts you may have written, since those scripts are executed using a different connection. You can write additional logic in your post-test script to clean up this data, but this might be a rather labor-intensive process. Another approach is to wrap your entire test (including the pre- and post-test scripts) in a transaction and rely on SQL Server's Distributed Transaction Coordinator (DTC) to roll back the entire set of operations.

A detailed example of wrapping your database unit test in a transaction using DTC can be found at http://msdn.microsoft.com/en-us/magazine/cc164243.aspx.

Group Series of Related Tests

Like any unit tests, database unit tests should be fairly constrained in scope to help you quickly pinpoint where problems might exist in your database. For example, you would never write one large database unit test that tests your entire database schema. Instead, you would write a series of smaller tests, each responsible for testing a piece of your database schema. This way, if a test fails, you can quickly correlate that test to the section of your database schema that must be fixed.

However, pieces of your database schema may be highly reliant on one another. For example, the process of fulfilling a customer order could first require that you receive a request from a customer, then that you verify your inventory, process payment, generate a shipment, update the inventory, and so on. You may wish to have one or more database unit tests for each step in this workflow so that, if a test fails, you can quickly pinpoint the broken step. But rather than cleaning up the database after every step, you can simply execute the tests in order, so that the expected completion state of one test becomes the expected beginning state of another.

You can use Visual Studio's built-in Ordered Test test type as a container for managing multiple database unit tests in a particular sequence. Ordered Tests are covered in Chapter 12. The downside of using an Ordered Test is that you won't be able to wrap the entire Ordered Test in a transaction as described in the preceding section, so you would need to write your own cleanup scripts or simply re-deploy your original test data after each end-to-end test.

Use a Variety of Approaches

An effective database test plan will likely employ several different approaches for validating the integrity and intended behavior of a database schema. Database unit testing with Visual Studio provides a very direct way of probing and validating your database schema, but it shouldn't be the only method that you employ. For example, you may want to author and execute unit tests directly against a Web application that, in turn, makes calls to a database. This ensures that the integration of your database with your application code works as intended. For example, you may discover that changing the shape or name of a table in your database schema causes certain database calls in your application to fail.

Another type of testing you may wish to employ is that of load testing the database. Load testing a database can ensure that a database will continue to perform adequately under stress, such as during a high volume of retail transactions during the holiday season. You can use Visual Studio to conduct database load testing by first creating database unit tests, and then adding these tests to a Visual Studio load test. (Load tests are described in Chapter 13.)

Your database testing plan may benefit from manual testing as well. For example, how does a user interface behave when it is connected to a back-end database filled with test data? Are text fields big enough to display long strings of data? What happens when a query (for example, `show all customer records`) returns many rows of data? Can the user easily navigate through multiple pages of data? (Manual testing is covered in Chapter 14.)

These are a few of the considerations you should plan for when building out your database test plan, and this list is by no means exhaustive. But by using Visual Studio, you can stage a test database, fill it with sample data, and utilize a variety of testing frameworks (for example, unit testing, load testing, and manual testing) to author and execute a wide range of tests with Visual Studio.

T-SQL Static Analysis

So far, you have seen how Visual Studio can help you develop, test, and deploy your database schema. Visual Studio can also help you improve the overall quality of your T-SQL scripts by using its built-in static code analysis engine. T-SQL static analysis can help you identify several potential problems with your scripts, such as performance bottlenecks, brittle queries and object references, or even poor naming conventions.

There are two ways to run T-SQL static analysis. You can right-click on your database project within Solution Explorer and select Run Code Analysis. Alternatively, you can enable code analysis to be run every time you build your project. Do this now by right-clicking your `MyDatabaseProject` project from within Solution Explorer and selecting Properties. Click on the Code Analysis tab and enable the checkbox labeled Enable Code Analysis on Build. Expand each of the ruleset nodes to see the full list of static analysis rules, as shown in Figure 10-27.

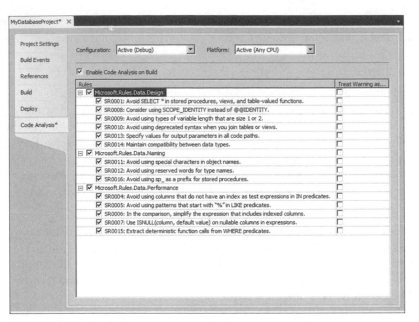

FIGURE 10-27

From this properties window, you can choose which static analysis rules will be run when your project is built. If you find that the number of warnings you receive on a project is overwhelming at first, disabling some rules is one way you can scope the warnings down to the ones you care the most about.

You can also enable the "Treat Warning as Error" checkbox to cause any failed rule to result in a build failure. By default, rules that fail will display a warning but will not prevent a build from succeeding. Treating static analysis rules as build errors can be an effective way of getting team members to take them more seriously. Lastly, static analysis can be run and enforced during automated builds, as discussed in Chapter 21.

Save your project settings and build your solution (press Ctrl+Shift+B, or click Build ➪ Build Solution). After your project is built, T-SQL static analysis will be run and the results will appear in the Error List (View ➪ Error List). Your output should resemble that of Figure 10-28.

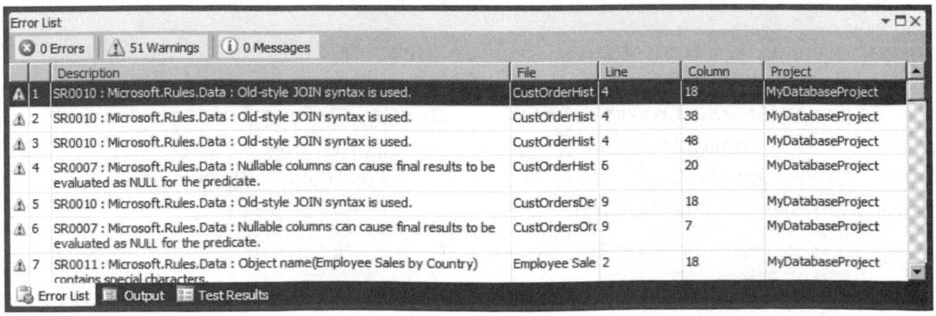

FIGURE 10-28

Start by fixing a file with a single, simple error. Click on the File column within the Error pane to sort this list of warnings based on the names of your T-SQL script files. Find the warning for the file named `CustOrdersDetail.proc.sql`, which indicates that the "Old-style JOIN syntax is used." Double-click on this warning to automatically open the offending T-SQL file. This also places the cursor at the line of script where this warning was discovered by the static analysis engine — although note that, depending on the type of rule, this won't always correspond to the exact place where the script must be updated.

One of the most valuable aspects of static analysis is that it not only finds problems in your scripts, but each warning is documented with additional information about the cause of the problem and suggestions on how to fix it. Right-click the warning for this file in the Error List and choose Show Error Help.

Read the help topic to understand why this script triggered this rule to fail, along with instructions on how to make the appropriate changes. Change this script to use the new SQL JOIN syntax as follows. Note that you are updating the FROM clause, and changing the WHERE clause to ON.

```
CREATE PROCEDURE CustOrdersDetail @OrderID int
AS
SELECT ProductName,
    UnitPrice=ROUND(Od.UnitPrice, 2),
    Quantity,
    Discount=CONVERT(int, Discount * 100),
    ExtendedPrice=ROUND(CONVERT(money, Quantity * (1 - Discount)
        * Od.UnitPrice), 2)
FROM Products AS P INNER JOIN [Order Details] AS Od
ON Od.ProductID = P.ProductID and Od.OrderID = @OrderID
```

Save this file and build your project again. This should cause the static analysis warning for this file to disappear. There are several such "Old-style JOIN" warnings that you could fix in this project, but since this is just a sample database, you can ignore the rest of these warnings.

Sometimes, static analysis rules can be fixed by using Visual Studio's database refactoring tools. Find the warning in "Alphabetical list of products.view.sql" with a description of "SR0001 : Microsoft.Design : The shape of the result set produced by a SELECT * statement will change if the underlying table or view structure changes." Double-click on this warning to open the file.

You can read the help for this static analysis warning to learn more about why using a wildcard (*) in a SELECT statement can be problematic. The fix is simple. From Schema View, expand Schemas ⇨ dbo ⇨ Views. Now, right-click on "Alphabetical list of products.view.sql" and click Refactor ⇨ Expand Wildcards. Preview and apply the changes. Note that the wildcard (*) is now replaced with the names of all of the columns from the Products table. While this produces a much longer script, this script is now more robust, since you have helped to isolate the results of this view from changes to the shape of the Products table. Replacing the wildcard also results in a slight performance improvement. Rebuild your project again and notice that this warning has disappeared.

You should also notice another warning for this file with a description of "SR0011 : Microsoft. Naming : Object name(Alphabetical list of products) contains special characters." This warning is occurring because there are whitespace characters within the name for this view. If you read the help for this warning, you will discover that this is a relatively low-priority warning. There's nothing technically wrong with using whitespace characters in the name of a view, but it does make it more difficult to reference, since you will need to encapsulate the name of the view in quotes (" ") whenever you reference it.

You can choose to resolve this warning by choosing Refactor ➪ Rename and giving this object a name that does not include whitespace characters. Or, you may decide that making this change introduces unnecessary risk into your database schema, which is not outweighed by the benefits of using a better naming convention.

For example, there might be applications that refer to this database view by its original name, and you don't want to risk breaking those applications. In that case, you can right-click the warning message and choose Suppress Static Code Analysis Message(s). When you choose to suppress a warning, an entry is added to a file called StaticCodeAnalysis.SuppressMessages.xml, and you will no longer receive this warning for this file. If you wish to enable this warning again in the future, simply delete the corresponding <SuppressedFile> entry from this file.

By utilizing static analysis for your T-SQL scripts, you can quickly identify ways of improving your overall database schema. As you can see from the list of warnings, even Microsoft could have benefited from having T-SQL static analysis capabilities when it originally shipped Northwind as a SQL Server database sample!

Additional Database Tools

Visual Studio also ships with a few other tools that may be useful when working with databases. The following sections examine these tools.

Redistributable Deployment Engine

Earlier in this chapter, you used Visual Studio to build and deploy your database project to a target database. This is a viable option when you have access to the target database. But there are times when you may want to package up your database schema so that someone else can perform the actual deployment.

For example, as a database developer, you may not have access to the production database, so you rely on a database administrator to deploy changes. In that example, your database administrator may not have Visual Studio installed. Or, maybe you sell packaged software to other organizations, and those organizations could be upgrading from various versions of your software. In that case, you want to defer the comparison of the source and target databases so that an appropriate script is generated based on the state of the target database.

These scenarios are enabled by Visual Studio's redistributable deployment engine. Visual Studio 2010 allows you to build and redistribute your database project along with the deployment engine so that it can be deployed later, such as by a database administrator or a customer of your packaged software. The deployment engine is responsible for comparing your target database with your database project and generating the appropriate deployment .sql script.

For this example, you will perform a deployment against the original Northwind database running on your local instance of SQL Server Express, but the steps would be identical if you were going to package this and deploy it on a remote machine.

Start by creating a folder for your redistributable package, such as `C:\DeployPackage`. Copy all of the files from `[Program Files]\Microsoft Visual Studio 10.0\VSTSDB\Deploy` to this folder (replace `[Program Files]` with the actual path to your program files directory). Next, copy all of the `.dll` files from `[Program Files]\Microsoft SQL Server Compact Edition\v3.5` to this folder.

> *Take care to ensure that you are only copying files during these steps, and not moving them, or else you can break existing Visual Studio and SQL Server functionality.*

You have now copied all of the files that make up Visual Studio's database deployment engine. The next step is to copy a built version of your database project. Return to Visual Studio and build your project (Build ➪ Build Solution). From Solution Explorer, right-click your database project and choose "Open Folder in Windows Explorer." Open the `sql\debug` folder.

This folder essentially contains a compiled version of your database project. The file `<ProjectName>.dbschema` is an XML representation of your database schema. The `.deploymanifest` file contains information from your project properties, such as the target database you were deploying and the database connection string. Previously, you were deploying to the `TestMyDatabaseProject` database, so, in a moment, you will override this value to target the `Northwind` database. Also note that the `Transaction.refactorlog` is included here, which is important to ensure the preservation of intent, as covered earlier in the section "Preservation of Intent."

Create a subfolder in your deployment folder to make it easier to organize these files. For this example, name the subfolder `NWv2`, so your folder will be something like `C:\DeployPackage\NWv2`. Copy the contents of the `sql\debug` folder into this subfolder.

You now have everything you need to deploy your database project to the original `Northwind` database. You could even copy the contents of this folder onto a memory stick or a network location, and use it from a remote machine, even if that machine didn't have Visual Studio installed. You could also invoke this deployment package from your application's installation program.

Open a command-prompt and navigate to your deployment folder (for example, `C:\DeployPackage`). The executable file at the heart of Visual Studio's redistributable deployment engine is called `VSDBCMD.EXE`. Type **VSDBCMD** and press Enter to see a list of command-line options. These options are further explained in the product documentation, and you will discover that you have a great deal of flexibility when invoking the deployment engine.

Now you will deploy your project to the `Northwind` database. Type the following and press Enter:

```
VSDBCMD /a:deploy /dd /Manifest:.\NWv2\MyDatabaseProject.deploymanifest
     /p:TargetDatabase=Northwind
```

Visual Studio will now analyze your target database (`Northwind`) against your source database (`MyDatabaseProject.dbschema`). Note that you did not need to specify the name of your

.dbschema file here because Visual Studio read this value from your .deploymanifest file. However, your .deploymanifest file currently points to the TestMyDatabaseProject target database. Hence, you overrode this value using the /p: option to point to Northwind instead. You could have used similar syntax to override the connection string or other values from the .deploymanifest file.

Also note that the /dd switch tells the deployment engine to deploy your database to your target immediately. If you had instead used /dd-, then it would generate a deployment .sql file for you to preview and make any changes to prior to deployment.

If you have followed this tutorial correctly, then this deployment will actually fail with the following error message:

```
*** TSD01268    .Net SqlClient Data Provider: Msg 547, Level 16, State 0, Line 1
 The ALTER TABLE statement conflicted with the CHECK constraint
"CK_PostalCodeLength". The conflict occurred in database "Northwind",
table "dbo.Clients", column 'PostalCode'.
```

This failure was caused by the constraint you added earlier, which requires that the PostalCode column is either five or ten characters in length. While this constraint is correct for addresses in the United States, it turns out that Northwind has non-U.S. data that causes this constraint to fail. This type of failure is one that is important to look out for, since your database is now in a half-deployed state. Some operations succeeded, such as renaming the Customers table to Clients. But once this failure was encountered, the deployment script halted. This error highlights the need to generate test data that realistically simulates that of your production database.

In this example, this problem is easily bypassed by simply removing the check constraint. Return to Visual Studio and, from Solution Explorer, expand MyDatabaseProject ⇨ Schema Objects ⇨ Schemas ⇨ dbo ⇨ Tables ⇨ Constraints. Right-click on Clients.CK_PostalCodeLength.sql and choose Delete. Now, rebuild your project (Build ⇨ Build Solution).

Next, you will need to re-copy your built project to your deployment folder. Copy the contents of sql\debug to your deployment subfolder (for example, C:\DeployPackage\NWv2\), overwriting the original files.

Return to the command prompt and run the same command you ran earlier. Your deployment should now succeed without any warnings or errors. You have successfully updated the Northwind database with the changes you modeled in production.

Schema Compare

Visual Studio allows you to perform ad hoc comparisons of schemas using the built-in Schema Compare tool. Click on Data ⇨ Schema Compare ⇨ New Schema Comparison. The New Schema Comparison dialog shown in Figure 10-29 allows you to decide which schemas to compare.

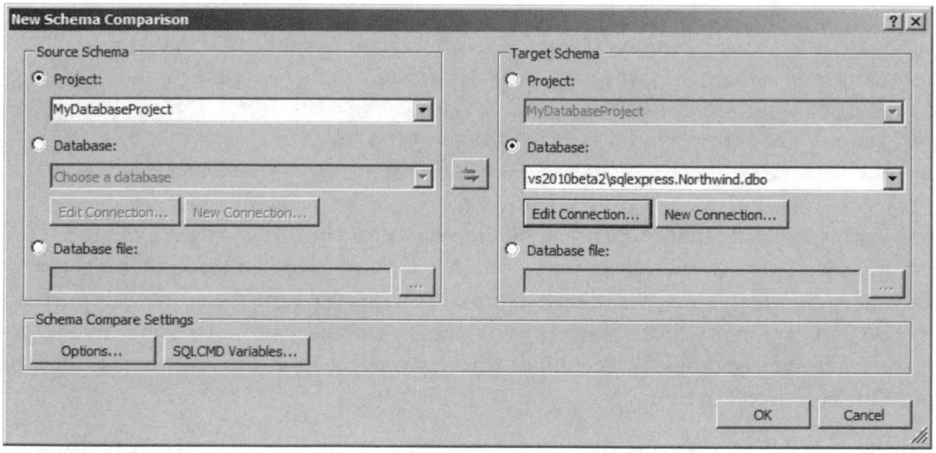

FIGURE 10-29

You can choose to compare any combination of database projects, live databases, or compiled database projects (.dbschema files). For your source database schema, select your MyDatabaseProject database. For your target schema, choose the Northwind database. Click OK.

Figure 10-30 shows the Schema Comparison results. This view allows you to quickly determine which differences exist between two schemas. You can even choose to use these results to produce a script that would modify the target database to resemble the source database.

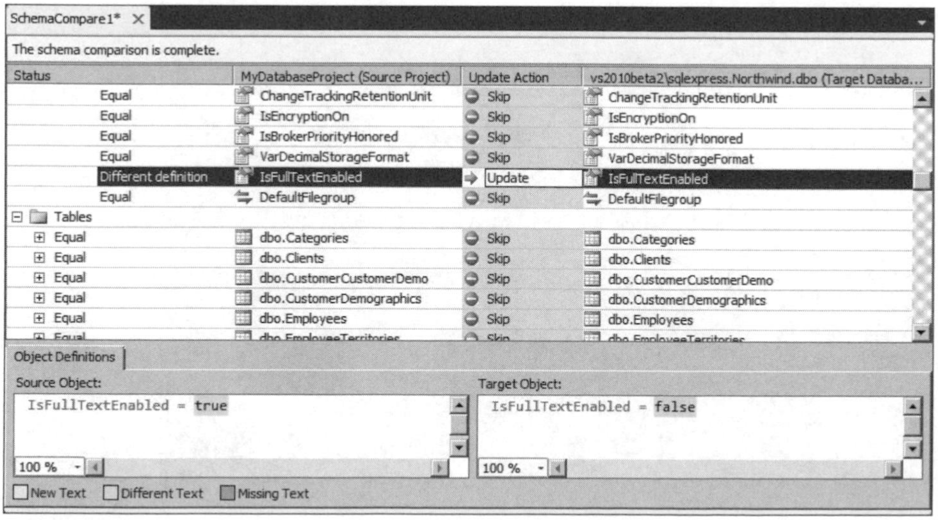

FIGURE 10-30

> *Be careful if you are using Schema Compare to generate change scripts. Schema Compare does not benefit from the refactoring transaction log required to maintain preservation of intent during certain refactoring operations (for example, renames or schema moves). If used improperly, data loss may occur.*

You might notice in this example that there are different values for the `IsFullTextEnabled` property of the database. You will encounter this difference if you are not running SQL Server Express with Advanced Services, since the other flavors of SQL Server Express do not support full text search. You can optionally disable this in your database project properties via the Project Settings tab. In the Catalog properties file section of this page, select Edit and remove the checkbox for the "Enable full text search" option.

The only other difference detected during the schema comparison should be that you are no longer specifying the properties for the MDF and LDF files. This difference is to be expected, and can be ignored.

Data Compare

Data Compare allows you to compare two live databases to detect differences that exist in rows of data. Click Data ➪ Data Compare ➪ New Data Comparison. The New Data Comparison dialog shown in Figure 10-31 allows you to choose two live databases to compare. Select `Northwind` as your source database and `TestMyDatabaseProject` as your target database. Click Finish.

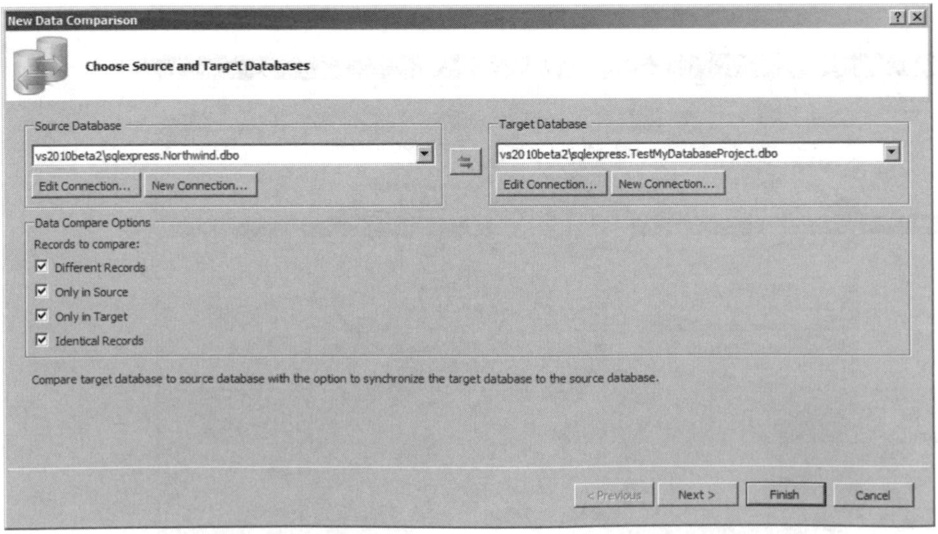

FIGURE 10-31

You can now see a table-by-table breakdown of the differences that exist in the data between the two tables, as shown in Figure 10-32.

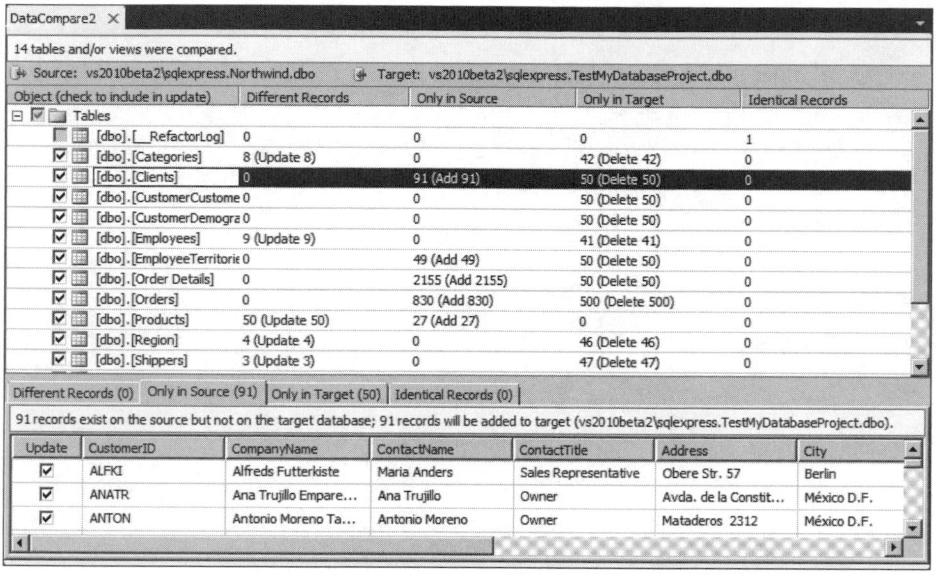

FIGURE 10-32

For this example, you should expect that all of the data would be different, since you generated pseudorandom test data for your test database. But you might encounter a real-world scenario where it is helpful to determine if data from a table in one database matches data from a table in another database. You can use this tool to detect any differences, and to quickly generate a `.sql` script for executing the changes necessary to make the data in your target database match the data in your source database.

SUMMARY

You have seen how Visual Studio 2010 can help you bring your database development lifecycle into the same toolset and process utilized by the rest of your software development team. With Visual Studio, you can develop changes to your database in an offline environment, test those changes, and automatically create scripts for deploying those changes. You can even version-control your database schema and enable parallel development by using a system such as Team Foundation Server. And you have explored some of the built-in tools Visual Studio offers for refactoring your database, analyzing schema dependencies, creating remote deployment packages, comparing schemas, and even comparing the data within two databases.

For many teams, this may represent a dramatic paradigm shift in the way database development is performed. This may require you to invest in significant changes to your process in the short term. But the longer-term results can pay dividends in terms of increased productivity for your developers, testers, and administrators, as well as the increased level of quality and predictability you can bring to your database development activities.

Chapter 11 explores some of the advanced debugging capabilities in Visual Studio 2010 that can be used to analyze code behavior and help fix bugs.

11

Introduction to IntelliTrace

WHAT'S IN THIS CHAPTER?

➤ Exploring the new IntelliTrace feature

➤ Understanding the events view and the call tree view

➤ Working with breakpoints

➤ Using the pinnable data tips

Many developers resent the fact that debugging has become one of the key traits in software development. Many developers have been known to spend a considerable amount of time simply on debugging. Adding salt to the wound are programming bugs where the behavior is not reproducible. In many instances, developers may wish there was a way to travel back in time to capture what happened, and then be able to wave a magic wand to debug the issue. That wish has now come true in Visual Studio 2010 Ultimate. (Not the magic wand part — that feature did not make the cut.)

Visual Studio 2010 introduces several new capabilities to help with the debugging experience, and to prevent bugs from getting into the system in the first place.

This chapter examines the feature called "IntelliTrace," which has debuted in Visual Studio 2010 Ultimate. In this chapter, you will learn how to use this feature to aid in your debugging effort, and to get to a faster resolution. This chapter also discusses the new capabilities for breakpoints and a cool sticky data tip feature.

DEBUGGING USING INTELLITRACE

In many cases, as a developer, you have discovered that debugging is a regular activity. It is also a task that could become monotonous. For example, you may have encountered a bug that the tester passed on to you, but one that you cannot reproduce. You may also have experienced the agony of stepping through one step past the point where the issue occurs, only to discover that it is time to start all over again. These are just a couple of common occurrences, and there are no doubt plenty more.

Visual Studio 2010 Ultimate includes new capabilities to address issues such as the famous "no repro" bug status. A key feature in this capability is the IntelliTrace feature. The key tactics used to address the non-reproducible bug are to capture as much information as possible while the bug is encountered, and to use the capability to leverage this information while debugging. The one feature that could top this would be for the bug to automatically resolve itself.

Let's take a deeper look at this new debugging feature.

In this chapter, examples will use "The Beer House" sample application to demonstrate the debugging features. You can download this sample application from the `http://thebeerhouse .codeplex.com` Web site. The sample application is used as an example in this chapter. You can use your own application to follow along and learn about the new debugging features.

Debugging Options

In Visual Studio 2010 Ultimate, the Debug menu has a new member called IntelliTrace, as shown in Figure 11-1. You use this new menu option to enable the intelligent tracing.

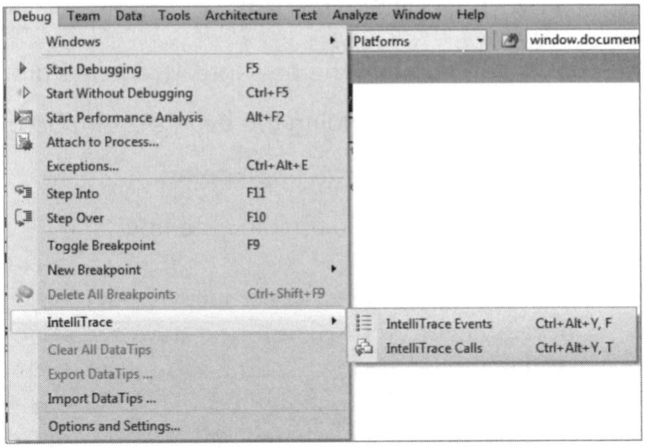

Let's start by looking at the Options and Settings dialog for configuring the IntelliTrace feature. Open the Debug Options window by clicking Debug ⇨ Options and Settings. In the resulting Options window, select the IntelliTrace section, as shown in Figure 11-2.

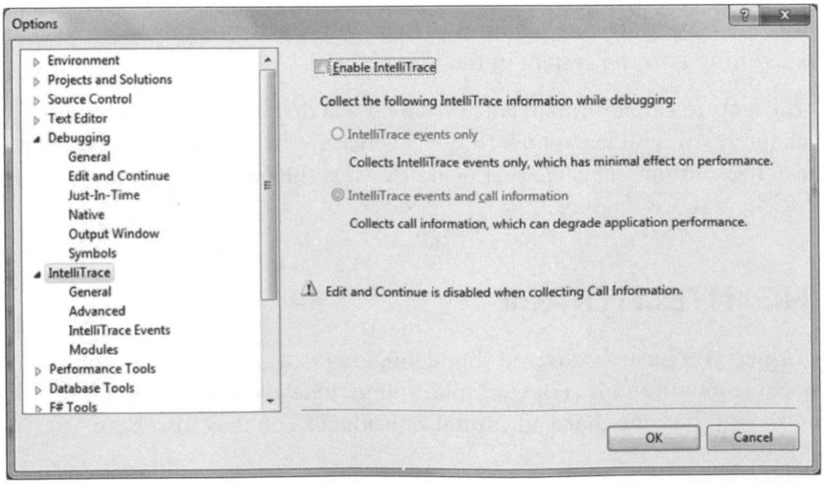

FIGURE 11-1

FIGURE 11-2

You should notice the following four configuration sections within the IntelliTrace option node:

➤   General

➤   Advanced

➤   IntelliTrace Events

➤   Modules

Let's look at the configurations available in each of these sections.

General

In the General section, you can enable IntelliTrace by clicking the checkbox labeled "Enable IntelliTrace." This checkbox allows you to enable (check) or disable (uncheck) IntelliTrace. In this window, you can also choose between the options to record events only or collect additional information that includes events, diagnostics, calls, and method level tracing. Of course, collecting more information means that a larger log file will be generated. As you can see in the Options window shown in Figure 11-2, collecting more information would have an impact on performance more so than merely collecting events.

Also, note that the "Edit and continue" option is disabled with the latter option. The option dialog will prompt you with this warning when you change the setting.

Advanced

The Advanced option provides two settings. As shown in Figure 11-3, you can set the location to store the generated log file, and specify the maximum size that the log file should be.

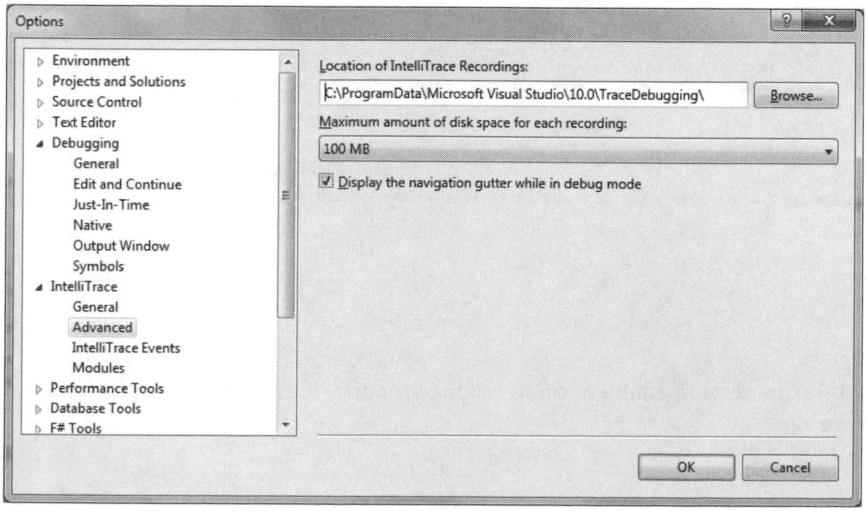

FIGURE 11-3

In addition, a checkbox at the bottom of the screen allows you to turn on or off the navigation gutter in Visual Studio. You'll learn more about the navigation gutter later in this chapter.

> *IntelliTrace works only with managed code debugging. Native code debugging is not supported at this time.*

IntelliTrace Events

As shown in Figure 11-4, the IntelliTrace Events section lists all the diagnostic events that are collected while debugging an application. The list of events is broken down by framework categories. Here you can select (that is, choose to collect) or deselect (choose not to collect) the diagnostic events shown on this list.

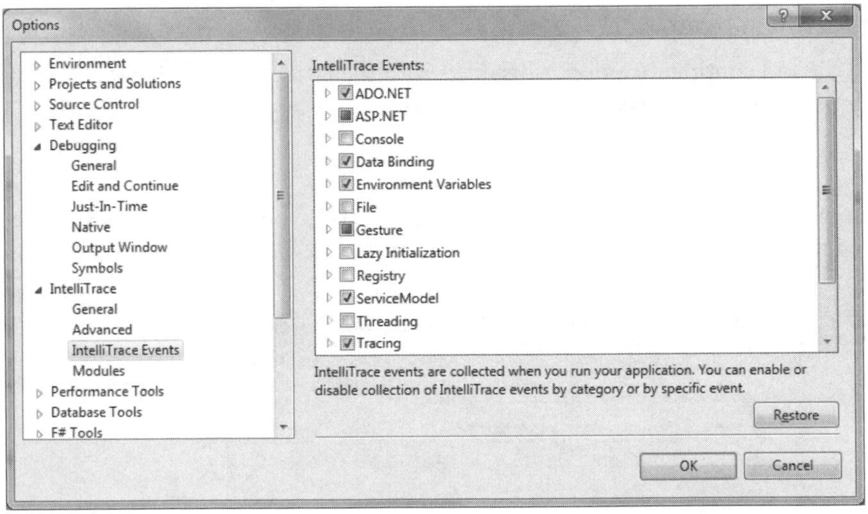

FIGURE 11-4

Modules

As shown in Figure 11-5, this section enables you to manage the list of modules for which data is collected during debugging.

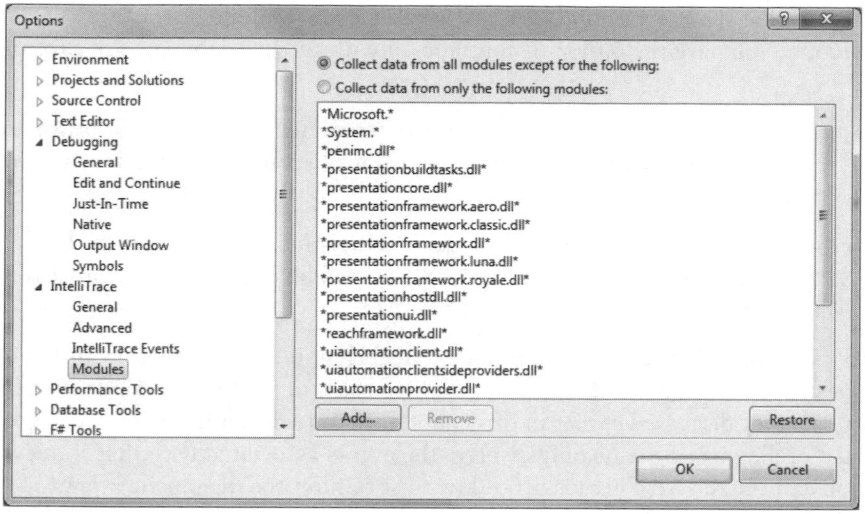

FIGURE 11-5

Here you can add new assemblies to collect debugging information, as well as exclude and remove assemblies for which you don't want to collect debugging information.

Events Recording

As you have learned, by enabling IntelliTrace and choosing the "events only" option, you have the option of recording several of the events occurring in your application, including user gestures, system calls, and exceptions. These events that are captured as they happen are presented in a history window.

To load the IntelliTrace window shown in Figure 11-6 with a list of events recorded, select Debug ⇨ Windows ⇨ IntelliTrace Events.

As you can see, the history shows events associated with several different modules, including application code. The highlighted event in Figure 11-6 shows a gesture, which, in this case, is a user action. The user has clicked a button to add an item to the shipping cart. As you would expect, exceptions will also be recorded in a similar fashion.

Note that this list is from a live debugging session. The last event in the list is a "Live

FIGURE 11-6

Event." The history shows that the execution hit a breakpoint in Line 36 in file ShoppingCart .aspx.cs. At this juncture, you have the option to continue on with the live debugging to capture additional events.

When you click on a particular event recording in this list, the associated source file will be loaded in the source window with the corresponding line highlighted. This becomes very handy when you are debugging an exception.

To locate a particular event or shorten the list of events, you can use the tools available in the IntelliTrace window. At the top of the window, you can find a search box. You can use this search box to short-list the events displayed in the window.

Additionally, you can incorporate a filter by using the All Categories and All Threads drop-down lists. The All Categories list shows the framework categories you saw in the Option window under the Diagnostic Events category discussed earlier in this chapter. If you select a framework category, you will see that the list of diagnostic events only displays the events associated with that framework category. Similarly, you can use the All Threads drop-down list to filter the diagnostic events.

Because of its low overhead (compared to recording the call information), the "events only" option is the default choice in Visual Studio 2010.

Debugging and Playback

Now that you understand what goes on when you choose to record events only, let's explore what goes on when you select the option to collect information about diagnostic events and call information (the second option presented to you on the Options screen shown in Figure 11-2).

If you are a sports fan, you may keep your DVR full of all sorts of recorded sports events. By recording the events on the DVR, you are able to pause, step back, and forward during the program to answer a phone, to take care of any distractions, or even to go back and watch a fantastic play that just took place.

A similar situation occurs in a live debugging session when you utilize IntelliTrace. You can now pause a live debugging session and review the events or calls. This new feature also allows you to play back the execution of an application from a past debugging session, which is certain to change the debugging experience once and for all. For example, a bug filed based on a test run of your application can now be attached with debugging information recorded during that test run. When you receive the attached debug file, you can run through the debugging file to review the events and calls, which could provide the missing information to identify and resolve a bug.

This section examines two new capabilities:

➤ Breaking, stepping back, or stepping forward a live debugging session

➤ Playing back a recorded debugging session

As shown in Figure 11-7, when you check the Enable IntelliTrace radio button in the Options window and select the second option to collect "IntelliTrace events and call information," you will get two warning messages. The first warning informs you that the changes won't take effect until you start a new debugging session. The second warning alerts you that the capability to "Edit and Continue" is disabled while capturing call information.

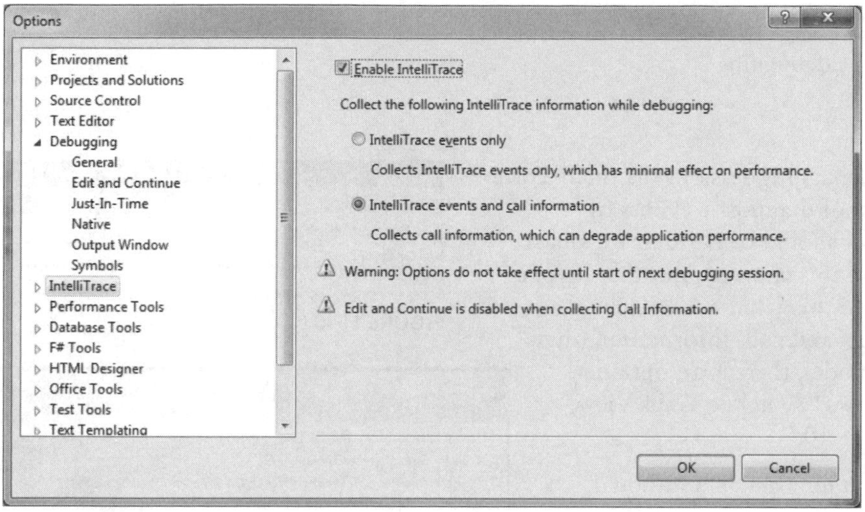

FIGURE 11-7

> *Selecting to collect diagnostic events and call information has an impact on the performance. So, use the "Events only" option if you don't need the playback capability.*

Once you select "Events and Call Information," you are then ready to take advantage of the playback capability.

Debug Navigation Bar

In Visual Studio, open "The Beer House" solution (or, alternatively, your own application). Set up the debugging option as described earlier to capture both events and call information.

Start a new debugging session in Visual Studio. You will see the IntelliTrace window, as shown in Figure 11-8. While the debugging is in progress, IntelliTrace is capturing the data. To view the data, you must pause the debugger. Click the "Break All" link to pause the debugger.

You should now see a new navigation bar in Visual Studio, as shown in Figure 11-9. The navigation bar contains icons that have the following five associated actions. (This list is ordered to match the order of the icons in the navigation bar.)

➤ Return to the caller

➤ Go to the prior call or the event

➤ Step in

FIGURE 11-8

FIGURE 11-9

➤ Go to the next call or the event

➤ Return to live debugging

Calls History

When pausing the debugging session, the IntelliTrace window shows a list of diagnostic events by default. This window should be familiar to you (see Figure 11-6 earlier in this chapter). But there is one important addition to this window. When you are capturing both events and calls information (that is, in the playback mode), there is an option at the top of the window, "Switch to Calls View," as shown in Figure 11-10.

With this option, you now get an additional view that shows the call tree, as shown in Figure 11-11.

The call tree view shows the sequence of execution steps in a tree view that you can now navigate through to get an understanding of what methods were called. This view also shows the entry and exit of functions, from the start of the application to the last step of the debugging session.

Trace Log file

The IntelliTrace Event view (Figure 11-6), and the calls history view (Figure 11-11) provide you with the capability to step back and analyze the execution history. The information presented by IntelliTrace in these two views is stored in a trace log file. As you learned earlier in this chapter, you specify the path to store this trace log file when you configure the Advanced area of the Options window (Figure 11-3).

FIGURE 11-10

FIGURE 11-11

As you can imagine, there are plenty of opportunities to make the debugging activity more productive. Some of the common scenarios include attaching the trace log file to a bug work item, to the build report on a failed build, and on a functional test run. When a trace log file is opened in Visual Studio, it shows a summary view, contains the threads list, and contains the exceptions list. For debugging a particular exception, you can double-click on the exception from the list to start debugging from the point this exception was thrown.

NEW FEATURES IN BREAKPOINTS

Breakpoints are a developer's friend when it comes to debugging. A breakpoint tells the debugger to stop executing at a certain point in the code. This enables the developer, for example, to get a handle on the various parameters, or to watch the execution carefully by going through the program one step at a time. Of course, most developers have gone "one step too many" while stepping through the code on several occasions. The "Debugging and Playback" section earlier in this chapter provided a glimpse of the new "time travel" capability that allows you to step back when this happens.

With breakpoints, you are stepping through the code and are able to debug the issues that you are trying to resolve. But there are invariably instances when you are at a loss in finding the cause of an issue that you are debugging.

When occasions like this crop up, you call for help. When you do that, you want to provide as much information as you can about the issue you are debugging and, if possible, hand off the breakpoints you have set as well. In Visual Studio 2010, you can now do just that.

Sharing Breakpoints

The Breakpoints window has now been enhanced to enable you to export and import breakpoints. Exporting breakpoints generates an XML file that can be shared with the rest of the team members.

To export or import breakpoints, you must first call up the Breakpoints window shown in Figure 11-12. You can do that by clicking Debug ⇨ Windows ⇨ Breakpoints or by pressing Ctrl + Alt + B.

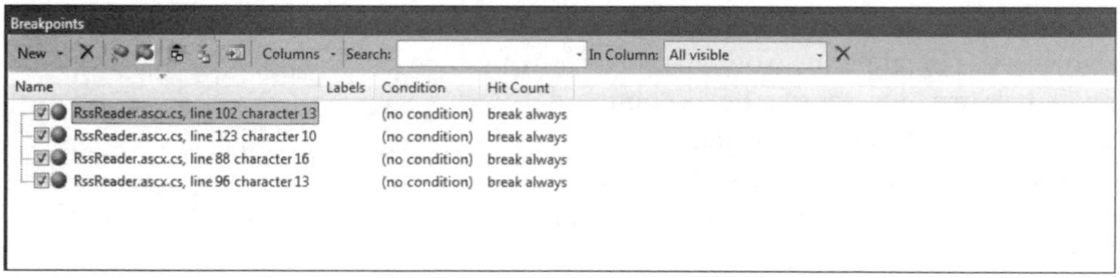

FIGURE 11-12

Click the "Export all breakpoints" menu item (the fifth icon from the left) from the Breakpoint window to open a Windows dialog to save all the breakpoints within the solution in a file with .xml extension.

You can share this file via email, on a shared drive, and so on, with the rest of your team, or you can attach it to the bug work item that you are investigating in the first place. If you attach it to the bug work item, whoever picks up this bug to work on will have the associated breakpoints file that you have just attached.

> *It would be convenient and useful to be able to export breakpoints and attach the file to the work item directly without having to do it in multiple steps. This is not possible to do in the 2010 version, but it may be a feature request for the next version of Visual Studio.*

To get the breakpoints added to the project, select the "Import breakpoints from a file" (the sixth icon from the left) menu item in the Breakpoints window and choose the file. This will add the breakpoints to the corresponding files within the solution.

This is indeed a nice little feature to help you share the breakpoints and possibly save some time for the developer who will be debugging an issue.

Labeling Breakpoints

Labeling breakpoints is similar to tagging. This will come handy if you have many breakpoints in your file and want to look at only a select few of the breakpoints.

You can label breakpoints from within the Breakpoints window shown in Figure 11-12. This window shows a list of breakpoints you set in the project. Right-click on a breakpoint to which you want add a label and select "Edit labels." This launches the "Edit breakpoint labels" window shown in Figure 11-13.

In the "Edit breakpoint labels" window, start by providing text for a new label and click the Add button to attach this label to the breakpoint. Note that you can add as many labels as you want to a breakpoint. You can also choose a label from the existing labels. Figure 11-13 shows three existing labels, with two of them associated with the selected breakpoint (as indicated by the checkmarks).

FIGURE 11-13

Now that you have set the labels, you can use them with the new search capabilities. In the Breakpoints window, type a label (for example, "red") in the Search box and press Enter. This will bring up only the breakpoints that have the labels "red."

You may want to label certain breakpoints that you are using to debug a particular bug with that bug work item ID or a description. Note that you can also export only breakpoints that were results of a label search. This will come in handy when you have numerous breakpoints and only want to export a subset of those breakpoints.

PINNABLE DATA TIPS

Breakpoints are definitely a key tool for debugging. Another often-used technique is physically watching variables, expressions, and more, during the debugging. Developers do this by using a watch list, a quick list, and a locals window. During the observation, the developer may track some of these by writing them down on a piece of paper and looking for values as they progress through the execution of code.

Instead of having to physically write down this tracking history, with Visual Studio 2010, developers may take advantage of the IDE automatically recording this information in the form of pinnable data tips.

In Visual Studio, if you hover over a variable or an expression, you will see a tool tip, as shown in Figure 11-14. This is called a *data tip*.

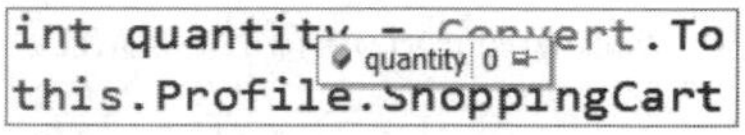

```
int quantity = Convert.To
this.Profile.ShoppingCart
```
      quantity 0

FIGURE 11-14

Note the pin icon to the right end of the tool tip in the Figure 11-14. This is new in Visual Studio 2010 and provides the capability to either stick the data tip on the screen, or let it float with the line of code with which it is associated.

To get a data tip pinned to the source, click the pin icon on the data tip. This results in the data tip being pinned to the right of the line of code, and a pin icon added to the gutter in the Visual Studio 2010 IDE.

Another way to get a data tip pinned to the source is by right-clicking on the expression you want to track, and selecting Expression '<<Name>>' ⇨ Pin To Source, as shown in Figure 11-15.

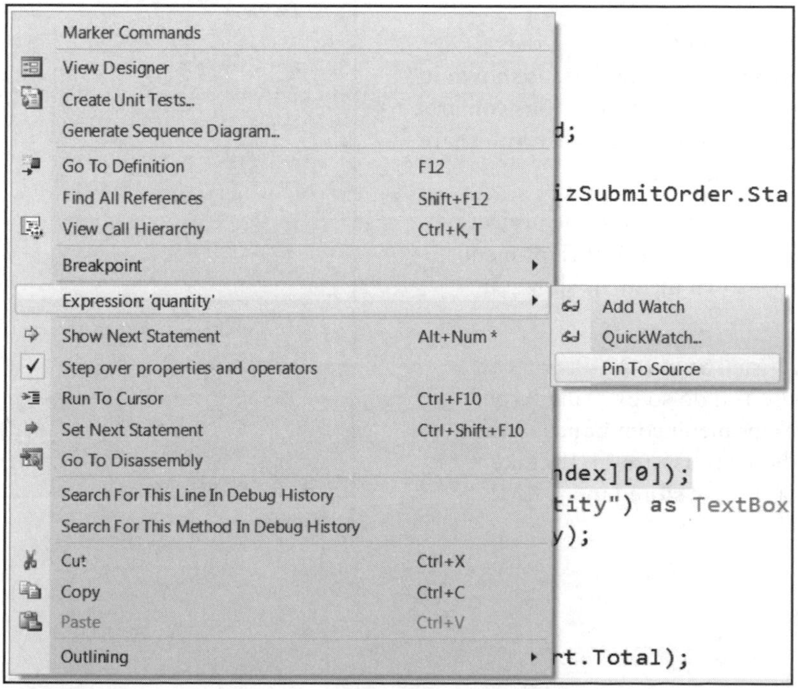

Marker Commands	
View Designer	
Create Unit Tests...	
Generate Sequence Diagram...	
Go To Definition	F12
Find All References	Shift+F12
View Call Hierarchy	Ctrl+K, T
Breakpoint	▶
Expression: 'quantity'	▶
Show Next Statement	Alt+Num *
Step over properties and operators	
Run To Cursor	Ctrl+F10
Set Next Statement	Ctrl+Shift+F10
Go To Disassembly	
Search For This Line In Debug History	
Search For This Method In Debug History	
Cut	Ctrl+X
Copy	Ctrl+C
Paste	Ctrl+V
Outlining	▶

Submenu for Expression: 'quantity':
- Add Watch
- QuickWatch...
- Pin To Source

FIGURE 11-15

If you pin the data tip like this, the data tip will stay visible all the time (not simply when you hover over the variable or expression), and will stay in line with the line to which it is pinned. When you scroll up or down on the source file, or when you switch to another file in the IDE, the data tip will disappear from the view.

In cases where you need to see the data tips at all time, instead of pinning the data tip, you want to unpin it. You do that by selecting the "Unpin from source" button from the data tip management menu bar, as shown in Figure 11-16. Hovering over a pinned data tip will bring the data tip management menu bar.

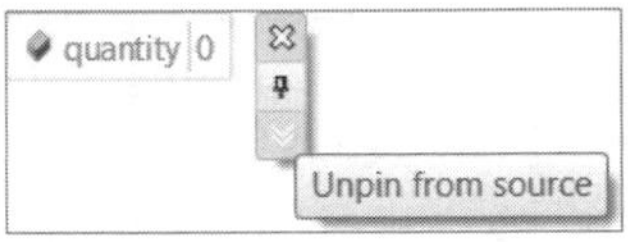

FIGURE 11-16

That will result in the data tip turning yellow (similar to a conventional sticky note). Now, even if you move around the source page, or move to another file, the data tip will be in sight for you.

You can also move this data tip outside the code window or to a second monitor. With this capability, you can have a collection of data tips (or watch lists) on a second monitor while you are working in a debugging session, essentially getting rid of the manual paper notes to keep track of variables.

FIGURE 11-17

Note that you can add expressions to a data tip by right-clicking on the data tip and choosing Add Expression. This will be useful if you want to track multiple dependent variables.

You can add a comment to the data tip by using the comment feature in the management menu bar, as shown in Figure 11-17. Adding a comment to the expressions you are tracking may prove to be helpful, especially when you share the data tips with your team members.

You can clear data tips (either all of them in the project or in the current file) by using the Clear All DataTips menu command in the Debug drop-down menu, as shown in Figure 11-18.

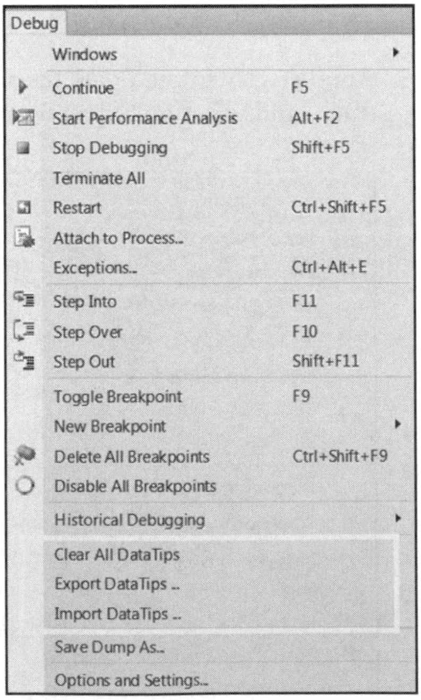

Similar to breakpoints, in Visual Studio 2010, you can export and import data tips. You do so by using Export DataTips and Import DataTips menu commands in the Debug drop-down menu shown in Figure 11-18. Like breakpoints, exported data tips are stored in an XML file format.

FIGURE 11-18

SUMMARY

This chapter took you on a quick tour of some of the new debugging capabilities in Visual Studio 2010. You learned how to configure the IntelliTrace feature, which lets developers travel back in time to analyze the execution history from a debugging session. This new capability is available in the Visual Studio 2010 Ultimate. You learned about the capability to record diagnostic events, and the capability to play back events from a live or previously executed debugging session.

This chapter also previewed the new features added to the Breakpoints window, such as labeling and the capability to export and import breakpoints. This neat little utility helps developers share breakpoints with fellow team members.

Finally, you learned about the enhancement of the data tip feature in the form of pinned data tips and sticky data tips. Coupled with the capabilities to add comments to data tips and to add expressions to data tips, this feature is going to save many sticky notes.

In Chapter 12, you will be introduced to the testing capabilities in Visual Studio 2010. You will learn about the various test types, diagnostic test adapters, and tools for working with tests. You will also learn about working with test results, ordered tests, and the test settings. Finally, you will learn about a cool new feature called "test impact analysis."

PART III
Tester

12

Introduction to Software Testing

WHAT'S IN THIS CHAPTER?

➤ Understand the different types of tests supported by Visual Studio 2010

➤ Learning about how to create, organize, and run tests within Visual Studio

➤ Publishing test results to Team Foundation Server

The next several chapters will introduce the testing functionality supported by Visual Studio 2010. Visual Studio provides support for authoring a wide range of tests, all designed to help you identify bugs in your software before your users do.

One of the most substantial investments Microsoft has made in Visual Studio 2010 is improved support for software testing. Microsoft has also focused considerably on *better integration* of those testing activities into the rest of the software development lifecycle, such as the handoff of detailed bug reports from a tester to a developer.

Perhaps the most notable addition to Visual Studio 2010 is the completely revamped support for authoring, executing, and managing *manual tests*. Manual testing — essentially just a form of testing that requires human input and validation — is usually performed by *generalist testers*, and is by far the most common type of testing conducted in the software development industry. Hence it's a natural extension of the Visual Studio family of products to support the generalist tester with better tools and testing frameworks. Manual testing is covered in detail in Chapter 14.

Visual Studio 2010 also introduces support for managing virtualized testing environments. Visual Studio Lab Management 2010 makes it possible to automatically spin up virtual machines for testing your software under a variety of configurations.

As testers discover them, they can easily file bugs, along with a pointer to a snapshot of the virtual environment that the developer can use to quickly analyze the state of the machine when the test case failed. Lab Management is covered in greater detail in Chapter 16.

ROLE-BASED TESTING TOOLS

The testing tools in Visual Studio 2010 are tailored for different testing-oriented roles generally found within software development and testing teams. Some individuals may perform more than one role, in which case a team member may use multiple tools.

➤ *Visual Studio Test Professional 2010* — The Test Professional product is primarily targeted at generalist testers who will be authoring, executing, and managing manual tests. It includes the Microsoft Test Manager and Microsoft Test Runner tools. These tools are introduced in more detail later in this chapter, and covered extensively in Chapter 14.

➤ *Visual Studio 2010 Premium* and *Visual Studio 2010 Ultimate* — The Premium and Ultimate editions of Visual Studio 2010 include functionality that is designed for specialist testers. A *specialist tester* is usually a software developer who focuses on writing software that is responsible for testing other software. Examples of duties that this role might perform include authoring tests that simulate large-scale load against a Web application, or converting manual test cases into automated tests that can be run without requiring human intervention. Visual Studio 2010 Premium includes the capabilities to write coded user interface (UI) tests. Visual Studio 2010 Ultimate includes all of the functionality from Premium, in addition to the capability to author Web performance tests and load tests. Visual Studio 2010 Ultimate also includes the functionality found in Visual Studio Test Professional 2010, effectively making Ultimate a superset of both Premium and Test Professional.

You will learn about the aforementioned test types next. For now, it is just important to know that testers who focus on manual testing can likely just purchase the less-expensive Test Professional product, whereas testers responsible for developing automated tests should look into either Premium or Ultimate. Team members responsible for managing and monitoring test plans (for example, test leads) may also use the Test Professional product to do so.

Note that Visual Studio 2010 Professional, Premium, and Ultimate all include the capability to author unit tests (see Chapter 7), as well as generic tests and ordered tests (covered later in this chapter). Premium and Ultimate also provide the capability of authoring database unit tests (see Chapter 10). For more information on the overall Visual Studio 2010 family of products, see the Introduction at the beginning of this book.

TYPES OF TESTS

Visual Studio 2010 provides support for authoring and executing a variety of test types, each with its own purpose for testing your applications. A successful test plan will likely include a mix of multiple types of tests from the following list:

➤ *Manual test* — A manual test simply requires a human to interact with an application, verify some expected result, and report on whether or not a test was successful. As you will see later, a manual test is the only type of test that is represented as a Visual Studio Team Foundation Server 2010 work item (a test case), instead of as a source code file. Manual tests are covered in detail in Chapter 14.

➤ *Manual test (text/Word format)* — This is a legacy test type from earlier editions of Visual Studio. It is simply a document containing a list of manual test steps that a tester should execute. If you have tests in this format, they will continue to work with Visual Studio 2010, but in order to benefit from the new manual testing tools and framework, you should consider migrating them to test cases, described in Chapter 14.

➤ *Coded UI test* — A coded UI test provides the capability to author tests that automatically interact with the user interface of an application, verify some expected result, and file bugs if an error is encountered. Since this whole process is automatic, it can be run very frequently, and without human interaction, but it is typically more expensive to author and maintain than a manual test would be. Coded UI tests are detailed in Chapter 15.

➤ *Unit tests* — These are low-level tests verifying that target application code functions as the developer expects. Unit tests are essentially code that tests other code. Unit testing is described in detail in Chapter 7.

➤ *Database unit test* — Visual Studio 2010 also provides the capability to write unit tests against database code (for example, T-SQL code within a SQL Server database). Database unit tests are covered in Chapter 10.

➤ *Web performance test* — A Web performance test is used to verify functionality or performance of a Web application. For example, you may create a Web performance test to verify that a user can create a new account on your site. This Web performance test could be one of a suite of Web performance tests that you run periodically to verify that your Web site is working as you expect. For more information on Web performance tests, see Chapter 13.

➤ *Load tests* — These tests verify that a target application will perform and scale as necessary. A target system is stressed by repeatedly executing a variety of tests. Visual Studio records details of the target system's performance and automatically generates reports from the data. Load tests are frequently based on sets of Web performance tests. However, even non-Web applications can be tested by selecting a number of unit tests to execute. For more information, see Chapter 13.

➤ *Generic tests* — These tests enable calling of alternative external testing systems, such as an existing suite of tests leveraging a third-party testing package. Results of those tests can be automatically parsed to determine success. This could range from something as simple as the result code from a console application to parsing the XML document exported from an external testing package. More information on working with generic tests can be found in the product documentation.

➤ *Ordered tests* — Essentially containers of other tests, these establish a specific order in which tests are executed, and enable the same test to be included more than once. For details, see the section "Using Ordered Tests," later in this chapter.

Sometimes, more than one test can be used to verify that a given piece of an application is behaving correctly. For example, both coded UI tests and Web performance tests can be used to verify the functionality of a Web application. But, as you become more familiar with coded UI tests versus Web performance tests, you will see that the former is better suited for validating functionality and UI layout, whereas the latter is better suited for checking performance and scalability (when used within a load test). You will get a better sense of which test to use in different situations in the detailed chapters for each test type.

DIAGNOSTIC DATA ADAPTERS

A key challenge with software testing is that of providing developers with enough information about a failing test so that the developer can adequately debug and fix the problem. How often have you seen bugs get resolved as "No Repro" because a developer wasn't able to reproduce a bug discovered by a tester? Unfortunately, the phrase "It works on my machine" has become an all-too-common part of the software development pop culture.

One of the major ways in which Microsoft is attempting to eliminate the "No Repro" problem in this release of Visual Studio is with *diagnostic data adapters*. A diagnostic data adapter is responsible for collecting information about one or more machines under test. The information collected from these diagnostic data adapters can then be attached to a bug, providing the developer with a rich amount of information with which to diagnose a problem.

Visual Studio 2010 ships with several diagnostic data adapters that can be enabled during test runs, including the following:

➤ *Action log and action recording* — This adapter is useful for manual tests. It can capture a log of exactly what steps testers took when they encountered a bug. For example, a developer studying the action log can determine that a tester clicked the Username textbox, typed "Brian," and then pressed the Enter key. A developer no longer has to guess about what testers were doing when they encountered a bug. Action recordings can also be used to fast-forward pieces of a manual test during subsequent test runs (see Chapter 14). The action recordings can even be used to automate a manual test by turning it into a coded UI test (see Chapter 15).

➤ *ASP.NET Profiler* — This data adapter can be used on remote machines when conducting a load test. It provides granular profiling information about an ASP.NET application, which can be used to more accurately diagnose performance bottlenecks. This data diagnostic adapter is available for use only with ASP.NET load tests.

➤ *Code coverage* — Code-coverage information can be used to determine which code paths are executed during an automated test. This can be analyzed later to determine if there are sections of code that are not being touched by your test plan, possibly indicating that additional test coverage is necessary. Code coverage is only available for automated tests, not for manual tests.

➤ *IntelliTrace* — IntelliTrace is a powerful way of capturing granular debugging information about a .NET application being tested. This information can then be loaded into Visual

Studio 2010 Ultimate by a developer to analyze exactly what was happening when a bug was encountered. For more information about working with IntelliTrace, see Chapter 11.

➤ *Event log* — This adapter can capture events that were written to the event log while a test was executing.

➤ *System information* — This adapter will gather system information and attach it to a bug. Now a developer no longer has to guess about the operating system version, 32- versus 64-bit, how much RAM, what version of browser, or other such critical information about the machines involved in a test run.

➤ *Test impact* — Test impact analysis is a powerful new feature of Visual Studio 2010 that analyzes which blocks of code are exercised by your tests. This data can later be used to help you determine which tests need to be re-run based on which blocks of code were changed in your application since the last time those tests were run. Test impact analysis can, therefore, help your test team focus on running the most important tests, based on which pieces of your application are churning. You will explore the benefits of test impact analysis with manual testing in Chapter 14, and with automated tests later in this chapter in the section "Test Impact View."

➤ *Video recorder* — The video recorder data adapter captures a recording of an application under test. This recording can help a developer diagnose problems with an application's UI, and can be used with both manual and automated tests (such as a coded UI test).

A diagnostic data adapter can also be used to impact a machine during a test. Visual Studio 2010 ships with one such adapter:

➤ *Network emulation* — The network emulation data adapter doesn't collect any data, but instead can be used to force a machine into behaving as if it had a slower network connection. For example, you may wish to simulate the experience that users in remote locations will have when connecting to your corporate network over a 56K modem link.

You can also create your own custom diagnostic data adapters. For example, you might be interested in capturing inbound network traffic on a given port that may be relevant to the behavior of your application. Or, you might want to author a custom adapter that impacts a machine, such as by rapidly reading from and writing to the hard disk in order to simulate heavy hard disk activity during a test. For information on creating a custom diagnostic data adapter, see the product documentation topic "Creating a Diagnostic Data Adapter to Collect Custom Data or Impact a Test System" at `http://msdn.microsoft.com/en-us/library/dd286743%28VS.100%29.aspx`.

> *There are limitations with using some diagnostic data adapters in certain configurations. For example, the code coverage adapter may not be used with manual tests, and may not be run in conjunction with the test impact or diagnostic trace adapters. For more information, consult the product documentation topic "Setting Up Machines and Diagnostic Information to be Collected Using Test Settings" at* `http://msdn.microsoft.com/en-us/library/dd286743%28VS.100%29.aspx`*.*

Using the right set of adapters can dramatically reduce the amount of time required to diagnose and solve a problem and can also reduce the back-and-forth communication required between a developer and a tester. You will discover how to configure diagnostic data adapters for manual tests in Chapter 14. Configuring diagnostic data adapters for automated tests within Visual Studio is covered later in this chapter.

MICROSOFT TEST MANAGER

Microsoft Test Manager is a new tool provided as part of the Visual Studio 2010 family of products. It provides a single environment from which to author and manage test cases, manage test plans, and define and manage your physical and virtual test environments (if using Lab Management). Figure 12-1 shows a typical view within Microsoft Test Manager.

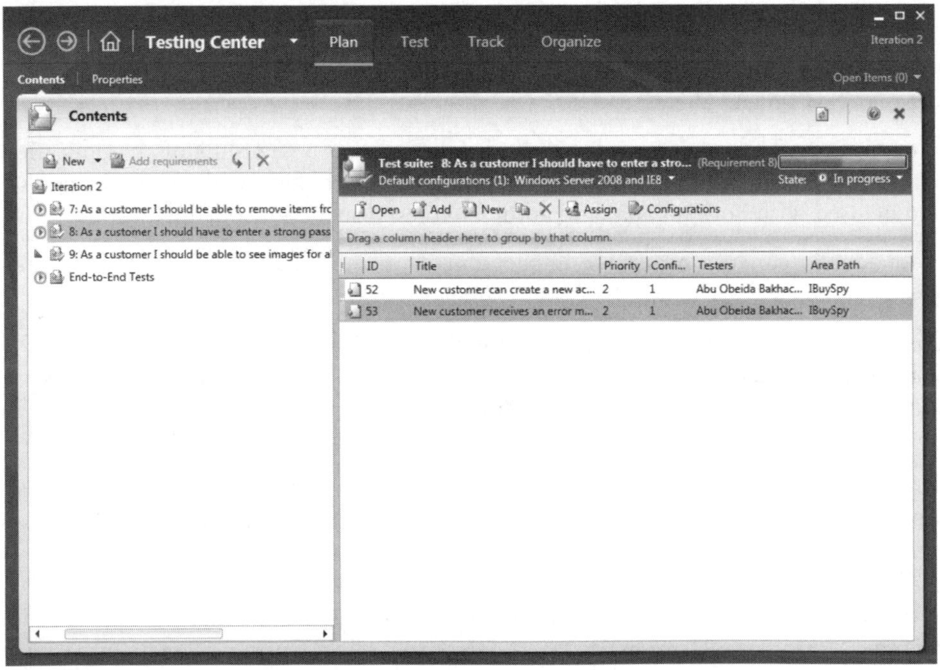

FIGURE 12-1

You will become familiar with using Microsoft Test Manager in Chapters 14 and 16.

> *Even if you aren't making use of the manual testing or lab management capabilities of Visual Studio 2010, you may wish to use Microsoft Test Manager to create and manage your test plans. As you will see in Chapter 14, test plans can include automated tests (for example, unit tests, coded UI tests, and so on), in addition to manual tests. Organizing automated tests into test plans is an effective way of tracking the overall status of your testing efforts.*

MANAGING AUTOMATED TESTS WITH VISUAL STUDIO

With the exception of manual tests (which are represented as work items within Team Foundation Server), all other test types within Visual Studio are stored as source code files. These tests are usually authored with Visual Studio, stored within source control (such as Team Foundation Server), and are tracked as essential artifacts of your development project. As your project grows, so should the suite of tests you write, which can help you verify the expanded functionality of your software.

Because these tests are so critical to project success, it is not uncommon for projects to have dozens, sometimes even hundreds or thousands, of tests. Fortunately, Visual Studio offers ways to organize and execute tests. In this chapter, you will learn how to use those features to work effectively with your application's tests, whether you have 5 or 5,000 tests to manage.

You will begin by learning about *test projects*, a special project type that you can use to contain your automated tests. You will learn about the creation of test projects, as well as the various options you can specify when a new test project is created.

Then, you will discover the Test View window and how to group your tests into test categories. Test categories offer effective ways to organize and execute the tests contained in your solutions.

You will learn about the management of test results. The Test Results window is described in detail. The files used to store test run results, called *TRX files*, are also discussed. You will learn how to export and import test run results and how to publish test run results to Team Foundation Server for tracking and reporting purposes.

Finally, an additional test type called an *ordered test* is introduced. Ordered tests are essentially containers of other tests, offering a convenient way to group and execute tests in a specified order.

Test Projects

Visual Studio offers a project template called a "Test Project." Projects of this type provide a convenient way to store automated tests. You may decide to have all of the tests in your test project be of one type, or you may mix different types of tests within the same test project.

Placing your tests in a test project has the additional benefit of keeping them separate from your implementation code, reducing the risk that you'll accidentally deploy test code to your production environment.

Creating a Test Project

There are a number of ways to create a new test project. You can create a test project before you create any tests, or you can create one as you are creating a new test.

To create a new test project within Visual Studio you can right-click on an existing solution and choose Add ⇨ New Project. You may also use the File menu by selecting Add ⇨ New Project. You will see the Add New Project dialog, as shown in Figure 12-2.

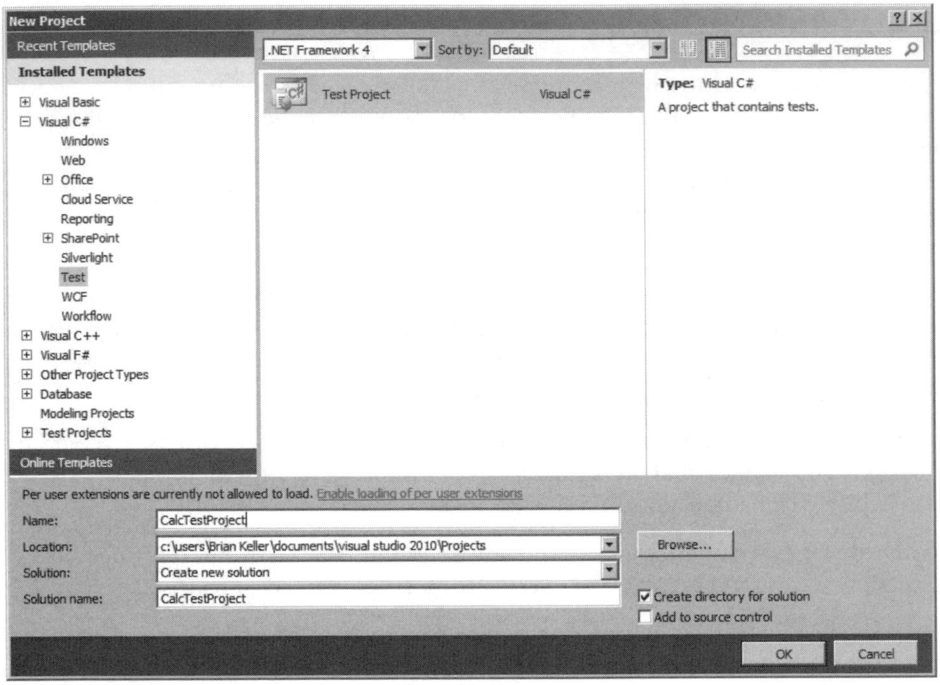

FIGURE 12-2

Under Installed Templates, choose the Test category under the language you wish to use for your tests (either Visual Basic or Visual C#). Select Test Project from the Templates list, and assign a name to your project. If you do not already have a solution, you will be able to create one here.

When creating tests, Visual Studio will offer to automatically create a test project for you if you do not already have one.

When your test project is created, Visual Studio adds three files to your solution's Solution Items folder. Two of these files are default *test settings*. These files have an extension of `.testsettings`. These files contain the various settings that determine how your tests will be executed. You can double-click on these file to display those settings. Test settings are covered later in this chapter in the "Test Settings" section.

The other file, known as the *test metadata file*, is also XML-based and is named `<ProjectName>` `.vsmdi`. This file stores information about your solution's test lists and links to any contained tests. Double-clicking this file will open the Test List Editor. Note, however, that test lists have been deprecated in this version of Visual Studio and replaced by test categories. Test categories are covered later in this chapter.

> *The one area of Visual Studio 2010 where test lists are still required is when working with Team Foundation Server check-in policies, which require test lists. If you find that you need to create a test list, see the product help topic titled "How to: Create a Test List."*

Setting Test Project Options

You may notice that the test project you have created is not empty. By default, a sample unit test file is included with your test project, and you can configure templates for other test types to be included by default as well. These can serve as a helpful starting point as you add your tests, but you can safely delete them if you choose. To change what types of files are added to a new test project, select Tools ⇨ Options. On the resulting Options dialog, expand the Test Tools category and select Test Project. You will see options as shown in Figure 12-3.

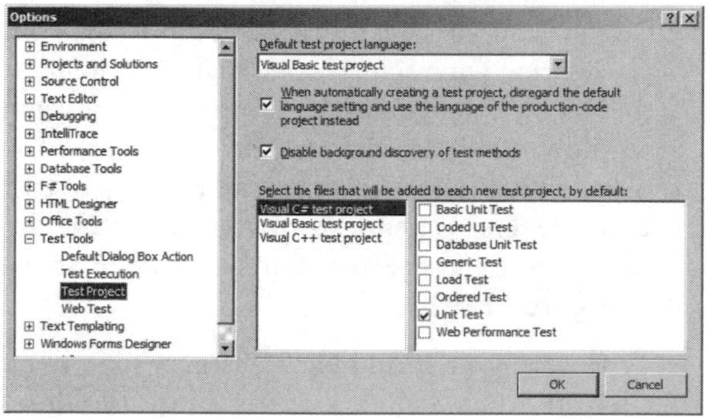

FIGURE 12-3

You may set the default language for new test projects using the drop-down list at the top. This setting will save you some time later, because you will not need to choose the language each time you create a new test project, though you always have the option to override this setting.

Below that, you will see a list of file types organized by test project language. Notice that several file types are already selected for you. The types of files that are automatically included can be specified by language type. For example, you may wish that Visual Basic test projects are always created empty, while your C# test projects include a sample unit test file. Select which files you wish to include, if any, and click OK.

Using Test Categories

As you start to use the variety of test types supported by Visual Studio, you may quickly find yourself with many tests in your solutions. Visual Studio projects can have hundreds or thousands of unit tests alone. Add suites of Web performance, load, and other tests and you could quickly have difficulty finding the right tests at the right time.

Fortunately, Visual Studio allows you to organize your tests using test categories. The Test View window is your main interface for organizing and executing your tests using test categories.

Test View

To access Test View, select Test ⇨ Windows ⇨ Test View, or click the Test View button on the Test Tools toolbar. You will then see a window similar to that shown in Figure 12-4.

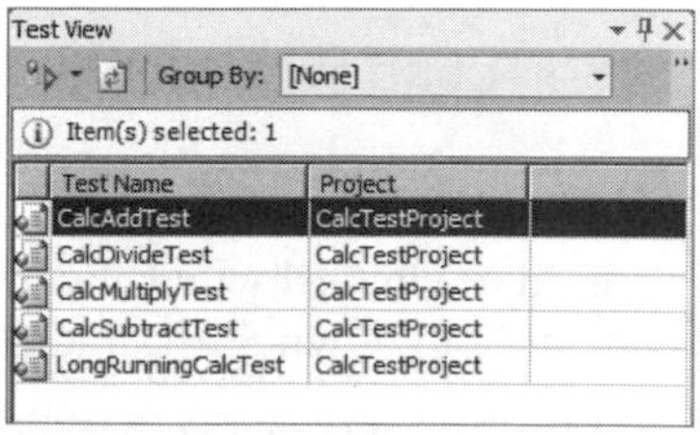

By default, Test View does not display the test categories property that you will use to classify your tests. To add this column, right-click on a test (or in the whitespace of this window), and select Add/Remove Columns. Add the Test Categories column and click OK.

FIGURE 12-4

The Test Categories column should now be visible within the Test View, but unless you have previously categorized your tests, this column will be empty. Categorize your first test by highlighting it from the Test View list and examining the Properties window (or right-click the test and select Properties, if your Properties window isn't already open). Find the Test Categories row and click the dotted ellipsis to open the Test Category editor shown in Figure 12-5.

Type **BVT** into the Add New Category textbox, and click on Add to define your first category. Click OK and notice that the test you selected now has a value of BVT in the Test Categories column of the Test View window. Note that you can assign a test to multiple categories if you wish.

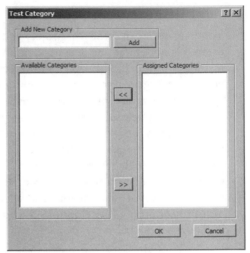

FIGURE 12-5

 The term BVT is short for "built verification test." A BVT should be an automated test that can run fairly quickly without user interaction or additional set-up work. BVTs can be used to help you quickly determine whether basic functionality is working. These can be run locally by a developer and can also be scripted to run as part of an automated build (see Chapter 21).

Double-click on that test to open the test within the code editor. You should notice that the test now has a new attribute denoting that it is part of the BVT category, such as the following:

```
[TestCategory("BVT"), TestMethod]
public void TestDivision()
...
```

You can also categorize a test by manually adding this attribute to the desired tests. If you use this approach, you must first save the file and then click the Refresh button within Test View for changes to take effect.

Selecting and Running Tests

Selecting and executing tests in Test View is simple. Just highlight one or more tests and click the Run Tests button. You can also right-click and choose Run Selection. To select multiple tests, hold down Ctrl while clicking on each test. To select a group of consecutive tests, click the first test, hold down Shift, and click on the last test.

The Run button also has a drop-down to select Debug Selection. Running your tests in debug mode can be helpful for debugging possible errors in your test logic. You can set breakpoints, add variables to your watch window, and perform all of the same debugging operations that you would against your actual application.

You can also filter the Test View by clicking the drop-down labeled [All Columns] and selecting the column you wish to filter by. Next, type the keyword that matches the filter you wish to apply. For example, you can select the Test Categories column, type **BVT,** and press Enter to show just the tests which are in a BVT category.

As the number of tests in your solution grows, test categories can be an effective means of focusing your test runs on the most important set of tests to run as you make routine code changes. Be sure to run all of your tests occasionally, but running all of your tests with every change can be time-consuming, and can interrupt your flow while programming. Later in this chapter, you will also learn how to discover which tests to run based on the most recent changes you made to your project (see the section, "Test Impact View").

> *You can also use the Test List Editor window to view, sort, filter, and manage your tests using test categories or test lists. But since test lists are deprecated in this release of Visual Studio, the recommended approach is to stick with the Test View window.*

Working with Test Results

This section shows how the Test Results window displays the progress and final outcome of test runs. You'll also learn about the secondary uses of the Test Results windows, including exporting and publishing test results.

Test Results Window

When a test run is started, the Test Results window is shown, displaying the current status of the run. Each test will update automatically, and you can use the control buttons to affect the run, even before it is complete. Click the Pause button to temporarily suspend test execution, or click Stop to abort the test run. Whether you pause or stop a run, you will be able to view the results of any completed tests.

As an example, Figure 12-6 shows the Test Results window for a sample test run of four unit tests.

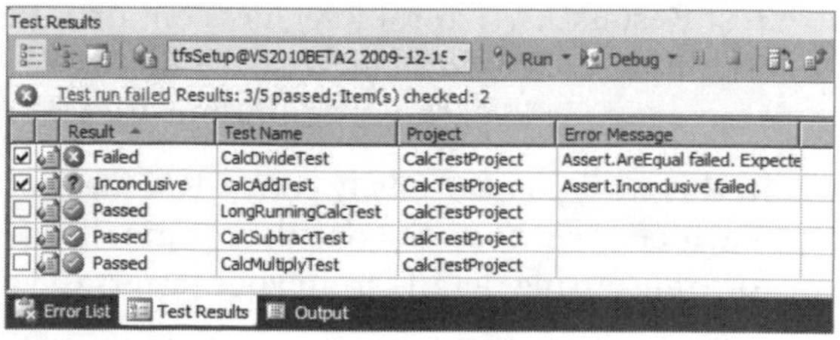

In Figure 12-6, the summary text says, "Results: 3/5 passed. Item(s) checked: 2." You can access additional details about the test run by clicking on the Run Details button on the Test Results toolbar (the fourth icon from the left). The Run Details will show details about the run start and stop time, the test settings used, and the user who submitted the run.

FIGURE 12-6

Simply double-click any test to see the detailed results for that test run. For tests that did not pass, you may see additional details such as the error message and a stack trace for the test failure. You can also right-click and choose Open Test to edit each test.

As you have seen with the Test View window, the Run button has a drop-down to select other options, including Debug.

You may notice that the Failed and Inconclusive test results automatically have their checkboxes checked, while the two tests that passed do not. This is to enable the quick rerunning of tests that did not pass. Simply click the Run button and the checked tests will be executed.

Sorting, Grouping, and Filtering Tests Results

The Test Results window supports exactly the same functionality for sorting, grouping, and filtering results that the Test View window does.

Click on any column header to sort by ascending value, and again for descending. You can also right-click and choose Add/Remove Columns to modify which columns are displayed.

You can use the Group By, Filter Column, and Filter Text fields on the right-hand side of the Test Results window's toolbar. For example, you might choose to filter your test results based on a particular test category.

Exporting Test Results

By default, whenever a test is run, statistics on that run are automatically stored in a file on disk. These files are XML files with an extension of .trx. These files are used to store information about which tests were run, when they ran, statistics on that run, and details about the results.

You can use the Test Results window to manually export test run results. To export all results from the current run, click the Export Results button. (By hovering your mouse cursor over the icons on the toolbar, you can see the tooltips indicating the names of each button.) You can choose to export a subset of test results, perhaps only for tests that failed, by pressing the arrow on the Export Results button and choosing Export Selected Test Results.

Note, however, that these files can contain a lot of data, especially if you have many tests or have any long-running load tests.

Using Test Results XML (TRX) Files

Test Results XML (or TRX) files contain all of the details for selected test runs. Visual Studio establishes a Windows file association for the .trx extension, so double-clicking on such a file will automatically load those results into Visual Studio, where the details can be viewed.

In this way, you can easily copy TRX files between systems to view results with full details on a machine other than the one that originally executed the tests. For example, you may find this useful for transferring details from your testers to your developers.

You can also use the Test Results window to manually import a TRX file to view its contents. Click the Import Test Results button on the Test Results toolbar and then select the correct TRX file. If the contained run is already loaded in the IDE, then you will see an error message. Otherwise, you will be able to view the results and details from that exported test run.

The following section describes a more powerful option available to you: *publishing*.

Publishing Results

Exporting test results will store the data in a local TRX file. However, if you have a Team Foundation Server instance configured, you can send those test results to it through a process called *publishing*.

Publishing your run data is vital to your project's success, because it enables your team to view and track testing metrics over time. Published data can be queried through various reports, such as Quality Indicators, Code Coverage Details, and Test Run Details. Publishing test results also allows you to create bugs that reference the results of your tests, including any diagnostic data collected during your test run.

Before you can publish results, you must be connected to a Team Foundation Server instance. In addition, that instance must have at least one Team Build definition configured because published results are associated with a specific build. Because run data is associated with a specific build, you can determine the quality of each build by reviewing the test run data for each to identify trends. Team Build is described in detail in Chapter 21.

To publish a test run, click the Publish button located near the center of the toolbar in the Test Results window. When you click this button, you will see the Publish Test Results dialog shown in Figure 12-7.

If the Publish button is disabled, ensure that you are connected to a Team Foundation instance, and that your team project has at least one build definition.

Choose one or more test runs to publish. You can then select the build with which to associate the run data. Finally, you can choose to include any code coverage data. Click OK and your results will be published. You will see the Publish View mode of the Test Results window, with details about each publication, including the status and any error message.

When your publication shows a status of Completed, your data has been saved to the operational store for your team project.

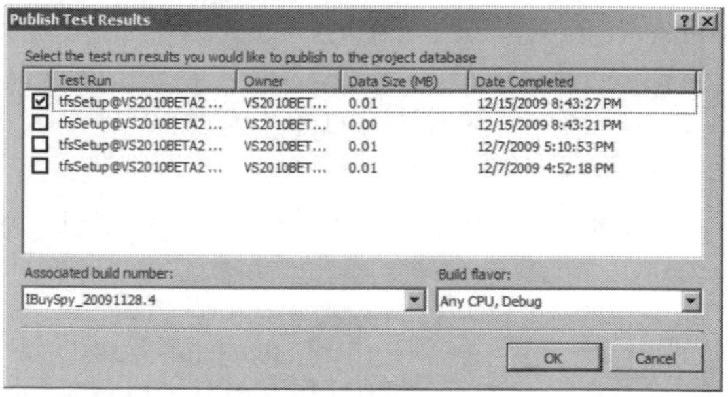

FIGURE 12-7

Published data is not immediately available for reporting. The data can be queried once it has been pulled into the data warehouse. This is done automatically at a frequency you can set in your Team Foundation Server instance.

You can also publish test run data from the command line using the MSTest console application. See Chapter 13 for more details on command-line testing.

Using Ordered Tests

You've already seen how test categories can be used to easily organize your tests. However, sometimes you need more control over the members of a test group. Another type of test that Visual Studio supports is the *ordered test*. An ordered test is simply composed of other logically related tests. You can add one or more tests as members of an ordered test. You can also arrange those tests to execute in a specific sequence. In addition, the same test can be added to an ordered test multiple times.

> *Don't feel constrained by the term "test" when creating your test suites. There may be perfectly valid cases when a "test" doesn't actually test anything. Perhaps you've created a utility method that erases your customer table. Create a unit test to call this method and add it to your ordered test wherever you need that table reset.*

Being able to specify the order of test execution (as well as including a test more than once) has a wide variety of applications. For example, you may have a Create User test that, after execution, adds a new user to your database. Your next test, Log User In, may rely on the existence of that new user. By ordering your tests, you ensure that the first test successfully creates the user before the second test attempts to log in that user.

Creating an Ordered Test

An ordered test is simply another type of test, so you create ordered tests much the same way as other tests. Right-click on your test project and select Add ➪ Ordered Test. You will see the Ordered Test Editor, as shown in Figure 12-8.

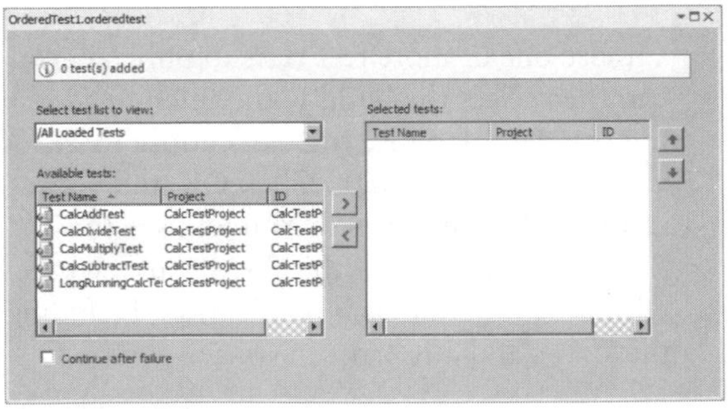

Using the right and left arrow buttons, add one or more of the tests to the ordered test. The list of tests includes the tests from all projects in the current solution. Multiple tests can be added at the same time by holding the Ctrl key while clicking on each test. As mentioned before, the same test can be added more than once.

FIGURE 12-8

You may order the execution of the contained tests by adjusting their position with the up and down arrow buttons. The test at the top of the list will be executed first, proceeding sequentially down the list.

One of the key features of an ordered test is that tests run one at a time in a specified sequence. Using the "Continue after failure" checkbox, you can indicate whether the ordered test continues to process remaining tests if a test should fail. By default, this is unchecked, indicating that the ordered test will abort when any test fails. Check the box to cause the ordered test to always execute all contained tests, regardless of success.

Ordered Test Properties

Find your ordered test in Test View. Right-click and select Properties. You will see the Properties window containing the values for your ordered test, similar to what is shown in Figure 12-9.

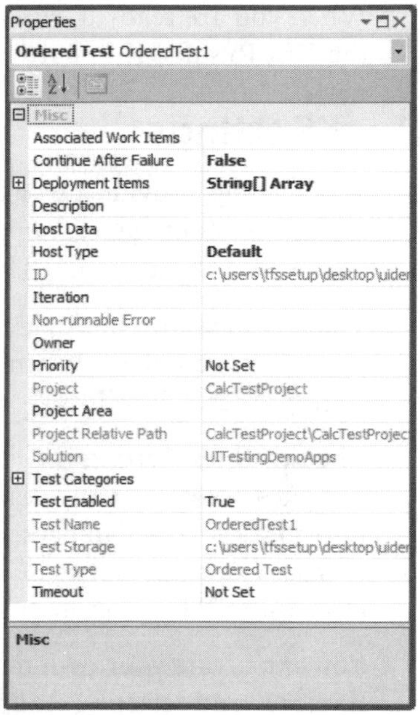

You can set the test's Description and temporarily disable the test via the Test Enabled property. Other properties include Timeout (which indicates how long the test should run before failing) and the Continue After Failure property, described in the previous section.

Executing and Analyzing Ordered Tests

An ordered test is executed just like other tests. You can use the Test View window. You can also use the command-line tool, MSTest.exe, as described in Chapter 14.

When executed from Visual Studio, the Test Results window will activate, displaying progress as the test is executing, and results when it is complete. The following example has an ordered test with four contained tests. As shown in Figure 12-10, the test has been run, but failed.

Notice that the Test Results window indicates "2/5 passed." The ordered test contained four inner tests, but the ordered test itself counts as a test with regard to success or failure. Right-click on the ordered test in the Test Results window and select View Test Results Details. The main window will display Common Results and Contained Tests.

The Common Results show the overall status of the ordered test, including the start and end time and the ultimate result.

However, in this case, you might be interested in finding out what happened with the individual tests contained in the ordered test. The Contained Tests section displays each of the contained tests, along with their type, name, result, and how long the test ran.

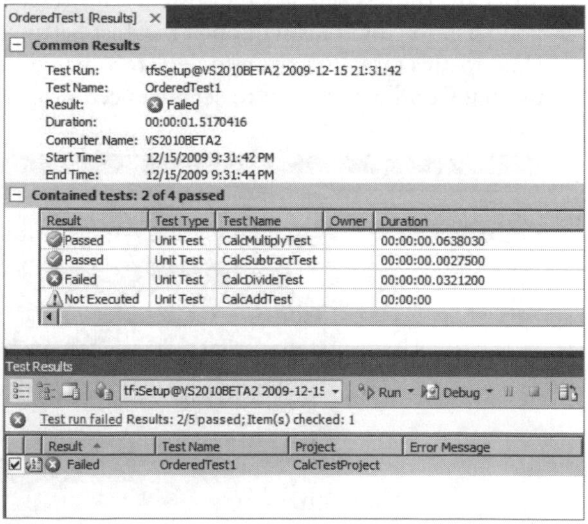

FIGURE 12-9

FIGURE 12-10

You can see that the first two tests have passed. However, the third test, CalcDivideTest, did not pass. Because the test's Continue After Failure property was set to False, the remaining fourth test was not executed. Double-click on any inner test to see details for that test. In this example, it probably would have been better to enable "Continue after failure," since these tests aren't strictly dependent on one another. However, if you are using ordered tests to represent (for example) a Web site workflow of account creation, account login, account activity, and account logout, then the rest of the tests in the sequence probably don't need to be run if the initial account creation fails.

When you are ready to run the test again, you can repeat the selection process via Test View, or use the Test Results' Run button.

Test Settings

Test settings provide a way of defining how tests are executed within Visual Studio. Such settings include timeout values, remote execution settings, and the diagnostic data adapters you wish to enable (see the section "Diagnostic Data Adapters," earlier in this chapter).

You can maintain multiple test settings files and switch among them based on the type of testing you wish to conduct. When you created your test project, Visual Studio created two default test settings files. Click Test ⇨ Select Active Test Settings to set the test setting that you want to use.

The Local test setting is designed to run with minimal overhead and produces smaller TRX files, but does not collect any diagnostic data. The Trace and Test Impact test setting enables the System information, Trace impact, and IntelliTrace data adapters. Consider using the Local test setting for everyday testing, and switch to the Trace and Test Impact test setting if you need to file a bug from test results. This way, additional diagnostic data will be available, along with the bug you are filing.

You can create your own test settings file by right-clicking on Solution Items within Solution Explorer and selecting Add ⇨ New Item. Under the installed templates, select Test Settings and provide your Test Settings file with a name. Click Add when finished.

You can edit test settings files by clicking Test ⇨ Edit Test Settings and selecting the settings file you wish to edit. This will open the Test Settings editor shown in Figure 12-11. The Data and Diagnostics tab allows you to declare which diagnostics data adapters should be enabled. You can use the Configure button to set advanced properties for some of the adapters.

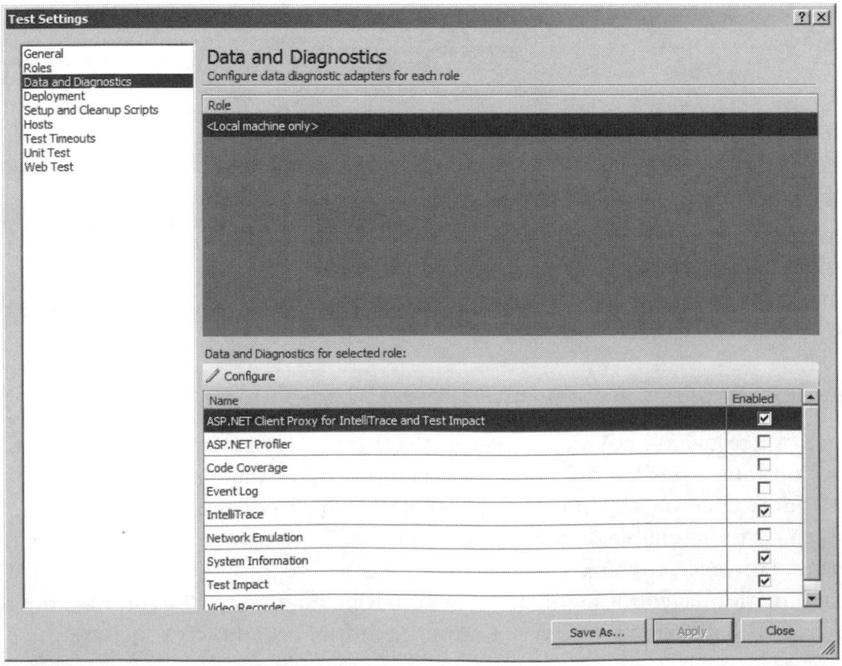

FIGURE 12-11

You can also configure test settings to collect data from remote machines that are part of your test environment. For example, you might be running a test locally that makes a call to an application running on a remote Web server. You can configure Visual Studio to collect data from both the local and remote machines. To do this, you would install a Test Agent on the remote machine(s) and connect these to a Test Controller. Then, use the Roles tab within the test settings editor. You will learn more about configure Test Controllers and Test Agents in Chapter 13.

Test Impact View

As the number of tests in your project grows, so will the amount of time it takes to run those tests. Running all of your tests every time you make changes to your code can hinder productivity. But choosing to not run tests frequently enough can cause code defects to go unnoticed.

One solution to this tradeoff lies in a new feature available in Visual Studio 2010 called *test impact analysis*. Test impact analysis can analyze managed code execution (such as C#, Visual Basic, managed C++) and keep track of which methods are executed when each test is run. By keeping track of which methods get called for each test, test impact analysis can then present a list of tests that you should consider running again when a given method or methods have changed.

To utilize test impact analysis you must first run your tests with the Test Impact diagnostic data adapter enabled in your test settings. See the previous section, "Test Settings," for more details on working with test settings and diagnostic data adapters. You should next run all of your tests with test impact analysis enabled in order to establish a baseline of test impact data.

Now, open the Test Impact View within Visual Studio by clicking Test ➪ Windows ➪ Test Impact View. The next time you build your project or solution, test impact analysis will examine the method(s) that have changed. Any tests that may be impacted by changes to your code since the last time the test was run (and passed) will be shown in the Test Impact View, as shown in Figure 12-12.

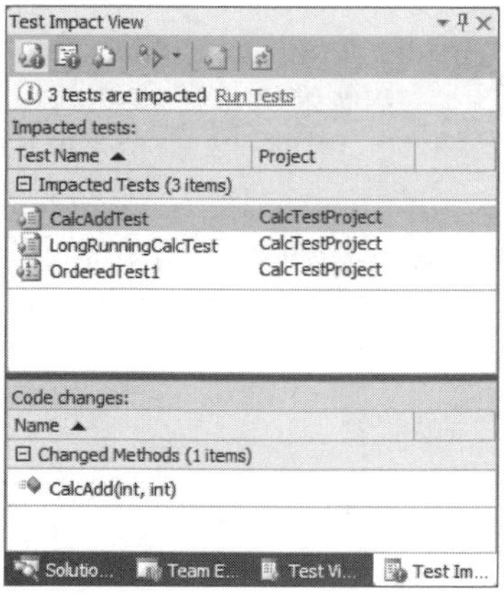

In this example, the `CalcAdd()` method has changed, and test impact analysis has detected that there are three tests within your solution that you should consider running again. You can choose to run only the impacted tests by clicking on the down arrow next to the Run Tests icon (the fourth icon from the left), and selecting Run All Impacted Tests. This will reset the baseline of test impact analysis data to indicate that all impacted tests have been run since the last time you made changes.

FIGURE 12-12

Test impact analysis is a powerful feature that can help improve code quality and developer productivity. But it shouldn't be used as a substitute for occasionally running all of the tests within your solution. Test impact analysis can't always catch all of the changes that may lead to entropy within your software project. For example, you may have tests that are driven by external data sources, or that interact with other systems outside of your solution. Since test impact analysis is only aware of the changes within the managed code in your solution, it is a good idea to routinely run the rest of your tests even if they don't appear in the Test Impact View.

In Chapter 14 you will learn how to utilize test impact analysis when deciding which manual tests to run.

SUMMARY

This chapter covered details about testing in Visual Studio 2010. You learned about the various types of tests, diagnostic data adapters, and tools for working with tests. You learned about test projects and how to configure the defaults for test projects you create.

You then learned about the Test View window and how to use test categories to group your tests.

You also learned how to work with the Test Results window, how to export and import test run results to TRX files, as well as how to publish those results to your Team Foundation Server instance for reporting and bug-filing purposes.

You learned about how to use ordered tests to group other tests together to be run as a unit. Contained tests are executed in a specified order, and you can optionally indicate that you want the test to abort when any test fails.

You learned about the important role that test settings play in determining how tests are run, and which data gets collected during test runs.

Finally, you learned how test impact analysis can help you focus on running the tests that are most likely to have been impacted based on recent changes to your source code.

The details covered in this chapter should prepare you to effectively manage and orchestrate the testing of your Visual Studio projects. Whether your project has just a few or many hundreds of tests, using the tools and techniques described in this chapter will help you to achieve success.

In Chapter 13, you will learn about how Web performance tests can be used to help speed up your Web applications. You will also learn how to simulate the results of hundreds (or even thousands) of users interacting with your Web application by using Visual Studio's load-testing capabilities.

13

Web Performance and Load Testing

WHAT'S IN THIS CHAPTER?

➤ Learning how to use Web performance tests to simulate user activity on your Web site

➤ Testing the capability of your Web site to accommodate multiple simultaneous users with load testing

➤ Understanding how to analyze the results of your Web performance tests and load tests to identify performance and scalability bottlenecks

This chapter continues coverage of the testing features of Visual Studio 2010 by describing Web performance and load tests.

With Web performance testing, you can easily build a suite of repeatable tests that can help you analyze the performance of your Web applications and identify potential bottlenecks. Visual Studio enables you to easily create a Web performance test by recording your actions as you use your Web application. In this chapter, you will learn how to create, edit, and run Web performance tests, and how to execute and analyze the results.

Sometimes you need more flexibility than a recorded Web performance test can offer. In this chapter, you will learn how to use coded Web performance tests to create flexible and powerful Web performance tests using Visual Basic or C# and how to leverage the Web performance testing framework.

Verifying that an application is ready for production involves additional analysis. How will your application behave when many people begin using it concurrently? The load-testing features of Visual Studio enable you to execute one or more tests repeatedly, tracking the performance of the target system. The second half of this chapter examines how to load test with the Load Test Wizard, and how to use the information Visual Studio collects to identify problems before users do.

Finally, because a single machine may not be able to generate enough load to simulate the number of users an application will have in production, you'll learn how to configure your environment to run *distributed load tests*. A distributed load test enables you to spread the work of creating user load across multiple machines, called *agents*. Details from each agent are collected by a controller machine, enabling you to see the overall performance of your application under stress.

WEB PERFORMANCE TESTS

Web performance tests enable verification that a Web application's behavior is correct. They issue an ordered series of HTTP/HTTPS requests against a target Web application, and analyze each response for expected behaviors. You can use the integrated Web Test Recorder to create a test by observing your interaction with a target Web site through a browser window. Once the test is recorded, you can use that Web performance test to consistently repeat those recorded actions against the target Web application.

Web performance tests offer automatic processing of redirects, dependent requests, and hidden fields, including `ViewState`. In addition, coded Web performance tests can be written in Visual Basic or C#, enabling you to take full advantage of the power and flexibility of these languages.

> *Although you will likely use Web performance tests with ASP.NET Web applications, you are not required to do so. In fact, while some features are specific to testing ASP.NET applications, any Web application can be tested via a Web performance test, including applications based on classic ASP or even non-Microsoft technologies.*

Later in this chapter, you will learn how to add your Web performance tests to load tests to ensure that a Web application behaves as expected when many users access it concurrently.

Web Performance Tests Versus Coded UI Tests

At first glance, the capabilities of Web performance tests may appear similar to those of coded user interface (UI) tests (see Chapter 15). But while some capabilities do overlap (for example, record and playback, response validation), the two types of tests are designed to achieve different testing goals and should be applied appropriately. Web performance tests should be used primarily for performance testing, and can be used as the basis for generating load tests. Coded UI tests should be used for ensuring proper UI behavior and layout. Coded UI tests cannot be easily used to conduct load testing. Conversely, while Web performance tests can be programmed to perform simple validation of responses, coded UI tests are much better suited for this task.

In versions of Visual Studio prior to 2010, Web performance tests were known simply as Web tests. The revised name reflects Microsoft's desire to position such tests as being more adequate for conducting performance testing, while UI validation is better suited to coded UI tests.

Creating a Sample Web Application

Before creating a Web performance test, you'll need a Web application to test. While you could create a Web performance test by interacting with any live Web site such as Microsoft.com, Facebook, or YouTube, those sites will change and will likely not be the same by the time you read this chapter. Therefore, the remainder of this chapter is based on a Web site created with the Personal Web Site Starter Kit.

The Personal Web Site Starter Kit is a sample ASP.NET application provided by Microsoft. The Personal Web Site Starter Kit first shipped with Visual Studio 2005 and ASP.NET 2.0, but there is a version which is compatible with Visual Studio 2010 and ASP.NET 4.0 at the Web site for this title. If you intend to follow along with the sample provided in this chapter, first visit www.wrox.com to download and install the Personal Web Site Starter Kit project template.

Once you have downloaded and installed the Personal Web Site Starter Kit project template, you must create an instance of this Web site. Open Visual Studio 2010 and click File ➪ New Web Site. Select the language you want to work in (Visual C# or Visual Basic). Choose Personal Web Site Starter Kit, enter the name **SampleWeb**, and then click OK.

Visual Studio will then create a new Web site, with full support for users and authentication and features such as a photo album, links, and a place for a resume.

This site will become the basis of some recorded Web performance tests. Later, you will assemble these Web performance tests into a load test in order to put stress on this site to determine how well it will perform when hundreds of friends and family members converge simultaneously to view your photos.

Creating Users for the Site

Before you create tests for your Web site, you must create a few users for the site. You'll do this using the Web Site Administration Tool that is included with ASP.NET applications created with Visual Studio.

Select Website ➪ ASP.NET Configuration. On the resulting page, select Security, and then Create or Manage Roles. Enter **Administrators** as the role name, and then click Add Role. Repeat this process to add a role named **Friends**.

The first time the site is run, the application start event will also create these roles for you.

You now have two roles into which users can be placed. Click the Security tab again, and then click Create user. You will then see the window shown in Figure 13-1.

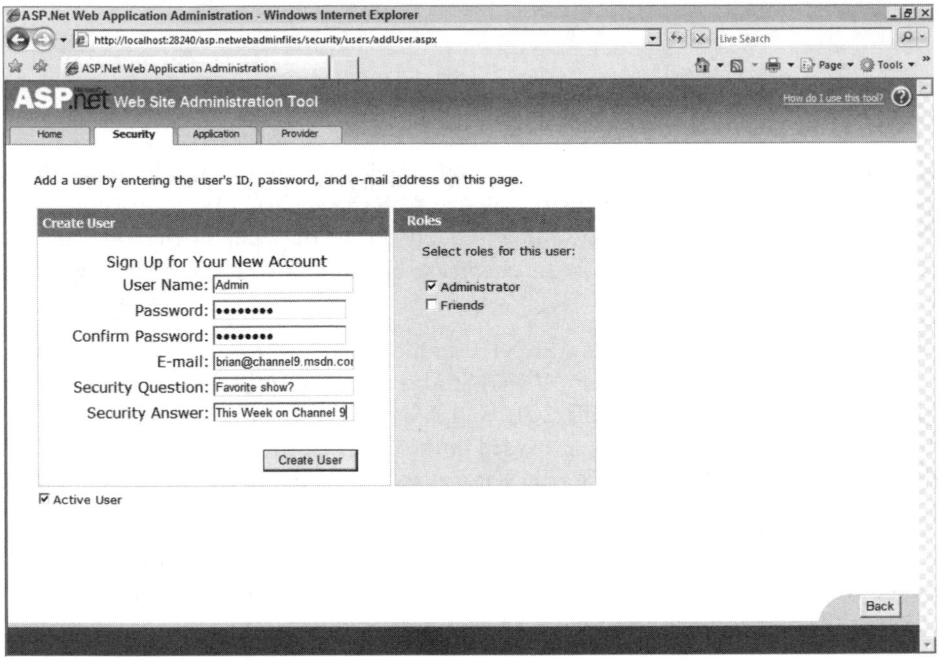

FIGURE 13-1

Your tests will assume the following users have been created:

➤ *Admin* — In the Administrator role

➤ *Sue* — In the Friends role

➤ *Daniel* — In the Friends role

➤ *Andrew* — In the Friends role

For purposes of this example, enter **@qwerty@** for the Password of each user, and any values you want for the E-mail and Security Question fields.

Configuring the Sample Application for Testing

It is common (but certainly not required) to run Web performance tests against a Web site hosted on the local development machine. If you are testing against a remote machine, you must create a virtual directory or Web site, and deploy your sample application. You may also choose to create a virtual directory on your local machine.

Visual Studio includes a feature called the ASP.NET Development Server. This is a lightweight Web server, similar to (but not the same as) IIS, that chooses a port and temporarily hosts a local ASP.NET application. The hosted application accepts only local requests, and is torn down when Visual Studio exits.

The Development Server defaults to selecting a random port each time the application is started. To execute Web performance tests, you'd have to manually adjust the port each time it was assigned. To address this, you have two options.

The first option is to select your ASP.NET project and choose the Properties window. Change the Use Dynamic Ports property to `false`, and then select a port number, such as 5000. You can then hard-code this port number into your local Web performance tests.

The second (and more flexible) option is to use a special value, called a *context parameter*, which will automatically adjust itself to match the server, port, and directory of the target Web application. You'll learn how to do this shortly.

Later in this chapter, you'll see that, unlike Web performance tests, load tests are typically run against sites hosted on machines other than those conducting tests.

Creating and Configuring Web Tests

There are three main methods for creating Web performance tests. The first (and, by far, the most common) is to use the Web Test Recorder. This is the recommended way of getting started with Web performance testing, and is the approach discussed in this chapter. The second method is to create a test manually, using the Web Test Editor to add each step. Using this approach is time-consuming and error-prone, but may be desired for fine-tuning Web performance tests. Finally, you can create a coded Web performance test that specifies each action via code, and offers a great deal of customization. You can also generate a coded Web performance test from an existing Web performance test. Coded Web performance tests are described later in this chapter.

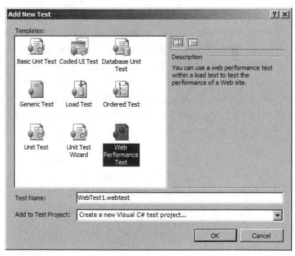

To create a new Web performance test, you may either create a test project beforehand, or allow one to be created for you. If you already have a test project, right-click it and select Add ➪ New Test. If you don't have a test project, choose Test ➪ New Test. You will see the Add New Test dialog, as shown in Figure 13-2.

FIGURE 13-2

You have several test types from which to choose. Select Web Performance Test and give your test a name. Web performance tests are stored as XML files with a `.webtest` extension.

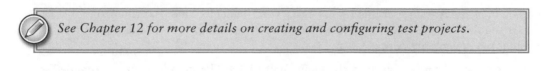

See Chapter 12 for more details on creating and configuring test projects.

After clicking OK, you will be prompted to provide a name for your new test project. For this example, use **SampleWebTestProject** and click Create.

> *Once you have a test project, you can quickly create other Web performance tests by right-clicking on your test project and selecting Add ⇨ Web Performance Test. This automatically creates a new Web performance test with default settings, named* WebTest1.webtest *(incrementing the number if that name already exists), and launches the Web Test Recorder within your browser.*

Recording a Web Performance Test

Once your Web performance test is created, an instance of Internet Explorer will be launched with an integrated Web Test Recorder docked window. Begin by typing the URL of the application you wish to test. For the SampleWeb application on a local machine, this will be something like http://localhost:5000/SampleWeb/default.aspx. Remember that supplying a port number is only necessary if you're using the built-in ASP.NET Development Server, and is generally not necessary when using IIS.

The ASP.NET Development Server must also be running before you can navigate to your site. If it isn't already running (as indicated by an icon in the taskbar notification area), you can start it by selecting your SampleWeb project in Visual Studio and pressing Ctrl + F5. This will build and launch your Personal Web Site project in a new browser instance. Take note of the URL being used, including the port number. You may now close this new browser instance (the Development Server will keep running) and return to the browser instance that was launched when you created a new Web test (with the Web Test Recorder docked window). Enter the URL for your Personal Web Site into this browser instance. Be sure to include the default.aspx portion of the URL (using the pattern shown in the previous paragraph).

> *If you don't see the Web Test Recorder within Internet Explorer at this time, then you might be encountering one of the known issues documented at Mike Taute's blog. See* http://tinyurl.com/9okwqp *for a list of troubleshooting steps and possible fixes.*

Recording a Web performance test is straightforward. Using your Web browser, simply use the Web application as if you were a normal user. Visual Studio automatically records your actions, saving them to the Web performance test.

First, log in as the Admin user (but do not check the "Remember me next time" option). The browser should refresh, showing a "Welcome Admin!" greeting. This is only a short test, so click Logout at the upper-right corner.

Your browser should now appear as shown in Figure 13-3. The steps have been expanded so you can see the details of the Form Post Parameters that were recorded automatically for you.

You'll learn more about these later in this chapter, but, for now, notice that the second request automatically includes `ViewState`, as well as the Username and Password form fields you used to log in.

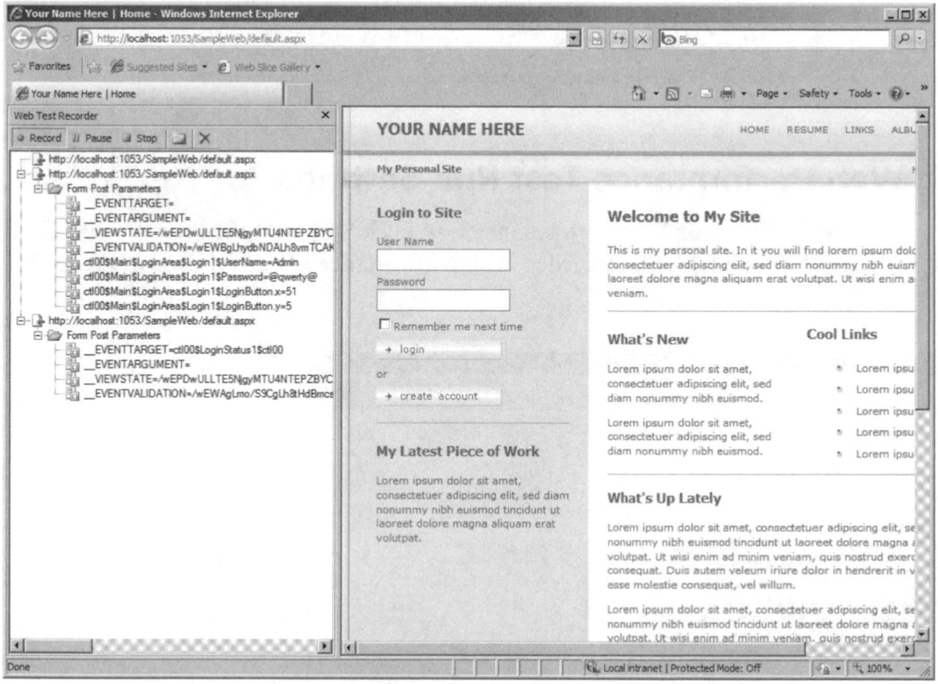

FIGURE 13-3

> *The Web Test Recorder will capture any HTTP/HTTPS traffic sent or received by your instance of Internet Explorer as soon as it is launched. This includes your browser's home page, and may include certain browser add-ins and toolbars that send data. For pristine recordings, you should set your Internet Explorer home page to be blank, and disable any add-ins or toolbars that generate excess noise.*

The Web Test Recorder provides several options that may be useful while recording. The Pause button in the upper-left corner temporarily suspends recording and timing of your interaction with the browser, enabling you to use the application or get a cup of coffee without affecting your Web performance test. You will learn more about the importance of timing of your Web performance test later, as this can affect playback conditions. Click the X button if you want to clear your recorded list. The other button, Add a Comment, enables you to add documentation to your Web performance test, perhaps at a complex step. These comments are very useful when you convert a Web performance test to a coded Web performance test, as you'll see later.

> *Calls to Web pages are normally composed of a main request followed by a number of dependent requests. These dependent requests are sent separately to obtain items such as graphics, script sources, and stylesheets. The Web Test Recorder does not display these dependent requests explicitly while recording. You'll see later that all dependent requests are determined and processed automatically when the Web test is run.*

Configuring Web Performance Test Run Settings

When you're finished recording your Web performance test, click Stop and the browser will close, displaying the Web Test Editor with your recorded Web performance test, as shown in Figure 13-4.

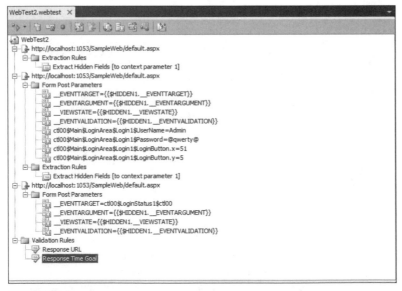

FIGURE 13-4

The Web Test Editor displays your test as a series of requests to be sent to the Web application. The first request is the initial page being loaded. The second request is the login request being sent. And the third request is the logout request.

Frequently, you'll need to use the Web Test Editor to change settings or add features to the tests you record. This may include adding validation, extracting data from Web responses, and reading data from a source. These topics are covered later in this chapter, but, for now, you'll use this test as recorded.

Parameterizing the Web Server

You may recall from the earlier section "Configuring the Sample Application for Testing," that using the ASP.NET Development Server, while convenient, poses a slight challenge because the port it uses is selected randomly with each run. While you could set your Web site to use a static port, there is a better solution.

Using the Web Test Editor, click on the toolbar button labeled Parameterize Web Servers. (You can hover your mouse cursor over each icon to see the name of each command.) You could also right-click on the Web test name and choose Parameterize Web Servers. In the resulting dialog, click the Change button. You will see the Change Web Server dialog, shown in Figure 13-5.

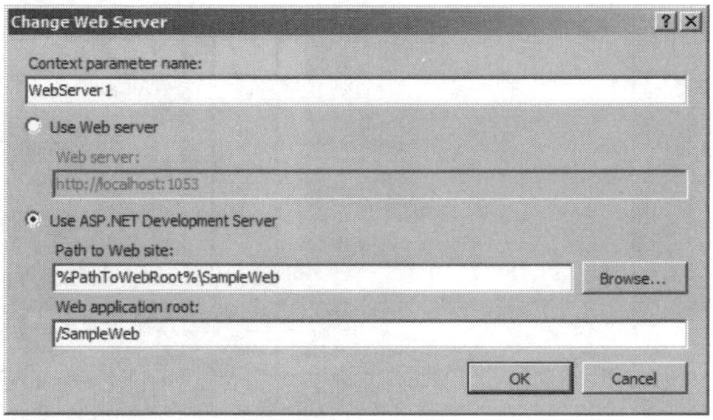

FIGURE 13-5

Use this dialog to configure your Web performance test to target a standard Web application service (such as IIS), or to use the ASP.NET Development Server. In this example, you are using the Development Server, so choose that option. The rest of the parameters are provided for you by default. The Web application root in this case is simply the name of the site, /SampleWeb. Click OK twice.

You will notice the Web Test Editor has automatically updated all request entries, replacing the static Web address with a reference to this context parameter, using the syntax {{WebServer1}}. In addition, the context parameter WebServer1 has been added at the bottom of the Web performance test under Context Parameters. (You'll see later in this chapter the effect of this on the sample Web performance test in Figure 13-10.)

> Context parameters (which are named variables that are available to each step in a Web performance test) are described in the section "Extraction Rules and Context Parameters," later in this chapter.

Now, you can run the Web performance test and Visual Studio will automatically find and connect to the port and address necessary when the ASP.NET Development Server is started. If the ASP.NET Development Server is not started, it will be launched automatically. If you have more than one target server or application, you can repeat this process as many times as necessary, creating additional context parameters.

Test Settings

Before you run a Web performance test, you may wish to review the settings that will be used for the test's runs. Choose Test ➪ Edit Test Settings ➪ Local. Select the Web Test entry from the list on the left side and you will see the options shown in Figure 13-6.

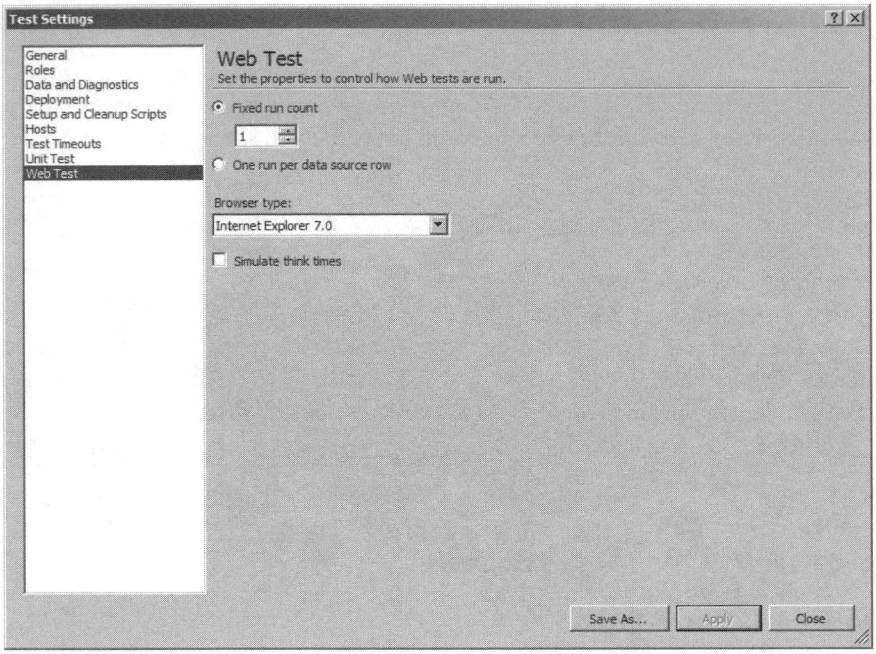

FIGURE 13-6

The option "Fixed run count" enables you to specify a specific number of times your Web performance tests will be executed when included in a test run. Running your test a few times (for example, three to ten times) can help eliminate errant performance timings caused by system issues on the client or server, and can help you derive a better estimate for how your Web site is actually performing. Note that you should not enter a large number here to simulate load through your Web performance test. Instead, you will want to create a load test (discussed later in this chapter) referencing your Web performance test. Also, if you assign a data source to your Web performance test, you may instead choose to run the Web performance test one time per entry in the selected data source. Data-driven Web performance tests are examined in detail later in this chapter.

The browser type setting enables you to simulate using one of a number of browsers as your Web performance test's client. This will automatically set the user agent field for requests sent to the Web performance test to simulate the selected browser. By default, this will be Internet Explorer, but you may select other browsers (such as Netscape or a Smartphone).

> Changing the browser type will not help you determine if your Web application will render as desired in a given browser type, since Web performance tests only examine HTTP/HTTPS responses and not the actual rendering of pages. Changing the browser type is only important if the Web application being tested is configured to respond differently based on the user agent sent by the requesting client. For example, a Web application may send a more lightweight user interface to a mobile device than it would to a desktop computer.

If you want to test more than one browser type, you'll need to run your Web performance test multiple times, selecting a different browser each time. However, you can also add your Web performance test to a load test and choose your desired browser distributions. This will cause each selected type to be simulated automatically. You'll learn how to do this in later in this chapter in the section "Load Tests."

The final option here, "Simulate think times," enables the use of delays in your Web performance test to simulate the normal time taken by users to read content, modify values, and decide on actions. When you recorded your Web performance test, the time it took for you to submit each request was recorded as the "think time" property of each step. If you turn this option on, that same delay will occur between the requests sent by the Web performance test to the Web application. Think times are disabled by default, causing all requests to be sent as quickly as possible to the Web server, resulting in a faster test. Later in this chapter, you will see that think times serve an important role in load tests.

Visual Studio also allows you to emulate different network speeds for your tests. From within Test Settings, select "Data and Diagnostics" on the left. Enable the Network Emulation adapter and click Configure. From here you can select a variety of network speeds (such as a dial-up 56K connection) to examine the effect that slower connection speeds have on your Web application.

Note that these settings affect every run of this Web performance test. These settings are ignored, however, when performing a load test. Later in this chapter, you will see that load tests have their own mechanism for configuring settings such as browser type, network speed, and the number of times a test should be run.

Running a Web Performance Test

To run a Web performance test, click the Run button (the leftmost button on the Web Test Editor toolbar, as shown in Figure 13-4). As with all other test types in Visual Studio, you can use the Test Manager and Test View windows to organize and execute tests. Chapter 12 provides full details on these windows.

You can also run Web performance tests from the command line. See the section "Command-Line Test Execution," later in this chapter.

Observing Test Execution and Results

When the test run is started, a window specific to that Web performance test execution will appear. If you are executing your Web performance test from the Web Test Editor window, you must click the Run button in this window to launch the test. The results will automatically be displayed, as shown in Figure 13-7. You may also choose to step through the Web performance test, one request at a time, by choosing Run Test (Pause Before Starting), available via the drop-down arrow attached to the Run button.

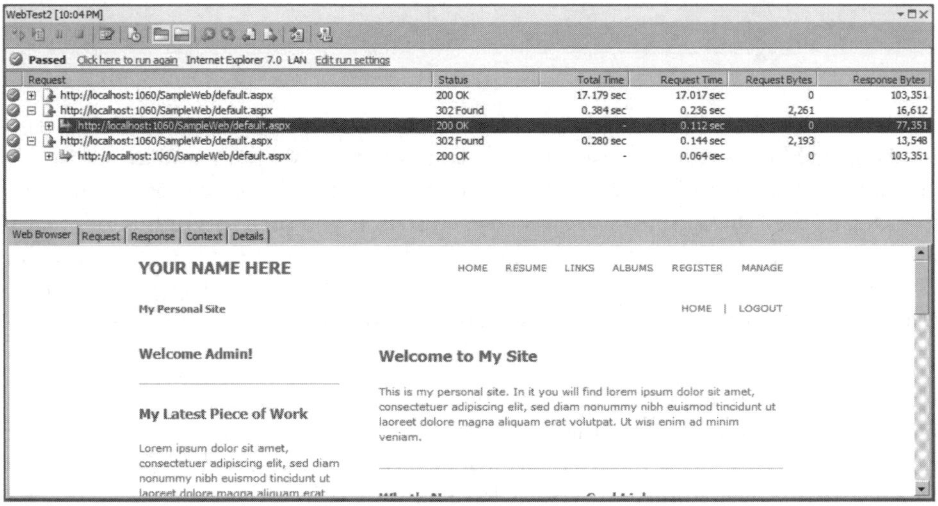

FIGURE 13-7

Note that if you choose to run your Web performance tests from Test View or Test Manager, the results will be summarized in the Test Results window, docked at the bottom of the screen. To see each Web performance test's execution details, as shown in Figure 13-7, double-click on the Web performance test's entry in the Test Results window.

This window displays the results of all interactions with the Web application. A toolbar, the overall test status, and two hyperlinked options are shown at the top. The first will rerun the Web performance test and the second allows you to change the browser type via the Web Test Run Settings dialog.

> *Changes made in this dialog will only affect the next run of the Web performance test and will not be saved for later runs. To make permanent changes, modify the test settings using Test ⇨ Edit Test Settings.*

Below that, each of the requests sent to the application are shown. You can expand each top-level request to see its dependent requests. These are automatically handled by the Web performance test system and can include calls to retrieve graphics, script sources, cascading stylesheets, and more.

Each item in this list shows the request target, as well as the response's status, time, and size. A green check indicates a successful request and response, whereas a red icon indicates failure.

Identifying which requests failed (and why) can be difficult if you have a large number of requests. Unfortunately, there is no summary view to see only failed requests with the reason for failure (for example, violating a validation rule). For large Web performance tests, you must scroll through all of the requests and open failed requests to see failure details.

The lower half of the window enables you to see full details for each request. The first tab, Web Browser, shows you the rendered version of the response. As you can see in Figure 13-7, the response includes "Welcome Admin!" text, indicating that you successfully logged in as the Admin account.

The Request tab shows the details of what was supplied to the Web application, including all headers and any request body, such as might be present when an HTTP POST is made.

Similarly, the Response tab shows all headers and the body of the response sent back from the Web application. Unlike the Web Browser tab, this detail is shown textually, even when binary data (such as an image) is returned.

The Context tab lists all of the context parameters and their values at the time of the selected request. Finally, the Details tab shows the status of any assigned validation and extraction rules. This tab also shows details about any exception thrown during that request. Context parameters and rules are described later in this chapter.

Editing a Web Performance Test

You'll often find that a recorded Web performance test is not sufficient to fully test your application's functionality. You can use the Web Test Editor, as shown in Figure 13-4, to further customize a Web performance test, adding comments, extraction rules, data sources, and other properties.

It is recommended that you run a recorded Web performance test once before attempting to edit it. This will verify that the test was recorded correctly. If you don't do this, you might not know whether a test is failing because it wasn't recorded correctly or because you introduced a bug through changes in the Web Test Editor.

Setting Request Properties

From within the Web Test Editor, right-click on a request and choose Properties. If the Properties window is already displayed, simply selecting a request will show its properties. You will be able to modify settings such as cache control, target URL, and whether the request automatically follows redirects.

The Properties window also offers a chance to modify the think time of each request. For example, perhaps a co-worker dropped by with a question while you were recording your Web performance test and you forgot to pause the recording. Use the Think Time property to adjust the delay to a more realistic value.

Adding Comments

Comments are useful for identifying the actions of a particular section of a Web performance test. In addition, when converting your Web performance test to a coded Web performance test, your comments will be preserved in code.

Because the requests in this example all refer to the same page, it is helpful to add comments to help distinguish them. Add a comment by right-clicking on the first request and choosing Insert Comment. Enter **Initial site request**. Comment to the second request as **Login** and the third request as **Logout**.

Adding Transactions

A *transaction* is used to monitor a group of logically connected steps in your Web performance test. A transaction can be tracked as a unit, giving details such as number of times invoked, request time, and total elapsed time.

> *Don't confuse Web performance test transactions with database transactions. While both are used for grouping actions, database transactions offer additional features beyond those of Web performance test transactions.*

To create a transaction, right-click a request and select Insert Transaction. You will be prompted to name the transaction and to select the start and end request from drop-down lists.

Transactions are primarily used when running Web performance tests under load with a load test. You will learn more about viewing transaction details in the section "Viewing and Interpreting Load Test Results," later in this chapter.

Extraction Rules and Context Parameters

Extraction rules are used to retrieve specific data from a Web response. This data is stored in *context parameters,* which live for the duration of the Web performance test. Context parameters can be read from and written to by any request in a Web performance test. For example, you could use an extraction rule to retrieve an order confirmation number, storing that in a context parameter. Then, subsequent steps in the test could access that order number, using it for verification or supplying it with later Web requests.

> *Context parameters are similar in concept to the* HttpContext.Items *collection from ASP.NET. In both cases, you can add names and values that can be accessed by any subsequent step. Whereas* HttpContext.Items *entries are valid for the duration of a single page request, Web performance test context parameters are accessible through a single Web performance test run.*

Referring to Figure 13-4, notice that the first request has an Extract Hidden Fields entry under Extraction Rules. This was added automatically when you recorded the Web performance test because the system recognized hidden fields in the first form you accessed. Those hidden fields are now available to subsequent requests via context parameters.

A number of context parameters are set automatically when you run a Web performance test, including the following:

➤ $TestDir — The working directory of the Web performance test.

➤ $WebTestIteration — The current run number. For example, this would be useful if you selected more than one run in the Test Settings and needed to differentiate the test runs.

➤ $ControllerName and $AgentName — Machine identifiers used when remotely executing Web performance tests. You'll learn more about this topic later in this chapter.

To add an extraction rule to a Web performance test, right-click on any request and select Add Extraction Rule. The dialog shown in Figure 13-8 will appear.

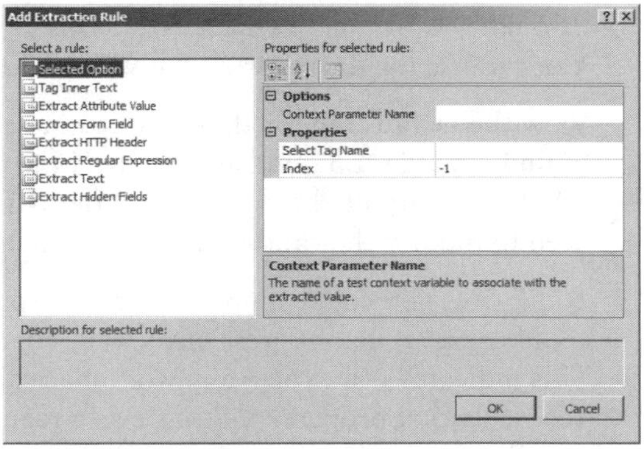

The built-in extraction rules can be used to extract any attribute, HTTP header, or response text. Use Extract Regular Expression to retrieve data that matches the supplied expression. Use Extract Hidden Fields to easily find and return a value contained in a hidden form field of a response. Extracted values are stored in context parameters whose names you define in the properties of each rule.

FIGURE 13-8

You can add your own custom extraction rules by creating classes that derive from the ExtractionRule class found in the Microsoft.VisualStudio.TestTools.WebTesting namespace.

Validation Rules

Generally, checking for valid Web application behavior involves more than just getting a response from the server. You must ensure that the content and behavior of that response is correct. Validation rules offer a way to verify that those requirements are met. For example, you may wish to verify that specific text appears on a page after an action, such as adding an item to a shopping cart. Validation rules are attached to a specific request, and will cause that request to show as failed if the requirement is not satisfied.

Let's add a validation rule to the test to ensure that the welcome message is displayed after you log in. Right-click on the second request and choose Add Validation Rule. You will see the dialog shown in Figure 13-9.

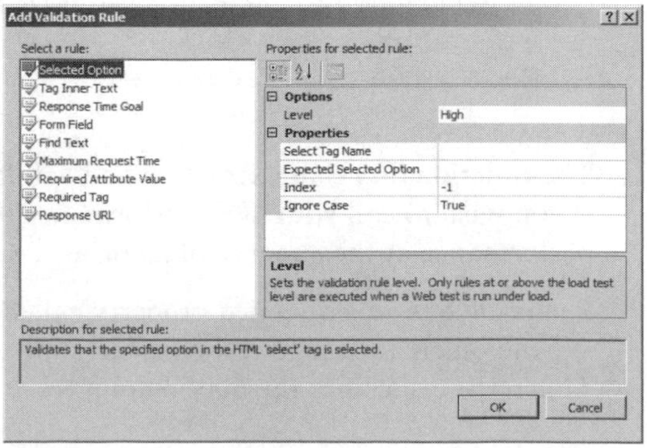

FIGURE 13-9

As with extraction rules, you can also create your own custom validation rules by inheriting from the base `ValidationRule` class, found in the `WebTestFramework` assembly, and have them appear in this dialog. Choose the Find Text rule and set the Find Text value to `Welcome Admin`. Set Ignore Case to `false`, and Pass If Text Found to `true`. This rule will search the Web application's response for a case-sensitive match on that text and will pass if found. Click OK and the Web performance test should appear as shown in Figure 13-10.

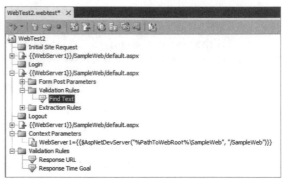

FIGURE 13-10

Verify that this works by running or stepping through the Web performance test. You should see that this test actually does not work as expected. You can use the details from the Web performance test's results to find out why.

View the Details tab for the second request. You'll see that the Find Text validation rule failed to find a match. Looking at the text of the response on the Response tab shows that instead of "Welcome Admin" being returned, there is a tab instead of a space between the words. You will need to modify the validation rule to match this text.

To fix this, you could simply replace the space in the Find Text parameter with a tab. However, you could use a regular expression as well. First, change the Find Text parameter to `Welcome\s+Admin`. This indicates you expect any whitespace characters between the words, not just a space character. To enable that property to behave as a regular expression, set the Use Regular Expression parameter to `true`.

Save your Web performance test and rerun it. The Web performance test should now pass.

> *Bear in mind is that the validation logic available within Web performance tests is not as sophisticated as that of coded UI tests (see Chapter 15). With coded UI tests, it is easier to confirm that a given string appears in the right location of a Web page, whereas with Web performance test validation rules, you are generally just checking to confirm that the string appears somewhere in the response.*

The functionality that extraction and validation rules provide comes at the expense of performance. If you wish to call your Web performance test from a load test, you might wish to improve performance at the expense of ignoring a number of extraction or validation rules.

Each rule has an associated property called `Level`. This can be set to Low, Medium, or High. When you create a load test, you can similarly specify a validation level of Low, Medium, or High. This setting specifies the maximum level of rule that will be executed when the load test runs.

For example, a validation level of Medium will run rules with a level of Low or Medium, but will exclude rules marked as High.

Data-Driven Web Performance Tests

You can satisfy many testing scenarios using the techniques described so far, but you can go beyond those techniques to easily create data-driven Web performance tests. A *data-driven Web performance test* connects to a data source and retrieves a set of data. Pieces of that data can be used in place of static settings for each request.

For example, in your Web performance test, you may wish to ensure that the login and logout processes work equally well for all of the configured users. You'll learn how to do this next.

Configuring a Data Source

You can configure your Web performance test to connect to a database (for example, SQL Server or Oracle), a comma-separated value (CSV) file, or an XML file. For this example, a CSV file will suffice. Using Notepad, create a new file and insert the following data:

```
Username,Password
Admin,@qwerty@
Sue,@qwerty@
Daniel,@qwerty@
Andrew,@qwerty@
```

Save this file as `Credentials.csv`.

The next step in creating a data-driven Web performance test is to specify your data source. Using the Web Test Editor, you can either right-click on the top node of your Web performance test and select Add Data Source, or click the Add Data Source button on the toolbar.

In the New Test Data Source Wizard, select CSV File and click Next. Browse to the `Credentials.csv` file you just created and click Next. You will see a preview of the data contained in this file. Note that the first row of your file was converted to the appropriate column headers for your data table. Click Finish. You will be prompted to make the CSV file a part of your test project. Click Yes to continue. When the data source is added, you will see it at the bottom of your Web performance test in the Web Test Editor, and the `Credentials.csv` file will be added to the Solution Explorer.

Expand the data source to see that there is a new table named `Credentials` in your Web Test Editor. Click this table and view the Properties window. Notice that one of the settings is Access Method. This has three valid settings:

➤ *Sequential* — Reads each record in first-to-last order from the source. This will loop back to the first record and continue reading if the test uses more iterations than the source has records.

➤ *Random* — Reads each record randomly from the source and, like sequential access, will continue reading as long as necessary.

➤ *Unique* — Reads each record in first-to-last order, but will do so only once.

Use this setting to determine how the data source will feed rows to the Web performance test. For this test, choose Sequential.

Binding to a Source

Several types of values can be bound to a data source, including form post and URL query parameters' names and values, HTTP headers, and file upload field names. Expand the second request in the Web Test Editor, expand Form Post Parameters, click the parameter for UserName, and view the Properties window. Click the down arrow that appears in the Value box.

You will then see the data-binding selector, as shown in Figure 13-11.

Expand your data source, choose the Credentials table, and then click on the Username column to bind to the value of this parameter. A database icon will appear in that property, indicating that it is a bound value. You can select the Unbind entry to remove any established data binding. Repeat this process for the Password parameter.

FIGURE 13-11

> *When binding to a database you may choose to bind to values from either a table or a view. Binding to the results of stored procedures is not supported for Web performance tests.*

Before you run your Web performance test, you must indicate that you want to run the test one time per row of data in the data source. Refer to the earlier section "Test Settings" and Figure 13-6. In the Web Tests section of your test settings, choose the "One run per data source row" option.

The next time you run your Web performance test, it will automatically read from the target data source, supplying the bound fields with data. The test will repeat one time for each row of data in the source. Your test should now fail, however, since you are still looking for the text "Welcome Admin" to appear after the login request is sent.

To fix this, you must modify your validation rule to look for welcome text corresponding to the user being authenticated. Select the Find Text validation rule and view the Properties window. Change the Find Text value to Welcome\s+{{DataSource1.Credentials#csv.Username}} and re-run your test. Your test should now pass again.

Coded Web Performance Tests

As flexible as Web performance tests are, there may be times when you need more control over the actions that are taken. Web performance tests are stored as XML files with .webtest extensions. Visual Studio uses this XML to generate the code that is executed when the Web performance test is run. You can tap into this process by creating a coded Web performance test, enabling you to execute a test from code instead of from XML.

Coded Web performance tests enable you to perform actions not possible with a standard Web performance test. For example, you can perform branching based on the responses received during a Web performance test or based on the values of a data-bound test. A coded Web performance test is limited only by your ability to write code. The language of the generated code is determined by the language of the test project that contains the source Web performance test.

A coded Web performance test is a class that inherits from either a base `WebTest` class for C# tests, or from a `ThreadedWebTest` base for Visual Basic tests. These classes can be found in the `Microsoft.VisualStudio.TestTools.WebTesting` namespace. All of the features available to Web performance tests that you create via the IDE are implemented in classes and methods contained in that namespace.

> While you always have the option to create a coded Web performance test by hand, the most common (and the recommended) method is to generate a coded Web performance test from a Web performance test that was recorded with the Web Test Recorder and then customize the code as needed.

You should familiarize yourself with coded Web performance tests by creating a number of different sample Web performance tests through the IDE and generating coded Web performance tests from them to learn how various Web performance test actions are accomplished with code.

Using the example Web performance test, click the Generate Code button on the Web Test Editor toolbar. You will be prompted to name the generated file. Open the generated file and review the generated code.

Here is a segment of the C# code that was generated from the example Web performance test (some calls have been removed for simplicity):

```
public override IEnumerator<WebTestRequest> GetRequestEnumerator()
{
    ...
    // Initial site request
    ...

    yield return request1;
    ...

    // Login
    ...
    WebTestRequest request2 = new
      WebTestRequest((this.Context["WebServer1"].ToString() +
      "/SampleWeb/default.aspx"));
    ...

    Request2.ThinkTime = 14;
    Request2.Method = "POST";
```

```
FormPostHttpBody request2Body = new FormPostHttpBody();
...
Request2Body.FormPostParameters.Add(
  "ctl00$Main$LoginArea$Login1$UserName",
  this.Context["DataSource1.Credentials#csv.Username"].ToString());

request2Body.FormPostParameters.Add(
  "ctl00$Main$LoginArea$Login1$Password",
  this.Context["DataSource1.Credentials#csv.Password"].ToString());
...

if ((this.Context.ValidationLevel >=
  Microsoft.VisualStudio.TestTools.WebTesting.ValidationLevel.High))
{
 ValidationRuleFindText validationRule3 = new ValidationRuleFindText();
 validationRule3.FindText = ("Welcome\\s+" +
   this.Context["DataSource1.Credentials#csv.Username"].ToString());
   validationRule3.IgnoreCase = false;
   validationRule3.UseRegularExpression = true;
   validationRule3.PassIfTextFound = true;
}
...
yield return request2;
...


// Logout
...
WebTestRequest request3 = new
  WebTestRequest((this.Context["WebServer1"].ToString() +
"/SampleWeb/default.aspx"));
Request3.Method = "POST";
...
yield return request3;
...
    }
```

This GetRequestEnumerator method uses the yield statement to provide WebTestRequest instances, one per HTTP request, back to the Web test system.

Visual Basic test projects generate slightly different code than C# tests because Visual Basic does not currently support iterators and the yield statement. Instead of having a GetRequestEnumerator method that yields WebTestRequest instances one at a time, there is a Run subroutine that uses the base ThreadedWebTest.Send method to execute each request.

Regardless of the language used, notice that the methods and properties are very similar to what you have already seen when creating and editing Web performance tests in the Web Test Editor. You'll also notice that the comments you added in the Web Test Editor appear as comments in the code, making it very easy to identify where each request begins.

Taking a closer look, you see that the Find Text validation rule you added earlier is now specified with code. First, the code checks the ValidationLevel context parameter to verify that you're including rules marked with a level of High. If so, the ValidationRuleFindText class is instantiated and the parameters you specified in the IDE are now set as properties of that instance. Finally, the instance's `Validate` method is registered with the request's `ValidateResponse` event, ensuring that the validator will execute at the appropriate time.

You can make any changes you wish and simply save the code file and rebuild. Your coded Web performance test will automatically appear alongside your other tests in Test Manager and Test View.

> *Another advantage of coded Web performance tests is protocol support. While normal Web performance tests can support both HTTP and HTTPS, they cannot use alternative protocols. A coded Web performance test can be used for other protocols, such as FTP.*

For detailed descriptions of the classes and members available to you in the `WebTesting` namespace, see Visual Studio's Help topic titled "Microsoft.VisualStudio.TestTools.WebTesting Namespace."

LOAD TESTS

Load tests are used to verify that your application will perform as expected while under the stress of multiple concurrent users. You configure the levels and types of load you wish to simulate and then execute the load test. A series of requests will be generated against the target application, and Visual Studio will monitor the system under test to determine how well it performs.

Load testing is most commonly used with Web performance tests to conduct smoke, load, and stress testing of ASP.NET applications. However, you are certainly not limited to this. Load tests are essentially lists of pointers to other tests, and they can include any other test type except for manual tests and coded UI tests.

For example, you could create a load test that includes a suite of unit tests. You could stress-test layers of business logic and database access code to determine how that code will behave when many users are accessing it concurrently, regardless of which application uses those layers.

As another example, ordered tests can be used to group a number of tests and define a specific order in which they will run. Because tests added to a load test are executed in a randomly selected order, you may find it useful to first group them with an ordered test, and then include that ordered test in the load test. You can find more information on ordered tests in Chapter 12.

Creating and Configuring Load Tests

The discussion in this section describes how to create a load test using the New Load Test Wizard. You'll examine many options that you can use to customize the behavior of your load tests.

As described earlier in this chapter in the section "Web Performance Tests," a test project is used to contain your tests, and, like Web performance tests, load tests are placed in test projects. You can either use the New Test option of the Test menu and specify a new or existing test project, or you can right-click on an existing test project and choose Add ➪ Load Test.

Whether from a test project or the Test menu, when you add a new load test, the New Load Test Wizard is started. This wizard will guide you through the many configuration options available for a load test.

Scenarios and Think Times

A load test is composed of one or more *scenarios*. A scenario is a grouping of Web performance and/or unit tests, along with a variety of preferences for user, browser, network, and other settings. Scenarios are used to group similar tests or usage environments. For example, you may wish to create a scenario for simulating the creation and submission of an expense report by your employees, whereby your users have LAN connectivity and all use Internet Explorer 7.0.

When the New Load Test Wizard is launched, the first screen describes the load test creation process. Click Next and you will be prompted to assign a name to your load test's first scenario, as shown in Figure 13-12.

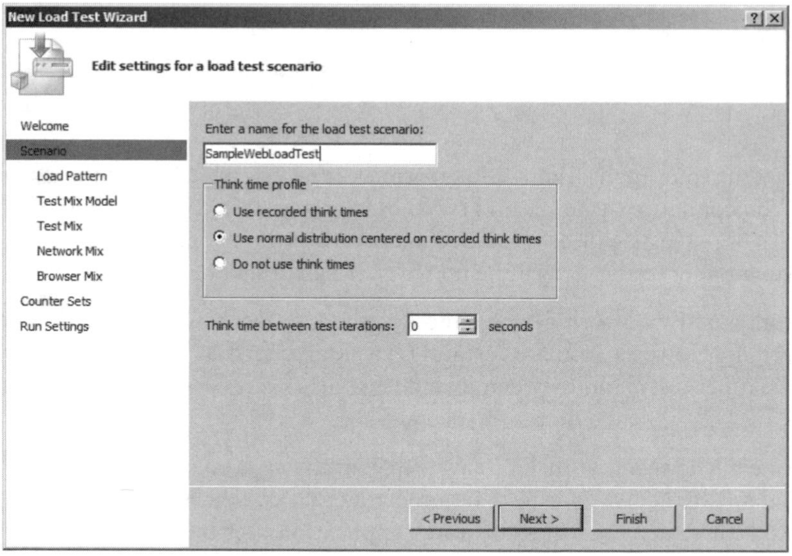

FIGURE 13-12

Note that the New Load Test Wizard only supports the creation of a single scenario in your load test, but you can easily add more scenarios with the Load Test Editor after you complete the wizard.

The second option on this page is to configure think times. You may recall from the earlier section "Web Performance Tests," that think time is a delay between each request, which can be used to approximate how long a user will pause to read, consider options, and enter data on a particular page. These times are stored with each of a Web performance test's requests. The think time profile panel enables you to turn these off or on.

If you enable think times, you can either use them as is, or apply a normal distribution that is centered around your recorded think times as a mean. The normal distribution is generally recommended if you want to simulate the most realistic user load, based on what you expect the average user to do. You can also configure the think time between test iterations to model a user who pauses after completing a task before moving to the next task.

You can click on any step on the left-hand side to jump to that page of the wizard or click Next to navigate through sequential pages.

Load Patterns

The next step is to define the load pattern for the scenario. The load pattern, shown in Figure 13-13, enables simulation of different types of user load.

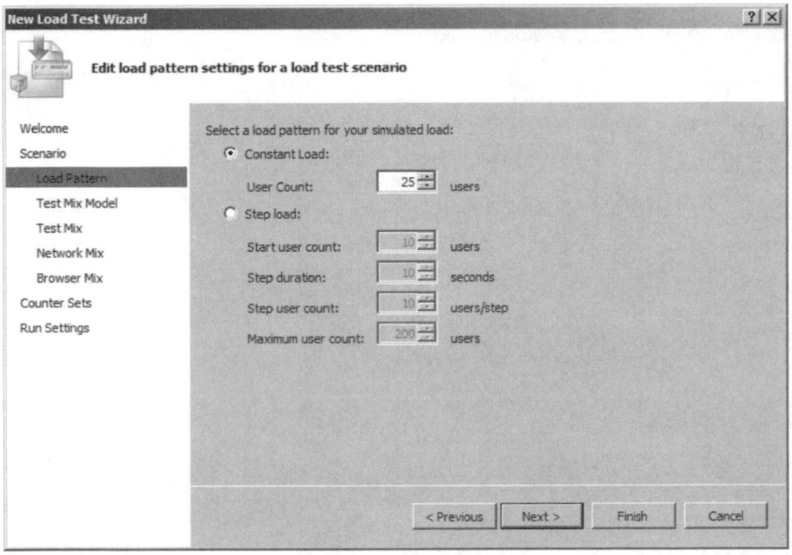

New Load Test Wizard	? X

Edit load pattern settings for a load test scenario

Welcome
Scenario
Load Pattern
Test Mix Model
Test Mix
Network Mix
Browser Mix
Counter Sets
Run Settings

Select a load pattern for your simulated load:

● Constant Load:

  User Count: 25 users

○ Step load:

  Start user count: 10 users

  Step duration: 10 seconds

  Step user count: 10 users/step

  Maximum user count: 200 users

< Previous | Next > | Finish | Cancel

FIGURE 13-13

In the wizard, you have two load pattern options: Constant and Step. A *constant load* enables you to define a number of users that will remain unchanged throughout the duration of the test. Use a constant load to analyze the performance of your application under a steady load of users. For example, you may specify a baseline test with 100 users. This load test could be executed prior to release to ensure that your established performance criteria remain satisfied.

A *step load* defines a starting and maximum user count. You also assign a step duration and a step user count. Every time the number of seconds specified in your step duration elapse, the number of users is incremented by the step count, unless the maximum number of users has been reached. Step loads are very useful for stress-testing your application, finding the maximum number of users your application will support before serious issues arise.

 A third type of load profile pattern, called "Goal Based," is available only through the Load Test Editor. See the section "Editing Load Tests," later in this chapter, for more details.

You should begin with a load test that has a small constant user load and a relatively short execution time. Once you have verified that the load test is configured and working correctly, increase the load and duration as you require.

Test Mix Model

The test mix model (shown in Figure 13-14) determines the frequency at which tests within your load test will be selected from among other tests within your load test. The test mix model allows you several options for realistically modeling user load. The options for test mix model are as follows:

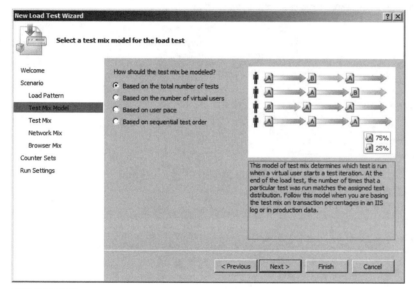

FIGURE 13-14

➤ *Based on the total number of tests* — This model allows you to assign a percentage to each test that dictates how many times it should be run. Each virtual user will run each test corresponding to the percentage assigned to that test. An example of where this might be useful is if you know that the average visitor views three photos on your Web site for every one comment that they leave on a photo. To model that scenario, you would create a test for viewing photos and a test for leaving comments, and assign them percentages of 75 percent and 25 percent, respectively.

➤ *Based on the number of virtual users* — This model allows you to assign a percentage of virtual users who should run each test. This model might be useful if you know that, at any given time, 80 percent of your visitors are browsing the catalog of your e-commerce Web site, 5 percent are registering for new accounts, and 15 percent are checking out.

➤ *Based on user pace* — This model executes each test a specified number of times per virtual user per hour. An example of a scenario where this might be useful is if you know that the average user checks email five times per hour, and looks at a stock portfolio once an hour. When using this test mix model, the think time between iterations value from the Scenario page of the wizard is ignored.

➤ *Based on sequential test order* — If you know that your users generally perform steps in a specific order (for example, logging in, then finding an item to purchase, then checking out) you can use this test mix model to simulate a sequential test behavior for all virtual users. This option is functionally equivalent to structuring your tests as ordered tests.

> *Don't worry if you are having a difficult time choosing a test mix model right now. You can always play with different test mix models later as you learn more about the expected behavior of your application's users. You may also discover that your application exhibits different usage patterns at different times of the day, during marketing promotions, or during some other seasonality.*

The option you select on this dialog will impact the options available to you on the next page of the wizard.

Test Mix

Now, select the tests to include in your scenario, along with the relative frequency with which they should run. Click the Add button and you will be presented with the Add Tests dialog shown in Figure 13-15.

By default, all of the tests (except manual tests and coded UI tests) in your solution will be displayed. You can constrain these to a specific test list with the "Select test list to view" drop-down. Select one or more tests and click OK. To keep this example simple, only add the Web performance test you created earlier in this chapter.

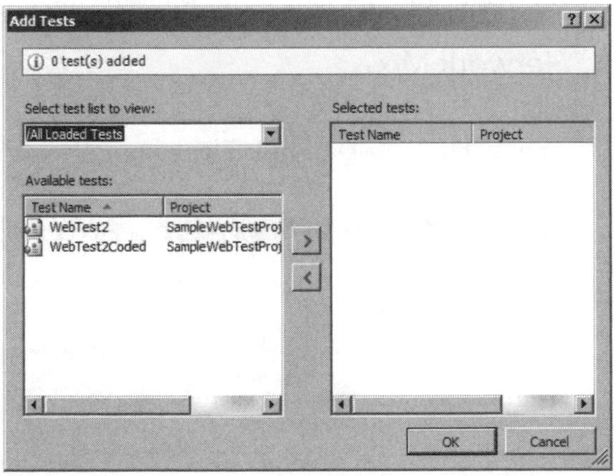

FIGURE 13-15

Next, you will return to the test mix step. Remember that this page will vary based on the test mix model you selected in the previous step. Figure 13-16 assumes that you selected "Based on the total number of tests" as your test mix model.

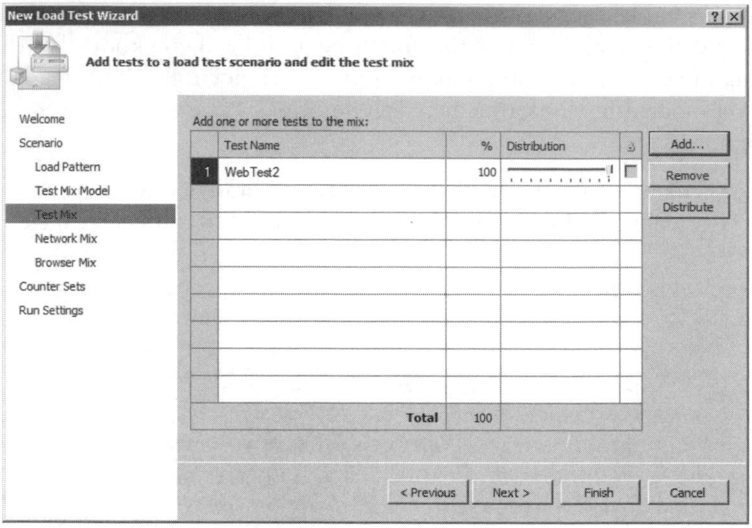

FIGURE 13-16

Use the sliders to assign the chance (in percentage) that a virtual user will select that test to execute. You may also type a number directly into the numeric fields. Use the lock checkbox in the far-right column to freeze tests at a certain number, while using the sliders to adjust the remaining "unlocked" test distributions. The Distribute button resets the percentages evenly between all tests. But, since you only have a single test in your test mix right now there is nothing else to configure on this page, and the slider will be disabled.

Network Mix

You can then specify the kinds of network connectivity you expect your users to have (such as LAN, Cable-DSL, and Dial-up). This step is shown in Figure 13-17.

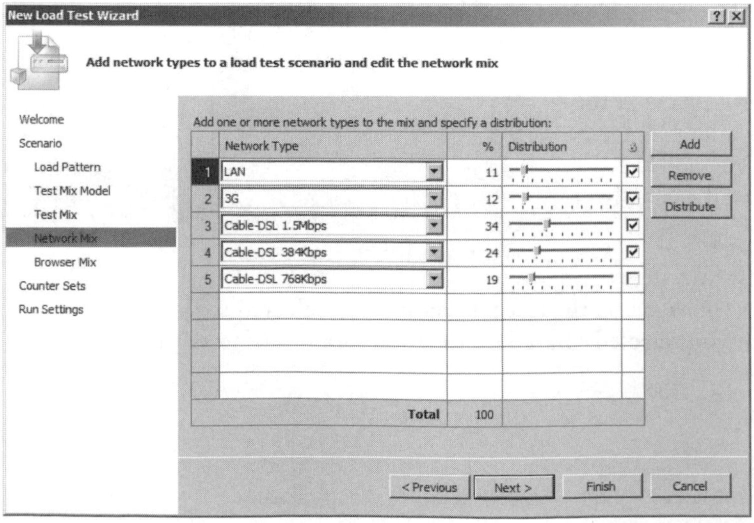

FIGURE 13-17

Like the test mix step described earlier, you can use sliders to adjust the percentages, lock a particular percent, or click the Distribute button to reset to an even distribution.

As with the test mix settings, each virtual user will select a browser type at random according to the percentages you set. A new browser type is selected each time a test is chosen for execution. This also applies to the browser mix described next.

Browser Mix

The next step (applicable only when Web performance tests are part of the load test) is to define the distribution of browser types that you wish to simulate. Visual Studio will then adjust the headers sent to the target application according to the selected browser for that user.

As shown in Figure 13-18, you may add one or more browser types, and then assign a percent distribution for their use.

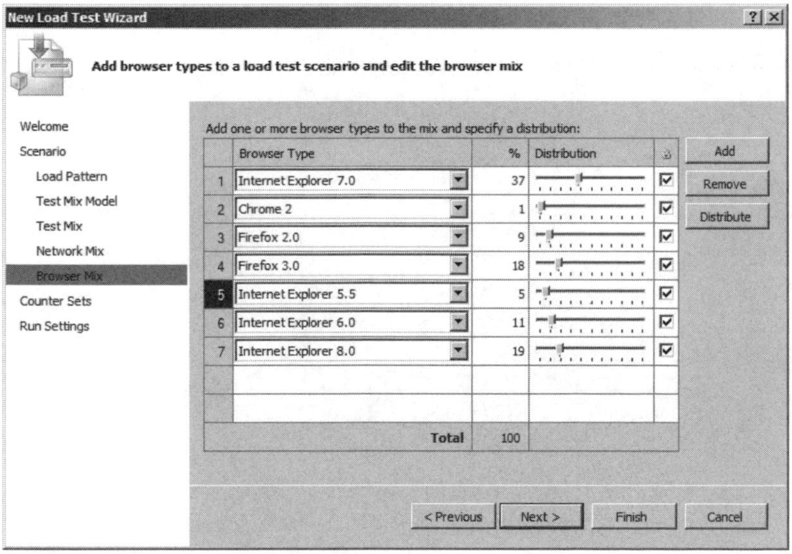

FIGURE 13-18

Performance Counter Sets

A vital part of load testing is the tracking of performance counters. You can configure your load test to observe and record the values of performance counters, even on remote machines. For example, your target application is probably hosted on a different machine from the one on which you're running the test. In addition, that machine may be calling to other machines for required services (such as databases or Web services). Counters from all of these machines can be collected and stored by Visual Studio.

A *counter set* is a group of related performance counters. All of the contained performance counters will be collected and recorded on the target machine when the load test is executed.

> *Once the wizard is complete, you can use the editor to create your own counter sets by right-clicking on Counter Sets and selecting Add Custom Counter Set. Right-click on the new counter set and choose Add Counters. Use the resulting dialog box to select the counters and instances you wish to include.*

Select machines and counter sets using the wizard step shown in Figure 13-19. Note that this step is optional. By default, performance counters are automatically collected and recorded for the machine running the load test. If no other machines are involved, simply click Next.

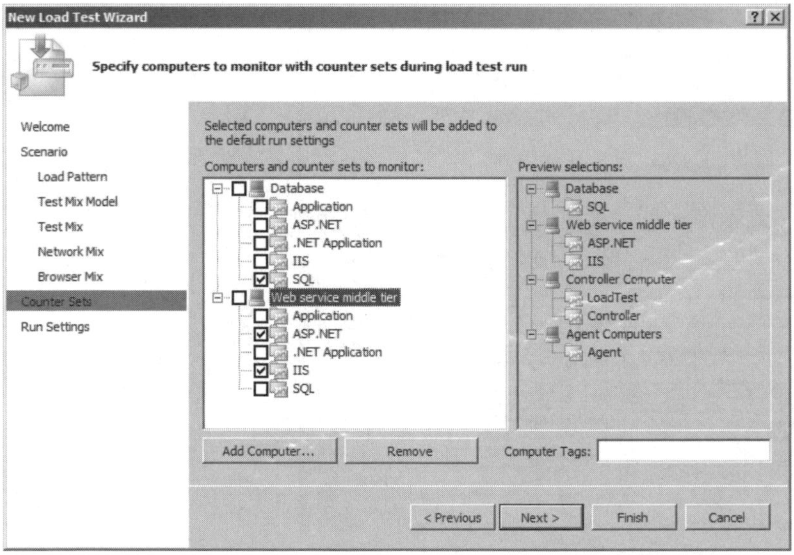

FIGURE 13-19

To add a machine to the list, click Add Computer and enter the name of the target machine. Then, check any counter sets you wish to track to enable collection of the associated performance counters from the target machine.

> *If you encounter errors when trying to collect performance counters from remote machines, be sure to visit Ed Glas's blog post on troubleshooting these problems at* `http://tinyurl.com/bp39hj`*.*

Run Settings

The final step in the New Load Test Wizard is to specify the test's run settings, as shown in Figure 13-20. A load test may have more than one run setting, but the New Load Test Wizard will only create one. In addition, run settings include more details than are visible through the wizard. These aspects of run settings are covered later in the section "Editing Load Tests."

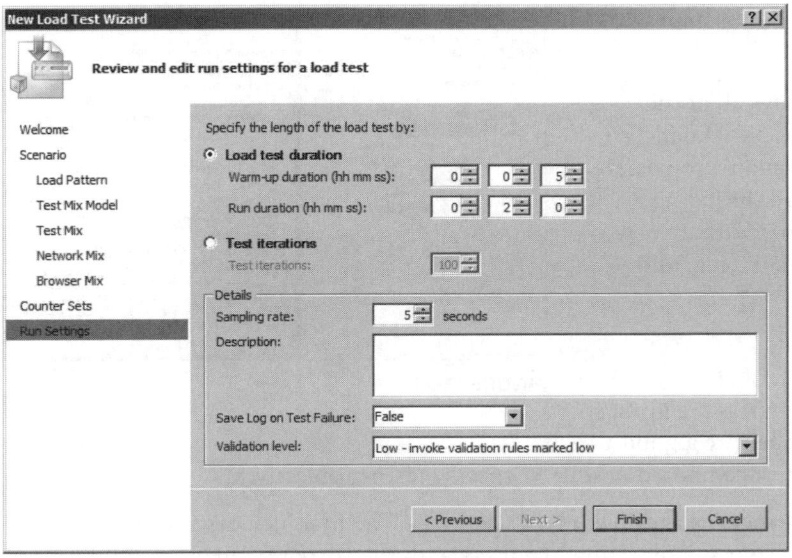

FIGURE 13-20

First, select the timing details for the test. "Warm-up duration" specifies a window of time during which (although the test is running) no information from the test is tracked. This gives the target application a chance to complete actions such as just-in-time (JIT) compilation or caching of resources. Once the warm-up period ends, data collection begins and will continue until the "Run duration" value has been reached.

The "Sampling rate" determines how often performance counters will be collected and recorded. A higher frequency (lower number) will produce more detail, but at the cost of a larger test result set and slightly higher strain on the target machines.

Any description you enter will be stored for the current run setting. Save Log on Test Failure specifies whether or not a load test log should be saved in the event that tests fail. Often, you will not want to save a log on test failure, since broken tests will skew the results for actual test performance.

Finally, the "Validation level" setting indicates which Web performance test validation rules should be executed. This is important, because the execution of validation rules is achieved at the expense of performance. In a stress test, you may be more interested in raw performance than you are that a set of validation rules pass. There are three options for validation level:

➤ *Low* — Only validation rules marked with Low level will be executed.

➤ *Medium* — Validation rules marked Low or Medium level will be executed.

➤ *High* — All validation rules will be executed.

Click Finish to complete the wizard and create the load test.

Editing Load Tests

After completing the New Load Test Wizard (or whenever you open an existing load test), you will see the Load Test Editor shown in Figure 13-21.

The Load Test Editor displays all of the settings you specified in the New Load Test Wizard. It allows access to more properties and options than the wizard, including the capability to add scenarios, create new run settings, configure SQL tracing, and much more.

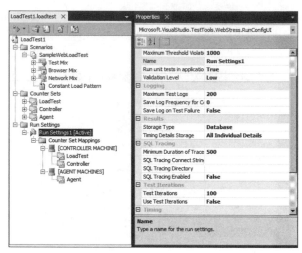

FIGURE 13-21

Adding Scenarios

As you've already seen, scenarios are groups of tests and user profiles. They are a good way to define a large load test composed of smaller specific testing objectives.

For example, you might create a load test with two scenarios. The first includes tests of the administrative functions of your site, including ten users with the corporate-mandated Internet Explorer 8.0 on a LAN. The other scenario tests the core features of your site, running with 90 users who have a variety of browsers and connections. Running these scenarios together under one load test enables you to more effectively gauge the overall behavior of your site under realistic usage.

The New Load Test Wizard generates load tests with a single scenario, but you can easily add more using the Load Test Editor. Right-click on the Scenarios node and choose Add Scenario. You will then be prompted to walk through the Add Scenario Wizard, which is simply a subset of the New Load Test Wizard that you've already seen.

Run Settings

Run settings, as shown on the right-hand side of Figure 13-21, specify such things as duration of the test run, where and if results data is stored, SQL tracing, and performance counter mappings.

A load test can have more than one run setting, but as with scenarios, the New Load Test Wizard only supports the creation of one. You might want multiple run settings to enable you to easily switch between different types of runs. For example, you could switch between a long-running test that runs all validation rules, and another shorter test that runs only those marked as Low level.

To add a new run setting, right-click on the Run Settings node (or the load test's root node) and choose Add Run Setting. You can then modify any property or add counter set mappings to this new run setting node.

SQL Tracing

You can gather tracing information from a target SQL Server instance though SQL Tracing. Enable SQL Tracing through the run settings of your load test. As shown in Figure 13-21, the SQL Tracing group has four settings.

First, set the SQL Tracing Enabled setting to True. Then click the SQL Tracking Connect String setting to make the ellipsis button appear. Click that button and configure the connection to the database you wish to trace.

Use the SQL Tracing Directory setting to specify the path or Universal Naming Convention (UNC) to the directory in which you want the SQL Trace details stored.

Finally, you can specify a minimum threshold for logging of SQL operations. The Minimum Duration of Traced SQL Operations setting specifies the minimum time (in milliseconds) that an operation must take in order for it to be recorded in the tracing file.

Goal-Based Load Profiles

As you saw in the New Load Test Wizard, you had two options for load profile patterns: Constant and Step. A third option, Goal Based, is only available through the Load Test Editor.

The goal-based pattern is used to raise or lower the user load over time until a specific performance counter range has been reached. This is an invaluable option when you want to determine the peak loads your application can withstand.

To access the load profile options, open your load test in the Load Test Editor and click on your current load profile, which will be either Constant Load Profile or Step Load Profile. In the Properties window, change the Pattern value to Goal Based. You should now see a window similar to Figure 13-22.

First, notice the User Count Limits section. This is similar to the step pattern in that you specify an initial and maximum user count, but you also specify a maximum

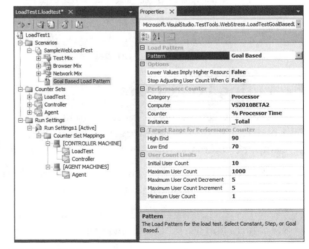

FIGURE 13-22

user count increment and decrement and minimum user count. The load test will dynamically adjust the current user count according to these settings in order to reach the goal performance counter threshold.

By default, the pattern will be configured against the % Processor Time performance counter. To change this, enter the category (for example, Memory, System, and so on), the computer from which it will be collected (leave this blank for the current machine), and the counter name and instance — which is applicable if you have multiple processors.

You must then tell the test about the performance counter you selected. First, identify the range you're trying to reach using the High-End and Low-End properties. Set the Lower Values Imply Higher Resource Utilization option if a lower counter value indicates system stress. For example, you would set this to True when using the system group's Available MBytes counter. Finally, you can tell the load test to remain at the current user load level when the goal is reached with the Stop Adjusting User Count When Goal Achieved option.

Storing Load Test Run Data

A load test run can collect a large amount of data. This includes performance counter information from one or more machines, details about which test passed, and durations of various actions. You may choose to store this information in a SQL Server database.

To select a results store, you must modify the load test's run settings. Refer back to Figure 13-21. The local run settings have been selected in the Load Test Editor. In the Results section of the Properties window is a setting called Storage Type, which can either be set to None or Database.

In order to use the Database option, you must first configure an instance of SQL Server or SQL Express using a database creation script. The script, LoadTestResultsRepository.sql, is found under the \Common7\IDE directory of your Visual Studio installation directory. You may run this script any way you choose, such as with Query Manager or SQL Server's SQLCMD utility.

Once created, the new LoadTest database can be used to store data from load tests running on the local machine or even remote machines. Running remote load tests is described later in this chapter in the section "Distributed Load Tests."

Executing Load Tests

There are several ways to execute a load test. You can use various windows in Visual Studio, the Load Test Editor, Test Manager and Test View, or you can use command-line tools. For details on using the command line, see the section "Command-Line Test Execution," later in this chapter.

In the Load Test Editor, you can click the Run button at the upper-left corner, or right-click on any load test setting node and select Run Load Test.

From the Test Manager and Test View windows, check or select one or more load tests and click the Run Tests button. In Test View, you may also right-click on a test and select Run Selection.

Viewing and Interpreting Load Test Results

If you ran your test from either Test Manager or Test View, you will see the status of your test in the Test Results window, as shown in Figure 13-23.

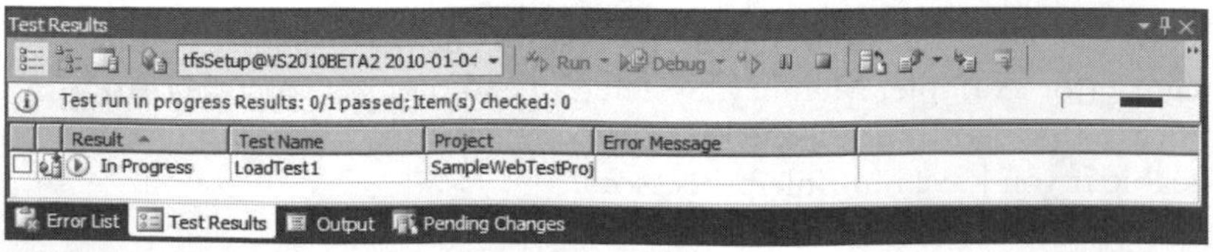

FIGURE 13-23

Once the status of your test is In Progress or Complete, you can double-click to see the Load Test Monitor window, shown in Figure 13-24. You may also right-click and choose View Test Results Details. When a load test is run from the Load Test Editor, the Test Results window is bypassed, immediately displaying the Load Test Monitor.

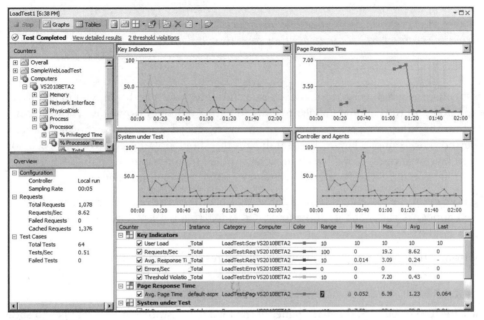

FIGURE 13-24

You can observe the progress of your test and then continue to use the same window to review results after the test has completed. If you have established a load test result store, then you will also be prompted to view additional details at the completion of the load test run (see the earlier section, "Storing Load Test Run Data").

At the top of the screen, just under the file tabs, is a toolbar with several view options. First, if you are viewing detailed information from a results store, you will have a Summary view that displays key information about your load test. The next two buttons allow you to select between Graphs and Tables view. The Details (available if you are viewing detailed information from a results store) provides a graphical view of virtual users over time. The Show Counters Panel and graph options buttons are used to change the way these components are displayed.

Graphs View

The most obvious feature of the Load Test Monitor is the set of four graphs, which is selected by default. These graphs plot a number of selected performance counters over the duration of the test.

The tree in the left-hand (Counter) pane shows a list of all available performance counters, grouped into a variety of sets — for example, by machine. Expand the nodes to reveal the tracked performance counters. Hover over a counter to see a plot of its values in the graph. Double-click on the counter to add it to the graph and legend.

> *Selecting performance counters and knowing what they represent can require experience. With so many available counters, it can be a daunting task to know when your application isn't performing at its best. Fortunately, Microsoft has applied its practices and recommendations to predefine threshold values for each performance counter to help indicate that something might be wrong.*

As the load test runs, the graph is updated at each snapshot interval. In addition, you may notice that some of the nodes in the Counters pane are marked with a red error or yellow warning icon. This indicates that the value of a performance counter has exceeded a predefined threshold and should be reviewed. For example, Figure 13-24 indicates threshold violations for the % Processor Time counter. In fact, you can see small warning icons in the graph itself at the points where the violations occurred. You'll use the Thresholds view to review these in a moment.

The list at the bottom of the screen is a legend that shows details of the selected counters. Those that are checked appear in the graph with the indicated color. If you select a counter, it will be displayed with a bold line.

Finally, the bottom-left (Overview) pane shows the overall results of the load test.

Tables View

When you click the Tables button, the main panel of the load test results window changes to show a drop-down list with a table. Use the drop-down list to view each of the available tables for the load test run. Each of these tables is described in the following sections.

Tests Table

This table goes beyond the detail of the Summary pane, listing all tests in your load test and providing summary statistics for each. Tests are listed by name and containing scenario for easy identification. You will see the total count of runs, pass/fail details, as well as tests per second and seconds per test metrics.

Pages Table

The Pages table shows all of the pages accessed during the load test. Included with each page are details of the containing scenario and Web performance test, along with performance metrics. The Total column shows the number of times that page was rendered during the test. The Page Time column reflects the average response time for each page. Page Time Goal and % Meeting Goal are used when a target response time was specified for that page. Finally, the Last Page Time shows the response time from the most recent request to that page.

Transactions Table

A *transaction* is a defined subset of steps tracked together in a Web performance test. For example, you can wrap the requests from the start to the end of your checkout process in a transaction named Checkout for easy tracking. For more details, see the section "Adding Transactions," earlier in this chapter.

In this table, you will see any defined transactions listed, along with the names of the containing scenario and Web performance test. Details include the count, response time, and elapsed time for each transaction.

SQL Trace Table

The SQL Trace table will only be enabled if you previously configured SQL Tracing for your load test. Details for doing that can be found in the earlier section "SQL Tracing."

This table shows the slowest SQL operations that occurred on the machine specified in your SQL Tracing settings. Note that only those operations that take longer than the Minimum Duration of Traced SQL Operations will appear.

By default, the operations are sorted with the slowest at the top of the list. You can view many details for each operation, including duration, start and end time, CPU, login name, and others.

Thresholds Table

The top of Figure 13-24 indicates that there are "2 threshold violations." You may either click on that text, or select the Threshold table to see the details. You will see a list similar to the one shown in Figure 13-25.

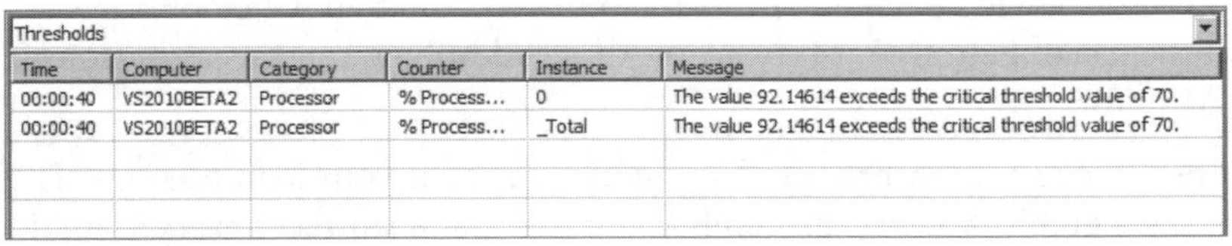

Thresholds					
Time	Computer	Category	Counter	Instance	Message
00:00:40	VS2010BETA2	Processor	% Process...	0	The value 92.14614 exceeds the critical threshold value of 70.
00:00:40	VS2010BETA2	Processor	% Process...	_Total	The value 92.14614 exceeds the critical threshold value of 70.

FIGURE 13-25

Each violation is listed according to the sampling time at which it occurred. You can see details about which counter on which machine failed, as well as a description of what the violating and threshold values were.

Errors Table

As with threshold violations, if your test encountered any errors, you will see a message such as "4 errors." Click on this text or the Errors table button to see a summary list of the errors. This will include the error type (such as Total or Exception) and the error's subtype. SubType will contain the specific Exception type encountered — for example, `FileNotFoundException`. Also shown are the count of each particular error and the message returned from the last occurrence of that error.

If you configured a database to store the load test results data, you can right-click on any entry and choose Errors. This will show the Load Test Errors window, as shown in Figure 13-26.

This table displays each instance of the error, including stack and details (if available), according to the time at which they occurred. Other information (such as the containing test, scenario, and Web request) is displayed when available.

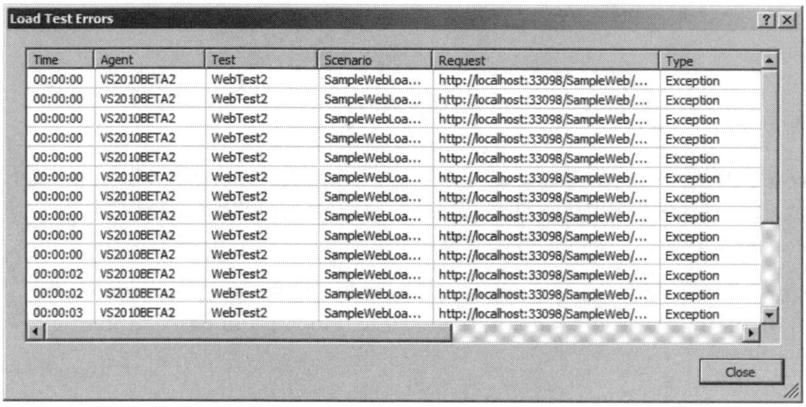

FIGURE 13-26

Detailed Results

If you are utilizing a load test results store (see the earlier section "Storing Load Test Run Data"), then you will have the option of viewing detailed results for your load test run. Click on View detailed results (shown at the top of Figure 13-24) to access these additional options as buttons on the top of the Load Test Monitor.

The Summary view provides a concise view of several key statistics about your load test run. The Detail view allows you to see a graph showing the number, duration, and status of every virtual user within your load test at any given point in time. This view can be helpful for pinpointing times when certain behaviors occur, such as a contention between two given virtual user sessions attempting to access the same functionality in your Web application. The Create Excel Report button allows you to export detailed results of your load test run into a spreadsheet for further analysis.

COMMAND-LINE TEST EXECUTION

To execute a Web performance or load test from the command line, first launch a Visual Studio 2010 command prompt. From the Start menu, select Programs ➪ Microsoft Visual Studio 2010 ➪ Visual Studio Tools ➪ Visual Studio Command Prompt (2010). This version of the command prompt sets environment variables that are useful for accessing Visual Studio utilities.

The MSTest.exe utility is found under the \Common7\IDE directory of your Visual Studio installation directory, but will be available from any directory when using the Visual Studio command prompt.

Executing Tests

From the directory that contains your solution, use the MSTest program to launch the test as follows:

```
MSTest /testcontainer:<Name>.<extension>
```

The target can be a Web performance test, a load test, or an assembly that contains tests such as unit tests. For example, to execute a load test named LoadTest1 in the SampleWebTestProject subfolder, enter the following command:

```
MSTest /testcontainer:SampleWebTestProject\LoadTest1.loadtest
```

This will execute the specified test(s) and display details, such as pass/fail, which run configuration was used, and where the result were stored.

Executing Test Lists

You can also run tests that are grouped into a test list. First, specify the /testmetadata:<filename> option to load the metadata file containing the test list definitions. Then, select the test list to execute with the /testlist:<listname> option.

Other Test Options

Remember that tests can have more than one test settings file. Specify a test settings file using the /testsettings:<filename> option.

By default, results are stored in an XML-based file called a *TRX file*. The default form is MSTest.MMDDYYYY.HHMMSS.trx. To store the run results in an alternate file, use the /resultsfile:<filename> option.

More options are available. To view them, run the following command:

```
MSTest /help
```

DISTRIBUTED LOAD TESTS

In larger-scale efforts, a single machine may not have enough power to simulate the number of users you need to generate the required stress on your application. Fortunately, Visual Studio 2010 load testing includes features supporting the execution of load tests in a distributed environment.

There are a number of roles that the machines play. *Client* machines are typically developer machines on which the load tests are created and selected for execution. The *controller* is the "headquarters" of the operation, coordinating the actions of one or more *agent* machines. The controller also collects the test results from each associated agent machine. The agent machines actually execute the load tests and provide details to the controller. The controller and agents are collectively referred to as a *test rig*.

There are no requirements for the location of the application under test. Generally, the application is installed either on one or more machines either outside the rig or locally on the agent machines, but the architecture of distributed testing is flexible.

Installing Controllers and Agents

Before using controllers and agents, you must install the required Windows services on each machine. The Visual Studio Agents 2010 package includes setup utilities for these services. This setup utility allows you to install the test controller and test agent.

Installing the test controller will install a Windows service for the controller, and will prompt you to assign a Windows account under which that service will run. Refrain from registering your test controller with a team project collection if you want to run load tests from Visual Studio. Enable "Configure for Load Testing" and select a SQL Server or SQL Server Express instance where you want to store your load test results.

Use the "Manage virtual user licenses" button to administer your licenses of load agent virtual user packs. Virtual user packs must be licensed based on the number of concurrent virtual users you wish to simulate. You will be unable to run load tests until you have assigned at least one virtual user pack to your test controller.

> *Install your controller and verify that the Visual Studio Test Controller Windows service is running before configuring your agent machines.*

After the controller service has been installed, run the Test Agent setup on each agent machine, specifying a user under whom the service should run and the name of the controller machine.

Your test controller and test agents can be configured later using the respective entries on the Start Menu under Programs ➪ Microsoft Visual Studio 2010. For additional instructions on configuring test controllers or test agents, consult the product documentation.

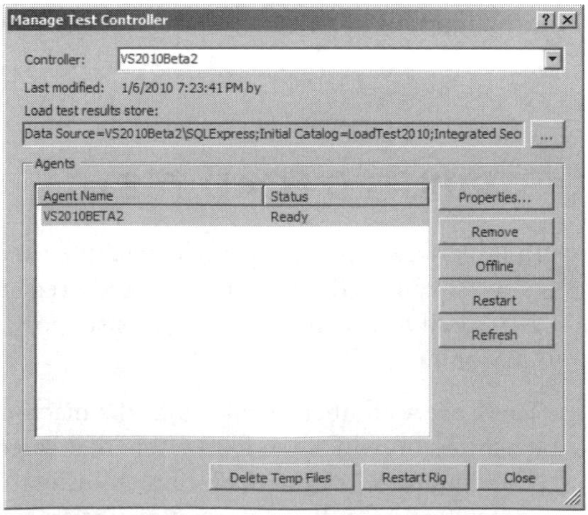

Configuring Controllers

Once you have run the installation packages on the controller and agent machine(s), configure the controller by choosing Test ➪ Manage Test Controllers. This can be done from any machine and does not need to be done on the controller machine itself. You will see the Manage Test Controller dialog, as shown in Figure 13-27.

FIGURE 13-27

Type the name of a machine in the Controller field and press Enter. Ensure that the machine you specify has had the required controller services installed. The Agents panel will then list any currently configured agents for that controller, along with each agent's status.

The "Load test results store" points to the repository you are using to store load test data. Click the ellipsis button to select and test a connection to your repository. If you have not already configured a repository, refer to the earlier section "Storing Load Test Run Data."

The Agents panel will show any test agents that have been registered with your test controller. Temporarily suspend an agent from the rig by clicking the Offline button. Restart the agent services on a target machine with the Restart button.

You also have options for clearing temporary log data and directories, as well as restarting the entire rig.

Configuring Agents

Using the Manage Test Controller dialog just described, select an agent and click the Properties button. You will be able to modify several settings, described in the following sections.

Weighting

When running a distributed load test, the load test being executed by the controller has a specific user load profile. This user load is then distributed to the agent machines according to their individual weightings.

For example, suppose two agents are running under a controller that is executing a load test with ten users. If the agents' weights are each 50, then five users will be sent to each agent.

IP Switching

This indicates the range of IP addresses to be used for calls from this agent to the target Web application.

Attributes

You may assign name-value attributes to each agent in order to later restrict which agent machines are selected to run tests. There are no restrictions on the names and values you can set.

You will learn how to leverage these attributes in the next section.

Test Settings

Once your controller and agents have been installed and configured, you are ready to execute a load test against them. You specify a controller for the test and agent properties in the test settings. You may recall seeing the test settings when we covered Web performance tests.

Open your test settings by choosing Test ➪ Edit Test Settings and selecting your active test settings file. Then, choose the Roles entry from the left-hand list. You should see the dialog shown in Figure 13-28.

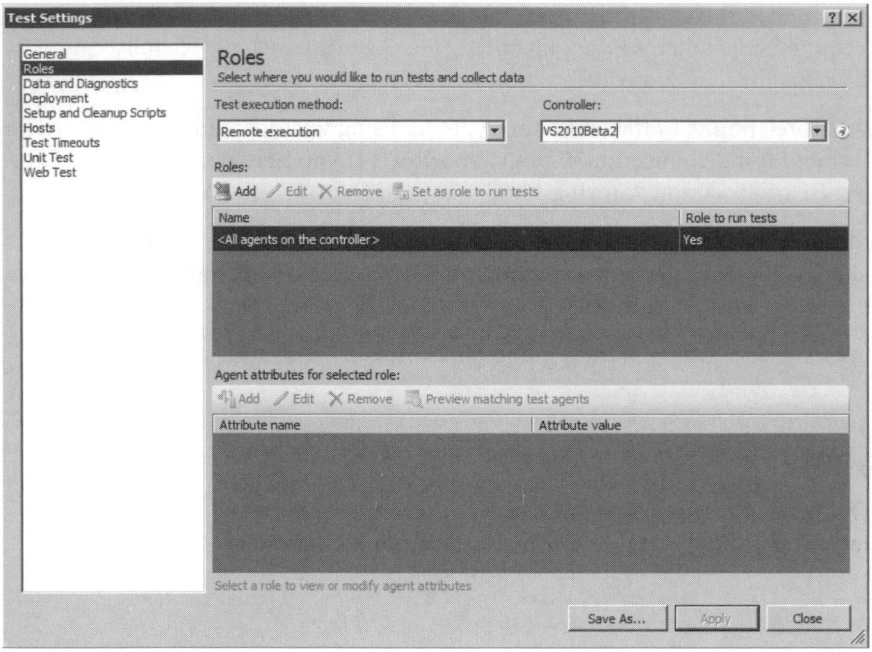

FIGURE 13-28

Under "Test execution method," choose Remote execution, and then enter or select the name of a valid controller machine.

The Roles panel and "Agent attributes for selected role" panel are used if you want to restrict the agents that will execute your tests to a subset of those registered with your test controller. Otherwise, all available agents will be utilized.

When you have finished making your changes, you may wish to create a new test settings file especially for remote execution. To do so, choose Save As and specify a new file.

Running a Distributed Load Test

Now that you have installed and configured your rig (a controller and at least one agent machine) and modified your test run configuration to target the controller, you may execute the load test. Execute the test using any one of the options described in the earlier section "Executing Load Tests," ensuring that the correct test settings have been selected (Test ➪ Select Active Test Settings).

The controller will then be signaled to begin the test. The controller will contact the (qualifying) agent machines and distribute tests and load to each. As each test completes, the controller collects test run details from each agent. When all agents have completed, the controller finalizes the test and the test run ends.

Viewing a Distributed Load Test

To view the progress of your distributed load test, open the Test Runs window via the Windows option under the Test menu. You will see a window similar to the one shown in Figure 13-29.

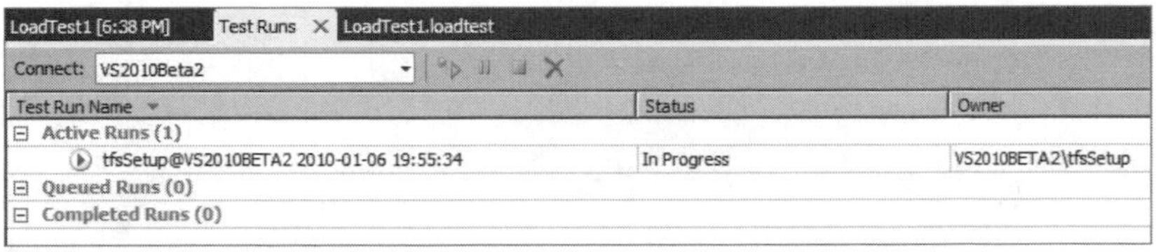

FIGURE 13-29

Select the controller from the Connect drop-down. The window will then show details of any running, waiting, and completed runs on that controller. You may also select a run and start, stop, or temporarily suspend its execution.

SUMMARY

This chapter described Web performance and load tests in detail. You first learned how to use the Web Test Recorder to easily record a new Web performance test. You then learned how to use the Web Test Editor to finely tune the Web performance test, adding features such as validation and extraction rules. You also looked at coded Web performance tests, which enable you to create very flexible tests.

The next section introduced load tests, which can be composed of any automated testing type, such as Web performance and unit tests. You learned how to use the New Load Test Wizard to create an initial load test. You then used the Load Test Editor to add scenarios, SQL tracing, and other options not available through the wizard. You also looked at various options for executing load tests, including the command-line tool MSTest.exe.

You then saw the power of the Load Test Monitor, used to graphically view performance counter details as well as errors, transactions, SQL operations, and more.

Finally, you learned how to run load tests in a distributed environment. You now know how to install and configure the controller and agent machines, and how to use the controller to parcel out load to the agent machines, collecting results in the test repository.

In Chapter 14, you will discover the powerful new capabilities of Visual Studio 2010 for creating and managing manual tests.

CONFER PROGRAMMER TO PROGRAMMER ABOUT THIS TOPIC.

Visit p2p.wrox.com

14

Manual Testing

WHAT'S IN THIS CHAPTER?

➤ Using Microsoft Test Manager to create and manage test plans

➤ Authoring manual tests and publishing the results

➤ Taking advantage of fast-forward for manual testing to speed up test runs

Across the software development industry, manual testing still makes up about 70 percent of the testing efforts as compared to creating automated tests, or specialized testing efforts such as performance and scale testing. Yet, manual testing has historically been overlooked by most software development tool vendors. Microsoft is seeking to change that disparity with Visual Studio 2010 by building an entirely new set of tools targeted specifically at the *generalist tester*. A generalist tester is a person who tests software manually by directly interacting with the software in the way a user might, and filing bugs when the tester encounters broken functionality or unexpected behavior.

In this chapter, you will learn how Visual Studio 2010 can make generalist testers more efficient at authoring, managing, and executing manual test cases. You will also gain an understanding of how the new testing framework in Visual Studio 2010 bridges the gap between testers and developers by capturing rich diagnostics during test runs, which can then be analyzed by developers to help them diagnose and resolve bugs.

MICROSOFT TEST MANAGER

Microsoft Test Manager is a new tool designed specifically for generalist testing teams. With Test Manager, you can create and manage test plans and test cases, author and execute manual tests, and file rich bugs. In Chapter 16, you will also see how Test Manager can be used to create and manage physical and virtual test environments.

Test Manager requires a connection to Visual Studio Team Foundation Server 2010. Team Foundation Server is used for storing all testing artifacts used by Test Manager, such as test plans, test cases, bugs, and the results of test runs. Test Manager also relies on the use of Team Foundation Build for building the software that you are testing.

FIGURE 14-1

The first time you start Microsoft Test Manager, you will be prompted to connect to Team Foundation Server, as shown in Figure 14-1. Type in the name of your server as provided by your Team Foundation Server administrator, and click Add. If your Team Foundation Server is configured for a non-standard port, type the server name as `servername:portnumber`. If your Team Foundation Server instance has been configured for a non-standard virtual application directory, you may need to supply the full URI path. Consult with your Team Foundation Server administrator for assistance. Click Add when you are finished.

Next, you will be prompted to connect to a team project, as shown in Figure 14-2. Select your team project and click "Connect now."

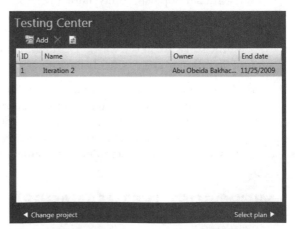

FIGURE 14-2

USING TEST PLANS

A *test plan* is used within Test Manager to manage your entire testing effort for a given iteration. This includes your test cases, test results, the configurations you plan to test (for example, different operating systems and Web browsers), and several other settings that you will learn about in this chapter.

You will usually have different test plans for different iterations of your application's development lifecycle. For example, early test plans may focus on testing core functionality, whereas future test plans may be targeted at fit-and-finish (such as layout, rendering, spelling, and so on).

FIGURE 14-3

If your team project doesn't already include a test plan, you will need to create one, as shown in Figure 14-3. Click on Add to create a new plan. Once created, select the plan and click "Select plan."

You are now ready to begin working with your test plan. If at any time you want to switch to a different test plan or Team Foundation Server instance, you can click on the name of your test plan in the upper-right hand corner of Test Manager.

You should spend a few minutes familiarizing yourself with the navigation menu at the top of Test Manager. Test Manager is divided into two *activity centers,* the Testing Center and the Lab Center, which can be toggled by clicking on the text for Testing Center. This chapter will focus on the Testing Center. (You will learn more about the Lab Center in Chapter 16.)

Each activity center consists of several *activities*. Activities can be accessed by clicking the headings for each activity center, then the subheadings underneath those headings. The Testing Center is divided into the following four main areas of activities:

➤ *Plan* — The Plan area is used to manage your overall test plan. This includes the plan's properties, as well as the individual test suites and test cases that make up your plan.

➤ *Test* — The Test area is used to view the list of test cases that are ready to be run. From here, you can launch test runs to execute test cases and save the results, file bugs, and so on.

➤ *Track* — The Track area allows you to change the build that you are currently testing. This tab also helps testers discover which tests might be most important to run, based on the build in use.

➤ *Organize* — The Organize area provides an easy way of accessing and modifying all of your test cases, test configurations, and other test plans.

You will learn more about these areas in the remainder of this chapter.

For now, let's focus on configuring the properties of your test plan. Click on Plan and then click on Properties. Test Manager then displays the test plan properties activity for your test plan, as shown in Figure 14-4.

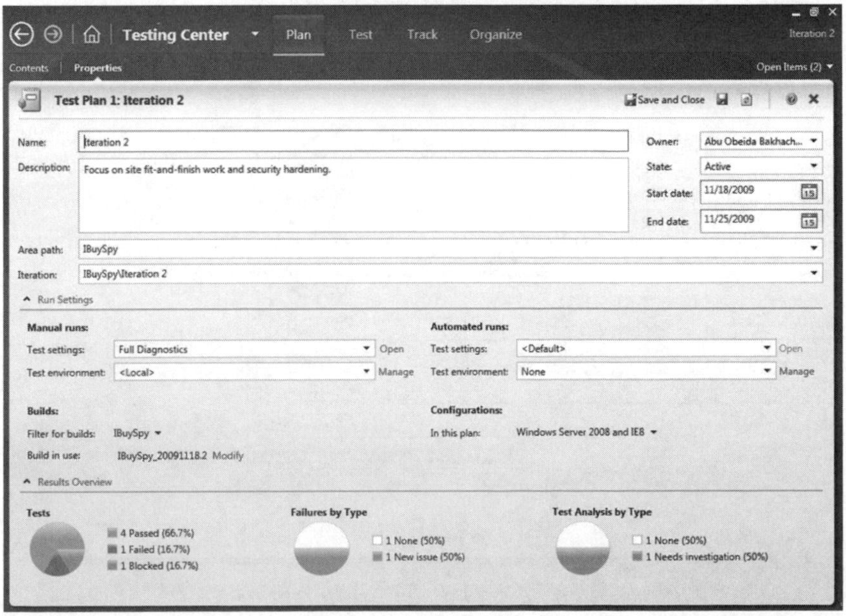

FIGURE 14-4

The upper portion of your test plan's properties includes metadata that you can use to describe the plan (such as name, description, and owner). This metadata can be useful for planning purposes, but it won't actually impact the functionality of your test plan. For example, setting your plan's State to Inactive or the Iteration Start Date to occur in the future won't prevent this plan from being used by testers. It's only useful for describing your plan.

Let's take a look at the rest of the properties you can set for your test plan.

Configuring Test Settings

Test settings define which data diagnostic adapters will be used when conducting your test runs. Data diagnostic adapters were introduced in Chapter 12. Data diagnostic adapters can collect data from the machines being tested or affect the machines being tested (such as by emulating a slower network connection). This data can be very useful for developers when they receive a bug by providing rich data about how the bug was encountered and even the state of the application at various points in time leading up to the bug discovery.

From within your plan properties, you can select the default test settings, which should be used for both manual and automated test runs. You can also create a new test setting entry, or modify existing test settings. You will learn more about test settings for automated runs in Chapter 16 when you learn about configuring test environments.

Figure 14-5 shows an example of test settings for manual runs. The "Data and Diagnostics" tab allows you to configure which data diagnostic adapters should be enabled when this test setting is used. Note that some data diagnostic adapters have additional options that can be configured (such as the maximum length for video recordings).

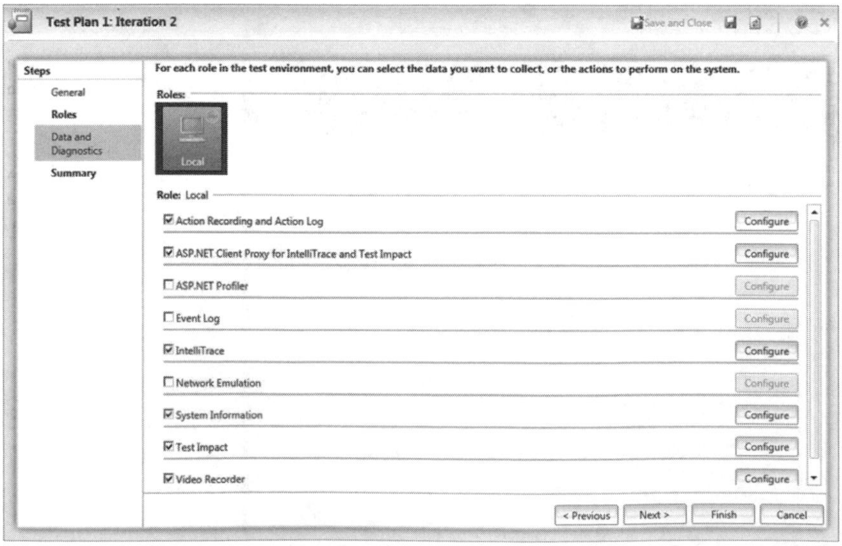

FIGURE 14-5

Chapter 12 provides more information on data diagnostic adapters.

Note that data diagnostic adapters have varying amounts of overhead, including start-up time, CPU usage, and storage space for the various artifacts that will be included with test results. Also note that some data diagnostic adapters cannot be used simultaneously with other data diagnostic adapters. The product documentation includes a matrix that explains this in greater detail.

It is a good practice for the testing team to work with the development team in defining which data diagnostic adapters should be enabled for each machine within the environment. This helps to ensure that developers have everything they need to diagnose a problem when they receive a bug, along with attachments from the test run.

This may result in creating two different test settings. One "lightweight" test setting can be used for everyday testing and to capture basic diagnostic information. Another "full" test setting can be used to collect any and all diagnostics that may eventually help a developer to troubleshoot an issue. If, after finding an issue using the "lightweight" test setting, a tester believes that additional diagnostic data might be useful to the developer, he or she can run the test again using the "full" test setting.

Using Builds

As your testing progresses, you will periodically select new builds with which to test. From your test plan's properties, you can first configure the filter for your builds to match the build definition (as defined in Team Foundation Build) and, optionally, the build quality to use as a filter from among all available builds.

For example, it is common to have a tester *scout* a build before the rest of the team tries the build. Scouting usually involves installing the software and running some initial tests to ensure that it's worth using by the rest of the team. Once a build is scouted, the status of that build can be changed to indicate that it's a suitable build candidate to be used by the rest of the team.

After you configure a build definition and filter, you can click on Modify to view the Assign Build dialog shown in Figure 14-6. Start by choosing with which build to begin testing and click "Assign to plan." Note that previous builds are no longer available to assign to your plan after you do this.

FIGURE 14-6

After you choose your initial build, you can view newer builds by using the "Available builds" drop-down. When examining a newer build, any work items (such as requirements or bugs) that have been changed since your currently selected build will be displayed in the lower portion of the dialog. This is determined by compiling a list of work items that are linked to changesets from all builds between the current build and the build you are considering.

> *Chapter 19 provides more information on changesets.*

This information can help you decide whether to continue testing with your existing build, or to switch to a newer build (by clicking on "Assign to plan"). For example, maybe your testing efforts for a given feature are blocked until a task is implemented or a bug is fixed. In Figure 14-6, you can see that one user story, three tasks, and two bugs have been impacted since the currently assigned build. Clicking on "Assign to plan" would update the test plan to use that newer build. Afterward, results from test runs would be recorded against this newer build.

> *Assigning a new build to a test plan affects the entire team working on that test plan. Also note that you can't assign builds older than the one you have already selected. For these reasons, carefully consider which newer builds to assign to your test plan.*

You can also access the Assign Build activity by clicking on Test, then Assign Build.

Analyzing Impacted Tests

Test impact analysis is a powerful feature that can help improve the productivity of testers by allowing them to quickly identify tests to re-run based on changes to code. Test impact analysis can be enabled to run in the background while tests are being executed. This feature records which sections of code get executed while each test is run. These tests can be automated tests (for example, unit tests, load tests, or coded UI tests) as well as manual tests, but the code you are analyzing must be managed code (that is, .NET Framework 2.0 and above).

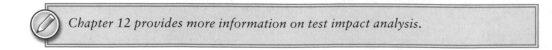

> *Chapter 12 provides more information on test impact analysis.*

To use this feature, click Track ➪ Recommended Tests to get to the Recommended Tests activity. Here, you can see a list of test cases that may have been impacted by recent changes to source code.

This activity works similarly to that of the Assign Build activity by comparing the results of your currently selected build to that of an older build. Use the Recommended Tests activity to quickly compile a list of tests that might be useful to re-run. To mark a test to be re-run, click that test (or select a range of tests), and then click the "Reset to active" button. This causes that test case to appear as Active from the Run Tests activity (which you will learn about later).

> *You should be careful not to rely too heavily on test impact analysis, since there are certain factors that may impact the tests not captured by test impact analysis. This includes changes to test data (which may result in different paths through a code base), and changes to other libraries or applications with which your test application interacts, but which aren't being analyzed by test impact analysis. For this reason, you should examine your test plan from multiple angles (for example test impact analysis, changes to work items, and so on) and routinely consider re-running all of your tests, regardless of whether they are known to have been impacted.*

Defining Test Configurations

Often, your software must be supported on a variety of hardware and software configurations. Correspondingly, your test plan should account for these configurations if they have the potential to impact the functionality or behavior of the application you are testing. Test Manager allows you to define *test configurations* to represent the matrix of environments that you want to test.

The test plan properties page allows you to select the default test configurations that should be applied to tests in your plan. You can override these defaults for an individual test case, but, by default, if you want all of your tests to be run on Windows Vista with Internet Explorer 7 and Windows 7 with Internet Explorer 8, you must specify that in your test plan properties.

Figure 14-7 shows the Test Configuration Manager that is used to build the matrix of test configurations you might wish to include in your test plan. Creating a new test configuration allows you to select one or more configuration variables (such as operating system and browser) and their assigned values.

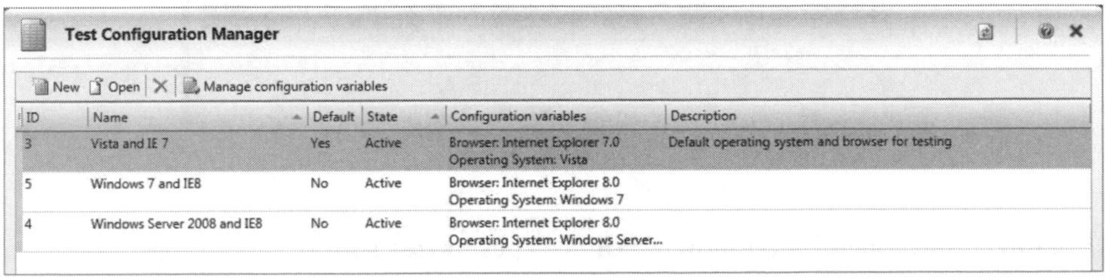

ID	Name	Default	State	Configuration variables	Description
3	Vista and IE 7	Yes	Active	Browser: Internet Explorer 7.0 Operating System: Vista	Default operating system and browser for testing
5	Windows 7 and IE8	No	Active	Browser: Internet Explorer 8.0 Operating System: Windows 7	
4	Windows Server 2008 and IE8	No	Active	Browser: Internet Explorer 8.0 Operating System: Windows Server...	

Test Configuration Manager

New Open X Manage configuration variables

FIGURE 14-7

Configuration variables for operating system and browser are provided to you by default. But you might want to create your own configuration variables, or modify the existing variables to include additional browser and operating system choices. You can do this by clicking on "Manage configuration variables." You can create configuration variables for anything that you want to track for your testing efforts. For example, maybe it's important to test with different operating system languages, service pack levels, or even keyboard layouts. All of these changes in the environment can be represented using configuration variables.

After you have created your configuration variables in Test Configuration Manager, click New to assign variables and their values to a test configuration. These test configurations can then be added to your test plan from within the Test Plan Properties activity.

In Chapter 16, you will learn how the new Lab Management feature of Visual Studio 2010 can be used to help you run tests in a variety of environments to quickly address a wide range of test configurations. For now, you will be running all of your tests locally.

Using Plan Contents

If you click Plan ➪ Contents, you can use the Contents planning activity to create and organize the *test cases* that make up your test plan. A test case is simply a set of interactions with a software application that are designed to validate application functionality or behavior. For example, you might have a test case that confirms that a new user can create an account within your application. Test cases are represented as work items in Team Foundation Server, and, correspondingly, in Test Manager. In this chapter, you will learn how to author test cases and manage them within your test plan. Figure 14-8 shows the Contents planning activity.

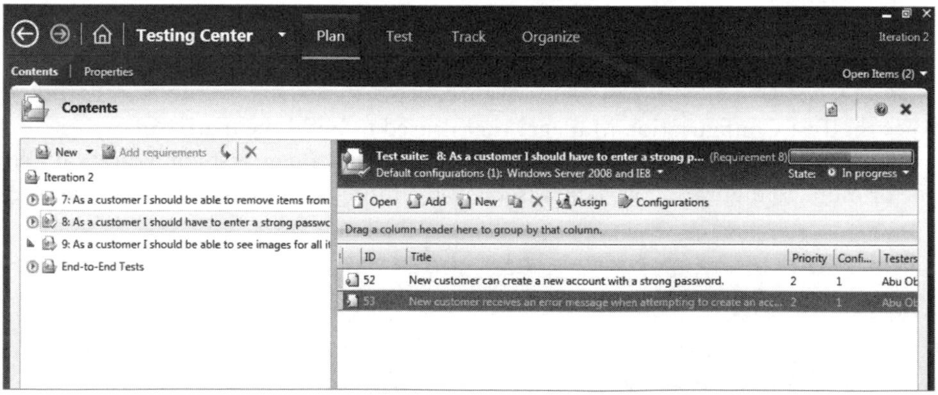

FIGURE 14-8

Test cases are organized into one of the following three types of *test suites*:

➤ *Requirements-based test suite* — This includes any test cases that are linked to requirement work items via a "Tests" relationship. For any given iteration of an application's development, you will usually want to start by adding all the requirements that are being implemented in that iteration. This way, you can create and execute test cases that verify an application is on track to deliver the promised functionality. Click on "Add requirements" to add a requirements-based test suite to your plan. You will be prompted to select the requirement to which to bind your suite.

➤ *Query-based test suite* — This allows you to specify a dynamic work item query for selecting test cases. For example, you might want to include all test cases with a priority of 1, even if they are for requirements that were implemented and tested in earlier iterations. This can help ensure that critical functionality that used to work doesn't break (or *regress*) as the application progresses. Click New ➪ "Query-based suite" to add this to your plan. You will be prompted to create the work item query to which to bind this suite. The sort order of the query will define the test order of the suite.

➤ *Static test suite* — This is simply a list of test cases that can be added manually to the suite. A static test suite can also be used as a container for other test suites, giving you a hierarchical option for organizing your tests. Click New ➪ Suite to add a static test suite to your plan.

You can also copy suites from other plans by clicking on the blue arrow. For example, when you create your Beta 2 test plan, you might want to carry forward some of the Beta 1 test suites.

If you highlight a test suite, you will see all of that test suite's test cases to the right. You will learn how to work with test cases next. For now, note that you can change the State of a test suite by clicking on the State drop-down. Test suites can have one of the following three valid states:

➤ *In planning* — This indicates that you are still authoring your test cases, and that they aren't yet ready to run.

➤ *In progress* — This means that test cases in this suite should be run by the testing team. Only test suites that are "In progress" will show up in the Test activity for testers to run. This is the default state for new test suites.

➤ *Completed* — This should be used when you no longer want to run the test cases that make up this suite. For example, if all of the test cases that make up this suite are passing for current builds, then you may deem it unnecessary to continue to run those tests.

Authoring Test Cases

You can add a test case to a requirements-based test suite or a static test suite by first highlighting that suite, and then clicking New or Add on the right side of the activity window. Click New to create a brand new test case, or Add to browse for an existing test case. When you are adding test cases to a requirements-based test case, a "Tests/Tested By" link will be made between your test case work item and the requirement work item.

Clicking on New will display a new test case form. Figure 14-9 shows a test case that has already been authored.

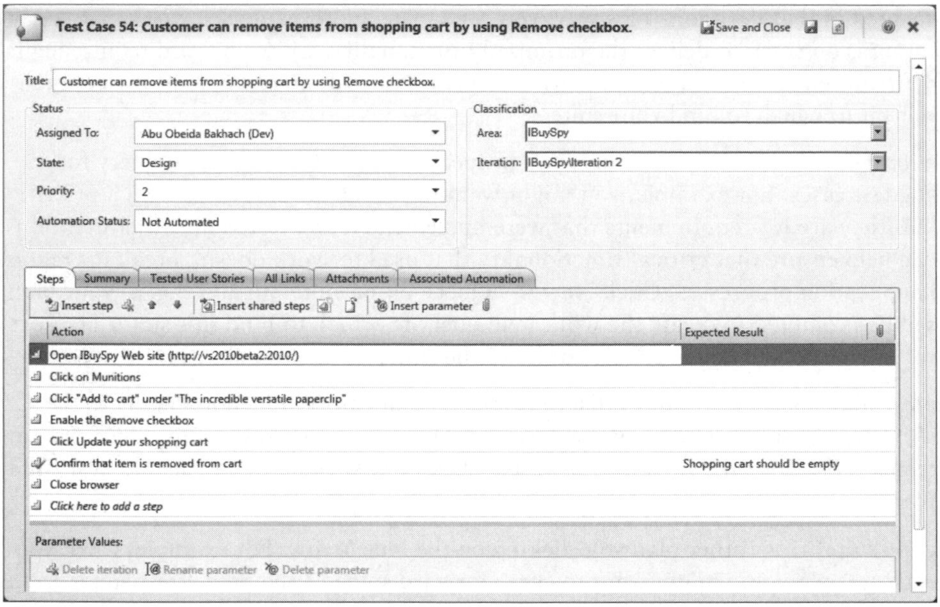

FIGURE 14-9

The top portion of this form should look familiar if you've worked with any other work items in Team Foundation Server before. But the Steps tab is where the test case form gets interesting, since this is where you can author the steps that a generalist tester should take when running this test case.

You can start by simply typing the actions that you want the tester to perform during the test case. Each step should go on a new row. You can place your cursor on a new row and begin typing, or press Enter when you are ready to type a new row. You can also use the toolbar to manage the insertion/deletion of steps or to move steps up or down in the list of test steps.

The Expected Result column is used to tell the tester what he or she should be verifying as the tester runs the test case. For example, after creating a new account, the tester should see a message indicating that the account creation was successful. Specifying an expected result changes the test step to be a *verification step*. The tester will be expected to report on the status of each verification step to indicate whether or not that test step was successful.

You can also add attachments (such as an image) to a test step to provide further instructions to a tester about what to do or what the tester should be verifying. To add an attachment, right-click on a test step and click "Manage test step attachments." You will be prompted to upload the files that you want to attach to this test step.

Finally, parameters can be used to provide different values for a test step. For example, you might want to test the process of creating a new user account by trying different values for username, password, and so on. Instead of writing a new test case for each set of values you want to test, you can simply parameterize a single test case with multiple values. Each row of data you specify will result in a separate iteration of the test case during a test run. To create a new parameter, use the "@" symbol within a test step preceding a variable name, as shown here:

```
Type @username and @password and click OK
```

This will create two new parameters, `username` and `password`, in the Parameter Values table at the bottom of the test case. You can then supply values for these parameters within the table. These values will be used later on when running the test. Each row of your Parameter Values table will correspond to a unique iteration when running this test case.

> *Parameter Values can also be used by coded UI tests, as you will see in Chapter 15.*

Using Shared Steps

There may be times when you have steps within your test plan that are repeated across multiple test cases. A good example of this is the process of creating an account, or signing into a Web site, before completing other steps within a test case. Instead of authoring (and maintaining) these common steps within each test case, you can utilize *shared steps*.

Shared steps allow you to author and maintain common test steps within a unique container. Like test cases, shared steps are also persisted as work items within Team Foundation Server. Shared steps are most valuable for protecting your test cases in the event that these common test steps change, such as if you modify the process of creating an account or signing into the application. Instead of needing to change these steps within multiple test cases, you can simply update the shared steps work item. Test cases that include those shared steps will be updated automatically. Action recordings, which you will learn about later, are also stored within shared steps. This means that you can update the action recordings for a set of shared steps in a single location, instead of needing to re-create the action recording for each test case that includes those shared steps.

To create shared test steps from within a test case, highlight the first step in the series of common steps that you wish to convert into shared steps. While pressing the Shift key, click on the last step in the list of steps that you wish to convert into shared steps. Now, right-click on this range of steps and select "Create shared steps," as shown in Figure 14-10.

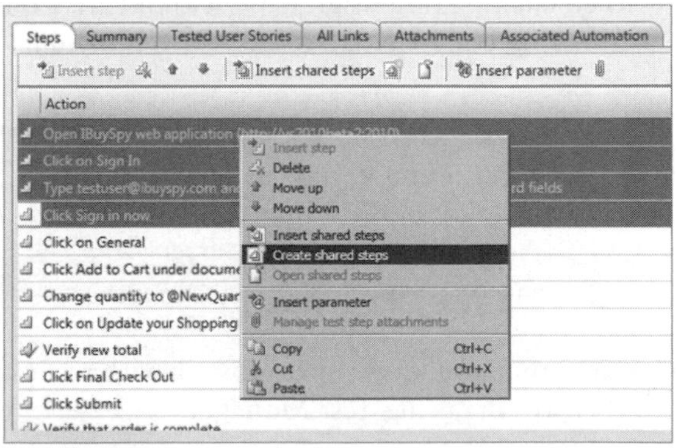

FIGURE 14-10

You will be prompted to give your shared steps a name. Afterward, the common steps in your test case will be collapsed into a single, bolded test step, as shown in Figure 14-11. You can open and edit shared steps by right-clicking on them and selecting "Open shared steps." You can also insert other shared steps by right-clicking and choosing "Insert shared steps."

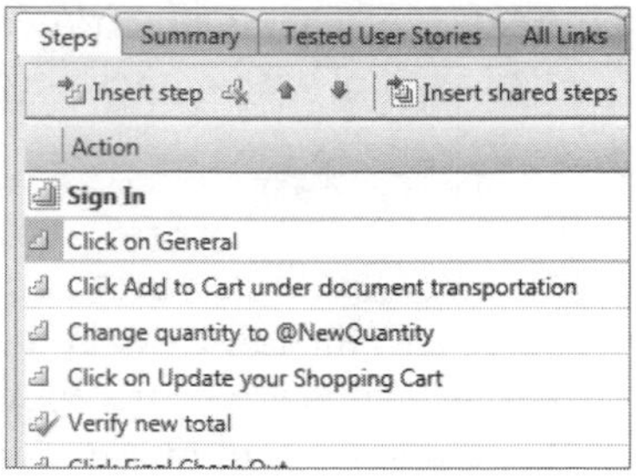

Assigning Configurations

Earlier, you learned how test configurations can be assigned to a test plan. This defines the default test configurations that all test cases in this test plan should utilize. However, you can override your test plan's test configurations setting for individual test cases, or for an individual test suite.

FIGURE 14-11

To override the test configuration for an individual test case, first select a test suite from within the Contents planning activity. Then select a test case from the right-hand pane of the activity. Click Configurations to display the Select Test Configurations activity shown in Figure 14-12. Click on "All configurations" to display the full list of configurations available. From here, you can select the test configurations that should be assigned to this test case.

FIGURE 14-12

To apply new test configurations to an entire test suite, right-click the test suite and choose "Select test configurations for all tests."

Assigning Testers

You can assign test cases to the testers who should run them. Do this by selecting a test suite and then clicking on Assign from within Plan Contents activity. The Assign Testers activity will appear, allowing you to assign test cases to individual testers.

> *Assigning testers to test cases is only used as a guide to help the test team divide up work. Test Manager won't prevent a tester from running test cases that are assigned to another tester.*

Now that you know how to work with test plans, it's time to learn how to run test cases and track their results using Test Manager.

RUNNING TESTS AND TRACKING RESULTS

Open the Run Tests activity (click Test ⇨ Run Tests) to see a view of your test suites and test cases, like that shown in Figure 14-13. The Run Tests activity is used to help you select which tests to run, and to track the status of previous test runs.

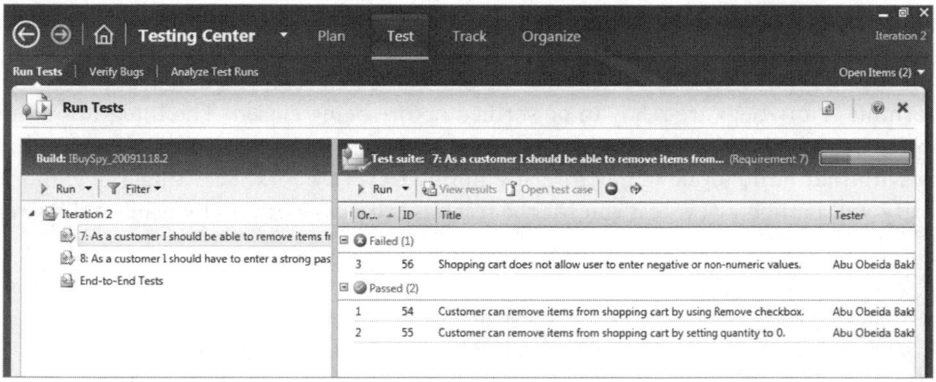

FIGURE 14-13

Any test suites that are set to a status of "In progress" will be shown along the left side of this activity pane. Along the right side of this activity pane you will see the test cases within the currently selected test suite.

Note that each test case may be listed multiple times if there are multiple test configurations assigned to that test case. You can use the Filter button to choose which test configurations you are ready to test. This way, you can show just the test configurations that you can support on the machine you are currently testing with.

This view also shows you the status of each test case from the last time it was run (passed, failed, or inclusive for tests that have not yet been run). Tests that are not ready to be run will be marked with a blocked icon. You might want to block certain test cases if they are not yet implemented in the current build you are using, or if you know that they will fail because they depend on other test cases that are failing. For example, a test case that relies on logging in as a new user account could fail if the test case for creating a new account is failing. You can toggle which test cases are blocked by using the "Block test" and "Reset test to active" buttons on the right-hand side of the activity pane.

You can learn more about previous runs for a test case by selecting that test case and clicking on "View results." You can also use the Analyze Test Runs activity (click Test ➪ Analyze Test Runs) to view a list of *test runs*, as shown in Figure 14-14. A test run is a continuous testing session during which one or more test cases are executed.

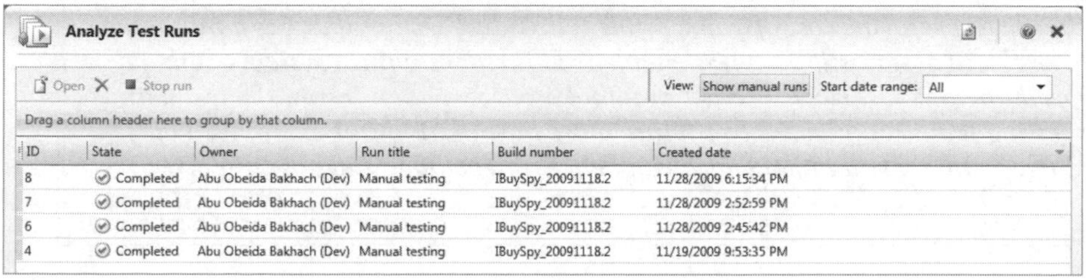

FIGURE 14-14

The My Bugs activity (click Test ⇨ My Bugs) displays a list of bugs that were either created by you, or assigned to you, as shown in Figure 14-15. If a developer has fixed a bug, he or she will usually assign it back to the tester to confirm that the bug can be closed. You can use this activity to determine if any bugs are ready to be verified before being closed. The Integration Build column will show you which build the bug fix has been checked in to so that you can ensure that you are testing with that build (or newer) before attempting to verify a fix. Selecting a bug and clicking on Verify will launch a new test run for the test case that was originally used to discover that bug.

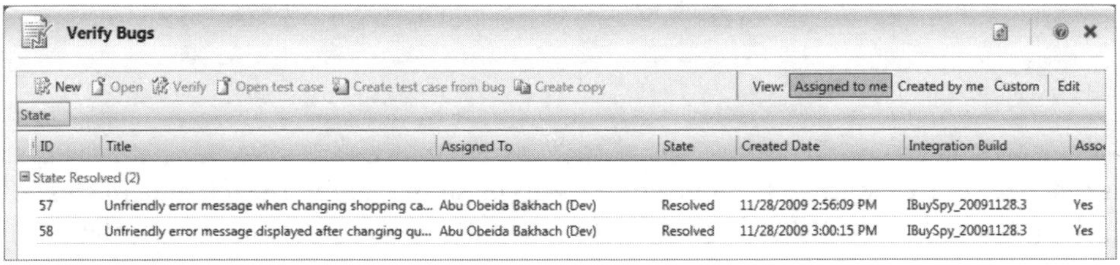

ID	Title	Assigned To	State	Created Date	Integration Build	Asso
⊟ State: Resolved (2)						
57	Unfriendly error message when changing shopping ca...	Abu Obeida Bakhach (Dev)	Resolved	11/28/2009 2:56:09 PM	IBuySpy_20091128.3	Yes
58	Unfriendly error message displayed after changing qu...	Abu Obeida Bakhach (Dev)	Resolved	11/28/2009 3:00:15 PM	IBuySpy_20091128.3	Yes

FIGURE 14-15

You can also construct a custom query from this view, such as to build a query composed of the bugs belonging to all of the members of your team.

Using Microsoft Test Runner

Microsoft Test Runner is used to exercise test runs. To start a test run, return to the Run Tests activity (Test ⇨ Run Tests) and select a test case that you want to run. You can also select a range of test cases to run by using pressing Shift-click or Ctrl-click. Click on Run above the list of test cases to begin a test run.

> *You can also run all of the active tests within a test suite by clicking on the Run icon located above the list of test suites. Click the down arrow next to the Run icon and choose "Run with options" if you want to override the test plan's default test settings, build, or test environment for your test run. For example, you may decide to perform most of your testing with a test setting that has a minimum number of data diagnostic adapters enabled. This can minimize system overhead and speed up your test runs. Then, if you find a bug, you can re-run the test with a test setting that is configured to capture more information (for example, a video recording, or IntelliTrace file), which can help the developer diagnose and fix the bug.*

Test Runner will be launched as shown in Figure 14-16. Test Runner is now ready to help you run the test cases that you selected for this run.

Test Runner allows you to record an *action recording* that can be used to "fast-forward" through test steps during future test runs. This feature is known as *fast-forward for manual testing.* Playing back an action recording can dramatically speed up a test run by performing actions far faster than a human could perform them. This can also make a generalist tester's job less mundane by allowing the tester to focus on examining an application for bugs, instead of following a mindless script of clicking and typing repeatedly. Action recordings can even be used as the basis for creating fully automated coded UI tests, as you will see in Chapter 15.

To create an action recording, select "Create action recording" and click on Start Test.

Test Runner will now open a list of test steps for the test case you are currently running, as shown in Figure 14-17. If a step has an Expected Result value, it will be shown here as well to help guide the tester about what he or she should be validating.

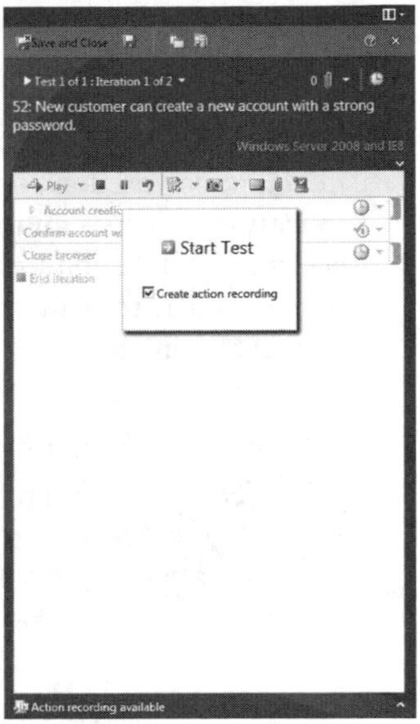

FIGURE 14-16

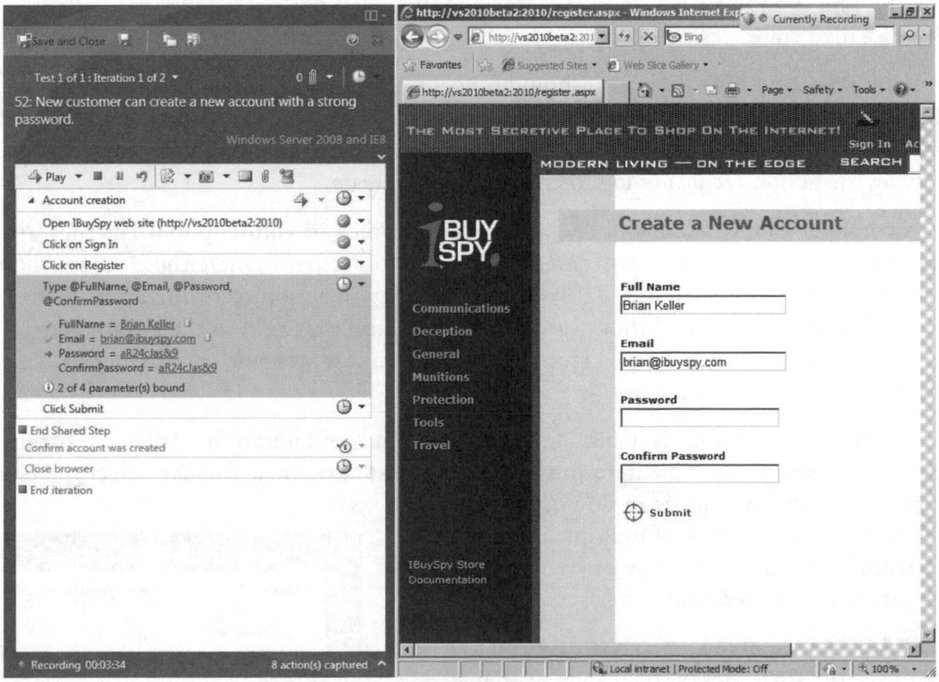

FIGURE 14-17

If you chose to create an action recording, then every interaction you have with the applications you are testing will be captured. To gather a clean recording, you should be careful not to perform steps that are not part of your test case. This includes launching other applications or interacting with the desktop. Interactions with the Test Runner user interface are excluded from your action recording by default, so you don't have to worry about these polluting your recording. You can exclude other applications (such as an instant messaging application) by configuring the test settings for Action Recording and Action Log, as shown in Figure 14-5. You can also use the Pause button on the Test Runner toolbar to pause the action recording, allowing you to interact with other applications before returning to your test run.

> *The capability for Microsoft Test Runner to capture action recordings is limited to the type of application being tested. See the "Supported Technology" section later on in this chapter for more information.*

As you are running a test case, you can report on whether each test step passes or fails. Do this by clicking on the drop-down to the right of each test step, or by using the keyboard shortcuts. By default, Windows Key + Shift + P will pass a test step, and Windows Key + Shift + F will fail a test step.

You are only required to report on the status of validation steps, those that are marked with a checkmark icon. Failing to indicate whether or not a validation step has passed will cause the test case to default to a failed state.

If you are capturing an action recording, you should report on the status of each test step as you perform it. This makes it possible for the action recording log to correlate individual test steps with the actions that they are composed of. This is important for playing back individual test steps later on, and when using the action recording log to create coded UI tests.

If your test has parameter values, these will be automatically copied to your clipboard as they are encountered in your test case. This way, you can simply place your cursor where these values should be entered and press Ctrl + V to paste them. If you are capturing an action recording, Test Runner will remember the field that you pasted those values into, and bind that field to the parameter. This binding will be used later during playback. Figure 14-17 shows a test step with parameter values being bound to fields on a Web application.

After you have finished running your test case iteration, click on "End iteration." If your test run included multiple test cases, or multiple iterations for a given test case, then you can select the next test case or iteration to run from the drop-down, as shown in Figure 14-18. A test case will consist of multiple iterations if you are using parameter values. Each row of your parameter values will generate a unique iteration.

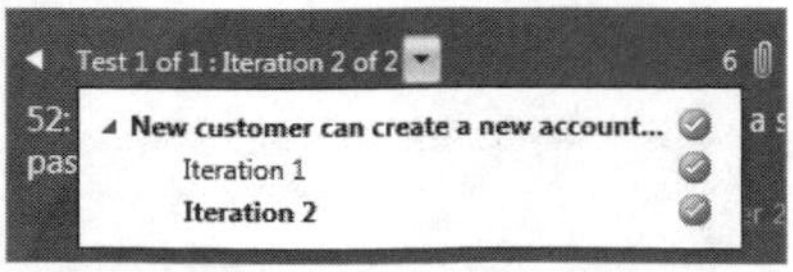

If an action recording is available for the test case you are running, you will see the text "Action recording available" at

FIGURE 14-18

the bottom of Test Runner. This means that you can use this action recording to play back one or more test steps.

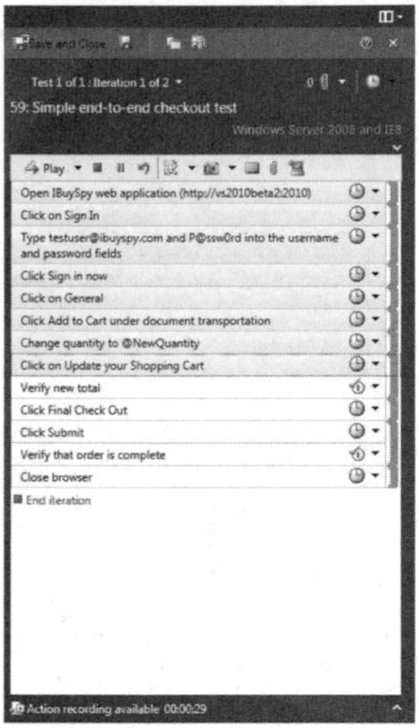

To play back an action recording, select the first step that you wish to play back. Then, press Shift and click on the last step that you want to play back. Now, click on Play, as shown in Figure 14-19.

Test Runner will begin playing back the actions that you recorded earlier. This includes launching applications, clicking on windows and controls, and entering values. It is important that you don't use your mouse or keyboard while this is being played back, or else you might interfere with the playback.

You can use action recordings to play back an entire test case or just sections of a test case. You can also launch playback multiple times within a test case, selecting a new range of test steps each time. Launching multiple times is helpful to give you a chance to inspect the application and verify that it's behaving properly. You may also choose to play back steps of the recording that you know work, and manually perform actions that may not match the last recording (such as if the user interface changed for a given set of steps). Depending on the type of user interface change, it may eventually become necessary to re-record the action recording for a test case.

FIGURE 14-19

Supported Technologies

Fast-forward for manual testing requires that your application be built using one of several supported technologies. The testing framework requires that it understands the underlying technology so that it can interact with the application being tested. The list of supported technologies is expected to grow over time, and Visual Studio 2010 offers an extensibility framework to allow third parties to build their own testing providers. However, if your application uses a technology for which there is not a testing provider available, you will be unable to benefit from fast-forward for manual testing.

> *For a complete list of supported technologies and caveats, consult the Visual Studio 2010 product documentation.*

Saving Test Results

The results of test runs conducted with Test Runner can be published to Team Foundation Server. When you are finished with a test run, click on Save and Close to save your test run results. You can alternatively abandon a test run by clicking on the X to close Test Runner. These test results can be viewed later from within Test Manager, as shown in Figure 14-20.

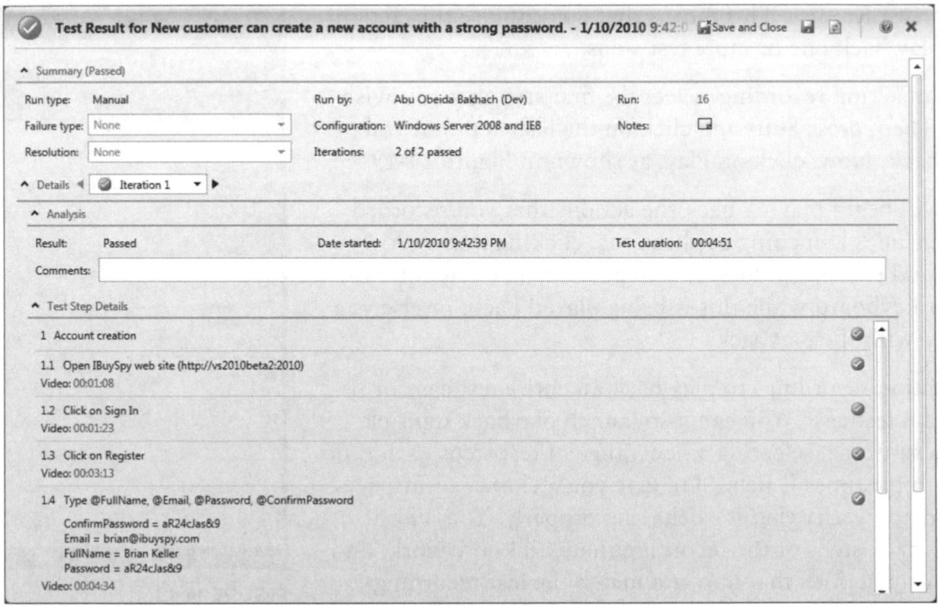

FIGURE 14-20

Depending on the test settings you are using, and whether you are capturing an action recording, you may have a variety of attachments included with your test runs. This might include a video recording, action recordings, system information, or any other artifacts that are captured by the data diagnostic adapters you have configured in your test settings. You can also capture additional information (such as screenshots or comments) by using the toolbar above the list of test steps within Test Runner.

Finally, you can use Test Runner to file bugs by clicking on the "Create bug" button. When you file a bug with Test Runner, all of the attachments from your test run will be included with the bug, making it easier for the developers to understand how your bug was discovered, and providing them with richer information that may be helpful for resolving the bug later on. For example, if you opted to capture an IntelliTrace file it will be included here. When the developer opens this bug, he or she can use this data to help diagnose and fix the bug more quickly.

> *Saving the results of a failed test run does not automatically file a bug. If you don't file a bug for a failed test, then the developer may never learn that there is a problem.*

RUNNING AUTOMATED TESTS

Over time, you may decide to add automated tests to your test plan. Automated tests are more expensive to author and maintain, but they have the benefit of being capable of running without manual interaction, making them suitable for quickly catching bugs caused by changes to source code. In Chapter 12 you learned how you can use Visual Studio to manage automated tests (such as unit tests, coded UI tests, and Web performance tests). But you can also manage automated tests as part of the same test plans that you use within Test Manager.

Automated tests can be run as part of your automated builds, and the status of those tests can be published along with the rest of the tests within your test plan. The main advantage of managing your automated tests along with your manual tests is that you can gain a consolidated view across your entire test plan of how your application's quality is trending.

To utilize automated tests within Test Manager, you must first create an automated test in Visual Studio 2010, and check it in as part of your Team Foundation Server source control. Next, from within Visual Studio 2010, open the work item corresponding to the test case that you wish to automate. Click on the Associated Automation tab, as shown in Figure 14-21.

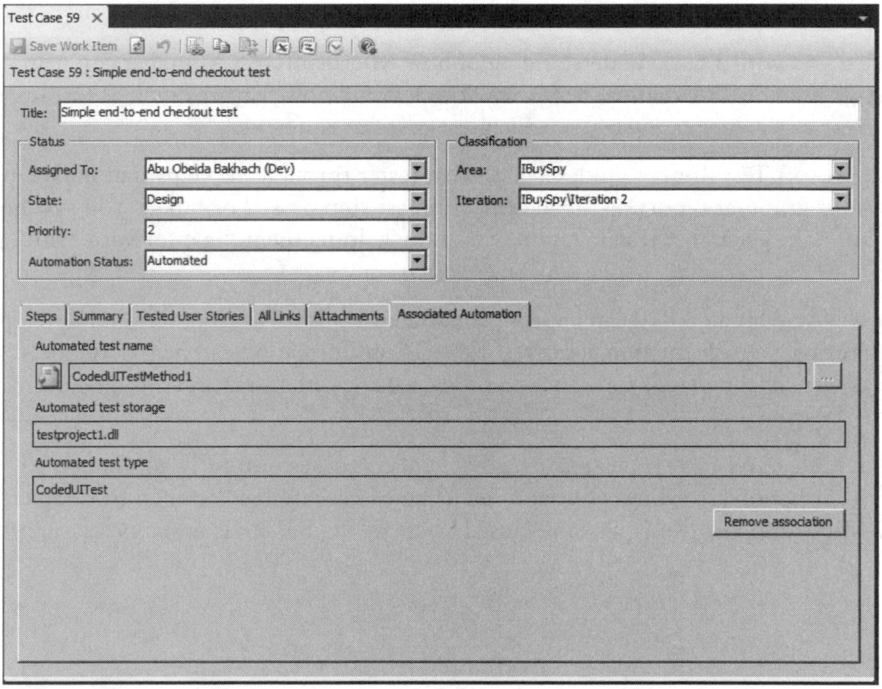

FIGURE 14-21

Use the ellipsis (. . .) to the right of the "Associated test name" field to browse for the automated test you wish to use when running this test case. Once selected, the rest of the fields on this form will be populated for you. Save the work item.

Now, when you run this test from within Test Manager, it will be run automatically without requiring user intervention. Additionally, if you configure Team Foundation Build to run this test as part of an automated build (see Chapter 21), then the status of this test will automatically be reported back to your test plan, so there is no need to run this test from within Test Manager unless you want to reproduce a test run.

You will learn how to create a coded UI test in Chapter 15. After creating a coded UI test, you may wish to revisit this topic to wire up your coded UI test as associated automation for an existing test case.

> *Before you can run automated tests within Test Manager for the first time, you must first define an automated test environment and automated test settings for your test plan. Test settings within Test Manager were first introduced in this chapter; automated test settings and test environments will be covered in greater detail in Chapter 16.*

SUMMARY

This chapter provided you with a basic understanding of how Microsoft Test Manager can help testers author, manage, and execute manual test plans. You learned how features such as test impact analysis and changesets can help you determine which test cases to run next.

You learned how Microsoft Test Runner guides a generalist tester through the steps that make up a test case, and allows for granular reporting of whether each test step passed or failed. You saw how action recordings can make generalist testers more efficient by helping them "fast forward" through ranges of test steps.

You also learned how Visual Studio 2010 can improve communications between testers and developers by automatically capturing rich information about test runs. This information can help developers understand how bugs were encountered, and can even provide them with information to help them more quickly resolve those bugs.

In Chapter 15, you will discover how you can convert manual test cases into fully automated UI tests by starting with the action recordings you captured using Microsoft Test Runner. In Chapter 16, you will learn how Microsoft Test Manager can be used to create virtual environments for running your tests.

15

Coded User Interface Testing

WHAT'S IN THIS CHAPTER?

➤ Understanding how coded UI tests can be used to create automated functional UI tests

➤ Learning how to create a coded UI test from scratch, or from existing action recordings

➤ Learning techniques for making coded UI tests more robust

In Chapter 14, you saw how Visual Studio 2010 has matured to provide first-class support for manual testing. Manual tests are relatively cheap to author, which makes them well-suited for testing your application while it's undergoing regular changes. As the user interface (UI) undergoes churn (perhaps because of usability feedback, or additional features being implemented), it's easy to update manual test cases to reflect those changes. After all, a manual test is essentially just a textual list of steps.

The downside of manual tests is that, by definition, they require human intervention to execute and validate. As an application grows, it may become cost-prohibitive to run every manual test for every build you're testing. The desire is to use automated tests that can be run routinely to help ensure application integrity, without requiring ongoing human testing resources. Visual Studio 2010 has introduced a new test type known as a *coded UI test,* which is designed for functional UI testing.

A coded UI test provides a mechanism to automatically execute and validate a test case. Unlike most other automated tests (such as unit tests), a coded UI test operates at the user-interface layer and "drives" the application in much the same manner as a human sitting in front of a mouse and keyboard would. A coded UI test can be programmed to validate elements of the UI at various points during the test to confirm that the application is behaving properly. For example, is the checkout total accurately reflected in the correct location on a form after adding a given number of items to the shopping cart?

Coded UI tests can be authored in C# or Visual Basic, and Visual Studio 2010 provides tools to help auto-generate much of this required code. Note that coded UI tests require that the application being tested was built using one of the supported technologies — for example, Windows Presentation Foundation (WPF), Windows Forms, HTML/AJAX, and so on. See the section "Supported Technologies," later in this chapter for more information.

In this chapter, you will learn how to work with coded UI tests. You will start by creating a simple coded UI test using the Coded UI Test Builder and adding some validation logic. Next, you will parameterize this test to run multiple times using different sets of input data. Lastly, you will discover how coded UI tests can be created using action recordings, which can be generated while running manual tests.

CREATING CODED UI TESTS USING THE CODED UI TEST BUILDER

One way of recording a coded UI test is to use the Coded UI Test Builder. By using the Test Builder, you can record a given path through an application, usually by emulating a scenario that you expect a user to perform. Along the way, you can add validation logic to ensure that the application is behaving correctly. The Test Builder is responsible for generating source code (in C# or Visual Basic) that represents the coded UI test. You can then customize this source code, such as to parameterize inputs and expected outputs for creating a data-driven test.

Setting up the Sample Application

The tutorial presented here utilizes a very simple WPF-based calculator. You can download this sample from this book's Web site at www.wrox.com. A version of the calculator written using Windows Forms is also available for you to try, although the source code and screenshots in this chapter will match that of the WPF version.

Begin by opening the solution for the SimpleWPFCalculator application. Press F5 to launch the application. You will notice that this is a very primitive application, but it will serve as a good example for learning how to work with coded UI tests. To use the application, simply enter an integer into each textbox and click the buttons corresponding to each math operation to generate the respective results, as shown in Figure 15-1. (In this example, the Subtract button was clicked.)

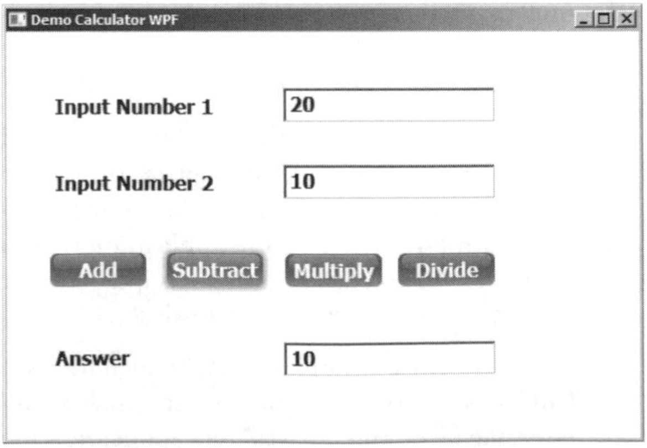

FIGURE 15-1

Create a desktop shortcut for your application to make it easier to launch when you are creating your tests. From within Windows Explorer, browse to the project directory where you unzipped the sample application. Open the SimpleWPFCalculator\bin\Debug folder and right-click on the `SimpleWPFCalculator.exe` file. Choose Create Shortcut, then drag the shortcut that is generated onto your computer's desktop. Confirm that double-clicking this shortcut launches the WPF calculator application.

Create a Test Project

Next, you will need a test project in which to house your coded UI test. Click File ➪ New ➪ Project, which will display the New Project dialog shown in Figure 15-2. Select Visual C# ➪ Test ➪ Test Project. Name your project `CodedUITestProject` and select "Add to solution" in the Solution drop-down box. Click OK when finished.

> *You may also choose Visual Basic as the language for your test project, but the sample code in this chapter will be showing a C# test project.*

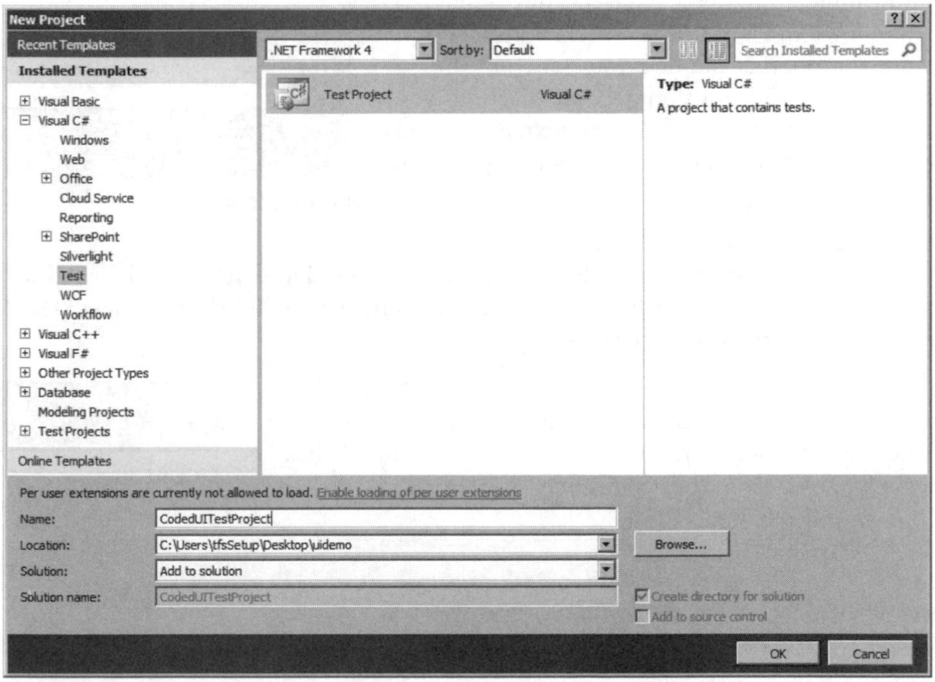

FIGURE 15-2

Add a Coded UI Test

You are now ready to add a coded UI test to your testing project. Right-click on the `CodedUITestProject` file from within Solution Explorer and choose Add ➪ Coded UI Test. A new file, `CodedUITest1.cs`, will be added to your solution. The dialog shown in Figure 15-3 will also appear, providing you with options for generating your test.

Choose the first option, "Record actions, edit UI map or add assertions." This option allows you to record a coded UI test from scratch by navigating through the application in the same manner that a user might. In the section "Creating Coded UI Tests Using Action Recordings," later this chapter, you will learn how to convert existing manual test cases into coded UI tests.

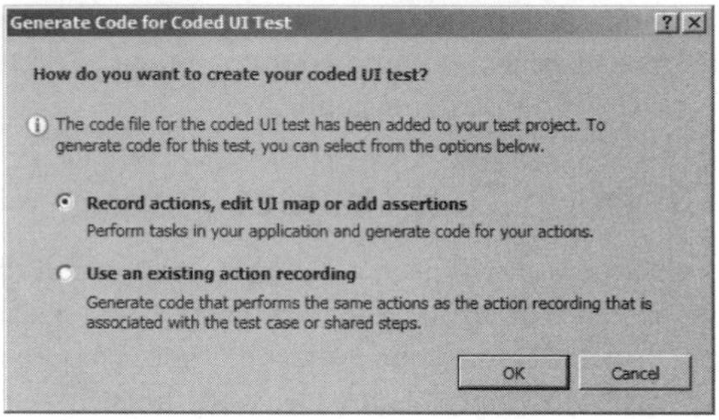

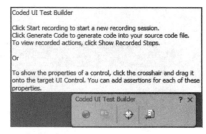

FIGURE 15-3

Visual Studio will now be minimized to make room for you to begin recording your test.

Coded UI Test Builder

The Coded UI Test Builder now appears in the lower-right of your screen, as shown in Figure 15-4. The Test Builder is, as the name implies, a tool that can help you construct your coded UI tests. It is responsible for both recording actions you perform (for example clicking buttons, typing text, and so on), and for identifying controls and their properties that you wish to validate.

FIGURE 15-4

Minimize any open applications so that you can clearly see your desktop and the shortcut to the WPF calculator application. However, don't launch the shortcut yet. Click the Record button (the red, round circle on the left end of the toolbar) of the Test Builder when you are ready to begin recording your test.

The Test Builder should now resemble Figure 15-5, which indicates that it is recording your actions. At any time, you can click Pause (the leftmost button) to instruct Test Builder to stop recording your actions, and click the Record button when you are ready to resume.

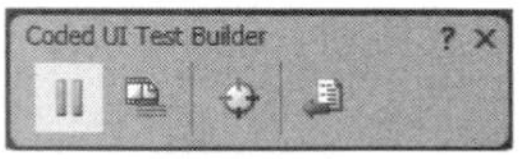

FIGURE 15-5

> Once you begin recording, Test Builder will capture any and all actions you perform, even if they aren't part of the application you are trying to test. For example, if you are recording a test and you respond to an instant message, or click the Start menu to launch an unrelated application, these actions will be captured. This may result in unnecessary playback steps when executing your coded UI tests, and could even cause your tests to fail unexpectedly. For this reason, you should take care to record your tests cleanly and close unrelated applications prior to recording your tests. You can also pause the Test Builder if you must perform unrelated actions during a test. Just be sure you do not interact with the application being tested while the Test Builder is paused. Doing so could cause the application you are testing to get into a state other than what it was in when you paused the Test Builder, and, hence, subsequent steps you record might fail on playback.

You are now ready to begin recording the coded UI test by using the application in the same manner you would expect a user to. Launch the WPF calculator application by double-clicking on the desktop shortcut you created earlier. Type **20** in the first textbox, then type **10** in the second textbox, and click the Add button.

You can visually inspect the actions that the Test Builder has captured by clicking on Show Recorded Steps (the second button from the left) of the Test Builder. The window shown in Figure 15-6 will appear, showing you an easy-to-read list of the steps you have performed while recording your test. Note that you can pin this window if you'd like to have it remain visible while you are recording.

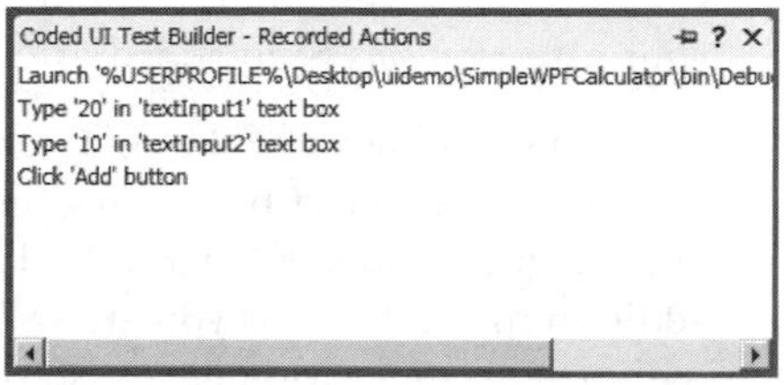

FIGURE 15-6

At this point in your test, you are ready to add some validation logic to confirm that the result of your addition operation is correct. But, before you add an assertion, you must convert the steps you have performed so far into source code. Do so by clicking on Generate Code (rightmost button) within the Test Builder.

The dialog shown in Figure 15-7 will prompt you for the name of the method you want to create within your coded UI test. You should use descriptive method names to make it easier to understand your generated code. Type **EnterDataAndClickAdd**; then click "Add and Generate" to resume building your coded UI test. The Test Builder will now convert your recorded steps into source code, which is then added to your Visual Studio project files. You will inspect this code later.

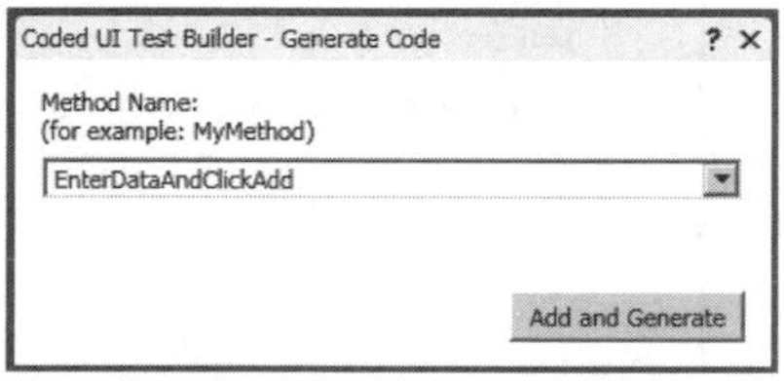

FIGURE 15-7

You can now add assertion logic to validate the properties of one or more controls. The Test Builder allows you to easily select the control you wish to validate. Do so by clicking and dragging the crosshair icon from the Test Builder onto the bottommost textbox of the calculator. As you hover over controls and windows of your desktop and applications, you will notice that they become highlighted to indicate which control you are selecting. Once you have selected the bottommost textbox of the calculator, release your mouse button.

The properties for the `TextAnswerEdit` textbox you have selected will be displayed as shown in Figure 15-8.

You can also use the up/down/left/right arrows of this dialog to navigate through the control hierarchy. You don't need to do so for this test, but this is helpful for controls that are difficult to select using the crosshairs, or invisible controls (such as a panel that may be used a container for other controls).

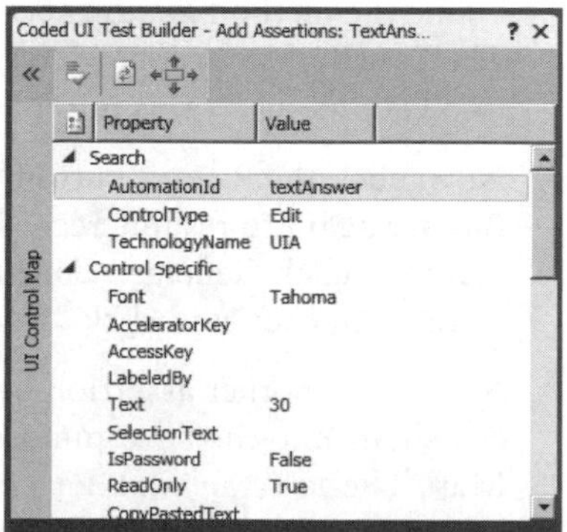

For this test, you want to confirm that the number 30 (the sum of 20 plus 10) is properly displayed in the textbox. In the list of properties for this control, you will see that the `Text` property has a value of `30`. Highlight this row, then click Add an Assertion (the second button from the left on

FIGURE 15-8

the toolbar). Figure 15-9 will appear, allowing you to define the behavior of your assertion. Click the Comparator drop-down to examine your assertion choices. Accept the default value (AreEqual) for Comparator and the current value (30) for Comparison Value. Click OK. The Test Builder will display a message indicating that your assertion has been added.

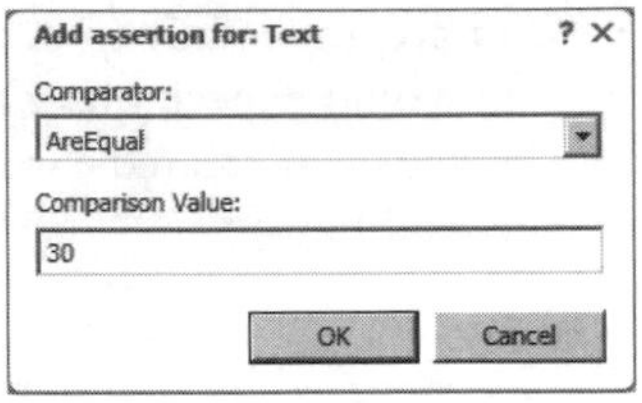

Add assertion for: Text ? ✕

Comparator:
AreEqual

Comparison Value:
30

OK   Cancel

FIGURE 15-9

You can examine all of the controls that have been captured as part of your coded UI test by clicking Show UI Control Map (the leftmost button on the toolbar). Figure 15-10 shows the controls that have been added so far. Note that, in addition to the controls you are validating via assertions, the controls you have used to navigate within your application have also been added here.

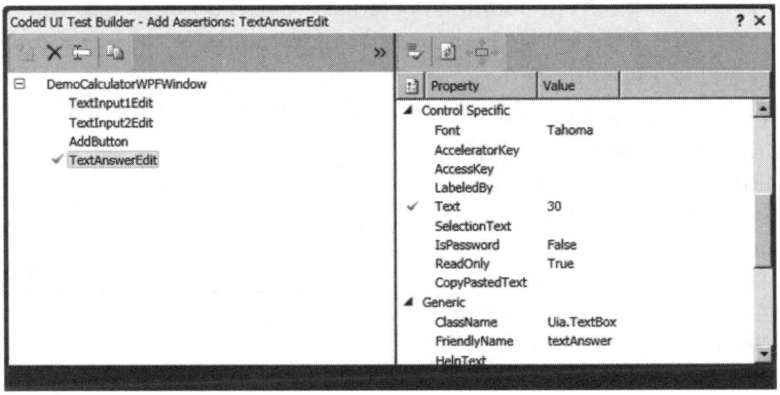

Coded UI Test Builder - Add Assertions: TextAnswerEdit ? ✕

Property	Value
▲ Control Specific	
Font	Tahoma
AcceleratorKey	
AccessKey	
LabeledBy	
✓ Text	30
SelectionText	
IsPassword	False
ReadOnly	True
CopyPastedText	
▲ Generic	
ClassName	Uia.TextBox
FriendlyName	textAnswer
HelpText	

DemoCalculatorWPFWindow
  TextInput1Edit
  TextInput2Edit
  AddButton
  ✓ TextAnswerEdit

FIGURE 15-10

Click Generate Code from within the Test Builder (the rightmost button) to codify the assertion you just added. The dialog shown in Figure 15-11 will appear, prompting you to name the method that will correspond to your assertion. Name the method `AssertAdd` and click "Add and Generate." The Test Builder will now convert the assertion you defined into C# and insert this into your test project.

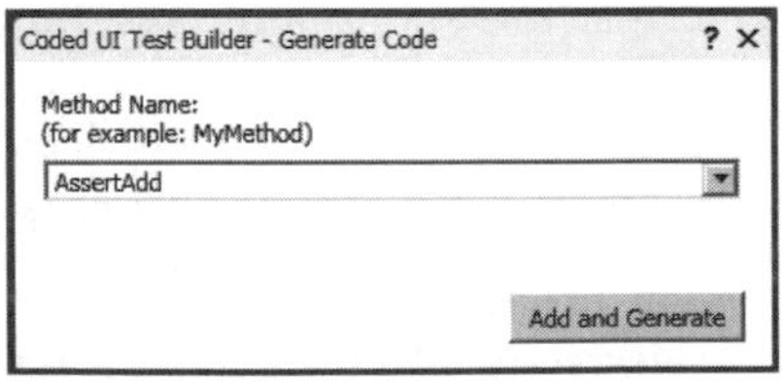

Coded UI Test Builder - Generate Code ? ✕

Method Name:
(for example: MyMethod)

AssertAdd

Add and Generate

FIGURE 15-11

Now, click the Record button (leftmost button) in the Test Builder again to resume recording your test case. Click on the Subtract button in the calculator, and then click Generate Code (the rightmost button) in the Test Builder. Name this method `ClickSubtract` and click "Add and Generate."

Now, add another assertion by following the same steps you followed earlier. After dragging the crosshair onto the bottommost textbox in the calculator, you will see the expanded UI Control Map. The `TextAnswerEdit` control should be highlighted. Select the `Text` property and add an assertion stating that this property should now be equal to 10. Click on Generate Code and name the assertion `AssertSubtract`.

Repeat these steps for the multiplication and division functions. Name the methods for clicking those buttons `ClickMultiply` and `ClickDivide`, respectively. Name the corresponding assertions `AssertMultiply` and `AssertDivide`. Once you are finished, close the Test Builder, which will return you to Visual Studio.

Generated Code

From within Visual Studio, you can now examine the code that was generated by the Test Builder while you were recording your test actions and assertions. The file `CodedUITest1.cs` is the main execution harness for your test, and calls all of the action and assertion methods you defined earlier, as shown here:

```
[TestMethod]
public void CodedUITestMethod1()
{
 this.UIMap.EnterDataAndClickAdd();
 this.UIMap.AssertAdd();
 this.UIMap.ClickSubtract();
 this.UIMap.AssertSubtract();
 this.UIMap.ClickMultiply();
 this.UIMap.AssertMultiply();
 this.UIMap.ClickDivide();
 this.UIMap.AssertDivide();
}
```

To better understand what each underlying method is actually doing, you can examine the partial class file named `UIMap.Designer.cs`. Right-click on the `EnterDataAndClickAdd` method call and select "Go to definition." This method is defined as follows:

```
/// <summary>
/// EnterDataAndClickAdd - Use 'EnterDataAndClickAddParams'
/// to pass parameters into this method.
/// </summary>
public void EnterDataAndClickAdd()
{
    #region Variable Declarations
    WpfEdit textInput1Edit = this.DemoCalculatorWPFWindow.TextInput1Edit;
    WpfEdit textInput2Edit = this.DemoCalculatorWPFWindow.TextInput2Edit;
    WpfButton addButton = this.DemoCalculatorWPFWindow.AddButton;
    #endregion

    // Launch '%USERPROFILE%\Desktop\codedui\uidemo\SimpleWPFCalculator\bin\Debug\'
        + 'SimpleWPFCalculator.exe'
    ApplicationUnderTest demoCalculatorWPFWindow = ApplicationUnderTest.Launch(
    this.EnterDataAndClickAddParams.DemoCalculatorWPFWindowExePath,
    this.EnterDataAndClickAddParams.DemoCalculatorWPFWindowAlternateExePath);

    // Type '20' in 'textInput1' text box
    textInput1Edit.Text = this.EnterDataAndClickAddParams.TextInput1EditText;
```

```
        // Type '10' in 'textInput2' text box
        textInput2Edit.Text = this.EnterDataAndClickAddParams.TextInput2EditText;

        // Click 'Add' button
        Mouse.Click(addButton, new Point(48, 15));
    }
```

This method is responsible for performing four distinct actions, as defined by the actions you recorded earlier. This method will first launch the application, then enter values into two textboxes, then click on the Add button. Notice, however, that the parameters for this method are defined elsewhere in this file. Scroll down to the class `EnterDataAndClickAddParams`:

```
    /// Parameters to be passed into 'EnterDataAndClickAdd'
    public class EnterDataAndClickAddParams
    {

        public string DemoCalculatorWPFWindowExePath =
        "C:\\Users\\administrator.ONEBOX\\Desktop\\codedui\\"
        + "uidemo\\SimpleWPFCalculator\\bin\\Debug\\SimpleWPFCalculator.exe";

        public string DemoCalculatorWPFWindowAlternateExePath =
        "%USERPROFILE%\\Desktop\\codedui\\uidemo\\SimpleWPFCalculator\\bin\\"
        + "Debug\\SimpleWPFCalculator.exe";

        public string TextInput1EditText = "20";

        public string TextInput2EditText = "10";
    }
```

The reason that the parameters are separated from the actual method doing the work is that this makes it easier to override the parameters with new values. This is very important when creating data-driven tests that will run multiple times, using different values each time. You will do this later in this chapter.

Notice that there are two slightly different values defined to describe from where the application under test will be launched, `DemoCalculatorWPFWindowExePath` and `DemoCalculatorWPFWindow AlternateExePath`. Whenever possible, Visual Studio will look for ways to make your tests more robust so that they are less prone to accidental failure. The actual values you have for your test will vary, based on where you stored your application. But, for this example, notice that Visual Studio stored both the absolute path to the executable and the relative path based on the `%USERPROFILE%` environment variable. This makes your tests more fault-tolerant in the event that your executable changes locations later on.

Also, notice that the Test Builder interpreted your test actions as launching an application executable, instead of double-clicking on that application's shortcut on your desktop. This is also a way of making your test more fault-tolerant. In the future, you might decide to delete or move the shortcut to the executable, but you are less likely to move the actual executable itself. Recording tests can be a relatively expensive investment, so Visual Studio will use tricks like this to make it less likely that you must re-record your tests later on.

Running Your Test

You are now ready to run your test and confirm that everything was properly recorded. Do so by returning to the `CodedUITest1.cs` file and right-clicking anywhere within the `CodedUITestMethod1()` code block. Select Run Tests. Avoid using your mouse or keyboard while the text executes. If you have recorded your test properly, the calculator will launch, the values 20 and 10 will be inserted into the textboxes, and each of the four operation buttons will be exercised. When finished, the test results will be displayed as shown in Figure 15-12.

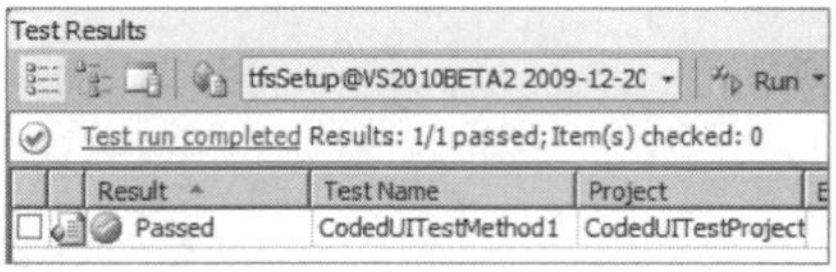

FIGURE 15-12

Congratulations! You have now authored your first coded UI test. But what if you want to test values other than 20 and 10? One approach would be to author new tests, each with their own values. But this would be very time-consuming. A better solution is to create a data-driven test by binding the values for this test case to a database or XML file.

Creating a Data-Driven Test

The process of creating a data-driven coded UI test is very similar to that of creating a data-driven unit test. Start by opening the Test View window (Test ⇨ Windows ⇨ Test View). If the Properties window isn't already shown, right-click `CodedUITestMethod1` from within the Test View and select Properties. Select the ellipsis for Data Connection String, as shown in Figure 15-13.

The New Test Data Source Wizard will launch, as shown in Figure 15-14. This wizard will help you bind your test to a database, an XML file, or a comma-separated value (CSV) file to use as a data source for creating a data-driven test. Select XML File and click Next.

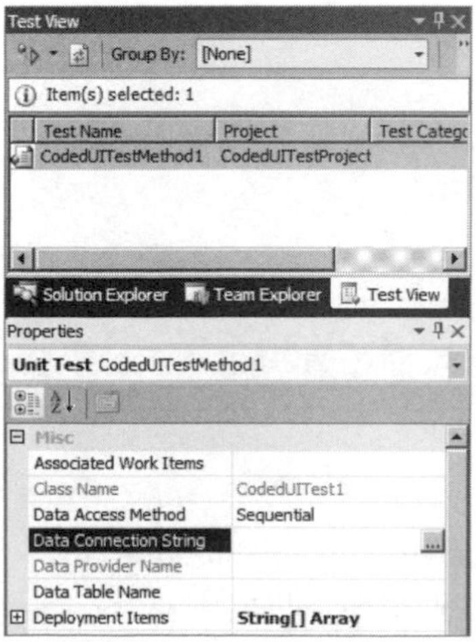

FIGURE 15-13

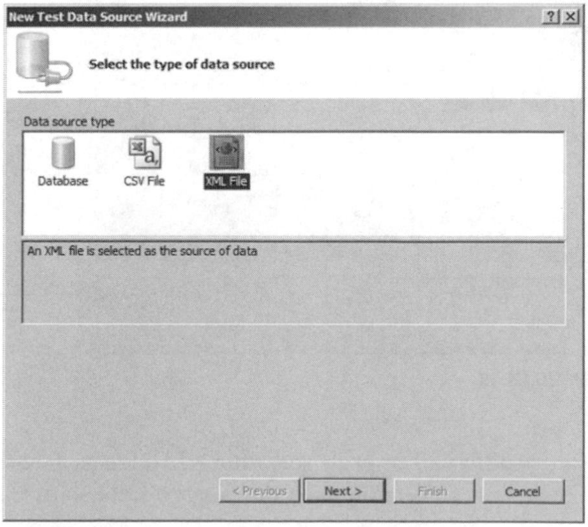

FIGURE 15-14

The sample application for this chapter includes an XML dataset named `calcdata.xml`. The contents of this file are as follows:

```
<?xml version="1.0" encoding="utf-8"?>
<DataContextData>
  <DataContextRow InputValue1 ="10"
                  InputValue2 ="2"
                  ExpectedAddAnswer ="12"
                  ExpectedSubtractAnswer="8"
                  ExpectedMultiplyAnswer="20"
                  ExpectedDivideAnswer="5"/>
  <DataContextRow InputValue1 ="20"
                  InputValue2 ="10"
                  ExpectedAddAnswer ="30"
                  ExpectedSubtractAnswer="10"
                  ExpectedMultiplyAnswer="200"
                  ExpectedDivideAnswer="2"/>
</DataContextData>
```

Use the wizard to browse to this file. A preview of the data contained in this file will be displayed, as shown in Figure 15-15. Click Next.

Lastly, highlight `DataContextRow` in the final dialog page, as shown in Figure 15-16, and click Finish.

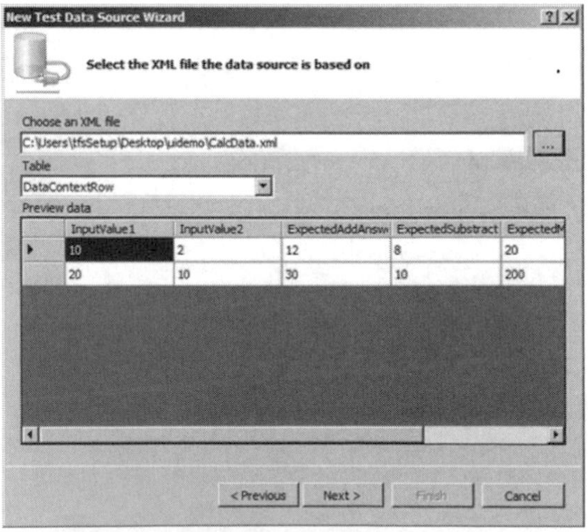

FIGURE 15-15

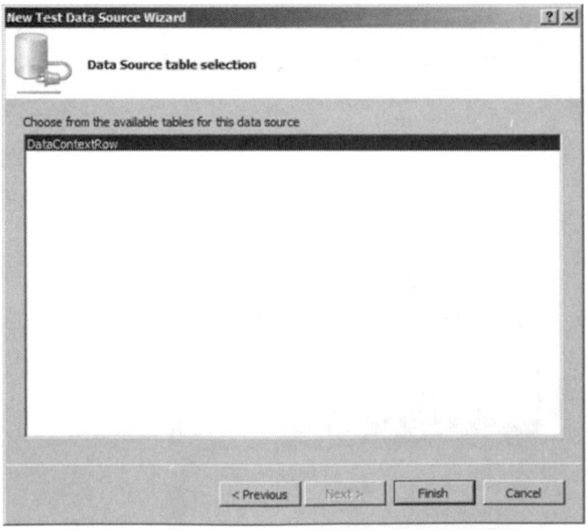

FIGURE 15-16

Visual Studio will offer to add your XML file as a deployment item within your solution. This makes it easy to version-control your test data source along with your tests. Click Yes.

You can now begin overriding the parameters that you recorded earlier by data-binding them to your XML data source. The architecture of coded UI tests makes it easy to do this from within one central location — the CodedUITest1.cs file. Modify the CodedUITest1 method by inserting the following highlighted lines.

```
this.UIMap.EnterDataAndClickAddParams.TextInput1EditText =
TestContext.DataRow["InputValue1"].ToString();
this.UIMap.EnterDataAndClickAddParams.TextInput2EditText =
TestContext.DataRow["InputValue2"].ToString();

this.UIMap.EnterDataAndClickAdd();
this.UIMap.AssertAddExpectedValues.TextAnswerEditText =
TestContext.DataRow["ExpectedAddAnswer"].ToString();
this.UIMap.AssertAdd();

this.UIMap.ClickSubtract();
this.UIMap.AssertSubtractExpectedValues.TextAnswerEditText =
TestContext.DataRow["ExpectedSubtractAnswer"].ToString();
this.UIMap.AssertSubtract();

this.UIMap.ClickMultiply();
this.UIMap.AssertMultiplyExpectedValues.TextAnswerEditText =
TestContext.DataRow["ExpectedMultiplyAnswer"].ToString();
this.UIMap.AssertMultiply();

this.UIMap.ClickDivide();
this.UIMap.AssertDivideExpectedValues.TextAnswerEditText =
TestContext.DataRow["ExpectedDivideAnswer"].ToString();
this.UIMap.AssertDivide();
```

The code you added will now override the values from each of the respective "ExpectedValues" methods within the UIMap.Designer.cs file by data binding the values to the corresponding columns within your XML data source.

Run your test again by right-clicking within your test method and selecting Run Tests. Your coded UI test will now execute twice — once for each row of the XML data source. When finished, the test results should indicate that 3/3 tests have passed successfully. This includes each data row, as well as the overall test.

You can now maintain the calcdata.xml file within your test project to add new rows of data. These rows will be used during future test runs, thus providing you with an easy way to grow your test coverage. Any time you make changes to calcdata.xml, you will need to rebuild your solution (Build ➪ Build Solution) in order to deploy the updated file.

Using the using() Clause

By now, you may have noticed that your test runs leave instances of the WPF calculator running once the tests have finished. You could have closed the calculator as the last step of your recorded test actions. The problem with this approach, however, is that if your test fails, then the remaining actions will not be executed.

You want a solution that will close the calculator every time, regardless of whether or not the test fails. Otherwise, your machine will become littered with multiple instances of the application you are testing. This can eventually bog down your test machine, and may even cause tests to fail if the application being tested can only include one running instance.

The solution to this problem is to wrap the application launch event with a `using` clause. The `using` clause will cause the application to automatically close once it has gone out of scope, regardless of whether or not the test passed.

Open the `EnterDataAndClickAdd` method within the `UIMap.Designer.cs` file. Cut (don't copy) the line that defines `ApplicationUnderTest`. Paste this line into the top of the `CodedUITestMethod1` method. You will need to further qualify the references within the method arguments to specify that the parameters live within the `UIMap` partial class. Finally, encapsulate the `ApplicationUnderTest` definition within a `using()` clause, and encapsulate the rest of the `CodedUITestMethod1` logic within curly braces, as shown here:

```
using (ApplicationUnderTest demoCalculatorWPFWindow =
ApplicationUnderTest.Launch
(this.UIMap.EnterDataAndClickAddParams.DemoCalculatorWPFWindowExePath,
this.UIMap.EnterDataAndClickAddParams.DemoCalculatorWPFWindowAlternateExePath))
{
 this.UIMap.EnterDataAndClickAddParams.TextInput1EditText =
 TestContext.DataRow["InputValue1"].ToString();
 …
 this.UIMap.AssertDivide();
}
```

Now, when you run this test, the calculator will automatically be closed after each test run, regardless of whether or not that run succeeded. You have now created a UI test that is fully automated, robust, and data-bound.

Enhanced Assertion Reporting

You can cause your tests to fail by changing the values in the `calcdata.xml` file (for example, 1 + 1 = 3). However, you may notice that the test results after each test run will only report that a test failed; it won't tell you which assertion (addition/subtraction/multiplication/division) was responsible for the test failing. For coded UI tests with multiple assertions, it can be useful to know more about exactly which assertion caused the test to fail. You can easily enhance the assertion reporting by adding an additional argument to each assertion call.

Open the `UIMap.Designer.cs` file and find the `Assert` call you wish to modify. Simply add a third argument with the text that you would like to show if an assertion fails. The following example will display "Addition failed" in the test results if the assertion for the addition step fails:

```
Assert.AreEqual(this.AssertAddExpectedValues.TextAnswerEditText,
textAnswerEdit.Text, "Addition failed");
```

> Note that a test will fail and abort immediately after the first assertion has failed. For example, if you see a message that the addition assertion failed, you still won't know whether or not the subtraction/multiplication/division operations are working properly. If you require more granular reporting of your test runs, it is advisable to create multiple coded UI tests, each verifying one unit of functionality.

Another way of creating such a test would be to utilize the action recording from an existing manual test.

CREATING CODED UI TESTS USING ACTION RECORDINGS

Creating a coded UI test from an existing manual test can be less time-consuming than recording a coded UI test from scratch. If your team is already creating manual test cases and associated action recordings, you can benefit from these artifacts when creating your coded UI tests.

For this section, it is assumed that you know how to create manual tests and their associated action recordings. For more information about manual testing, see Chapter 14.

Start by creating a test like the one shown in Figure 15-17. For simplicity, this test will only be validating that the addition and subtraction functions of the calculator work properly. You can easily extend this test to support multiplication and division if you want. Also note that this test uses parameterized values for the inputs and expected results.

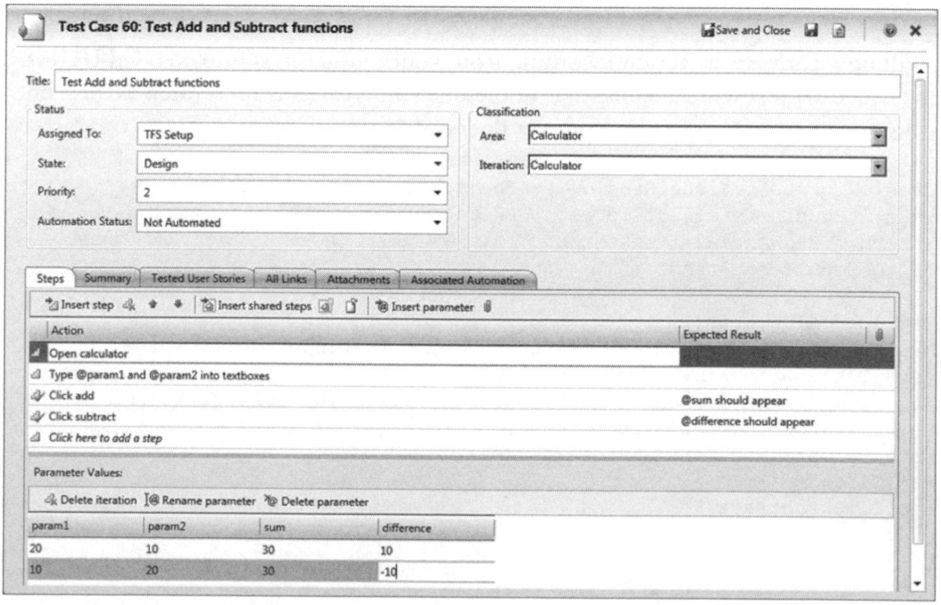

FIGURE 15-17

Now, run this manual test and create an action recording for it. Be sure to mark each test step as Pass while you are recording so that your actions get properly associated with each test step.

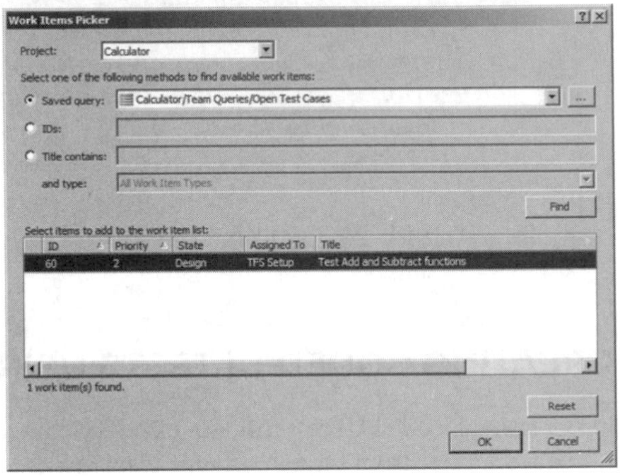

Now that the manual test has been created, along with an associated action recording, you are ready to convert this into a coded UI test. Create a new test project (or you can use the one you created earlier in this chapter). Right-click the project and add a coded UI test. The dialog shown in Figure 15-3 will appear again. This time, select "Use an existing action recording."

The Work Items Picker shown in Figure 15-18 allows you to select the test case work item from which you want to create a coded UI test. Find and select the work item you created earlier for your manual test case, and then click OK.

FIGURE 15-18

> The test case work item has a field called Automation Status. You may wish to instruct your test team to set this value to Planned when test cases are ready for a developer to convert into a coded UI test. You can then create a query to use from the Work Items Picker to find test cases whose Automation Status is equal to Planned.

Visual Studio will now convert the action recording from your manual test into a coded UI test. The structure of this coded UI test will resemble that of the one you created from scratch earlier, but there are a few key differences. Here is the code for CodedUITestMethod1:

```
[DataSource("Microsoft.VisualStudio.TestTools.DataSource.TestCase",
"http://vsts:8080/tfs/defaultcollection;WPF Calculator", "1",
DataAccessMethod.Sequential), TestMethod]
public void CodedUITestMethod1()
{
  this.UIMap.Opencalculator();
  this.UIMap.Typeparam1andparam2intotextboxesParams.TextInput1EditText =
  TestContext.DataRow["param1"].ToString();
  this.UIMap.Typeparam1andparam2intotextboxesParams.TextInput2EditText =
  TestContext.DataRow["param2"].ToString();
  this.UIMap.Typeparam1andparam2intotextboxes();
  this.UIMap.Clickadd();
  this.UIMap.Clicksubtract();
}
```

> *The path to your Team Foundation Server instance in the* `[DataSource]` *attribute will likely vary from that listed here.*

First, notice the attribute on this test method that is data-binding it to the parameter values stored in the test case work item you created. This means that you can update the test parameters centrally from within the work item without needing to maintain a separate database or XML file as you did earlier. This makes it easier for generalist testers (who may not work with source control within Visual Studio) to update test case data.

Next, notice that the names of the method calls in this test method match the text that was used for each test step in the manual test. This makes it easy to see exactly which method call corresponds to each part of the test execution.

Finally, you may notice that this coded UI test doesn't contain any assertions yet. Manual tests rely on human beings to perform validation of the intended UI behavior, so, in order to automate this validation, you must update this code.

Add a new line after the `Clickadd()` method call. Right-click on this empty line and select Generate Code ⇨ Record actions, edit UI map, or edit assertions. Alternately, you can access this menu via Test ⇨ Generate Code, as shown in Figure 15-19.

FIGURE 15-19

The Coded UI Test Builder will appear again as shown earlier in Figure 15-4. Open the calculator application and use the crosshair to select the bottommost textbox, as you did earlier. Add an assertion on the `Text` property of the `TextAnswerEdit` textbox. The assertion should be "Are Equal" and the comparison value will be empty. After you have added this, click Generate Code and name your assertion method `AssertAdd2`. Click "Add and Generate."

> *The reason you are naming this method* `AssertAdd2` *(as opposed to simply* `AssertAdd`*) is to avoid naming conflicts with the assertion method you created earlier in this chapter. If you are using a new test project, then this naming distinction is not necessary.*

Add another assertion on the same control/property, but this time, name it `AssertSubtract2`. Close the Coded UI Test Builder when you are finished. Visual Studio will open again, and you will notice that two assert method calls have been added to your coded UI test method. Rearrange the method calls so that the assertions appear after their respective action method calls. When finished, your test method should contain the following lines:

```
this.UIMap.Clickadd();
this.UIMap.AssertAdd2();
this.UIMap.Clicksubtract();
this.UIMap.AssertSubtract2();
```

You will now need to data-bind the parameters used by the assertions to the parameters stored within your test case. Add the following highlighted lines to your test method:

```
this.UIMap.Clickadd();
this.UIMap.AssertAddExpectedValues.TextAnswerEditText =
TestContext.DataRow["sum"].ToString();
this.UIMap.AssertAdd();
this.UIMap.AssertSubtractExpectedValues.TextAnswerEditText =
TestContext.DataRow["difference"].ToString();
this.UIMap.Clicksubtract();
this.UIMap.AssertSubtract();
```

You can now run your test by right-clicking within the test method and clicking Run Tests. Your test should run once for each data row within your test case's parameter value table. Try manipulating the parameters in your test case and run your coded UI test again to see the data-binding relationship.

You may wish to further enhance this coded UI test by following the steps outlined earlier in the sections, "Using the using() Clause" and "Enhanced Assertion Reporting."

You can also add your coded UI test as associated automation for the original manual test case. By associating the test case with the automated test, the automated test can be run as part of your test plan, and tracked along with the rest of your test cases. Chapter 14 provides more details on how to create this association.

SUPPORTED TECHNOLOGIES

Coded UI tests require that your application be built using one of several supported technologies. The coded UI testing framework requires that it understands the underlying technology so that it can interact with the application being tested. The list of supported technologies is expected to grow over time, and Visual Studio 2010 offers an extensibility framework to allow third parties to build their own testing providers. However, if your application uses a technology for which there is not a testing provider available, you will be unable to author coded UI tests for it.

 For a complete list of supported technologies and caveats, consult the Visual Studio 2010 product documentation.

SUMMARY

Coded UI tests provided a powerful way of crafting automated tests for functional UI testing of your applications. In this chapter, you saw how you can either create a coded UI test from scratch, by interacting with an application the way you expect a user would, or from an existing action recording, thus leveraging some of the work already done by your testing team.

You also learned how you can enhance your coded UI tests by data-binding them to create multiple test runs out of the same set of test steps. Finally, you learned how to use the `using` clause and additional assertion arguments to further enhance your coded UI tests.

In Chapter 16, you will learn about how Visual Studio Lab Management 2010 can be used to help you establish virtual test labs. Virtual test labs are a powerful way of managing multiple environments with which to stage builds of your software, run automated and manual tests, and help developers reproduce and diagnose bugs.

16

Lab Management

WHAT'S IN THIS CHAPTER?

➤ Understanding the capabilities of Visual Studio 2010 Lab Management

➤ Using Lab Management to run tests, capture bugs, and share snapshots

➤ Configuring end-to-end build-deploy-test workflows with Lab Management

As software development projects become more complex, so do the environments in which that software will run. Such an environment could consist of multiple machines, specific firewall (and other security) settings, databases, and a variety of other configurations that could impact the way in which your software behaves.

To effectively test software, testers must create a test environment that simulates the production environment. Traditionally, this could require securing several dedicated physical machines and developing a potentially labor-intensive process for staging those machines on a regular basis with new builds of your software. And, given the variety of possible configurations, it's usually necessary to have multiple test environments in order to find problems that may arise when you ship your software to customers running different environments, each with his or her own unique configurations.

With the rising popularity and availability of virtualization technology, many testing teams have begun to turn to virtualization to make better use of hardware and to more efficiently stage testing environments. But, despite the advances in virtualization, there are still several challenges related to the process of managing a virtual test lab, which can make this a costly and time-consuming endeavor.

Visual Studio Lab Management 2010 addresses the challenge of working with such virtual test lab environments. Lab Management integrates with Team Foundation Server 2010 to provide the following capabilities:

➤ Creation, management, and teardown of environments consisting of one or more virtual machines (VMs).

➤ Automated deployment of builds into virtual environments.

➤ Execution of manual and automated tests across virtual environments.

➤ Use of snapshots to enable environments to be quickly restored to a given state (such as immediately after a new build of software is deployed or when a new bug is discovered). Snapshots can then be shared between testers and developers to help diagnose and fix bugs.

➤ Network isolation of virtualized environments, allowing clones of environments without fear of IP address collisions or naming conflicts with other machines on your network.

In this chapter, you will learn how Visual Studio Lab Management 2010 can be used to take advantage of these capabilities.

LAB MANAGEMENT INFRASTRUCTURE

Visual Studio Lab Management 2010 is licensed separately from Team Foundation Server 2010. Once licensed, it can be installed as an additional capability and enabled for use with a Team Foundation Server 2010 instance. Installation and administration of Lab Management is covered extensively in the product documentation and won't be covered in this book, but a few key concepts will be introduced here.

Lab Management includes a license for Microsoft System Center Virtual Machine Manager (SCVMM) 2008 which provides many of the VM administration capabilities required for your test lab. Lab Management includes the SCVMM license you will need for setting up your virtual test lab. SCVMM, in turn, relies on Windows Server 2008 Hyper-V as the low-level virtualization technology.

 While SCVMM itself does allow for the management of VMware-based VMs, VMware is not yet supported for use with Lab Management.

SCVMM uses a *library server* to store copies of VMs, which can then later be deployed to a *VM host group* (made up of one or more *VM hosts*). A library server is essentially a file server that SCVMM is aware of and has read/write access to. Each library server can contain one or more *library shares*, which is basically a shared folder.

A library server can contain *VM templates* that enable you to customize a VM at the time of deployment. This allows you to specify such settings as machine name, domain or workgroup membership, and product key. VM templates are a powerful tool for building out your test lab, since they provide the most control over how VMs are deployed.

Golden Images

While setting up your test lab, you will need to consider the VM configurations on which you will need to test your software. For example, maybe your software needs to be tested to run in environments containing machines running Windows 7, Windows Server 2008, and Windows Server 2008 R2. You should also consider which other prerequisite software must be installed, such as Internet Information Server (IIS) or database engines such as SQL Server.

The installation guidance for Lab Management refers to the concept of using *golden images* for populating your library server. A golden image is a VM or VM template that contains all of the prerequisites necessary for testing your software. In the previous example, you might configure a golden image for each operating system version that will eventually be involved in your test environments.

Agents

Agents can be installed on VMs to provide additional capabilities that are helpful in deployment, testing, and network isolation with your virtual environments. Three types of agents can be installed:

> A *build agent* allows a VM to participate in Team Foundation Build workflows. This includes the capability to deploy new builds to your VMs and to execute post-build deployment scripts.

> A *test agent* enables manual or automated tests (such as unit tests, coded UI tests, or Web performance tests) to be executed on your VMs.

> A *lab agent* enables network isolation capabilities for a VM environment. With network isolation enabled, you don't have to worry about VMs in your test lab conflicting (name or IP address) with other machines on your network. This makes it possible to have multiple virtual environments with the same IP address and/or machine name without needing to set up dedicated networks for each one.

If you plan on taking advantage of agents in your test lab, you should install those agents on your golden image prior to storing that golden image in your VM library.

The preceding descriptions should provide you with a basic understanding of what is necessary to configure the infrastructure required for taking advantage of Lab Management. But it is by no means a substitute for the detailed product documentation. Your test lab administrator should carefully consult the product documentation for instructions on configuring and optimizing your Lab Management infrastructure. Once configured, you can benefit by using Lab Management as detailed in the remainder of this chapter.

VIRTUAL ENVIRONMENTS

A *virtual environment* consists of one or more VMs that can be deployed and managed together. An environment usually contains all of the VMs necessary to run a set of test cases. For example, an environment could consist of a database server and a Web server, each running Windows Server 2008. A separate virtual environment might also contain similarly configured database and Web servers, but use Windows Server 2003 to offer expanded test coverage.

The first step in creating a virtual environment with Lab Management is to define the VMs or VM templates that will make up your environment. You will use Microsoft Test Manager, introduced in Chapter 14, to do this. Before completing this step, you must have one or more golden images (VMs or templates) stored in your SCVMM library.

Click Start ➪ All Programs ➪ Microsoft Visual Studio 2010 ➪ Microsoft Test Manager. If this is your first time launching Microsoft Test Manager, you may need to define which Team Foundation Server instance and team project you are connecting to. When connected, open the Lab Center, then click Library ➪ Virtual Machines and Templates. The Virtual Machines and Templates activity appears, as shown in Figure 16-1.

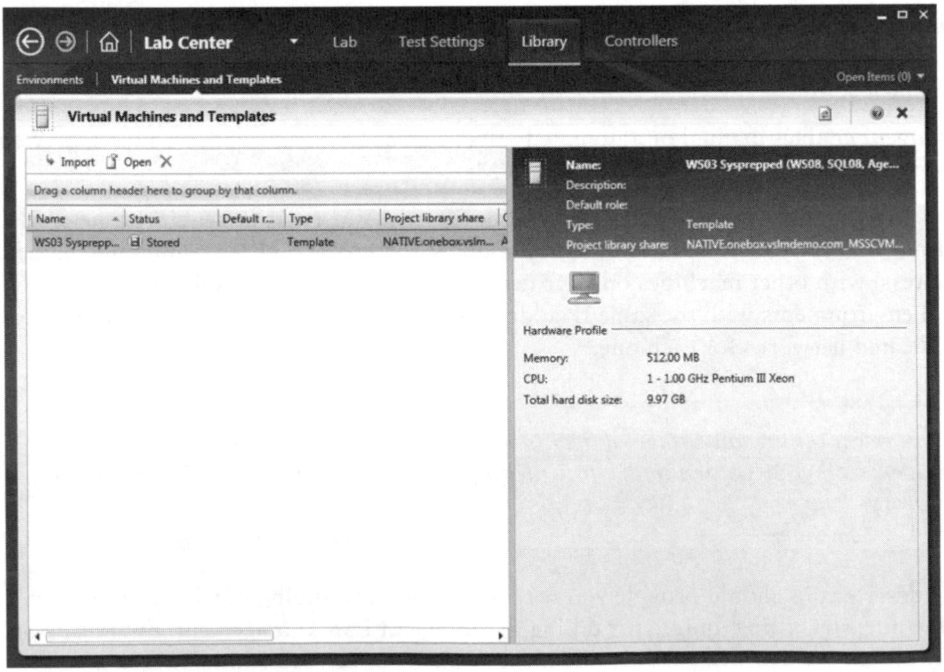

FIGURE 16-1

From here, you can manage all of the VMs and templates that are available to the team project you are connected to. To add a new VM, click the Import button in the upper-left area of the screen.

Begin by defining the path to your new VM or VM template. This path defines the location within the SCVMM library server where your VM or template is stored. Use the Browse button to explore the library server path(s) defined in SCVMM.

Next, provide a name for your VM or template. You can optionally provide a description (useful for describing what's installed on this VM or VM template), along with a default role (discussed later in this chapter).

The "Machine properties" tab shown allows you to specify default parameters that will be used when your VM is deployed (such as the amount of RAM that should be assigned to your VM when deployed). If you are using a VM template, then the "OS profile" tab is available, allowing you to define additional parameters (such as the machine name, domain or workgroup membership, and product key). You can use the "Machine tags" tab to construct advanced deployment workflows.

Clicking Next will display a summary of your actions. Click Finish and your VM or template will now be listed in the Virtual Machines and Templates activity within Test Manager.

> *You can repeat this process for defining as many VMs and VM templates as you want. You can even use the same VM template from your SCVMM library as the basis for multiple VMs or templates within Test Manager (such as to specify various default parameters).*

Once you have configured one or more VMs or templates, you are ready to define a virtual environment. Click Library ➪ Environments. From the Environments activity shown in Figure 16-2, you can assemble one or more VMs or templates into an environment that can later be deployed to a VM host group.

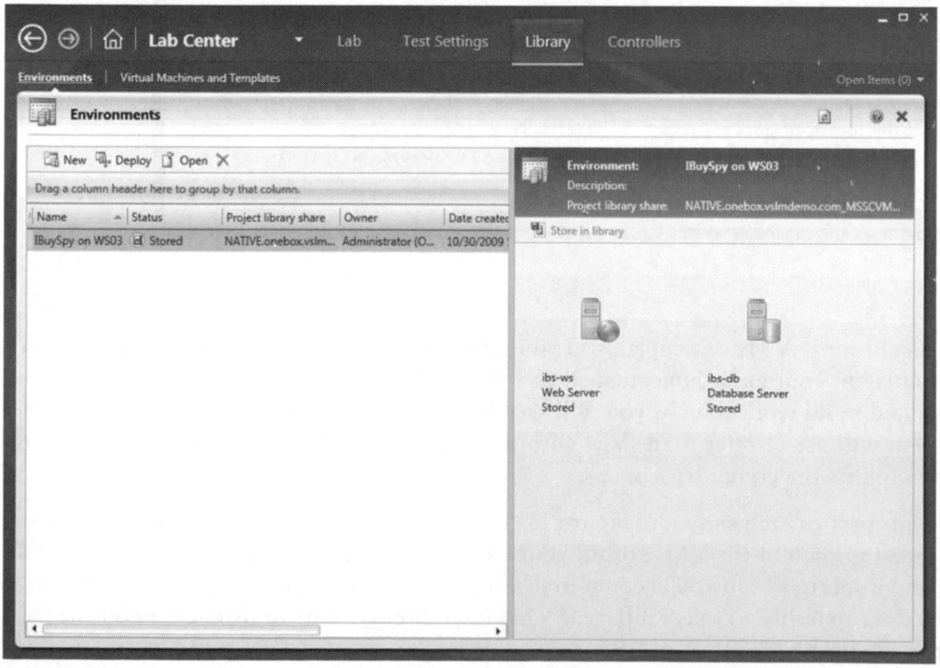

FIGURE 16-2

Click New to create a new virtual environment. You can provide a name and description for your environment. You can also specify the location on the SCVMM library server where the environment definition should be stored, along with environment tags that can be used for defining advanced build workflows.

The Machines tab shown in Figure 16-3 is where you can begin constructing your virtual environment based on the VMs or templates you defined earlier. To do this, first select a VM or template from the list of VMs and templates on the right side of the screen. Next, select "Add to environment." This will add the VM to the environment on the left side of the screen. You can add the same VM template multiple times, if desired.

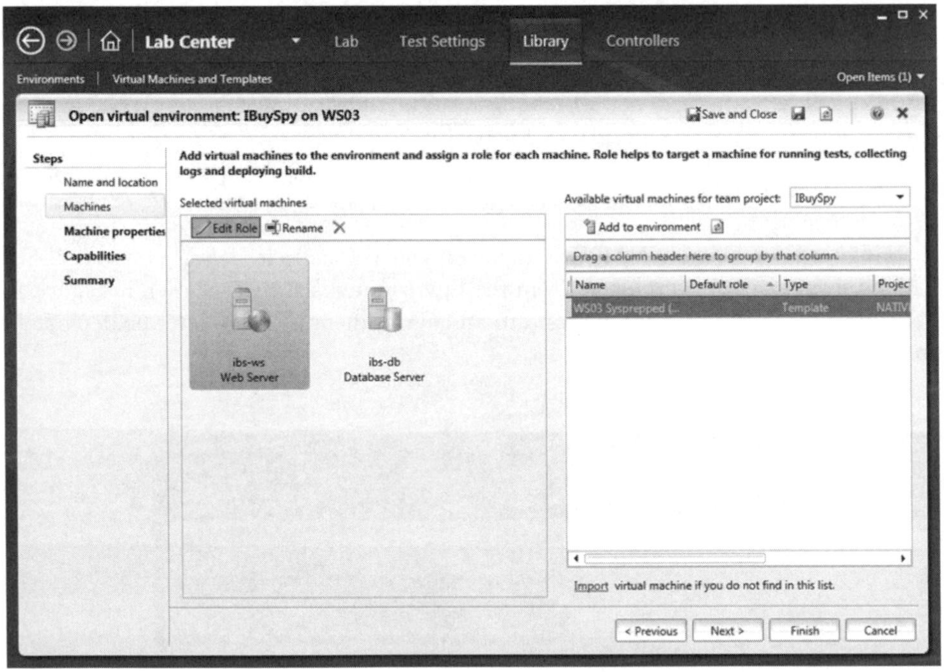

FIGURE 16-3

After adding one or more VMs or templates to your environment, you can then specify which role these machines play in your environment (such as a Web server or database server). Roles are used by test settings and build workflows as you will see later on. You can also specify the name that Lab Management will use to refer to the VM within the environment. Note that this name is not necessarily the same as the computer name.

The "Machine properties" tab shown in Figure 16-4 allows you to define the parameters that should be assigned to each of the VMs within your environment. This screen should look similar to the "Machine properties" tab you encountered when defining a VM or template, except that it also includes the capability to select different VMs in your environment by clicking on the role icons across the top of the screen. Any machine properties you defined earlier will be shown here as default values and can be overridden in this step.

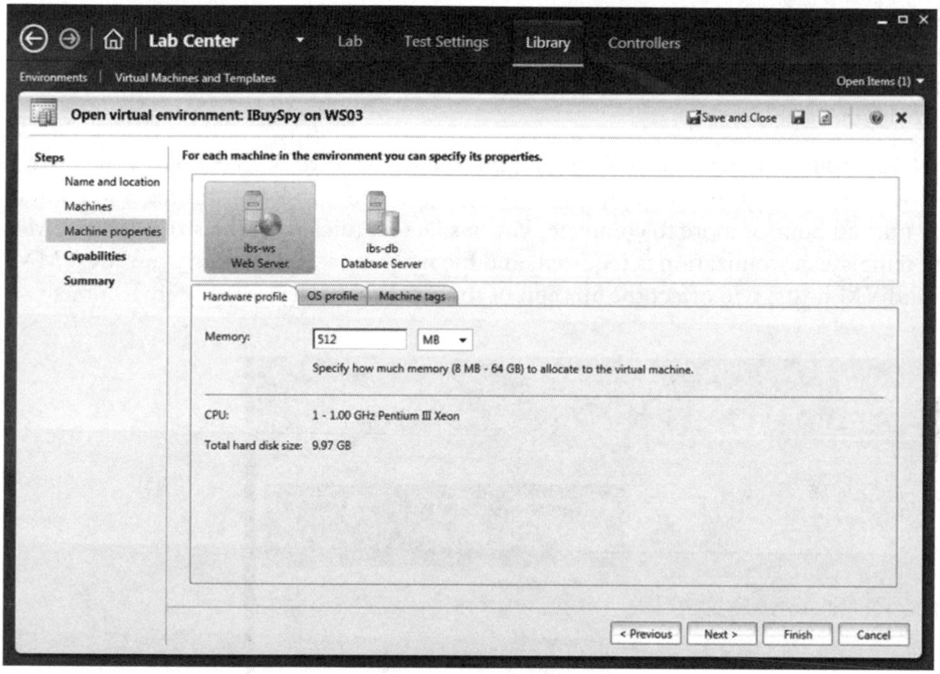

FIGURE 16-4

The Capabilities tab shown allows you to describe which agents are installed on the VMs within your environment. For build agents and test agents, you will also define the build and test controllers that should be used with those agents. If you are unsure of what values to use here, consult with your Lab Management administrator.

The Summary tab describes your selections. Click Finish to finalize your environment definition.

Once your virtual environment is defined, it will show up in the list of available environments in your library, as shown in Figure 16-2. Once your virtual environment is defined, it is ready to deploy. Select the environment within your library and click the Deploy button in the upper-left of the screen. The "Deploy environment" dialog shown in Figure 16-5 will appear.

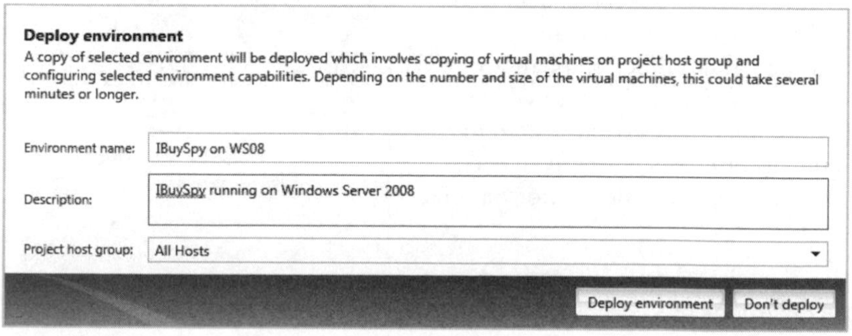

FIGURE 16-5

From this dialog, you can provide a name and a description for what will become a running instance of your virtual environment. You can also specify the SCVMM VM host group to where you want to deploy your environment. Click "Deploy environment" to begin the virtual environment deployment process.

From the Lab ⇨ Environments activity, you can monitor the status of your virtual environment as it is deployed, as shown in Figure 16-6. Deploying a virtual environment is a long-running operation that can potentially take an hour or more to complete. Various factors (including the size of your VMs, whether or not template customization is required, and the network speed between your SCVMM library server and VM hosts) will affect the amount of time it takes to deploy your environment.

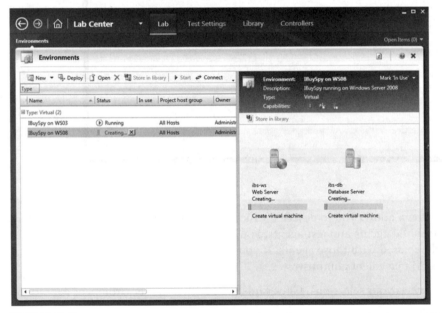

FIGURE 16-6

Once deployed, your virtual environment can be managed from the Lab ⇨ Environments activity. This includes starting, stopping, and pausing the virtual environment. Figure 16-7 shows an environment that has been deployed and is currently running. The Capabilities icons indicate which of your agents is running and online. You can hover your mouse over each capabilities icon to discover which icon corresponds to each capability. Any errors related to the VMs within your environment, or errors with any agents, will be displayed here as well, along with more information describing the error.

You can right-click on a running virtual environment and select Connect to open the Environment Viewer shown in Figure 16-8. The Environment Viewer allows you to interact with the VMs running within your environment.

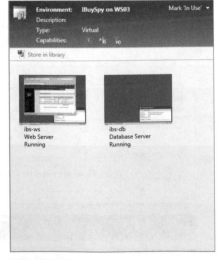

FIGURE 16-7

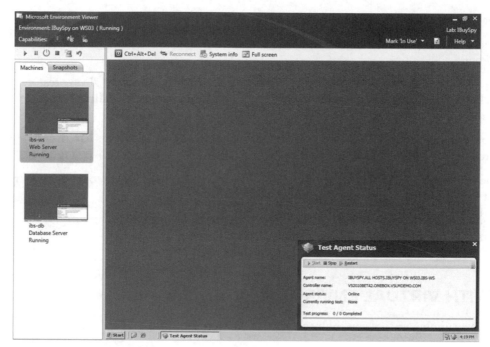

FIGURE 16-8

From the Environment Viewer you can also stop, start, and pause the running environment, see the status of agents running on the VMs (in the upper-left corner), and mark an environment as "In use" (upper-right corner). This signals to other members of your team that you are using the environment and they should not attempt to connect to it.

The "System info" button allows you to view properties of the running VMs (such as the fully qualified machine name). This can be useful information for connecting to the VM from outside of the environment (such as when using a Web browser on a client machine to connect to a Web site running within your virtual environment).

You can also manage *snapshots* for your environment from here by clicking on the Snapshots tab on the left side of the screen, as shown in Figure 16-9. Snapshots allow you to save the state of an environment at any point in time, and likewise to restore the state of an environment by restoring a snapshot. Lab Management allows you to create a snapshot of an entire environment at once, although you can create a snapshot of individual VMs a few seconds apart, so this may have an impact on transactions that were in process when you started the synchronization.

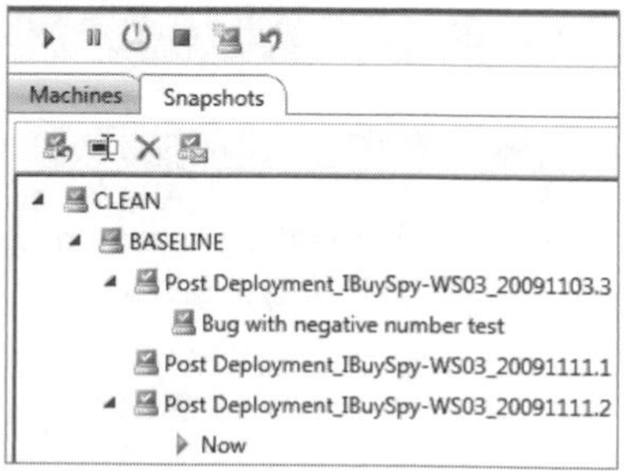

FIGURE 16-9

Snapshots have the following useful applications:

➤ A snapshot can provide a clean "baseline" state that can be used prior to installing each new build.

➤ Snapshots can be created after installing a new build, providing a way to always restore to a known state prior to any tests being executed that may potentially "dirty" an environment.

➤ Snapshots can be created by testers when they find a bug. These snapshots can then be shared with the development team to help them diagnose the bug and deliver a fix.

From the Snapshots tab you can create new snapshots, rename them, delete them, or restore your environment to an existing snapshot.

Now that you understand the basics of creating, deploying, and working with running environments, it's time to explore software testing with virtual environments.

TESTING WITH VIRTUAL ENVIRONMENTS

Once you have a running virtual environment, you can use it to run your tests.

Create New Test Settings

In Chapter 14, you configured test settings to define which diagnostics data to collect as you ran your tests (such as video, IntelliTrace files, and action logs). But now that you are going to run tests with an environment, you may want to create a new test setting that specifies how data should be collected from each machine within your environment. This step is optional, but can provide valuable diagnostics data to your developers when bugs are discovered.

> *To define a test setting that collects data from remote machines, you must have installed and configured test agents on the VMs within your environment.*

From within Test Manager, click on Testing Center ➪ Plan ➪ Properties. Your test plan properties will be displayed, as shown in Figure 16-10.

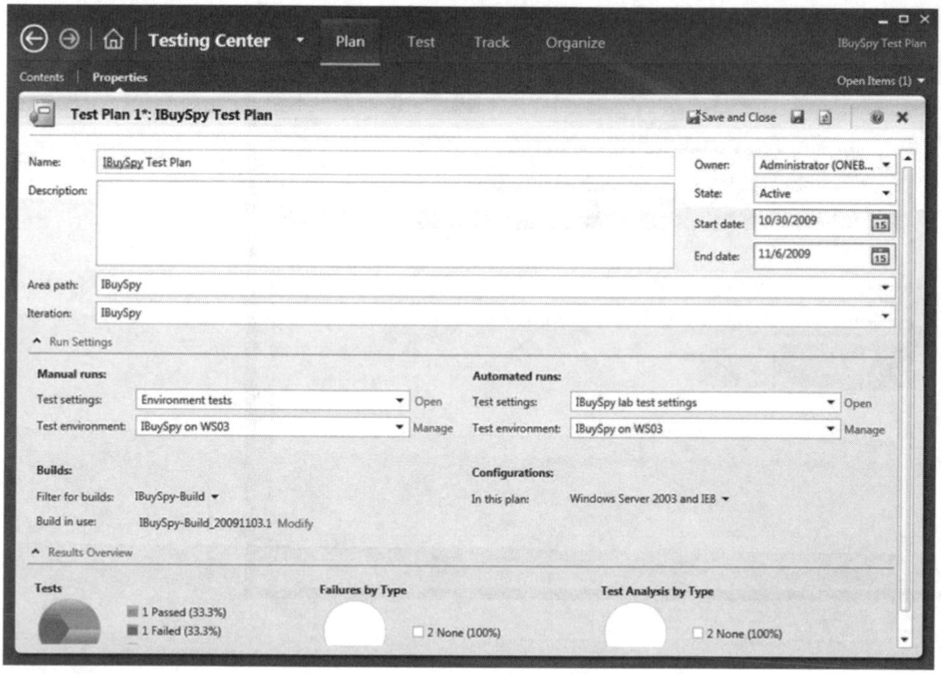

FIGURE 16-10

> The discussion in this section assumes that you have already configured your first test plan as described in Chapter 14.

From within your test plan properties, create a new test settings definition (Manual Runs ⇨ Test Settings ⇨ New). Provide a name and (optionally) a description for your new test settings. Click Next.

The Roles tab shown in Figure 16-11 allows you to select the virtual environment for which you want to define test settings. When defining test settings for automated tests, you can also select the role from where automated tests will be run. When configuring manual tests, the tests are always run from the local machine where Test Manager is running. After selecting your environment, click Next.

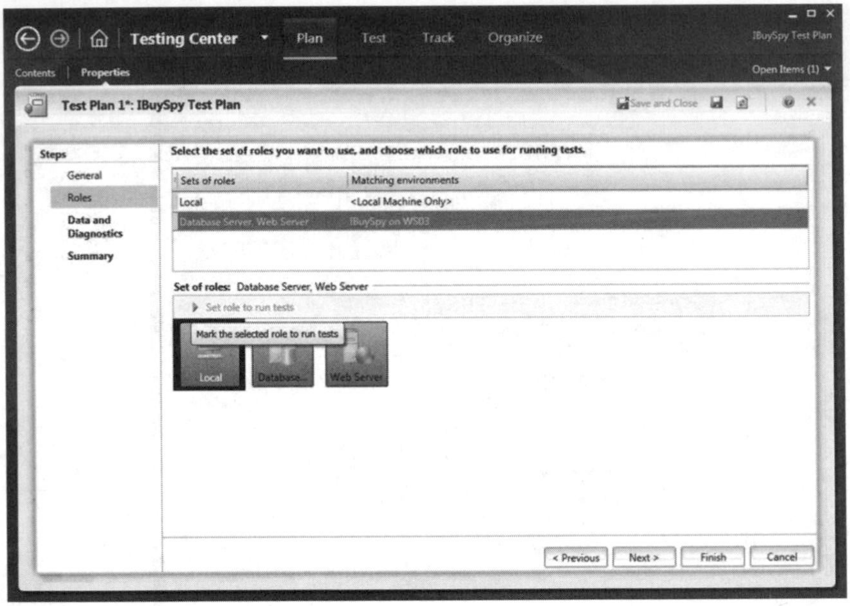

FIGURE 16-11

The Data and Diagnostics tab shown in Figure 16-12 allows you to define the individual diagnostics data adapters that will be used for each machine within your virtual environment. Data diagnostics adapters were covered in detail in Chapter 14. From here, you can configure the adapters for each machine within your environment.

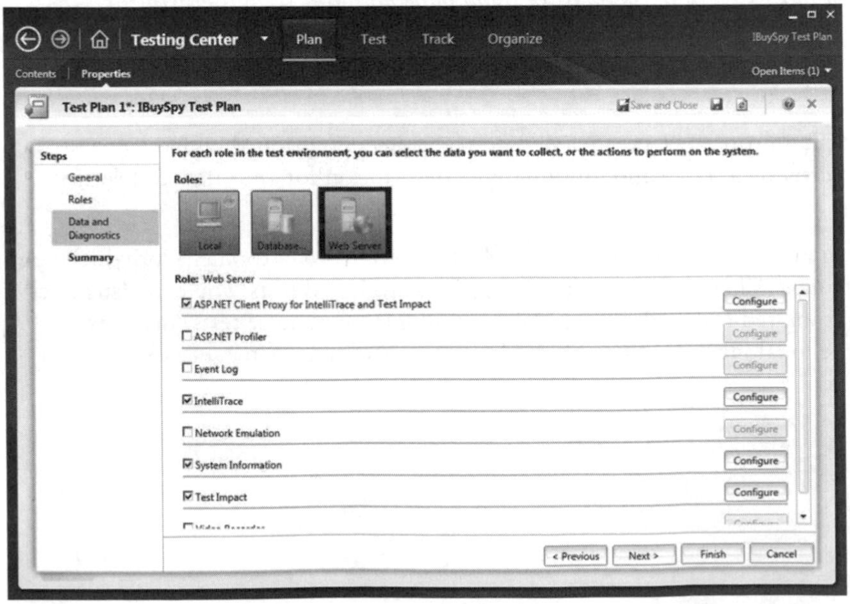

FIGURE 16-12

> *Action logs and recordings can only be enabled on the local machine where Test Manager is running.*

Run Manual Tests with an Environment

Run a test case as you normally would by clicking on the Test ⇨ "Run tests" activity.

> *The discussion in this section assumes that you have already created one or more test cases as defined in Chapter 14.*

Select a test case that you want to run with your environment and click Run ⇨ "Run with options."

The Run Options dialog shown in Figure 16-13 appears, allowing you to select the test settings and environment with which you want to run your test. If your manual test has associated automated tests (such as a coded UI test) and your test plan is associated with a build definition, then you can also opt to run this test as an automated test. For now, if your test has associated automated tests, just select the "Run all the tests manually" checkbox.

If you defined new test settings for collecting data from your environment, select it here. Also, select your running environment from the Environment drop-down. Click Run and this will launch your test run and the Microsoft Test Runner.

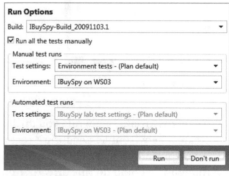

FIGURE 16-13

Once the Microsoft Test Runner is open, you can click the "Connect to environment button" (shown in Figure 16-14) to open the Environment Viewer for your environment.

FIGURE 16-14

Once the Environment Viewer is open, you can then begin running your test just like you would run any other manual test. You may wish to use the Snapshots tab to restore the environment to a known state (such as immediately after a given build was deployed). As needed, you can even switch among multiple machines within your environment if your test case requires it. Figure 16-15 shows a test case being run with a virtual environment.

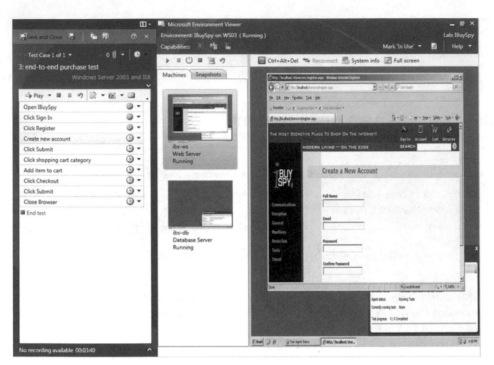

FIGURE 16-15

If you discover a bug while you are testing, you may wish to create an environment snapshot that can be shared with the development team to help them diagnose the problem. Even though you could do this directly from within the Environment Viewer, a better way is to do so is from within the Microsoft Test Runner. This automatically attaches a pointer to the environment snapshot to the test results.

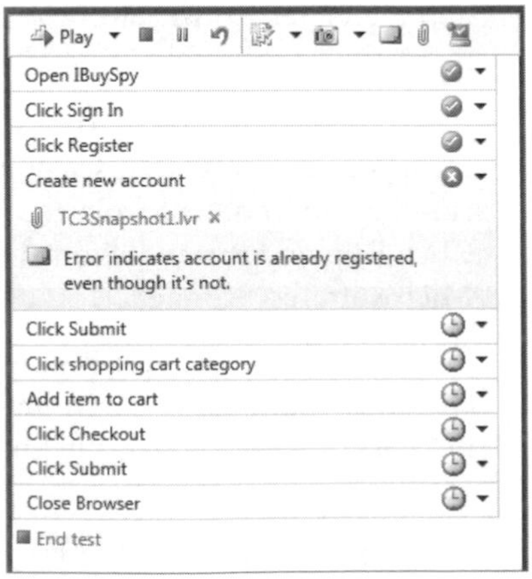

To create an environment snapshot with Microsoft Test Runner, click the rightmost icon along the Microsoft Test Runner toolbar (shown in the upper-right corner of Figure 16-16). This creates a new snapshot of the environment and saves an .lvr file to your test results. The .lvr file is a pointer to the environment snapshot that can be opened later to restore your environment to this snapshot.

FIGURE 16-16

Click the "Create bug" icon within the Microsoft Test Runner to create a new bug along with your test results (hover your mouse over the toolbar icons to discover the Create Bug icon). Figure 16-17 shows the new bug creation form, along with a reference to the .lvr file created earlier.

When reviewing this bug later, a developer can open the .lvr file simply by clicking on it, provided the developer has Test Manager installed. The dialog shown in Figure 16-18 will appear when an .lvr file is opened. This dialog gives you the option of connecting to the running environment as-is, or restoring the environment to the state it was in when the snapshot was created.

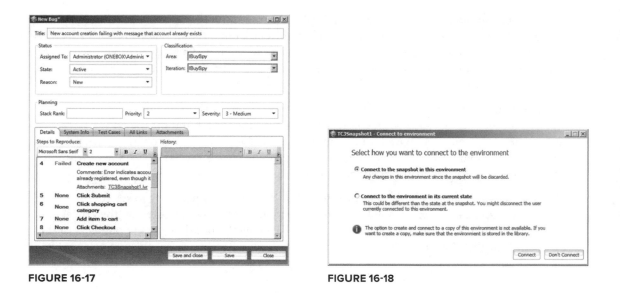

FIGURE 16-17   **FIGURE 16-18**

You may want to create copies of your running environment so that multiple people can be working with their own copies of a virtual environment. This is especially helpful when a tester finds a bug and wants to create a snapshot for the development team to use in diagnosing the problem.

To do this, the tester should shut down the environment after creating a bug with a snapshot. From the Lab Center ⇨ Lab ⇨ Environments activity, right-click the virtual environment and select "Store in library." Depending on the performance of your Lab Management servers and the size of your environment, this may be a long-running operation.

Once a copy of the environment has been stored in the SCVMM library, Figure 16-18 will include an option for the developer to connect to a copy of the environment from where the .lvr *file was created.*

You have now seen how you can take advantage of virtual environments when running manual tests. You can use a similar process for running manual tests that have associated automation (such as coded UI tests and unit tests). You can also run such tests as part of an automated end-to-end build-deploy-test workflow. You will learn how to configure this next.

AUTOMATED BUILD-DEPLOY-TEST WITH VIRTUAL ENVIRONMENTS

The true power of Lab Management comes to life when combined with the automated build, deployment, and testing capabilities of Team Foundation Build. As new builds are produced by the development team, they can be automatically deployed into one or more virtual environments. A snapshot can be created from the environment, thus providing the testing team with a baseline for running any manual tests against an environment with that build. Then, any automated tests can be run automatically, thus providing valuable data about any possible regressions in your test plan. This entire workflow can take place without any manual intervention.

Team Foundation Build is covered in detail in Chapter 21, but this discussion will provide an overview of the settings used when configuring Team Foundation Build for use with a virtual environment. Certain steps within the Team Foundation Build configuration are omitted, since they are covered in Chapter 21. This example assumes that you have a virtual environment with both build agents and test agents installed and configured.

The first step in creating a build definition for use with Lab Management is to select `LabDefaultTemplate.xaml` as the Build process template. This is configured on the Process tab of your build definition. Selecting this template will change the Build process parameters to those shown in Figure 16-19. Next, you define the Lab Workflow Parameters by clicking on the ellipsis in the Workflow settings row.

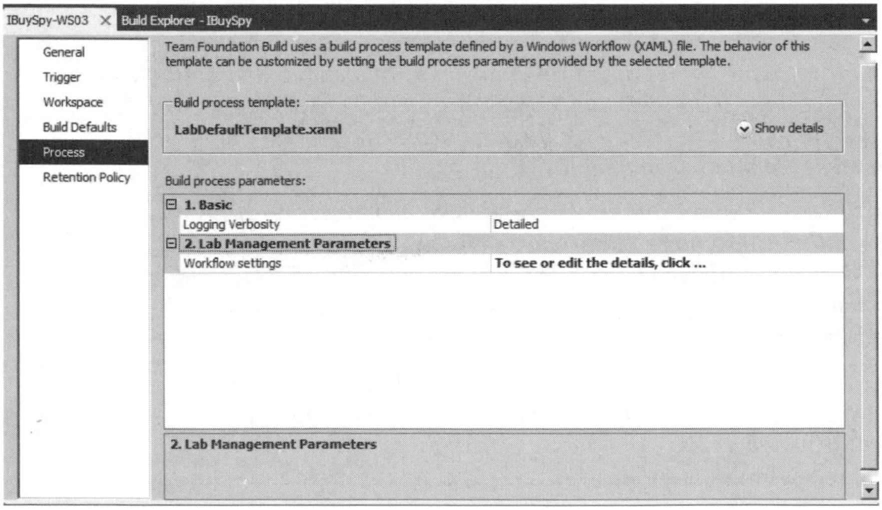

FIGURE 16-19

As shown in Figure 16-20, the first page of the Lab Workflow Parameters wizard allows you to define which virtual environment should be used as part of your build workflow. You can choose to use an environment that is already running on a VM host group. Keep in mind that deploying a new environment can be a long-running operation and may take an hour or more to complete, whereas using a running lab environment will be much faster.

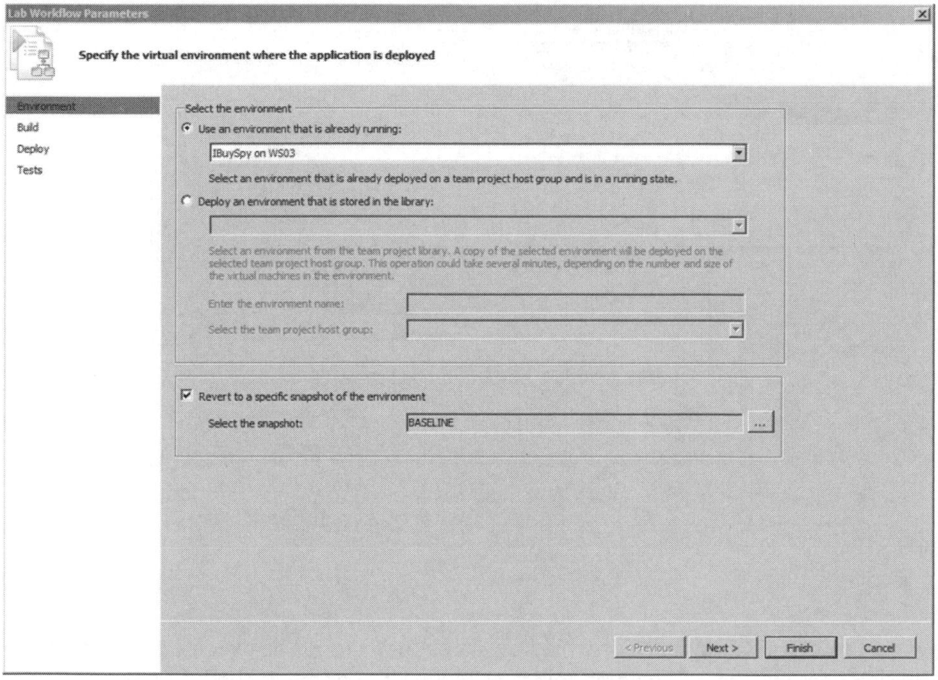

FIGURE 16-20

You can also choose to restore the environment to an environment snapshot prior to proceeding with the workflow. This is useful for establishing a clean baseline for your lab environment before attempting to install a new build or running any tests.

The Build page of the Lab Workflow Parameters wizard defines which build of your software should be used. You can rely on another build definition to create a new build, or you can select an existing build that was generated by another build definition. You can also point to a specific location where your software build resides, even if it wasn't created using Team Foundation Build.

As shown in Figure 16-21, the Deploy page of the Lab Workflow Parameters wizard allows you to specify how a build should be deployed within one or more VMs running in a virtual environment.

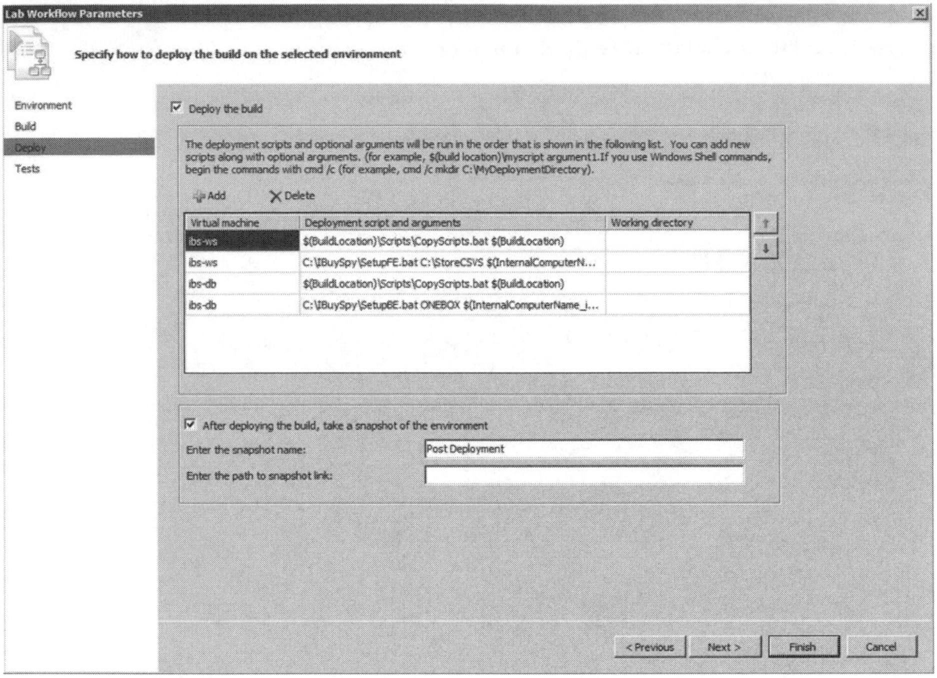

FIGURE 16-21

The grid allows you to define a sequence of workflow steps that should be executed in order during the build deployment phase. The first column specifies the name of the VM within the lab environment that defines where the given deployment step should be run. Note that this is not the computer name, but is the name of the VM which was provided when you configured the environment.

The second column specifies the command that should be run as part of that workflow step. This might include copying files to a Web server directory, running an `.msi` file, or even running a batch file. You can use the following variable names here to parameterize your commands.

➤ `$(BuildLocation)` — This resolves to the location that your build is initially copied to by Team Foundation Build.

➤ `$(InternalComputerName_VM-name)` — This resolves to the hostname of the VM within the environment. For example, this macro would return `mywebserver` for a VM whose fully qualified domain name (FQDN) is `mywebserver.contoso.com`. To use this command, replace *VM-name* with the name of the VM as defined within your environment. This variable is especially useful when you don't always know the machine name of the VMs within your environment, but your deployment scripts rely on those names. As an example, you might need to update a configuration file in your Web application to use the machine name of the database server in your environment.

➤ `$(ComputerName_VM-name)` — This returns the FQDN of the VM within the environment. To use this command, replace *VM-name* with the name of the VM, as defined within your environment. Typically, the FQDN of a machine is a concatenation of its hostname and its domain suffix. As an example, the FQDN for a VM with a hostname of `mywebserver` in the `contoso.com` domain would be `mywebserver.contoso.com`. Note that when using network isolation, `$(InternalComputerName_`*VM-name*`)` will be the same for a VM in each copy of a given virtual environment but its FQDN will be different. As an example, for a VM with hostname `mywebserver` in a network isolated environment, this macro would return `VSLM_`*<uid>*`.contoso.com` where *<uid>* is a unique alphanumeric identifier. This value can be important when using network isolation, where the `InternalComputerName` will be the same on each copy of a given virtual environment.

Finally, after deploying a build, you can create a new snapshot of the environment by enabling the bottom checkbox and providing a name with which to preface such snapshot names. This will then create new snapshots with names based on the build name and build number such as those in Figure 16-9.

The Tests page of the Lab Workflow Parameters wizard allows you to run any automated tests that you may have in your test plan. Your test cases will need to have associated automation (such as coded UI tests or unit tests). After builds are deployed, these tests will be run automatically, and the test results will be published to your test plan. You will need to specify automated test settings as defined earlier.

PHYSICAL ENVIRONMENTS

The focus of this chapter has been on virtual environments, and virtual environments offer many advantages over physical environments such as using snapshots, as well as better resource utilization. But there may be times when the tests you need to run can't take advantage of virtual environments, such as when your tests rely on specialized hardware that isn't supported by virtual environments.

A *physical environment* can be defined to run tests remotely and collect diagnostics data. The first step in defining a physical environment is to install a test agent on each machine that will make up your physical environment. Those test agents then must be registered with a test controller associated with your team project collection.

Next, you can define a physical environment from within Test Manager. Open Lab Center ⇨ Lab ⇨ Environments as shown in Figure 16-6. Click on New ⇨ Physical Environment. You can define a physical environment similarly to the way you defined a virtual environment, but without the capability to provide customizations such as RAM, computer name, and domain and workgroup memberships.

Finally, you can define new test settings for your physical environment by following the same steps you did earlier in this chapter for a virtual environment. This allows you to define which data is collected when running your tests.

Then, run tests by specifying an environment like you did earlier in this chapter with a virtual environment. You won't be able to connect to your physical environments by using the Environment Viewer like you would with tests running in a virtual environment, but you can use a technology such as Remote Desktop to achieve similar results.

SUMMARY

In this chapter, you have seen how Lab Management can be used to help create and manage VMs running within a virtual test lab. You learned how to create new environments and define which diagnostic data should be collected on various machines as tests are run on those environments. You learned the benefits of snapshots and how to work with them and share them among team members.

You also learned how an end-to-end workflow can be established to automatically build and deploy your software, then run automated tests within those virtual environments.

Finally, you learned about how physical environments can be used when virtual environments are not an option.

In the next several chapters, you will gain an in-depth understanding of Team Foundation Server, and the central role it plays when performing application lifecycle management with Visual Studio 2010. The examination begins with an overview of Team Foundation Server in Chapter 17.

PART IV
Team Foundation Server

17

Introduction to Team Foundation Server

WHAT'S IN THIS CHAPTER?

➤ What is Team Foundation Server

➤ Team Foundation Server Core Concepts

➤ How to Access Team Foundation Server

➤ What's New in Team Foundation Server 2010

➤ Adopting Team Foundation Server

This chapter introduces you to Microsoft Visual Studio Team Foundation Server 2010. Here you will learn what it is for, the key concepts needed when using it, and how to connect to Team Foundation Server.

For those who are already familiar with Team Foundation Server from previous versions, the discussion in this chapter highlights areas that are new or have changed substantially. However, because understanding the legacy of a technology is always helpful, this chapter also includes some of the history of the Team Foundation Server product, which will help explain how it became what it is today. This chapter will also examine some best practices and strategies for adopting Team Foundation Server in your organization.

Later chapters will go into more depth with an examination of the architecture of the Team Foundation Server product. There you will learn about version control, including a whole chapter dedicated to branch and merge strategies. Another chapter concentrates on the Build Automation capabilities provided by Team Foundation Server, since they have been growing in functionality as the product matures, and this release has some particularly significant functionality.

WHAT IS TEAM FOUNDATION SERVER?

Developing software is difficult, a fact that is repeatedly proven by how many projects fail. An essential factor in the success of any software development team is how well the members of the team communicate with each other and with the people who wanted the software developed in the first place.

Microsoft Visual Studio 2010 Team Foundation Server provides the core collaboration functionality for your software development teams in a very tightly integrated product. The functionality provided by Team Foundation Server includes the following:

➤ Project management

➤ Work item tracking (WIT)

➤ Version control

➤ Test case management

➤ Build automation

➤ Reporting

Team Foundation Server is a separate server product. Logically, Team Foundation Server is made up of the following two tiers, which can be physically deployed across one or many machines:

➤ *Application tier* — The application tier primarily consists of a set of Web services with which the client machines communicate by using a highly optimized Web service-based protocol.

➤ *Data tier* — The data tier is made up of a SQL Server database containing the database logic of the Team Foundation Server application, along with the data for your Team Foundation Server instance. The data stored in the database is used by Team Foundation Server's reporting functionality. All the data stored in Team Foundation Server is stored in this SQL Server database, thus making it easy to back up.

Team Foundation Server was designed with extensibility in mind. There is a comprehensive .NET API for integrating with Team Foundation Server and a set of events that allow outside tools to integrate with Team Foundation Server as first-class citizens. The same .NET programming model and event system is used by Microsoft itself in the construction of Team Foundation Server, as well as the client integrations into Visual Studio.

TEAM FOUNDATION SERVER CORE CONCEPTS

Let's take a look at some of the core concepts that are critical to understanding Team Foundation Server, some of which are new in the Visual Studio 2010 release. If you have been using previous versions of Team Foundation Server for a while, then you might want to skip to the section "What's New in Team Foundation Server 2010," later in this chapter.

Figure 17-1 provides an overview of the Team Foundation Server components.

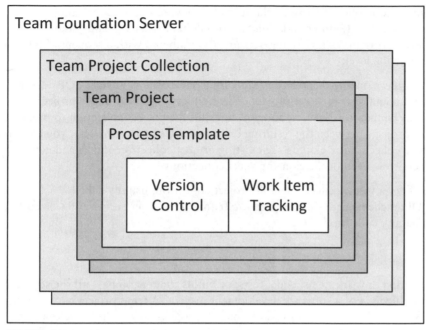

FIGURE 17-1

Team Foundation Application Tier

The *Team Foundation Application Tier* is a slightly modified concept in Team Foundation Server 2010. It refers to the running Web application that is handling all requests for data from the Team Foundation Server and is, therefore, often referred to as simply the Team Foundation Server. You refer to your Team Foundation Server by name or URL (that is, `tfsserver` or `http://tfsserver:8080/tfs`) when Team Foundation Server is installed in the default virtual directory in IIS on the default port.

Because of load-balancing capabilities introduced in Team Foundation Server 2010, this server can be split across several actual servers making up a Team Foundation Server Farm. Each machine has the Team Foundation application tier components installed and pointing to the Team Foundation Server data tier.

Team Foundation Server can scale to support a very large number of active users, depending on the hardware supporting it. Therefore, for most organizations, the Team Foundation Server Instances tend to be scoped by who pays for the installation and operation of the instance.

Team Project Collection

A *team project collection* is another new concept in Team Foundation Server 2010. This is a container for team projects. Each server has one or many team project collections, and a project collection can have zero or more team projects.

In many ways, the team project collection can be thought of as having many of the same characteristics as older versions of Team Foundation Server. Global security groups take effect at the project collection level. Work items and changesets are all numbered with a sequential ID that is unique at the project collection level.

A team project collection has a one-to-one relationship with a database instance in SQL Server. Therefore, you can back up and restore at the project collection level. You can move project collections between Team Foundation Servers, and you can split the project collection to break up the distribution of team projects between the resulting collections. Using this process, you can move a team project into a new collection by cloning the existing project collection and then deleting the appropriate team projects from each of the cloned project collections.

Each Team Foundation Server instance has a default project collection, usually called `DefaultCollection`. Older clients that were created for Team Foundation Server 2008 or 2005 will only be able to see the default collection.

Team Project

A *team project* is a collection of work items, code, tests, or builds that encompass all the separate tools that are used in the lifecycle of a software development project. A team project can contain any number of Visual Studio solutions or projects, or, indeed, projects from other development environments. A team project is usually a fairly long-running thing with multiple areas and iterations of work.

You need at least one team project to start working with Team Foundation Server. When the team project is created, the following are also created by default:

➤ Team project Web site

➤ Document library

➤ Path in version control

➤ Default work items

➤ Stock reports

> *It is not possible to rename a team project once created. Also, the number of team projects in the team project collection has a performance impact on the system, so you do not want to have too many (less than 250). Therefore, you want to think carefully before creating a new team project.*
>
> *It is often useful to experiment with Team Foundation Server features in a sandboxed test instance of Team Foundation Server. Many people download the Team Foundation Server Trial Virtual PC image from Microsoft for this purpose, but some organizations have enterprise-wide test instances of Team Foundation Server for people to experiment in.*

The granularity that you chose for your team project has important implications for how you structure your work and when you move from one team project to another.

Team projects are intended to represent the largest unit of work in your organization. For example, in Microsoft Developer Division, the whole of the Visual Studio 2010 release lives in a single team project with Team Foundation Server as an area of that project.

A team project has a single process template, and changes made to the process template of a running team project affect that team project only. The default reports and work item queries are all scoped by team project, making it easy to track and find work for that team project as an entity.

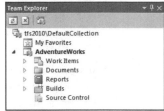

FIGURE 17-2

As shown in Figure 17-2, the following are also linked to the team project that they belong to and, in general, are difficult to move between team projects:

➤ *Work Items* — Each work item is attached to the team project and uses the process template assigned to it. For this reason, it is not possible to move a work item from one team project to another, although you may copy the work item between projects in the same project collection and include a link to the source work item for reference.

➤ *Document Libraries* — The team project optionally refers to a project Web site based on Windows SharePoint Services (WSS). The document libraries in this Web site are linked to this project, and all the documents, projects plans, process guidance, or other non-deliverable assets contained in the document library therefore correspond to the team project.

➤ *Reports* — All the reports created as part of one of the stock process templates are scoped to the team project level, making it easy to determine the progress of work inside that team project.

➤ *Builds* — Each build definition is tied to a team project, as are the build controllers and build agents performing the builds.

➤ *Version Control* — All items stored in version control must be stored under a team project node in the repository. All settings for version control (such as check-in policies, check-in notes, and multiple check-out support) are controlled at the team project level.

➤ *Classifications* — A team project is typically broken up into areas and iterations. An *area* is typically a functional area of the code that may have a subset of the whole team typically working on it. For example, a particular application may be broken into tiers — the Web tier, application tier and database tier. It is common that a feature or requirement may impact all tiers of the application, but a task or bug may just affect a small area of the code. Therefore, areas are organized hierarchically so that a feature could be assigned to the whole application in the team project, but an ASP.NET form development task may be assigned to a child area. *Iterations* are similarly organized. For Version 1 of the application, you may split development into several phases and, in each phase, have several short iterations (or *sprints*). These can be organized hierarchically in the iterations section.

SCOPE OF A TEAM PROJECT

In general, a Team Project is "bigger than you think." A good way of thinking about what needs to be grouped into a single team project is to think about the impact of a typical requirement for your software development project. If the requirement would affect the ASP.NET front end, Java middleware, and SQL database repository, then all these projects and teams of developers probably want to be working in the same team project.

Following are three general areas that are used when scoping a team project, but every organization is different, and yours might need to combine these aspects when deciding on your approach:

➤ Application

➤ Release

➤ Team

For some organizations, it makes sense to only have a single team project in a single project collection. Others may have more than a hundred.

TEAM PROJECT PER APPLICATION

In general, this is the most common approach when scoping Team Projects and probably the position you should first consider. Generally, requirements are addressed by the entire application, and a group of people are assigned to work on it. The applications typically have a long lifecycle, going from inception, active development into the support, and then finally end-of-life phases.

TEAM PROJECT PER RELEASE

This is the methodology adopted by Microsoft Developer Division as they develop Visual Studio. It is useful for very large teams working on long-running projects. After every major release (such as Visual Studio 2010), you create a new team project. At this point in time, you can carry out changes that might have come about from your post-release review. You might take the opportunity to re-organize your version control tree, improve process templates, and copy over work items from the previous release that didn't make it.

This methodology tends to be suited to large independent software vendors (ISVs) working with products with a very long lifetime. In these cases, it is generally safer to start as a team project per application and then move to a team project per release if required to make reporting easier.

TEAM PROJECT PER TEAM

For smaller teams (less than 50) where the number of people working on the team tends to stay fairly static but the applications they work on are in a constant state of flux, the team project per team approach may be most suitable. This is most often seen in consulting-style organizations where the same group of people may be responsible for delivering applications to clients with rapid turnaround. If your team members are often working on more than one project at a time, the same team or subset of the team works together on those projects over time, or if the project lifecycle is measured in months rather than years, then you may want to consider this approach.

Process Template

An important fact about software development projects is that there is no single process that is suitable for delivering all types of solutions to all types of business with all types of teams. Therefore, Team Foundation Server was designed from the ground up to be flexible in how you want your teams to work.

The *process template* is a set of XML files that provide the details of how you would like your process to work. Microsoft provides the following two process templates with the default installation of Team Foundation Server:

➤ *Microsoft Solutions Framework (MSF) for Agile Software Development* — This is a lightweight template designed for teams following a delivery process based on Agile Software Development. User needs are tracked by "User Story" work items, as well as types for Bugs, Issues, Tasks, and Test Cases. In general, the work items have a simple state progression from active to resolved to closed. It is also an excellent starting point for people who want to customize a process to fit with their development organization.

➤ *MSF for Capability Maturity Model Integration (CMMI) Process Improvement* — This is a more heavyweight template designed for teams with more heavyweight process requirements — that is, those that typically have longer lifecycles and possible governance requirements that the process template would help fulfill. Note that if your organization is striving for CMMI compliance, then you should not consider this template as your only choice, but still evaluate the possibilities offered by the MSF for Agile Software Development template among others.

In addition to the templates installed by default, many more are available to download online. If you have an existing process in your organization, it is possible to create a custom process template to match the process.

To obtain information about additional process templates available from Microsoft and its partners, see http://go.microsoft.com/fwlink/?LinkId=80608. *For information on Open Source and community-driven process templates for Team Foundation Server, see* http://templex.codeplex.com.

Once you have created a team project with a process template, it is possible to modify all aspects of it while the project is in flight, including work item types, fields, states, and so on. This was another critical design decision taken by Microsoft in designing Team Foundation Server, because Microsoft recognized that the best teams are those that continually improve and adapt their processes, and that, as the project continues, more is learned about the domain, as well as the strengths and weaknesses of the team.

The following areas can be configured using a standard process template during the project creation process:

➤   *Work item tracking (WIT)* — You can define the initial work item types, team project queries, and create some initial work items to provide guidance for someone creating the team project on what to do next.

➤   *Classifications* — You can define the initial areas and iterations for a project. This is often useful to define the high-level aspects for the project (such as delivery phases), and to allow more detailed iterations to be created as children of the high-level phases once they are known.

➤   *SharePoint* — If a SharePoint-based project Web site is to be created as part of the team project, then you can control on which site template the project will be based, what features should be activated, which document libraries are created, what folders should be in those libraries and even some template files to include.

➤   *Version control* — This defines the initial security groups and permissions for the team project path in version control, what check-in notes to request, whether multiple users can check out a file at the same time, and whether users should automatically get the latest version of a file as they check out the file.

➤   *Reports* — This includes the folders and reports to create in the reports site for the team project.

➤   *Groups and permissions* — This includes the new Team Foundation Server security groups to create for the team project, as well as permissions to apply to each group specified.

➤   *Build* — This includes the default build processes to use for new build definitions, as well as the build permissions to give to each of the groups.

➤   *Lab* — This includes the default lab processes to use, as well as the lab permissions to give to each of the groups.

➤   *Test management* — This includes the default test configurations, variables, settings, and resolution states.

Chapter 23 provides a more in-depth look at process templates.

Work Item Tracking

Work items in Team Foundation Server are things like requirements, bugs, issues, and test cases. In other words, these are the items of work that your organization needs to track to manage the delivery of a software development project.

The work item tracking system is highly extensible. You can control which fields are presented to the user, which fields are rolled up into the reporting data-warehouse, how the work item looks, what states the work item can be in, and how to transition from one state to the next.

All work items share certain common fields such as an ID, Status, and Title. As shown in Figure 17-3, they have a full history of changes recorded to every field in the work item and by whom. You can also link work items, files, Web pages or other elements in Team Foundation Server.

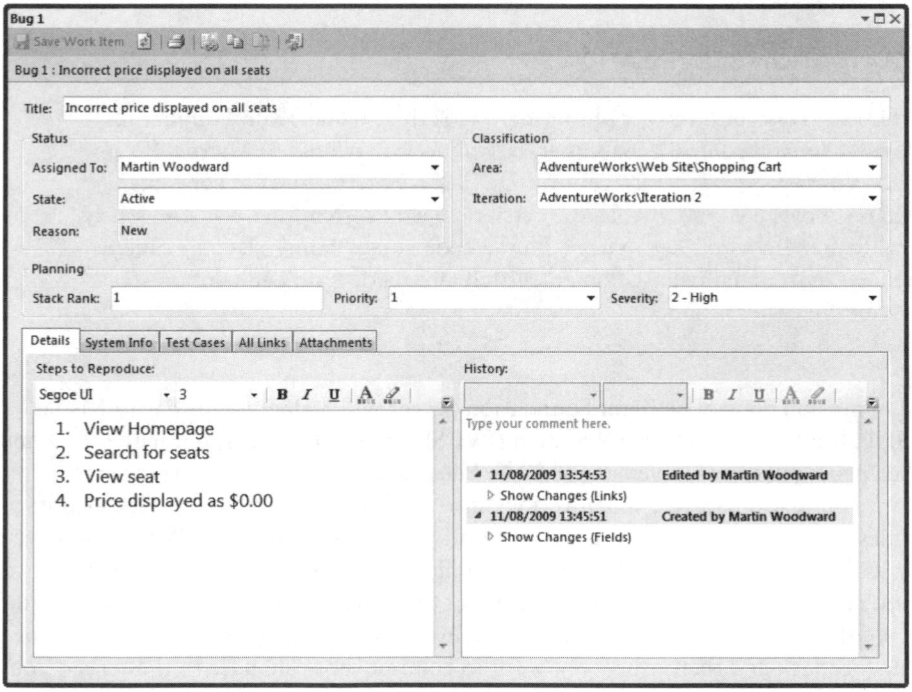

FIGURE 17-3

The work item type definitions are all configurable at the team project level. The work item types are created as part of the process template during project creation, but they can be modified as the team project is in flight. Changing the work item types in one team project does not affect those in another team project, even if they were created using the same process template.

Obtaining help in understanding how to use the particular work items in a team project is relatively simple. You simply right-click the work items node in Team Explorer, right-click the work item form itself, or click the process guidance button in the toolbar of the work item.

All data about the work item is stored in the Team Foundation Server database. Any file attachments are also stored in the database.

> *You will learn more about work items in Chapters 22 through 26, all of which are included in Part V of this book.*

Version Control

Team Foundation Server includes a full enterprise-class, centralized version control system that has been designed from the ground up to work well in environments that are spread across a wide geographical area over high latency, low-bandwidth connections.

> **TEAM FOUNDATION SERVER AND VSS**
>
> An important misconception to get out of the way is that, while Team Foundation Server provides version control capabilities, it is in no way related to Microsoft's previous version control system, Visual SourceSafe (VSS). In terms of core concepts, it actually shares more in common with the version control system that was previously used internally in Microsoft, a product with the code name "Source Depot." Team Foundation Server is actually based on an entirely new code base and contains features not found in either product.

The basic model of version control in Team Foundation Server will feel very familiar to Visual SourceSafe (VSS), Polytron Version Control System (PVCS), or Perforce users, but may take some getting used to for people used to Subversion or CVS. Files are stored in a centralized server repository in Team Foundation Server. When you want to work on a copy of those files locally, you must "Get" the files to download them from the server to your local workspace. When you have the files locally, they will all be read-only. Before you edit a file, it must be "checked out" from version control. When you check out a file, the client will contact the server to ensure that it is still available for check-out. If so, the file will be marked as writeable in your local file system. You make your changes to the file (or files), and then, when you want to commit those changes to the server, you "check in" the files to Team Foundation Server.

By default, Team Foundation Server allows multiple people to edit the same text-based files at the same time. This is particularly useful for `.sln`, `.vbproj`, and `.csproj` files in a Visual Studio project. When you go to check the file in to the server, if the latest version of that file is newer than the one you checked out, then you will be prompted to merge your changes with the changes made by your colleague(s). At the time of check-out, you may specify that you wish to "lock" the file so that it cannot be edited by others until you release the lock — usually by checking the file back in again. This setting can be made the default by a user with administration privileges on the team project. However, it is recommended that you allow for concurrent editing of files if your organization permits this.

When you check out a file in your workspace, you are checking out the version of the file that you have downloaded to your machine. Therefore, it is important to get into the habit of regularly doing a "Get Latest" on your project to ensure that you are working against the latest version of the code for your team. If you wish, you may set Visual Studio to automatically download the latest version of the code as it is checking out a file (the behavior more familiar to VSS users). The reason this is not the default behavior is that two files that are dependent on each other may have been checked in at the same time. However, you are only editing one of them.

The tight IDE means that if you are making changes in your code editor, then it will (by default) automatically check out files when needed, perform renames, and so on. However, if you must work outside of the IDE, then you must ensure that you check files out before editing them and manually add any new files that you create.

> *Chapter 19 provides more in-depth information about version control.*

Team Foundation Server version control contains the following features:

➤ *Atomic check-ins* — Changes you make to the files are batched up into a "changeset." When you check in the files in a changeset, they are taken as a single atomic transaction. If a single file cannot be checked in (for example, because of a merge conflict), then the whole changeset it not committed. Only once the whole changeset has been successfully applied do any of the files become the latest version. This way, you can ensure the consistency of your code base.

➤ *Associate check-ins with work items* — When you perform a check-in, you may associate that changeset with one or more work items. In this way, you are able to get full traceability of requirements from the initial feature desired by the user, to the tasks required to create it, to the check-ins into version control that were required to implement the feature. This information is also surfaced in the work item that you linked to, as well as being passed into the reporting system in Team Foundation Server.

➤ *Branching and merging* — Team Foundation Server supports a full path space branching model. If you desire parallel development on a code base, then you can create a branch of the code in two separate places in the version control repository, and then merge changes that have been applied to one branch into the other. Substantial improvements have been made to the branch and merge support in Team Foundation Server 2010.

> *Chapter 20 provides more information about branching and merging in Team Foundation Server.*

➤ *Shelving* — This includes the capability to store files on the server without committing them to the main version control repository. This is useful in a couple of different scenarios. You may want to back up changes made on your local machine to the server if you are going to be working on the files for more than a few hours or if you need to work on a different task temporarily and resume later. Another scenario is when you want to copy changes from one machine to another without checking them in (for example, to have a colleague verify your changes).

➤ *Labeling* — In Team Foundation Server, you can tag a set of files at a particular version with a textual label. This is useful for indicating which files were included in a certain build or which files are ready to move to your quality assurance (QA) process. Note that, in Team Foundation Server, labels are always editable. Provided you have permission, you may add or remove files from that label at any time.

➤ *Concurrent check-outs* — Also known as the Edit-Merge-Commit model, by default, multiple people may edit a file at the same time. If a file were modified while you were working on it, then you would be prompted to merge the changes with the latest version of the file.

➤ *Follow history* — If you rename a file or branch it, then you are able to view the history of that file before it was renamed or branched. You can also follow the history of a file from before it was branched or merged.

➤ *Check-in policies* — When performing a check-in, Team Foundation Server provides the capability for the client to run code to validate that the check-in should be allowed. This includes performing actions such as checking that the change is associated with a work item, checking that the code passes static code analysis rules, and so on. Check-in policies are also an extension point in Team Foundation Server so that you can create your own, should you wish to do so.

➤ *Check-in notes* — In some organizations, it is necessary to capture metadata about a check-in (such as the code reviewer, or a reference to a third-party system). In other version control systems, this is frequently accomplished by requiring the check-in comment follow certain un-enforced conventions. Team Foundation Server provides check-in note functionality to capture this metadata. A team project administrator may add or remove check-in notes at the team project level, as well as make a particular check-in note mandatory.

➤ *Team Foundation Server proxy* — Frequently, organizations have regional development centers separated from the main development offices or the data center hosting the Team Foundation Server environment. When a "Get" is performed from version control, files are downloaded to the client machine. In the remote office environment, this often means that the same files are downloaded over the wide-area network (WAN) to every client machine involved in the development. Team Foundation Server provides an optional proxy server that may be installed in these remote offices. In those scenarios, the clients may be configured to perform the download via the proxy so that the proxy may cache the downloaded files at the remote location. In that way, the majority of the developers in the remote office will be downloading files from the proxy server local to them, thus removing traffic from the WAN and improving performance.

Team Build

Team Foundation Server provides a fully featured build automation server to allow you to standardize the build infrastructure for your team. Team builds are set up in the system as a *build definition*. You provide the build definition with information as to *what* you want build — that is, the folders or files in Team Foundation Server version control that contain the sources to be built, and the projects or solutions in those folders to build. You also specify through one of the following trigger controls *when* to perform the build:

➤ *Manual* — A build must be manually queued by a person or by third-party integration code. This is useful for ad-hoc builds or builds that deploy into a particular environment after completion (such as a QA environment).

➤ *Continuous integration* — This enables you to perform a build on every check-in to version control affecting the folders or files specified previously.

➤ *Rolling builds* — This is similar to the continuous integration trigger. However, check-ins are grouped together so that all the changes within a defined time period (say, 30 minutes) are included in the build. This is the default style of build used by some other continuous integration build servers, such as the popular Open Source build server CruiseControl.NET.

➤ *Gated check-ins* — This trigger forces the client to submit the check-in as a shelveset, rather than checking the code directly into the main code development area. The build is then performed and only if the code passes the build (along with any verification tests) will that code then be checked in. This is useful with very large development teams, but introduces an additional step to check-in, which may affect the agility of smaller teams.

➤ *Scheduled builds* — This enables you to configure a time on particular days of the week that a build should be performed (such as daily or nightly builds).

You tell the build definition *how* to perform the build by specifying a build process to follow. In Team Foundation Server 2010, these processes are defined as a Windows Workflow 4.0 XAML file.

You provide *where* you would like the build to be performed (that is, the build controller machine that will execute the build Windows Workflow process file), and *where* you would like the results of the build to be staged for deployment. The staging location must be a Windows file share using full Universal Naming Conventions (UNCs) (that is, \\server\share).

Finally, you can optionally set up a retention policy for the builds. If you are performing continuous integration-style builds or daily builds, then you can quickly consume a large amount of disk space storing the build results, including all the binaries created, deployment files, and so on. The retention policy can be set to only keep a defined number of the last builds for each type of build result (such as failed or successful builds). At any time, you may manually select a build to be excluded from this retention policy by marking the build as "Retain Indefinitely."

 Chapter 21 provides more information on the build automation capabilities.

ACCESSING TEAM FOUNDATION SERVER

There are many ways for a developer to interact with the core services in Team Foundation Server, including the following:

- ➤ Visual Studio
- ➤ Team Foundation Server Administration Console
- ➤ Web access
- ➤ Microsoft Excel
- ➤ Microsoft Project
- ➤ Eclipse-based development environments
- ➤ Command-line tools
- ➤ Third-party integrations

The following sections examine each of these, including the functionality they provide and basic usage.

> **TEAM FOUNDATION SERVER LICENSING**
>
> You must ensure that you are licensed to connect to Team Foundation Server. In general, for Team Foundation Server, this means that you need to have a Client Access License (CAL), which is typically included with the MSDN subscription, or can be purchased separately for people without MSDN. It is your responsibility to ensure that you have the correct licenses required to cover your usage of Team Foundation Server. If in doubt, contact your Team Foundation Server administrator. If your organization needs help understanding its licensing needs, then contact your local Microsoft representative for licensing assistance.

Accessing Team Foundation Server from Visual Studio

Team Foundation Server functionality is installed as a standard part of the install of a Visual Studio team edition. However, you may also access Team Foundation Server from Visual Studio Standard or Professional editions by installing the Microsoft Visual Studio Team Explorer. This is available on the Team Foundation Server media in the `tfc` directory, or available as a separate download. You can tell if you have the Team Foundation Server integration installed into Visual Studio by going to View, and looking for Team Explorer, as shown in Figure 17-4.

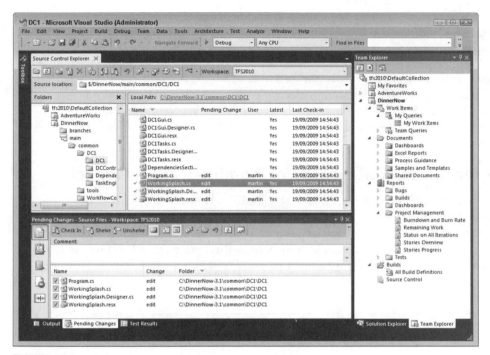

FIGURE 17-4

Assuming that a team project has been created for you by your Team Foundation Server administrator, to connect to your Team Foundation Server, click on the Connect to Team Project button. If your desired server is not available in the Servers drop-down then, click the Servers button, and then click the Add button to connect to your Team Foundation Server. As shown in Figure 17-5, you can enter the server name or provide the full URL given to you by your Team Foundation Server administrator.

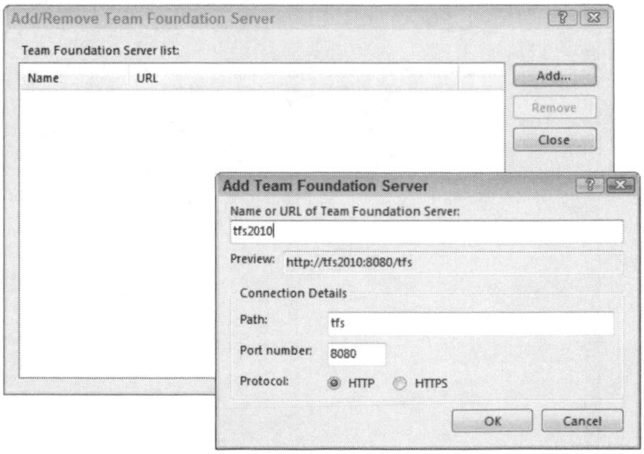

Once you have added the server, select the project collection that contains your team

FIGURE 17-5

projects, and select the team projects that you want to work on. Your Team Explorer window will now be populated with the team projects. If you expand each project, you will see additional nodes for different elements accessible from Visual Studio (such as work items, SharePoint documents libraries, reports, and version control).

If you have additional nodes for each team project, then this is probably because you have the Team Foundation Server power tools installed on your machine. This excellent set of tools is provided by the team at Microsoft to further enhance your Team Foundation Server experience. The Team Explorer, like most parts of Team Foundation Server, is extensible, so you can install extensions that take advantage of this or even create your own.

Using the Team Foundation Server Administration Console

The Team Foundation Administration Console (Figure 17-6) is installed as part of the Team Foundation Server installation and is available on the application tier machines by default. It allows you to configure your application tiers, project collections and define you SharePoint Web applications, reporting services locations, as well as administer your Team Lab functionality. In addition, the proxy server and Team Foundation Build controllers can be configured from this console.

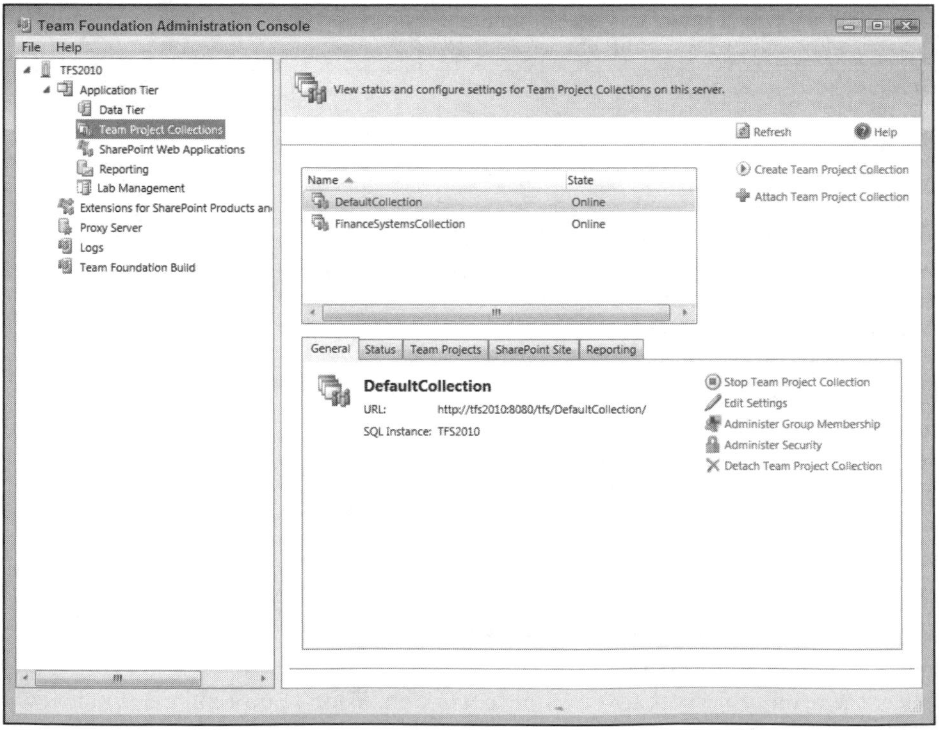

FIGURE 17-6

Accessing Team Foundation Server through a Web Browser

In Team Foundation Server 2010, a Web-based client to Team Foundation Server is installed by default on the application tier machine into the `web` subdirectory of the Team Foundation Server virtual path (that is, `http://tfs2010:8080/tfs/web`).

The Web client (Figure 17-7) is ideal for users who do not wish to install a dedicated Team Foundation Server client on their machines. At a high level, it offers the following functionality from the browser:

➤ Create and edit work items and work item queries

➤ Manage areas and iterations

➤ Read-only access to version control

➤ Queue and manage build definitions

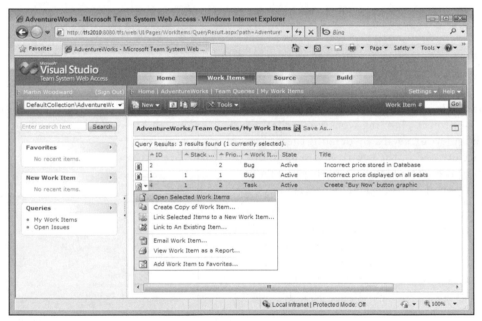

FIGURE 17-7

Using Team Foundation Server in Microsoft Excel

As part of the Team Explorer installation, integration into Microsoft Excel is provided by default. This allows the capability to add and edit work items directly from Excel spreadsheets, as shown in Figure 17-8.

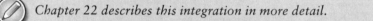

FIGURE 17-8

Chapter 22 describes this integration in more detail.

A new feature in Team Foundation Server 2010 is a powerful set of project planning workbooks that can be customized for your needs. By default, these workbooks are created in the `Excel Reports` folder (Figure 17-9) of the team document library, available via the project portal or from the Documents node in Team Explorer.

Another way that Excel can be used with Team Foundation Server is to connect to the SQL Server Reporting Services data warehouse and create custom reports. This is a great tool for mining data about your team, but also a good way of prototyping reports that you might wish to include in your project.

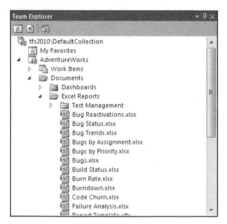

FIGURE 17-9

Chapter 24 contains more information on the reporting and analysis functionality available using Excel.

Using Team Foundation Server in Microsoft Project

An integration is added to Microsoft Project as part of the Team Explorer installation. This provides the capability to add and edit work items directly from Microsoft Project and to view data about the progress of these work items, as shown in Figure 17-10.

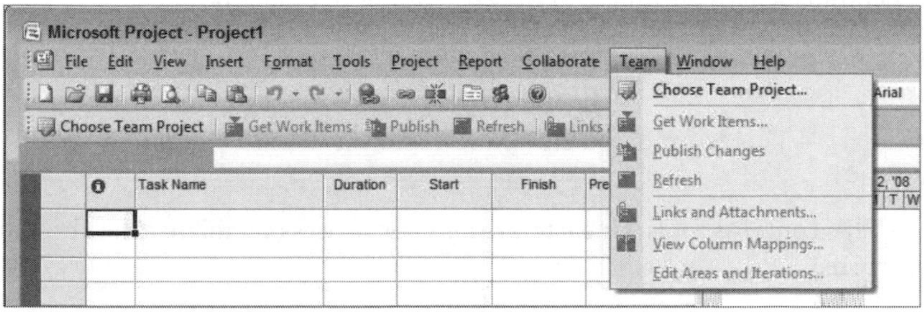

FIGURE 17-10

Chapter 22 describes this integration in more detail.

Command-Line Tools for Team Foundation Server

Team Foundation Server includes a set of command-line tools as part of the Team Explorer installation. The following commands-line tools are available from a Visual Studio 2010 command prompt:

➤ `tf.exe` — This provides full access to Team Foundation Server version control functionality, including features in Team Foundation Server that are not exposed via the Visual Studio integration.

➤ `TFSBuild.exe` — This enables you to create and work with build definitions and builds.

➤ `TFSDeleteProject.exe` — This is a command-line tool that helps you delete a team project from a team project collection.

➤ `TFSFieldMapping.exe` — This is a utility used to change or customize the mappings used by the Microsoft Project integration when working with the work items in your team project.

➤ `TFSLabConfig.exe` — This is a command-line tool used to manage the lab services by Visual Studio Team Lab Management 2010.

> *Chapter 16 provides more information on Visual Studio Team Lab Management.*

➤ `TFSSecurity.exe` — This tool enables you to view or edit groups, users, and permissions in Team Foundation Server.

In addition, the following commands are installed on the application tier machine:

➤ `TFSConfig.exe` — This enables you to view and edit configuration settings for Team Foundation Server.

➤ `SetupWarehouse.exe` — This is a tool to help you re-build the Team Foundation Server data warehouse.

➤ `WitAdmin.exe` — This contains tools for customizing your process template after the team project has been created.

> *Chapter 23 provides more information about customizing your process template.*

> *For more information and full reference information on the command-line tools available for Team Foundation Server, see* `http://msdn.microsoft.com/en-us/library/ms253088(VS.100).aspx`.

Accessing Team Foundation Server from Eclipse

For members of the team who are using Eclipse-based IDEs (including IBM Rational Application Developer or Adobe Flex), full access to the Team Foundation Server capabilities are now available from Microsoft. The Eclipse integration was previously available via a third-party company called Teamprise, but the technology was acquired by Microsoft and made available as part of the 2010 release.

As you can see in Figure 17-11, at a high level, the Eclipse integration provides all the same functionality that a developer inside Visual Studio would utilize, including the following:

➤ Full version control integration (check-out, check-in, history, branch, merge, label, synchronize, and so on)

➤ Full work item tracking (create, edit work items, and work item queried)

➤ Full team build integration (create, edit, and manage builds and build definitions)

➤ Access to team reports and documents

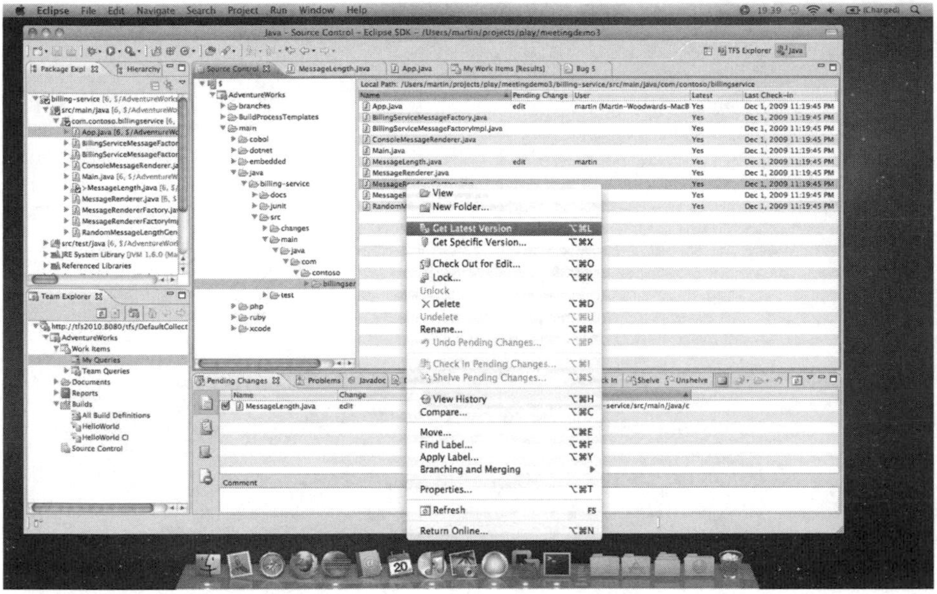

FIGURE 17-11

> *Check-in policies for the cross-platform and Eclipse clients must be separately configured inside that client. Also, the Java build extensions power tool is required to integrate with Ant or Maven 2 build processes that are common in Java environments.*

Visual Studio, the Team Foundation Server Administration Console, or the command-line tools must still be used for Team Foundation Server and team project administrative functionality (such as creating team projects, managing security permissions, and so on).

Windows Explorer Integration with Team Foundation Server

As part of the Team Foundation Server power tools, a Windows Explorer shell extension is available as an optional installation (Figure 17-12). This provides access to the basic version control functionality of Team Foundation Server from a standard Windows Explorer window and is most useful when working with Team Foundation Server version control outside of Visual Studio or Eclipse.

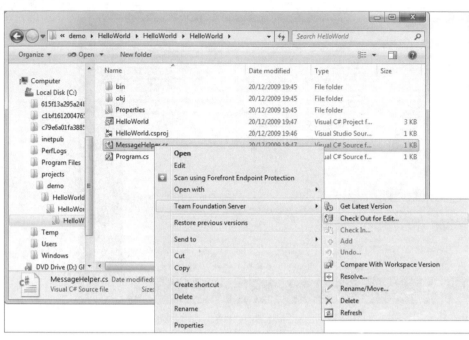

FIGURE 17-12

Access to Team Foundation Server via other Third-Party Integrations

Team Foundation Server supports a rich and vibrant third-party eco-system. As discussed previously, the same .NET object model used by Microsoft to talk to Team Foundation Server from Visual Studio is also available for developers in third-party companies to integrate with. Integrations are available into other parts of the Microsoft Office suite (such as Word and Outlook). In addition, many development tools now integrate with Team Foundation Server using the extensibility hooks provided by Microsoft.

WHAT'S NEW IN TEAM FOUNDATION SERVER 2010

Team Foundation Server 2010 is the most significant release of Team Foundation Server since the launch of the product with Team Foundation Server 2005. As this book demonstrates, it is a big release with considerable new functionality and improvements across the board. While many of these features are explained throughout this book, if you have used a previous version of Team Foundation Server, then the features described in the following sections will be new to you.

Project Management

The biggest change in the project management area is that work items are now hierarchical — you can have child and parent links between work items. You can also customize work item links. In addition, you can have hierarchical queries so that a tree of work item results can be displayed. Queries can be organized into sub-folders, and permissions can be assigned as to who can view and modify team queries.

There are several new work item controls both to enhance functionality in regular work items and support the new test functionality. The Excel and Project integrations have both also seen significant improvements, especially in the capability to modify the formatting and layout of data, while providing the capability to round-trip data.

There are several new Agile Development Process planning workbooks available by default, significant usability improvements to the default reports and SharePoint Web parts added to access work item information directly from the project portal. Dashboards have been introduced that can make use of additional functionality available when running the project portal on a full Microsoft Office SharePoint Server (MOSS) over and above the features available using a standard WSS site.

Version Control

The most visual addition here is that branches are now treated as first-class objects in version control. A significant new UI has been added to assist management and visualization of branches. History and labeling have undergone huge changes, including the capability to view labels from the history view and the capability to view history of a merged file.

Rollback support is provided, along with the capability to share a workspace between users on the same machine.

> *There have been significant changes in the underlying version control model employed by Team Foundation Server 2010 that are particularly noticeable when renames and merges are performed. For more information on the changes, the reasons behind the changes, and how the changes, present themselves in the UI, take a look at the blog post at* `http://blogs.msdn.com/mitrik/archive/2009/05/28/changing-to-slot-mode-in-tfs-2010-version-control.aspx`.

Build

The build automation system has undergone huge revisions in Team Foundation Server 2010. The first change you will notice is the new and improved build report. However, probably the most significant change is that the build is now based around Windows Workflow 4.0. You now have the capability to use build agent pooling, gated and buddy builds, and integration with source and symbol servers.

> *Chapter 21 provides more information on builds.*

Administration

The installation and general administration experience of Team Foundation Server is now drastically improved and simplified. The SharePoint and reporting services components are now optional. Team Foundation Server supports the use of network local balancing in front of Team Foundation Server application tier machines. The new project collection concept allows for collection move, archive, backup, and restore, independent of other collections running on the server.

There is a dedicated administration console in Team Foundation Server. Team Foundation Server 2010 can also now be installed on 64-bit server operating systems, and the clients all work on 64-bit client systems (including an AnyCPU-compatible .NET object model).

ADOPTING TEAM FOUNDATION SERVER

The value from Team Foundation Server is realized when it is utilized in a team. Therefore, ensuring a successful Team Foundation Server adoption requires cooperation from many people in your organization. The following sections should help you avoid some common pitfalls and provide you with some suggestions on where to start with what may seem like a large and daunting product.

Hosting Team Foundation Server

For the team to have trust in Team Foundation Server, you must be sure that it is there when they need it and that it performs as well as possible. For organizations that depend on creating software, your version control and work item tracking repositories are critical to getting your work done. Therefore, those features should be treated on the same level as other mission-critical applications in the organization.

The Team Foundation Server infrastructure is a production environment for your company. Ideally, it should be hosted on a server with adequate resources (both physical memory and disk space). If hosted in a virtual environment, then you should ensure that the host machine has sufficient resources to handle the load of all guest machines.

When planning upgrades, configuration changes, or when performing training, you should use a test Team Foundation Server environment. For some organizations, the test requirements justify the purchase of a hardware platform equivalent to the production environment.

However, for many scenarios, simply using a virtual Team Foundation Server environment will provide a suitable environment for testing. These virtual environments are especially useful when developing a new process template, or testing work item process modifications. Microsoft provides an evaluation version of Team Foundation Server pre-configured as a virtual hard disk (VHD) file. This is frequently used as a test bed for work item modifications and new process templates.

Adoption Plan

When introducing any new tooling into a large organization, it is important that you address the key pain points first. For many companies, traceability of work through the development lifecycle is often an area that is being poorly addressed by existing tooling. For others, the version control system being used may be out-of-date and poorly performing. It is, therefore, usually the work item tracking or version control components that people first start using when adopting Team Foundation Server.

Luckily, Team Foundation Server is flexible enough that you can still get value from the product when only using one or two components of the system. Once you have adopted both version control and work item tracking, the next area to tackle to gain most benefit is likely to be Team Foundation Build. By automating your build system and increasing the frequency of integration, you reduce the amount of unknown pain that always occurs when integrating components together to form a product.

The key is to be gradually removing the unknown and unpredictable elements from the software delivery process, all the time looking for wasted effort that can be cut out.

Automating the builds not only means that the build and packaging process becomes less error-prone, it also means that the feedback loop of requirements traceability is completed. You are now able to track work from the time that it is captured, all the way through to a change to the source code of the product, and into the build that contains those changes.

After a period of time, you will have built up a repository of historical data in your Team Foundation Server data warehouse, and you can start to make use of the reporting features to predict if you will be finished when you expect (that is, if the amount of estimated work remaining on the system is reducing at the required rate). You will also be able to drill into areas that you might want to improve — for example, which parts of the code are causing the most bugs.

It is after a period of getting used to the tooling that you then want to look at your process templates and ensure that all the necessary data is being captured — but, equally, that all the work item types and transitions are required. If there are unnecessary steps, then consider removing them. If you notice problems because of a particular issue, consider modifying the process to add a safety net.

It is important to adjust the process not only to fit the team and organization, but also to ensure that you only adjust your processes when you need to, and not just because you can.

Check-in policies represent a key area where Team Foundation Server administrations have a temptation to go overboard at first. Check-in policies prevent checking in of code that doesn't meet with the requirements programmatically defined in the check-in policy. However, each policy has a performance penalty for the whole team, not only in running the policy on each check-in, but also in ensuring that the policy will pass before checking in the code.

If you notice that a problem you have is that developers are not checking in code in small iterative changes, then this is not going to be easily remedied by introducing a check-in policy — the policy alone will provide some discouragement for checking in. Therefore, check-in policies should be introduced over time and when the need is identified by the whole team.

SUMMARY

This chapter introduced Team Foundation Server and discussed its role in bringing the team together when developing an application. You learned about some of the core concepts at the heart of Team Foundation Server, different ways to access the data in your organization's server, and what is new in the 2010 release of the product. Finally, you learned about some points that you should bear in mind when planning your Team Foundation Server deployment.

Chapter 18 digs deeper into the architecture of Team Foundation Server to learn about the components making up the product. In addition to gaining an understanding of the areas that have been radically improved in the 2010 release, you will gain insight into how the product fits together, and which configuration of Team Foundation Server will best fit the needs of your organization.

18

Team Foundation Architecture

WHAT'S IN THIS CHAPTER?

➤ Understanding Team Foundation Server logical architecture

➤ Understanding Team Foundation Server physical architecture

➤ Taking a look at deployment scenarios

➤ Upgrading Team Foundation Server

As discussed in Chapter 17, Visual Studio Team Foundation Server 2010 contains a variety of features you can use to manage your software development projects. From working item tracking to version control to reporting, Team Foundation Server provides all the tools needed to make software projects successful.

Team Foundation Server is based on a modern, service-oriented, three-tier architecture comprised of a client, an application tier, and a data tier. The application tier is facilitated by an ASP.NET Web server hosted in an IIS6 or IIS7 environment. The data tier is supported by SQL 2008. The architecture of Team Foundation Server is optimized around the following basic assumptions:

➤ A high-bandwidth connection exists between the application and data tier.

➤ The application-tier and data-tier servers can co-exist on the same side of a switch, which limits the impact their traffic has on the overall network.

➤ Clients may talk to the application tier beyond the switch in possibly remote locations.

➤ A combination of low-bandwidth and high-bandwidth connections exists between the clients and the application tier.

The general architecture of Team Foundation Server stayed relatively constant between Team Foundation Server 2005 and Team Foundation Server 2008. However, all applications need to evolve, and this is exactly what has happened with the most recent release. Team Foundation Server has undergone some significant architectural changes, designed to help ease and strengthen the management of team projects.

This chapter examines some of the enhancements and changes to the Team Foundation Server architecture. The discussion begins by looking at the old logical architecture of Team Foundation Server 2008, and contrasting it with the new logical architecture of Visual Studio Team Foundation Server 2010. After that, the chapter examines the physical architecture, and the new hardware and software requirements. Some of the different deployment scenarios for Team Foundation Server are considered, and the chapter wraps up with a brief overview of the two main clients used to access Team Foundation Server.

TEAM FOUNDATION SERVER LOGICAL ARCHITECTURE

When talking about Team Foundation Server, both the physical architecture and the logical architecture must be considered. It is easier to start with the logical architecture, because there are multiple ways to configure the physical architecture, as will be shown later in this chapter. The logical architecture of Visual Studio Team Foundation Server 2010 has changed significantly from previous versions.

First, let's briefly cover the logical architecture of Team Foundation Server 2008. This will provide a basis for understanding some of the changes in Visual Studio Team Foundation Server 2010.

Figure 18-1 shows the logical architecture of Team Foundation Server 2008.

Application Tier   Data Tier

| Relational Database (Team Projects) | Data Warehouse |

FIGURE 18-1

Team Foundation Server is a Web application consisting of multiple Web services running on the application tier. These Web services drive all the functionality of Team Foundation Server. You have the capability to create your own applications to run against these Web services (for example, creating your own application to access the work item tracking system or the version control system). But that is not advised.

Instead, you should make use of the Team Foundation Server Object Model. This object model is an application programming interface (API) into Team Foundation Server. While the Web services can and will change from one version of Team Foundation Server to the next, the object model will always remain similar or will at least degrade gracefully. You can be fairly confident that if an application is built against the Team Foundation Server Object Model, it will easily port to new versions of Team Foundation Server with minimal changes. The same cannot be said for applications written directly against the Team Foundation Server Web services.

The application tier is where most of the work in Team Foundation Server starts. That is where all the processing for accessing the work item tracking and version control systems happens, as well as monitoring and tracking of build and report information.

On the data tier, Team Foundation formerly used SQL Server 2005 or 2008. The data tier is composed of multiple relational databases and a data warehouse. Team project information is stored in the relational databases, and, at scheduled intervals, the information from the relational databases is pulled into the data warehouse. Having all the data from Team Foundation Server reside in SQL Server made backup and restore of the Team Foundation Server as easy as running a nightly backup of the database server.

However, the architecture of Team Foundation Server 2008 was not without its problems. There was no good way to group team projects into a kind of organizational structure. The only possible option for that was to have a separate Team Foundation Server for every group you wanted to collect. This was not feasible from an expense or a maintainability viewpoint. There was no way to restore a particular team project in the event of a catastrophe with that team project. You could restore the entire Team Foundation Server database to a point in time, but that would affect all the team projects on that server. Again, this was not the best solution.

Since the data tier was just SQL Server, you were able to use database clustering and mirroring for maintaining uptime on the data tier. However, there was no equivalent option on the application tier. The closest option available was the ability to have a warm standby Team Foundation Server. If the main application tier suddenly went down, you could turn on the standby server, run some configuration commands, and within few minutes have a new application tier up and running.

There were no options for network load balancing against the application tier. And finally, the application tier was still a 32-bit application. While 64-bit SQL Server 2005 and 2008 were supported, the application tier itself could only be installed on a 32-bit version of the operating system.

While all of these issues may not have been completely addressed, a majority of them have been taken into account in the new architecture of Visual Studio Team Foundation Server 2010.

Now, let's look at the new logical architecture of Visual Studio Team Foundation Server 2010, as shown in Figure 18-2.

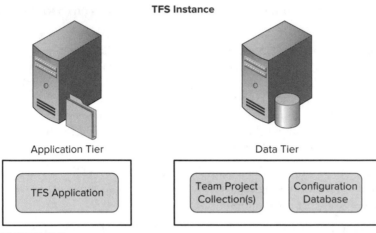

FIGURE 18-2

The new logical architecture still uses all the old concepts (such as having an application tier and a data tier), but some of the concepts (especially relating to the application tier) have changed significantly. The best way to understand all the changes is to break them down into individual pieces. Let's start with the changes to team projects and work our way out.

Team Project Collections

As discussed in Chapter 17, in Visual Studio Team Foundation Server 2010, the concept of a team project remains relatively unchanged. The team project is still the "bucket" where all the stuff related to your project (work items, source code, reports, and so on) is stored. In Team Foundation Server, team projects have become lighter-weight, easier to organize, and easier to manage. All of this is facilitated through the concept of *team project collections*.

A team project collection, at its core, is simply a way to group team projects together. By grouping team projects together, it's easier to take advantage of certain features across team projects, such as branching and merging, and atomic check-ins. In effect, a team project collection is similar to an instance of Team Foundation Server 2008 — that is, a container of different team projects. Where with Team Foundation Server 2008 you would have to spin up a separate server to create a new collection of team projects, with Visual Studio Team Foundation Server 2010, all that is needed to create a separate group is to create a new team project collection. The concept is very similar to SharePoint Site Collections and SharePoint Sites (for those familiar with SharePoint architectures).

Team project collections provide a nice isolation mechanism for keeping team projects separated. For example, let's assume there are two teams: Team A and Team B. Team A and Team B both develop widgets, and they have a team project for each widget they create. They want to host all these team projects on Team Foundation Server, but want to isolate each group's team projects.

To do so, they would create a team project collection for each team. Team A would connect to their team project collection, which contains only the team projects for Team A. Team B would connect to their team project collection, which contains only the team projects for Team B. Work items and version control changesets for Team B would all be numbered sequentially for that project collection. Changes made to the projects in Team A's project collection would have no impact on the Team B users.

On the database server, each team project collection is housed in its own database. This makes the team project collection a manageable unit for administration. For this reason, it is important that all the team projects in a team project collection be tightly coupled, because many operations will be performed at the team project collection level, not the team project level. Backup, restore, and move operations are carried out at the team project collection level, and are not available at the team project level. A single team project cannot be restored from a database backup. However, the capability to restore individual team project collections now minimizes the impact that a database restore will have on the rest of the team project in a Team Foundation Server, because only the team projects in the team project collection being restored will be affected.

As mentioned earlier, team project collections are very similar to an instance of Team Foundation Server 2008. As such, they have some of the same limitations:

➤ No branching, merging, or sharing of code between team project collections

➤ No backup or restore of individual team projects in a team project collection

➤ No atomic operations (such as check-ins) can happen across team project collections

Some serious thought should go into how to organize your team projects in collections before you begin with Team Foundation Server. Before creating a new team project, consider all the artifacts that will be part of the project, and the purpose of the team project, to see if it belongs in the current team project collection, or if a new collection should be created.

> *For more information, see the Scaling Team Foundation Server 2010 whitepaper at* `http://go.microsoft.com/?linkid=9707136`.

A single Team Foundation Server can support many team project collections (hundreds or thousands, depending on physical resources available, such as database disk space). However, the number of "active" team project collections available on the server is less, in the order of 150-200 active collections per SQL instance. Note that as you can host project collections on different SQL instance you can increase this for a Team Foundation Server instance. For example, if you have your project collections split across 3 SQL instances, then you could get up to 600 active team project collections.

When a user connects to a project collection that is not active, Team Foundation Server will spin up all the resources and database connections necessary to connect the application tier to that project collections database. Those resources will continue to be occupied until there are no connections to that project collection for a given period of time (usually around 5 minutes). After that time, the project collection will go dormant, and the application-tier resources will be freed up. This means that project collections are an excellent way of handling projects that get archived.

At some point, even the best thought-out plans must be changed. With some work, it is possible to move a team project into a new project collection. But it is not possible to merge two team project collections, or move team projects from one collection into an existing one.

Team Foundation Server Farm

The introduction of the Team Foundation Server Farm is another big architectural change in the 2010 release. In the past, you were able to share the load of the Team Foundation Server application across an application-tier machine, database server, SharePoint server, reporting services server, and so on. However, you could only have a single machine that was the application tier, which had obvious downsides for ensuring availability of the Team Foundation Server application.

With Team Foundation Server 2010, you can configure multiple Team Foundation Server application-tier machines to service the same set of team project collections, and those application tiers can sit behind a network load-balancing device to not only share the load of in inbound requests, but also to allow for a better availability story. Any one of the application-tier machines can fail, and the farm will continue to operate without significant user interruption. This also improves the capability when performing such tasks as operating system patches, which can be done in a standard rolling manner (that is, take an application-tier machine offline, patch, and then return back into the pool).

In addition to the application-tier scale out support, now each project collection may point to a different SQL Server instance when storing its data. Because each project collections database is independent, SQL Server administrators have a great degree of flexibility in how they wish to manage their SQL resources. A single project collection may be easily suspended while its database is moved to a different SQL instance without affecting the other project collections. This gives SQL administrators the capability to manage capacity, retire old servers, and so on.

Team Foundation Server Application

The Team Foundation Server application is an ASP.NET Web application running on the Team Foundation Server application tier. Its main purpose is to perform operations on the team project collections. The Team Foundation Server application uses the Configuration Database (more on this later) to store its configuration information and information about which team project collections the Team Foundation Server application is responsible for.

On each application tier, there is one configuration server instance running, and all application-tier state is stored in the databases. Each Team Foundation Server application can host multiple team project collections. A request can come for one of the multiple team project collections and be handled by any one of the application instances in a Team Foundation Server Farm.

Having the configuration server instance manage all the services for one or more team project collections allows for centralized administration to be built directly into the framework. This allows for many new options not available in previous version of Team Foundation Server, including the following:

➤ The capability to start, stop, and pause a Team Foundation Server application or team project collection

➤ Capability to move project collections between application tiers

Earlier in this section, the Configuration Database was mentioned. The Configuration Database is a SQL Server database containing the configuration information about the Team Foundation

Server application and the collections managed by it. Examples of the information stored in the Configuration Database include the following:

➤ The team project collection map

➤ SQL Server access information

➤ Logging data

The main benefit of the Configuration Database is that it allows administrators to make global changes to the Team Foundation Server application, and apply those changes to all the team project collections managed by the Team Foundation Server application. That way, the administrator does not have to touch each individual team project and team project collection in order to make changes.

The Configuration Server has a set of public APIs for interacting with it.

> *For more information see the MSDN help on the* `Microsoft.TeamFoundation` `.Client` *namespace* (`http://msdn.microsoft.com/en-us/library/microsoft` `.teamfoundation.client.aspx`) *under the class* `TfsConfigurationServer`. *Note that this class was called* `TeamFoundationApplicationInstance` *in early beta versions of Team Foundation Server 2010, in case you find any old examples still referring to that name.*

Team Foundation Server Instance

Thus far, you have learned about some of the specific new features and changes for both the application tier and the data tier. Now, let's step back and define the concept of what actually is a Team Foundation Server instance.

At its most basic form, a Team Foundation Server instance is a Team Foundation Server application tier (or multiple applications in a Team Foundation Server Farm) that handles requests for sets of team project collections. The SQL Server databases that contain the data associated with these team project collections are also part of the Team Foundation Server instance. A Team Foundation Server instance can be made up of one or more physical servers. Ancillary servers (such as the SharePoint portal or Reporting Services servers) are also often considered to make up the Team Foundation Server instance, despite their being somewhat separate.

Most users will need only one Team Foundation Server instance, but there are times when multiple instances may be needed. For example, an enterprise organization may have an IT organization that is split by division. Each division might want its own Team Foundation Server instance in order to have separate operations, management, and security policies.

Because of the new improvements in load balancing and scalability in Team Foundation Server 2010, along with the introduction of team project collections, the decision whether to have multiple Team Foundation Server instances is usually a financial one in larger enterprises. Say that Department A paid for all the servers and so on, and, therefore, Department B may not use "their" instance. Because Team Foundation Server offers a level of scalability and requires very little management overhead, there has been a significant movement inside IT-focused organizations for Team Foundation Server resources to be managed by a central IT organization (much like the Exchange email services) with centralized billing of that capability. This also ensures that the Team Foundation Server instance is treated with the same importance as any other production system.

PHYSICAL ARCHITECTURE

You have multiple options when configuring your Team Foundation Server deployments. You can deploy all the components (Team Foundation Server application, SQL Server, Reporting Services, and Windows SharePoint Services) onto one machine. This is called a *single-server installation* and should work fine for a total number of users of 450 or less. In general, single-server installations are the easiest installations.

For more than 450 users, a *multi-server installation* should be considered. There are several flavors of multi-server installations. At its most basic, there are two servers. One server is the data tier, running SQL Server, and the other is the application tier, running Team Foundation Server, Reporting Services, and Windows SharePoint Services.

Your organization may have an existing SharePoint Portal Server, and/or SQL Server Reporting Services Server that it wants to use in conjunction with Team Foundation Server. For that scenario, you would then have a physical server for running Team Foundation Server Web Services, a physical server for running the SQL Server databases, and separate servers for running SharePoint Portal Server and Reporting Services.

For high-availability scenarios, clustering of machines is available at each point in the architecture. As previously discussed, the Team Foundation Server application-tier machines can be located behind a network load-balancing device. The SQL Server instances referred to by the Team Foundation Server application and project collections can also be clustered.

Hardware Requirements

Table 18-1 shows the hardware requirements for a single-server installation, where the application tier and data tier reside on the same physical machine. However, keep in mind that these numbers are estimates, and, obviously, the more hardware you can throw at a problem, the better.

TABLE 18-1: Hardware Requirements for Single-Server Installation

NUMBER OF USERS	CPU	HARD DISK	MEMORY
Less than 20 users	One 2.2 GHz processor	8 GB	1 GB
20 to 250 users	One 3.6 GHz processor	230 GB	2 GB
250 to 450 users	Two 2.9 GHz processors	500 GB	4 GB

For a multi-server installation (where you have distinct physical servers for the application tier and the data tier), Table 18-2 lists the application-tier hardware requirements.

TABLE 18-2: Application-Tier Hardware Requirements

NUMBER OF USERS	CPU	HARD DISK	MEMORY
450 to 2,200 users	Two 2.8 GHz processors	Dual Drives or Drive Array; 31 GB and 136 GB	4 GB
2,200 to 3,600 users	Four 2.2 GHz processors	Dual Drives or Drive Array; 31 GB and 136 GB	4 GB

Table 18-3 lists the data-tier hardware requirements.

TABLE 18-3: Data-Tier Hardware Requirements

NUMBER OF USERS	CPU	HARD DISK	MEMORY
450 to 2,200 users	Four 2.6 GHz processors	Dual Drives or Drive Array; 480 GB and 3.75 TB	8 GB
2,200 to 3,600 users	Eight 2.6 GHz processors	Dual Drives or Drive Array; 480 GB and 3.75 TB	16 GB

Keep in mind that the application tier may be hosting Windows SharePoint Services and/or SQL Server Reporting Services, in addition to Team Foundation Server. This might require you to bump your hardware numbers in some form or fashion.

Virtualization is a hot topic these days. Virtualization allows you to buy a large server, and then virtually host several different servers on one physical machine, allowing an organization to make the most of a physical machine's resources. There are some pieces of the Team Foundation Server environment that can be safely hosted in a virtual environment, and some that should never be virtualized.

Ideally, the following pieces should be installed on physical servers:

➤   SQL Server 2008 Database Engine

➤   SQL Server Reporting Services

➤   SQL Server Analysis Services

SQL Server is the foundation for holding all the information regarding Team Foundation Server. Should it become corrupted, the entire Team Foundation Server system will go down. To minimize the chances of database corruption, you should avoid hosting SQL Server 2008 in a virtualized environment.

The following can be safely installed in a virtualized environment with minimum to no impact on the Team Foundation Server system:

➤   Team Foundation Server application tier

➤   Windows SharePoint Services

➤   Team Foundation Build servers

Software Requirements

Visual Studio Team Foundation Server 2010 can be installed on the following operating systems:

➤ Windows Server 2003 Datacenter Edition with Service Pack 2

➤ Windows Server 2003 Enterprise Edition with Service Pack 2

➤ Windows Server 2003 Standard Edition with Service Pack 2

➤ Windows Server 2003 R2 Datacenter Edition with Service Pack 2

➤ Windows Server 2003 R2 Enterprise Edition with Service Pack 2

➤ Windows Server 2003 R2 Standard Edition with Service Pack 2

➤ Windows Server 2008

➤ Windows Server 2008 R2

➤ Windows Vista

➤ Windows 7

Visual Studio Team Foundation Server 2010 can be installed on both 32-bit and 64-bit versions of any of the listed operating systems. (Previous versions were only available on 32-bit operating systems, but this restriction has been removed in the 2010 release.) Keep in mind, however, that Team Foundation Server does not support Itanium-based systems.

Team Foundation Server requires SQL Server 2008. During the beta phase, there was a lot of debate over whether to make Visual Studio 2010 Team Foundation Server backward compatible with SQL Server 2005, but, in the end, the capability to use many of the new features in SQL Server 2008 won out. The following editions of SQL Server 2008 are supported:

➤ SQL Server 2008 Standard Edition

➤ SQL Server 2008 Enterprise Edition

➤ SQL Server 2008 Express Edition

If you are installing Team Foundation Server's databases onto an existing database server, ensure that the existing database server is configured correctly. Consult the Team Foundation Server Installation Guide (available online at `http://msdn.microsoft.com`) for more information on this.

Team Foundation Server optionally uses SharePoint products to create its team project portal. If you want the application tier to also host the portal site, then Windows SharePoint Services 3.0 can be installed on the application tier as part of the application install. If you want the portal site to be on a different server, there are two options:

➤ Install Windows SharePoint Services 3.0 on a separate server.

➤ Use Microsoft Office SharePoint Server, either an existing installation or a fresh install.

Again, consult the Team Foundation Server Installation Guide for more information.

DEPLOYMENT SCENARIOS

Once the decision has been made to use Team Foundation Server 2010, the next step is to actually get it deployed and working in your organization. A good bit of planning must take place before the actual installation can occur:

➤ What sort of installation will you need — single-server or multi-server?

➤ Will you make use of existing servers and software (such as a pre-existing SQL Server 2008 server, or a pre-existing SharePoint Portal Server 2007 server)?

➤ Will you attempt the installation yourself, or bring in a consultant who specializes in Visual Studio Team Foundation Server?

➤ Will you use a vanilla, out-of-the-box installation of Team Foundation Server, or do you want to customize it to fit your specific needs?

The place to start preparing for your deployment is with the Team Foundation Server Installation Guide. This guide gives you in-depth, detailed information on how to plan and implement the installation of your Team Foundation Server. It is so detailed that it even provides step-by-step instructions for every step of the install, down to exactly what needs to be clicked on every screen of every installation program. The installation guide can be downloaded from the Microsoft Web site. Always ensure that you have the latest version of the Installation Guide, because it is updated from time to time to account for bug fixes and service packs.

If problems are encountered during the installation and deployment, one of the best resources to turn to is the MSDN forums (http://forums.microsoft.com/msdn). There are a specific set of forums dedicated to Visual Studio Application Lifecycle Management (ALM) topics and Team Foundation Server, and a specific discussion group for installation and deployment issues. The forums are constantly monitored by both members of the product team from Microsoft, as well as recognized experts in the field and other interested, knowledgeable people. The forums are your best source for quickly finding answers to any of your deployment problems.

Once Team Foundation Server is installed in your organization, a typical enterprise will need a quarter to half an administrator resource/operations person to handle any day-to-day operations related to Team Foundation Server. Some of these operations include initial configuration, backing up and restoring data, and handling security permissions. A good resource for your administrators is the Team Foundation Administrator Guide. This free reference, also available from the Microsoft Web site, is a treasure trove of information. It contains detailed information on all the scenarios discussed next, and more, including walkthroughs. It also covers administrative information related to all the different pieces of Team Foundation Server (such as SharePoint and SQL Server). As with the Installation Guide, check the Microsoft Web site to ensure that you have the latest version of the Administrator Guide.

There are five main scenarios to consider when planning a deployment of Team Foundation Server:

➤ Individuals and small teams

➤ Small companies

➤ Large enterprises

➤ Hosting organizations

➤ Upgrading from a previous version of Team Foundation Server

Individuals and Small Teams

Team Foundation Server now supports a basic installation mode. In this mode, no SharePoint portal or reporting services are set up for the server. In addition, a SQL Express-based data tier can be created by the installer itself, rather than using an existing SQL instance. Also, on more recent operating systems (such as Windows Vista, Windows 7, or Windows Server 2008), if IIS is not installed, then the installer can install it and configure the required prerequisites.

This, combined with the fact that Team Foundation Server can be installed on a client machine (such as a Windows 7 desktop) or a machine with other applications running on it (such as Small Business Server, or even Windows Home Server), means that Team Foundation Server is, more than ever, suitable for use by individual software developers or small teams. A basic install of Team Foundation Server using SQL Express can be backed up and restored to a "full" install of Team Foundation Server running against a standard full SQL Server-based database instance, and the portal and reporting systems configured. Therefore, the basic installation mode is a great way to get started with Team Foundation Server.

Small Shops

For smaller shops, with a total number of Team Foundation Server users of 450 or less, a single-server installation should be sufficient. All the components of Team Foundation Server can be installed on a single server. Figure 18-3 shows an example of the architecture for a small shop.

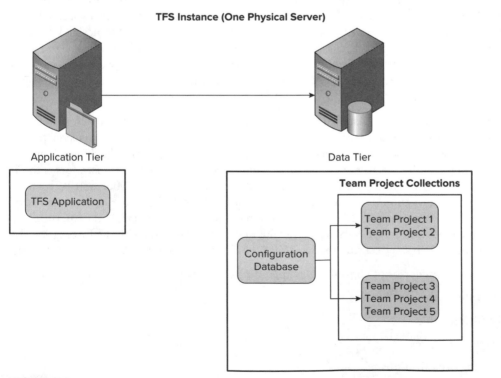

FIGURE 18-3

The small shop has one physical server. (For server specifications, see the earlier section in this chapter "Hardware Requirements.") The physical server contains only one Team Foundation Server instance. The application tier and the data tier are both installed on the same physical server. There is one application tier, containing one Team Foundation Server application. On the data tier, there is one Configuration Database. There can be one or more team project collections, with each team project collection maintaining up to 500 team projects.

Single-server installations (and, by extension, small shop deployments) are usually the easiest to perform, even for someone who has never installed Team Foundation Server before. All the different components of Team Foundation Server (including SharePoint and SQL Server) will be installed fresh on the target machine. Read the Team Foundation Server Installation Guide carefully, ensure that you follow the step-by-step instructions, and take your time. You should have minimal problems with the installation.

Large Enterprises

For a large number of Team Foundation Server users (450 or more), or for large enterprises in general, a multi-server installation will probably be required. The large enterprise scenario has the potential to be the most complex install, but also the most common for large enterprises. Figure 18-4 shows an example of the architecture for a large enterprise.

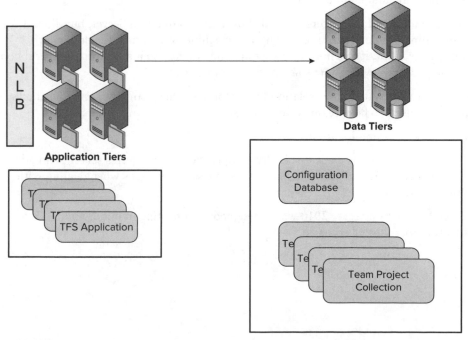

FIGURE 18-4

The large enterprise deployment is made up of multiple physical servers. This deployment includes one or more application-tier servers, each with its own Team Foundation Server application. Network load balancers can be used to balance the load across these multiple application tiers. There are multiple data tiers with multiple team project collections. These multiple data tiers can all reside on one physical SQL Server machine, or can be spread across multiple machines with project collections having their databases located on separate SQL instances. For high-availability requirements, those instances can be clustered, if required.

Large enterprises may already have servers running SQL Server 2008 and SharePoint, and may want to leverage their existing investment in those infrastructures. Team Foundation Server allows that to happen in a multi-server installation. Again, the Installation Guide is your best friend in this scenario, because it walks you through all the different combinations that would be available to large enterprises.

As well as adding data-tier machines into your environment, Team Foundation Server allows you to add additional Team Foundation Server application tiers to an existing deployment, allowing you to scale out capacity as needed.

Hosted Environments

One of the major goals of the architecture redesign of Team Foundation Server was to allow for Team Foundation Server to work in a hosted environment. With Team Foundation Server 2008, there was a large demand for running Team Foundation Server in a hosted environment — in effect, outsourcing the installation and maintenance.

Organizations wanted to use all the features provided by Team Foundation Server, but did not want the overhead of installing or administrating the physical machine. While this was possible with Team Foundation Server 2008, it was not easy to set up, and you had to jump through several hoops to make it work correctly. Following were some of the main issues:

➤ No support for encapsulation or isolation for customers other than new server instances (making it expensive to host Team Foundation Server).

➤ No central area for administration.

➤ Creation of team projects is a client-side-driven operation, and requires server farm administration privileges in SharePoint, which creates some security issues when dealing with shared infrastructure.

Visual Studio Team Foundation Server 2010 was redesigned with hosting in mind. Figure 18-5 shows the architecture for a hosted scenario.

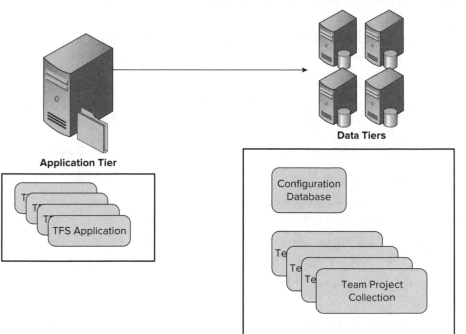

Hosted Team Foundation Server (Multiple TFS Instances)

Application Tier

TFS Application

Data Tiers

Configuration Database

Team Project Collection

FIGURE 18-5

The goal of a hosted environment is to facilitate hardware sharing and, therefore, reduce the cost per transaction. This environment starts out with one instance, and has as many customers as possible sharing project collections and security settings for customer isolation. They begin by scaling out this instance by first using network load balancing of the application tier and multiple SQL Server instances for project collections. Then, if performance starts to degrade, that may expand out to multiple instances of Team Foundation Server.

Making it easier to install and configure Team Foundation Server in a hosted environment will contribute significantly to increasing its adoption in the application lifecycle management space. Not every company is currently ready to entrust their source code and work items into the cloud with a hosted solution. But hosting is particularly attractive to smaller companies, start-ups and non-IT-focused organizations that do not wish to invest the hardware infrastructure costs required in hosting themselves.

However, the same features that make hosting in the cloud possible also make it easier for large enterprises to centralize hosting of Team Foundation Server resources inside the company, allowing the organization to make dramatic cost savings in terms of development infrastructure at the same time as reducing the training and support requirements by having a common environment for all teams to use.

Upgrading from Older Team Foundation Server Versions

For customers who have existing installations of Team Foundation Server 2005 or 2008, the upgrade story is going to be of keen interest. The upgrade path in Team Foundation Server 2010 is a major upgrade requiring some reading up, planning, and practice — but one that is well-supported.

> *The best place to find out more information is the Team Foundation Server 2010 Installation Guide, available on the Team Foundation Server installation media, or you may download a more up-to-date version from MSDN.*

When you are upgrading you may wish to also consider the following:

➤ Do you wish to take the opportunity to upgrade operating systems (that is, from Windows Server 2003 32-bit to the latest Windows Server 2008 R2 64-bit)?

➤ You must upgrade to SQL Server 2008 for your data tier if you are currently running on a SQL Server 2005 database.

➤ What additional tools do you use and what customizations have you made to Team Foundation Server?

➤ Do you wish to change the architecture of your Team Foundation Server installation to take advantage of new features and scenarios available to you with Team Foundation Server 2010?

➤ Have you made plenty of back-ups and have a suitable roll-back plan if the upgrade does not run smoothly?

There are two major paths available to you when upgrading to Visual Studio Team Foundation Server 2010:

➤ In-place upgrade

➤ Migration upgrade

In-Place Upgrade

An *in-place upgrade* is one in which you are using the same set of hardware with the same operating system version that is running the current Team Foundation Server instance. In this scenario, you basically uninstall the existing Team Foundation Server application from the application-tier machine, and install the new version, pointing it at the existing database data. This will enable you to run the upgrade wizard, which will take care of making all the database schema changes necessary.

For example, if you have a single-server installation, you would uninstall the Team Foundation Server application, upgrade to SQL Server 2008 (including Reporting Services and Analysis Services, if applicable), Upgrade to Windows SharePoint Services 3.0 SP1 or later, run the Team Foundation Server 2010 Setup, and select Upgrade from Previous Version.

Migration Upgrade

A *migration upgrade* is one in which you are using a separate, duplicate set of hardware to perform the upgrade. In this scenario, you basically create a new set of servers with all the prerequisites installed (IIS, SQL Server, Windows SharePoint Services, and so on). You then copy the existing Team Foundation Server-related databases over to the new database server, install the Team Foundation Server application, and call the upgrade wizard.

Choosing the Appropriate Path

For small Team Foundation Server installations that are well backed up, or for ones with a constrained budget for new hardware, then an in-place upgrade may well be the easiest solution. If your installation is pretty much a standard Team Foundation Server installation, then everything should work as planned. However, it would be recommended to test this first in a virtualized copy of your production system. You should also ensure that you have adequate back-ups and a tested roll-back plan in case the upgrade process does not go smoothly.

The migration path gives the greatest flexibility and allows you to do plenty of testing beforehand. It also gives you the opportunity to upgrade your server infrastructure to the latest versions available, and to a 64-bit environment, giving you plenty of room for growth in the future. The final benefit of the migration path is that the fall-back plan is very straightforward. Should anything go awry during the upgrade process, you can fall back to the existing hardware, and resume using the old Team Foundation Server installation.

Additional Tasks

Once you have performed the upgrade, there are a number of additional tasks that you may want to perform that are well documented in the Team Foundation Server Installation Guide. For example, you may want to update your process template to enable features introduced in the new process templates in 2010 (such as hierarchical work items and to enable the new test tools), and you may also want to convert some branch folders into fully fledge branches in Team Foundation Server version control.

SUMMARY

This chapter has shown how the architecture of Visual Studio Team Foundation Server 2010 has changed significantly from its previous versions, but for the better. You learned about the original architecture of Team Foundation Server 2008, and some issues that arose from that architecture.

This chapter examined the new Team Foundation Server 2010 architecture, explaining new concepts such as team project collections and the configuration database.

You learned about the physical hardware required to install Team Foundation Server, as well as the software needed. The discussion touched upon the different deployment scenarios for Team Foundation Server, from small shops to large enterprises, and touched on the upgrade path from previous version of Team Foundation Server.

Chapter 19 takes a deeper look at the version control features available in Team Foundation Server, and what new functionality has been introduced in Team Foundation Server 2010.

19

Team Foundation Version Control

WHAT'S IN THIS CHAPTER?

- ➤ Understanding Team Foundation version control

- ➤ Setting up version control

- ➤ Using the Source Control Explorer

- ➤ Understanding basic version control operations

- ➤ Understanding check-in policies

- ➤ Viewing the history of files and folders

- ➤ Understanding labels

- ➤ Understanding shelvesets

- ➤ Understanding to branching and merging

- ➤ Getting to know command-line tools

If you are a developer or a tester, you are basically living in a world of source code. When you have more than one person working on a project, versioning becomes an issue. If two developers work on the same assembly, how do you merge their code together? How do you prevent accidentally overwriting files? Incredibly, many organizations still use file shares to store source code. Others push Microsoft Visual SourceSafe to the limit with 150 active users or more, or use third-party solutions or Open Source solutions that integrate poorly with Visual Studio.

One of the key features of Visual Studio Team Foundation Server 2010 is its version control management system. It offers a number of features, including the capability to branch, merge, and shelve your source code, atomic check-ins, policies, security — all the features you would expect from an enterprise version control solution. The core engine for this tool is Microsoft SQL Server 2008. As such, the performance of Team Foundation version control will greatly depend on your server's hardware and the size of your SQL Server 2008 database.

> *You'll notice that the title of the feature is Team Foundation "version control." However, when you start using the feature, a lot of the tools and windows will say "source control," such as in the "Source Control Explorer." The version control title is there to indicate that the product can handle much more than source code. You can upload manual tests, work products, build files — anything you want, really.*

Once you install Visual Studio Team Explorer 2010 alongside Visual Studio 2010, you will get access to a nicely integrated Source Control Explorer. You can also manipulate the version control system using the Team Foundation command-line client called tf.exe. In this chapter, you will learn how to use both tools.

If you have used version control in Team Foundation Server 2005/2008, then you are in for a nice surprise. While all the original features are still there, many of them have been updated or enhanced. There are new tools for visualizing branching and to assist with merging, including better conflict-resolution tools. Branches are now considered to be first-class citizens, and have their own security permissions.

In this chapter, you will learn about features such as branching and merging, checking in and checking out code, setting check-in policies, and temporarily shelving your code for easy access at a later date. The Team Foundation version control system also supports a number of other features, such as atomic check-ins, workspaces, and changesets, all of which will be covered in this chapter.

> *One of the common misconceptions about Team Foundation version control is that it is a new version of Microsoft Visual SourceSafe (VSS). This is completely untrue — Team Foundation version control was written from scratch. And, unlike SourceSafe, it has been designed to scale well to a large number of developers (more than 2,000). They are completely different products.*

TEAM FOUNDATION VERSION CONTROL AND VISUAL SOURCESAFE (VSS) 2005

As Visual SourceSafe (VSS) 2005 reaches end of mainstream support in 2011 and extended support will end in 2016, no new versions of the product will be released. With the 2010 release of Team Foundation Server, Microsoft has made several changes to both the product and its licensing to make it suitable for all sizes of development teams.

Team Foundation version control is part of a greater Software Configuration Management (SCM) solution. Unlike VSS, Team Foundation version control is designed to scale to large development teams and can support distributed and outsourced teams in remote locations. Plus, you will avoid problems such as the occasional corruption of your source code files (since the data is written to a real database, rather than flat files).

Like VSS before it, Team Foundation Server is now available in all MSDN subscriptions including Visual Studio. Retail prices for the product work out around the same or even less than VSS. Therefore, it is now time to consider moving away from any existing VSS databases towards Team Foundation Server.

SETTING UP VERSION CONTROL

Assuming that you've never used a version control system, where do you start? Even if you have used other version control systems, how do you effectively set up and use Team Foundation version control? Let's walk you through the process step-by-step.

When you create a new team project (by clicking on File ➪ New ➪ New Team Project — you have to be connected to a Team Foundation Server for this option to show up), you will be provided a series of options. You'll get two version control options to set up a new parent folder, as shown in Figure 19-1.

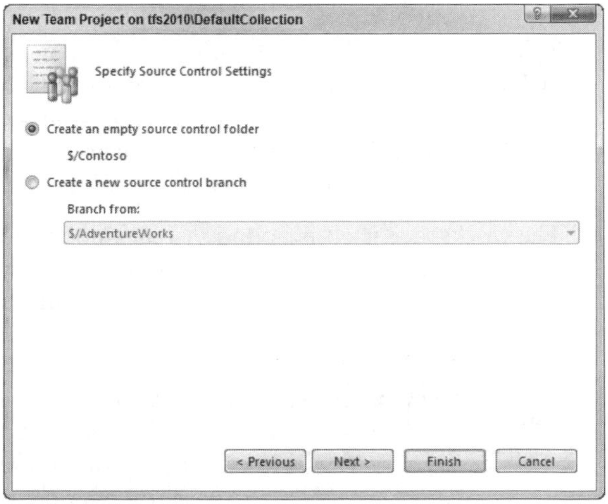

In this window, you have the following two options:

FIGURE 19-1

➤ You can create a brand-new parent version control folder (based on the name of your project). For most occasions, you will choose this option.

➤ You can create a branch based on a pre-existing project. This option is especially compelling if you want to create another version of an existing application or implement a new process to develop an existing application.

Setting up Security Roles

Before you start using the version control features of Team Foundation Server, you should determine who on your team will take on the responsibility of an administrator. The rest of the individuals on your team will be typically classified as contributors. Keep in mind that the way you organize your roles should be determined by a matter of convenience and organizational requirements.

The following roles and responsibilities are configured appropriately for a large organization:

➤ *Team project administrator* — The team project administrator is responsible for setting up version control permissions for each contributor (either directly, or through the IT staff). He or she also sets the security and policies for your code check-in and co-ordinates with the build team.

➤ *Development or test lead* — The lead could be granted certain additional permissions above a contributor, but still less than an administrator.

➤ *Contributor* — The contributor's role is as an end user, to check in and check out code, shelve and create changesets. Typically, you would assign this role to a tester or developer.

Setting up Your Workspace

Think of a *workspace* as your personal sandbox to work on source code. A workspace is the bridge between code on the server and your client machine. A workspace has one or many folders mapped in Team Foundation version control with your local file system. Whenever you check out code, the code from the repository is placed in your workspace, and vice-versa. The core advantage is isolation — workspaces allow you to work on an application without affecting any changes the rest of your team might be making.

The workspace itself is bound to a machine and owner. If you move to a different machine you have to create a new workspace. Files checked out in your workspace live on the associated machine only. This is an important difference to keep in mind with some other version control systems.

> *There are two primary restrictions in setting up your workspaces. You can't map two local folders to one folder in the repository. Likewise, you can't map two repository folders to a single local folder. As a rule of thumb, stick to one local folder mapped to a single folder in the version control system.*

To set up a new workspace, click on File ⇨ Source Control ⇨ Workspaces. You'll then see the Manage Workspaces window, as shown in Figure 19-2.

The next step involves adding a new workspace. Note that within each workspace, you can create several one-to-one mappings between local folders and repository folders. Click the Add button on this window to open the Add Workspace window, as shown in Figure 19-3.

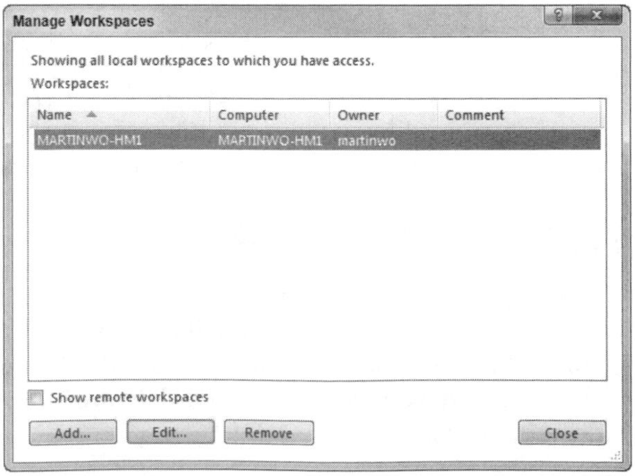

FIGURE 19-2

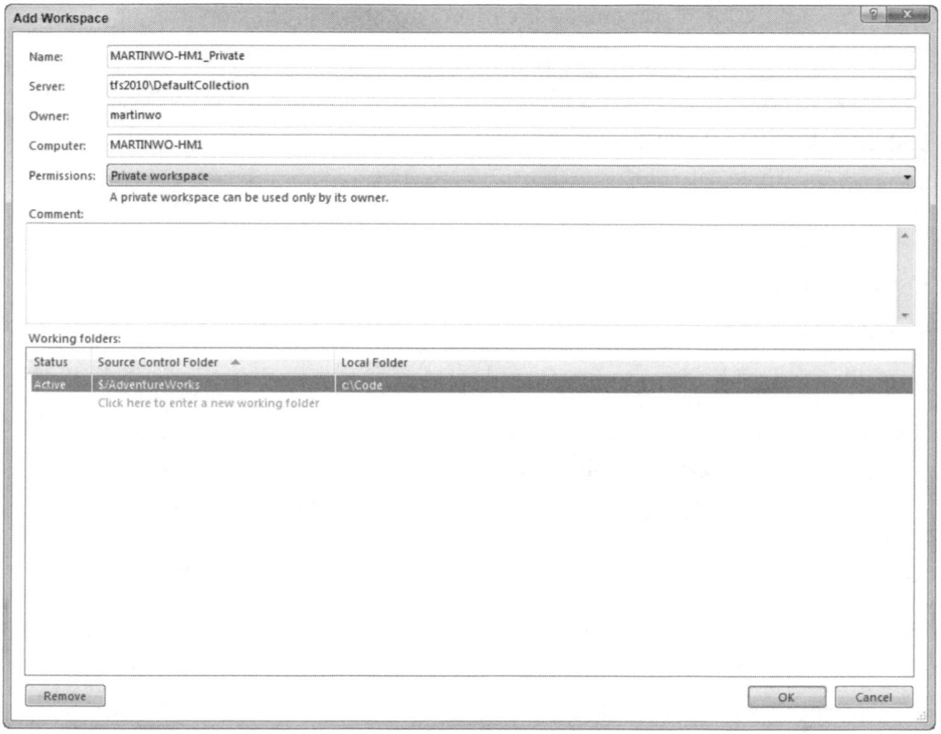

FIGURE 19-3

In the example shown in Figure 19-3, the `Code` folder on the local `c:` drive will synchronize with the `VSTS2010` folder in Team Foundation version control.

> *Notice that you have a Status field next to the Source Control Folder path. There are two statuses that can be set: Active and Cloaked. When you cloak a folder, you exclude it from certain synchronization tasks (such as add, get, and others). Note that cloaking is not an alternative to deleting a workspace. It's a way to cut down on the amount of disk space used, as well as bandwidth for files that you don't have an interest in or need for. It will also provide better performance because only Active mappings are synchronized.*

USING THE SOURCE CONTROL EXPLORER

The Source Control Explorer is similar to other explorers in Visual Studio. It enables you to browse and manage entire projects and individual folders in the repository. You can add and delete files; check in, check out, and view any of your pending changes; and view the status your local code compared to the code in Team Foundation version control. Think of it as your master control area for all tasks related to source code management. Following are some of the important tasks it will allow you to do:

➤ Create shelvesets

➤ Lock and unlock files and folders

➤ Resolve conflicts

➤ Branch and merge

➤ View historical data

➤ Compare files and folders

➤ Label your files and folders

> *As you will learn later in this chapter, a* shelveset *is a collection of changes stored in a "shelf," or area, to temporarily store your source code without committing it to the repository.*

Many of these topics will be examined later in this chapter. To access the Source Code Explorer, simply click View ➪ Other Windows ➪ Source Control Explorer.

Another way you can open your source code is by clicking File ➪ Source Control ➪ Open from Source Control. Visual Studio will then prompt you to connect to the Team Foundation Server and select the source code repository of your choice if you are not connected.

Figure 19-4 shows the Source Control Explorer interface. It is divided into three main areas: the source tree view on the left (which enables you to navigate and select source files from your project), the details view on the right, and the "Source location" bar. The Workspace drop-down list enables you to easily jump from one workspace to another.

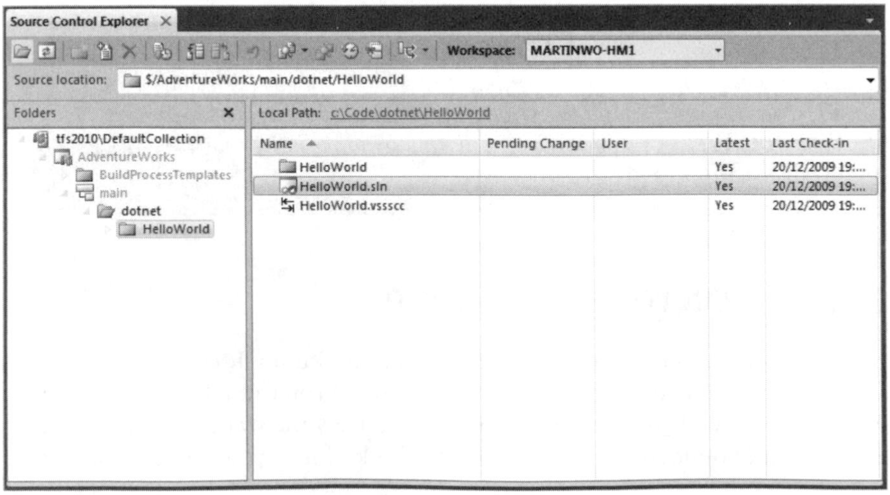

FIGURE 19-4

Workspaces

When you create a project or solution, you can automatically add it to Source Control, as shown in Figure 19-5. Note that a workspace is created *only* if you don't already have one. Think of the workspace as your local copy of the source files and folders contained on the server. It enables you to work on an application without affecting any changes the rest of your team might be making.

Each of the changes you make to these files will be pending until you check them in or undo them. Once they are checked in, they will be committed into the main repository.

You can manipulate your workspace from the GUI by selecting File ⇨ Source Control ⇨ Workspaces. You can also manipulate it using the Team Foundation command-line tool. For example, to create a new workspace, simply type the following command:

FIGURE 19-5

```
> tf.exe workspace /new MobileExplorerProject
```

In the preceding example, a new workspace is created called `MobileExplorerProject`. Anyone can create his or her own workspaces, but you must be logged in as an administrator to create and assign workspaces for other people.

Table 19-1 describes common workspace options.

TABLE 19-1: Common Workspace Options

WORKSPACE OPTIONS	DESCRIPTION
/comment	Tag a workspace with a comment
/computer	Specify the target computer for the workspace
/delete	Delete a workspace
/new	Create a new workspace
/newname	Rename an existing workspace
/newowner	Change the owner of the workspace
/noprompt	Execute workspace commands without prompts
/permission	Set the workspace permission: Private, Public-Limited, or Public
/template	Specify a workspace to be used as a template to create brand-new workspaces

The `workspaces` (plural) command provides you with a holistic view of the workspaces on your Team Foundation Server. Note that the `workspaces` command will update the local cache file. It will cause the server to update its user cache when /updateUserName is used. The /updateComputerName option will change the computer name that is associated with the workspace on the server.

Table 19-2 describes `Workspaces` options.

TABLE 19-2: Workspaces Options

WORKSPACES OPTIONS	DESCRIPTION
/computer	Indicate what workspaces you want to view or manipulate from the repository, filtered by computer name.
/format	Specify the format in which you would like to see the reports. You have two possible values at your disposal: `Brief` or `Detailed`. The default value is `Brief`.
/owner	Specify the creator of the workspace.
/collection	Specify the name or URL of the Team Foundation Server project collection.
/updateComputerName	Instruct Team Foundation Server to refresh because the client computer has changed name. It is typically written out as `/updateComputerName:oldComputerName`. The `oldComputerName` is the name that the computer had previously.
/updateUserName	Instruct Team Foundation Server to refresh because one (or more) network users have changed names.

In addition to the command line, you can also use Visual Studio to manage your workspaces. Figure 19-6 shows the Manage Workspaces window. You can access this window by clicking File ⇨ Source Control ⇨ Workspaces, or by selecting "Workspaces…" in the Workspaces drop-down from the Source Control Explorer toolbar.

From this window, you can add new workspaces, edit existing workspaces, or remove old workspaces. Click the Add button to display the Add Workspace window, as shown in Figure 19-7.

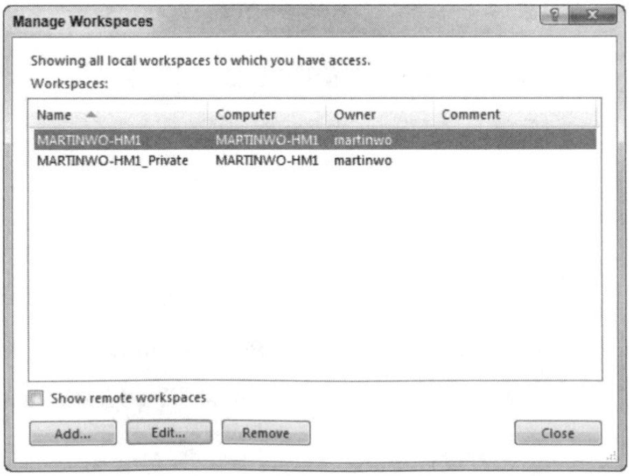

FIGURE 19-6

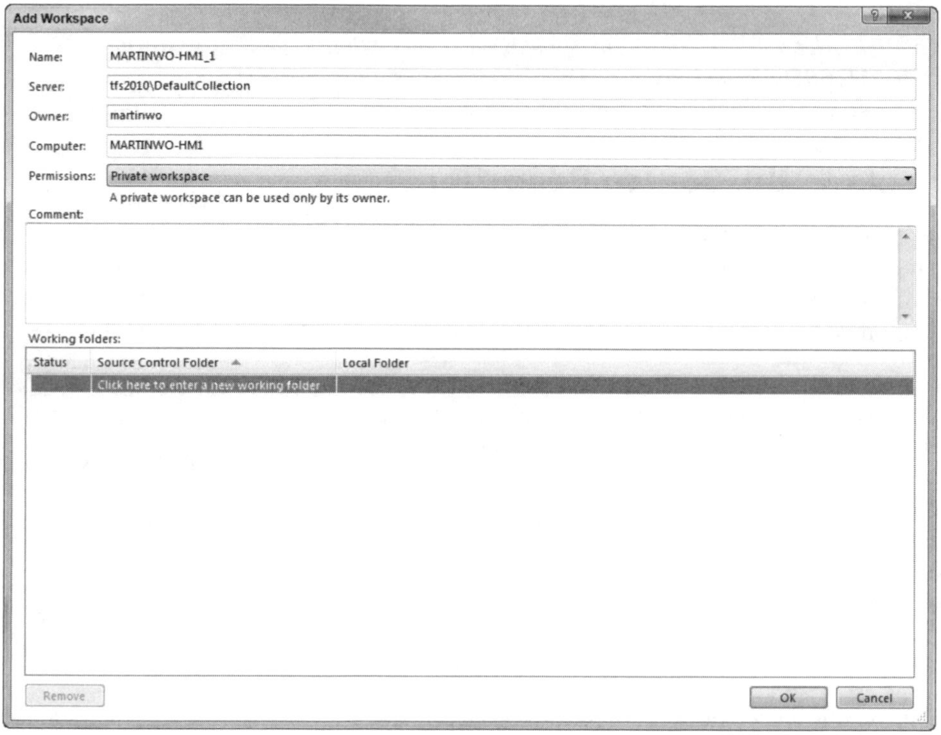

FIGURE 19-7

Visual Studio Team Foundation Server 2010 has added a new feature called *permissions* to workspaces. This feature allows you to control access to a workspace.

Table 19-3 shows the different permission features available.

TABLE 19-3: Permission Features

PERMISSION	DESCRIPTION
Private workspace	A private workspace can be used only by its owner.
Public workspace (limited)	A limited public workspace can be used by any valid user, but only the workspace owner can check in or administer the workspace.
Public Workspace	A fully public workspace can be used, checked in, and administered by any valid user.

Public workspaces now make it easier for teams to collaborate when sharing a single machine. One specific example would be merging bug fixes into a mainline branch. By utilizing a public workspace, multiple team members can work together on a common machine to resolve merge conflicts, thereby making the merge process run faster and smoother.

> *A "Private workspace" was the only type of workspace that Team Foundation Server 2005/2008 allowed.*

Adding Projects to the Source Repository

Once you have created workspaces, you can import the associated source files into the repository. The process of putting code in Team Foundation Server is called *checking in*. (You'll learn more about the check-in/check-out process in the next section.) To open the "Add to Source Control" window, simply right-click on your solution in the Solution Explorer and select "Add Solution to Source Control."

First, select which Team Foundation Server team project and workspace you want to use. Also, enter a name for the solution folder (it will default to the name of the solution). Click the Advanced button to invoke a window in which you can specify the locations for the solution and project files, as shown in Figure 19-8.

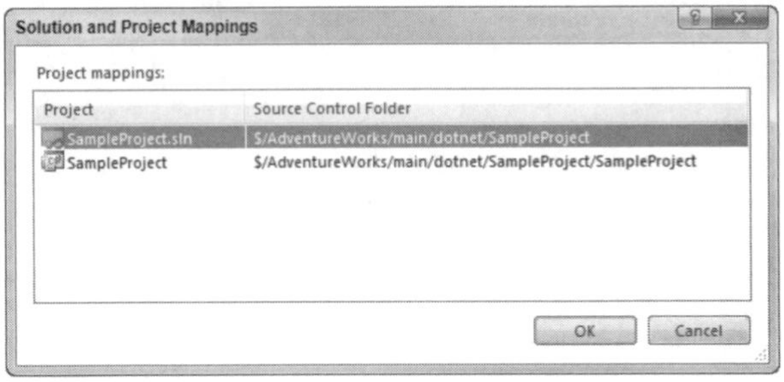

Solution and Project Mappings

Project mappings:

Project	Source Control Folder
SampleProject.sln	$/AdventureWorks/main/dotnet/SampleProject
SampleProject	$/AdventureWorks/main/dotnet/SampleProject/SampleProject

OK   Cancel

FIGURE 19-8

Click the OK button on this window. Then, click OK again, and your solution will be marked as a pending change to Team Foundation version control. However, your solution has not yet been officially "added" into the version control system.

In the next section, you will learn how to check in and check out code from the source repository. You also find out about changesets and how to configure team check-in policies.

CHECK-IN AND CHECK-OUT

Daily check-ins and check-outs are an essential part of a developer's workflow. *Checking out* simply means that you are operating with the files you already have in your personal workspace. *Checking in* refers to items that are re-inserted into the repository. The source code is represented as a tree structure, with branches and other logical elements.

> *Unlike VSS, Team Foundation version control does not necessarily retrieve the latest version of files from the source repository when performing a check. Team Foundation version control, by default, checks out the version of the file that you had in your workspace, and then will warn you to merge with the latest version when performing a check-in. This is an important point to consider.*

Checking In an Item

A *changeset* contains all of the information related to a check-in, such as work item links, revisions, notes, policies, and owner and date/time details. Team Foundation version control bundles all of the information together into this logical container. A changeset is created once you check code into the repository, and, as a container, it reflects only the changes you checked in at a particular time and date. You can also view it as the state of the repository at a particular time and date. The usefulness of a changeset comes from the fact that you can, on a very atomic level, return to any point in time and troubleshoot your code.

> *Team Foundation Server contains four types of artifacts: work items, changesets, source code files, and builds. For example, you can associate a work item to a source code file. You can also link builds to work items if you wish. This is a really powerful concept. Imagine that you are having trouble with a build. You can automatically call up the changeset with the problem code. You can also generate a work item to get a developer to fix the problem. The integration possibilities are endless.*

All developers forget to check in their code at one point or another. You can implement automatic check-ins by changing the environment settings in your project. Specifically, you can check an option called "Check-in Everything When Closing a Solution or Project."

The Pending Changes window enables you to view all of the checked-out files in your project. After your solution has been added to version control, the window shown in Figure 19-9 will appear on the bottom half of the screen. You can also access this window via the View ⇨ Other Windows ⇨ Pending Changes.

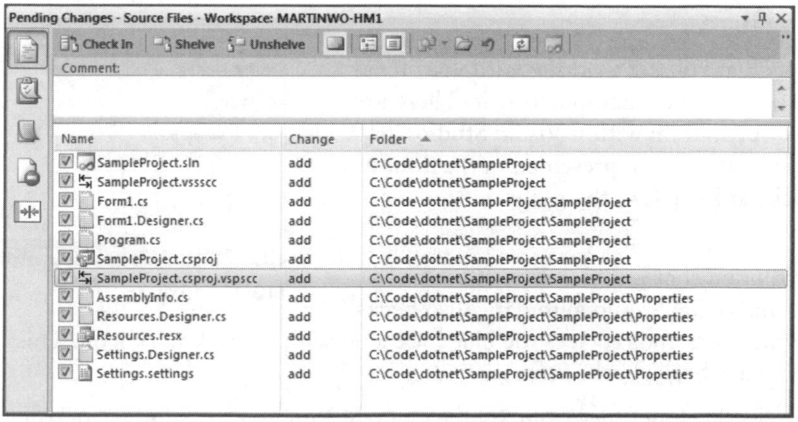

FIGURE 19-9

To check in your changes, select the files you wish to check in from the bottom pane, then click the Check In button. Assuming no check-in polices are being violated, your code will be added to Team Foundation version control.

But that is just the beginning of what you can do on this window. There is a toolbar called the *channel* on the left-hand side of the window. Selecting an item in the channel changes the contents of the pending changes window, increasing its functionality and allowing you to take full advantage of the different features in Team Foundation Server. Following are the channel options (in order from top to bottom):

➤ *Source Files* — This is the default channel option. This channel option allows you to select the files you want to check in, add a comment to the changeset, check in the changeset, or shelve/unshelve the changeset.

➤ *Work Items* — Team Foundation version control is integrated with the work item tracking system. This integration allows you to associate a changeset with one or more work items. This channel option allows you to run work item queries, and select the work items to associate with this changeset.

➤ *Check-in Notes* — Check-in notes are free-form text fields that can be associated with a changeset. These fields can be required or optional. For example, you may require code reviews of all code before it is checked into version control. You can specify a Code Reviewer check-in note and make it required, so that someone must enter his or her name into the field before the changeset can be checked in.

➤ *Policy Warnings* — This channel will show any check-in policies that you are currently violating. Check-in polices are discussed later in this chapter.

➤ *Conflicts* — This channel is new to Visual Studio 2010. This channel is used to handle any conflicts or issues during the check-in process, such as trying to check in a file when a newer version exists on the server.

Checking Out an Item

Checking out an item means that you are working with your local repository for the purpose of editing or manipulating it. There are several ways you can check out an item within Visual Studio 2010. Items that are under version control are represented in the Solution Explorer with small padlocks at the left of the program icon, as shown in Figure 19-10.

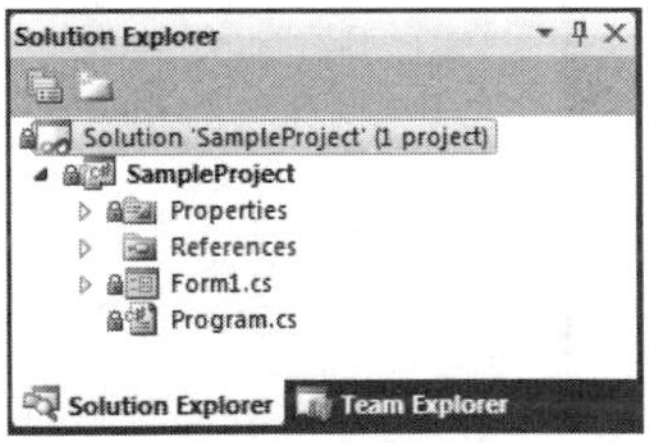

FIGURE 19-10

To check out an item in a solution that is under version control, simply open and edit the item. Visual Studio automatically checks out the item as you begin your edits and replaces the blue lock icon with a checkmark icon. This visually confirms that the file has been checked out.

You also have the capability to check out files from Source Control Explorer. In Source Control Explorer, find the file or files you want to check out, right-click on them, and select "Check Out for Edit." This opens the Check-Out window. In this window (in addition to selecting/deselecting which files you want to check out), you can specify a Lock Type for the files you are checking out. Following are the three lock options you can configure:

➤ *Check-In* — This option allows other users to check out the files, but they can't check them in.

➤ *Check-Out* — This option prevents other users from checking in/out the corresponding source files.

➤ *Unchanged* — This option allows other users to pend changes to the source files and keeps any existing locks on the files.

Creating and Administering Check-In Policies

Check-in policies provide a way for the team and individuals to effectively manage quality and workflow to the source management process used by the team. To configure your check-in policies, right-click on your Team Foundation project and select Team Project Settings ➪ Source Control. Under the Check-in Policy tab (Figure 19-11), you will find several options for modifying the check-in policies.

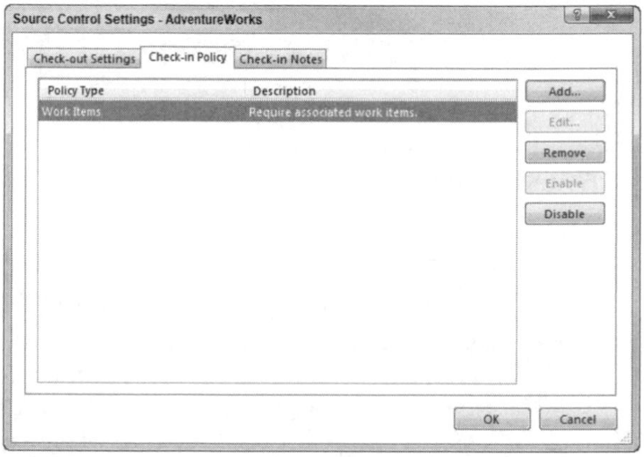

If you click the Add button in the Source Control Settings dialog box (see Figure 19-11), you will be prompted to select a check-in policy type. Select one of the four options shown in Figure 19-12 and click the OK button. Following are the default policy types included in Team Foundation version control:

FIGURE 19-11

➤ *Builds* — This option requires that the last build of the project was successful. If it was not, then new changes cannot be checked in until the offending code has been fixed.

➤ *Code Analysis* — This option adds a static code analysis quality check before source code can be inserted into the code repository. The code analysis check will be dependent on the project-level settings. For example, if you selected code analysis for C/C++ in your project, the engine will automatically use that test as a "quality gate" (or quality assurance) before code is reintroduced into the source.

➤ *Testing Policy* — You can apply testing policies to check the correctness of your code before it is checked in. For example, you may want to require unit testing to verify the default values in your application. For more information about testing policies, see the chapters in Part III of the book.

➤ *Work Items* — You may want to require that a work item must be associated with every check-in. That way, changes can be documented, which will make it easier to track any problems.

Once the check-in policy has been created, try checking in code without complying with the new policies. The Policy Failure window shown in Figure 19-13 will appear. At this point, you will have the option to override the policy requirement and comment on the failure.

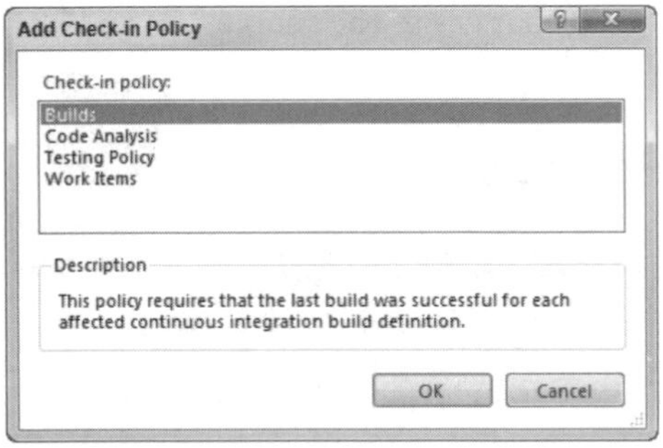

FIGURE 19-12

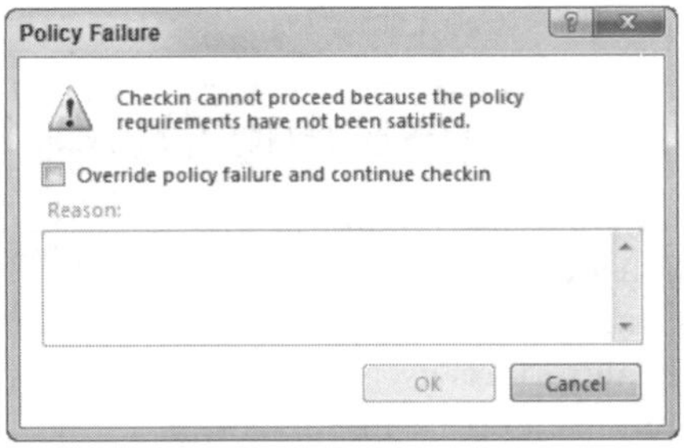

FIGURE 19-13

> *Overriding the check-in policy should only be done when absolutely necessary; otherwise, it will start to negate the reason for introducing the policy in the first place. The check-in policy overrides are reported into the data warehouse so that these can be acted on by the team. If it is found that a particular check-in policy is frequently overridden, then you may way to question why it is enabled in the first place. If a particular individual or group of individuals is found to be frequently overriding a check-in policy, then you may want to consult with them to help them understand the reason that the policy is in place.*

Viewing History

Viewing the history of files, folders, and changesets has been updated and enhanced in Visual Studio 2010. While previous versions of Visual Studio allowed you to view the history of a file or a folder, the experience was less than satisfying. The old history window was a docked tool window in Visual Studio, and, while it served its purpose, it did not help the user visualize and understand the changes that were taking place in the version control system. As such, the history window was redesigned to help users more fully understand the history of changes made in Team Foundation version control.

To view the history of a file or folder, in Source Control Explorer, right-click on the file or folder, and select View History from the context menu. This opens a new document tab, as shown in Figure 19-14.

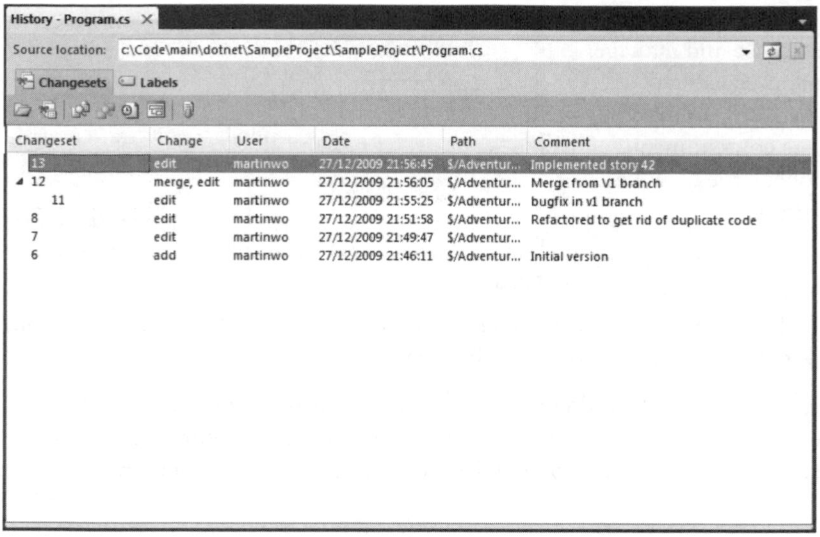

FIGURE 19-14

The new History window is now a tabbed document window in Visual Studio. This allows you to open multiple History windows for research, something that was not possible in previous versions of Visual Studio. Notice that the window has two sub-tabs: Changesets and Labels. The History window now gives you a view of both the changesets associated with the file or folder, as well as any labels.

You have several options from the Changeset sub-tab. You can select a changeset and click the View button to view the file version for that particular changeset. You can click the Changeset Details button to view the details for a particular changeset, including all the files that make up the changeset and any associated work items. You can compare two different versions of a file or folder to see the differences. Clicking the Annotate button allows you to see, line by line, who made what changes to a particular file.

Finally, you can select a changeset and click the Get This Version button. This will replace the current version of this file in your workspace with the selected version, enabling you to easily return to an earlier version of a file.

The History window also allows you to track the changes across multiple branches, merges and renames. This will be discussed later in this chapter.

Labeling Files

A *label* is a marker that can be attached to files and folders in Team Foundation version control. This marker allows all the files and folders labeled together to be retrieved as one collective unit. Labeling was available in previous versions of Visual Studio, but it had some issues. Labeling an item could sometimes be a tedious and complex process, and labeling a large number of files could be very slow.

With Visual Studio 2010, labeling has been updated to make it easier to use and manage. To create a new label, in Source Control Explorer, right-click on the file or folder you want to label, and from the context menu, select Apply Label. This opens the New Label window, as shown in Figure 19-15.

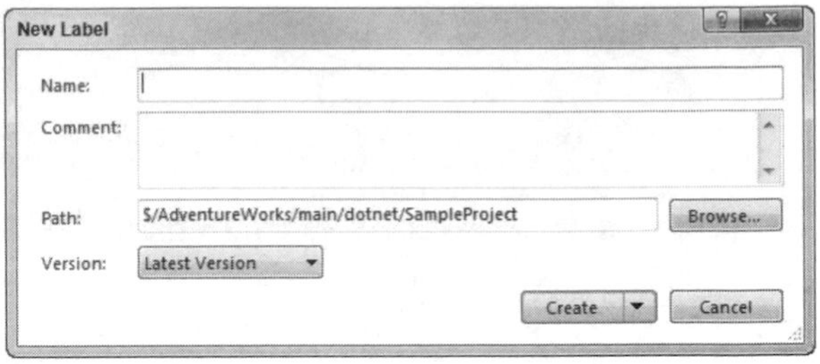

In this window, you can enter the label name and a comment. You can also select the version that you want to label. You can choose to label by Changeset, Date, Label, Latest Version, or Workspace Version. Click the Create button to create the label.

FIGURE 19-15

Notice next that the Create button is a drop-down arrow. Clicking the arrow provides you with two options. You can create the label as is, or you can create the label and then edit it. If you select Create and Edit, the label will be created, and you will be presented a new tab, as shown in Figure 19-16.

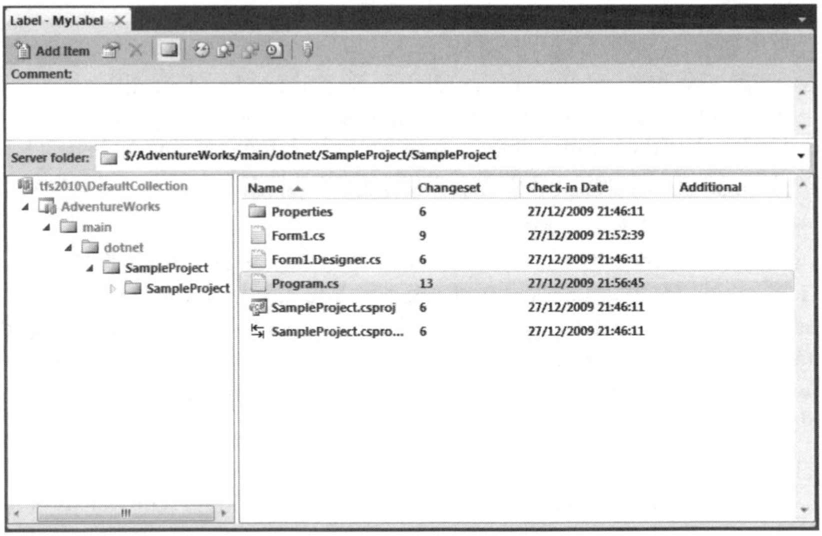

FIGURE 19-16

This tab allows you to make multiple changes to the label. You can add new files to the label. You can change the version of a file that the label is currently applied to. And you can remove files from the label. All of this is made easily accessible by using a tree-view control. Managing labels in Visual Studio 2010 is now a much easier process.

SHELVING

There are times when you won't be ready to commit your source code into the core repository. For example, say that you are working on solving a bug and you want to share the changes you have made with a colleague to get their assistance on a particular issue. *Shelving* enables you to store files and code aside on a temporary basis. The collections of stored pending changes that haven't been committed to the server are called *shelvesets*.

> The security settings for a shelveset are determined by the item permissions. You must have read and pending change permission for the item changes you wish to unshelve.

The process of creating a shelveset is fast and easy. To begin, access the Pending Changes window by clicking View ➪ Other Windows ➪ Pending Changes. In the Pending Changes window, select the items you want to shelve, and click the Shelve button.

The Shelve dialog box appears with the files you have selected. (Be sure to give it a descriptive name to differentiate it from the other shelvesets.) You now have the option of unchecking the items, preserving pending changes locally, or clicking the Shelve button. You also have the option of evaluating policies and check-in notes before shelving.

Shelvesets contain the same level of information as a changeset, including associated work items, comments, and check-in notes. Keep in mind that, unlike with a changeset, the changes are not versioned. Shelvesets can be permanently deleted (which is something you can't do with changesets). You can't link directly to a shelveset from a work item, and policies can't be enforced on shelving.

When would you want to use this feature? There are a few scenarios. Say that a project manager asks you to drop what you are doing and work on a bug fix. Your current work can be set aside temporarily. Say that you have code that isn't quite ready to be checked in, but needs a code review. You can shelve your pending changes to allow other team members to work with it. Shelving is also useful as a backup mechanism, and is used as a way to reassign unfinished code to another team member.

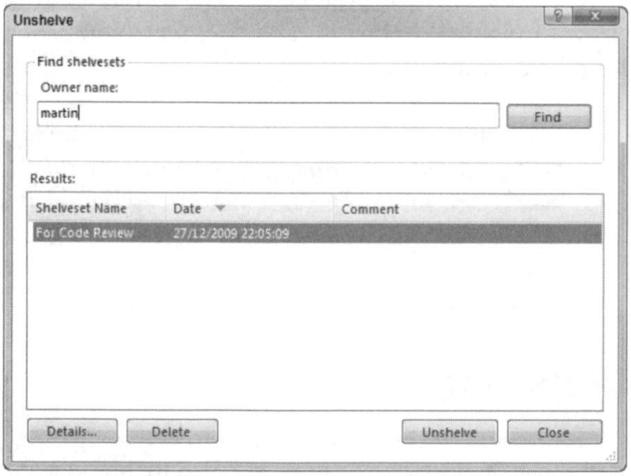

Unshelving source files is as easy as shelving them. First, bring up the Pending Changes window and click the Unshelve button. The Unshelve window appears with the option to select an owner and the name of a shelveset (Figure 19-17). You also have the option of deleting shelvesets or reading more details.

FIGURE 19-17

Once you select a shelveset, you then have the option of preserving the shelveset on the server. You can also choose whether you want to restore the work items and check in. When you unshelve your code, all the pending check-in information is also restored. If you made any changes to your workspace (for example, renamed or moved a folder in your workspace), the unshelved folder will also be renamed and moved. Shelved files that are marked for deletion are deleted in the workspace.

BRANCHING AND MERGING

Branching and merging are two important functions of any version control system. During the process of building a piece of software, you may find the need to release a stable version for beta testing, or you may want to work in parallel on bug fixes without interrupting the main development process. To better manage this process, you can create many development versions of the same code base (called *branching*) and re-integrate them into the main tree (*merging*).

You might have heard of the terms *forward integration* and *reverse integration*. In the context of branching and merging, forward integration is the process of merging changes from the main development line into a branch. Reverse integration is the complete opposite — you integrate or merge the changes in your branches back down to the main branch. Figure 19-18 shows a few common scenarios you might encounter where you would need branching and merging.

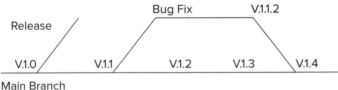

FIGURE 19-18

A branch was created from version 1.0 of the application to create a release or preview version for customers or beta testers. In version 1.1, a critical bug was found, and a separate branch was created with incremental fixes. The fixes were completed in version 1.1.1.2 and reintegrated into version 1.4 of the main branch.

> *Chapter 20 dives deeper into several of the more popular ways to use branching and merging. That chapter examines both the concepts around those strategies, and how to configure Team Foundation Server to implement these strategies.*

Branching

Branching enables you not only to create copies of your source files, but also maintain a history of your changes in case you want to do a merge in the future. You can use the Source Control Explorer to navigate between different branches. To create a branch, simply right-click on the folder or branch containing your solution in the Source Control Explorer. Select Branch and Merging, and then Branch from the context menu. The dialog box shown in Figure 19-19 will appear on screen.

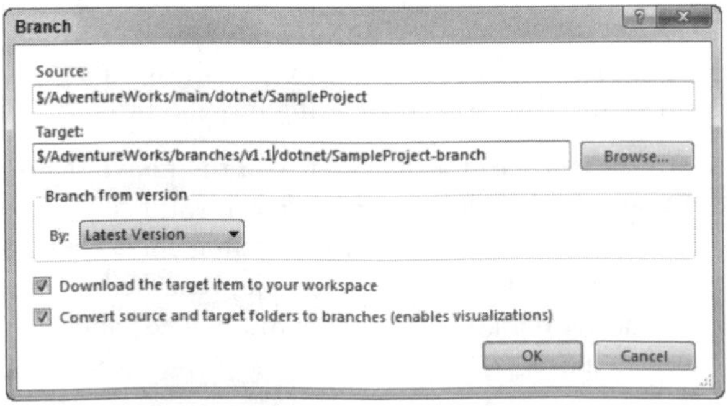

FIGURE 19-19

The Branch dialog box has several options. The Target field enables you to set the name of your branch. The "Branch from version" option enables you to select which version of the branch you would like to use (the latest version or an older version). You can opt to create a local copy of a branch by selecting the "Download the target item to your workspace" option. It will download the newly created branch files to your workspace.

At this point, the branch has only been pended to Team Foundation version control. To complete the branch process, open the Pending Changes window and click the Check-In button.

Note that a faster way to create the branch is to right-click on a folder that is marked as a branch (denoted by a separate branch icon in Source Control Explorer). Creating a branch of a branch will bring up a separate dialog as shown in Figure 19-20. When you press the branch button, the files will be branched and checked in with a single server operation. Not only does this save you the check-in step, the process is significantly faster when performing a branch of several thousands of files.

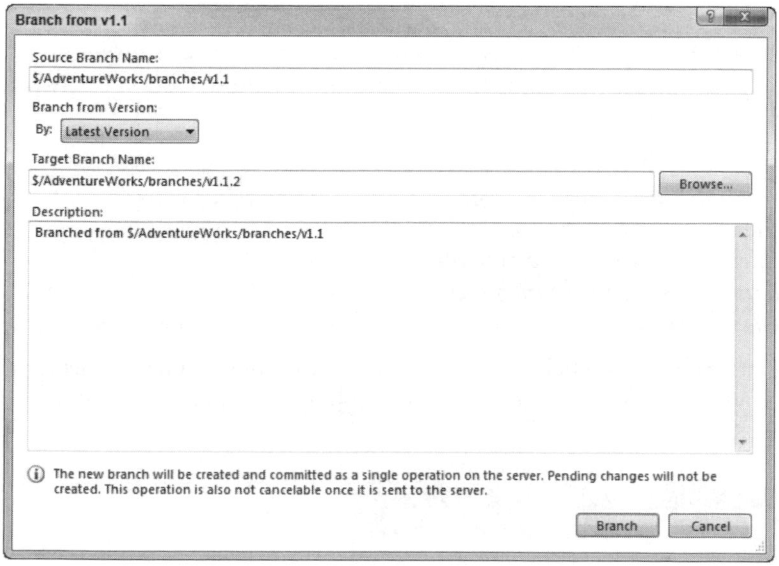

FIGURE 19-20

One of the great new features regarding branching in Visual Studio 2010 is the capability to do branch visualization. In earlier versions of Visual Studio, there was no nice, clear, concise way to view branch information. This issue was addressed in Visual Studio 2010. To take advantage of this, the first step is to turn your branched folders into Branch objects. To do this, right-click on the branched folder in Source Control Explorer, select Branching and Merging, then "Convert Folder to Branch." This opens the Convert Folder to Branch window, as shown in Figure 19-21.

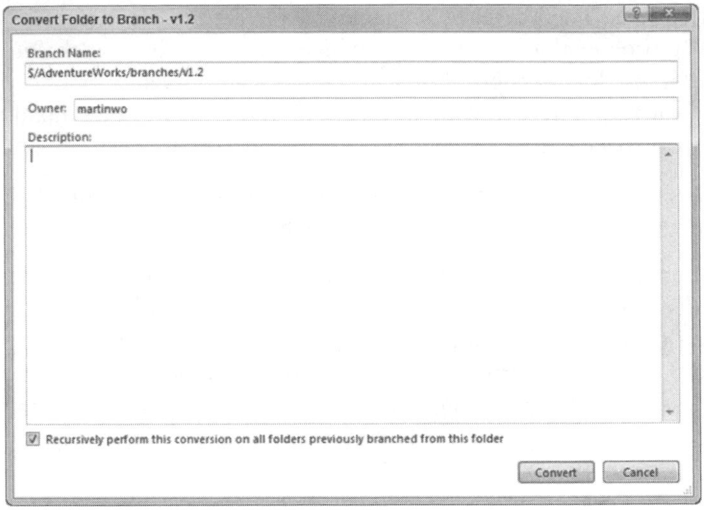

FIGURE 19-21

One nice feature of this window is the capability to recursively perform this conversion for all branched child folders. If you have an extensive branching structure, this allows you to easily turn all the child folders into Branch objects.

> *Turning a folder in version control into a Branch object does not affect your capability to check items in and out. You still access the information in version control using the folder metaphor. Converting the folder to a Branch object simply allows you to make use of the branch visualization options.*

To visualize your branching structure, right-click on a branch. From the context menu, select Branching and Merging, then View Hierarchy. A new document tab named Hierarchy will open, as shown in Figure 19-22.

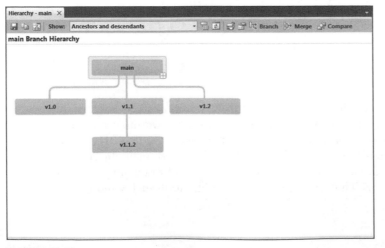

FIGURE 19-22

This tab provides a nice hierarchical view of the branching structure that has been implemented in Team Foundation version control. You can easily tell which branches are parents and children of other branches.

From this tab, you can save this visualization out to a graphics file to share with others. Using the drop-down box, you can adjust the view of the hierarchy in the tab. You can also select a branch in the visualization, open it, compare it to another branch, branch it again, or merge the branch back into its parent.

Merging

Merging means to combine changes from two or more branches. This functionality is very useful for teams of developers working in parallel. During a merge, many changes are integrated, including add/edit/delete operations. If there are merge conflicts between branches, you can resolve them in a variety of ways, including the use of a diff-merge tool.

There are two ways you can merge files: using the Source Control Explorer and via the command line. You can also specify whether you want to incorporate all the changes or just specific versions.

When you merge, Team Foundation version control uses the history behind the scenes to find files and folders that have been changed in another branch. Changes that don't exist in the target branch will be merged. If any of the files or folders has been changed in the target branch, a merge conflict will occur.

You can access the Merge Wizard in the Source Control Explorer by right-clicking the folder that you want to merge. If you click Branching and Merging, and then the Merge option on the context menu, you will be presented with the Source Control Merge Wizard, as shown in Figure 19-23.

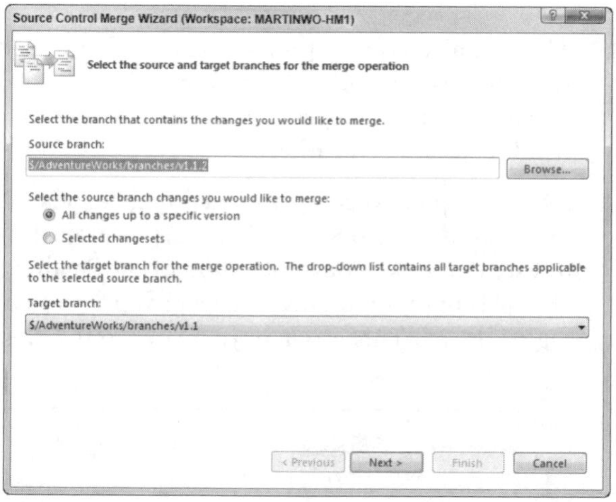

FIGURE 19-23

The Source Control Merge Wizard presents you with a preset list of target branches you can merge to and offers you the option to commit all changes in the source branch or only selected changes. Once you click the Next button, you will be presented with the option to select the changes you want to merge. Once all of the options have been set, all you must do is click the Finish button to execute the merge process.

Visual Studio 2010 also provides you with a graphical way to perform the merge process, as well as with the capability to drag and drop changesets across branches. When viewing the history of an object in the version control system (as discussed previously), one of the options on the History tab is the Track Changeset option. Right-clicking on a changeset and selecting Track Changeset opens the Changeset Tracking tab for that particular changeset. By clicking the Timeline Tracking button on this tab, you are able to view the different branches in version control, and see how a changeset has migrated between those branches, as shown in Figure 19-24.

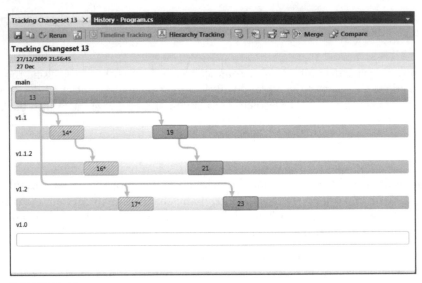

FIGURE 19-24

This is a nice visualization because you can easily tell whether a particular changeset has been fully or partially merged into a branch. You can also perform merges from this view by dragging and dropping a changeset from one branch to another. Performing this action will open the Merge window (described earlier).

As you begin branching and merging, at some point in time, you will encounter conflicts that must be resolved. Visual Studio 2010 has revamped its conflict-resolution mechanism to make it simpler to use. In the previous discussion of the Pending Changes window, you learned about the different channels of that window. A new channel on that window is the Conflicts channel, shown in Figure 19-25. This is where you work to resolve any conflicts related to a merge.

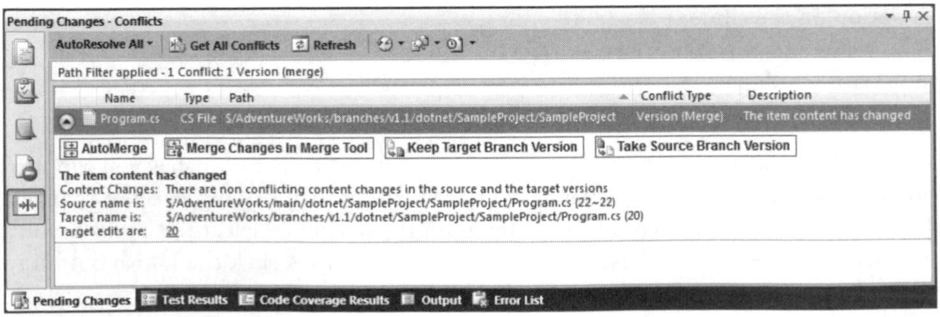

FIGURE 19-25

COMMAND-LINE TOOLS

You can manipulate any part of the version control system using the Team Foundation command-line tool. The tool itself is called `tf.exe` (short for Team Foundation). For example, to create a new workspace, simply type the following command:

```
> tf.exe workspace /new MobileExplorerProject
```

In the preceding example, a new workspace is created, called `MobileExplorerProject`. You can exercise a great deal of control over the version control system using the tool. For example, you can manipulate workspaces, permissions, changesets, labels, and much more.

You can also use the command-line tool to monitor how long files have been checked out. To get a report about the changes in your workspace, simply type the following:

```
> tf.exe status /collection:http://YourTFSServerName:8080/tfs/
    YourProjectCollection /format:detailed
```

The Team Foundation version control command-line tool will enable you to perform operations that you can't perform using the Source Control Explorer. One such operation is a rollback to a previous changeset. You may have the occasion where you need to roll back your version control system to a previous changeset version. This is not possible using Source Control Explorer, but can be done using the command-line tool, as shown here:

```
> tf.exe rollback /changeset:27~23
```

The previous command tells Team Foundation version control to roll back from changeset 27 to changeset 23.

To view a list of all possible commands using the command-line tool, run the following command:

```
> tf.exe /?
```

This will provide a list of all options, along with some help information. You can also refer to the MSDN online documentation for more information.

SUMMARY

In this chapter, you found out the core differences between Visual SourceSafe and Team Foundation version control. You examined the configuration options for Team Foundation version control.

You found out how to use the Source Control Explorer and how to check in and check out code, showing you the concepts of workspaces and changesets. You learned how to view the history of files and apply labels. The chapter also covered advanced concepts such and branching, merging, and shelving, including the new visualization tools available in Visual Studio 2010.

Version control is an important tool to help you manage your development process by providing an effective way of organizing your source code. In Chapter 20, you will learn some branching and merging strategy best practices, and how to configure Team Foundation Server to implement those strategies.

20

Branching and Merging

WHAT'S IN THIS CHAPTER?

➤   Understanding branching and merging

➤   Looking at common branching strategies

➤   Walking through a basic branching plan implementation using Team Foundation Server 2010

One of the biggest problems that developers of software projects encounter is the understanding of the software that is being built. How are all the different aspects of your software project organized and accounted for? Does everyone understand the organization of the code base and the ramifications of making certain changes?

Many people are afraid of branching in version control, because of the additional complications that this brings into the management of your files. Do your developers know when they are allowed to create a code branch, and when they are supposed to merge their changes back into the MAIN line? If not, you are asking for certain trouble as team members begin modifying the code.

There are trade-offs with any branching and merging strategy. The biggest trade-off is in the areas of risk versus productivity. Developers sometimes look at branching as having a low overhead, and don't see anything wrong with creating a branch of the code any time they must make a change. The capability to quickly and easily create branches can make developers more productive. However, creating branches in an ad hoc manner also adds more risk to your project.

One of the major risk areas surrounding branching is merging changes from branches back into the MAIN line. The more branches you have, the more merging that must occur, the more complex the merging may be, and the more chance for introducing errors into the merge process.

Don't just jump into branching because you have heard it is a good idea. You must have a plan, strategy, and reason for creating branches and performing merges. When creating your branching/ merging strategy, ask yourself the question, "How does this branch support my development project?" Before creating any branch, you should be able to justify why you are wanting to branch. The same goes for merging as well.

This chapter is all about branching and merging strategies with Visual Studio Team Foundation Server 2010. The discussion begins by covering some of the basic terminology around branching and merging. Next, you will take a tour of some of the common branching strategies. And then you'll learn some details about two branching strategies as used with Visual Studio Team Foundation Server 2010. While most branching strategies can be implemented with Team Foundation Server, these two strategies are easy to use for people new to branching and merging, as well as people who have been using branching and merging for a while.

These strategies help to show you the features and tools inside Team Foundation Server supporting branching and merging, and, therefore, they should help you to understand how to apply any other branching strategy with the product. However, do not take those strategies as strategies recommended by the authors for all projects all the time. You must first understand the concepts of branching and merging, learn what support the tooling gives you, and then decide on a branching strategy suitable for your situation at the current time.

> For more general branching guidance, also consult the excellent Visual Studio TFS Branching Guide 2010, freely available from `http://tfsbranchingguideiii .codeplex.com`.

UNDERSTANDING BRANCHING AND MERGING

There is a lot of terminology involved with configuration management, branching, and merging, which can be daunting to people new to it. To be able to really understand branching and merging, there are several terms that must be defined.

Software Configuration Management

Branching and merging is just one aspect of a larger topic referred to as Software Configuration Management (SCM).In his book *Software Engineering: A Practitioner's Approach* (New York: McGraw-Hill Science/Engineering/Math, 2009), Roger Pressman defined SCM as "a set of activities designed to control change by identifying the work products that are likely to change, establishing relationships among them, defining mechanisms for managing different versions of these work products, controlling the changes imposed, and auditing and reporting on the changes made."

SCM is important because it helps all the members of the team collaborate and communicate more effectively.

It's apparent that SCM covers a large range of topics, all of which Visual Studio and Team Foundation Server help to address.

Basic Definitions

Following are some definitions of basic terms used when discussing branching and merging:

➤ *Branch* — The easiest way to think about branching is that, when you branch your code, you are making a copy of it. And, in Team Foundation Server, that is exactly what you are doing — you are making a copy of your files. When you branch your files in Team Foundation Server, you create a separate physical copy of the files in a different location. You can then work on this branch, and when you are ready, you can merge your changes back with the original folder.

➤ *Merge* — This is the process of taking all the different branches, and combining them back into one code base. The main reason for this is to create a stable MAIN line of code that can be used for testing and release management. When you branch your code from the MAIN line, there is a relationship path established between the MAIN line and the branch. During the merge process, the files from the MAIN line are compared to the files in the branch. If possible, any changes will be integrated automatically. There will be occasions where the changes must be manually integrated. When you merge code from the parent branch into the child branch to push changes that have been made in that parent branch into the child branch, this is called a *forward integration* (FI). When you merge code from the child branch back into the parent branch to pull all the changes back into the parent branch that have been done in the child, then this is called a *reverse integration* (RI).

➤ *Baseless merge* — This is the process of merging items that are not directly branched from each other. While this process is available in Team Foundation Server 2010, it can lead to a confusing number of conflicts, and is generally not considered a good practice.

➤ *Release* — At some point, you are going to want to move your code from your development environment to its next stage, be that quality assurance or general release. A release is defined as a distribution of your code for some specific purpose, such as quality assurance testing or general availability to your clients.

COMMON BRANCHING STRATEGIES

As you can imagine, there are many different ideas and strategies involving how to branch your source code. All of them have their good points and bad points. You will find that different people will defend their branching strategies with a religious fervor.

This section examines popular branching strategies that are currently being used.

No Branching

Let's start with the most common and basic branching strategy, which is not to branch at all! Believe it or not, this is a valid branching strategy, and one that is perfectly suitable in many situations. Remember that the first rule of branching is to only create branches when you need them. This strategy is the easiest to understand, but is not a particularly interesting one to examine in detail in a chapter all about branching. Therefore it is included here to help to build off this strategy into other strategies.

Figure 20-1 shows an example of no branching.

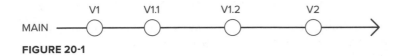

FIGURE 20-1

In this branching strategy, you only have one area of code, the MAIN line. All development is done directly against this code base. Code files are checked in and out directly from the MAIN line. As bugs are found, they are fixed and checked into this line.

When a release is ready, it is labeled (V1, V1.1, and so on) and development continues on this line toward the next release.

Note that you are still working in a MAIN branch. This means that if you want to introduce branches later on, then the option is still open to you. If you are not sure if you need to have a more complex branching strategy, start by creating a MAIN branch, and then you know you can create more if (and when) you need them. When creating a branch, you can specify a Label, Date, or Changeset to create the branch from. Therefore, you can create branches later for the code as it was at the V1 release if you find you need to.

This strategy is okay for a small team that is consistently working on the same codebase, a team that only releases and supports a single version of the application at any one time. That said, managing the release process in this way can mean that you have long periods of time when no development can be carried out, because the code base is being stabilized ready for a release.

The key thing about branching is that it enables parallel development on a code base. Even for a one-person development shop, some of the other branching strategies discussed here may be useful.

Branch Per Release

Branching per release is the second most common branching strategies used. The idea is to create branches that hold all the code for a particular release, as shown in Figure 20-2.

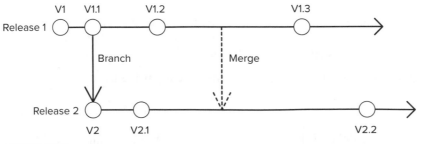

FIGURE 20-2

Each release of the software has its own branch. As you can see from Figure 20-2, Release 1 starts off on its own. Around the time of the release of Version 1.1, coding begins on Release 2. At that point, Release 2 is branched off of Release 1. Release 1 and Release 2 continue their development process. Occasionally, bugs or other critical fixes are merged from the Release 1 branch into the

Release 2 branch, but this is rarely done. And, in general, when a release is discontinued, the branch for that release is just abandoned.

Branch per release is easy to understand because people are familiar with the concept of labeling the source code on a particular release, and this is just taking that one step further. It allows you to easily get the code that is running in a particular version of the application, and is well-suited to organizations that need to support more than one version of an application that is running in production at any given time. However, for each release, there is still no more parallelism of development than in the standard "no branching" strategy.

Code Promotion Branching

Code promotion branching (or *promotion level branching*) breaks your branches off into different promotion levels, as shown in Figure 20-3.

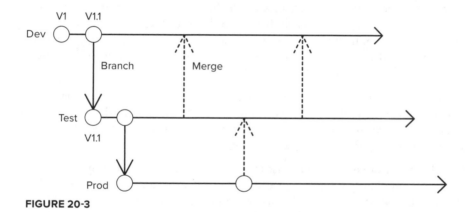

FIGURE 20-3

The initial development begins on the Dev line. Once the Dev line thinks Version 1.1 is complete, it is branched to the Test line. As bugs are found during testing, they are fixed in the Test branch, and merged back into the Dev branch.

Once the code has been tested, and is deemed ready to be released, it is branched again, this time from the Test line to the Production (Prod) line. In the Prod branch, the code base is stabilized and readied for release. Once it has been released, any final changes that were made are merged back into the Test and Dev branches.

This branching model is well-suited to controlled environments that have a single version of the application running in production at any one time. It allows development to continue in the Dev branch while stabilization is occurring in the in Test branch, and also allows you a very high degree of visibility of changes moving over to production.

Branch Per Feature

Branching per feature is used to isolate specific features into separate branches, thereby avoiding overlapping with other features. Figure 20-4 shows an example of branching per feature.

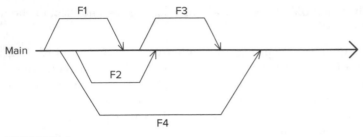

FIGURE 20-4

From the MAIN line, different branches are created depending on the feature. In Figure 20-4, you can see that, during the development cycle, four different branches were created: F1, F2, F3, F4. Each branch was created for a different feature. The feature was completed, and then the results were merged back into the MAIN line.

If you decide to use branching per feature, be sure to keep the life of your feature branches as short as possible, and ensure that you merge your changes back into the MAIN line as soon as you are finished. If you allow your feature branch to become stale (that is, old), then the merging process could become more complex, and undo any productivity gain you might have had by using this branching strategy.

If a feature is particularly long running, or has overlapping elements to another feature that has been completed, then you may want to merge changes from the MAIN branch into the feature branch (that is, have a forward integration) so that the code in your feature branch is updated with the latest code from the Main branch.

The advantage of branch per feature is that it increases the parallelism of your development. Multiple teams can split off and work on separate features at the same time. You are free to ship regular releases of code from your Main branch because you know the code in that branch is well-tested and features only get added to that branch once they are finished.

The downside is that you must ensure the areas that are being worked on are well-isolated. Otherwise, there will be a large number of conflicts when merging features together back into the MAIN branch. This only tends to be suitable for large code bases with a big team working on them. For smaller teams and codebases, the lack of isolation when implementing features, and the lack of resources to work on a particular feature, often mean that dealing with the problems of merging the code back together will offset productivity gains obtained from working in parallel.

That said, it is still sometimes useful to conduct a feature branch even in a small team when two or more developers must work on a particular feature that may be disruptive to the rest of the team during the development, or if there is a high risk associated with the feature being achievable and the developer(s) want to experiment in isolation from the rest of the team.

BASIC BRANCHING PLAN

So far, you have learned a lot of theory concerning branching and merging. You have learned what branching and merging are, and about some of the different branching models that you can implement.

Now, let's put some of this theory into action. This section and the next, "Advanced Branching Plan," discuss how to implement two different branching scenarios using Team Foundation Version Control.

Let's begin with a basic simple branching plan, which provides a good starting point for anyone who is new to branching.

Scenario

For this example, let's say that an organization has decided to install and use Team Foundation Server 2010 for version control needs. The organization has been reading a lot about software configuration management, best practices applicable to the use of version control, and has decided that it must implement some sort of branching strategy with Team Foundation Server 2010.

Currently, the development process in the organization is plagued by problems and inefficiency. Code is being checked in that has not been accurately tested, and there is usually a very lengthy process involved in releasing a version of an application, during which time everything is "frozen" and no one is allowed to make changes. This leads to developers who can't work on anything, which is very inefficient. This organization is hoping that, by implementing a good basic configuration management plan, it will be able to remove some of the inefficiencies from the process.

The Plan

Figure 20-5 shows the basic branching plan that the organization has decided to adopt.

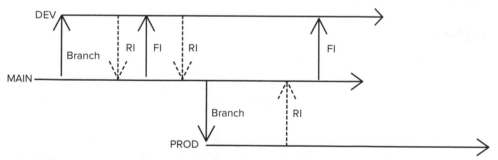

FIGURE 20-5

The following will be the three branches:

➤ MAIN — This is the MAIN line of the code, where all the testing and quality assurance will take place. As such, it must remain very stable. Nightly builds will be run against this branch, to ensure that no code has been checked in that breaks the MAIN line.

➤ DEV — This is a branch of the MAIN branch, which is used by the developers for writing code. Changes on the MAIN branch are forward-integrated (represented as FI in Figure 20-5) into this branch and, at certain milestones (such as the end of an iteration/sprint in an agile methodology), changes from the DEV branch are reverse-integrated (represented as RI) into the MAIN branch.

➤ PROD — This is the production/release branch. Once the code in the MAIN branch has reached a certain milestone, and it is time to release the application, this branch is created. This branch is where the final clean-up and stabilization of the code takes place. Once the release occurs, the branch is marked as read-only, and any changes made to the branch are reverse-integrated back into the MAIN branch.

Let's say that you have been hired to implement this process. You would start by creating the MAIN branch, and loading the existing code base (V1.0) into it. Next, you would branch that code base into the DEV branch. At that point, development work will begin in the DEV branch on V2.0. Developers will begin writing code, and checking it in and out.

At the end of the first iteration, there are no priority 1 bugs left in the DEV branch, and the code will be reverse-integrated (represented in Figure 20-5 as RI) back to the MAIN branch. The code is demonstrated to the project sponsor and real business users also use it. Any important bugs or minor changes based on feedback from the project sponsor that are found will be fixed in this branch. Once testing is completed, it is decided that this iteration is not ready for release yet until additional features (or user stories) have been implemented. All the changes from the MAIN branch are forward-integrated (represented in Figure 20-5 as FI) to the DEV branch, and development continues.

The next iteration is completed in the DEV branch and it is once again reverse-integrated back into the MAIN branch. More testing is performed, and the business decides that it is ready to be released. A new branch called PROD is created from the MAIN branch. In the PROD branch, any remaining issues are ironed out, and any show-stopping bugs are fixed. Once the code is ready, it is released. The PROD branch is set to read-only, and all the bug fixes and stabilization changes are reverse-integrated back into the MAIN branch. Those changes are then forward-integrated into the DEV branch, to be used as development begins on the next release.

Implementation

Now, let's see how to implement this scenario.

You would start off by creating a new team project in Team Foundation Server 2010. This will create an area in the version control system for storing your code. For this example, create a team project named MyProduct.

From within Team Explorer, double-click the Source Control icon to open the Source Control Explorer window. In the Source Control Explorer window, click the New Folder button and add a folder under the MyProduct team project called MAIN. You check in the source for V1.0 of your application (AcmeApp), and load it into the MAIN folder in version control. The easiest way to do this is to open the application in Visual Studio, right-click on the solution, and select "Add Solution to Version Control." A wizard will walk you through the process.

Once you have added the solution to the version control system, you must still check it in. To do this, you open the Pending Changes window, ensure that all your solution files are selected, and click the Check In button.

At this point, you have now added V1.0 of the application to the MAIN branch and the Source Control Explorer looks as shown in Figure 20-6.

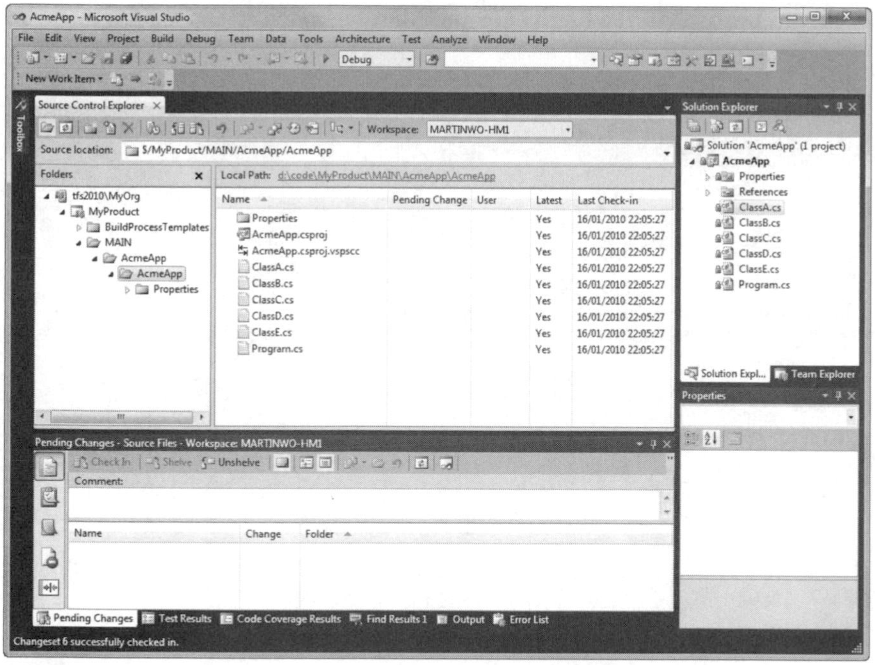

FIGURE 20-6

Before proceeding any further, you must tell Team Foundation Server 2010 which of these folders should be treated as branches. Right-click on the MAIN folder to view the options in the context menu, as shown in Figure 20-7.

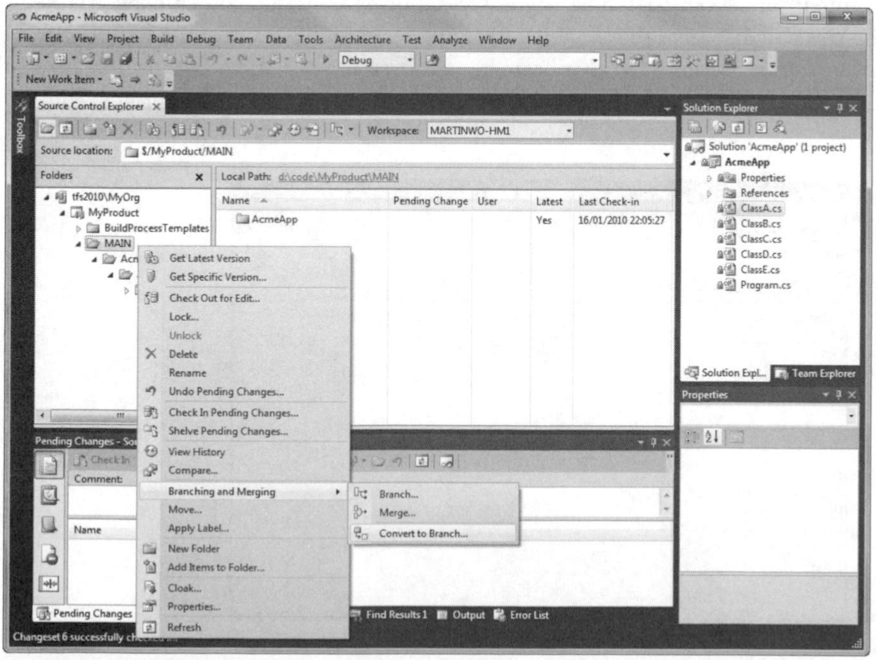

FIGURE 20-7

Selecting "Convert Folder to Branch" in the Branching and Merging menu opens the window shown in Figure 20-8.

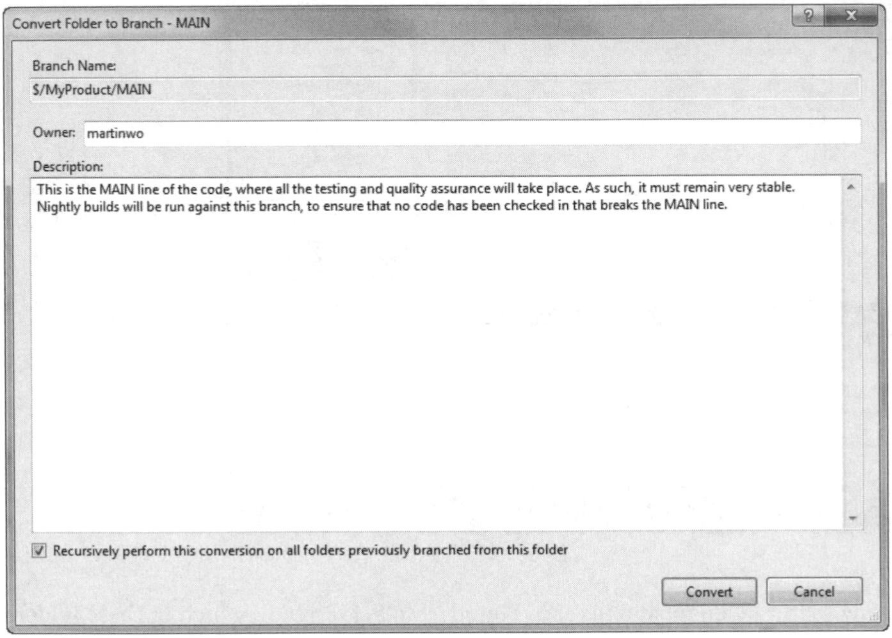

FIGURE 20-8

Branches in Team Foundation Server 2010 have owners. So, in this window, you can specify the owner of the branch. You can also give the branch a description (which is recommended). Click the Convert button, and the folder is converted to a branch, as shown in see Figure 20-9. You can see the folder icon has been changed to a branch icon, giving a visual indication that this is now a branch.

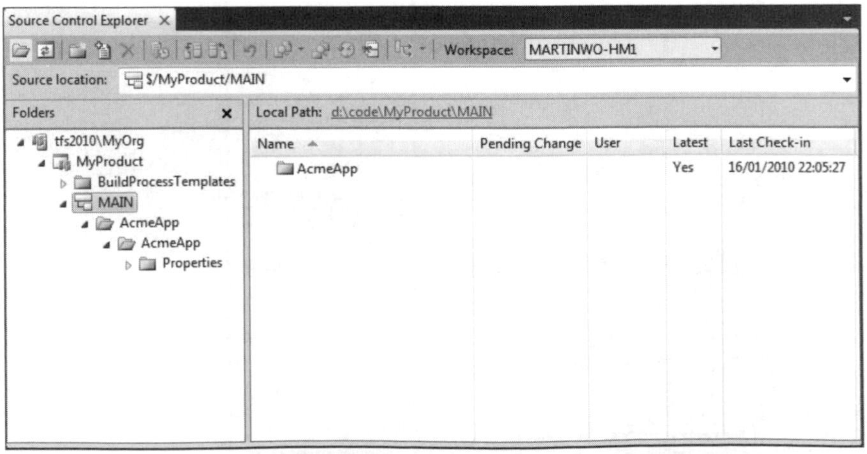

FIGURE 20-9

Now, to begin development on the first iteration of V2.0 of the application you take the V1.0 code from the MAIN branch, and create a DEV branch. You right-click on the MAIN branch and, from the context menu, select Branching and Merging ➪ Branch. This opens the Branching Wizard, shown in Figure 20-10.

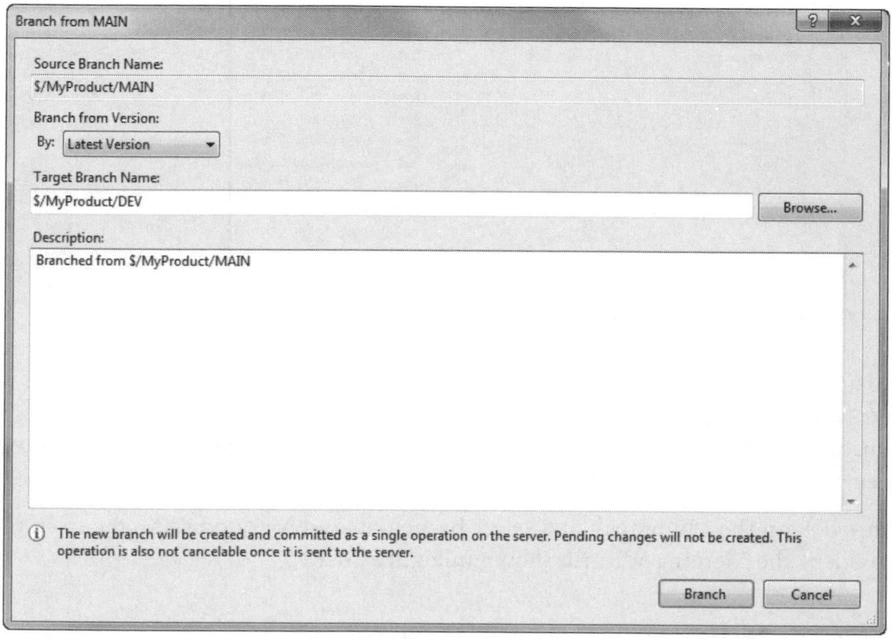

FIGURE 20-10

You want to branch by the latest version, which takes the latest version of the code from MAIN and branches it into DEV. You'll need to specify the target branch name as shown in the figure. The Description will default for you (as shown in the figure), but you should always add more description as to the purpose of your branch.

This description is used as the description of the branch, as well as the comment on the changeset when creating this branch in source control. Note that creating a branch in this way does all the work on the server in a single operation, which is very efficient — especially if you are branching a large code-base containing thousands of files. It does not create all the individual file branch operations on your machine, or download the new branch to your machine as part of this branch operation.

Figure 20-11 shows how things look in Source Control Explorer:

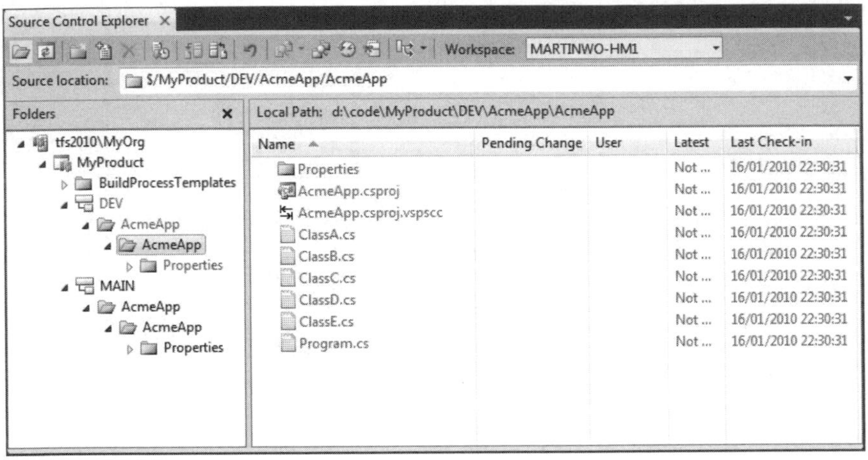

FIGURE 20-11

At this point, you are ready to begin work on your first iteration of the application. The developers get the code from the DEV branch and begin to make changes. At the end of the iteration, you now want to reverse-integrate changes back into the MAIN branch for testing.

To do this, you right-click on the DEV branch and select Branching and Merging ➪ Merge from the context menu. This opens the Merging Wizard, shown in Figure 20-12.

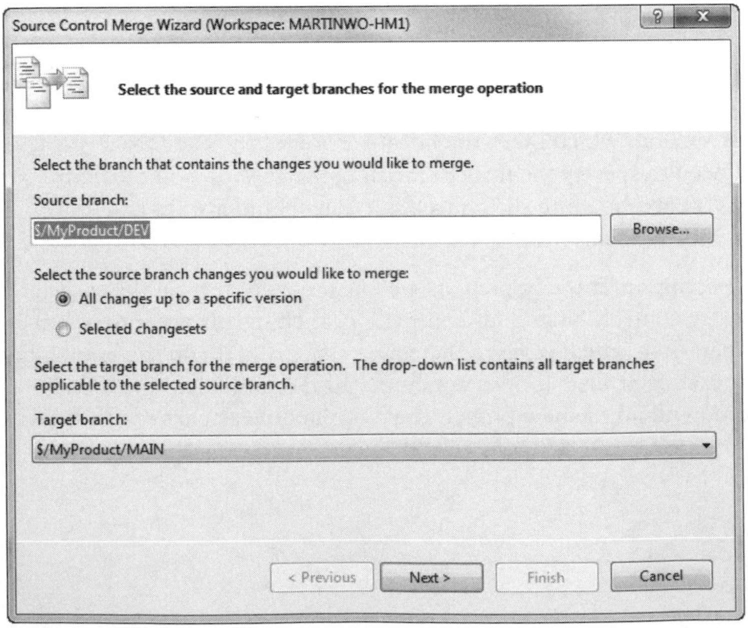

FIGURE 20-12

The "Source branch" contains the changes that you want to merge, in this case, the code from DEV. The "Target branch" contains the branch where you want to merge the changes. This drop-down box will default to the branch that DEV was created from, in this case, the MAIN branch. You can also choose whether to merge all the changesets up to a specific version or to merge just a selected range of changesets (called a *cherry-picked merge*).

You want to merge all the changes that were made so far, so you select the first radio button; then click the Next button. This takes you to the second page of the merge process (Figure 20-13).

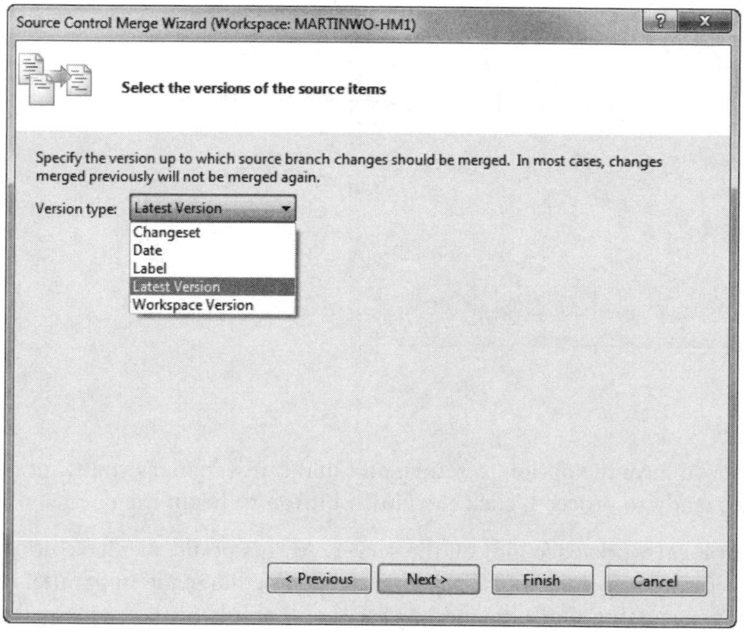

FIGURE 20-13

On this step of the wizard, you specify which version of "Source branch" changes should be merged into the "Target branch." You have several different options:

➤ *Changeset* — You can merge up to a specific changeset in the version control system.

➤ *Date* — You can merge all changes up to a particular date/time.

➤ *Label* — If you have applied labels to your code in the version control system, you can grab specific labels and merge the code associated with those labels.

➤ *Latest Version* — This gets the latest version of your code and merges it.

➤ *Workspace Version* — This takes the code at the version you have in your local workspace and merges it.

You want to merge all the code changes you have made so far, so you select Latest Version from the drop-down list, and click the Next button. This takes you to the final step of the wizard, which is a confirmation page (Figure 20-14).

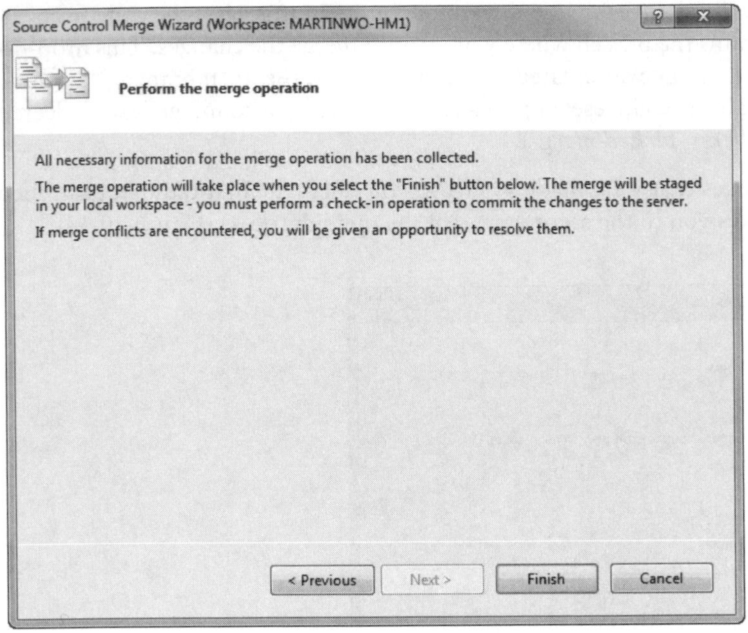

FIGURE 20-14

By clicking the Previous button, you have the option to return and make any changes you want to the merge process. Once you are ready to proceed, click the Finish button to begin the merge.

The merge itself happens in your local workspace, not on the server. At this point, you have no merge conflicts (because all the editing was done in the DEV branch — no edits made in parallel in the MAIN branch), so the merge is successful. Once the merge process is complete, all the merged changes are located on your local machine, in your workspace.

To finish the actual merge, you must check the merged changes in your workspace into version control. Figure 20-15 shows the Pending Changes window with the merged changes waiting to be checked in.

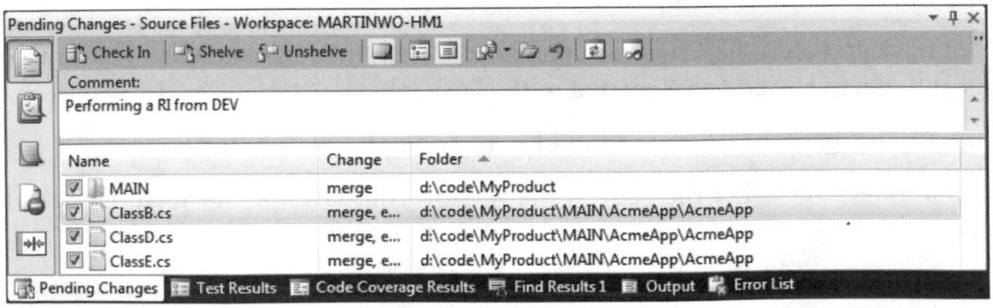

FIGURE 20-15

It is good practice to review the changeset with all the merges in place, and to compare the files with the latest version in version control for that file to ensure you are merging what you expect to. In addition, if you have a set of unit tests available, it is often useful to execute those to ensure that the system is working as expected, and will build correctly.

Because you can see from your source control history that all changes were made in the DEV branch and no parallel edits have been made in the MAIN branch, it is safe for you to check your merge in.

You click the Check In button in the pending changes view to check these merges into Team Foundation Version Control.

Once the code has been checked into the MAIN branch, you demo the application to your project sponsor and some business users. Some important bugs are found and the business users have feedback regarding wording in a particular area. These changes are made in the MAIN branch, and the business is suitably impressed about how responsive you are being to their needs. At the end of this phase, it is determined that more features are needed before you can release the product into production. All the bug fixes that have occurred in the MAIN branch must now be merged back into the DEV branch.

While the demo and associated changes were occurring in the MAIN branch, development continued on in the DEV branch. So, you can expect there to be some conflicts between the two branches that you must resolve as part of the merge process.

You start the merge process as you did previously, but this time, you select the MAIN branch, right-click on it, and select Branching and Merging ⇨ Merge. The Merge Wizard opens, as shown in Figure 20-16.

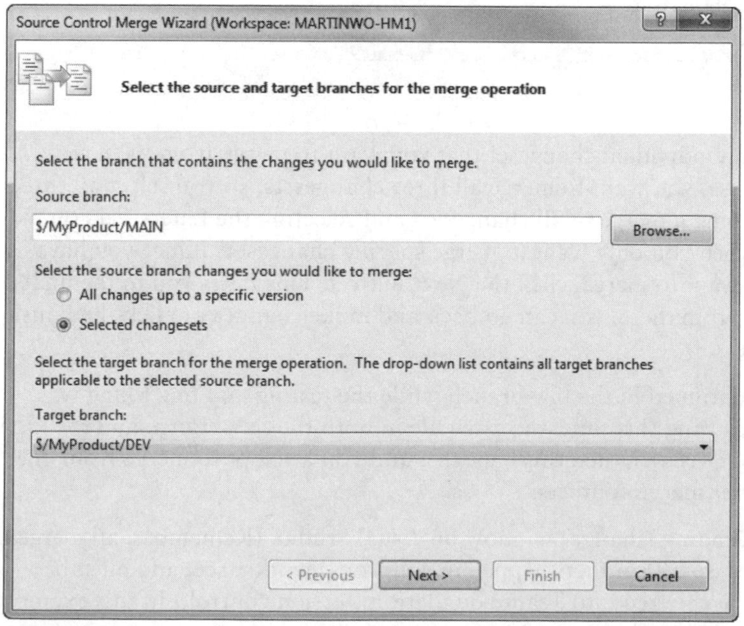

FIGURE 20-16

Notice how the source and target branches are different from the previous merge. For this merge, the source branch is the MAIN branch, while the target branch is the DEV branch. For this merge, you want to move a selected range of changesets (which represent the bug fixes) back into the DEV branch, so you select the "Selected changesets" radio button, and then click Next.

The Merge Wizard now shows a different second screen (Figure 20-17) from what it showed in the previous merge.

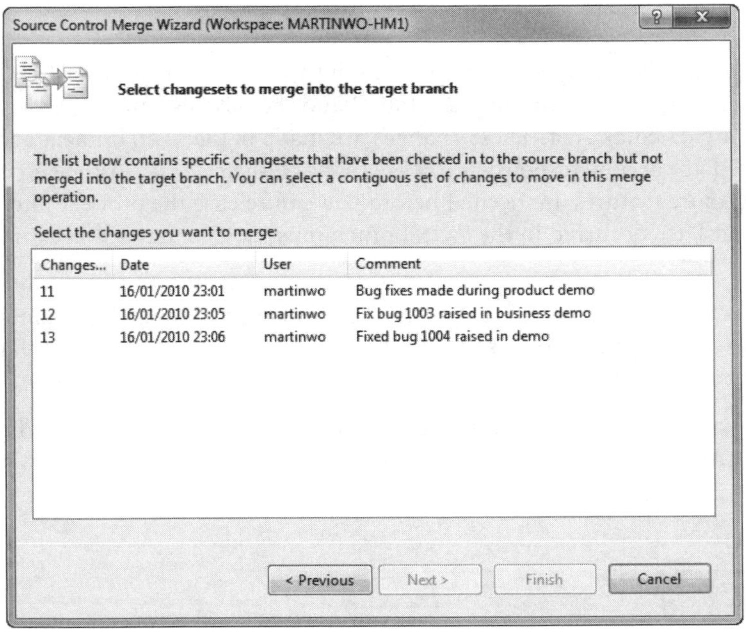

FIGURE 20-17

On this screen, you can select an individual changeset that you want to merge from MAIN to DEV, or a range of changesets. In this case, you want to merge all three changesets, so you select all three. This is, in effect, the same as doing a merge of all changesets and selecting the Latest Version. However, there will be times when you only want to merge specific changesets. Once you have selected all the changesets you want to merge, click the Next button. This takes you to the final window of the Merge Wizard. From there, you can go back and make changes or click the Finish button to start the merge process.

Remember, development has continued in the DEV branch while the testing and bug fixing was occurring in the MAIN branch. During this time, the same file in both the DEV branch and the MAIN branch has been modified (ClassA.cs). When this happens, and you attempt to merge from one branch to another, you encounter merge conflicts.

Merge conflicts appear in the Pending Changes window of Visual Studio. (Remember, all merges happen in your local workspace, so all conflicts happen in your local workspace, and must be resolved there before they can be checked into Team Foundation Version control.) In this example, you have one merge conflicts, as shown in Figure 20-18.

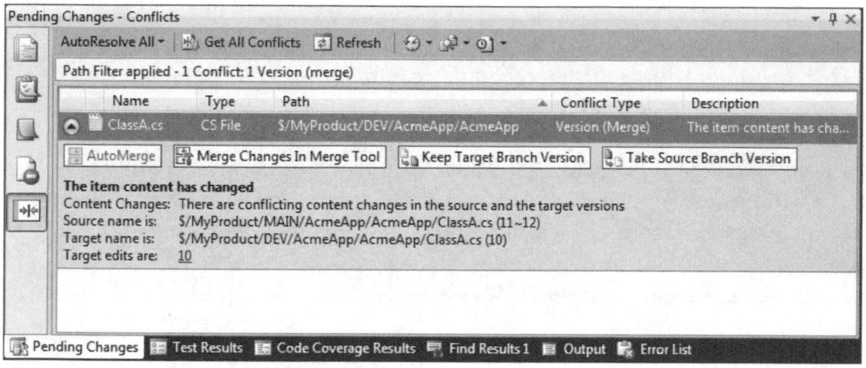

FIGURE 20-18

To resolve the conflict, you use the Merge Tool that comes with Visual Studio 2010. In the Pending Changes window, you click the "Merge Changes in Merge Tool" button. This opens the default merge tool, shown in Figure 20-19.

FIGURE 20-19

> As well as the one that ships with Visual Studio, there are a number of commercial, free, or Open Source diff/merge tools available that you may want to choose from. You can change the merge tool used by Visual Studio by going into the Options menu of Visual Studio. Go to Source Control ⇨ Visual Studio Team Foundation Server. Click the Configure User Tools button. You can then configure them in Visual Studio to use for compare (diff) or merge operations. You even choose to have different tools to use for different file types (as identified by their extensions).

Using the built-in merge tool, you can navigate to each conflict found in the file. Once you have analyzed the conflict, you select which version of the code to include in the final file by clicking on it in the upper-left or upper-right pane (or both, if you want both changes). You can even edit the resulting file directly in the merge tool if you need to. You can see the results of our merging process displayed in the bottom pane. Figure 20-20 shows the results of the merge.

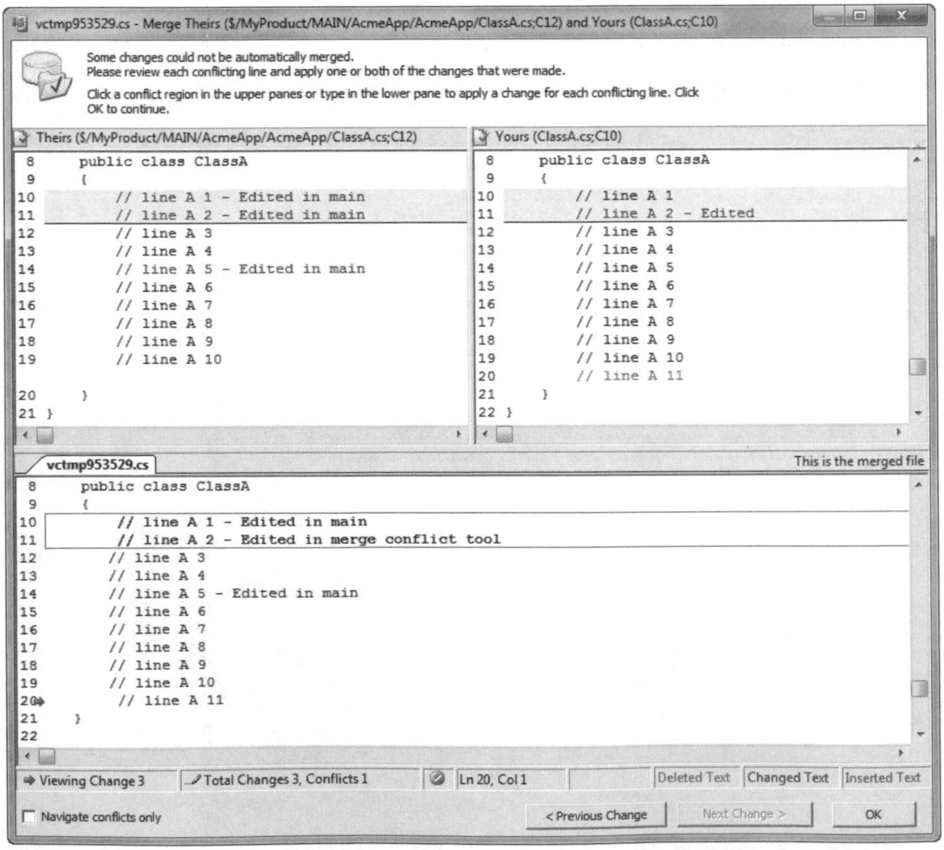

FIGURE 20-20

Once you are finished with the merges for this file, you click the OK button to save your changes and return to the Pending Changes window. As you resolve each conflict, they are removed from the Conflicts channel in the Pending Changes window.

In addition to using the merge tool, you have three other options for performing merges of this type of conflict:

➤ *AutoMerge* — If the changes in the two files can be merged into a single file without overwriting each other, the AutoMerge button will be enabled. Clicking this button will automatically merge the two files.

➤ *Keep Target Branch Version* — This will keep the version of the file from the target branch (in this case, the DEV branch).

➤ *Take Source Branch Version* — This will use the version of the file from the source branch (in this case, the MAIN branch)

Now you are finished resolving all the merge conflicts, you click the Check In button on the Pending Changes window to complete the merge process back to the DEV branch.

At this point, development continues in the DEV branch. Once the next iteration is finished, the code is merged back into the MAIN branch. Another round of testing and bug fixes occur in the MAIN branch, and it is decided that the product is ready to be released.

A new branch is created off the MAIN branch called PROD. Figure 20-21 shows the branching window from MAIN to PROD, and Figure 20-22 shows how things look in Source Control Explorer after the branching is complete.

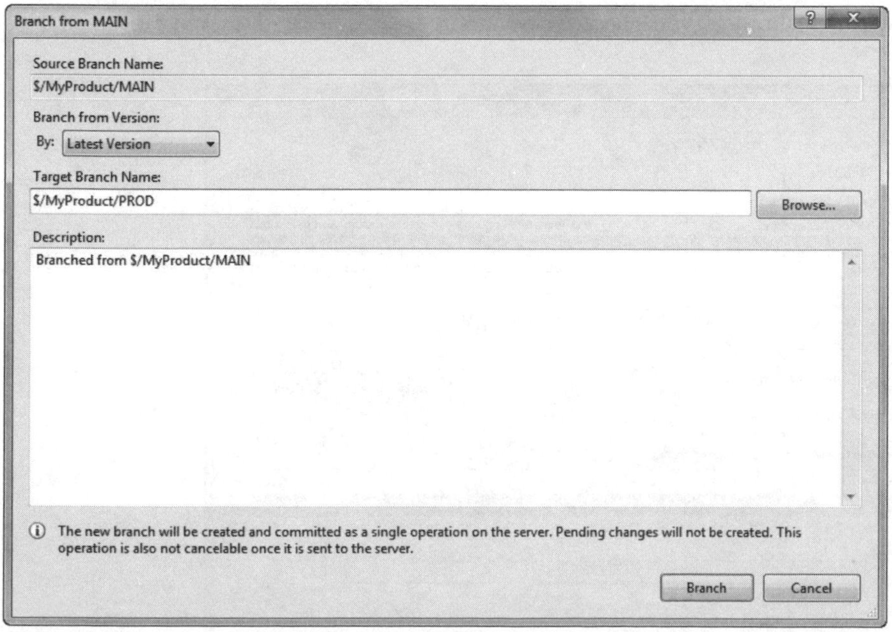

FIGURE 20-21

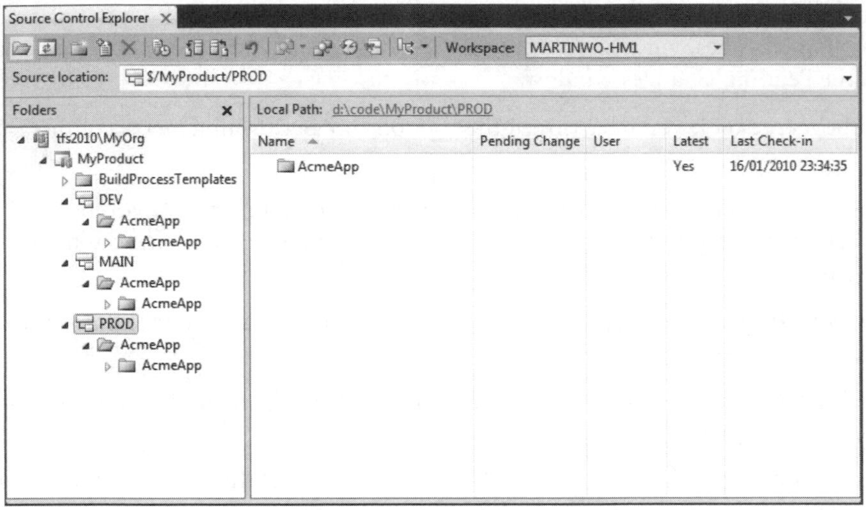

FIGURE 20-22

At this point, the code is stabilized in the PROD branch for release. Final show-stopping bugs are found and resolved. Finally, the code is ready to be released. At this point, all the bug fixes from the PROD branch are merged back into the MAIN branch, and then into the DEV branch, to be incorporated into the V3.0 development that is ongoing.

As a final step, the PROD branch is set to read-only to ensure that no one accidentally edits this code, and so that you always have an accurate representation of what code is running in production. You right-click on the PROD branch in Source Control Explorer and select Properties. This opens the Properties window for the branch. You select the permissions section, as shown in Figure 20-23.

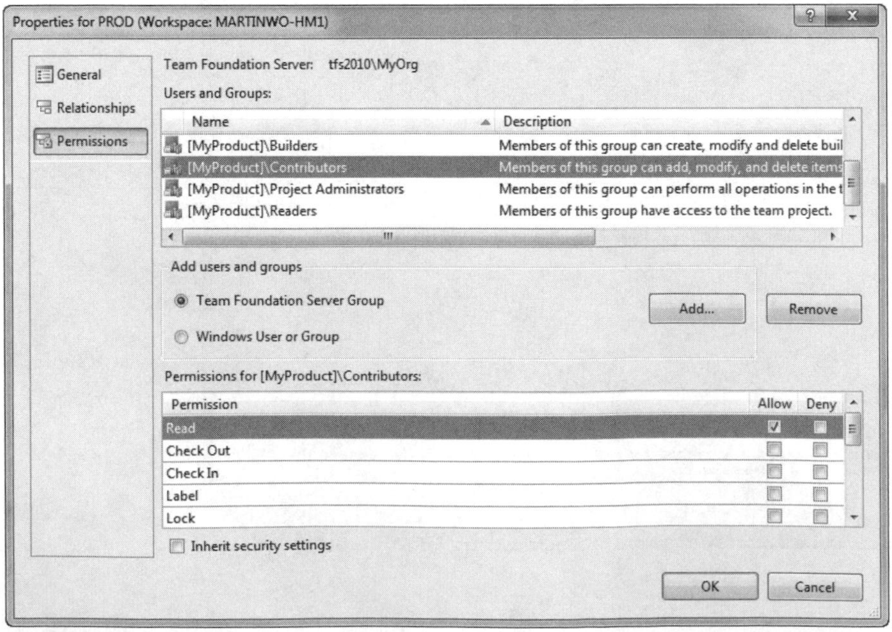

FIGURE 20-23

To make this branch read-only, you un-check the "Inherit security settings" check box on the bottom of the dialog. Then you select each group listed in the "Users and Groups" pane. In the Permission pane below, you remove all permissions, and then click Allow to set Read permissions.

> *Do not modify the permissions for the Team Project Collection Administrators. If you do, they won't be able to come back into this branch and turn off read-only permissions, if that were needed in the future.*

Let's take a quick look at how this branch structure would show using the new Branching Visualization features of Team Foundation Server 2010. You right-click on the MAIN branch, and select Branching and Merging ➪ View Hierarchy. The results are shown in Figure 20-24.

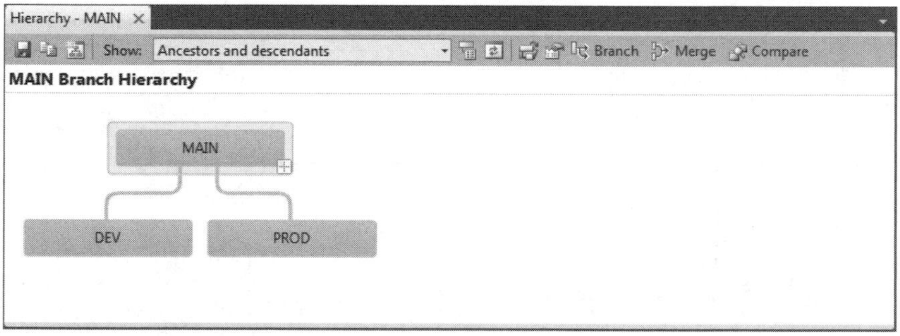

FIGURE 20-24

> *Note that you could have done your merge operations by drag/dropping one branch to the other in this view, which is often a more convenient and easy-to-remember way of ensuring that you have the correct Source and Target branches.*

ADVANCED BRANCHING PLAN

In the previous section, you saw how to implement a simple branching plan using Team Foundation 2010 Version Control. That plan will be more than satisfactory for a number of scenarios. But your organization may require a configuration management strategy that is more granular.

For example, in addition to just releasing your software, your organization may also create software patches for previously released versions of the application, while also working on the next version of the application. The basic branching plan presented previously does not lend itself to creating, integrating, and releasing these patches. What you need is a configuration management plan that is a little more advanced.

Scenario

For this example, let's say that an organization has decided to install and use Team Foundation Server 2010 for version control needs. The organization has past experience using a version control system, but is interested in using Team Foundation Server 2010 for its version control, work item tracking, and reporting capabilities. This organization releases software patches for its released software, while continuing development work on the next version of its product. The organization plans to implement a new branching strategy with the Team Foundation Server 2010 implementation to support this process.

The Plan

Figure 20-25 shows the basic branching plan that the organization has decided to adopt:

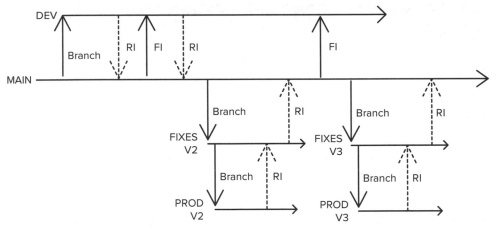

FIGURE 20-25

There will be four types of branches:

> MAIN — This is the MAIN line of the code, where all the testing and quality assurance will take place. As such, it must remain very stable. Nightly builds will be run against this branch, to ensure that no code has been checked in that breaks the MAIN line.

> DEV — This is a branch of the MAIN branch, which is used by the developers for writing code. Changes on the MAIN branch are forward-integrated into this branch, and, at certain milestones, changes from the DEV branch are reverse-integrated into the MAIN branch. The organization may create multiple DEV branches for different teams, or may decide to implement feature branching, or some other branching strategy, off the DEV branch.

> FIXES — This is a branch of the MAIN branch. Once the code in the MAIN branch has reached a milestone, and it is time to release the application, this branch is created, along with the PROD branch. Each version of the application (V1, V2, V3, and so on) will have

its own FIXES branch. This branch is where any software patches for this version of the application will be created. Those software patches can then be released from this branch and also integrated into the appropriate PROD branch, as well as the MAIN branch.

➤ PROD — This is a branch of the FIXES branch. Once the code in the MAIN branch has reached a milestone, and it is time to release the application, this branch is created, along with the FIXES branch. This branch is where the final clean-up and stabilization of the code takes place. Once the release occurs, the branch is marked as read-only, and any changes made to the branch are reverse-integrated back into the MAIN branch.

The organization starts by creating the MAIN branch, and loading the existing code base (V1.0) into it. Next, the organization branches that code base into the DEV branch. At that point, development work will begin in the DEV branch on V2.0. Developers will begin writing code and checking it in and out.

Once a stability milestone has been hit for V2.0 in the DEV branch, the code will be reverse-integrated (RI) back to the MAIN branch. Testing will be performed on the code in the MAIN branch, and any bugs that are found will be fixed in this branch. Once testing is completed, it is decided that V2.0 is not ready for release yet. All the bug fixes from the MAIN branch are forward-integrated (FI) to the DEV branch, and development continues.

Once the DEV branch hits another milestone for V2.0, it once again reverse-integrates its changes back to the MAIN branch. More testing is performed, and it is decided that V2.0 is ready to be released. Two new branches are now created: FIXES (which branches from the MAIN branch) and PROD (which branches from the FIXES branch).

In the PROD branch, the code is stabilized and any show-stopping bugs are fixed. Once the code is ready, it is released. The PROD branch is set to read-only, and all the bug fixes and stabilization changes are reverse-integrated back into the FIXES and MAIN branch. Those changes are then forward-integrated into the DEV branch, to be used as V3.0 begins development.

As fixes are needed to the V2.0 release, those fixes are created and released in the FIXES branch (remember, the PROD branch has been set to read-only now). Those fixes are then integrated back into the MAIN and DEV branches.

Implementation

The implementation of this plan is very similar to the implementation of the basic plan, but combined with elements of the Branch By Release model and Code Promotion model. In this implementation, you have the addition of the FIXES branch between the MAIN branch and the PROD branch. Just remember, when you are ready to create a production release, create a branch from MAIN to FIXES, and then a branch from FIXES to PROD. This will preserve the branch hierarchy for this configuration management strategy.

Merges may be performed from parent to child and child to parent — one up, one down. If you accidentally created the PROD branch from the MAIN branch, then, to merge changes from FIXES to PROD, you would first have to go via the MAIN branch. By creating PROD as a branch of FIXES, you can work as per your plan.

SUMMARY

As you can see from this chapter, software configuration management, and branching and merging strategies, can become very complex, depending on the needs of the organization. This chapter familiarized you with software configuration management and defined the different terms related to configuration management. Next, the chapter examined some of the different branching and merging strategies that are in use today.

The discussion then moved on to show how to implement a basic branching strategy using Team Foundation Server 2010 and how to use the tools provided with Team Foundation Server and Visual Studio to perform branch and merge operations. Also discussed was a slightly more complex branching strategy, showing that you can create hybrid branching models to meet the needs of your organization from the basic branch strategies outlined at the beginning of the chapter.

Chapter 21 examines how you ensure the code quality of each of these branches via the use of the build automation tools provided by Team Foundation Server 2010.

21

Team Foundation Build

WHAT'S IN THIS CHAPTER?

➤ Getting to know build automation

➤ Introducing Team Foundation Build

➤ Looking at what's new in Team Foundation Server 2010

➤ Understanding the Team Foundation Build architecture

➤ Working with Builds

➤ Understanding the Team Build process

➤ Customizing the Team Build process

This chapter examines the build automation capabilities of Team Foundation Server — what is provided out-of-the-box, how to use it, and how to customize it to suit your organizational requirements. But first let's take a quick look at build automation in general.

After version control, automating the build is the second most important thing you can do to improve the quality of your software.

Only once the parts of your application come together, can you tell if your application works and does what it is supposed to. Assembling the parts of an application is often a complex, time-consuming, and error-prone process. There are so many parts to building the application that without an automated build, the activity usually falls to one or two individuals on the team who know the secret. Without an automated build, even they sometimes get it wrong, with show-stopping consequences that are often discovered very late, making any mistakes expensive to fix.

Imagine having to recall an entire manufacturing run of a DVD because you missed an important file. Worse still, imagine accidentally including the source code for your application in a Web distribution, or leaving embarrassing test data in the application when it was deployed to production. All these things made headlines when they happened to organizations building software, yet they could have easily been avoided.

Integration of software components is the difficult part. Teams work on their features in isolation, making various assumptions about how other parts of the system function. Only once the parts are assembled together do the assumptions get tested. If you integrate early and often, these integrations get tested as soon as possible in the development process — therefore reducing the cost of fixing the inevitable issues.

It should be trivial for everyone involved in the project to run a copy of the latest build. Only then can you tell if your software works and does what it is supposed to. Only then can you tell if you are going to have your product ready on time. A regular, automated build is the heartbeat of your team.

In Visual Studio 2010, a developer is usually able to run his or her application by pressing the infamous F5 key to run the code in debug mode. This assembles the code together on the local workstation and executes it. This makes it trivial for the developer to test his or part of the code base. But what it doesn't do is ensure that the code works with all the latest changes committed by other members of the team. In addition, pressing the F5 key simply compiles the code ready for manual testing. As part of an automated build, you can also run full a suite of automated tests, giving you a high degree of confidence that no changes that have been introduced have broken something elsewhere.

Pressing the F5 key is easy for a developer. You want your automated build to make it just as easy to run your application — if not easier.

TEAM FOUNDATION BUILD

Build automation is so important to the quality of the software development process that Visual Studio Team Foundation Server 2010 provides build services as part of the core platform, as shown in Figure 21-1.

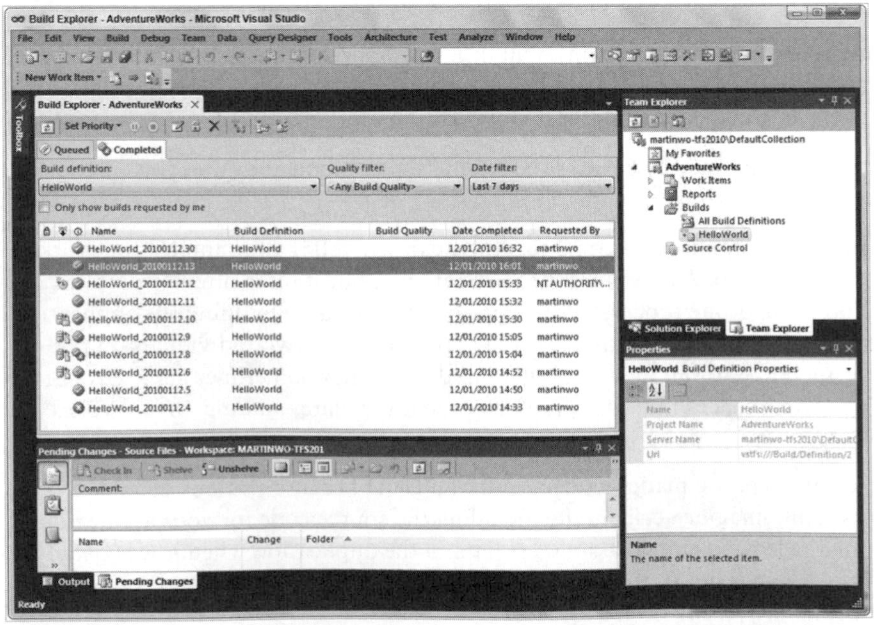

FIGURE 21-1

> *Chapter 17 provides more information on the other services offered by Team Foundation Server (including version control, work item tracking, and reporting).*

The build services provided by Team Foundation Server offer an enterprise-class, distributed build platform. Utilization of the build services is done inside the development environment in which the code is being created (either in Visual Studio or Eclipse). Information on the build services is tightly integrated with the version control, work item tracking, and the testing features provided by Team Foundation Server.

In addition, data obtained from the build system is fed into the Team Foundation Server data warehouse, thus allowing for the analysis of historical reports and trends. The build services provide notifications on build events using the standard Team Foundation Server eventing mechanisms, which means that email alerts can easily be sent to the team regarding build status. As part of the standard installation in Visual Studio 2010, the Build Notification Tool is installed alongside Visual Studio, which can provide the capability for additional build notifications via the application that runs in the system notification area.

Team Foundation Server provides a number of ways to trigger the build. Builds may be started by a manual request, automatically triggered by a check-in into Team Foundation Server version control, or run on a specified schedule. Team Foundation Server 2010 also introduces a new concept called gated check-ins. A gated check-in means that a developer's changes must successfully build on the build server when merged with the latest code from version control before the code is then checked in on behalf of the user.

Team Foundation Build also has a full .NET-based API. This is the same API used by the Visual Studio integration and the build notification tool. It provides you with deep integration into the build services. Combined with the build events, there is a highly extensible platform to integrate any additional systems that you can imagine.

BRIAN THE BUILD BUNNY

Some integrations with Team Foundation Server are more imaginative than others. A popular way of encouraging the team to pay attention to the current state of the build is to create creative and eye-catching build status notification mechanisms. While wall displays and lava lamps are a popular way of communicating this information to the team, one of the authors of this book has even gone so far as to connect a talking, moving robot rabbit into Team Foundation Server. For more information on this project (including a prize-winning YouTube video and full source code), see http://www.woodwardweb.com/gadgets/brian_the_build_1.html.

WHAT'S NEW IN TEAM FOUNDATION BUILD 2010

The build services offered by Team Foundation Server have been changed significantly since the initial version in Team Foundation Server 2005.

In the first version, Team Foundation Build was based heavily on MSBuild, along with a build server machine called the *build agent*. All configuration of the build was done by editing files stored in version control.

In the 2008 release, build management was greatly improved with the capability to trigger builds automatically, queue builds, and manage builds. This second version introduced the Build Definition as a Team Foundation Server entity in its own right that contained various configuration data about the build (such as the build name, workspace definition, default build agent, drop location, and build trigger). The file describing how to do the build (the TFSBuild.proj file) was still based on MSBuild.

The 2010 release continues much of the work done in 2008, with some notable changes that include the following:

- ➤ Windows Workflow 4.0
- ➤ Gated check-ins
- ➤ Private builds
- ➤ Build notifications
- ➤ Build controller
- ➤ Properties exposed for common customizations
- ➤ Integration with symbol and source server
- ➤ Enhanced build deletion options

Windows Workflow 4.0

MSBuild is a great language for compiling and managing build dependencies, but has many limitations when used as the language to manage the entire build process. Because of the use of dependency trees between the MSBuild targets, if you want to work out what actually happens in an MSBuild script, you must follow the full dependency tree backward, rather than reading the code from top to bottom, like you can with a regular programming or scripting language.

Also, there is no way to conduct MSBuild targets in parallel over multiple machines and wait for the results from all those targets to finish before moving to the next step. With Windows Workflow, you have the advantages of being able to read from top to bottom (Figure 21-2), being able to parallelize work across multiple machines, and having a good visual editing experience.

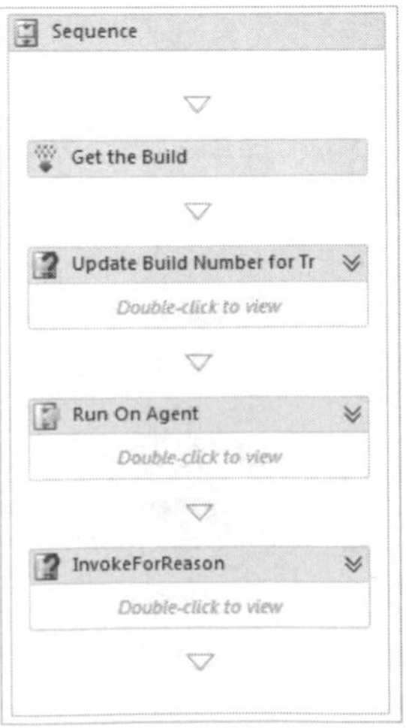

FIGURE 21-2

MSBuild is not completely dispensed with, however. For example, when compilation is required, MSBuild is invoked by the Windows Workflow. For builds created in a Visual Studio 2008 client, or builds that existed while performing a server upgrade, the Windows Workflow process is simply a thin wrapper around the existing MSBuild file (`TFSBuild.proj`).

Gated Check-ins

As previously discussed, having a frequent automated build is one of the most important things you can do to improve your software development process. The key is to ensure that the latest code in your repository always compiles and runs, and that it passes any associated automated tests. Once you have your working build, the team must ensure that it stays good.

For very large teams, this can be an issue. Imagine that a good developer might check something in that breaks the build once a year. If you have 500 people working on code bases, you quickly get into a situation where the build is breaking twice a day, every day. In these circumstances, configuring a build as a gated check-in may help.

A *gated check-in* means that, rather than checking the code in to version control, the code is submitted as a shelveset. The build server then takes the latest code, merges that with the changes contained in your shelveset, and performs the build. If the build is successful, the changes in your shelveset will be checked in automatically on your behalf by the build server.

> *Chapter 19 provides more information on shelvesets. For more information on gated check-ins, see the discussion in "Trigger Section," later in this chapter.*

Private Builds

To prevent the checking in of changes that would fail the build, it is a best practice to perform a get-latest before checking the code in, and then building and testing on the developers' machines to ensure that the code still works as expected. There are times, however, when developers may want to test that their changes work on the build server as well as just locally — for example, if they are checking in a change to the installer that is created as part of the build, or perhaps the developer needs a signed binary to test and the code signing certificates are only installed on the build machine.

Thankfully, *private builds* enable you to manually queue a build. But, at the time the build is queued, rather than building with the latest version of the source, you can build with the latest version of the source, merged with the shelveset that you create. These types of *private builds* sometimes also go by the name "buddy builds," especially inside Microsoft.

In this way, a private build is similar to a gated check-in, only the code is not automatically checked in as part of the build, nor is building in this manner enforced.

Build Controller

In Team Foundation Server 2005 and Team Foundation Server 2008, builds were performed on a single machine — the *build agent*. For a particular build definition, you could specify a default build agent. However, this did not allow for the build to be assigned to a pool of agents or for the build to be performed over multiple machines. This is solved in Team Foundation Server 2010 by introducing a new level of abstraction — the *build controller.*

Build controllers are allocated to Project Collections, and a default controller is given to a build definition. Multiple build agents can then be assigned to the build controller, and, by default, the controller will send new builds to the least-busy agent in the pool.

Build Notifications

Previously available as a power tool in Team Foundation Server 2008, the *build notification* application is now included in the main product as part of the installation of the Microsoft Team Explorer. This application runs in the system notification tray, and can be configured to notify you of build events (such as passed or failed builds).

Properties Exposed for Common Customizations

The new Windows Workflow-based build has also allowed for properties used to customize the build to be exposed in the user interface when creating a build definition or when queuing a new build. Also, additional properties have been introduced to control behavior that previously would have required extensive customization of the build process (such as custom build number formatting), as shown in Figure 21-3.

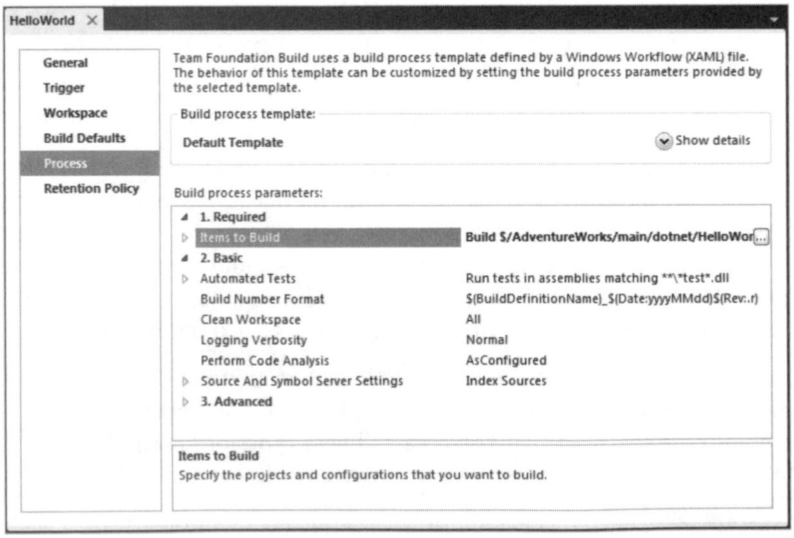

FIGURE 21-3

Integration with Symbol and Source Server

The default build process in Team Foundation Server 2010 includes a step to index source code and publish symbols to a symbol server in the organization.

A *symbol server* is simply a file share that is used to store the symbols for your executable binaries. Visual Studio can then be configured with details of this server. From then on, when debugging code live or using the advanced historical debugging features, Visual Studio is able to take you directly to the version of the source code from which the binary was generated, regardless of which version of the code that you have on your local system at that time. The configuration of the symbol server is performed by adding the symbol server details as a process parameter on the build configuration.

Enhanced Build Deletion Options

In previous versions of Team Foundation Server, when the build was deleted, all details of the build were removed, as well as the binaries, from the drop location. In Team Foundation Server 2010, you are now presented with a number of options for the data you wish to delete with the build (Figure 21-4), bringing build deletion more in line with deletion in version control.

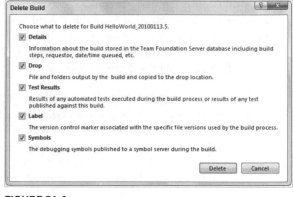

FIGURE 21-4

TEAM FOUNDATION BUILD ARCHITECTURE

As shown in Figure 21-5, several logical components are used as part of the Team Foundation Build services.

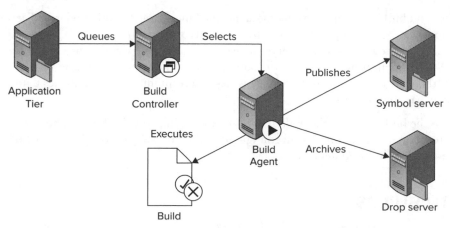

FIGURE 21-5

When a build is triggered, the Application tier sends a request to a server called the *build controller* using the Web services hosted by the build service to queue the build. The controller then downloads the build's Windows Workflow-based process and executes it. By default, this is then allocated to the next available build agent in the controller's pool of agents.

The *build agent* is the machine that actually executes the main portion of the build process as coded in the build's workflow — including calling MSBuild to perform the actual compilation step. It then archives the build results (that is, your executable binaries or your Web site) to a Windows file share provided as the *drop location*, and publishes symbols to the symbol server (if configured).

The build controller and the build agent services are provided by the Visual Studio Team Foundation Build service host installed from the Team Foundation Server installation media. IIS is not required on the build controller or build agent machines because the build service host uses the Windows Communication Framework (WCF) to host the Web services. The build controller and build agent are configured using the Team Foundation Server Administration Tool.

> *For information on how to install and configure the Team Foundation Server Build service, see the Team Foundation Server Installation Guide. The guide is included in the install media for Team Foundation Server. However, the latest version is published at* `http://go.microsoft.com/fwlink/?LinkId=127730`. *Microsoft continues to update the guide download to include extra guidance or any new issues that surface. Therefore, it is always worth working from the downloaded version.*
>
> *After you download the installation guide, you cannot view its contents unless you right-click the* `.chm` *file, click Properties, and then click Unblock. As an alternative, you can double-click the* `.chm` *file to open the Open File-Security Warning dialog box, clear the "Always ask before opening this file" check box, and then click Open.*

The build controller and build agent may live on the same machine as the Team Foundation Server Application tier. However, because a build is typically very CPU and disk I/O intensive, the build agent should at least be located on a separate server to avoid affecting the performance of the main Team Foundation Server application. If you run the build agent on the same machine as Team Foundation Server, this may cause some performance issues if certain intensive diagnostics data collectors are used as part of the build.

The actual details of the build (such as the build name, what to build, when to build it, how to build it, and what to do with the results) are all configured in the *build definition*. The results of individual builds are called the *build details*.

WORKING WITH BUILDS

This section examines working with team builds in Visual Studio. Figure 21-6 shows the key windows that you will need to use.

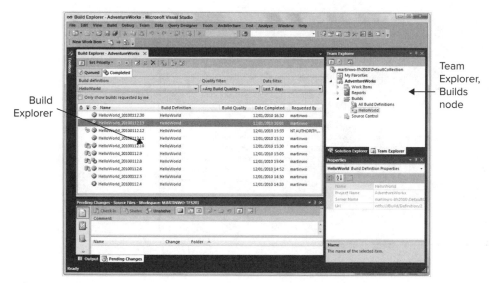

FIGURE 21-6

Team Explorer

You should already be familiar with the Team Explorer view (accessed in Visual Studio through View ⇨ Team Explorer).

Team Explorer contains a Builds node that provides you with access to all the functionality you need to interact with the build services in Team Foundation Server. Right-clicking on the Builds node in Team Explorer enables you to create a build and provides you with additional functionality that will be discussed later in this chapter. Listed under the Builds node are all the defined build definitions for that team project. Double-clicking on one of these will open the Build Explorer for that build definition.

Build Explorer

The Build Explorer view (accessed in Visual Studio through Build ⇨ View Builds) enables you to see all the builds that are currently executing (or awaiting execution) in the Queued tab, and those that have run on the system in the Completed tab.

Queued Builds

From the Queued tab of the Build Explorer (Figure 21-7), you can pause or change the priority of builds that are currently awaiting execution. You can also cancel paused builds or stop builds that are currently executing.

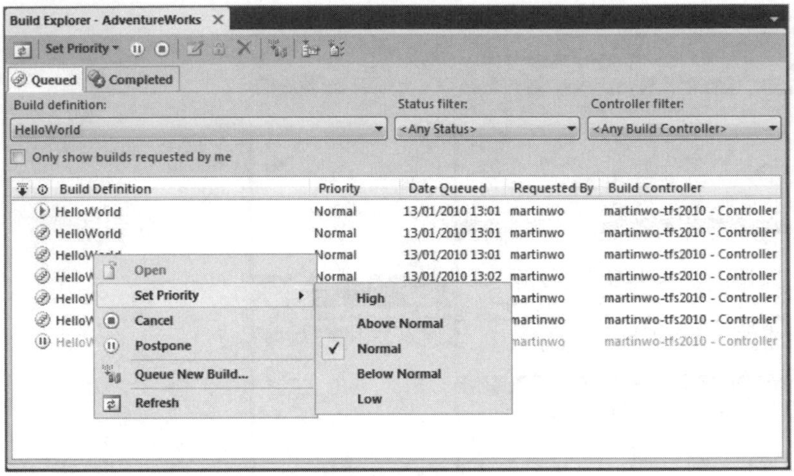

FIGURE 21-7

Completed Builds

From the Completed tab of the Build Explorer (Figure 21-8), you can view the build details, delete the build details, or set the quality of the build.

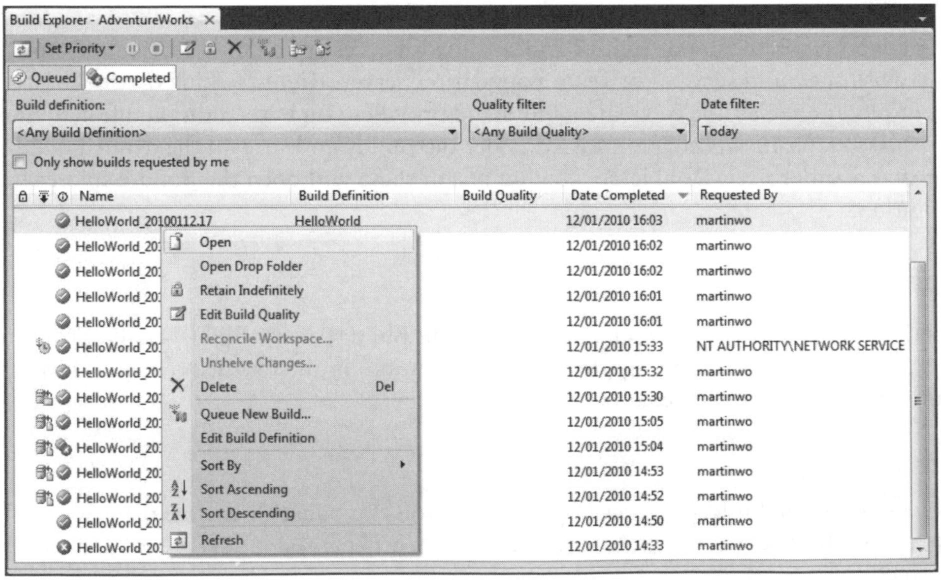

FIGURE 21-8

The *build quality* is a text string allocated to particular builds to denote the quality of that particular build (that is, "Released," "Ready for Test," and so on). In addition, you may mark the build with Retain Indefinitely to exclude it from any automatic retention policies on the build definition. You also have the option to Reconcile Workspace with the build, which is useful for a gated or private build because it will remove any pending changes that you may still have that were checked in on your behalf as part of the build.

Build Details View

When you double-click on a build in the Build Explorer, you see a report of the build details, as shown in Figure 21-9.

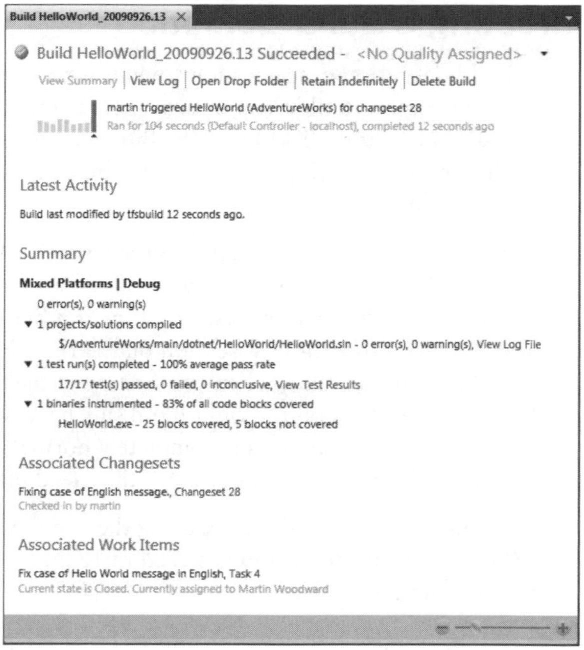

While the build is executing, the build details view shows the build log, and it periodically refreshes automatically to show the latest results of the build. A small bar chart in the top left-hand corner displays the currently executing build time against previous builds, which can give you an indication of how long the build might run.

FIGURE 21-9

As the build progresses, more information is added to the build log. The information forms a hierarchical tree, and the duration of each completed step is displayed in the top right-hand side. For steps that create additional log files (such as calling MSBuild to perform the actual compilation of the code), you are able to click on the report to download it from the drop location and view it inside Visual Studio.

Once the build has completed, you will see the build summary view showing all the projects, compilations, tests runs, as well as any unit test results, code coverage, or test impact data. You will also see information regarding the changesets included in the build since the last successful build of that build definition, along with any work items associated with those changesets when they were checked in.

In this way, you can start to see how full requirements traceability is obtained in Team Foundation Server, from the requirement being logged as a work item through to the development task to implement the requirement, to the change in source code to implement that task, and then, finally, the build of the software that includes that check-in. All the data is passed into the Team Foundation Server data warehouse to allow historical trend analysis and reporting.

From the build details view, you are able to open the drop folder in Windows Explorer to access the outputs of your build. You may modify the build quality assigned to that build, mark it to be retained indefinitely, or delete the build and associated results.

Creating a Build Definition

A build definition describes how, what, when, and where to perform your build. You create a new team build definition by right-clicking on the Builds node in Team Explorer, and selecting New Build Definition, as shown in Figure 21-10.

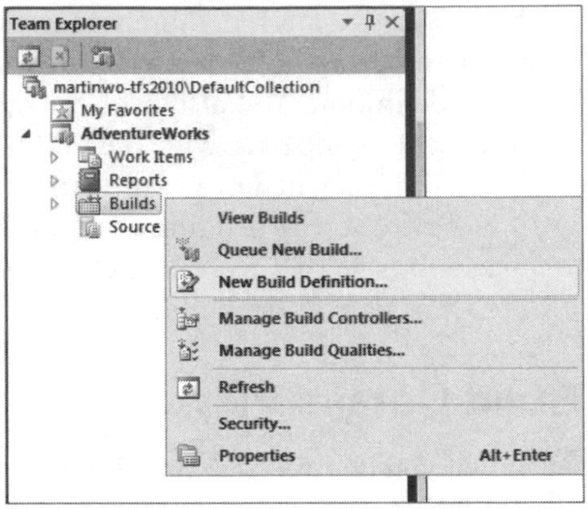

You then see a new build definition form inside Visual Studio. The form is split into two parts — a set of areas on the left-hand side that basically function like tabs, and the main area for that section on the right-hand side. You'll notice that, when you first open the dialog, a few of the sections on the right-hand side have warnings associated with them, this is completely normal. These

FIGURE 21-10

warnings are just to highlight areas that need information before the definition can be saved.

You can save the definition by using the usual mechanisms (File ➪ Save, or Ctrl+S, and so on). When saved, the definition is stored in Team Foundation Server, and will appear in the Builds node for all team members.

General Section

First, you must click to bring up the General section. Then you must give the build definition a name, and, optionally, a description, as shown in Figure 21-11. Note that, in current versions of Team Foundation Server, builds may not be organized into a hierarchy — but are simply listed alphabetically. Therefore, you might want to adopt a naming convention for your build definitions if you have multiple build definitions in your team project.

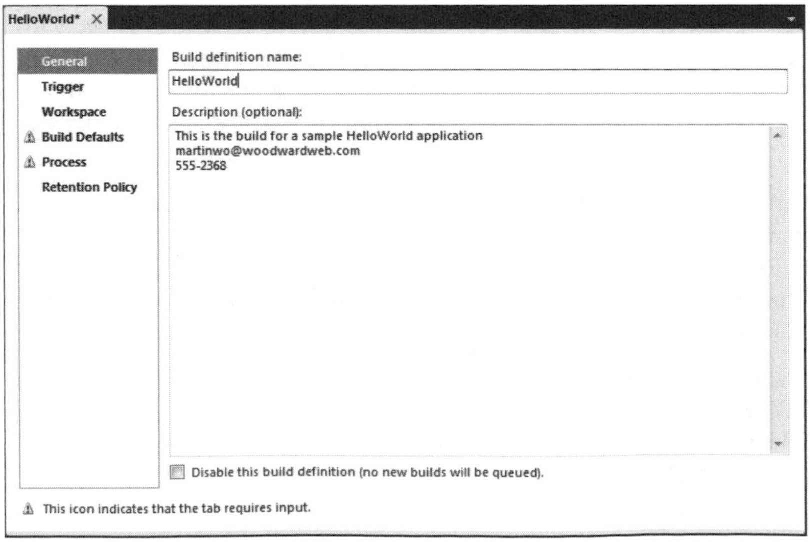

FIGURE 21-11

For the description of your project, you should provide a short, one-line summary of what the build is for, and contact details for the owner or "build master" for the build. The first three lines of the build description are displayed in other dialogs in Team Foundation Server before scrolling is required. Therefore, this important information should be placed at the top so that people working with the builds can see what the build is for and who to contact for questions.

Trigger Section

Located in the Trigger section, the build trigger tells Team Foundation Server *when* to perform a build. As shown in Figure 21-12, there are a number of triggers available, including the following:

➤ Manual

➤ Continuous Integration

➤ Rolling Builds

➤ Gated Check-in

➤ Schedule

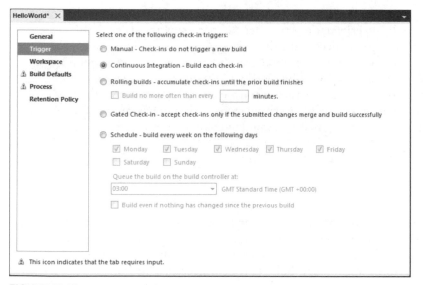

FIGURE 21-12

Manual

When you configure a build for a Manual trigger, the build will only run when explicitly queued, by using the user interface, by using the command line (that is, `tfsbuild.exe`), or by using the Team Foundation Server .NET object model. Manually triggered builds were the only option available in Team Foundation Server 2005.

Continuous Integration

In Team Foundation Server, the Continuous Integration trigger is one that queues a build for every check-in performed on the areas of code that you define as related to your build. (The "Workspace" section, later in this chapter, provides more information on defining those areas.)

Check-ins to Team Foundation Server are a discrete, atomic transaction represented by a changeset. By re-building the system for every changeset, you can easily determine which change broke the build (as well as who checked in that change). The downside to this is that there are, obviously, a lot of builds performed. Therefore, it is essential that build times are kept short to ensure rapid and frequent feedback to the development team as to the status of the current code base.

MARTIN FOWLER ON CONTINUOUS INTEGRATION

The term *continuous integration (CI)* emerged from agile software development methodologies such as Extreme Programming (XP) at the turn of the millennium. Martin Fowler's paper on continuous integration from 2000 is still worth reading today at `http://www.martinfowler.com/articles/continuousIntegration .html`.

Note that, as originally described, the term refers to increasing the speed and quality of software delivery by decreasing the integration times, and not simply the practice of performing a build for every check-in. Many of the practices expounded by Fowler's paper are supported by tooling in Visual Studio 2010 Team Foundation Server — not simply this one small feature of the build services. However, the term "continuous integration" has come to be synonymous with building after a check-in has occurred and is, therefore, used by Team Foundation Server as the name for this type of trigger.

Rolling Builds

Rolling Builds are similar to the Continuous Integration trigger in that a check-in will trigger a build. However, rather than building on every check-in, rolling builds will batch several check-ins together to ensure that the build server never becomes backlogged — and optionally setting a minimum time interval between which a new build may be triggered. This is the type of trigger that may be familiar to those who have experience with the Open Source build servers CruiseControl and CruiseControl.NET.

Performing rolling builds has the advantage of reducing the number of builds performed, which helps to reduce the number of builds queued at peak times (and, therefore, the time before the results of an individual developer's check-ins are known). However, it has the disadvantage of grouping changes together, therefore making it more difficult to determine the check-in responsible for the build failure. For this reason, many people stick with the Continuous Integration trigger, and instead focus efforts on increasing the speed of the build or the number of build agents available to perform the build.

Gated Check-in

A Gated Check-in trigger means that check-ins to the areas of version control covered by the build are not allowed by the server until a build has been performed and passed successfully. This means that when users attempt to check in a file, they are presented with the dialog shown in Figure 21-13.

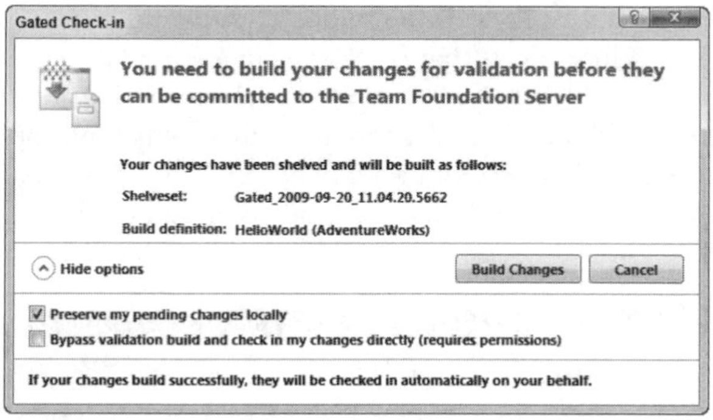

The changes are stored as a shelveset in version control. The build server takes the shelved changes and merges those changes with the latest version of code from version

FIGURE 21-13

control before performing the build. In the event of a successful build, the changes are then checked into the build server, and the user is notified via the build notification tool in the system notification area. At this point, the user may "reconcile" his or her workspace to remove the pending changes that were committed as part of the build from the current pending changes list.

Because of the automatic merge process that is performed by the build server, it is important to realize that the actual code committed by the gated check-in may differ from the code submitted as part of the shelveset.

If you have two build definitions with overlapping workspace mappings that both have Gated Check-in triggers, the user will get to pick which one gets built to verify his or her changes at the time of check-in. In addition, even though Team Foundation Server 2010 has build agent pooling features, only one build of a gated check-in may be executed at a time to prevent conflicting merges from being submitted.

Schedule

Builds may be triggered by a particular schedule — that is, a daily or nightly build. Note that a single time may be specified for each build definition for the chosen days of the week — repeated weekly. Also note that, in the case of a nightly build, the build time should be set outside of any backup or other regular maintenance jobs.

The time for a scheduled build is actually converted into the time zone for the Application tier when the build definition is saved. But this is always displayed in the time zone of the user's machine when editing the build definition in Visual Studio. For this reason, there can be some slight confusion as to the actual build time during periods where Daylight Savings Time is in operation in one of the time zones and not the other.

Workspace

The Workspace section allows you to define the working folder mappings that should be used for your build. These working folder mappings not only determine where on disk the files should be located but also which files on the server are considered relevant to the build.

The default working folder mapping for a new build definition is given as mapping the root of the team project (that is, `$/Adventureworks`) to the sources directory represented by the environment variable (`$(SourceDir)`), as shown in Figure 21-14. This is almost always too broad for your build, and includes too many files, which not only slows down the build (because more files must be downloaded from version control), but also means that some check-ins to the project risk triggering a build even though they do not affect the results of the build.

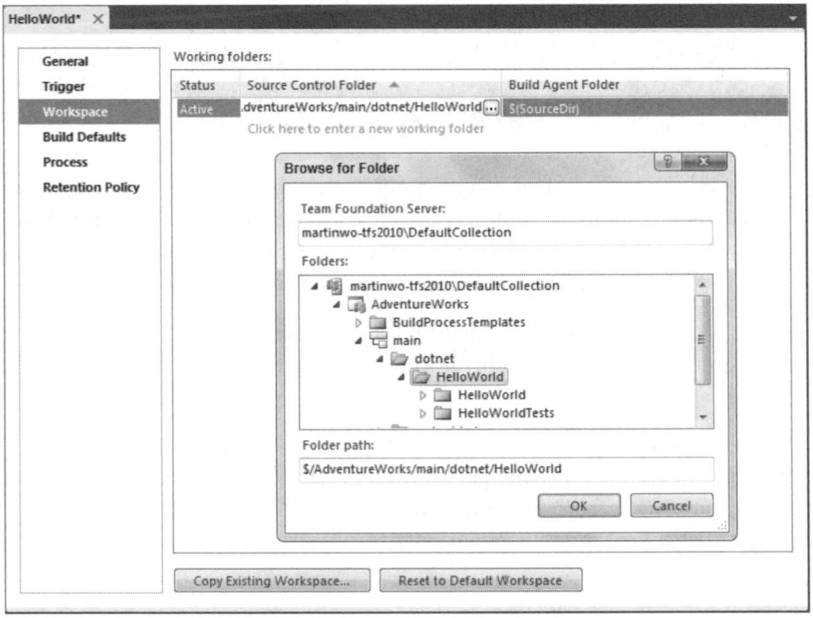

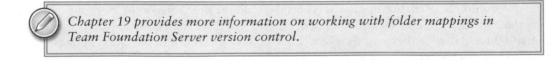

FIGURE 21-14

Therefore, you should immediately modify the server path of the build to only include the files you need. You may also make use of cloaked working folder mappings to exclude certain subfolders or files from a working folder mapping.

> *Chapter 19 provides more information on working with folder mappings in Team Foundation Server version control.*

Build Defaults

On the Build Defaults section shown in Figure 21-15, you specify which build controller you would like to use for the definition and where to copy the outputs from your build.

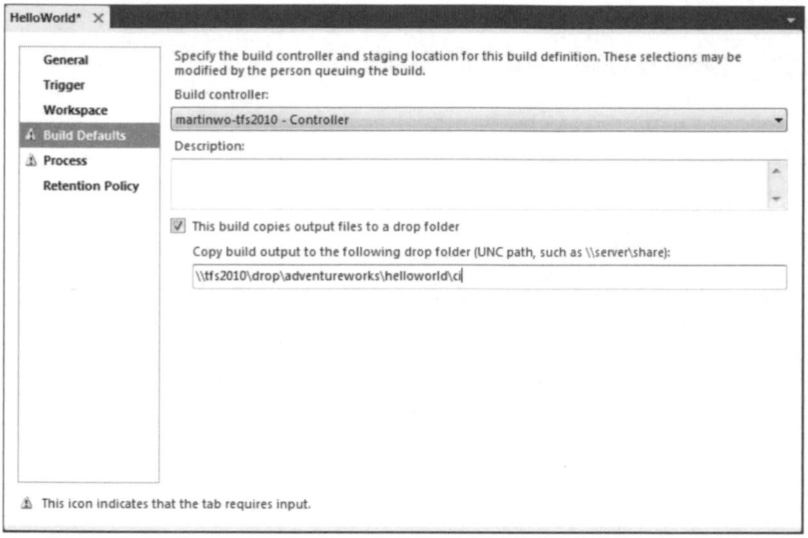

FIGURE 21-15

In Team Foundation Server 2010, build controllers and build agents are responsible for notifying the Team Foundation Server application of their existence as they are installed. If you have no build controllers available in the controller drop-down, then your Team Foundation Server administrator must install a build controller (and build agent) using the Team Foundation Server Setup media, and configure it to point to your project collection. The description field displays the description given to the build controller, and it is not editable from this dialog.

The "drop folder" location must be a Windows file share on the network to which the user running the build agent services has access. There is a limit (inherited from the .NET base class libraries) of 260 characters for the full path of all files copied to the drop folder location, so you should ensure that your server and share names are as short as possible, leaving you with the maximum space for your output. That being said, you should put your builds in directories corresponding to the build definition inside your drop folder location to help keep them organized.

Process

When talking to a Team Foundation Server 2010 server, you will be required to select which process should be used to perform the build. These processes are Windows Workflow 4.0-based processes. The initial list of processes are defined by the process template used, and can then be added to from the Process section. Each process has a number of easily customizable properties that are designed to be used to alter the behavior of that process. Processes with mandatory inputs are marked with a warning triangle when the build definition is created, as shown in Figure 21-16.

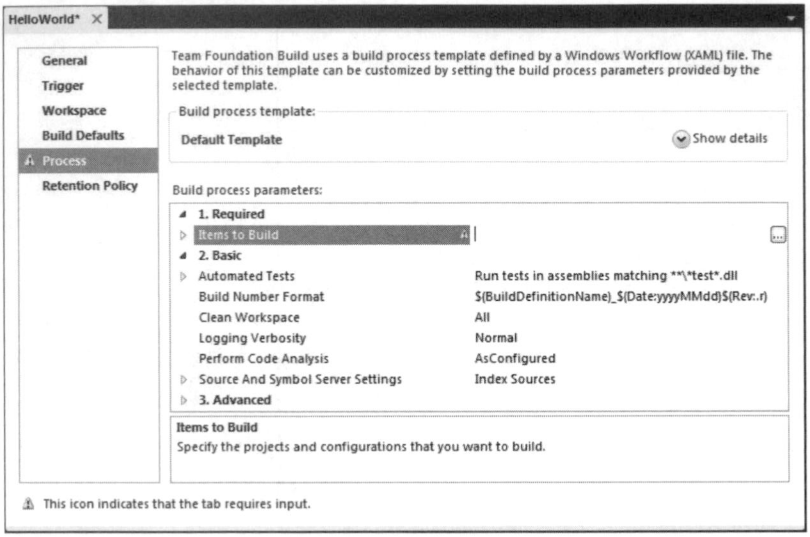

FIGURE 21-16

From this section, you may edit and customize the build process. (For more information on this, see the section "Team Build Process," later in this chapter.)

For the creation of a basic team project using the `DefaultTemplate`, the only property that you must initially configure is which solution or project to build. Simply click on the "Projects to Build" property and click the ". . ." button to add your solution or project to the list, as shown in Figure 21-17.

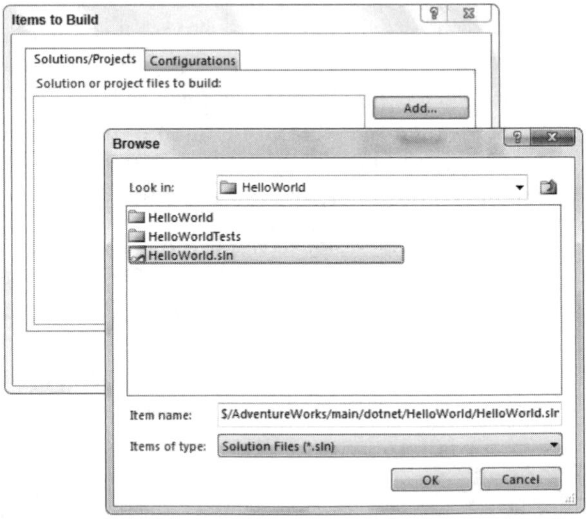

FIGURE 21-17

Retention Policy

Once you start automating builds, you quickly end up with a lot of build results in your archive. Finding the build that you are looking for can get complicated — not to mention the disk space required to store all the build results. Team Foundation Server has automatic retention policies to help with this, as displayed in the Retention Policy section shown in Figure 21-18.

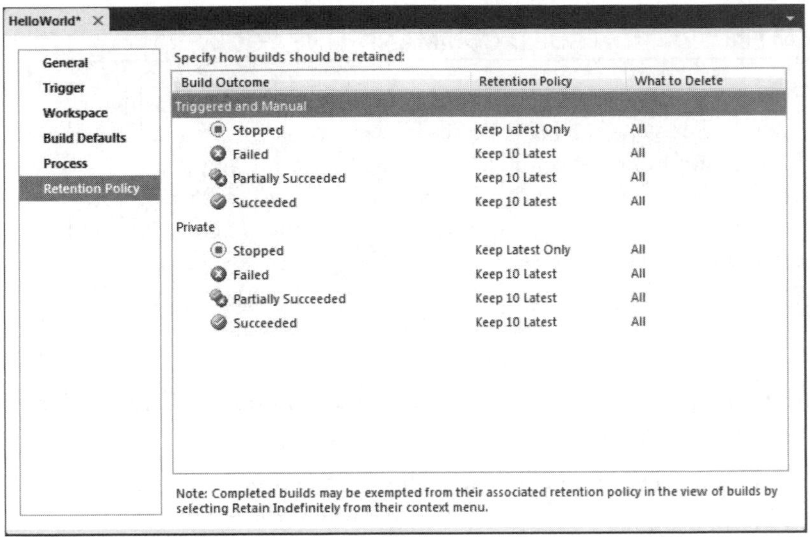

FIGURE 21-18

The retention policies determine, for each build result type, how many of those results you would like to keep by default. Note that, at any time, you can mark a build with the Retain Indefinitely Retention Policy from the build details context menu in the Build Explorer view. Marking a build as Retain Indefinitely means that it will be excluded from these automatic retention policies.

There are separate retention policies to control the team builds that are triggered or manually queued from the private builds of individual developers. Changing the private build retention policy affects all the developers performing private builds on that build definition — not just the developer editing the setting.

Queuing a Build

Whenever you create a new build definition, you should manually queue the build the first time to ensure that it is working as desired. The first successful build for a build definition also acts as the baseline for that build. Every build from that point on will record the changesets included since the last successful build for that definition. This information is stored in the build detail for each build, and reported into the Team Foundation Server data warehouse, thus allowing for historical trends over time.

A build can be manually invoked from the Builds node in Team Explorer by using the `TFSBuild .exe` command-line tool, or by using the Team Foundation Server .NET object model. Alternatively, the build might be triggered using one of the triggers defined earlier in this chapter (such as on a check-in into version control or on a specified schedule).

> ## USING THE TEAM FOUNDATION BUILD COMMAND-LINE TOOL
>
> Microsoft Team Explorer installs a number of command-line tools, one of which is the TFSBuild command. The TFSBuild command can be used to perform a limited number of Team Foundation Build tasks and is also useful in scripting scenarios where full access to the Team Foundation .NET object model is not required. For more information on the TFSBuild command, open a Visual Studio 2010 command prompt and type **TFSBuild help**, or visit http://msdn.microsoft.com/en-us/library/aa337622.aspx.

To manually queue a build in Visual Studio, right-click on the build definition in Team Explorer and select Queue New Build, as shown in Figure 21-19.

You will then be presented with the Queue Build dialog, as shown in Figure 21-20. The build definition is pre-selected in the build definition drop-down at the top of the dialog, and its description is displayed underneath.

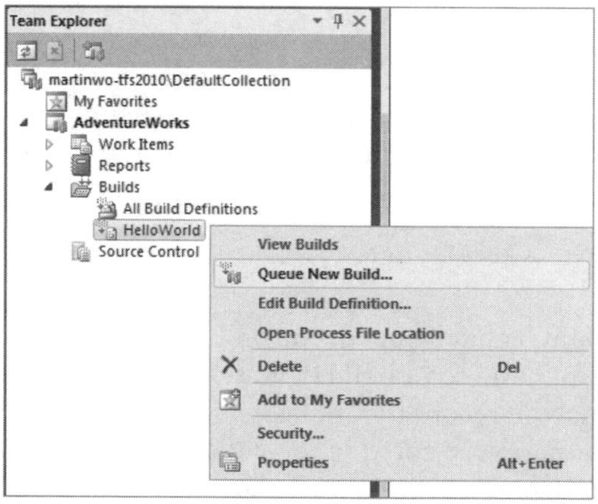

FIGURE 21-19

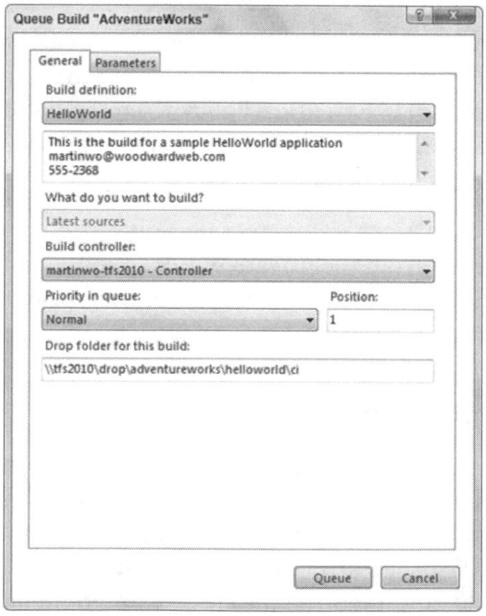

FIGURE 21-20

When you manually queue a build, you have options of selecting an alternative build controller (if one is available), adjusting the priority of the build, and modifying the drop folder location to be different from the default. Based on the selected queue priority, you will also be given an indication of the current position in the queue that your build would get if it were submitted.

There is also a tab called Parameters that is new for builds queued on a Team Foundation Server 2010 server. Here you will find all the customizable properties defined for the process, allowing you to alter the value of that property for this single invocation of the build.

Private Builds

A new feature in Team Foundation Server 2010 is the capability to adjust what you want to build from the General tab in the Queue Build dialog (Figure 21-21). You can either build from the latest version in source control at the time that the build is submitted to the queue, or you can take the latest version and apply a specified shelveset to the build before it is performed.

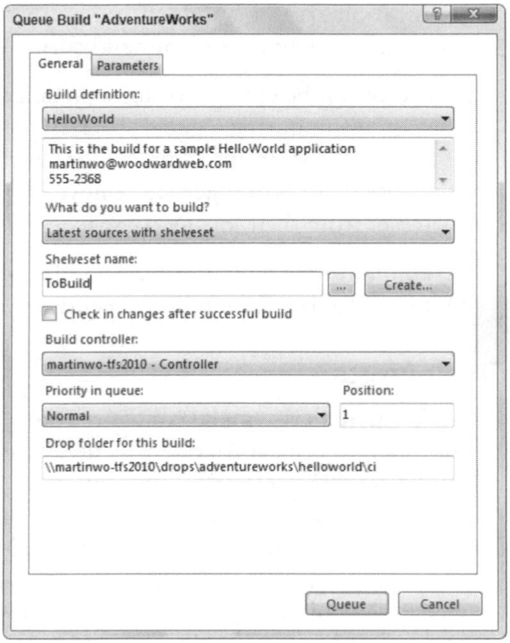

If you decide to perform a build that includes a shelveset of your changes not yet checked in to version control, this is called a *private build,* which can sometimes be referred to as a *buddy build.*

Private builds are useful when you want to check that you are including all the changes necessary to successfully perform the build on a different machine before you commit your changes to version control. Another use for them is when you may not have all the dependencies to perform that particular build definition on your local machine (such as a code signing certificate installed), but you want to test that your code functions correctly when built with those dependencies.

In many ways, a private build is similar to a gated check-in, apart from the fact that your changes are not automatically checked in to version control after a successful build.

Private builds do not follow the same build numbering mechanism defined for the regular team builds, and have separate retention policies. The build results for a private build are displayed to the developer who is invoking the private build, not to the whole team.

FIGURE 21-21

Build Notifications

Team Foundation Server exposes a powerful eventing model and .NET-based API that allows for custom integrations of any imaginable application or device for notification of build results—from standard email alerts to lava lamps, confetti-filled leaf blowers, and even talking robot rabbits. However, two main notification systems are exposed to the developer out of the box— the build notification tool and email alerts.

Build Notification Tool

The build notification tool used to be provided as a power tool, but now ships with the main application. As shown in Figure 21-22, it is a small application that runs in the system

FIGURE 21-22

notification area of Windows and notifies the end user of build events via an Outlook style pop-up message in the bottom right-hand corner of the screen.

This tool can be configured to automatically start when you log in to Windows. However, it will always be run during a gated check-in process so that the developers will be aware of the status of the build containing their changes. If the build is a success, the developers will easily be able to reconcile their workspaces to remove any pending changes that were included in the gated check-in shelveset from their local workspace.

To configure the build notification tool, right-click on the icon while the tool is running and select Options. To quit the application entirely, right-click on the icon and select Exit.

Email Alerts

Basic email alerts can be configured from the Team ➪ Project Alerts menu in Visual Studio once the selected team project has been highlighted in Team Explorer. Using the interface shown in Figure 21-23, email alerts can be enabled when a build quality changes, when any build completes, or when builds are initiated by the developer.

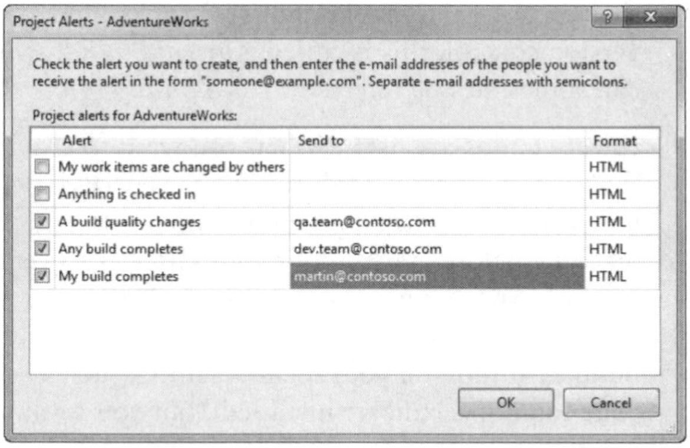

In the Team Foundation Power Tools, a more flexible Alerts Editor is available as an additional Alerts node on the Team Explorer. This provides a greater degree of control over which events and what events values cause an email alert to be dispatched.

Project Alerts - AdventureWorks

Check the alert you want to create, and then enter the e-mail addresses of the people you want to receive the alert in the form "someone@example.com". Separate e-mail addresses with semicolons.

Project alerts for AdventureWorks:

Alert	Send to	Format
☐ My work items are changed by others		HTML
☐ Anything is checked in		HTML
☑ A build quality changes	qa.team@contoso.com	HTML
☑ Any build completes	dev.team@contoso.com	HTML
☑ My build completes	martin@contoso.com	HTML

OK   Cancel

FIGURE 21-23

Emails can be sent to any email address, including team aliases, provided the Team Foundation Server Application tier is configured with the correct SMTP server details to send the messages. However, the email alerts belong to the user who created the alert, and that user must delete or edit the alert through the Visual Studio interface.

On the Team Foundation Server Application tier machine, the `BisSubscribe.exe` command is available in the `Team Foundation Server\Tools` folder, and can be used to script the creation of project alerts for a team project.

TEAM BUILD PROCESS

The process controlling the end-to-end build process in Team Foundation Server is described in a Windows Workflow 4.0 XAML file. The build process templates are created as part of the project creation process, and are defined in the process template.

In the MSF Agile and MSF CMMI processes, the following build processes are included:

➤ `DefaultTemplate` — This is the default template to be used for most new builds created for Team Foundation Server 2010. This is the template that is the primary focus of discussion in the remainder of this chapter.

➤ UpgradeTemplate — This is the default template for builds upgraded from Team Foundation Server 2008, or builds created using Visual Studio 2008. Basically, it performs some housekeeping, and then just wraps the call to the legacy TFSBuild.proj file for an MSBuild-based build configuration.

In addition, the LabDefaultTemplate build process template is also installed for the Lab Management functionality by the Lab section of the MSF processes.

> *Chapter 16 provides more information on Lab Management functionality in Visual Studio 2010.*

All the build process templates are stored as files in version control, allowing for quick and easy auditing of any changes to the process used to perform the build. By default, these are stored in a folder called TeambuildProcessTemplates at the root of the team project in version control, but may be located inside your team project branch structure, if that's more convenient.

The majority of the remainder of this chapter focuses on the DefaultTemplate — how it works, how to use it, and how to modify it.

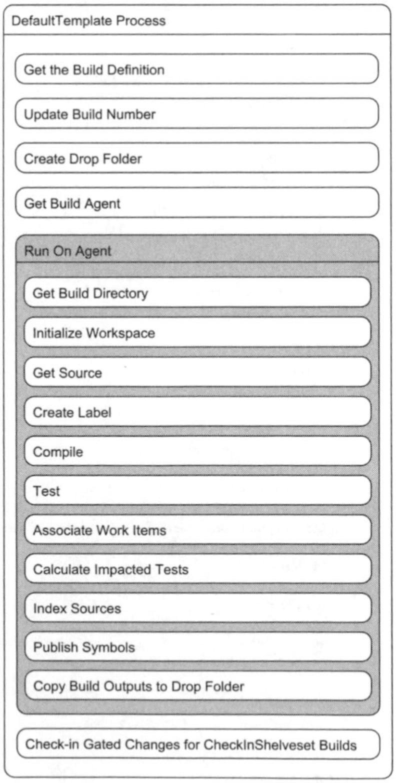

DefaultTemplate Process

The DefaultTemplate is used for most new, un-customized build definitions. The process followed is outlined at a high level in Figure 21-24, but can be explored in detail by opening the DefaultTemplate.xaml file from version control inside Visual Studio.

On the build controller, the build number is calculated and the drop location for the build created. Then, the build agent is calculated and the majority of the rest of the process is performed on the selected agent from the controllers build agent pool.

The working directory for the build is determined by using the build agent working directory setting as defined in the Build Agent Properties dialog. Then, the workspace is created (if required) and source downloaded from version control. The version that is downloaded is usually the changeset that represented the latest version in the project collection at the time the build was triggered. If a subsequent change has been made while the build was queued, this change is not included. The files that were downloaded are then labeled in version control with the build number.

Next, the process calls MSBuild to perform the actual compilation of the desired project files for the configuration, and then any specified automated tests are executed. Next, the build agent looks at the changesets included since the last

FIGURE 21-24

successful build of the build definition, and records any work items that were associated with those check-ins. For work items that were marked as resolved during check-in, the Fixed-In Build field for the work item is updated with the current build number.

From the files changed since the last successful build, the build agent then calculates which tests have been affected, and records them. The source code is then indexed and linked with the symbols that are published to the symbol server (if provided). Finally, on the build agent, the output from the build is copied over to the drop folder location previously created by the controller.

The process then moves back to the controller for the final step, which, for a build with a Gated Check-in trigger, is to check in the shelveset that contained the modified files included in the build.

Build Process Parameters

The build process templates are configured to make a number of parameters visible in the user interface in either the Build Definition editor or the Queue Build dialog (or both). These parameters (Figure 21-25) are provided to control the behavior of the selected build process.

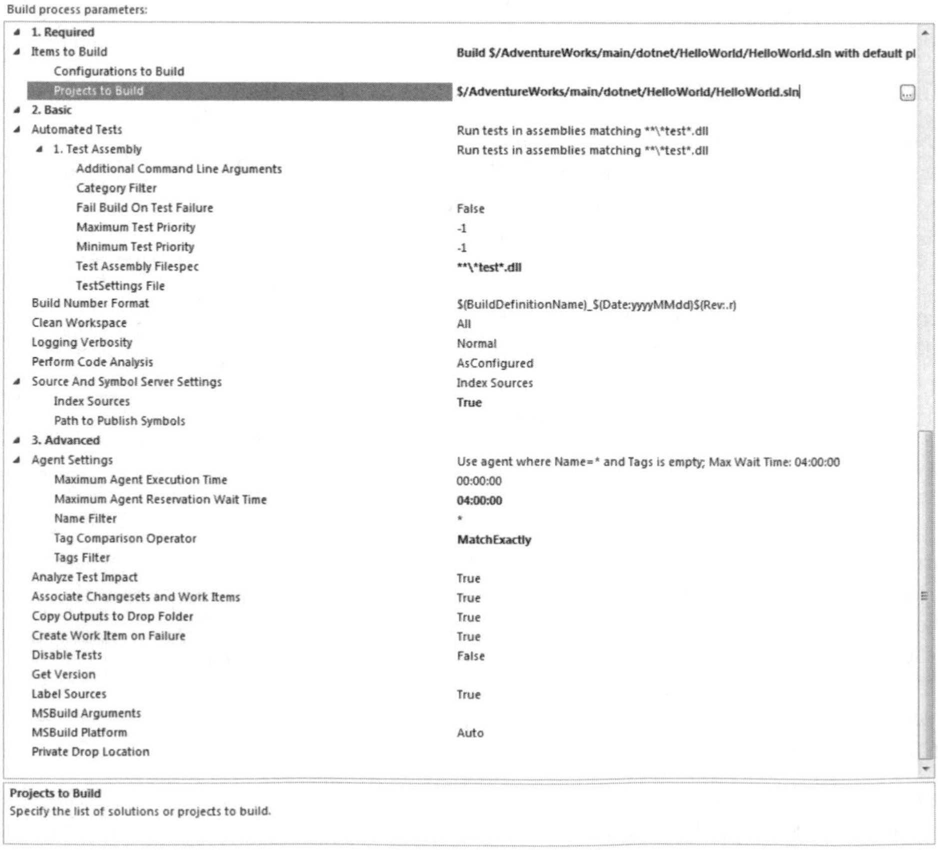

FIGURE 21-25

When you create the build definition, you set one of these parameters, "Items to Build," to be the solution file that you want to build. However, there are many other parameters provided for you to adjust the behavior of the template. If you select one of the parameters, additional information is displayed about the parameter in the comments box at the bottom of the process parameter table.

In the default process templates, these parameters are broken down into three categories: Required, Basic, and Advanced. Some of these parameters are worth calling out in this chapter, and are examined in the following discussions. However, it is worth familiarizing yourself with all the parameters and what they do.

Configurations to Build

The default Visual Studio build configuration to use is the default build configuration for your solution. To modify the configuration, use the Configurations dialog that is available when you press the ". . ." button in the Configurations To Build parameter under Required, Items to Build.

> **SOLUTION CONFIGURATIONS**
>
> Team Foundation Build typically deals with *solution configurations*. These allow you to specify a named collection of project-level platforms and configurations that should be built. For more information on solution configurations, see the blog post from Aaron Hallberg of the Team Foundation Build team at Microsoft, located at http://blogs.msdn.com/aaronhallberg/archive/2007/06/25/solution-configurations.aspx.

Logging Verbosity

By default, only messages above normal priority get included in the build log. However, you can adjust the logging priority to change the level of detail recorded. The more detailed the log, the slower the build will be performed, and the longer it will take to download build data to Visual Studio.

When diagnosing build problems, it is often useful to manually queue a build with this property set to Diagnostic. In that way, the log priority is only set for a single run of the build, rather than for all builds from that definition. The logging verbosity parameter can be found in the Basic category.

Agent Settings

Agent Settings can be found in the Advanced category of parameters. As well as limits for how long a build can run or wait for an available build agent, the Agent Settings group of process parameters includes both the Name Filter and Tags Filter. Together, these are used to determine on which build agent the build will be executed. If multiple build agents match the agent requirements, then the agent with the least number of build agents running will execute the build.

Specifying the Name of a build agent allows you to force it to run on a particular machine. You can also adopt a naming convention for your build agents, and then use wildcards in the Name Filter to assign builds to a pool containing a subset of all the build agents for the project collection (for example, "ProjectX*" for all build agents assigned to "ProjectX").

A more flexible way you can limit which build agents are used for a build is to make use of the tagging feature for build agents. From the build agent properties dialog, you can assign *tags* (which are a set of text strings) to an agent to denote certain features. For example, you could use "CodeSign" if you have the project's code signing certificate installed on the machine, "Datacenter1" if it is located in your main data center, or "Ireland" if the build server is located in your remote office in Ireland. You can then filter on which tags are required for your build agent by using the Tags Filter in the Agent Requirements, and then only agents with that tag will be used.

To edit the tags on a particular agent, you can use the Team Foundation Server Administration Console on the build agent machine itself, or you can right-click on the Builds node in Visual Studio and select Build Controllers. You then select your build agent and click the Properties button. You will then be presented with the Build Agent Properties dialog shown in Figure 21-26, and, provided you have sufficient permissions, you will be able to edit the assigned tags.

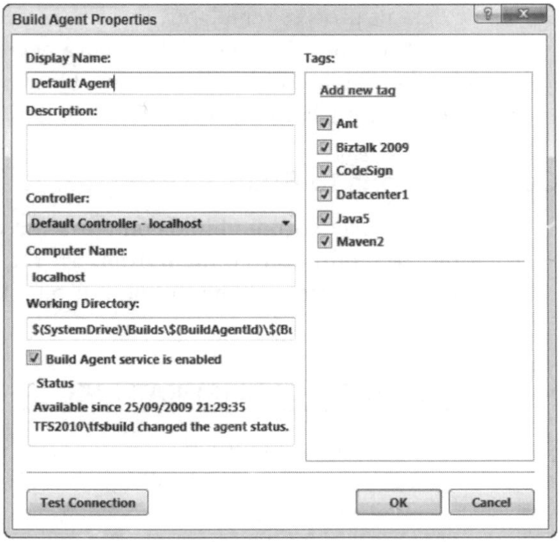

FIGURE 21-26

Clean Workspace

By default the Clean Workspace parameter is set to All, meaning that all existing build outputs and sources for that build definition will be deleted for every build. Although this is the safest option, it is also the slowest, because all the files must be downloaded from version control, and everything re-built for every build, regardless of what has changed.

If you have a lot of source files (or some very large files in your source), then you could set the value of this parameter to Outputs. This will simply delete the build outputs every time the build is performed, and only get the files that have changed between builds from version control.

If you set the value of the parameter to None, then neither the sources nor the build outputs will be deleted at the start of a build. Only the files that have changed in version control will be downloaded each time, and only the things that have changed will be recompiled as part of the build. Because not a lot of things usually change between builds, this will normally give your builds a significant performance boost by taking much less time to complete. It is also often useful for things such as ASP.NET-based Web sites, where you might want to subsequently only publish the items that have changed to your public Web site to minimize the upgrade impact for new versions.

However, if you have customized your build process and you make any of the source files writable for some reason (for example, to modify the AssemblyInfo files to contain your version number), or if your customized build process assumes a clean output directory, then you may run into issues with altering the default value of the Clean Workspace. So, use with caution.

Build Number Format

By default, Team Foundation Server numbers the builds in the format `$(BuildDefinitionName)_` `$(Date:yyyyMMdd)$(Rev:.r)`. For example, in `HelloWorld_20090927.5`, the "5" is the fifth build executed for that build definition on that day. Build numbers must be unique across a team project, and this format serves as a good default. However, it is often not the format that people want.

Thankfully, in Team Foundation Server 2010, editing the build number is very easy using the Build Number Format parameter. When you edit the Build Number Format parameter, you are presented with a dialog, similar to Figure 21-27, that gives you the format string, a preview of what a build number of that format will look like when generated, and a set of macro strings that can be used in the format. Clicking on each macro will give you more information about its behavior in the command section at the bottom of the dialog.

FIGURE 21-27

A common number format to use is `$(BuildDefinitionName)_V1.0.0$(Rev:.r)`, where you are currently working on version 1.0.0 of the product, and the `$(Rev:.r)` macro translates to an incrementing number that makes the build number unique.

Path to Publish Symbols

The `DefaultTemplate` in Team Foundation Server 2010 includes a step to index source code and publish symbols to a symbol server in the organization. As mentioned earlier in this chapter, a symbol server is simply a file share that is used to store the symbols for your executable binaries. Visual Studio can then be configured with details of this server. From then on, when debugging code live, or using the advanced historical debugging features, Visual Studio is able to take you directly to the version of the source code from which the binary was generated, regardless of which version of the code that you have on your local system at that time.

The configuration of the symbol server is performed by adding the UNC file path of the share to be used as the symbol sever in the "Path to Publish Symbols" process parameter under "Basic, Source and Symbol Server Settings."

Automated Tests

In the basic category of process parameters, you are able to configure automated tests that should run as part of the build using the Automated Tests parameter. By default, a new build will run all unit tests in assemblies matching the pattern `*test*.dll`. This means that, if you have created some unit tests in a companion test project called `HelloWorldTests`, for example, then they will be run automatically.

Pressing the "..." button will open the Automated Tests dialog shown in Figure 21-28, where you can add additional tests to run, or edit the test configuration.

If you select the existing test configuration and click Edit, the Add/Edit Test dialog shown in Figure 21-29 will be displayed, allowing you to edit aspects of your test run. For example, you can configure it to fail the build on test failure, run a particular set of test lists, modify the test category criteria, specify which priority range of tests that you wish to run, specify the command-line arguments, or provide a test settings file to use when executing the tests.

FIGURE 21-28

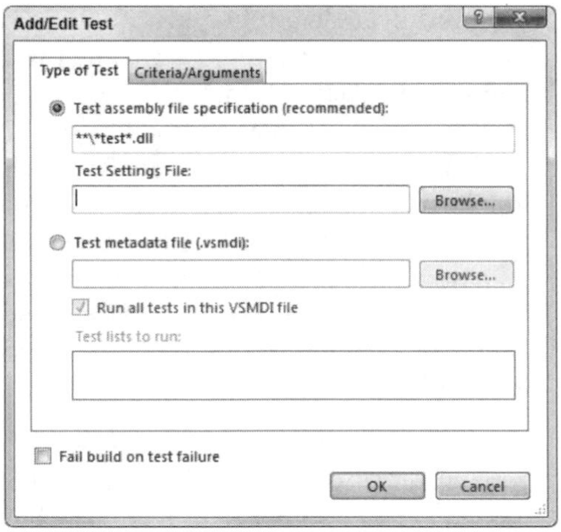

FIGURE 21-29

Your Visual Studio solution can contain a number of `.testsettings` files to control the behavior of the test environment and to enable configuration settings (such as code coverage or the test impact analysis, as part of the test run).

If you have unit tests as part of your automated build, then it may be very useful to enable code coverage and to test impact analysis as part of the build. Code coverage tracks how much of your application code is being tested by the unit tests. Test impact analysis determines which tests were affected by the changes committed into version control as part of that build — giving your testers an idea of which tests should be revisited when testing the build.

To enable code coverage and test impact analysis, it is best to create a new test settings file specifically for your build server settings. Open the `Local.testsettings` file in the Solution Items. Then, change the name to `Build Server` and click the Save As button, to save it as something like `BuildServer.testsettings`.

Open the build server test settings file, and, in the Data and Diagnostics section, check both the Code Coverage and Test Impact options, as shown in Figure 21-30.

With the Code Coverage option selected, click the Configure button to enable code coverage on the assemblies that make up your product (that is, not your unit tests), as shown in Figure 21-31.

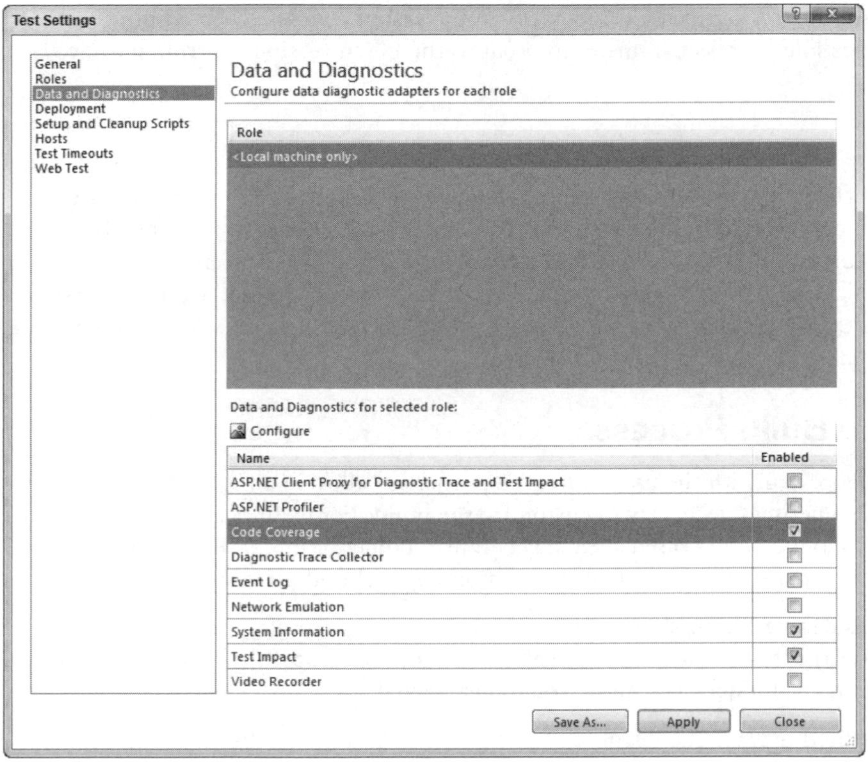

FIGURE 21-30

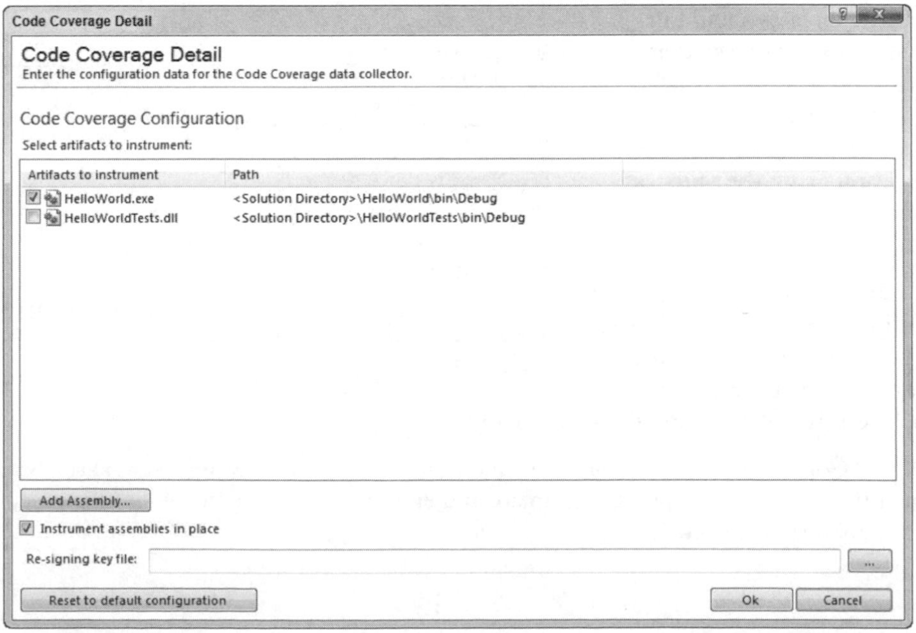

FIGURE 21-31

Once configured, save the test settings file and check in to version control. Then edit the Test Container TestSettings File process parameter to point to the file in version control, and save the build definition.

Get Version

Builds are usually performed with the latest sources from version control. However, occasionally you may want to perform a build of the source at a particular date, changeset, or label. In those circumstances, you can modify the Get Version process parameter. This is usually done as you queue the build by clicking on the Parameters tab. The value provided should be a valid version specification such as C1234 for changeset 1234, D2008-04-22T17:37 for a date/time, or LmyLabel for a label called myLabel.

Customizing the Build Process

While the DefaultTemplate with the pre-configured properties allows you to perform common build scenarios, it is sometimes necessary to customize the build. For example, if you wanted to parallelize parts of the build across build agents, generate documentation, or even create MSI installers and ISO disk images, you would need to customize the build process.

The remainder of this chapter discusses the basics of customizing the build process. To comprehensively cover this topic could easy take a whole book, but hopefully this will be enough to familiarize you with the techniques and allow you to get started.

Your processes are stored in version control. Therefore, to access them, you could easily just open the file from Source Control Explorer and start editing. However, customized process templates should be stored in a file with a new name so that others in your team project may create a build using the DefaultTemplate, if required. This also allows you to experiment with a build definition using your process template while the team continues to work with the DefaultTemplate.

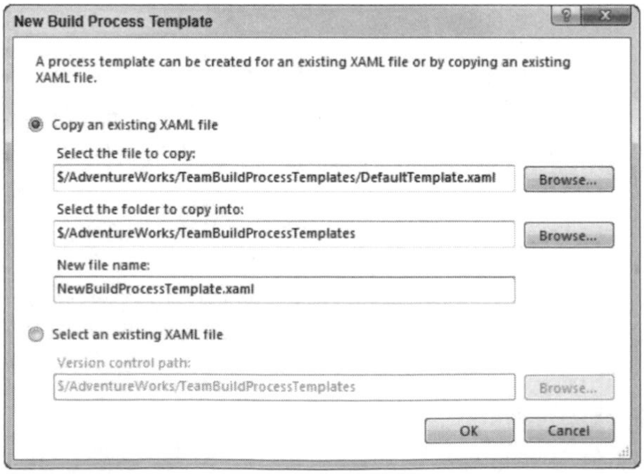

FIGURE 21-32

To create a new build process template, start by editing the build definition. In the Process section of the dialog, click the New button toward the top of the screen. This brings up the New Build Process Template dialog shown in Figure 21-32.

In the dialog, select "Copy an existing XAML file" and point it at DefaultTeamplate.xaml. Select the folder in which to create the new process template and enter the new filename — in this case, let's use NewBuildProcessTemplate.xaml.

This will create the file in version control. You must save your build definition to make it use the new build process template from now on. You then perform a Get Latest on the build process template in Source Control Explorer, so that you can open the file for editing inside Visual Studio (Figure 21-33).

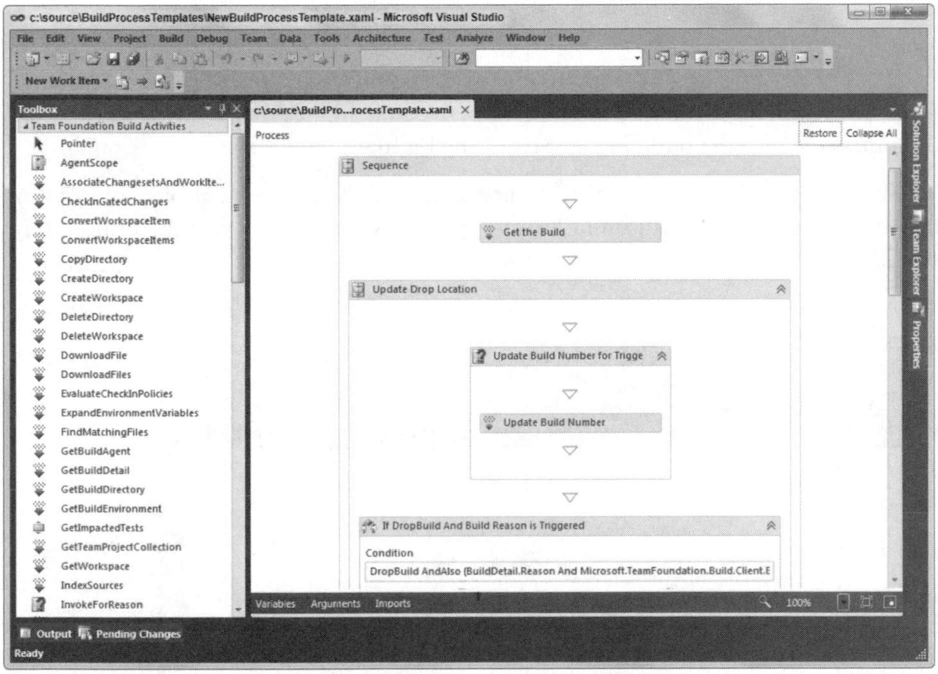

FIGURE 21-33

It is important to remember that the team build process templates are simply Windows Workflow activity XAML files — the same as if you had created your own workflow activity project in Visual Studio.

Team Foundation Server ships with a set of additional workflow activities related to the build process in the assembly `Microsoft.TeamFoundation.Build.Workflow`. This includes all the build-related activities called by the build process templates that ship with the product, along with several other activities that are useful when performing common build customization.

When you edit the build process, you have exactly the same design time features available as if you were editing any other workflow activity, including a full graphical designer tool.

DON'T FORGET TO CHECK IN YOUR BUILD PROCESS TEMPLATE

It is important to remember that your process template file is just a Workflow Activity XAML file checked in to version control. The build will use the latest version of that file at run-time. However, both the build definition editor and the Queue Build dialog base what they display on the latest version of the process template that is checked in to version control, not the version you have locally. While this is obvious, it is surprisingly easy to forget. You will not be alone if you get caught on this as you start experimenting with customizing build processes.

Adding Workflow Activities

You can drag and drop activities from the toolbox into your new build process template. To begin, let's simply add a message into the build log as part of the build.

Locate the `WriteBuildMessage` activity in the toolbox under the Team Foundation Build Activities section and drag it over into the Overall Build Process, placing it above the "Get the Build" step, as shown in Figure 21-34.

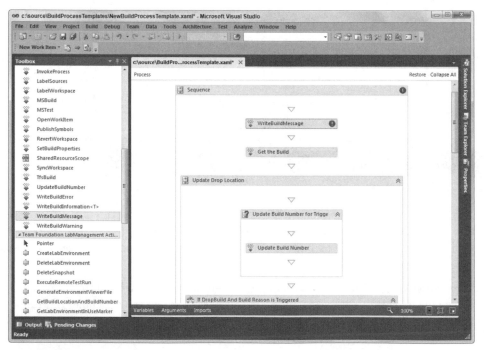

FIGURE 21-34

In the properties for the build step, shown in the lower-right of Figure 21-35, change the DisplayName to `Log Welcome Message`. Change the Importance to `Microsoft.TeamFoundation .Build.Client.BuildMessageImportance.High`, and set the Message to `"Welcome to my customized build process"`. Note the quotes in the message — you are actually entering a piece of VB.NET code that evaluates to the string required for the message.

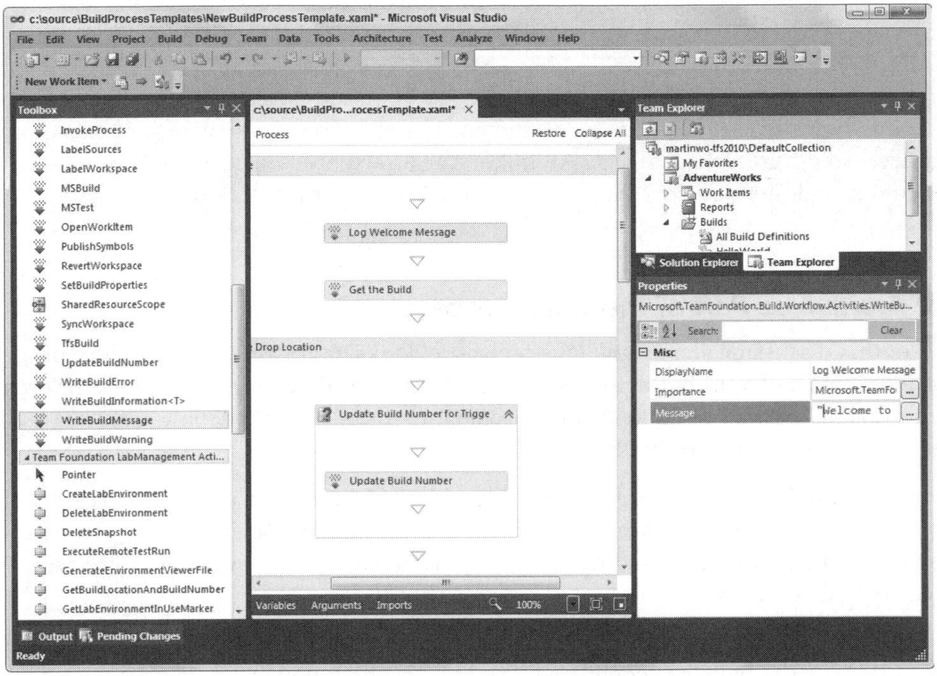

FIGURE 21-35

Now, remember to save the customized process template XAML file and check it in to Team Foundation Server from the Pending Changes view. Then, queue a build using your new process template. If you look at the build log (as shown in Figure 21-36), you should see your message.

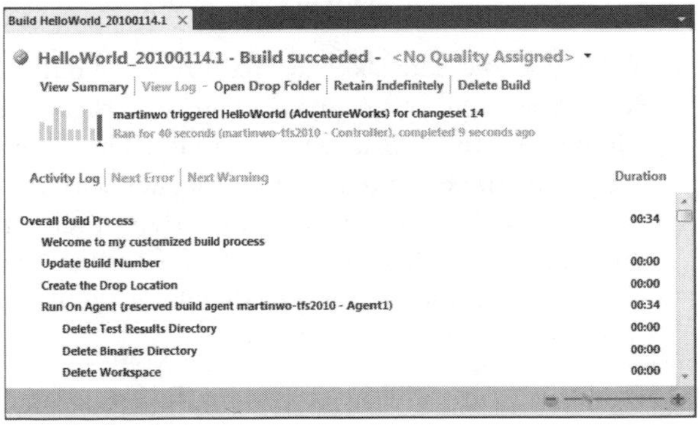

If you do not see your message, then verify the following:

➤ That you set the importance of the message to High

➤ That you checked in your template into version control

➤ That your build definition is configured to use the process template

➤ That you have saved your build definition

FIGURE 21-36

Extending the build process is now just an extension of this, but with increased complexity. Obviously, adding things to the build log alone is not particularly useful (except, perhaps, for debugging why something else is not working). Let's instead invoke a process from the build.

> **NAVIGATING AROUND THE BUILD PROCESS**
>
> Once you start working with the build process in the Windows Workflow process editor, you will notice that there are many embedded steps. To get a view of the high level steps, press the Collapse All link in the top right-hand corner of the process editor, and then you can double-click on each section to drill down.

Creating a ZIP Archive as Part of the Build Process

The remainder of this discussion about build customization looks at creating a ZIP archive of the build binaries. As part of your build process, you may want to package your binaries, or even source files, into various formats to make them convenient to distribute and deploy. Creating a ZIP archive of files is a handy method for making them easy to download.

For this particular example, let's use 7-zip, which is a popular Open Source utility for manipulating archives. Along with a Windows interface, it also includes a command-line utility, `7z.exe`, that you will invoke as part of the build. You can download 7-zip from `www.7-zip.org/`; the software is available under the L-GPL license.

The command that you want to execute will be to create a new `ZIP` archive from the contents of the `Binaries` directory after the build has completed. It will be in the following format:

```
7z.exe a -bd -r -tzip output.zip -r
        c:\Builds\1\AdventureWorks\HelloWorld\Binaries\*
```

You want to create the `zip` archive on the build agent. Double-click on the "Run On Agent" activity at the root of the build process, then double-click on the "Try Compile, Test and Associate Changesets and Work Items" activity. This activity is where the actual compilation of your project is done by the build agent. The "Sequence in the Try" block is where that activity is done, and the "Finally" block contains the activity that copies the results of your build from the `Binaries` directory to the drop location. You want the "Package Binaries" activity to occur at the end of a successful build process, so double-click on the "Sequence" in the Try block to see the main compilation steps.

From the Control Flow section of the Toolbox, drag a new "If" activity to the end of your sequence. Call it "If Compilation Successful," as shown in Figure 21-37, and add the following condition:

```
BuildDetail.CompilationStatus =
        Microsoft.TeamFoundation.Build.Client.BuildPhaseStatus.Succeeded
```

You have now created an "If" block that will run when the build has had a clean compile phase. Double-click on the "If" block, and then drag a new "Sequence" over to the "Then" section of the "If" block. Call it "Package Binaries," as shown in Figure 21-38.

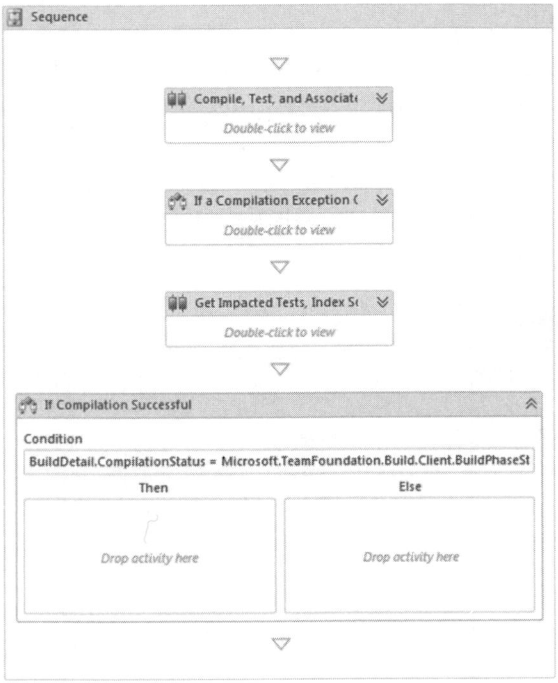

FIGURE 21-37

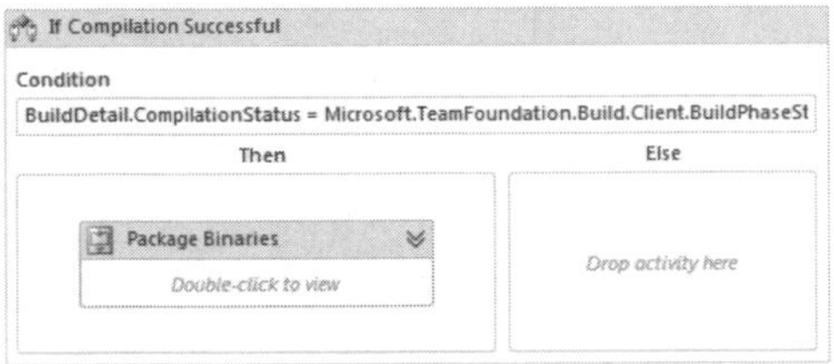

FIGURE 21-38

Double-click on the "Package Binaries" sequence. Then drag in a new `InvokeProcess` activity from the Team Foundation Build section of the Toolbox. Give it a display name of "Invoke 7zip."

STORING TOOLS IN VERSION CONTROL

It is considered good practice to make your builds as easily repeatable as possible, and, in general, this means avoiding the assumption that certain applications or files will be pre-installed on the build agent machines, whenever possible. Therefore, when using tools like 7-zip as part of the build, you can check those binaries into version control to allow you to run the command on the build agent without having to install it first.

You can include your tools as part of the project that you are building, or you can create a section in version control that stores all your common tools, and then

continues

(continued)

add a working folder mapping as part of your build definition so that the tools are downloaded as part of the "Get of source" done at the start of running on the build agent.

In the example shown in the discussion, you have checked in 7z.exe, along with its associated files (7z.dll, Licence.txt, and copying.txt) into a folder called 7zip inside a tools folder you created as part of the project.

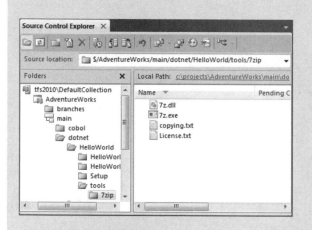

You are then able to reference these tools by giving a path relative to the tools directory.

In the FileName, enter a fully qualified path to find the 7-zip executable, which, in this case, is the following:

```
String.Format("{0}\7zip\7z.exe", System.IO.Path.Combine
    (SourcesDirectory, "tools"))
```

In the Argument section, give the command-line arguments to pass to the 7-zip command, as shown here:

```
String.Format("a -bd -y -tzip {0} {1}/* -r",
    Path.Combine(BinariesDirectory, "output,zip"), BinariesDirectory)
```

Save this template and check it in to version control. Then manually queue a build. After the build completes, you should find a zip file called output.zip in your build drop folder location containing the contents of your Binaries directory.

While this will actually execute the process for you, you are not handling error messages or logging the results of the command, which will make it difficult to debug. To log the standard output and standard errors of the process to the build log, double-click on "Invoke 7zip process." Drag a WriteBuildMessage activity into the Handle Standard Output section. Set the Message to be stdOutput. Drag a `WriteBuildError` activity to the "Handle Error Output" section and set the message to be `errOutput`.

> *Note that, under the default logging conditions, you do not see build messages with an importance of* Normal. *Therefore, to view the output of the 7-zip process, you should manually queue a build and set the Logging Verbosity process parameter to Diagnostic.*

If you look at the XAML that you have just created using the visual designer, the section you have edited looks something like the following:

Available for
download on
Wrox.com

```xml
<If Condition="[BuildDetail.CompilationStatus =
      Microsoft.TeamFoundation.Build.Client.BuildPhaseStatus.Succeeded]"
    DisplayName="If Compilation Successful">
  <If.Then>
    <Sequence DisplayName="Package Binaries">
      <mtbwa:InvokeProcess
          Arguments="[String.Format(&quot;a -bd -y -tzip {0} {1}/* -r&quot;,
              Path.Combine(BinariesDirectory, &quot;output.zip&quot;)
              ,BinariesDirectory)]"
          DisplayName="Invoke 7zip"
          FileName="[String.Format(&quot;{0}\7zip\7z.exe&quot;
              ,System.IO.Path.Combine(SourcesDirectory, &quot;tools&quot;))]">
        <mtbwa:InvokeProcess.ErrorDataReceived>
          <ActivityAction x:TypeArguments="x:String">
            <ActivityAction.Argument>
              <DelegateInArgument x:TypeArguments="x:String" Name="errOutput" />
            </ActivityAction.Argument>
            <mtbwa:WriteBuildError Message="[errOutput]" />
          </ActivityAction>
        </mtbwa:InvokeProcess.ErrorDataReceived>
        <mtbwa:InvokeProcess.OutputDataReceived>
          <ActivityAction x:TypeArguments="x:String">
            <ActivityAction.Argument>
              <DelegateInArgument x:TypeArguments="x:String" Name="stdOutput" />
            </ActivityAction.Argument>
            <mtbwa:WriteBuildMessage Message="[stdOutput]"
              mva:VisualBasic.Settings="Assembly references and
                  imported namespaces serialized as XML namespaces" />
          </ActivityAction>
        </mtbwa:InvokeProcess.OutputDataReceived>
      </mtbwa:InvokeProcess>
    </Sequence>
  </If.Then>
</If>
```

Code Snippet [464265 snippet1.txt]

While the visual designer is a good way of discovering and adjusting the build process, you will need to get a high degree of familiarity with the XAML that is generated. Therefore, it is worth spending a little time now reading through and understanding the XAML created, and how it matches up against what is seen in the designer.

For the most robust handling when invoking processes, you should also check the exit code of the process. For most processes, an exit code of 0 means that everything has worked, with other error codes indicating an error. To check this, create an `Int32` variable in the "Package Binaries" sequence called `exitCode`. Set `exitCode` as the `Result` of the `InvokeProcess` activity. Then drag a new "Switch" block into the workflow to check the values of the exit code and log an appropriate message. The resulting XAML should look something like the following:

```
<If Condition="[BuildDetail.CompilationStatus =
      Microsoft.TeamFoundation.Build.Client.BuildPhaseStatus.Succeeded]"
    DisplayName="If Compilation Successful">
  <If.Then>
    <Sequence DisplayName="Package Binaries">
      <Sequence.Variables>
        <Variable x:TypeArguments="x:Int32" Name="exitCode" />
      </Sequence.Variables>
      <mtbwa:InvokeProcess
        Arguments="[String.Format(&quot;a -bd -y -tzip {0} {1}/* -r&quot;,
            Path.Combine(BinariesDirectory, &quot;output.zip&quot;),
            BinariesDirectory)]"
        DisplayName="Invoke 7zip"
        FileName="[String.Format(&quot;{0}\7zip\7z.exe&quot;,
            System.IO.Path.Combine(SourcesDirectory, &quot;tools&quot;))]"
        Result="[exitCode]">
        <mtbwa:InvokeProcess.ErrorDataReceived>
          <ActivityAction x:TypeArguments="x:String">
            <ActivityAction.Argument>
              <DelegateInArgument x:TypeArguments="x:String" Name="errOutput" />
            </ActivityAction.Argument>
            <mtbwa:WriteBuildError Message="[errOutput]" />
          </ActivityAction>
        </mtbwa:InvokeProcess.ErrorDataReceived>
        <mtbwa:InvokeProcess.OutputDataReceived>
          <ActivityAction x:TypeArguments="x:String">
            <ActivityAction.Argument>
              <DelegateInArgument x:TypeArguments="x:String" Name="stdOutput" />
            </ActivityAction.Argument>
            <mtbwa:WriteBuildMessage
              Message="[stdOutput]"
              mva:VisualBasic.Settings="Assembly references and
                  imported namespaces serialized as XML namespaces" />
          </ActivityAction>
        </mtbwa:InvokeProcess.OutputDataReceived>
      </mtbwa:InvokeProcess>
      <Switch x:TypeArguments="x:Int32" Expression="[exitCode]">
        <Switch.Default>
          <mtbwa:WriteBuildError Message="[String.Format(&quot;Known exit code {0}
              from 7z.exe&quot;, exitCode)]" />
        </Switch.Default>
```

```
      <mtbwa:WriteBuildMessage x:Key="0"
         Importance="[Microsoft.TeamFoundation.Build.Client.
            BuildMessageImportance.High]"
         Message="[String.Format(&quot;Binary Archive '{0}' created.&quot;,
            &quot;output.zip&quot;)]"
         mva:VisualBasic.Settings="Assembly references
            and imported namespaces serialized as XML namespaces" />
      <mtbwa:WriteBuildWarning x:Key="1" Message="Non fatal error occured when
         running 7z.exe" />
      <mtbwa:WriteBuildError x:Key="2" Message="Fatal error running 7z.exe" />
      <mtbwa:WriteBuildError x:Key="7" Message="Command line error for 7z.exe" />
      <mtbwa:WriteBuildError x:Key="8" Message="Not enough memory to perform
         binary archive" />
      <mtbwa:WriteBuildError x:Key="255" Message="Process terminated" />
    </Switch>
  </Sequence>
</If.Then>
```

Code Snippet [464265 snippet2.txt]

Customizing Process Parameters

When you start to customize the build process, it is good to be able to re-use your build process templates. That way, you would hard-code as little as possible into the build to allow it to be adapted for use by other build definitions in your organization.

You have full access to be able to add your own properties so that they appear in the user interface when editing the build definition or queuing a new build. To add a new property and make it appear in the user interface, you would follow two steps:

1. You create the process argument.

2. You create the metadata that is used when displaying the argument in the Team Foundation build dialogs.

Creating the Process Argument

In the workflow designer, click on the Arguments section at the bottom of the designer. Scroll to the bottom of the arguments and click on the Create Argument section. Enter a name, direction ("In" for process parameters), argument type, and any default value. For this example, create two parameters — one to control the type of archive created (`ArchiveFormat`) and one to control the archive filename (`ArchiveOutputFile`), as shown in Figure 21-39.

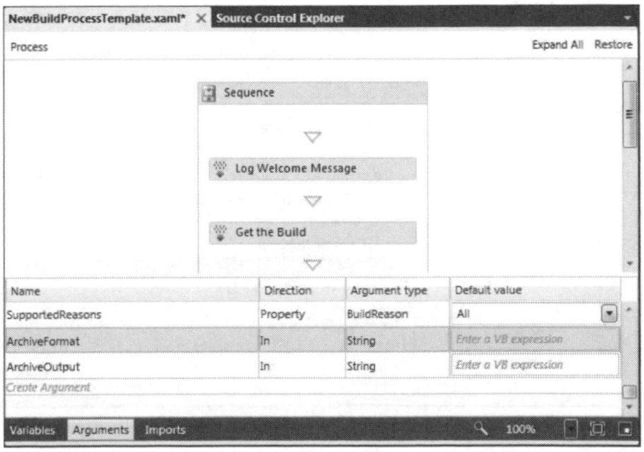

FIGURE 21-39

Creating Process Parameter Metadata

Next, you must create the metadata used to display the arguments in the Team Foundation build dialogs. In the Arguments section, find the argument called Metadata, which is a collection of all the metadata required for the process parameters. Click on the . . . button to open the Process Parameter Metadata Editor shown in Figure 21-40.

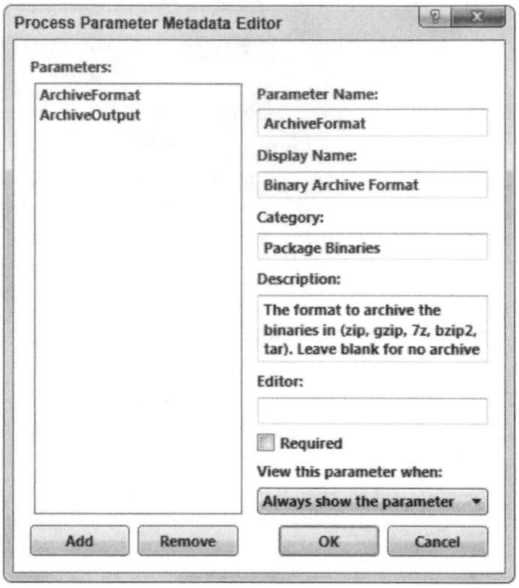

Add new parameters for each of the process arguments. Give them a suitable Display Name and Description. Set the Category to be Package Binaries so that they show in their own section of the process parameters. Also, set the "View this parameter when" field to be "Always show the parameter" so that it displays in both the build editing and the queue build dialog.

Click OK in the Process Parameter Metadata Editor. Save the build process template and check in to version control.

FIGURE 21-40

Right-click on the build definition in Team Explorer and select Edit Build Definition. Go to the Process section; your process parameters should now be displayed, as shown in Figure 21-41. Set the Binary Archive Output File to be `output.zip` and the Binary Archive Format to be `zip`, and then save the build definition.

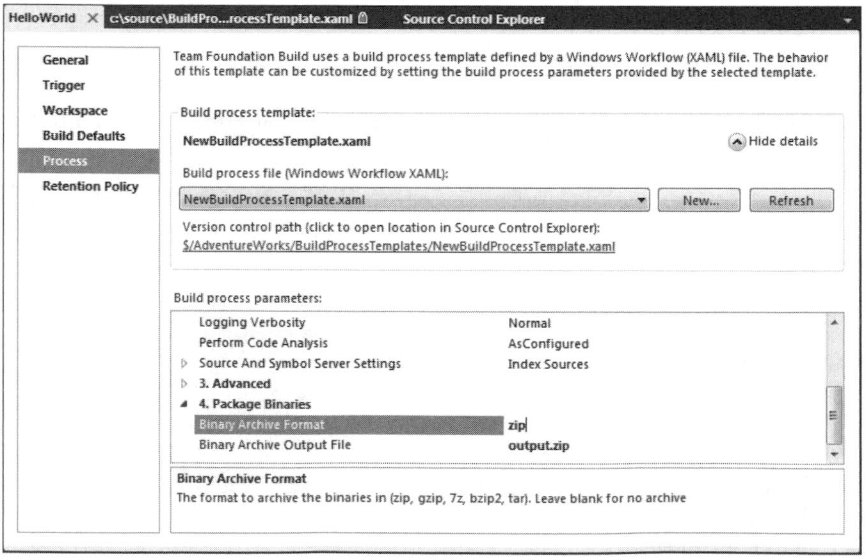

FIGURE 21-41

Now that you have created your process parameters, you want to make use of them. Taking the earlier example of creating a `zip` archive of the build binaries, let's now customize the process to make use of the new parameters.

The parameters appear in the workflow as variables that you can access. The designer has full Intellisense when writing functions, and you should see the new parameters appear when you start typing.

In the custom build template, replace occurrences where you have hard-coded the string `output.zip` and the archive type of `zip`. Also, add an "If" block into the package binaries sequence so that you only run 7-zip if an archive type has been specified — that is, an "If" block with the condition `Not String.IsNullOrEmpty(ArchiveFormat)` as shown in Figure 21-42.

The XAML created for this step should now look like the following:

FIGURE 21-42

```xml
<If Condition="[BuildDetail.CompilationStatus =
    Microsoft.TeamFoundation.Build.Client.BuildPhaseStatus.Succeeded]"
  DisplayName="If Compilation Successful">
  <If.Then>
    <Sequence DisplayName="Package Binaries">
      <Sequence.Variables>
        <Variable x:TypeArguments="x:Int32" Name="exitCode" />
      </Sequence.Variables>
      <If Condition="[Not String.IsNullOrEmpty(ArchiveFormat)]"
        DisplayName="If ArchiveFormat Specified">
        <If.Then>
          <Sequence DisplayName="Run 7zip">
            <mtbwa:InvokeProcess
              Arguments="[String.Format(&quot;a -bd -y -t{0} {1} {2}/* -r&quot;,
                  ArchiveFormat, Path.Combine(BinariesDirectory,
                  ArchiveOutput), BinariesDirectory)]"
              DisplayName="Invoke 7zip"
              FileName="[String.Format(&quot;{0}\7zip\7z.exe&quot;,
                  System.IO.Path.Combine(SourcesDirectory, &quot;tools&quot;))]"
              Result="[exitCode]">
              <mtbwa:InvokeProcess.ErrorDataReceived>
                <ActivityAction x:TypeArguments="x:String">
                  <ActivityAction.Argument>
                    <DelegateInArgument x:TypeArguments="x:String" Name=
                        "errOutput" />
```

```xml
              </ActivityAction.Argument>
              <mtbwa:WriteBuildError Message="[errOutput]" />
            </ActivityAction>
          </mtbwa:InvokeProcess.ErrorDataReceived>
          <mtbwa:InvokeProcess.OutputDataReceived>
            <ActivityAction x:TypeArguments="x:String">
              <ActivityAction.Argument>
                <DelegateInArgument x:TypeArguments="x:String" Name=
                    "stdOutput" />
              </ActivityAction.Argument>
              <mtbwa:WriteBuildMessage
                Message="[stdOutput]"
                mva:VisualBasic.Settings="Assembly references
                      and imported namespaces serialized as XML namespaces" />
            </ActivityAction>
          </mtbwa:InvokeProcess.OutputDataReceived>
        </mtbwa:InvokeProcess>
        <Switch x:TypeArguments="x:Int32" DisplayName="Check Exit Code of
            Process" Expression="[exitCode]">
          <Switch.Default>
            <mtbwa:WriteBuildError Message="[String.Format(&quot;Known exit
                code {0} from 7z.exe&quot;, exitCode)]" />
          </Switch.Default>
          <mtbwa:WriteBuildMessage x:Key="0"
            Importance="[Microsoft.TeamFoundation.
                Build.Client.BuildMessageImportance.High]"
            Message="[String.Format(&quot;Binary Archive '{0}'
                created.&quot;, &quot;output.zip&quot;)]"
            mva:VisualBasic.Settings="Assembly references
                  and imported namespaces serialized as XML namespaces" />
          <mtbwa:WriteBuildWarning x:Key="1" Message="Non fatal error
              occured when running 7z.exe" />
          <mtbwa:WriteBuildError x:Key="2" Message="Fatal error
              running 7z.exe" />
          <mtbwa:WriteBuildError x:Key="7" Message="Command line
              error for 7z.exe" />
          <mtbwa:WriteBuildError x:Key="8" Message="Not enough memory to
              perform binary archive" />
          <mtbwa:WriteBuildError x:Key="255" Message="Process terminated" />
        </Switch>
      </Sequence>
    </If.Then>
  </If>
</Sequence>
</If.Then>
```

Code Snippet [464265 snippet3.txt]

Now you have made this archive step part of a re-usable build process template. For builds that do not need binary archiving, just leave the archive file format to the default blank value. However, if you decide that you want an archive, you can set the archive type property and output file values, and then that functionality is automatically enabled.

Custom Workflow Activities

While it is possible to edit the process template to build up increased functionality, sometimes you may want to collect common workflow activities in a custom, re-usable Workflow Activity Library. Also, sometimes you might not want to simply build activities out of other activities, but execute some of your own .NET code.

For example, when creating the `zip` archive file discussed previously, rather than invoking the 7-zip process, you might want to create a custom activity that uses code from an Open Source archiving library, such as `SharZipLib`, to perform the `zip` functionality without requiring the 7-zip tool to be downloaded or installed.

You can create your own Windows Workflow activity libraries in .NET 4.0, build them a compiled assembly containing your activities, and then use them in your build process. The Team Build workflow activities themselves are provided in this way.

There are four main ways to author a new activity:

➤ Write a new `CodeActivity`

➤ Write a new `NativeActivty`

➤ Compose your custom activity in XAML

➤ Compose your custom activity in code

The first two ways involve creating code using the Windows Workflow libraries. While not incredibly complicated, it does require some exposure and knowledge of Windows Workflow programming, and a proper treatment of this is, therefore, outside the scope of this book. However, for an example of creating a build Code Activity, see the blog post from Jim Lamb, Program Manager of the Team Foundation Build team at Microsoft on the Web at `http://blogs.msdn` `.com/jimlamb/archive/2009/11/18/how-to-create-a-custom-workflow-activity-for-tfs-` `build-2010.aspx`.

The next two ways involve creating a new activity from existing activities. This is the best approach to take, when possible, for a few reasons. It re-uses well-tested code. The activities created are automatically cancelable by the workflow run-time, meaning that a build created with your activity can be stopped cleanly. They can be easily tracked as they execute. And, finally, the process is comparatively easy.

A custom-composed activity is basically what you created previously when you were customizing the build process. By putting this into a Workflow Activity assembly, you are just making those activities re-usable by other build process templates as a compiled assembly.

So, let's create a custom activity. To get started, create a new Windows Workflow `ActivityLibrary` project in Visual Studio. Add references to `Microsoft.TeamFoundation.Build.Workflow` in `ProgramFiles\Microsoft Visual Studio 10\Common7\IDE\PrivateAssemblies` and to `Microsoft.TeamFoundation.Build.Client` in `ReferenceAssemblies`. This will allow you to use the Team Foundation Server build activities in addition the standard Workflow 4.0 activities. To get this to build correctly, you might need to change the project's target framework to .NET Framework 4, rather than the .NET Framework Client Profile default.

You can then copy/paste the Run 7zip sequence from your earlier build process customization and refactor it to introduce some new activity arguments, as shown in Figure 21-43.

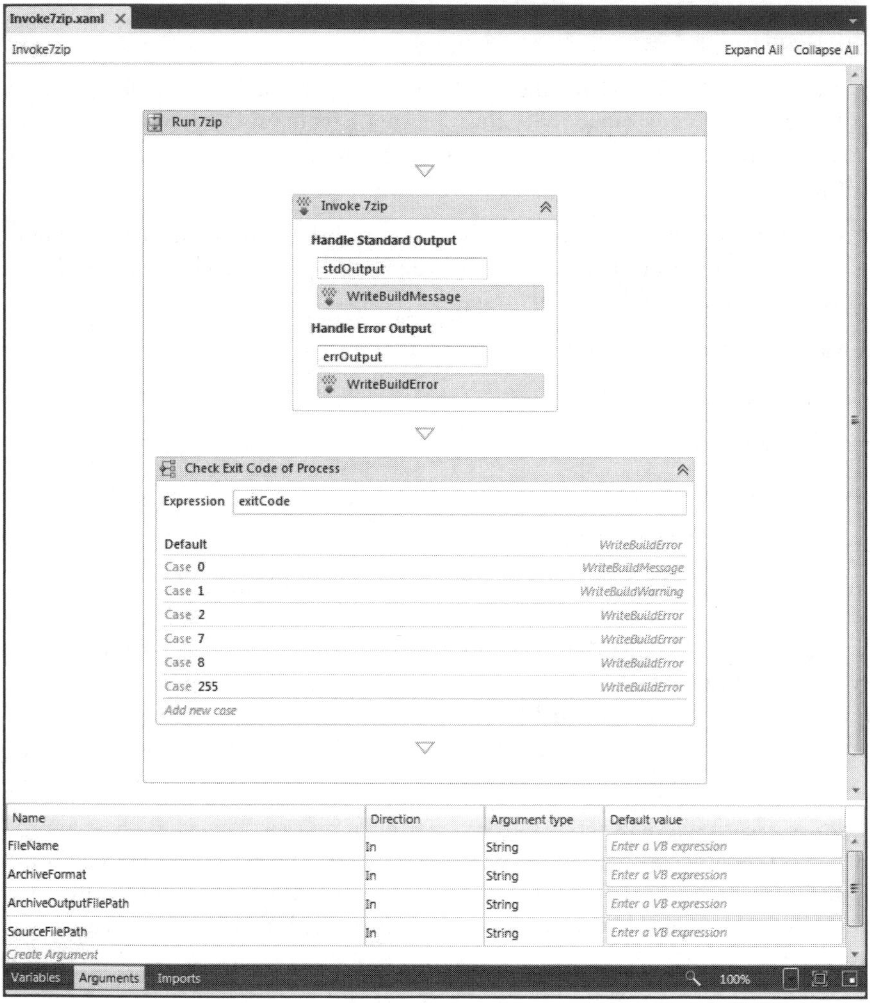

FIGURE 21-43

The XAML code behind the changes in the designer looks as follows:

Available for download on Wrox.com

```
<Activity mc:Ignorable="sap" x:Class="CustomBuildActivities.Invoke7zip"
  xmlns="http://schemas.microsoft.com/netfx/2009/xaml/activities"
  xmlns:mc="http://schemas.openxmlformats.org/markup-compatibility/2006"
  xmlns:mt="clr-namespace:Microsoft.TeamFoundation;
       assembly=Microsoft.TeamFoundation.Common"
  xmlns:mtbc="clr-namespace:Microsoft.TeamFoundation.Build.Client;
       assembly=Microsoft.TeamFoundation.Build.Client"
  xmlns:mtbw="clr-namespace:Microsoft.TeamFoundation.Build.Workflow;
```

```
      assembly=Microsoft.TeamFoundation.Build.Workflow"
xmlns:mtbwa="clr-namespace:Microsoft.TeamFoundation.Build.Workflow.Activities;
      assembly=Microsoft.TeamFoundation.Build.Workflow"
xmlns:mtbwt="clr-namespace:Microsoft.TeamFoundation.Build.Workflow.Tracking;
      assembly=Microsoft.TeamFoundation.Build.Workflow"
xmlns:mttbb="clr-namespace:Microsoft.TeamFoundation.TestImpact.
      BuildIntegration.BuildActivities;assembly=
      Microsoft.TeamFoundation.TestImpact.BuildIntegration"
xmlns:mtvc="clr-namespace:Microsoft.TeamFoundation.VersionControl.Client;
      assembly=Microsoft.TeamFoundation.VersionControl.Client"
xmlns:mtvc1="clr-namespace:Microsoft.TeamFoundation.VersionControl.Common;
      assembly=Microsoft.TeamFoundation.VersionControl.Common"
xmlns:mv="clr-namespace:Microsoft.VisualBasic;assembly=System"
xmlns:mva="clr-namespace:Microsoft.VisualBasic.Activities;
      assembly=System.Activities"
xmlns:s="clr-namespace:System;assembly=mscorlib"
xmlns:s1="clr-namespace:System;assembly=System"
xmlns:s2="clr-namespace:System;assembly=System.Core"
xmlns:s3="clr-namespace:System;assembly=System.ServiceModel"
xmlns:s4="clr-namespace:System;assembly=System.ComponentModel.Composition"
xmlns:s5="clr-namespace:System;assembly=System.Xml"
xmlns:sa="clr-namespace:System.Activities;assembly=System.Activities"
xmlns:sad="clr-namespace:System.Activities.Debugger;assembly=System.Activities"
xmlns:sap="http://schemas.microsoft.com/netfx/2009/xaml/activities/presentation"
xmlns:scg="clr-namespace:System.Collections.Generic;assembly=mscorlib"
xmlns:scg1="clr-namespace:System.Collections.Generic;assembly=System"
xmlns:scg2="clr-namespace:System.Collections.Generic;
      assembly=System.ServiceModel"
xmlns:scg3="clr-namespace:System.Collections.Generic;assembly=System.Core"
xmlns:sd="clr-namespace:System.Data;assembly=System.Data"
xmlns:si="clr-namespace:System.IO;assembly=mscorlib"
xmlns:si1="clr-namespace:System.IO;assembly=System"
xmlns:si2="clr-namespace:System.IO;assembly=System.Core"
xmlns:si3="clr-namespace:System.IO;assembly=WindowsBase"
xmlns:si4="clr-namespace:System.IO;assembly=System.ServiceModel"
xmlns:sl="clr-namespace:System.Linq;assembly=System.Core"
xmlns:st="clr-namespace:System.Text;assembly=mscorlib"
xmlns:x="http://schemas.microsoft.com/winfx/2006/xaml">
<x:Members>
  <x:Property Name="FileName" Type="InArgument(x:String)" />
  <x:Property Name="ArchiveFormat" Type="InArgument(x:String)" />
  <x:Property Name="ArchiveOutputFilePath" Type="InArgument(x:String)" />
  <x:Property Name="SourceFilePath" Type="InArgument(x:String)" />
</x:Members>
<mva:VisualBasic.Settings>Assembly references and imported namespaces
      for internal implementation</mva:VisualBasic.Settings>
<Sequence DisplayName="Run 7zip"
  sad:XamlDebuggerXmlReader.FileName="C:\code\
      CustomBuildActivities\CustomBuildActivities\Invoke7zip.xaml">
  <Sequence.Variables>
    <Variable x:TypeArguments="x:Int32" Name="exitCode" />
  </Sequence.Variables>
  <mtbwa:InvokeProcess
    Arguments="[String.Format(&quot;a -bd -y -t{0} {1} {2}/* -r&quot;,
```

```xml
          ArchiveFormat, ArchiveOutputFilePath, SourceFilePath)]"
      DisplayName="Invoke 7zip"
      FileName="[String.Format(&quot;{0}\7zip\7z.exe&quot;, FileName)]"
      Result="[exitCode]">
      <mtbwa:InvokeProcess.ErrorDataReceived>
        <ActivityAction x:TypeArguments="x:String">
          <ActivityAction.Argument>
            <DelegateInArgument x:TypeArguments="x:String" Name="errOutput" />
          </ActivityAction.Argument>
          <mtbwa:WriteBuildError Message="[errOutput]" />
        </ActivityAction>
      </mtbwa:InvokeProcess.ErrorDataReceived>
      <mtbwa:InvokeProcess.OutputDataReceived>
        <ActivityAction x:TypeArguments="x:String">
          <ActivityAction.Argument>
            <DelegateInArgument x:TypeArguments="x:String" Name="stdOutput" />
          </ActivityAction.Argument>
          <mtbwa:WriteBuildMessage
            Message="[stdOutput]"
            mva:VisualBasic.Settings="Assembly references and imported
                namespaces serialized as XML namespaces" />
        </ActivityAction>
      </mtbwa:InvokeProcess.OutputDataReceived>
    </mtbwa:InvokeProcess>
    <Switch x:TypeArguments="x:Int32"
      DisplayName="Check Exit Code of Process"
      Expression="[exitCode]">
      <Switch.Default>
        <mtbwa:WriteBuildError Message="[String.Format(&quot;Known exit
            code {0} from 7z.exe&quot;, exitCode)]" />
      </Switch.Default>
      <mtbwa:WriteBuildMessage x:Key="0"
        Importance="[Microsoft.TeamFoundation.Build.Client.
            BuildMessageImportance.High]"
        Message="[String.Format(&quot;Binary Archive '{0}' created.&quot;,
            &quot;output.zip&quot;)]"
        mva:VisualBasic.Settings="Assembly references and imported namespaces
            serialized as XML namespaces" />
      <mtbwa:WriteBuildWarning x:Key="1" Message="Non fatal error occured when
          running 7z.exe" />
      <mtbwa:WriteBuildError x:Key="2" Message="Fatal error running 7z.exe" />
      <mtbwa:WriteBuildError x:Key="7" Message="Command line error for 7z.exe" />
      <mtbwa:WriteBuildError x:Key="8" Message="Not enough memory to
          perform binary archive" />
      <mtbwa:WriteBuildError x:Key="255" Message="Process terminated" />
    </Switch>
  </Sequence>
</Activity>
```

Code Snippet [464265 Invoke7zip.xaml]

As previously discussed, you could also create this in pure code. In this case, you could derive directly from `System .Activities.Activity<T>`. But, as you can see in Figure 21-44, `CodeActivity<T>` and `NativeActivity<T>` are provided as base classes that are used when building an activity that contains more functionality than just a composition of other activities.

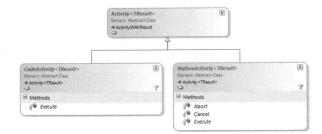

FIGURE 21-44

Regardless of how you create your custom activities, you must be able to configure the build controller and build agents so that they are able to locate the compiled Workflow Activity Library assemblies. To do this, you must check in the compiled assembly into a folder in version control. Then, you point the build controller to this folder by right-clicking on the Builds node in Team Explorer. Select Manage Build Controllers, select the controller, and then click Properties. You will then be presented with the Build Controller Properties dialog, shown in Figure 21-45, where you can browse version control to provide the custom assembly path.

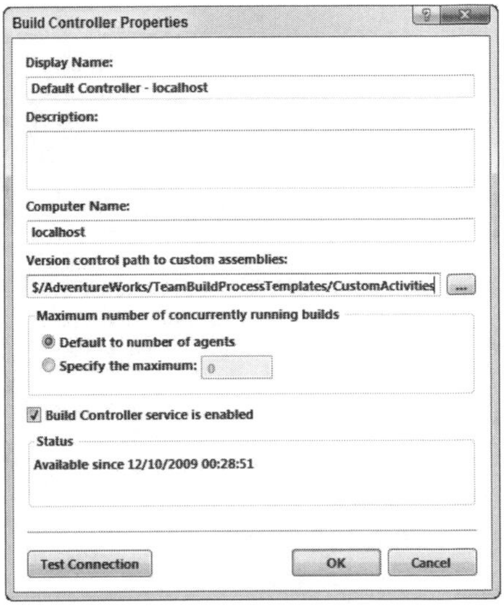

SUMMARY

FIGURE 21-45

In this chapter, you gained an understanding of the build services provided by Team Foundation Server 2010, and how they have been enhanced from previous versions.

You learned how to create build definitions, trigger builds, and view and manage build results. You also learned how the new Windows Workflow-based build process works and how to perform common customizations.

Finally, you learned how to further customize the build process yourself, using the example of creating a `zip` archive as part of the build process.

In Chapter 22, you will learn about the project management capabilities of Team Foundation Server. In Chapter 23, you will learn about the process templates governing the way in which work is done in Team Foundation Server for your team project, including which build process templates should be provided.

PART V
Project/Process Management

Introduction to Project Management

WHAT'S IN THIS CHAPTER?

➤ Exploring project management capabilities in Team Foundation Server

➤ Learning about Team Project

➤ Learning how to use work items to plan your project

➤ Understanding work items and how you can track work

➤ Learning how to use Microsoft Project and Microsoft Excel to manage work items in Team Foundation Server

Software development is a team sport. The players in a software development team include developers, testers, business analysts, project managers, and more.

In American football, a quarterback is leader of the team on the field and has multiple tasks at hand — the most obvious being the handling of the football. A quarterback should be able to communicate clearly to his teammates the plan for the next play, call an audible depending on the opposing team's defensive formations, change routes on-the-fly if his assigned receivers are double-teamed by the opposition, and manage the game clock effectively and efficiently. This is just a sample list of a quarterback's responsibilities.

You could infer that there are similarities between the responsibilities of a quarterback and the role of a project manager in a software development team. There are clear parallels in that a project manager should communicate the task at hand clearly to the team, be able to change the project plan based on changes caused by requirement changes or resource issues, be able to reassign tasks if a particular team member is blocked, and manage the overall schedule and scope. While a quarterback's responsibilities are sometimes tested in a matter of few seconds during a particular play, thankfully it is not that dramatic in a project manager's world.

The point here is that a project manager is a key player and a leader of the software team, and has a huge impact on the success or failure of the project.

While we're on the subject of success and failure, it may be worth mentioning that a 2004 report from Standish Group estimates an overall software project success rate of 34 percent. In other words, two thirds of software projects have failed to meet the needs of the stakeholders. It is rather a gloomy assessment. A quick search on the Internet will result in several reports and research papers on the factors contributing to the failures. Could you attribute all of this project success or failure to a project manager? Not quite. Remember, software development is a team sport. So, the entire team must play their roles in successfully completing a project, with the project manager as the orchestrator.

Having the right information at the right time is critical to understanding the various aspects of the project, including schedule, scope, risks, resource issues, and so on. As the famous saying goes, "Garbage in means garbage out."

Obviously, information plays a key role here. You no doubt know that having binders full of process controls for the team to follow, and a gazillion tools/logs to capture the information, is only a deterrent, and does not help in capturing the information.

Here are some of the common tasks that are performed repeatedly by project managers:

➤ Help define scenarios and customer requirements to map out the features of the software application, and ensure that these features provide business value within a limited budget.

➤ Create a set of iteration plans based on milestones.

➤ Work with team members to define and schedule development and test tasks to successfully implement each scenario.

➤ Orchestrate work flow, facilitate communication within your development team, and manage relationships.

➤ Continuously monitor the status of the project to avoid bottlenecks and identify possible risks.

In Visual Studio 2010 and Team Foundation Server 2010, there are capabilities/features to accomplish many of these things. Not only can you create and monitor project plans, Team Foundation Server 2010 provides a set of tools and the infrastructure to help you communicate and collaborate with other team members, automatically aggregate and collect project health metrics, and centralize all project management operations. Project managers can now choose to interact with a project on Team Foundation Server using a variety of tools, including Microsoft Excel, Microsoft Project, or Visual Studio 2010 Team Explorer. You can pick the tool you feel most comfortable with, and run with it. The same is true if you are a developer, or an architect, or a tester. You can choose one of the Visual Studio editions, or Excel, or Team Explorer to integrate with Team Foundation Server 2010.

TEAM PROJECT SETUP AND CONFIGURATION

Team Foundation Server provides a set of capabilities to aid in better planning, scheduling, managing scope, communication, reporting and analysis, and continuous process improvement. These capabilities include the following:

➤ *Team project* — Stores and organizes data about the entire software development lifecycle of a project, including work items, code, tests, reports and more. It's the topic of the next section of this chapter.

➤ *Team Project Collection* — A new concept introduced in Team Foundation Server 2010, this is a container for multiple team projects. See Chapter 17 for more information on team collections.

➤ *Process template* — This is a set of XML files that defines the process used by a team project. This includes work item types, fields and workflow, reports, and more. See Chapter 23 for details.

➤ *Process guidance* — This is a narrative guidance for the two process templates. See Chapter 23 for more on this.

➤ *Work item tracking* — Work items represent requirements, tests, and bugs in Team Foundation Server. The tracking of these work items (including the state, the assignment, and information contained within) is key to managing the project. You will learn more about work items and work item tracking in Chapters 22 through 26 of the book.

➤ *Project portal/dashboards* — Dashboards provide a one-stop view for team members. This includes a snapshot of work items assigned to a particular team member, reports, and more. This is explored in more detail in Chapter 24.

➤ *Microsoft Project and Microsoft Excel integration* — With this integration, team members can access information in Team Foundation without having to use Visual Studio. More on this later in this chapter.

➤ *Planning workbooks* — Team Foundation Server 2010 introduced two new planning workbooks to help Agile teams manage their backlogs both at the project level, and at the iteration level. See Chapter 25 for details.

➤ *Reporting* — Team Foundation Server leverages the wealth of data captured throughout the lifecycle of a project, and presents it in various reports. There are sets of reports included with each of the two process templates, and you can modify existing reports, or add new reports. See Chapter 24 for more on this.

Creating a Team Project

The basis for all projects in Team Foundation Server is the team project. The team project holds information about every step of the software development lifecycle in a central repository within the Team Foundation Server. This includes requirements, scheduling, source code, build, quality, and resources.

There are important differences between a team project and a Visual Studio project — in fact, some people get confused about the meaning of these project types. The Team Explorer enables you to navigate and manage all elements of your team project, including your development team, the SharePoint team portal, source code repository, work item database, documents, reports, and templates.

Not every new project in your organization will require a new team project. If the new project is part of a larger organizational effort, or you are continuing a new phase of an existing effort, then you are probably looking at joining an existing team project instead of a creating a new one. Obviously, creating a new team project means that you will have the flexibility to choose the process you want to use, customize work items based on the needs of the project, have a project portal specific to that team project, and so on. These items all have one-to-one dependency with the team project.

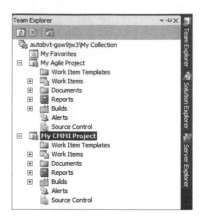

FIGURE 22-1

Figure 22-1 shows two team projects (MyAgileProject and MyCMMIProject) as displayed in Team Explorer.

> ✎ *Chapter 17 provides a detailed overview of Team Explorer.*

Before examining the anatomy of a team project, let's create a new team project. Here is what you need to know before you start:

➤ The name for your team project.

➤ The process that you are going to use with this team project.

> ✎ *Chapter 23 provides more detail on a Visual Studio Team Foundation Server 2010 process template.*

➤ A description for the team project.

➤ Source control needs for your project.

➤ Portal site needs for your project.

> ✖ *Be sure to connect to a Team Foundation Server before creating a team project. Note that the team project name or the process template cannot be changed once the team project is created. It is important that you make these selections after careful consideration of the team's requirements for the project.*

New Team Project

To create a new project, select File ➪ New Team Project from the Visual Studio menu. The New Team Project Wizard appears, as shown in Figure 22-2, prompting you to enter a name for your project. Alternatively, you can launch the wizard by right-clicking your server name in the Team Explorer and selecting New Team Project. Name your project and click Next.

Next, select a process template (see Figure 22-3). Team Foundation Server comes with two process templates: MSF (Microsoft Foundation) for Agile Software Development v5.0, and MSF for CMMI (Capability Maturity Model Integration) Process Improvement v5.0.

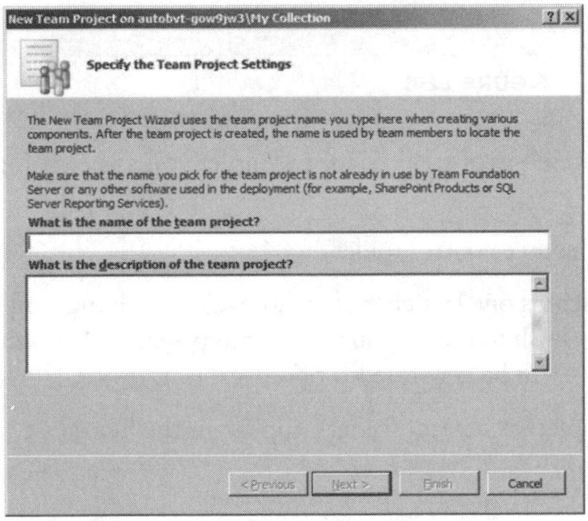

FIGURE 22-2

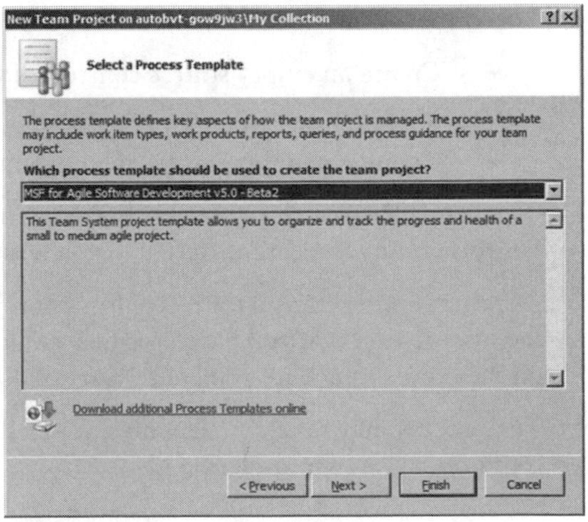

FIGURE 22-3

You should choose the process template that best fits your team's need. For this example, select the MSF Process for Agile Development template. You can obviously customize the template and associate artifacts along the way, but there is not an easy way to change to the process template of an existing team project. Note the link on this dialog window, which points to an online Web page with links to other available process templates. For more information on Process Templates, see Chapter 23.

The next step is to choose the site setting. If you have set up SharePoint integration with Team Foundation Server, then a portal site based on SharePoint can be created for the team project. (Refer to Chapter 17 for more on this integration.) As you can see in Figure 22-4, you can elect to create a SharePoint site. Use the Configure option to specify where you want the site to be created.

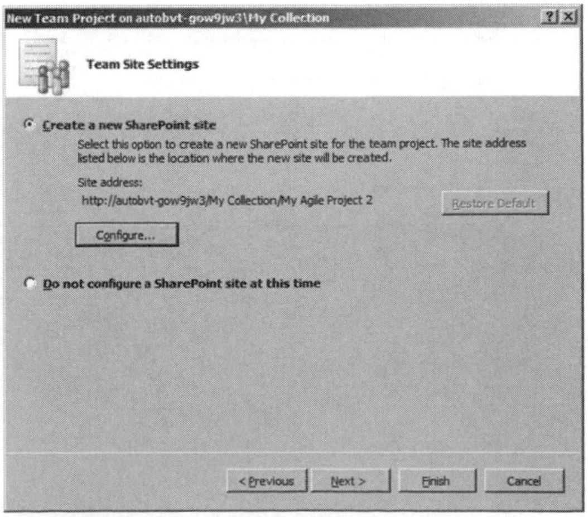

FIGURE 22-4

You also have the option to not create a SharePoint site. You can use the Project Portal Settings dialog shown in Figure 22-5 to change this selection. As you can see, there is an option to point to an existing Web site instead of a new portal site. You can do the same for process guidance as well. For example, you can use the same process guidance site for more than one team project.

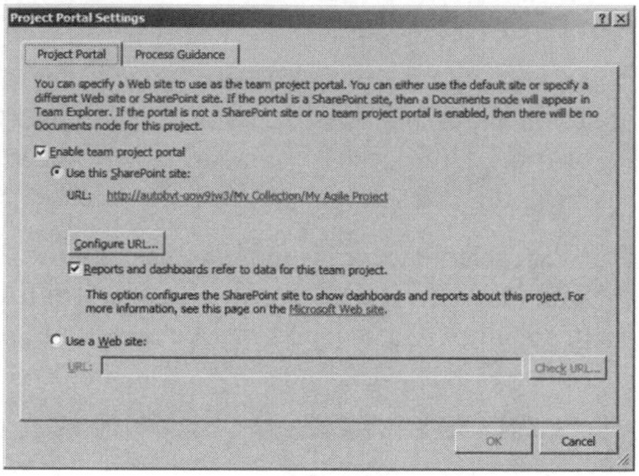

FIGURE 22-5

The next step in the configuration (Figure 22-6) is to set the preliminary source control options. There are two choices:

➤ Create an empty source control folder for your project.

➤ Create a new branch from an existing source control tree (if, for example, you are creating a project that is derived from another).

For this example, select the option to create an empty source control folder.

Clicking Next takes you to the confirmation page. Here is one last chance to go back and change any of the information that you have specified so far. Click Finish to create your new team project. Depending on the process template you chose, a set of documents will be generated for your project.

The process may take a little while. When it is completed, several folders appear in the Team Explorer, as shown in Figure 22-7.

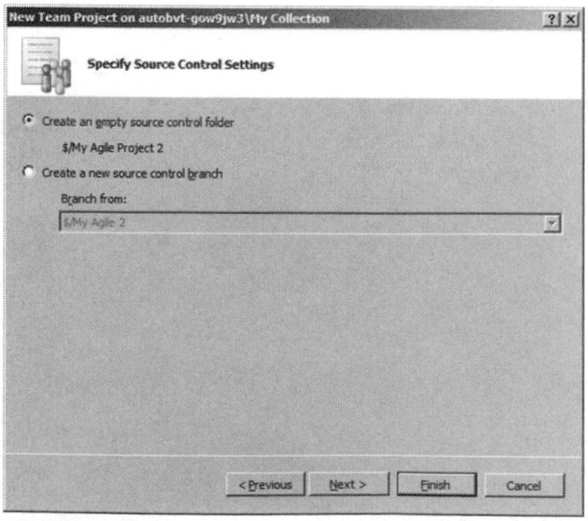

FIGURE 22-6

FIGURE 22-7

Your team project tree has five primary nodes:

➤ *Work Items* — This includes predefined queries and custom queries to list the work items associated with your project.

➤ *Documents* — This includes Process Guidance, Excel Reports, Samples and Templates, and Shared Documents to help you map out your development process.

➤ *Reports* — This includes a variety of reports grouped into several folders.

➤ *Builds* — This provides access to a variety of build definitions, including custom types.

➤ *Source Control* — This provides easy access to your source code tree via the Source Control Explorer.

Connecting to the Team Foundation Server

The team project becomes the gateway to every member of the project team. For those team members familiar with Visual Studio, Team Explorer and the various nodes should be familiar.

Before you can start working with a team project, you must first connect to your Team Foundation Server. Team Explorer enables you to connect to different instances of Team Foundation Server and manage the associated projects. The easiest way to connect to Team Foundation Server is by clicking Tools ➪ Connect to Team Foundation Server. If the Team Explorer isn't showing up, you can bring it up by clicking View ➪ Team Explorer.

Once you connect to the server, a window will appear to help you manage your server, team project collection, and team projects. Figure 22-8 shows the "Connect to Team Foundation Server" window. Notice that the team projects have checkmarks next to them. This enables you to pick the team project to which you want to attach and, hence, show in the Team Explorer.

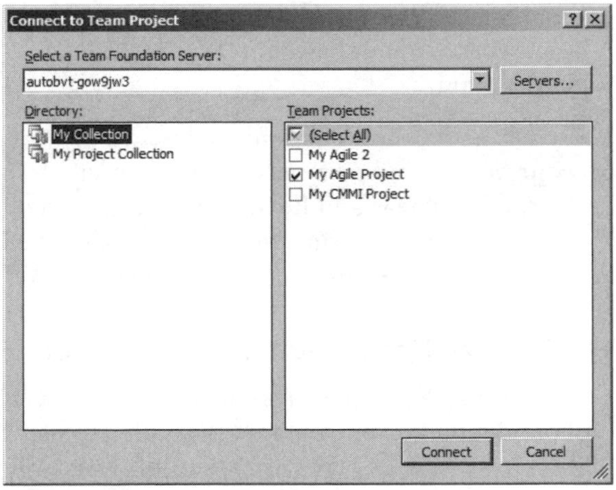

Also, you can remove the team project from the Team Explorer by right-clicking on the team project name and clicking "Remove," or simply selecting the team project and pressing the Delete key. Note that this action does not delete the team project, but only removes it from the Team Explorer. You can add it back to the Team Explorer at a later time if you choose to.

FIGURE 22-8

Structuring Your Project

Once you have created a project, you must be able to configure it to fit your needs. As a project manager, you want to ensure that the team members have access to the team project and associated artifacts (such as reports) that are critical to their jobs. You, as a project manager, will work with your administrator to manage the project security settings.

One of the easiest ways of organizing work items in your project is by grouping them together logically. In Team Foundation Server, you can use Iterations and Areas. Many software projects (particularly involving teams using Agile Methods) develop software in iterations. It makes sense to organize work items in iterations, rather than having teams wade through a huge pool of work items for each project.

To access the Areas and Iterations feature, right-click on your team project and then select Team Project Settings ⇨ Areas and Iterations.

Click on the Iterations tab and you'll notice that there are already predefined iterations in place: Iteration 1, Iteration 2, and Iteration 3, as shown in Figure 22-9. You can rename these to whatever you like.

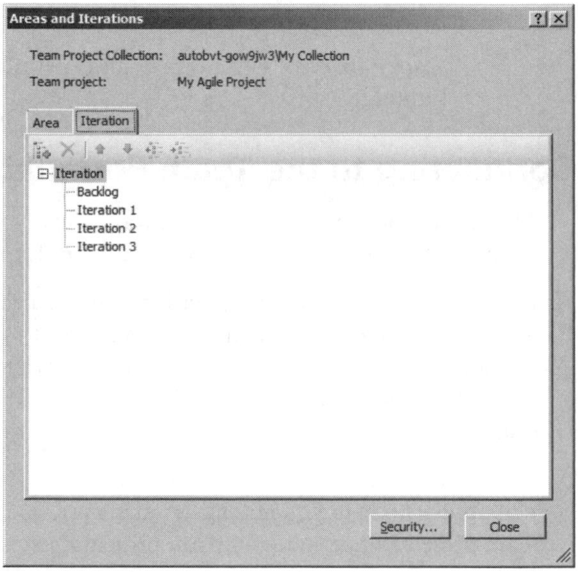

Areas offer another way of organizing and classifying your work. Think of Areas as another word for "categories." You can define your own custom areas and assign work to them. Then, it is quite easy to filter the work by area. Areas also can be used to manage and group work by teams or sub-teams. For example, there could be sections of a project that will only be worked by a small set of team members; areas can be used to set off that work without having to expose it to the larger team.

To access the Areas options, right-click on your project and then select Team Project Settings ⇨ Areas and Iterations. To create a collection of areas, start by right-clicking on the root area node and selecting New. A sub-node called "Area 0" will appear right below the root node. You can rename this node to whatever you like.

FIGURE 22-9

Working with the Team Project Portal

The team project portal is the window to a wealth of information about team projects. In Team Foundation Server, you have the option to use the team project portal based on Windows SharePoint Services (WSS), or the new Microsoft Office SharePoint Services (MOSS) based dashboards with Excel services reports. You will learn more about portals, dashboards, and reports in Chapter 24.

PLANNING YOUR PROJECT

With the creation of your team project and associated configurations (including permissions and source control settings), you now have the necessary infrastructure to start and structure your project. As a project manager, one of your key activities is to build a project plan and continue with the planning throughout the project, as changes appear along the way. Obviously, the method or technique you use may vary depending on the methodology you use. Whether you are an Agile team doing just enough planning and continuously changing the plans as you embrace change, a team that lays out a detailed plan upfront and monitors and modifies it as change happens, or somewhere in between, the activity of planning is every bit as important. To quote Dwight D. Eisenhower, "Plans are nothing; planning is everything."

Work items are the key entities that take the form of requirements, bugs, test cases, and so on. Regardless of the tool you use, the work items are created and stored in the centralized data store of Team Foundation Server. (Chapter 19 provides more information on this.) What this means is that the team members can choose the tool they are most comfortable with, and still have access to the task lists defined as part of the work breakdown structure. For example, a project manager may opt to use Microsoft Excel to define and modify the work breakdown structure, whereas a developer or a tester may opt to use a work item form from within Visual Studio.

> *If you rather enjoy the comfort of your Outlook application while working with Team Foundation Server work items, there are couple of third-party tools that integrate Team Foundation Server and Microsoft Outlook. Check out* `http://www.teamcompanion.com` *and* `http://www.personifydesign.com/products/teamlook/teamlook.aspx` *for these third-party tools.*

ALL THINGS WORK ITEMS

Work items are the drivers behind Team Foundation Server's work management and project-tracking capabilities. In this section, you'll learn a little about work item internals, including what they are, how to create and manage work items in your projects, using work item queries, and how to create custom work item types (WITs).

Understanding a Work Item

Work items are the core entities in Team Foundation Server that represent requirements, bugs, issues, test cases, risks, and more. Work items capture and provide the information that powers the reports.

In Team Foundation Server, the type of work items depend on the process template you use. Each of the process templates will have a set of work items. For example, the Agile template that ships in Team Foundation Server 2010 has the following work items:

- ➤ User Story
- ➤ Task
- ➤ Issue
- ➤ Bug
- ➤ Test Case
- ➤ Shared Step Set

> *For more on these work item types in the Agile template, refer to Chapter 23.*

All of the work items in your project are stored in the work item database and, hence, form the basis for the reports used to gauge the progress of a project.

Table 22-1 describes some of the common fields found in work items. (Note that this is, by no means, an exhaustive list.)

TABLE 22-1: Common Fields Found in Work Items

NAME	DESCRIPTION
ID	Uniquely identifies each work item within the work item database.
State	Describes the status of a work item. The initial state varies by the work item type. For example, it is "Active" for a new "User Story" work item in the Agile template.
Type	The type of work item. Depending on the process template you select, several work item types are made available within a team project, such as User Story, Bug, Test Case and so on.
Priority	Indicates the priority order for your work items. This enables your team members to prioritize their workloads and rank work items in order of importance.
Title	The title of the work item. Ensure that you create a descriptive title, because it is the first thing you will see when you design a Work Item Query. For example, simply writing "Bug" will not help you assess the type or importance of the bug in the system.
Assigned To	Identifies the team member to whom the work item is assigned. You can change the value of this field when you want to reassign a work item to another team member.

Work items can also contain durations (including a start date and finish date), descriptions, work estimates, and more. You can also associate a work item with an area and an iteration. For example, if you are doing iterative development, you want to assign work items (such as requirement, use case, story, and so on) to the corresponding iteration.

In simple terms, a work item is a collection of fields with information necessary to carry out various activities in project management, be it development or testing or issue identification. Collections of these fields are grouped into types of work items. Work items are represented in a form with the respective fields, and any associated validations and rules. For example, certain fields may be read-only, and certain other fields may only become editable based on a certain value entered in another field.

Figure 22-10 shows the work item is displayed within Visual Studio.

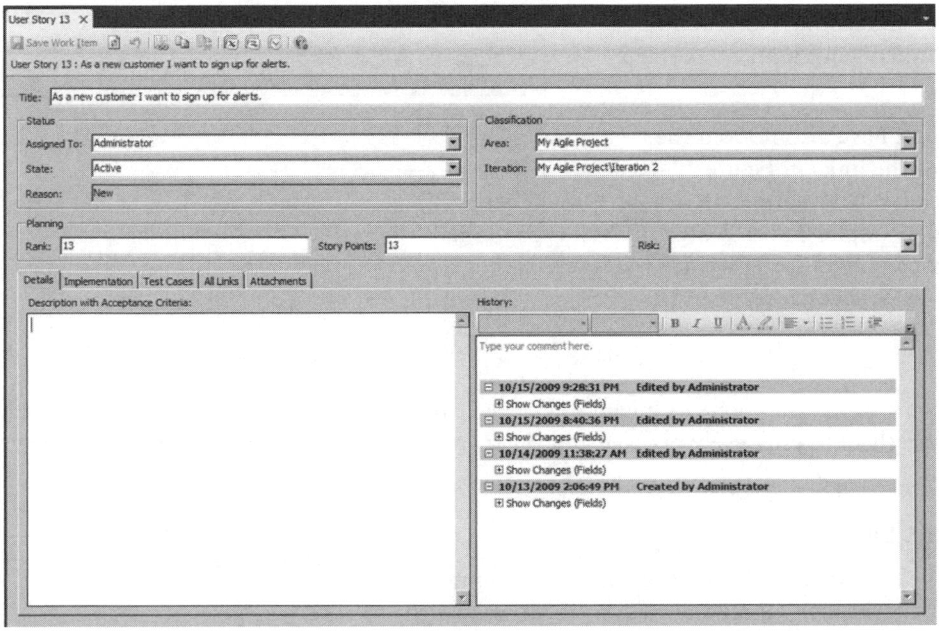

FIGURE 22-10

Earlier, you learned about areas and iterations. As you can see in Figure 22-10, work items have fields for choosing areas and iterations. You will select the appropriate values for these two fields to group work as needed.

Work Item Links and Link Types

Work item links and relationships have undergone a major facelift in this new version of Team Foundation Server. In the previous version of Team Foundation Server, work item lists were essentially a flat list with simple linking between one work item and another. This was not particularly useful when you were dealing with relationships that were more defined (such as a parent-child or predecessor-successor type relationships), nor when you were building a tiered list with grouped work items.

Enter Team Foundation Server 2010. The prayers of those wishing for hierarchical work items have been granted. Not only that; now, out-of-the-box work items support several link types, and allow you to add custom link types as well.

In Figure 22-11, you see a list of link types. This window shows a dialog to add a linked work item from an existing work item.

It is easy to add a linked work item by right-clicking on the work item you want to add a link to, and choosing whether you want to add a link to an existing work item or create a new linked work item, as shown in Figure 22-12.

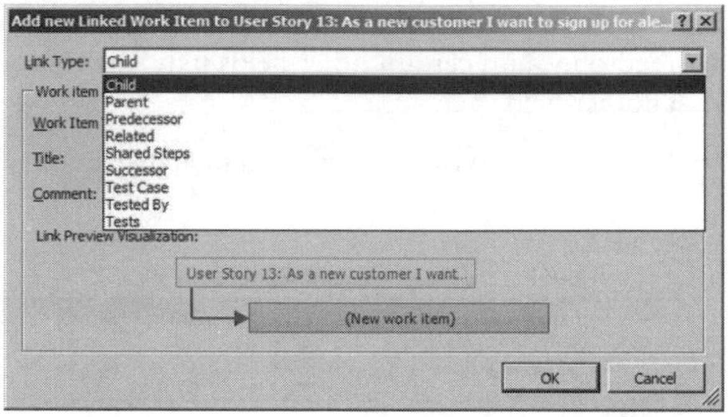

Curious eyes will have also noticed the visualization of the links in Figure 22-11. This provides a quick visual preview of what the relationship looks like. For example, if you change the link type in the drop-down from "Child" to "Parent," you'll see that the visualization changes accordingly.

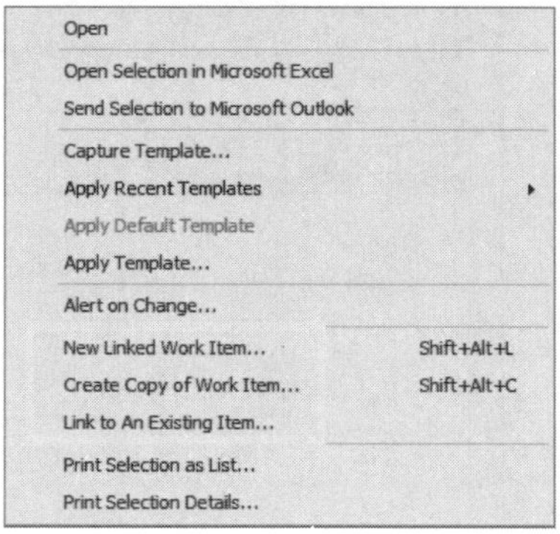

FIGURE 22-11

Link Types

Let's look at some of the common work item link types, and how you can use them to effectively manage and track your project.

Related Items Link

FIGURE 22-12

You will use the "Related item" link type to create a simple and straightforward relationship between one or more work items. You will typically use this to link work items of same level (such as two Requirements work items or two Features work items). Note that, by using this type, you are not creating a hierarchy. When you migrate over work items that are linked from team projects in prior versions of Team Foundation Server, these links will, by default, be made into a Related link in Team Foundation Server 2010.

Parent-Child Link

These two link types bring the much-awaited hierarchical work items to Team Foundation Server. You will use these two link types to create a tiered set of work items.

For example, a user story will be completed by finishing a set of task work items. For this, you would create a user story work item and set of child task work items that are associated with the particular user story work item. Note that each work item can have only one parent, but a parent can have many child work items. Figure 22-13 shows a work item with a set of linked work items.

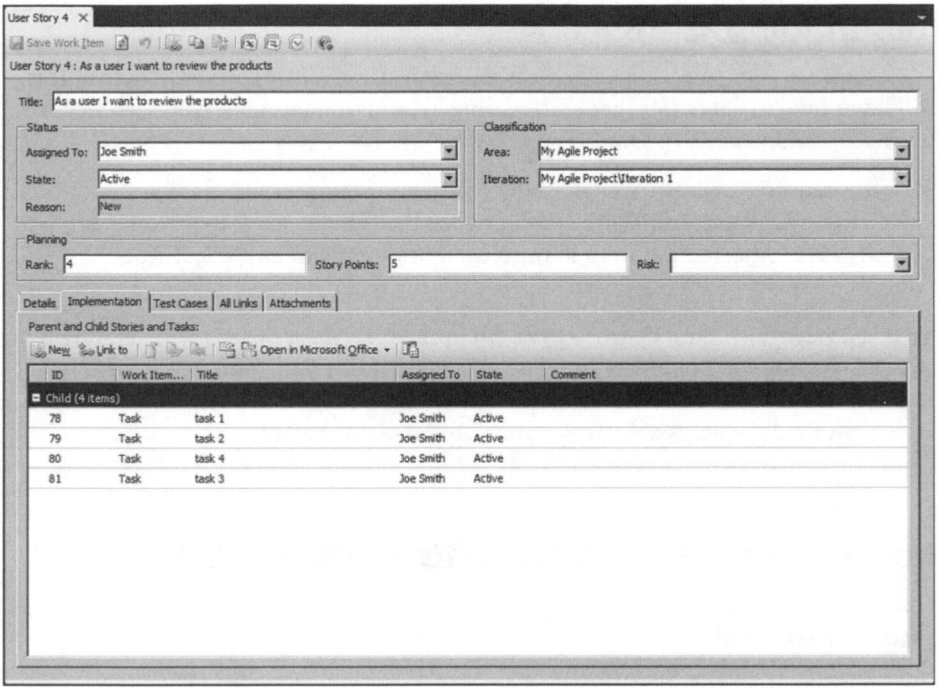

FIGURE 22-13

As you can see, the work item displays information such as the ID, Title, who it is assigned to, and so on. There are also a few tabs that are included in this work item. Note that the tabs, and any information within these tabs, vary by the work item type.

Figure 22-13 shows the details in the Implementation tab, which contains the associated work items. This user story work item contains four task work items as its child work items. If you open one of the child work items, you will see the parent work item in the Implementation tab.

Predecessor-Successor Link

As the name suggests, you will use these link types to create a sequential dependency. For example, if there is a task or feature that must be completed prior to starting another task or feature, then you will use this link type to express that dependency.

Creating and Updating Work Items

In this section, you will see how to create and edit work items using Visual Studio. Later in this chapter, you will learn how to carry out these tasks using Team Foundation Server Web Access, Microsoft Office Excel, and Microsoft Office Project.

To create a new work item from within Visual Studio, go to your team project in Team Explorer. Right-click Work Items, and select Add Work Item. Choose the type of work item you want to create. You can also click the Team option in the Visual Studio menu and select Add Work Item.

If you choose to add a new "User Story" work item, fill in the New User Story form, as shown in Figure 22-14. As you see, the Title field has template text filled in for you. This is the form to define the user, the user's actions, and the goals. The new "User Story" work item will be saved in the work item store, and will be accessible to everyone on the team project.

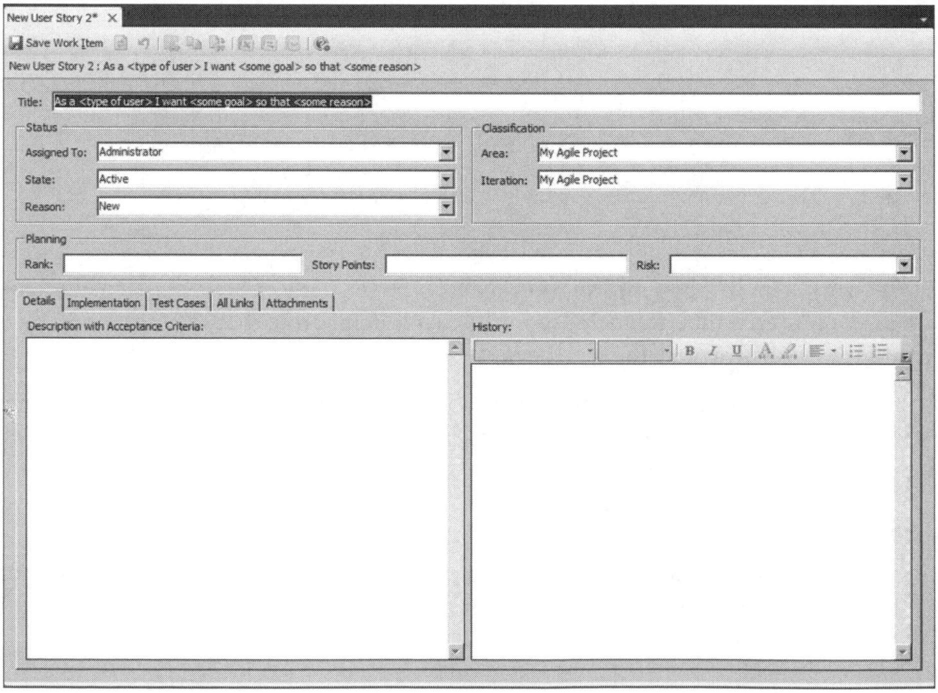

FIGURE 22-14

To edit a work item, you can go to that particular work item if you know the ID; or, in Team Explorer, your can pick a query to find the work item. For example, double-click the Work Items ➪ Team Queries ➪ Open Work Items query. A split window will appear, with a work item list on the top, and a preview pane at the bottom.

As soon as you select a work item in the top pane, you can edit the work item in the bottom pane. Make the changes to the selected work item, and click Save Work Item to save these changes to the work item data store.

Once the changes are saved, you will see that the History information is updated with an entry for the latest change that you made. This will include the date and time stamp for the changes that were made, the user that made the changes, and the fields that were changed, including the original value and the new value. This information is quite valuable for the entire team. As a project manager, you can monitor these changes and, if there are questions that are based on these changes, you know who to ask, because that information is captured automatically.

Work Item Queries

Now that you know how to create a work item, edit a work item, and add links to a work item, the next step is to understand how to track the work items throughout the project lifecycle. Tracking the status of the work items (and, hence, the progress of the project) is a chore that project managers do regularly.

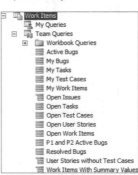

Pre-Defined Work Item Queries

You will use the work item queries to get a view into the status of the various work items. Team projects contain a `Work Items` folder with two sub folders titled `My Queries` and `Team Queries`. The `Team Queries` folder contains several predefined work item queries that are based on the process template of the team project. Figure 22-15 shows the list of queries in a team project based on the Agile Process template.

FIGURE 22-15

> *A subfolder called* `Workbook Queries` *in* `Team Queries` *is discussed in more detail in Chapter 26.*

To get the results of a Work Item Query, you can simply double-click the corresponding query in the Team Explorer window.

Let's look at the Open User Stories query by right-clicking on it and selecting the Edit Query option. This will load the query editor with the split pane. The top pane will display the query itself, with the results of the query displayed in the bottom pane, as shown in Figure 22-16.

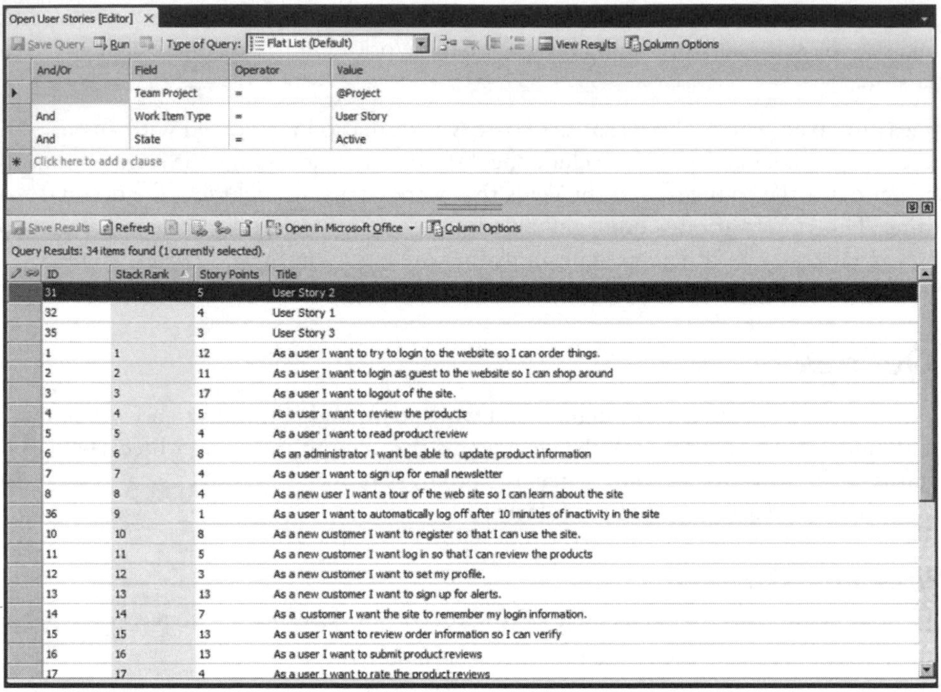

FIGURE 22-16

As you see in the query editor, the Open User Stories query uses three clauses to pull in work items that are User Stories from the current team project with a state that is not Closed. You could modify the clauses in the query editor to tweak the results. For example, if you want to restrict the query to pull only work items assigned to a certain team member, you could do so by adding a clause using the field Assigned To.

In Figure 22-16, you see the "Type of Query" field in the query editor. There are three types of queries:

➤ Flat List

➤ Work Items and Direct Links

➤ Tree

For the Open User Stories query, this field is set to Flat List. That is the default option for work item queries. This query results in 34 items, as shown in the bottom pane in Figure 22-16. To get a list of work items linked work items, change the query type to "Work Items and Direct Links." As you see in Figure 22-17, this query now brings a total of 74 items, including 34 top-level items and 40 linked items.

Open User Stories [Editor]* ✕

Save Query Run | Type of Query: Work Items and Direct Links ▾ | View Results Column Options

And/Or	Field	Operator	Value
	Team Project	=	@Project
And	Work Item Type	=	User Story
And	State	=	Active
*	Click here to add a clause		

And linked work items that match the query below:

And/Or	Field	Operator	Value
	Work Item Type	=	[Any]
*	Click here to add a clause		

− Linking Filters

Top level work items:
- Return all top level work items
- Only return items that have the specified links
- Only return items that do not have the specified links

Types of links:
- Return links of any type
- Return selected link types:
  - ☐ Affected By
  - ☐ Affects
  - ☐ Child
  - ☐ Parent

Save Results Refresh | Open in Microsoft Office ▾ Column Options

Query Results: 74 items found (34 top level, 40 linked items, 1 currently selected).

ID	Link Type	Stack Rank	Story Points	Title
41	Child			Task 4
42	Child			Task 3
43	Child			Task 2
44	Child			Task 1
2		2	11	⊟ As a user I want to login as guest to the website so I can shop around
31	Child		5	User Story 2
32	Child		4	User Story 1
35	Child		3	User Story 3
3		3	17	⊟ As a user I want to logout of the site.
36	Child	9	1	As a user I want to automatically log off after 10 minutes of inactivity in the site
4		4	5	⊟ As a user I want to review the products
78	Child			task 1
79	Child			task 2
80	Child			task 4
81	Child			task 3
5		5	4	⊟ As a user I want to read product review
82	Child			task 1

FIGURE 22-17

You can refine this list further by using the linking filters. You could choose to return work items with any type of links (which is the result shown in Figure 22-17), or you can only return work items with specific types of link. You could also choose to return only work items that either have or don't have a specified type of link. This type of query is very helpful when you want to find a list of requirements without any test cases, user stories without any associated tasks, and so on.

Creating a New Work Item Query

To create a Work Item Query, go to the Team Explorer pane. Right-click on Work Items, and select Add Query. In the query editor, simply change the And/Or, Field, Operator, and Value fields.

Once you save a query, you will be prompted to do one of the following:

➤ *Make it visible to everyone on the team* — If you choose to make it visible to everyone on your team, the query will appear in the Team Queries folder in Team Explorer (and everyone on your team will be able to run it).

➤ *Make it visible only to yourself* — If you choose to save it for yourself, it will appear in the My Queries folder in Team Explorer (and it will not be visible to the rest of your team).

Personal queries are useful to organize your work items in useful views (for example, all the personal tasks that were assigned by a particular project manager).

➤ *Save it as a file* — If you are working on a customized process template, the Save as a File option is useful to extract queries as WIQ files.

USING MS OFFICE WITH TEAM FOUNDATION SERVER

You probably are not thinking about (or used to thinking about) Visual Studio when it comes to project planning. And that does not have to change. With Visual Studio Team Foundation Server 2010, you have at least three ways to build and manage your work breakdown structure:

➤ Using Team Explorer within Visual Studio

➤ Using Microsoft Office Project

➤ Using Microsoft Office Excel

This section examines the integration between Microsoft Office Project/Office Excel and Team Foundation Server. Obviously, these are two very popular and commonly used Microsoft tools for laying out a work breakdown structure and managing the tasks throughout the lifecycle of the project.

> *Chapter 25 provides more information on the use of Excel for managing prod-uct backlog and iteration backlog for an agile team.*

Figure 22-18 from the Team Foundation Server help documentation shows the integration between Team Foundation Server, and Microsoft Office Project and Microsoft Office Excel. As you can see, the Work Item Add-in is the key connector. You get this when you install Team Explorer or one of the Visual Studio 2010 editions on your computer.

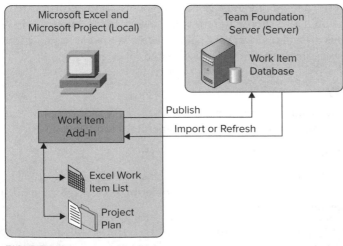

FIGURE 22-18

Office Project and Team Foundation Server

In Microsoft Office Project, you see a team project menu item and a toolbar with team-related actions, as shown in Figure 22-19.

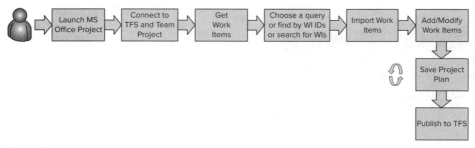

FIGURE 22-19

You start by connecting to a team project.

Once you connect to the team project, you create the project plan with a detailed list of requirements, schedule, resources, and so on.

Figure 22-20 shows a pictorial representation of a flow to connect to Team Foundation Server and manage work items.

FIGURE 22-20

Field Types

The mapping between the fields in the work item in Team Foundation Server and the fields in Microsoft Project are defined in a field mapping file, which is an XML file that is specific to a team project. It can be modified by using `TFSFieldMapping` utility. You will use this command-line utility to download the mapping file of your team project, make changes as necessary, and upload the file to the team project. It is important that the mappings between the fields in the Team Foundation Server Work Item database and Microsoft Project are compatible.

Using Office Project to Create a Project

Let us start by attaching to an existing team project. Launch Microsoft Project and click "Choose team project" from the toolbar. In the "Connect to Team Foundation Server" window, verify that the Team Foundation Server name is correct and select a team project. Then, click OK to connect to this project.

You will notice that a few new columns show up in Project after the connection has been established. By default, Microsoft Project uses the Gantt view. In this split view of Gantt chart and task sheet, the field labels are updated to reflect the labels used in Team Foundation Server work items. In this view, read-only fields are marked, and fields with predefined values in Team Foundation Server will have a drop-down attached to them for selection. There are fields in Microsoft Project that are not stored in Team Foundation Server work items, so saving the Microsoft Project plan is a good idea.

In addition, if you have certain tasks that you are not going to track in Team Foundation Server (such as getting a contract in place, budget approval, vendor selection activities, and so on), you can still have them in the same project plan, but mark the field "Publish and Refresh" as No. This will prevent this line item from being published or overwritten during the synchronization with Team Foundation Server work items.

Obviously, as project manager, you will lay out a high-level project plan and let the team members work on filling in the details (including detailed requirements, a breakdown into development and architecture tasks, and testing-related tasks). These tasks could be entered by the business analyst, developer, architect, and testers, using the Team Explorer within Visual Studio. You can pull these work items into Microsoft Project and into your project plan by clicking on the Get Work Items option in the toolbar.

This will launch the Get Work Items dialog, as shown in Figure 22-21.

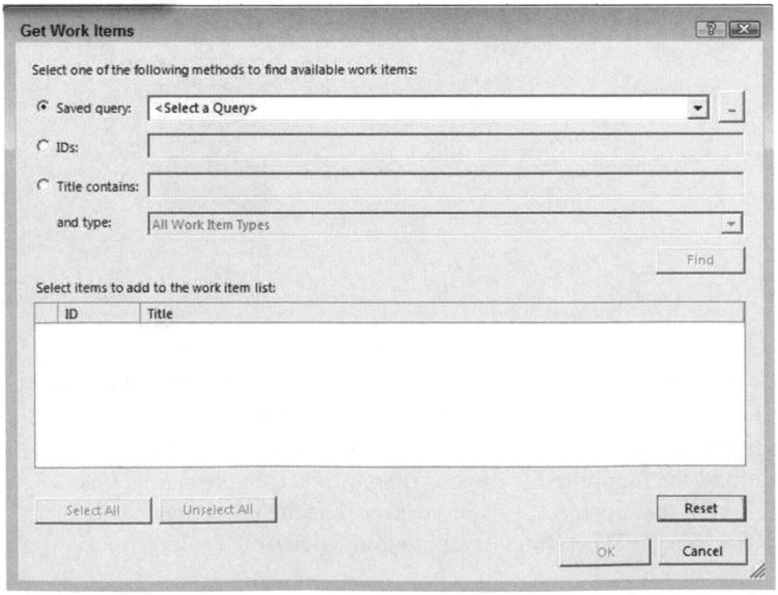

FIGURE 22-21

From this dialog, you have the following three ways to pull work items into Microsoft Project:

➤ By using a saved query from within Team Foundation Server (which is a frequently used option to pull in a set of work items from Team Foundation Server)

➤ By specifying the ID or IDs of the few work items (if you are looking to pull particular work items)

➤ By specifying a keyword in a work item title, and the type of work item

Regardless of the option you choose, you click the Find button to locate the work items based on your selections. Then you have the choice of selecting a particular work item (or all work items) from the results window, and bringing those into Microsoft Project.

As an alternate way to get these work items into Microsoft Project, start in the Team Explorer and run the query that you are interested in. Once you get the results of this query, you will see a menu item to open the results in Microsoft Project or Microsoft Excel, or to send the query in an email to Microsoft Outlook.

Once you have the requirements and tasks in the project plan, the next step is to organize the plan with dependencies, a summary, and subtasks.

You could create summary tasks and subtasks from within Microsoft Project using the indent and outdent capabilities, or you could use the "Links and Attachments" option from the team project toolbar. Note that if you use the "Links and Attachments" option to create summary tasks and subtasks, these relationships/links are stored in the Team Foundation Server database. To see this relationship in the Microsoft Project plan, you must publish these changes and do a refresh of these work items from Team Foundation Server.

In MS Project, you can define your work breakdown structure with summary and sub tasks. After you are finished organizing the project plan, publish the work items to Team Foundation Server by clicking the Publish button in the toolbar. To avoid conflicts with changes, synchronize the project plan in Microsoft Project with Team Foundation Server on a regular basis.

In Visual Studio 2010, with the hierarchical support, the list of work items retains the parent-child relationships established in MS Project. Figure 22-22 shows the list of work items in a tree view with parent-child relationships.

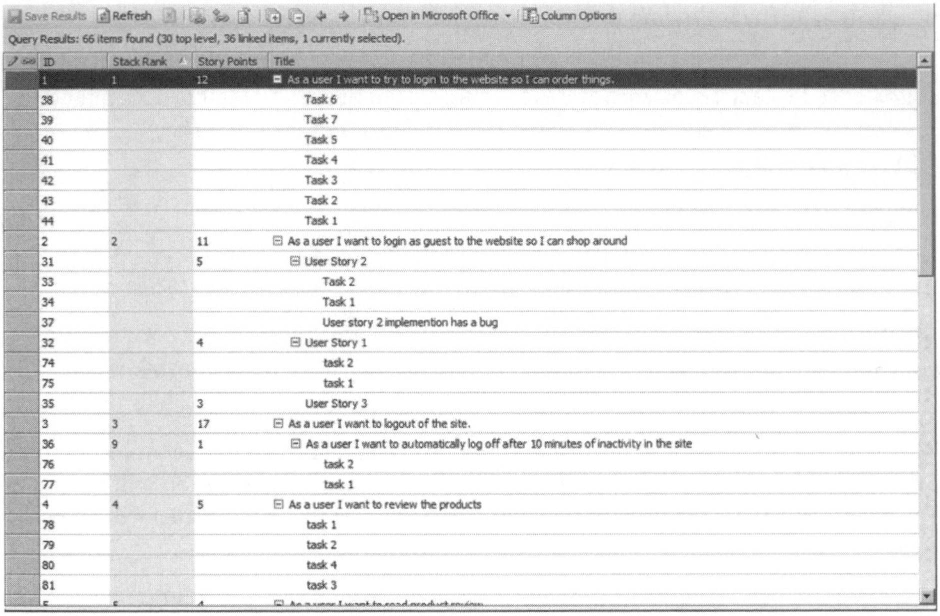

FIGURE 22-22

This linking and hierarchical capability for work items was one of the most often requested features in Team Foundation Server, and it is now available in the 2010 version.

You can continue to work with your project plan offline while not connected to Team Foundation Server or a team project. Once you have completed making necessary changes, you can reconnect to Team Foundation Server and the team project, and perform a "Publish" to get the changes in. If there were any conflicts in changes, you will get validation errors that you need to take care of prior to completing the publish. If you have not made any changes to the plan while you were offline, you can simply pull in the latest set of work items by reconnecting to Team Foundation Server and the team project and performing a "Refresh."

There are certain operational differences between Office Project and Team Foundation. The Team Foundation Server help document captures these differences, as shown in Table 22-2.

TABLE 22-2: Differences Between Office Project and Team Foundation Server

COMPONENT	OFFICE PROJECT	TEAM FOUNDATION SERVER	RECOMMENDED ACTIONS
Team project calendar	Maintains a team project calendar week that specifies workday length, weekends, and holidays.	Has no concept of a calendar week, so it cannot track days when work does not take place.	Use Microsoft Project to manage project schedules, and use this feature.
Task constraints and dependencies	Allows you to specify task dependencies, dependency types, and lead and lag times that specify the scheduling relationships between tasks.	Tracks predecessor-successor dependencies as work item links for context, but it does not track dependency types, lead and lag times, or work item constraints.	Use Microsoft Project to manage and update changes to dependencies and constraints.
Start and finish dates and tracking hours worked	Constraints applied to tasks dictate when tasks can start or when they must finish. A change made to the number of hours worked automatically recalculates remaining work and finish dates.	Stores estimated, completed, remaining work, and start and finish dates, but it does not recalculate the fields when updates are made. For example, if you use Team Explorer to increase the duration of a task, Team Foundation Server does not update the finish date.	Use Microsoft Project to manage and update changes to the start and finish dates, and to update calculated fields for completed and remaining work.
Resource assignments	Supports allocating multiple resources to a task.	Allows only one resource to be assigned to a task.	In Microsoft Project, assign only one resource to a task. Break tasks into subtasks in order to allocate them to more than one resource.

continues

TABLE 22-2 *(continued)*

COMPONENT	OFFICE PROJECT	TEAM FOUNDATION SERVER	RECOMMENDED ACTIONS
Publish and refresh	Changes made to tasks in Microsoft Project must be published to be seen in Team Foundation Server.	Changes made to work items in Team Foundation Server must be refreshed in Microsoft Project to be seen.	In Microsoft Project, only publish those tasks that you want to also track in Team Foundation Server. You do this by setting the Publish and Refresh field as needed. Publish and refresh the project plan frequently to avoid data conflicts.

Source: VSTS Help Files

In summary, as a project manager, you can continue to work in the familiar environment of Microsoft Project to build a project plan, schedule resources, set dependencies, publish a baseline, and track progress against the baseline. With Team Foundation Server integration, now you have opened up the plan to the entire team. The team members can add tasks, estimates, work completed, and so on, with the tool that they are accustomed to (such as Visual Studio).

Office Excel and Team Foundation Server

This section examines the integration between Microsoft Office Excel and Team Foundation Server. Microsoft Excel is a popular tool among many project managers and team members that is used to manage tasks lists and resources. Figure 22-18 shows the integration between Team Foundation Server, and Microsoft Project and Microsoft Excel. The Work Item Add-in makes a new Team tab appear in Excel, as shown in Figure 22-23.

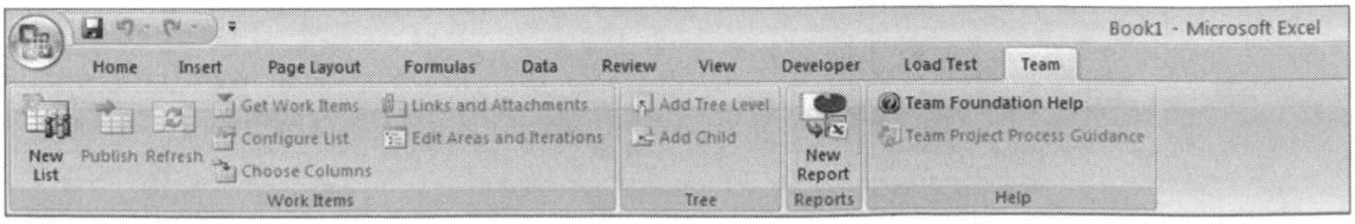

FIGURE 22-23

Figure 22-24 shows one sequence of connecting to a Team Foundation Server team project and managing work items from within Microsoft Excel.

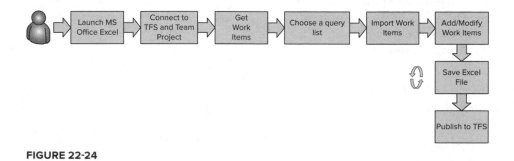

FIGURE 22-24

Using Excel to Plan a Project

Let's start by connecting to the team project. To do so, select the New List menu item from the Team tab. That will bring up the Connect to Team Foundation Server dialog. This is a familiar drill, so select the Team Foundation Server and the team project to connect to. Once connected to the team project, you will be presented with a New List dialog, as shown in Figure 22-25.

FIGURE 22-25

Following are the two options to choose from to build the work item list:

➤   *Query List* — A query list is tied to a particular Work Item Query in Team Foundation Server. (That is, the query list will bring the results of a Work Item Query into Microsoft Excel as a list.) This could be a flat or tree list, depending on the query itself. When you refresh the query list, any changes or items that are not in Team Foundation Server will be overwritten with the results from the query.

➤   *Input List* — An input list is not tied to a particular query in Team Foundation Server. You can build a plan/list by using one or more queries, and by hand-picking work items. You could also add items to this list that are not tracked in Team Foundation Server, and not have worry about losing these items when refreshing the work item list.

Using the Input List Option

For now, choose the "Input list" option to build a plan using Microsoft Excel. That builds a table with a set of columns.

Obviously, what you have is an empty table. So, let's pull a list of work items into this spreadsheet. Click Get Work Items on the Team tab and select the "Open User Stories" query for the Saved Query. This will load the spreadsheet with the Open User Story work items from Team Foundation Server, as shown in Figure 22-26.

With support for hierarchical and linked work items, comes two new menu items: Add Tree Level and Add Child.

Let's use these two new menu options to understand how it works. Click Add Tree Level. This will change the list to the Tree View, add additional columns such as "Title 2" and "Title 3," and pull in any associated child work items, as shown in Figure 22-27.

Project: My Agile Project **Server:** autobvt-gow9jw3\My Collection **Query:** [None] **List type:** Flat

ID	Title	Work Item Type	State	Reason	Assigned To
31	User Story 2	User Story	Active	New	John Doe
32	User Story 1	User Story	Active	New	Sally Smith
35	User Story 3	User Story	Active	New	Joe Smith
1	As a user I wa	User Story	Active	New	John Doe
2	As a user I wa	User Story	Active	New	John Doe
3	As a user I wa	User Story	Active	New	John Doe
4	As a user I wa	User Story	Active	New	Joe Smith
5	As a user I wa	User Story	Active	New	Joe Smith
6	As an admini:	User Story	Active	New	Joe Smith
7	As a user I wa	User Story	Active	New	Sally Smith
8	As a new use	User Story	Active	New	Sally Smith
36	As a user I wa	User Story	Active	New	John Doe
10	As a new cust	User Story	Active	New	Administrator
11	As a new cust	User Story	Active	New	Administrator
12	As a new cust	User Story	Active	New	Administrator
13	As a new cust	User Story	Active	New	Administrator
14	As a custome	User Story	Active	New	Administrator
15	As a user I wa	User Story	Active	New	Administrator
16	As a user I wa	User Story	Active	New	Administrator
17	As a user I wa	User Story	Active	New	Administrator
18	As an admini:	User Story	Active	New	Administrator
19	As an admini:	User Story	Active	New	Administrator
20	As a user I wa	User Story	Active	New	Administrator
21	As a user I wa	User Story	Active	New	Administrator
22	As a user I wa	User Story	Active	New	Administrator
23	As a user I wa	User Story	Active	New	Administrator
24	As a user I wa	User Story	Active	New	Administrator
25	As a user I wa	User Story	Active	New	Administrator
26	As a user I wa	User Story	Active	New	Administrator
27	As a user I w:	User Story	Active	New	Administrator
28	As a administ	User Story	Active	New	Administrator
29	As a user I wa	User Story	Active	New	Administrator
30	As a user I wa	User Story	Active	New	Administrator
9	As a administ	User Story	Active	New	Administrator

FIGURE 22-26

Project: My Agile Project **Server:** autobvt-gow9jw3\My Collection **Query:** [None] **List type:** Tree

ID	Title 1	Title 2	Title 3	Title 4	Work Item Type	State	Reason	Assigned To
1	As a user I want to try to login to the website so I can order things.				User Story	Active	New	John Doe
38		Task 6			Task	Active	New	John Doe
39		Task 7			Task	Active	New	John Doe
40		Task 5			Task	Active	New	John Doe
41		Task 4			Task	Active	New	John Doe
42		Task 3			Task	Active	New	John Doe
43		Task 2			Task	Active	New	John Doe
44		Task 1			Task	Active	New	John Doe
2	As a user I want to login as guest to the website so I can shop around				User Story	Active	New	John Doe
31		User Story 2			User Story	Active	New	John Doe
33			Task 2		Task	Active	New	John Doe
34			Task 1		Task	Active	New	John Doe
37			User story 2 implemention has a bug		Bug	Active	New	John Doe
32		User Story 1			User Story	Active	New	Sally Smith
74			task 2		Task	Active	New	Sally Smith
75			task 1		Task	Active	New	Sally Smith
35		User Story 3			User Story	Active	New	Joe Smith
3	As a user I want to logout of the site.				User Story	Active	New	John Doe
36		As a user I want to automatically log off after 10 minutes of			User Story	Active	New	John Doe
76			task 2		Task	Active	New	John Doe
77			task 1		Task	Active	New	John Doe
4	As a user I want to review the products				User Story	Active	New	Joe Smith
78		task 1			Task	Active	New	Joe Smith
79		task 2			Task	Active	New	Joe Smith
80		task 4			Task	Active	New	Joe Smith
81		task 3			Task	Active	New	Joe Smith
5	As a user I want to read product review				User Story	Active	New	Joe Smith
82		task 1			Task	Active	New	Joe Smith
83		task 2			Task	Active	New	Joe Smith
84		task 3			Task	Active	New	Joe Smith
6	As an administrator I want be able to update product information				User Story	Active	New	Joe Smith
85		task 1			Task	Active	New	Joe Smith
86		task 2			Task	Active	New	Joe Smith
87		task 3			Task	Active	New	Joe Smith
88		task 4			Task	Active	New	Joe Smith
89		task 5			Task	Active	New	Joe Smith

FIGURE 22-27

On the other hand, if you wanted to add more child items to an existing parent item, you would use the Add Child menu item. Select the row with the work item to which you want to add the child item, and click Add Child. This will insert a blank row to provide the details of this new child item.

Click Publish and this new child item with the "Parent-Child" link is now committed to the Team Foundation Server work item data store. You can verify that by running a query from within Team Explorer if you like.

> *There are some common conditions that could result in an error when working tree lists in Microsoft Excel. See the help document, "How to: Resolve Invalid Links in an Office Excel List Tree," for more information on how to resolve these common tree list errors.*

SUMMARY

This chapter took a quick tour of some of the capabilities of Team Foundation Server to aid in managing software projects. Communication is a key element, and one that ensures a great flow of information within the team, as well as to the various stakeholders (both business and technical). Team Foundation Server not only provides the common repository to store and mine this information, but also provides integration with various tools that are commonly used by different members of a software team.

You learned how to create a team project, and to manage security and access to the team project. You learned how to use commonly used project management tools such as Microsoft Project and Microsoft Excel to create, manage, and update a project plan by leveraging the integration between these tools and Team Foundation Server.

The process you choose to follow as part of your team development is critical to the team. So is the ability to understand the metrics based on the information gathered throughout the lifecycle. Understanding the status of the project using reports, customizing or building additional reports, and the capability to have a dashboard that has the common set of data and reports that informs the team members of the current status and the task at hand, are very valuable during the course of the project. These topics will be the focus of upcoming chapters.

Chapter 23 kicks off that discussion by examining process templates.

Process Templates

WHAT'S IN THIS CHAPTER?

➤ Understanding the process template and its components

➤ Learning about the MSF for Agile Software Development
v5.0 template

➤ Learning about the MSF for CMMI Process Improvement
v5.0 template

A *process* is a method or a system used by teams while developing software applications. Most of us have had our fair share of experience working on projects using the waterfall method. And there is no shortage of other documented processes as well. A quick search online could get you a list of various development processes. These processes rely on the members of the team to comprehend the value that this process offers, and to follow the steps or procedures laid out by these processes.

As most of us could attest, many times the processes that were documented in binders and handed off to team members stayed largely untouched. You might argue that this was because of the sheer complexity of the process itself, or because of the amount of context-switching required by the team members to adhere to some of these processes. The list of potential reasons goes on. Sam Guckenheimer and Juan Perez, in their book *Software Engineering with Microsoft Visual Studio Team System* (Upper Saddle River, N.J: Addison-Wesley Professional, 2006), talk about the fact that most processes and tools force a one-size-fits-all approach, and hence, do not factor in the varying needs of teams.

Visual Studio 2010 Ultimate edition and Team Foundation Server 2010 provide a customizable environment for teams to choose and adopt a process (and set of practices) that matches the needs of the team, and does so by integrating the process enactment within the tool. This reduces context-switching enormously, and significantly raises the probability of process adherence by team members.

Process templates provide the fabric that brings together the key components of Visual Studio Team Foundation Server 2010 for process enactment. As a colleague used to describe it, process templates are the files to get Team Foundation Server configured to fit the way your team works well.

This chapter looks into the various components of a process template. The discussion in this chapter helps you understand the process templates that ship with Team Foundation Server and reviews a few of the process templates that are available from partners and the community.

UNDERSTANDING A PROCESS TEMPLATE

Process templates are built around the concept that a process should enable you rather than hinder you. If you implement too little of a process, you must expend significant effort to stay on track. The inroads you make on a project will fully depend on the organizational skills of your team. The infrastructure will not support or enforce your process. Too much process inhibits productivity and velocity.

Process templates in Team Foundation Server 2010 provide a way to introduce the process to the entire team without getting in the way. When you create a new team project, process templates are used to set up the work items, work item queries, several shared documents, dashboards, reports, and more.

Figure 23-1 shows the contents of the Microsoft Solutions Framework (MSF) for Agile Software Development process template in a folder view. As you can see, it contains the various key elements for a team project, including work item tracking, version control, reports, and so on. A process template is a collection of files, including XML files, documents, and spreadsheets.

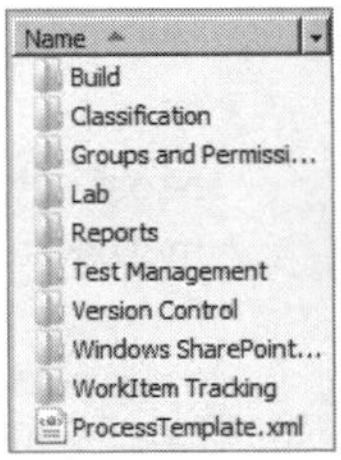

FIGURE 23-1

Team Foundation Server process templates contain components to support a software development process. As mentioned earlier, while setting up a new team project, a process template is used to create and configure the various parts of the team project, including the following:

- ➤ Work items
    - ➤ Work item types and definitions
    - ➤ Link types
- ➤ Work item queries
- ➤ Team project portal
- ➤ Project documents
    - ➤ Samples and templates
    - ➤ Planning workbooks

➤ Groups and permissions

➤ Reports that are included in a particular template

➤ Work item field and Microsoft Project field mappings

➤ Predefined areas and iterations

➤ Version control settings (including check-in policy settings)

PROCESS TEMPLATES OUT OF THE BOX

Team Foundation Server 2010 ships with two process templates out of the box:

➤ MSF for Agile Software Development v5.0

➤ MSF for Capability Maturity Model Integration (CMMI) Process Improvement v5.0

As mentioned earlier, for many teams, one of these two templates will serve as a starting point. Obviously, one size does not fit all, and that is especially true for software development processes, but teams can customize the process template to meet their specific needs.

See Chapter 26 for details on process template customization. It is advisable to start from one of the pre-defined process templates (that is, either of the two shipped in the box, or one from a partner or the community, as described later in this chapter). Your custom in-house processes (usually a combination of an established development process and policies, processes, and conventions used within your own company) can also be integrated into Team Foundation Server process template. That means you can work within a recognizable framework, making it easy for your team to adapt to Team Foundation Server.

Let's start by looking at the two process templates shipped in the box.

MSF for Agile Software Development

Agile development has gained significant momentum in the recent years. From the famous meeting at a resort in Utah that led to the Agile Manifesto (see www.agilemanifesto.org) to the broad adoption of eXtreme Programming (XP) and Scrum, agile development techniques have become mainstream in the software development world.

XP (with its focus on engineering practices) and Scrum (with its focus on project management practices) complement each other. Agile techniques are no longer just a favorite of developers, but also a favorite of many project managers, business analysts, and users. A quick search of agile development on the Web will provide you with a significant amount of literature to read on this topic.

Microsoft has many internal teams (including teams building Visual Studio and the Microsoft patterns and practices team) using agile methodologies and processes, including XP, Scrum, Feature-Driven Development (FDD), and other agile techniques and practices.

> The "Microsoft patterns & practices: Agile Development Showcase" page has links to content and videos at http://msdn.microsoft.com/en-us/practices/dd128747.aspx.

MSF for Agile Software Development process template is primarily designed for an agile development team. Following are a few key characteristics of this process:

➤ *Open communication between team members* — Freely sharing information within the team is a marker of project success. The work item tracking, reports, and dashboards all work together to open channels within your team.

➤ *Shared vision* — Everyone on your team must have the same vision of the project.

➤ *Agility and adaptation* — The capability to document every possible event that might occur within a software development project would result in volumes of documentation. Adaptation uses mindsets and principles as a basis for dealing with unlikely or infrequent events.

➤ *Focus on the customer* — Communicating with the customer is key to achieving the business goals in any software project.

➤ *People come first* — Tools and processes will only get you so far. The most important factor in any project is the people involved — your team members. Team Foundation Server increases the productivity of your team by organizing your process in a central team portal, tracking workflow using work items, and providing an easy work environment by facilitating process through tool-process integration. If you want a project to succeed, the best thing you can do is create an empowering environment for your team.

➤ *End-to-end quality* — Quality can be achieved using the iterative process and tests to maintain the highest levels of security and performance. You can also enforce quality by setting tool-driven *quality gates* in your development process. Quality gates are policies that ensure that your code meets a certain standard (mostly through extensive testing) before it can be checked into the source tree.

➤ *Frequent deployment* — The best software products are designed out of a need to maintain the highest level of quality. Highly iterative processes and frequent testing will help in reaching that goal. The product should be used internally and fit the customer's requirements. Tools such as the Unit Test Framework and Team Foundation Build can drive your team to reach a high caliber of quality.

➤ *Customize template to your needs* — As explained earlier, the process templates are designed to provide you with a base template. There is no doubt that guidance is required for any successful project, but you have the option to integrate as much or as little as you want.

Figure 23-2 shows the main page of the MSF for Agile Software Development process guidance.

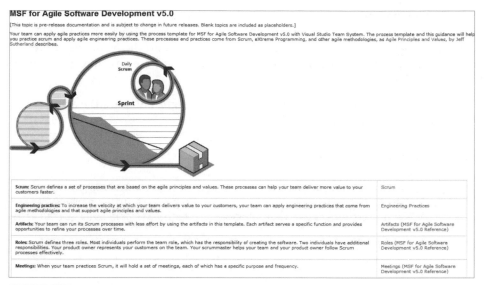

FIGURE 23-2

What you see in Figure 23-2 is the view of the process guidance within a browser. You will learn more about this later in the chapter, in the section "Process Guidance."

New Features of MSF for Agile Software Development

MSF for Agile Software Development has gone through a major overhaul in Team Foundation Server 2010. MSF for Agile Software Development v4.2 and prior versions had terminologies and guidance that were different from the terminologies and guidance used by agile teams, or that were familiar to agile practitioners. The Microsoft product team heard this feedback from the community and made significant changes to the template to make it a good base template for agile teams.

The MSF for Agile Software Development v5.0 template in Team Foundation Server 2010 has several new additions, including work item types (for example, user story work item), reports (for example, burndown), and planning workbooks (for example, product planning and iteration planning) that are familiar to users of agile practices and planning workbooks. That is on top of the new features of Team Foundation Server 2010, including the hierarchical work items and work item links. These new capabilities make the agile template very useful and compelling for agile teams.

Migrating to the Process Templates in 2010

There is not a way to migrate existing projects that use one of the process templates from Team Foundation Server 2008 to the new process templates in Team Foundation Server 2010. There are many fundamental changes to the new template. Obviously, the best way to take advantage of these new capabilities is to start with a new team project based on this new template.

In cases where you want to leverage some of these new capabilities, there is not an automated way to accomplish this. But you can take advantage of some of these features by performing a series of manual steps. The blog post at `http://blogs.msdn.com/allclark/archive/2009/10/13/` `enabling-new-application-lifecycle-management-features-for-visual-studio-2010-` `beta-2-in-upgraded-team-projects.aspx` shows how you can enable the planning workbooks, reports, lab management, and test management on team projects that were upgraded from an earlier version of Team Foundation Server.

Table 23-1 shows a quick summary of changes between MSF for Agile Software Development in Team Foundation Server 2008 and Team Foundation Server 2010.

TABLE 23-1: Differences in MSF Agile Software Development

FEATURE	MSF FOR AGILE SOFTWARE DEVELOPMENT V4.2 (TEAM FOUNDATION SERVER 2008 VERSION)	MSF FOR AGILE SOFTWARE DEVELOPMENT V5.0 (TEAM FOUNDATION SERVER 2010 VERSION)
Work Items	Scenario	User Story
	Task	Task
	Bug	Bug
		Issue
	Risks	Removed in 2010
	Quality of Service Requirements	Removed in 2010
		Shared Step
		Test Case
Link Types	None	Parent/Child
		Tests/Tested By
Reports	RDL reports	Both RDL and Excel reports. (RDL reports have undergone a major revision in 2010.)
Planning workbooks	Not available	Product Planning and Iteration Planning workbook
Dashboards	Team Portal	Two versions of portal — Windows SharePoint Services (WSS) and Microsoft Office SharePoint Server (MOSS) based.

Work Items

Team Foundation Server uses work items to track assignments and work. Work items are the key entities that represent the work; hence, the data associated with work items is used to track and monitor project progress.

See Chapter 22 for more information on work items and work items tracking.

MSF for Agile Software Development v5.0 contains six work item types:

➤ User Story

➤ Task

➤ Bug

➤ Issue

➤ Test Case

➤ Shared Steps

User Story

User stories are no strangers to software teams using agile techniques. User stories made sticky notes and index cards must-haves in an agile team's toolbox. Often, a team room may be decorated with sticky notes and index cards showing user stories on the story wall.

User stories are a representation of customer requirements similar to use cases but different in the amount of information captured. Agile teams value communication with a customer. Rather than trying to capture every edge scenario of a requirement on a piece of paper, many teams have started using small-sized index cards and sticky notes instead of regular office printer paper to capture the user requirements. The level of information captured in a user story provides enough detail for the development team to estimate the cost for implementing the user story.

Mike Cohn's book, User Stories Applied: For Agile Software Development *(Upper Saddle River, N.J.: Addison Wesley, 2004) is a great book on user stories. Particularly, Chapter 7 and Chapter 12 will be helpful, both if you are new to user stories or if you have been using user stories in your projects and need a refresher.*

Obviously, user stories in the form of sticky notes on a wall do not work well when you have teams that are geographically distributed. With its integrated work items tracking system and the associated backlog worksheets, Visual Studio Team Foundation Server 2010 helps the whole team get on the same page with respect to project status. There are also partner tools that integrate with Team Foundation Server to provide a digital story wall that can be used by teams dispersed across geographical boundaries.

> *A few implementations of story boards are integrated with Team Foundation Server. These story boards (or story walls) provide an experience closer to the physical story boards, which scales quiet well, even for distributed teams. Following are two Microsoft partner Web sites that provide examples of such implementations:*
>
> ➤ *Scrum Task Board by Conchango* (`http://scrumforteamsystem.com/en/TaskBoard/Default.aspx`)
>
> ➤ *Urban Turtle Planning/Task Board* (`http://www.urbanturtle.com/`)

A user story work item captures information including a title, description, priority, stack rank and story points. The title field of the user story work item has a template to describe the user story. The format of the title field is "As a <type of user> I want <some goal> so that <some reason>."

The implementation of a user story is captured using child tasks that are associated with the user story. As you can see in the example shown in Figure 23-3, there are several user stories with associated child tasks.

ID	Work Item Type	Link Type	Stack Rank ⌐	Story Points	Title
7	User Story		7	2	⊟ As a customer I should be able to remove items from my shopping car cart.
36	Task	Child			Design UI for item removal
37	Task	Child			Bind cart removal function to back end
9	User Story		9	9	⊟ As a customer I should be able to see images for all items.
40	Task	Child			Update database to point to actual images
41	Task	Child			Upload images for all products
42	Task	Child			Update web site to include new product images.
10	User Story		10	6	⊟ As a store administrator I should be able to track all open orders.
43	Task	Child			Create database view to group together all open orders
44	Task	Child			Implement web front-end for viewing all open orders
45	Task	Child			Design web front-end for viewing all open orders
11	User Story		11	2	⊟ As a store administrator I should be able to examine contact details for a customer.
46	Task	Child			Design web front-end for viewing customer details
47	Task	Child			Implement web front-end for viewing customer details
12	User Story		12	2	⊟ As a store administrator I should be able to cancel or modify an open order.
48	Task	Child			Design web front-end for modifying an open order
49	Task	Child			Implement web front-end for modifying an open order
50	Task	Child			Create stored procedure for modifying an open customer order

FIGURE 23-3

A user story work item has the following three states:

➤ Active

➤ Resolved

➤ Closed

A user story work item also has the following five tabs:

➤ *Details* — This tab provides the information that you would typically write down on a index card or sticky note, including the acceptance criteria for this user requirement.

➤ *Implementation* — This tab shows the list of related work items, including the parent and child work items. Typically, task work items that are used to implement a user story would be listed here. (Task work items are discussed in more detail later in this chapter.) You could also add a link to an existing work item, or add a new linked work item from within this tab.

➤ *Test Cases* — This tab shows the list of test case work items that are used to test a particular user story. You could also link to an existing test case work item, or add a new test case work item that is testing the user story. This link between test cases and user stories shows the test coverage of user stories.

Chapter 12 provides more information on test cases.

➤ *All Links* — This tab shows all the links to other work items.

➤ *Attachments* — You can use this tab to attach any associated documents (such as wireframes, mockups, and so on).

Task

You create *task* work items within a project to assign and complete work. Tasks provide the implementation details for a user story. A task work item has the following two states:

➤ *Active* — Once a new task work item is created, it is automatically set to the Active state. The Active state denotes that there are work requirements that must be completed. Tasks can be reassigned to other team members.

➤ *Closed* — This state means that a task has been completed. Development tasks are completed once code updates have been implemented. Test tasks are completed when all tests have been executed for a specific feature or component.

Bug

A *bug* is a work item used to track and monitor problems within a software product. To be effective, a bug must be well-documented, including the steps to reproduce the issue. From the work item, the impact of the bug should be easily and clearly recognized.

In MSF for Agile Software Development v5.0 template, bugs have the following three states:

➤ *Active* — This is the default state of a bug. An active bug means that the bug has been documented, but not yet dealt with.

➤ *Resolved* — A Resolved state means that a bug has been handled by a developer or tester. Once resolved, a bug can be classified as "Fixed" or included "By Design."

➤ *Closed* — A Closed status means that the bug has been completely dealt with, including a verification process.

The Reason field value, combined with the state, gives you a better sense for the status of a bug. The Reason field values will depend on the value of the state field. For example, a bug with a Closed state could be put into Active state, and the Reason field would contain the following two values to choose from:

➤ Reactivated

➤ Regression

Similarly, a bug in the Active state could be changed to a Resolved state, and Reason field would show the following six values:

➤ As Designed

➤ Cannot Reproduce

➤ Deferred

➤ Duplicate

➤ Fixed

➤ Obsolete

Unfortunately, the Reason field does not include the value "Undocumented Feature." When a bug is moved to a closed state from a resolved state, the Resolved Reason field (which is a read-only field) will show the reason the bug was closed.

A bug work item has the following tabs (in addition to fields such as priority, severity, stack rank, and effort estimates):

➤ Details

➤ System Info

➤ Test Cases

➤ All Links

➤ Attachments

The information captured in a bug work item goes a long way toward an understanding of the problem and then finding a fix to address the bug. Visual Studio Ultimate 2010 provides key capabilities to enhance the quality of information that could be captured when reporting a bug. This should help in getting past the "No repro" scenario.

The capabilities start with simple additions such as rich text capabilities to highlight text in the bug work item. But the major additions include the capability to collect data on a test execution, and attaching that data automatically to a bug work item. This includes a list of steps to reproduce a bug. These steps can be marked green to indicate a successful execution of a step, or red if it resulted in a failure.

There is also a link to a video file with the location index to show you the steps as followed by a tester. This should help you understand exactly what happened as the test case was executed to validate a particular feature of the system. This step-by-step walkthrough is available in the Details tab of the bug work item.

The trace log from IntelliTrace could also be attached to a bug work item to help in debugging.

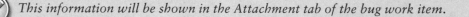

Chapter 11 provides more information on IntelliTrace.

Visual Studio 2010 gets this information from a new tool introduced in 2010 called the *Test and Lab Manager.* This tool provides vital information to make the bug easy to reproduce, and hence, increase the probability of finding a resolution quickly.

This information will be shown in the Attachment tab of the bug work item.

In addition, important information about the system under test will be captured in the Systems Tab. This includes the build in which the bug was found, which OS was used, which OS version was used, and so on.

The "All links" tab contains all the linked work items.

Issue

An *issue* work item captures obstacles or items that must be addressed during the current (or future) iteration. An issue could result in associated work items such as tasks or bugs, but not necessarily. It could simply be used to track an item that the team needs to address. For example, an issue could be dealing with an external dependency, availability of a subject matter expert (SME) on a project, implementation decisions for future reference, and so on.

An issue work item has only two states:

➤ Active

➤ Closed

In addition to capturing the details, links, and any attachments, you could also specify a due date for the issue work item.

Test Case

A *test case* work item captures a series of steps that make up a test to verify a feature, a set of features, or part of a feature. The Steps tab in the test case work item contains the series of actions to be performed and the expected result for each of the actions.

The Tested Stories tab shows the list of user stories that this test case is testing. This association gives you the capability to generate a report on test coverage of user stories.

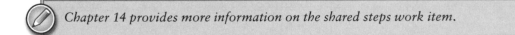

Chapter 14 provides more information on test case work items.

Shared Steps

You create a series of steps in the test case work item that are used to walk through and verify a feature or functionality. But there are often steps (such as visiting the home page, logging in to the application, and logging out of the application) that are repeated prior to executing the steps unique for the feature you are testing.

A *shared steps* work item is used to capture these steps that are repeated often. As the name states, steps created in this work item can be shared across several test cases. In the test case work item, you could use the Insert Shared Steps action to include a shared step work item as part of the test case.

Chapter 14 provides more information on the shared steps work item.

Process Guidance

In Team Foundation Server 2010, the process guidance is now entirely available online and integrated into MSDN. In the 2008 version, the process guidance files were part of the process template, and the Microsoft product development team chose to integrate the guidance and make it available online on MSDN. This choice was made for multiple reasons, including discoverability, integration between guidance topics with online help content, and the capability to share the guidance among multiple team projects.

Note that the guidance is also available in an offline version in the form of a wiki library. You will make the changes to the location of the process guidance (that is, either the wiki library, or the MSDN Web site) using the project portal settings.

Reports

Team Foundation Server reports are the window through which you look into the progress of the project. There are several reports that are available out-of-the-box. The MSF for Agile Software Development v5.0 template includes the following RDL reports. In 2010, the reports are categorized and presented in groups as shown here:

- ➤ Project Management
  - ➤ Burn down and Burn Rate
  - ➤ Remaining Work
  - ➤ Status on All Iterations
  - ➤ Stories Overview
  - ➤ Stories Progress

- ➤ Tests
    - ➤ Test Case Readiness
    - ➤ Test Plan Progress
- ➤ Bugs
    - ➤ Bug Status
    - ➤ Bug Trends
    - ➤ Reactivations
- ➤ Builds
    - ➤ Build Quality Indicators
    - ➤ Build Success Over Time
    - ➤ Build Summary
- ➤ Dashboards
    - ➤ Burn Rate
    - ➤ Burndown

Several of these reports are used commonly by agile teams, including Burndown and Remaining Work.

> *Chapter 24 provides more details for each of these reports, and also examines how to add new reports and customize existing reports.*

In addition to the SQL reporting services report listed previously, Team Foundation Server 2010 provides a set of very useful Microsoft Excel reports, as shown in Figure 23-4.

Agile Planning Workbooks

The MSF for Agile Software Development v5.0 includes two agile planning workbooks:

- ➤ One to organize, estimate, and manage user stories in the product backlog
- ➤ Another to analyze a user story, break it down into tasks, estimate tasks, and plan the work for the iteration

The Product planning workbook and the Iteration planning workbook provide a template that aids in both levels of planning.

```
Excel Reports
  Test Management
  Bug Progress.xlsx
  Bug Reactivations.xlsx
  Bug Trends.xlsx
  Bugs by Assignment.xlsx
  Bugs by Priority.xlsx
  Build Status.xlsx
  Burndown.xlsx
  Code Churn.xlsx
  Code Coverage.xlsx
  Failure Analysis.xlsx
  Issue Trends.xlsx
  Report Template.xltx
  Task Progress.xlsx
  Test Activity.xlsx
  Test Case Readiness.xlsx
  Test Plan Progress.xlsx
  User Story Progress.xlsx
  User Story Test Status.xlsx
```

FIGURE 23-4

Chapter 25 discusses these two workbooks in detail.

Samples and Templates

You might find several of the sample documents and templates included in the MSF for Agile Software Development template useful in your project. For example, having a retrospective meeting following each iteration (and following a release) helps agile teams get a report of how the particular iteration (or release) went. Typically, retrospectives are used by agile teams to discuss what worked well and what didn't, thus identifying the root cause of issues, and the steps that must be taken to address these issues.

In the `Samples and Templates` folder under the team project, you will find a document template for iteration retrospective that you can use during your retrospective meeting, as well as a sample retrospective document for reference. Figure 23-5 shows the `Samples and Templates` folder, and the various documents contained in this folder.

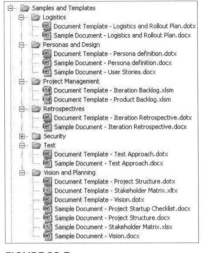

FIGURE 23-5

MSF for CMMI Process Improvement v5.0

Team Foundation Server includes a template called MSF for Capability Maturity Model Integration (CMMI) Process Improvement. CMMI was originally developed by the Carnegie Mellon Software Engineering Institute (www.sei.cmu.edu/cmmi/) to assess defense, aerospace, and government contractors in a regulated environment. The MSF version of CMMI is partially based on the work of W. Edwards Deming, a renowned statistician in the area of quality control and statistical process.

Deming popularized statistical process control in the field of business and manufacturing in his *theory of profound knowledge.* To properly implement process controls, you must be able to identify the difference between *common cause variations (CCVs)* and *special cause variations (SCVs).* CCVs are natural fluctuations found in any process. SCVs are caused by special occurrences, environmental factors, and problems that affect a process. The challenge as a project manager is to correctly identify an instance of a SCV and reduce it. Complicating this goal is the fact that these variations usually occur on a random basis.

The reporting component of Team Foundation Server provides visual metrics to measure factors such as project health. These charts can help you determine whether the Upper Control Limits (UCLs) and Lower Control Limits (LCLs) are within operational boundaries. Figure 23-6 illustrates the two types of variation, and the attainment of process improvement.

Statistical Process Control

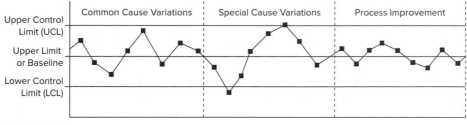

FIGURE 23-6

Process within a project is vitally important to bring down costs and increase productivity, which is why you are first selecting a process template to create a team project in Team Foundation Server.

System and hardware engineering processes have matured over the decades. Relative to manufacturing, software engineering is still in its infancy. CMMI is based on quality assurance ideas that came out of manufacturing. This makes sense from an operational perspective — most hardware manufacturing companies rely on software on the production line. For that reason, there are many varieties of CMMI specifications.

In a nutshell, CMMI is used to track the maturity of any software design organization, from requirements to validation. The CMMI has six maturity capability levels outlined in Table 23-2.

TABLE 23-2: CMMI Maturity Capability Levels

LEVEL	MATURITY	DESCRIPTION
0	Incomplete Process	
1	Performed Process	You have little to no controls in your project. The outcome is unpredictable and reactive. Frequent instances of SCVs. All of the process areas for performed process have been implemented and work gets done. However, the planning and implementation of process has not yet been completed.
2	Managed Process	You have satisfied all of the requirements for the implementation of a managed process. Work is implemented by skilled employees according to policies. Processes are driven according to specific goals such as quality and cost. Planning and review are baked into the process. You are managing your process.
3	Defined Process	In the defined process, you have a set of standard processes (or processes that satisfy a process area) within your organization that can be adapted according to specific needs.

continues

TABLE 23-2 *(continued)*

LEVEL	MATURITY	DESCRIPTION
4	Quantitatively Managed Process	All aspects of a project are quantitatively measured and controlled. Both your operational and project processes are within normal control limits.
5	Optimizing Process	CMMI Level 5 focuses on constant process improvement and the reduction of SCVs. The project process is under constant improvement.

> *There are two models for implementing CMMI: the* continuous model *and the* staged model. *In the continuous model, elements such as engineering, support, project management, and process management are each composed of a set number of process areas.* A process area *is a description of activities for building a planned approach for improvement. Using the staged model, the process areas are set up according to the six maturity levels. The MSF for CMMI Process Improvement template was designed to support the staged model.*

Capability Level 3

The CMMI template included in Team Foundation Server is designed to help you accelerate the appraisal to Level 3 compliance. The CMMI specifications are quite detailed (more than 700 pages long). Here are the characteristics of CMMI Level 3 (boiled down to three main points):

➤ CMMI Level 3 is customized to the organization's set of standard processes according to the organization's guidelines.

➤ CMMI Level 3 has a process description that is constantly maintained. This is implemented in Team Foundation Server using work items and iterations.

➤ CMMI Level 3 must contribute work products, metrics, and other process improvement information to the organization's process assets. Process templates and the Project Site enable project managers to share metrics and documents with the rest of the team.

Business Analysts, and Project and Release Managers

Business analysts and managers can benefit from utilizing pre-established planning and management processes based on lessons learned and best practices. Projects contain templates and historical metrics that apply regardless of what project you are working on, which help in the estimation phase of the project. You can detect and reduce defects early in the process and before you ship. From a business perspective, you can establish a project schedule and measure costs, which enables you to negotiate better contracts with your clients.

Developers, Testers, and Architects

CMMI Level 3 provides a solid process framework for developers, testers, and architects. With process, the knowledge and experience gathered during the project is quantifiable. This means that any lessons learned can help improve the process, bugs are avoided, and code is enhanced. All of this information can then be leveraged on future projects. This also builds processes that are derived from best practices, much like MSF is derived from Microsoft's collective experience.

In a process-driven environment, the roles and tools are better defined because it is a more detail-oriented methodology. This helps team members stay focused within your organization. CMMI provides a focus on process and project management — in fact, the entire team shares the responsibility of making decisions, managing risk, and shaping and meeting requirements. CMMI emphasizes training and integrated teams to create an environment that facilitates the integration of end-to-end features, and a verification process to lower bugs and keep the project on track in terms of QA and feature requirements.

CMMI Level 3 Versus MSF for CMMI Process Improvement

Formal processes have a reputation of being too bureaucratic and lacking agility. The traditional way of planning software is using the waterfall method. The plan is central to the process, and usually a lot of ceremony is attached to the handing off of the project (for example, a project plan sent to developers for a coding phase).

MSF enables your team to operate at CMMI Level 3. The MSF for CMMI Process Improvement template adds work items such as requirement, risk, change requests, and issues. The MSF for CMMI Process Improvement template also includes a set of reports to help monitor and track the project.

The MSF for CMMI Process Improvement template is designed to be flexible. In fact, The MSF for CMMI Process Improvement template out of the box will not "auto-magically" transform an organization into Level 3 — it must be augmented with training. If you need a formal process architecture, MSF for CMMI Process Improvement template provides a light and flexible meta-framework that you can customize to your needs.

The MSF for CMMI Process Improvement template provides an example of an agile interpretation of CMMI when, more often than not, the interpretation is traditional, waterfall, command-and-control, and documentation centric. It is designed to be light, with almost no overhead or bureaucracy. David J. Anderson (one of Microsoft's leading architects for the CMMI for Process Improvement Framework) describes this hybrid in his book *Agile Management for Software Engineering* (Upper Saddle River, N.J.: Prentice Hall, 2003) as "the Learning Organization Maturity Model." The CMMI version of MSF has the following characteristics:

➤ It is geared toward larger-scale projects with a greater emphasis on breaking a project into phases and groups. MSF for Agile Software Development, conversely, is designed for smaller groups with quicker iterations.

➤ It is designed to conform to a process, rather than plans and specifications. Process improvement is implemented in two ways: by reducing variations within baseline operating conditions and by instituting constant improvement using cyclical process structures.

➤ It does not support project management artifacts by default, such as time tracking. However, the specification can be extended to include *earned value (EV)*, the *critical path method (CPM)*, and other enterprise project management features into the framework.

➤ Everyone on the development team is responsible for issue and risk management. The goal is to eliminate special cause variation.

➤ The MSF for CMMI Process Improvement template focuses on automation through Team Foundation Server's toolset and the CMMI appraisal model via the reporting tools to measure quality, velocity, and productivity.

➤ All team members are empowered to make decisions and take responsibility for the success of a project. This includes status meetings and log, risk, and operations reviews.

➤ All software development contains constraints. They include time, personnel, functionality, resources, and budget. The MSF for CMMI Process Improvement template has the means to help you buffer uncertainties (SCVs) within your project, and measure events and activities outside the scope of your project. The MSF for CMMI model is geared to reduce variation.

➤ The MSF for CMMI Process Improvement template expands on CMMI with the concepts of release management, risk management, and iterative cycles.

➤ It includes custom work items, reports, and process guidance. Like the MSF for Agile Software Development template, the framework is highly extensible and customizable.

➤ This version of MSF uses metrics such as remaining work (or cumulative flow) and burn down (measuring work completed to track project health).

Work Items

MSF for CMMI Process Improvement template v5.0 has the following work item types:

➤ Requirement

➤ Change Request

➤ Task

➤ Review

➤ Bug

➤ Issue

➤ Risk

➤ Test Case

➤ Shared Steps

These are essentially the same set of work items from the v4.2 template, with the addition of two new work items (Test Case and Shared Steps).

Process Guidance

In Team Foundation Server 2010, the process guidance is integrated and made available on MSDN for online viewing. The guidance for MSF for CMMI Process Improvement v5.0 is available at `http://msdn.microsoft.com/en-us/library/dd997574(VS.100).aspx`.

Reports

Team Foundation Server reports are the window through which you look at the progress of the project. There are several reports that are available out-of-the-box. The MSF for CMMI Process Improvement v5.0 template includes the following RDL reports. In 2010, the reports are categorized and presented in groups as shown here:

➤ Project Management

    ➤ Burn down and Burn Rate

    ➤ Remaining Work

    ➤ Requirements Overview

    ➤ Requirements Progress

    ➤ Status on All Iterations

➤ Tests

    ➤ Test Case Readiness

    ➤ Test Plan Progress

➤ Bugs

    ➤ Bug Status

    ➤ Bug Trends

    ➤ Reactivations

➤ Builds

    ➤ Build Quality Indicators

    ➤ Build Success Over Time

    ➤ Build Summary

➤ Dashboards

    ➤ Remaining Work

> *Chapter 24 provides more details for each of these reports, and also examines how to add new reports and customize existing reports.*

In addition to the SQL reporting services report listed previously, Team Foundation Server 2010 provides a set of very useful Microsoft Excel reports as shown in Figure 23-7.

PARTNER AND COMMUNITY TEMPLATES

In addition to the two process templates shipped with Team Foundation Server, there are additional process templates available from Microsoft partners and the community. This demonstrates the ability to customize Visual Studio Team Foundation Server to enact the process/methodology of your choice.

FIGURE 23-7

 Chapter 26 provides more information about the tool and the techniques to customize process templates.

Table 23-3 shows a list of some of the process templates from partners and the community. Refer to `http://msdn.microsoft.com/process` for more information on third-party process templates.

TABLE 23-3: Partner and Community Process Templates

NAME	DESCRIPTION
Scrum for Team System	Conchango (`www.scrumforteamsystem.com`), a Microsoft Partner, provides a template based on the Scrum methodology for Team Foundation Server. Very popular among agile teams, this template provides a nice integration between the popular Scrum methodology and Visual Studio Team Foundation Server.
Feature Driven Development	Cognizant (`www.cognizant.com/html/contacts/downloadRequest .asp?linkID=CognizantFDDEval`), a Microsoft partner, integrates Visual Studio Team System with FDD.
Lightweight Scrum	This community-driven template (available at `http://vstsscrum .codeplex.com`) provides a simple integration of Scrum and Visual Studio Team Foundation Server.

NAME	DESCRIPTION
Microsoft Process Template (MPT)	This process template (available at `http://mpt.codeplex.com`) is used by teams within Microsoft. This template includes all the work items, queries, and reports used by Microsoft product teams. This was recently released to CodePlex, which serves as the repository for community-generated process templates and tools.
Templex	This project (available at `http://temple.codeplex.com`) was created by the community in CodePlex.

> *Check out a series of blog posts on how the Team Foundation Server team uses the MPT internally. Start with the first post of this series at* `http://blogs.msdn.com/teams_wit_tools/archive/2008/03/27/how-microsoft-devdiv-uses-tfs-chapter-1-our-process.aspx`.

SUMMARY

Process Templates are a key component of Team Foundation Server and Visual Studio Application Lifecycle Management. The templates configure the team project and set the infrastructure that enables the team to adhere to certain process and practices. Process and associated guidance were available to software teams, but, in most cases, it existed outside the tool used by team members, or it was so complex that it was a non-starter for many teams. By integrating the process into the tooling, Team Foundation Server helps the team be more successful in adhering to these practices, and ultimately in delivering the value that is critical to the business.

The choice of the process template (whether between the two templates shipped with Team Foundation Server, or a template available from a third party or the community, or even a customized version) will largely depend on the environment of your team and the processes and practices that are in use. If your current practices are reflected closely in one of the process templates, it is recommended that you start with that template, and customize as needed. You will find more information on process customization in Chapter 26. Remember that the key here is to start with a good base template, and evolve it on an on-going basis.

In this chapter, you learned about process templates and their components. You also learned about the two process templates that are shipping with Visual Studio Team Foundation Server 2010: MSF for Agile Software Development and MSF for CMMI Process Improvement. This chapter discussed the various parts of these two process templates, including work items, reports, and documents.

Chapter 24 delves into the reports, portals, and dashboards that are key to monitoring and tracking projects.

24

Using Reports, Portals, and Dashboards

WHAT'S IN THIS CHAPTER?

➤ Understanding Team Foundation Server data stores

➤ Understanding the tools available to manage reports

➤ Creating and customizing reports using Excel

➤ Creating RDL reports with Report Designer and Report Builder

➤ Understanding project portals and dashboards

Capturing information throughout the project is critical not only to project managers but to all team members alike. Equally important is the capability to analyze the information that was captured and understand it. With Visual Studio Team Foundation Server 2010, the mundane tasks associated with capturing is mostly automated, and gives crucial time back to the team to focus on building software rather than capturing information associated with building it.

Team Foundation Server also provides powerful features used to analyze the data and understand it. Tracking a project and monitoring it throughout its lifecycle is now made easier with Team Foundation Server Reporting and the dashboards. (Dashboards serve the purpose of providing useful information in an easy-to-consume form.)

This chapter examines the reporting capabilities of Team Foundation Server, working with reports, customizing reports, and the reviewing of reports shipped out-of-the box. In addition, this chapter looks into the new dashboards introduced in Visual Studio Team Foundation Server 2010 and team project portal as a way to stay up to date with the status of the project and the team.

Let's start with the reporting capabilities of Visual Studio Team Foundation Server 2010.

TEAM FOUNDATION SERVER REPORTING

Reporting is one of the most powerful features of Team Foundation Server. Right from the first release of Team Foundation Server (that is, Team Foundation Server 2005), the central repository and the reports have been cornerstones for software development teams and the management team alike. Any data stored in the Team Foundation Server repository can be viewed as a report, which enables you to view and organize project metrics very easily. This includes work item tracking, build reports, version control stats, test results, quality indicators (performance and code coverage), and overall project health reports. Team Foundation Server ships with set of reports out-of-the-box (more on that later), but you can also create custom reports.

The reporting tools are not only useful for project managers, but also for team members in every role. For example, a developer can look at test results and hone in on specific bugs. Testers can look at a report to identify the work complete for testing, and so on.

Before looking into the details of reports, how to create custom reports, or the tools available to create reports, let's first look at how Team Foundation Server stores data. As you see in Figure 24-1, there are essentially three different data stores that Team Foundation Server uses:

➤ Team Foundation Server operational store

➤ Team Foundation Server data warehouse

➤ Team Foundation Server OLAP cube

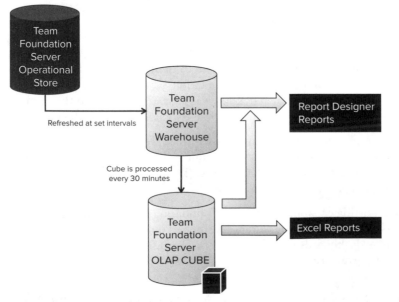

FIGURE 24-1

Team Foundation Server Operational Store

The Team Foundation Server operational store is a set of databases for storing information, including source control, build reports, test results, work item tracing, and so on. These are relational databases and they handle all live data. Hence, they are optimized for speed and performance. Multiple databases serve as the operational store, including the `TFS_Configuration` database and the various databases for the team project collections. Typically, you don't have to deal with (or understand) the structure of this set of databases. You will not go against this store to do reporting, for example.

Team Foundation Server Data Warehouse

Team Foundation Server data warehouse is specifically designed for querying and reporting, unlike the operational store that is designed for transactions. The schema of the warehouse is much easier to understand.

Team Foundation Server data warehouse gets the data from the operational stores on regularly set intervals. There are adapters for each of the databases in the operation store that take care of pushing the data into the warehouse. In Team Foundation Server 2008, by default, the refresh interval was 3600 seconds (that is, 60 minutes). Of course, you could change the interval using a controller service. In Team Foundation Server 2010, the update from the operational store to the warehouse is based on various events. When an event fires up, the corresponding adapter will be scheduled to execute and refresh the data in the warehouse. The interval for this execution is configurable.

In Team Foundation Server 2010, you will use the warehouse control service to change the refresh interval. Go to `http://<TFS Server Name:port>>/tfs/TeamFoundation/Administration/v3.0/WarehouseControlService.asmx`. You must have the permission to update the warehouse setting to access this service. The `WarehouseControlWebService` has the following operations available:

➤ `BringAnalysisProcessingOnline`

➤ `BringWarehouseProcessingOnline`

➤ `ChangeSetting`

➤ `GetJobProperties`

➤ `GetProcessingStatus`

➤ `GetSettings`

➤ `ProcessAnalysisDatabase`

➤ `ProcessWarehouse`

➤ `SetAnalysisJobEnabledState`

➤ `SetWarehouseJobEnabledState`

➤ TakeAnalysisProcessingOffline

➤ TakeWarehouseProcessingOffline

In the `ControllerService` page, if you choose the operation `GetSettings`, it will show you the various processing jobs, its default value, and its current value. As you can see, the frequency with which the warehouse data refresh jobs are running is set to 120 seconds (or 2 minutes).

Team Foundation Server OLAP Cube

The star schema of the warehouse is suitable for analyzing the data. But, as you get into reports that require aggregated values, the warehouse may not be the best choice. The aggregation of values can become slow, depending on the volume of the rows.

Enter the Team Foundation Server OLAP cube. This is a multi-dimensional database that aggregates data for better analysis. Hence, you can correlate data based on the different metrics (that is, work items, build, test, and so on). Team Foundation Server OLAP cube gets the data from warehouse on preset interval. A scheduled job runs every 30 minutes to refresh the data in the cube from the warehouse, as shown in the settings in Figure 24-2. Also note that a full processing of the analysis database is scheduled to run on a daily basis, as indicated by the interval of "86400" seconds (or 24 hours) for the `FullProcessIntervalSeconds` setting.

```xml
<?xml version="1.0" encoding="utf-8" ?>
<WarehouseSettings xmlns:xsi="http://www.w3.org/2001/XMLSchema-instance" xmlns:xsd="http://www.w3.org/2001/XMLSchema"
  xmlns="http://schemas.microsoft.com/TeamFoundation/2005/06/Services/Controller/03">
- <RunIntervalSeconds 120scription="Frequency with which TFS Warehouse Data Sync jobs are running. Measured in seconds." DefaultValue="120">
    <Value>120</Value>
  </RunIntervalSeconds>
- <IncrementalProcessIntervalSeconds Description="Frequency with which Analysis Database is updated. Measured in seconds." DefaultValue="1800">
    <Value>1800</Value>
  </IncrementalProcessIntervalSeconds>
- <FullProcessIntervalSeconds Description="Frequency with which Analysis Database is fully processed. Measured in seconds." DefaultValue="86400">
    <Value>86400</Value>
  </FullProcessIntervalSeconds>
- <DailyFullProcessingTime Description="Time of the day when the full cube process is started. By default it is set to midnight." DefaultValue="02:00:00.0000000-
    08:00">
    <Value>02:00:00.0000000-08:00</Value>
  </DailyFullProcessingTime>
- <MaxParallelASProcessingCommands Description="Used by Analysis Services processing. Indicates the maximum number of commands in parallel. If set to 0,
    the instance of Microsoft SQL Server Analysis Services determines an optimal number based on the number of processors available on the computer."
    DefaultValue="0">
    <Value>0</Value>
  </MaxParallelASProcessingCommands>
- <SchemaUpdateWaitSeconds Description="This timeout is used by jobs trying to acquire an exclusive access to the warehouse resources during the Schema
    Change stage. SchemaUpdateWaitSeconds is how long a job will be waiting in the Running state for the exclusive access to call
    IWarehouseAdapter.SchemaChange() or to perform Analysis Database schema update. If the timeout expires before the Schema Change is finished,
    the job quits and try at a later (scheduled) time." DefaultValue="3600">
    <Value>3600</Value>
  </SchemaUpdateWaitSeconds>
- <DataUpdateWaitSeconds Description="This timeout is used by jobs to acquire a shared access to the warehouse resources during the Data Change stage.
    DataUpdateWaitSeconds is how long a job will be waiting in the Running state for another adapter making Schema changes or for Analysis Processing
    job changing Analysis Database schema. If the timeout expires before the Schema Change is finished, the job quits and try at a later (scheduled) time."
    DefaultValue="3600">
    <Value>3600</Value>
  </DataUpdateWaitSeconds>
- <WarehouseCommandSqlTimeout Description="Timeout used for acquiring an exclusive access to a warehouse resource." DefaultValue="3600">
    <Value>3600</Value>
  </WarehouseCommandSqlTimeout>
- <AnalysisServicesProcessingTimeout Description="How long to wait for an Analysis Services processing call to complete. Measured in seconds."
    DefaultValue="86400">
    <Value>86400</Value>
  </AnalysisServicesProcessingTimeout>
</WarehouseSettings>
```

FIGURE 24-2

The data in the cube can then be used by a variety of client tools, including Microsoft Excel and SQL Report Designer.

The cube consists of measures and dimensions. A *measure* is a numeric value that can be aggregated. *Dimensions* provide a way to summarize measures and categorize them based on additional metrics. Figure 24-3 shows the available measures and dimensions in the Team Foundation Server Analysis database.

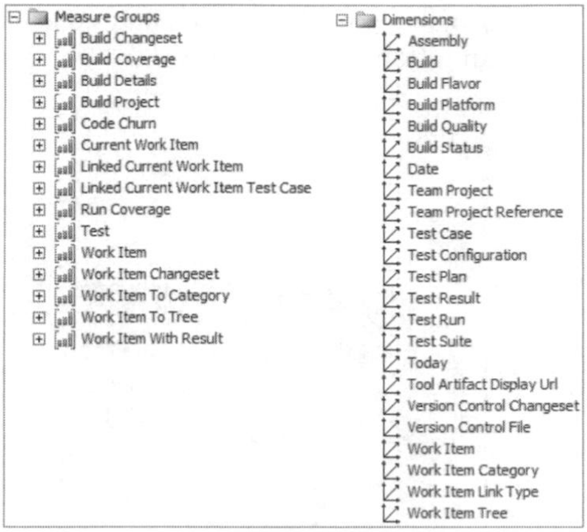

FIGURE 24-3

> *The blog post at* http://blogs.msdn.com/sunder/archive/2009/10/19/team-foundation-server-2010-cube-schema-changes-in-beta-2.aspx *provides information on changes to the cube between the 2008 and 2010 versions.*

WORKING WITH TEAM FOUNDATION SERVER REPORTS

Team Foundation Server includes two sets of reports in its process template: Microsoft Excel Reports and SQL Reporting Services Reports. There are about 35 reports in the two process templates that ship with Team Foundation Server. From a project management perspective, one of the great advantages of using Team Foundation Server is that you don't have to manually correlate data from a host of third-party sources. The available reports are readily available in a dashboard (or portal).

You'll learn more about the reports shipped with the two process templates later in this chapter. But first, let's start by looking at the tools you will use to create Team Foundation Server reports.

Tools to Create Reports

You can use any tool that can connect to a data warehouse or an analysis database to create a report. Following are the two primary tools to create reports from Team Foundation Server by connecting to either the Team Foundation Server data warehouse or the Team Foundation Server OLAP cube:

- ➤ Microsoft Office Excel
- ➤ Report Designer and Report Builder

> *You can also now use the work item queries to create a Microsoft Excel Report, which is discussed in more detail later in this chapter.*

Figure 24-4 shows a quick map of which of these two tools is appropriate against which Team Foundation Server data store.

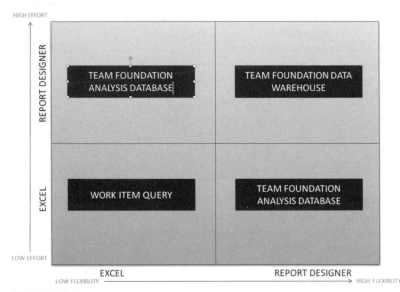

FIGURE 24-4

As you see, you can use the work item queries and Team Foundation Server Analysis database with Microsoft Excel and use Team Foundation Server analysis database and the data warehouse with the Report Designer.

Let's dive in and create some reports.

> To create reports, you need read access to the databases that makes up the warehouse and the cube. You can get access to either the warehouse or the cube or both. That will depend on the data store you will be using and the type of reports you want to create. The administrator of the database can grant you the read access. Refer to the help documentation at `http://msdn.microsoft` `.com/en-us/library/ms252477(VS.100).aspx` for information on permissions needed to access the warehouse and the analysis database.

Working with Microsoft Excel Reports

As mentioned earlier, you can use Microsoft Excel to create reports from either the Team Foundation Server OLAP cube, or by using the work item queries. The latter is new in Team Foundation Server 2010, and a very popular addition in 2010. But let's first look at the steps to create a Microsoft Excel report from the cube. This should be familiar to you if you have created similar reports in Team Foundation Server 2008. The key advantage with the Microsoft Excel reports is the simplicity of using a pivot table, and connecting it to the cube to generate a report.

Creating Microsoft Excel Reports Using Data in the OLAP Cube

First, ensure that you have read access to the OLAP cube. Follow these steps to create a quick pivot table report using Microsoft Excel:

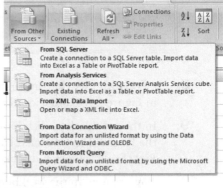

1. Open Microsoft Office Excel.

2. Select the Data tab from the ribbon.

3. Click on From Other Sources and select From Analysis Services, as shown in Figure 24-5.

4. That should bring up the Data Connection Wizard.

5. Provide the server name and credentials, and then click Next.

FIGURE 24-5

6. That will bring up the "Select Database and Table" dialog, as shown in Figure 24-6.

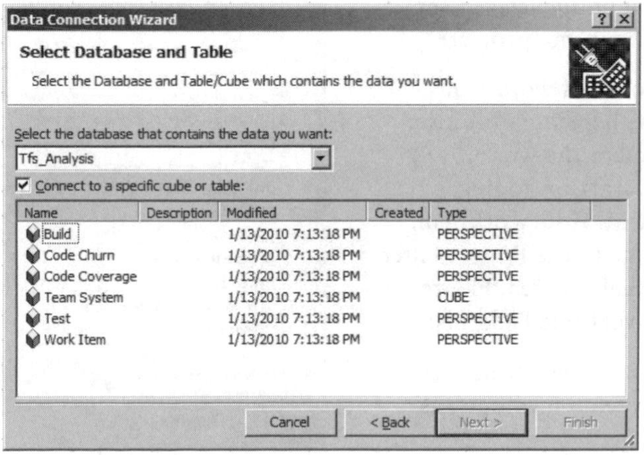

FIGURE 24-6

7. In the drop-down that reads, "Select the database that contains the data you want," select Tfs_Analysis. The interesting part is the list of perspectives and cube. As you see in Figure 24-6, the TFS_Analysis database has a cube named "TeamSystem." It is essentially a representation of the entire warehouse, and contains about 15 measure groups and 23 dimensions. That is one powerful (but complex) cube. If you must depend on the data from the various measure groups and dimensions for your report, then you must endure the complexity. On the other hand, if you are only interested in a small portion of the cube, you could turn your attention to one of the 5 available perspectives. Note that perspectives are only available with SQL Server Enterprise Edition. The other editions do not support perspectives, and, hence, you will have to use the "Team System" cube to create reports.

> Perspectives *are subsets of cubes that provide application- or business-specific views into the cubes. In other words, perspectives provide a simplified view of the cube for specific purposes. In Tfs_Analysis, there are perspectives specific to build, test results, work items, code churn, and code coverage.*

8. Choose the Work Item perspective from the list in Figure 24-6 and click Next.

9. In the next dialog, click Finish to get you to the Import Data dialog. Leave the selection as PivotTable Report and click OK.

10. You are now in the workbook with a list of fields from the Current Work Item perspective. You can now build a report using any of these fields in the work item.

This example will show you how to create a report that answers the question, "How many active user story or task work items are there in my project?"

To do that, you must know the count of work items of type user story and task and with a state of Active. You can list that by the team member the work items are assigned to. To do that, start by adding Work Item Count to the Values area. Add WorkItem.WorkItemType and WorkItem.State to the Report Filter area and AssignedTo to the Row Labels area. Figure 24-7 shows the selection in the PivotTable Field List.

This results in a simple report that shows the active user story and task work items by team members, as shown in Figure 24-8.

This is not a particularly fancy report, but you get the point. By choosing the appropriate perspective or the "Team System" cube, as well as the fields that you need for the pivot table, you could create a report in a fairly simple manner. The focus should be on choosing the right source. So, it might be helpful for you to familiarize yourself with the perspectives provided in the warehouse.

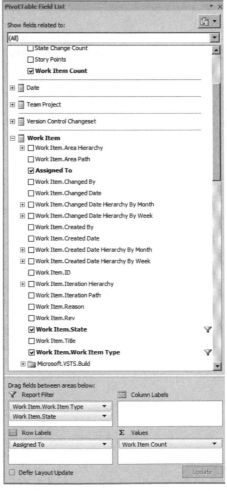

FIGURE 24-7

FIGURE 24-8

For more information on the various perspectives provided in the Team Foundation Server warehouse and the details on each one of them, refer to the Team Foundation Server help documentation at `http://msdn.microsoft.com/ en-us/library/ms244691(VS.100).aspx.`

Customizing a Microsoft Excel Report

You don't necessarily start with a brand new report every time. In many cases, you may simply modify an existing report to get the data that you are looking for. In Team Explorer, you will find existing Microsoft Excel reports in the team project under Documents ⇨ Excel Reports, as shown in Figure 24-9.

To customize a report, first choose the Microsoft Excel report that you want to modify. Open the report in Microsoft Excel by double-clicking on the report filename in Team Explorer.

FIGURE 24-9

If you get a security warning in Microsoft Excel that says, "Data connections have been disabled," click the Options button to get the Microsoft Office Security Options window. You may have to change the selection from "Help protect me from unknown content (recommended)" to "Enable this content."

Once you have the report open in Microsoft Excel, click on the report cell to open the PivotTable Field List window (see Figure 24-7) and the toolbar. You will use this field list to make necessary changes to the report. After you are finished with changes, you can either save them locally, or publish them so others can see the updated report. You will learn about the different publishing options later in this chapter.

Creating Microsoft Excel Reports Using Work Item Query

Work item queries provide an easy way to retrieve information about work items in Team Foundation Server 2010. The Team Queries folder contains queries shared by everyone. The My Queries folder contains queries that only you can use. Chapter 22 provides more detail on work item queries.

In Team Foundation Server 2010, you can now use these work item queries to create a Microsoft Excel report, and do so quickly. Not only can you create Microsoft Excel reports, but you can also share them with the team by publishing them. Creating reports using work item queries is a very popular feature in Visual Studio Team Foundation Server 2010. It provides a quick-and-easy way to turn work item queries into reports.

Let's look at how to create one. In Team Explorer, expand your Team Project node and the Work Items node. Let's create a report out of a team query. Expand the Team Query node. Right-click on the work item query and that will bring up the menu shown in Figure 24-10.

As you can see in Figure 24-10, you have the option called "Create Report in Microsoft Excel," and, you guessed it, that is the option you will be selecting. That should launch Microsoft Excel. The first thing that happens is that Microsoft Excel translates the work item query into data that Microsoft Excel can use to generate reports. After that, it presents a New Work Item Report window, as shown in Figure 24-11.

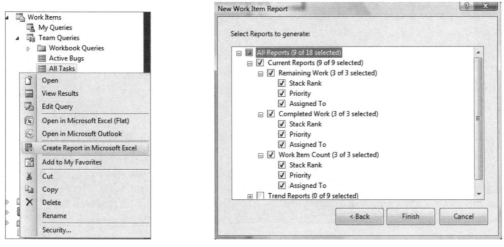

FIGURE 24-10   **FIGURE 24-11**

There are two buckets of reports, Current Reports and Trend Reports, with nine reports in each. To understand where these reports come from, let's look at the query and the results shown in Figure 24-12.

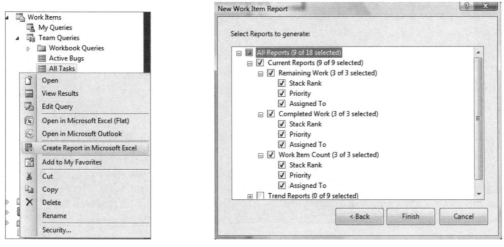

FIGURE 24-12

Obviously, because you are looking at the All Tasks query, the query clause is simple enough in listing every work item under the team project of work item type Task. The result of this query returns the following fields:

➤ ID

➤ Stack Rank

➤ Priority

➤ Assigned To

➤ Remaining Work

➤ Completed Work

➤ Title

You get reports on the values that can be aggregated, such as Remaining Work, Completed Work, and the default Work Item count. Each of these reports also has variations based on attributes such as the Stack Rank, Priority, and Assigned To fields — hence, the nine reports that you see in Figure 24-11. The trend reports are based on the work item history data.

Now, let's get back to Microsoft Excel for generating the reports. From the New Work Item Report dialog (Figure 24-11), select the reports you want to see generated, or select them all. Click Finish and Microsoft Excel will begin working on the reports. When the report generation is completed, you will see a Microsoft Excel workbook with 19 worksheets — 1 worksheet with the table of contents (as shown in Figure 24-13) and 18 worksheets for each of the 18 reports.

Each of these reports is a pivot table report. You can customize these reports by modifying the fields using the PivotTable Field List dialog, as shown in Figure 24-7.

Publishing Microsoft Excel Reports

Now that you understand the basics of creating and customizing Microsoft Excel reports that are based on the data from Team Foundation Server OLAP cube and the work item queries, let's look at the options you have to publish them. Obviously, you do not have to worry about publishing if you don't have to share the reports you create. In that case, you can simply save them locally. But it is highly likely that you will be sharing reports with the rest of the team.

The publishing options for Microsoft Excel reports depend on whether you have Microsoft Office SharePoint Server (MOSS) Enterprise running your dashboard/portals, or Windows SharePoint Services (WSS) for your portals. Table 24-1 summarizes the capabilities for MOSS Enterprise users versus WSS users.

Table of Contents

Current Reports:
  Remaining Work
    Stack Rank
    Priority
    Assigned To
  Completed Work
    Stack Rank
    Priority
    Assigned To
  Work Item Count
    Stack Rank
    Priority
    Assigned To

Trend Reports:
  Remaining Work
    Stack Rank
    Priority
    Assigned To
  Completed Work
    Stack Rank
    Priority
    Assigned To
  Work Item Count
    Stack Rank
    Priority
    Assigned To

FIGURE 24-13

TABLE 24-1: MOSS Enterprise Versus WSS/SharePoint

FEATURE	MOSS ENTERPRISE	WSS/SHAREPOINT
Team site	Portal with six dashboards.	Portal with two dashboards.
Reports	Dashboard uses Excel reports.	Dashboard uses Report Definition Language (RDL) Reports.
Viewing Microsoft Excel reports	Viewable as Web parts.	Open in Microsoft Excel from the document library.
Microsoft Excel reports are available in	Team Explorer under Documents ➪ Excel Reports.	Team Explorer under Documents ➪ Excel Reports.
Creating new Microsoft Excel reports	From Microsoft Excel, create a new report and publish it to Excel Services. Make it available on the dashboard using the New Excel Report button from the dashboard.	From Microsoft Excel, create a new report and save it to the document library.
Publishing Microsoft Excel reports	Publish to Excel Services and make the report available in the dashboard by using the Excel Web Access Web part.	Save the report to the document library and view it in Microsoft Excel.
Dashboards	A set of dashboards (for example, Work Progress, Product quality, test progress, and so on) are created as part of the Team Project setup.	Excel reports are not available. RDL reports are presented in Web parts.

Publishing to a Document Library

You could publish a report to the shared documents from Team Explorer, or you could use the WSS portal site and upload the document.

To upload it from Team Explorer, get to the folder you want to upload the new report to. In this example, let's upload a new report, "Current Work Item count by state." To do that, first find the Excel Reports folder under Team Project ➪ Documents ➪ Excel Reports. Then, right-click on the Excel Reports folder and select Upload Document from the menu.

You can then select the Microsoft Excel report that you have saved locally and upload it. After you have done so, refresh the team project and voilá, the new report appears in the Team Explorer.

You could also upload the Microsoft Excel report from outside Team Explorer. To do that, open up the Team Project portal. Once in the project portal, click on Excel Reports link on the right navigation bar and upload the report to this folder, as shown in Figure 24-14.

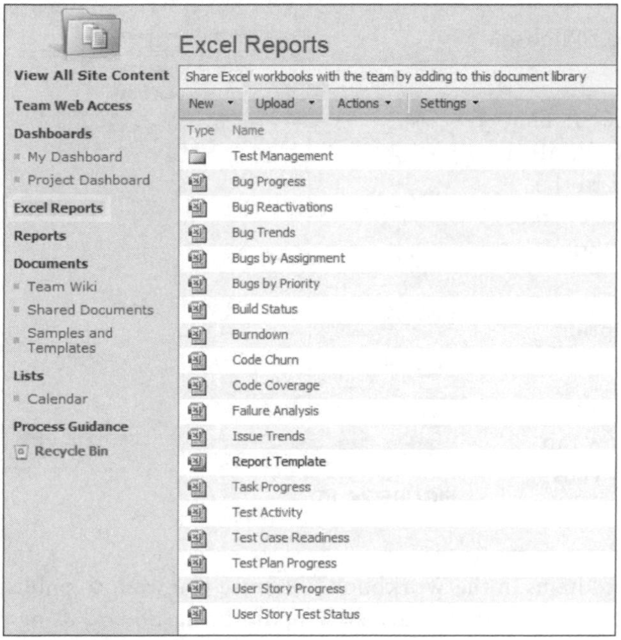

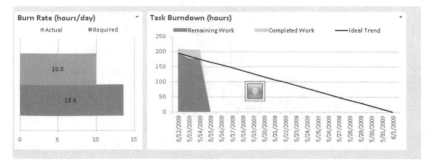

Excel Reports

Share Excel workbooks with the team by adding to this document library

View All Site Content
Team Web Access
Dashboards
  My Dashboard
  Project Dashboard
Excel Reports
Reports
Documents
  Team Wiki
  Shared Documents
  Samples and Templates
Lists
  Calendar
Process Guidance
  Recycle Bin

New · Upload · Actions · Settings ·

Type | Name
- Test Management
- Bug Progress
- Bug Reactivations
- Bug Trends
- Bugs by Assignment
- Bugs by Priority
- Build Status
- Burndown
- Code Churn
- Code Coverage
- Failure Analysis
- Issue Trends
- Report Template
- Task Progress
- Test Activity
- Test Case Readiness
- Test Plan Progress
- User Story Progress
- User Story Test Status

FIGURE 24-14

Publishing to Excel Services

A project portal is a SharePoint site. You will learn more about the portals and dashboards later in this chapter. If you are running MOSS 2007 Enterprise, then you have access to Excel Services. You can publish Microsoft Excel reports to Excel Services. Doing so provides the option to display the Microsoft Excel report using the Excel Web Access Web part in the dashboard. This allows you to easily and quickly create Microsoft Excel reports and share them broadly with the team using dashboards.

Figure 24-15 shows a portion of a dashboard with two Microsoft Excel reports displayed using Excel Web Access Web parts. Let's review the steps to publish a Microsoft Excel report and make it viewable in the dashboard.

FIGURE 24-15

First, start with a Microsoft Excel report. Create a
Microsoft Excel report following the steps described
earlier in this chapter, or open an already created
Microsoft Excel report.

Click the Microsoft Office button and select Publish,
as shown in Figure 24-16.

Select Excel Services from the Publish menu. That
will bring up the familiar Save As dialog. Verify
that the path information is correctly set to the
Team Project path. If not, change it to the correct
path. Then, click on the Excel Services Option
button.

Now you will be in the Excel Services Option
dialog.

In this window, there are two tabs: Show and
Parameters. You will only be using the Show tab
here. The Parameters tab is used to specify cells
that you can provide value to while viewing the
Microsoft Excel report.

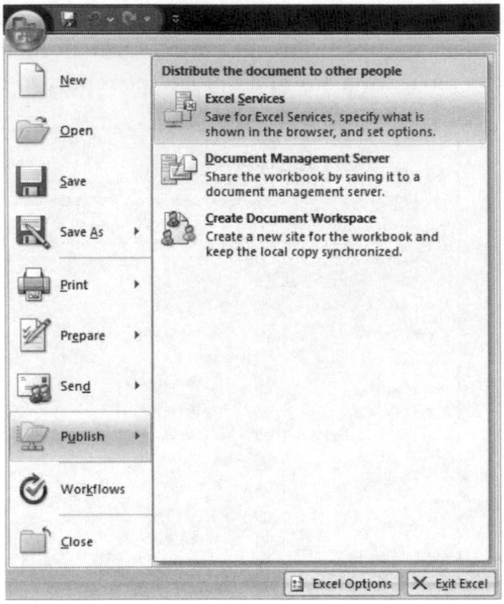

FIGURE 24-16

In the Entire Workbook drop-down, select "Items in the Workbook" because you want to publish
the Microsoft Excel report to Excel Services and have the chart show up in the dashboard using the
Excel Web Access part. You don't want the entire spreadsheet to show up in the dashboard, but
rather just the short version. Selecting "Items in the Workbook" changes the view in the box below
the drop-down. Now you have the capability to select all charts or individual charts, as well as all
pivot tables or individual pivot tables. In this example, you only have one chart and one pivot table.
Select All Charts, as shown in Figure 24-17.

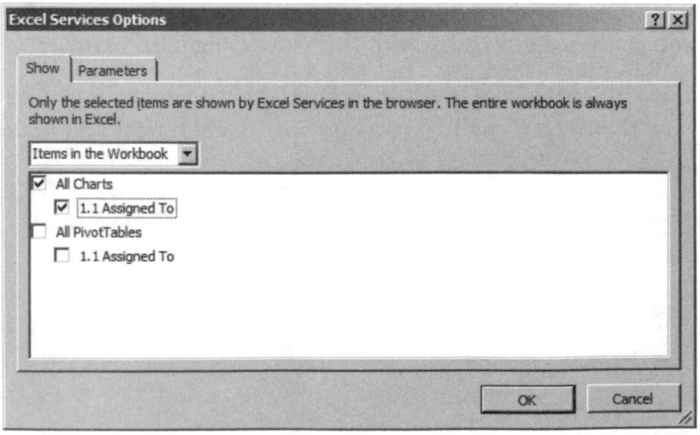

FIGURE 24-17

Click OK in this window and then Save to publish the Microsoft Excel report. Now you are finished with the publishing.

The next step is to add the report to the dashboard. To launch the dashboard, in Team Explorer, right-click on the team project name and select Show Project Portal. That will open the project portal in the browser. Select Excel Reports from the left navigation, as shown in Figure 24-14.

This will bring up the list of Microsoft Excel reports, including the new report you just published, as shown in Figure 24-18.

You now want to get this report onto the dashboard. From the Dashboards list, select the dashboard to which you want to add this report. As shown in Figure 24-14, you can choose between My Dashboard or the Project Dashboard. In this example, select the Project Dashboard.

To add the new report to this dashboard, click Site Actions on the top right-hand corner and select Edit Page.

🗀	Test Management
🖹	Bug Progress
🖹	Bug Reactivations
🖹	Bug Trends
🖹	Bugs by Assignment
🖹	Bugs by Priority
🖹	Build Status
🖹	Burndown
🖹	Code Churn
🖹	Code Coverage
🖹	Failure Analysis
🖹	Issue Trends
🖹	Remaining Work by Team Members ! NEW
🖹	Report Template
🖹	Task Progress
🖹	Test Activity
🖹	Test Case Readiness
🖹	Test Plan Progress
🖹	User Story Progress
🖹	User Story Test Status

FIGURE 24-18

If you have worked with SharePoint sites and Web parts, then the next few steps will be very familiar to you. You will add a new Web part to this page by clicking the Add Web Part button in the Footer section.

That will bring up the "Add Web Parts to Footer" window. You will use an Excel Web Access Web part, so select that Web part and click Add.

That adds the Excel Web Access Web part to the dashboard page. The next step is to select a workbook that you want to display in this Web part. In this example, that would be the "Remaining Work Items by Team Member" workbook (see Figure 24-14). So, select that workbook. You do that by specifying the details in the tool pane. There is obviously lots of information that you can provide in this tool pane. Following are the two fields that you will update here:

➤ Workbook

➤ Title

Click OK on the tool pane window and exit the edit mode to see this report displayed in the dashboard.

Microsoft Excel reports are truly going to make it easy for team members get the data and metrics that they want from Team Foundation Server. The capability to create report from a work item query is a great addition to the reporting capability in Team Foundation Server. Couple that with the Microsoft Excel services and dashboards, and now no one can complain about not having the right information at the right time.

Working with RDL Reports

This section briefly examines the tools available to create and customize Report Definition Language (RDL) reports. Team Foundation Server 2010 includes set of RDL reports out-of-the-box, and the reports vary by the type of process template you choose to use for your project. You'll learn about the list of these reports later in this chapter.

There are two tools available to work with RDL reports:

➤ Report Builder

➤ Report Designer

Report Builder

The Report Builder 2.0 tool has full support for SQL Reporting Services. It's designed for business analysts and developers who wish to create custom reports quickly and easily. You can download the tool from `http://www.microsoft.com/downloads/details.aspx?FamilyID=9f783224-9871-4eea-b1d5-f3140a253db6&displaylang=en#filelist`. With this tool, you can work with RDL files, make necessary changes, and save it as an RDL file. This file can then be used, for example, using the Report Designer.

Once you have the tool installed, launch the report builder and start by connecting the report server. (For example, `http://<<Server instance name/reportserver>>`.) It is probably easier to start with an existing report and customize it than it is to create one from scratch.

To edit an existing report, you start by selecting the reports folder in the report server, then the team project collection, followed by the actual team project. This will bring the up the folders with the reports, and you will choose the report for customization from one of these folders. Figure 24-19 shows the "Stories Overview" report in the Report Builder 2.0 tool.

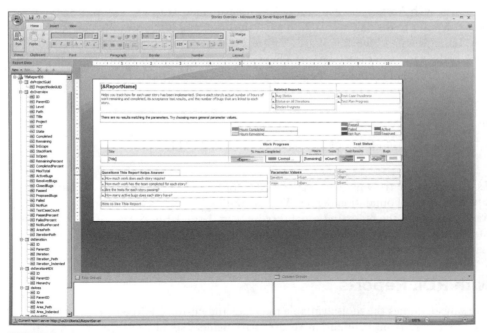

FIGURE 24-19

The report data pane has the parameters, data set, and the built-in fields that you will work with to modify the report.

 SQL Server Developer Center on MSDN has several how-to topics on Report Builder 2.0. For more information, see http://msdn.microsoft.com/en-us/ library/dd220513.aspx.

Report Designer

This is an add-on that is installed with SQL Server Client Tools.

 Note you also have the "Business Intelligence Development Studio" that you can use to create and work with reports.

After you install it, you will have access to a new project type called Business Intelligence Projects. This will have a template called Report Server Project. You will use this project to set up a report project in Visual Studio. Once you have the project set up, you can start adding new reports from within Visual Studio.

Follow these steps to work on an existing report:

1. Create a Report Server project as described previously.

2. In the Solution Explorer, you will see two folders named Shared Data Sources and Reports created.

3. Right-click on Shared Data Sources, and select "Add a Data Source."

4. In the Shared Data Source Properties window, provide a name for the data source and select Microsoft SQL Server Analysis Services as the type.

5. Click the Edit button to specify the connection information. In the Connection Properties dialog, specify the server name and select Tfs_Analysis as the database name. You may want to test the connection to this database before proceeding.

Now that you have set the data source, the next thing to do is to get the report you want to modify. To do that, you must save the RDL file into this project. To do that, follow these steps:

1. Go to the team project report site. (From within Team Explorer, right-click on the Reports folder under the team project, and select Show Report Site.)

2. Select the report you want to edit.

3. Go to the Properties tab from the report page.

4. In the Properties page, select Edit and save the .rdl file.

With the report file saved, switch back to Visual Studio and to the Report Project. In Solution Explorer, right-click the `Reports` folder and select "Add an existing item." At this point, you want to add to this project the `.rdl` file you saved in the prior step.

Now, you will see the report file added to the Solution Explorer. Double-click the report file to open it in the designer, as shown in Figure 24-20. This probably looks familiar, because it is very similar to the view you saw in Figure 24-19, which was using the Report Builder 2.0 tool.

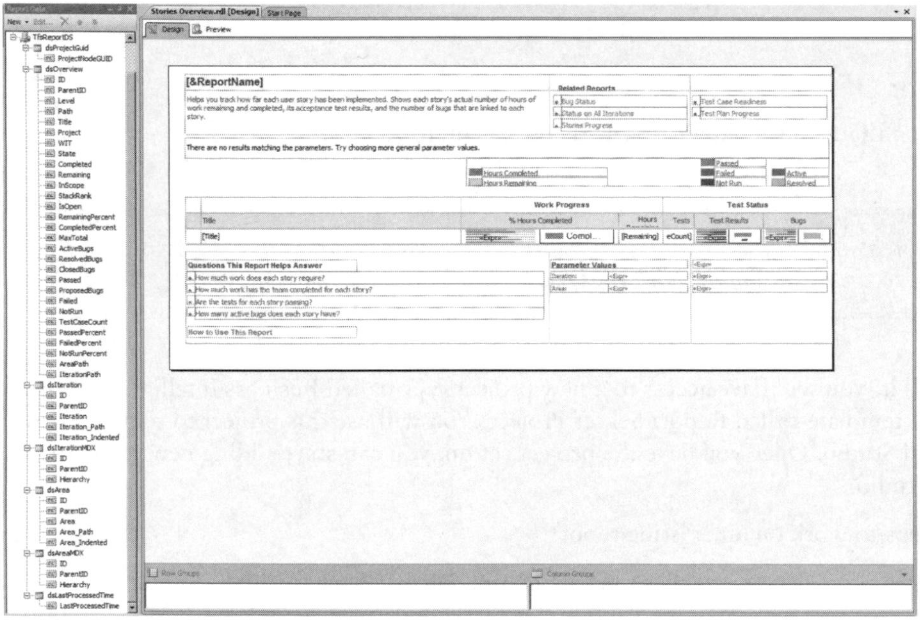

FIGURE 24-20

Check out the MSDN article "Creating and Customizing TFS Reports," at `http://msdn.microsoft.com/en-us/library/aa337239(SQL.90).aspx` *for detailed information on how to create and customize RDL reports using Report Designer.*

For the reports you have created for Team Foundation Server 2008, refer to the following blog posts to learn about the steps to upgrade them over to Team Foundation Server 2010.

➤ `http://www.socha.com/blogs/john/2009/05/upgrading-visual-studio-team-foundation.html`

➤ `http://www.socha.com/blogs/john/2009/10/upgrading-team-foundation-server-2008.html`

Reports Out-of-the-Box

As you learned in Chapter 23, Team Foundation Server includes two process templates — one for teams practicing agile techniques, and the other for teams requiring a more formal process in CMMI. This section takes a look at the reports included in each of these two templates.

Reports Included in the Team Foundation Server Process Templates

As discussed in Chapter 23, the MSF for Agile Software Development template has been significantly updated to get the terminologies and practices in line with mainstream agile methodologies. That applies to the reports as well. If you are a practitioner of agile methods, you are probably aware of reports such as a work burndown and remaining work. These two reports are among the 15 shipped with the MFS for Agile Software Development template.

MSF for CMMI Process Improvement template also includes a set of SQL Reporting Services reports and Excel reports. Obviously, the user story-related reports are based on the "Requirements work item" in the CMMI template.

In Team Foundation Server 2010, reports are logically grouped, and are available in specific folders. Table 24-2 shows the SQL Reporting Services reports available out-of-the-box in the Team Foundation Server process templates.

TABLE 24-2: SQL Reporting Services Reports

GROUP	REPORT NAME	DESCRIPTION
BUGS	Bug Status	Helps you track the team's progress toward resolving bugs. Shows the number of bugs in each state over time, a breakdown of bugs by priority or severity, and the number of bugs that are assigned to each team member.
	Bug Trends	Helps you track the rate at which the team is discovering and resolving bugs. Shows a moving average of bugs discovered and resolved over time.
	Reactivations	Helps you track how effectively the team is resolving bugs. Shows the number of bugs that the team resolved over time in relation to the number of bugs that the team resolved and later re-activated.
BUILDS	Build Quality Indicators	Helps you track how close the completed code is to release quality. Shows test coverage, code churn, and bug counts.
	Build Success Over Time	Helps you track changes in the quality of the code that the team has checked in. Shows test results for the last build of each day.
	Build Summary	Helps you determine the status of each build. Shows a list of builds with test results, test coverage, code churn, and quality notes.

continues

TABLE 24-2 *(continued)*

GROUP	REPORT NAME	DESCRIPTION
PROJECT MANAGEMENT	Burndown and Burn Rate	Helps you track the team's progress toward completing the work in iteration. Shows how many hours of work the team has completed, how many hours remain, the rate of progress, and the work assigned to each team member.
	Remaining Work	Helps you track the team's progress. Shows the total number of hours of work in an iteration and the team's progress toward completing it.
	Status on All Iterations	Helps you track the team's performance over successive iterations. Shows each iteration's original estimates for the number of hours of work, the actual numbers of hours of work that the team completed, the number of hours of work that remain, and the number of bugs.
	Stories Overview (or Requirements Overview in the CMMI template)	Helps you track how far each user story has been implemented. Shows each story's actual number of hours of work remaining and completed, its acceptance test results, and the number of bugs that are linked to each story.
	Stories Progress (or Requirements Progress in the CMMI template)	Helps you track recent progress for each user story. Shows each story's remaining, completed, and recently completed work.
TESTS	Test Case Readiness	Helps you track how many test cases are ready to be run. Shows the number of test cases in each state of preparation.
	Test Plan Progress	Helps you track the progress of your test plans. Shows the results of running the tests over time.

The reports shown in Table 24-2 are all available as RDL reports. You can view them by going to the team project report site. By default, you will get to a page with the various report folders. Select the folder and click on the individual report to view it. Figure 24-21 shows the "Stories Progress" report under the Project Management folder.

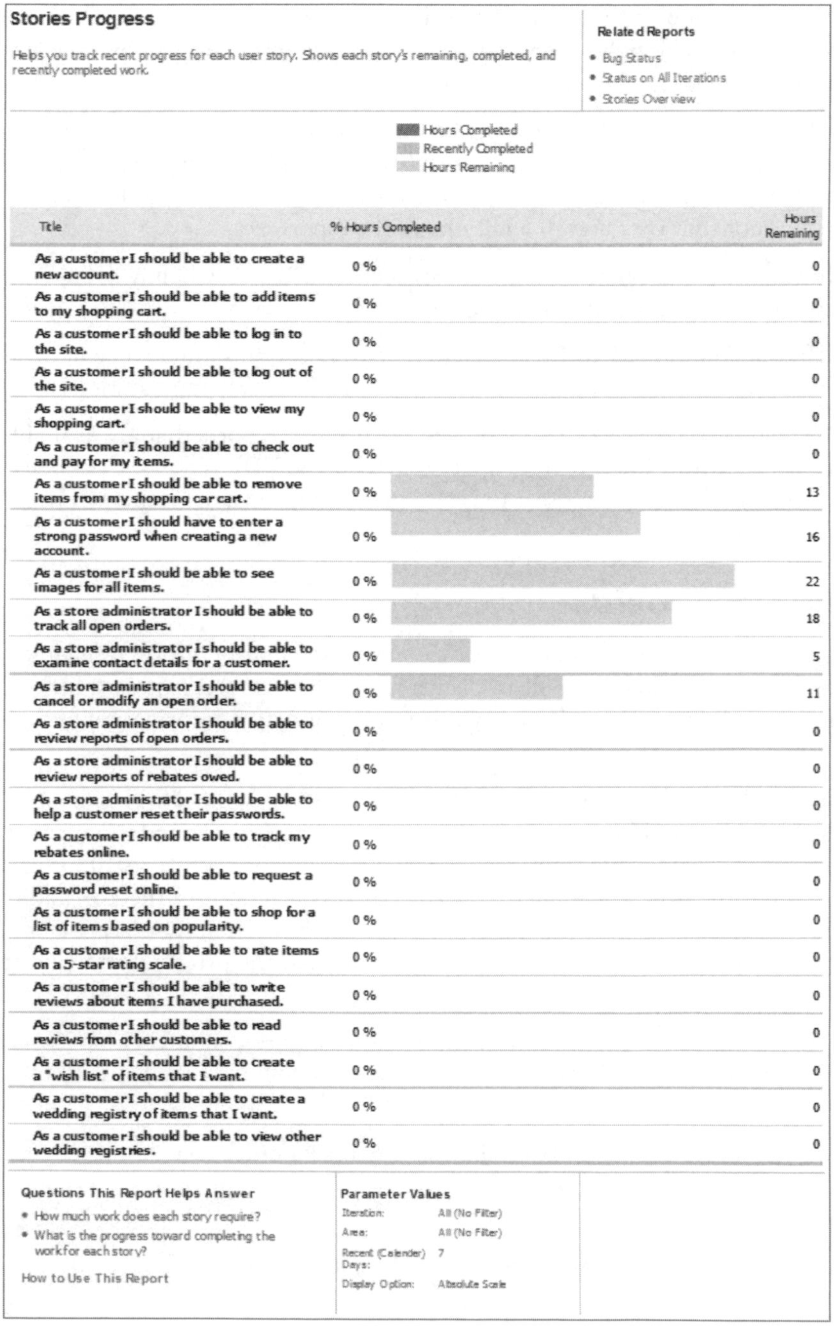

Stories Progress

Helps you track recent progress for each user story. Shows each story's remaining, completed, and recently completed work.

Related Reports
- Bug Status
- Status on All Iterations
- Stories Overview

Hours Completed
Recently Completed
Hours Remaining

Title	% Hours Completed	Hours Remaining
As a customer I should be able to create a new account.	0 %	0
As a customer I should be able to add items to my shopping cart.	0 %	0
As a customer I should be able to log in to the site.	0 %	0
As a customer I should be able to log out of the site.	0 %	0
As a customer I should be able to view my shopping cart.	0 %	0
As a customer I should be able to check out and pay for my items.	0 %	0
As a customer I should be able to remove items from my shopping car cart.	0 %	13
As a customer I should have to enter a strong password when creating a new account.	0 %	16
As a customer I should be able to see images for all items.	0 %	22
As a store administrator I should be able to track all open orders.	0 %	18
As a store administrator I should be able to examine contact details for a customer.	0 %	5
As a store administrator I should be able to cancel or modify an open order.	0 %	11
As a store administrator I should be able to review reports of open orders.	0 %	0
As a store administrator I should be able to review reports of rebates owed.	0 %	0
As a store administrator I should be able to help a customer reset their passwords.	0 %	0
As a customer I should be able to track my rebates online.	0 %	0
As a customer I should be able to request a password reset online.	0 %	0
As a customer I should be able to shop for a list of items based on popularity.	0 %	0
As a customer I should be able to rate items on a 5-star rating scale.	0 %	0
As a customer I should be able to write reviews about items I have purchased.	0 %	0
As a customer I should be able to read reviews from other customers.	0 %	0
As a customer I should be able to create a "wish list" of items that I want.	0 %	0
As a customer I should be able to create a wedding registry of items that I want.	0 %	0
As a customer I should be able to view other wedding registries.	0 %	0

Questions This Report Helps Answer
- How much work does each story require?
- What is the progress toward completing the work for each story?

How to Use This Report

Parameter Values

Iteration:	All (No Filter)
Area:	All (No Filter)
Recent (Calendar) Days:	7
Display Option:	Absolute Scale

FIGURE 24-21

If you are thinking the reports are looking different than what you are used to seeing in Team Foundation Server 2008, you would be right. The reports have undergone changes both on visual appeal and the information it provides.

Some of the reports are composite reports that show data from multiple reports. This helps to get a snapshot of the progress without having to view multiple reports. The "Burndown and Burn Rate" report under the "Project Management" report folder is one such composite report. There are also a couple of minor (but very useful) additions to the report:

➤   On the top-right corner, you see the Related Reports section. It's a very handy list to reference in case you want to get additional information.

➤   In the bottom left, the Questions This Report Helps Answer section should come in handy to aid in understanding the report and how to use the report in answering questions.

In addition to these RDL reports, there are also a set of Microsoft Excel reports that are available out-of-the-box. Some of the Microsoft Excel reports are the same as the RDL reports, but there are additional ones as well. You will find the Microsoft Excel reports under the Documents ➪ Excel Reports folder in the team project.

Project Portals and Dashboards

One of the key features of Team Foundation Server is the capability to capture information, and, more importantly, make that information available to the team and the management with little or no overhead. *Project portals* and *dashboards* play a key role in disseminating information to the entire team.

Project portals should be familiar to the users of Team Foundation Server 2008. This has gone through a face lift in the 2010 version. However, dashboards are new in Team Foundation Server 2010. A project portal serves as the one-stop information portal for your project. In 2010, project portals include several new dashboards. The number of dashboards you get out-of-the-box and the type of reports displayed in these dashboards depend on whether you have MOSS Enterprise or WSS site associated with your team project. This section takes a quick look at the project portal and the dashboards.

Let's start with the portal. To access the portal, from within Team Explorer, right-click on the team project name and select Show Project Portal. That will launch the browser and load the project portal page.

This screen has changed quite a bit from its 2008 version, so let's take a quick tour of this page.

Left Navigation Pane

Let's start from the left navigation and look at significant features in the portal.

Team Web Access

This is a link to the Team Foundation Server Web Access. Team Web Access provides a Web-based interface to connect to Team Foundation Server and manage a team project. Team Web Access is customizable, and provides many capabilities that are available through Team Explorer, including the following:

➤ Managing Work Items

➤ Managing Work Item Queries

➤ Work with version control

➤ Work with builds (start, stop, and queue build)

➤ Access documents and reports

Dashboards

Dashboards are new in Team Foundation Server 2010. Out-of-the-box, Team Foundation Server includes the following six dashboards:

➤ Burndown

➤ Quality

➤ Bugs

➤ Test

➤ Build

➤ My Dashboard

These dashboards are only available if the team project portal is associated with a MOSS enterprise site. Dashboards use two kinds of SharePoint Web parts to display the information. It uses Excel Web Access Web part to display Excel reports and uses Team Web Access Web part to display work item query results. You will see examples of these later in this section.

Each of these dashboards is essentially a collection of reports that provide relevant information particular to that dashboard. For example, Figure 24-22 shows the Burndown dashboard. This dashboard presents the following four reports:

➤ Task Burndown

➤ Task Progress

➤ User Story Progress

➤ Issue Trend

With the information from these four reports, Burndown dashboard helps you get a quick snapshot of how the project is coming along. By looking at the Task Burndown chart in Figure 24-22, you can get a sense for how the team is progressing against the ideal trend line. In this example, the team is on track to complete. This dashboard also shows the issues trend. You obviously don't want the active issues to trend high. In this example, the issues trend looks fine, with many resolved or closed issues, and the active issues line trending low. Don't you simply enjoy sample projects where all the metrics look just the way you want them to be?

Note that each of these dashboards is customizable based on your need, or you can add a new dashboard if you want to track a different set of information that does not fit into the existing dashboards. With the exception of My Dashboard, all other dashboards use Excel reports, and, hence, the Excel Web Access Web part.

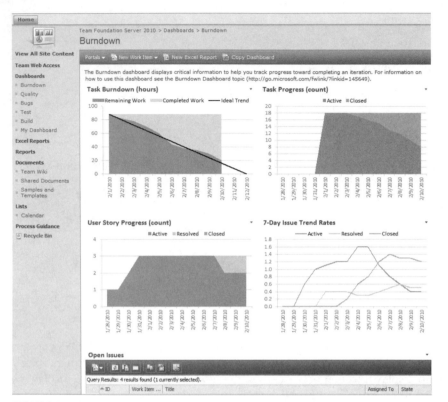

FIGURE 24-22

My Dashboard uses the Team Web Access Web part to show results from various work item queries. This dashboard could serve as the view of your "TODO" list. It provides you with a view of the team bugs, tasks, and issues that are assigned to you, as shown in Figure 24-23.

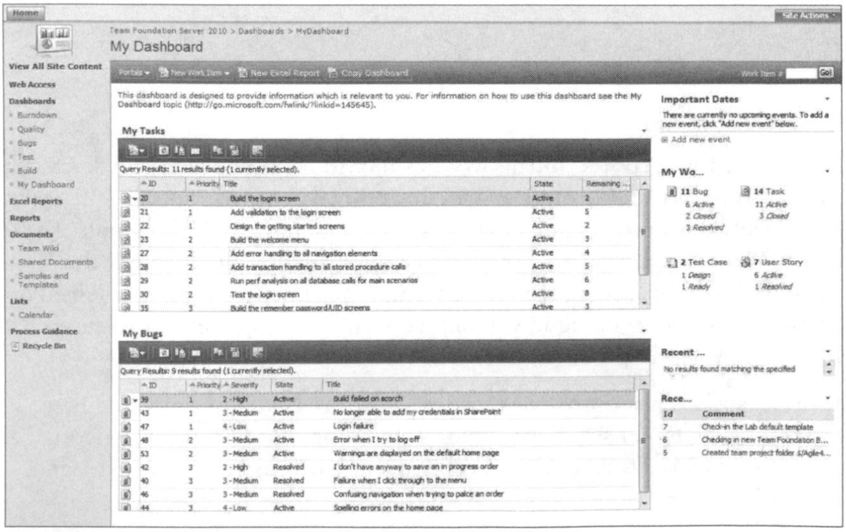

FIGURE 24-23

Obviously, you could edit the queries that are attached to these Web parts, or add additional Web parts to modify this dashboard to fit your need and the information that you would like to see in this dashboard.

If you do not have a MOSS Enterprise-based site associated with your team project, and instead have a WSS site associated with the project, you get the following two dashboards in the portal:

➤ *My Dashboard* — This is the same as what has been previously described.

➤ *Project Dashboard* — This dashboard contains the following three main sections:

  ➤ Task Burndown RDL report presented in a Page Viewer Web part

  ➤ Burn Rate RDL report presented in a Page Viewer Web part

  ➤ Results of the Product Backlog query presented in the Team Web Access Web part

Excel Reports

The next menu item on the left navigation is the "Excel Reports." Clicking on this link will load the list of Microsoft Excel reports that are available in this team project.

Reports

This links to the Report Manager page. In this page, you will see the folders that the various reports are grouped under.

Documents

This has three links:

➤ *Wiki page* — Wiki page is a site to collaborate with your team by sharing information, design artifacts, a knowledge base, and so on. It is a simple wiki site that is set up as part of the portal-creation process that you can use to suit the needs of your team. Refer to the "How to use this wiki site" document in the wiki pages for more information on this.

➤ *Shared Documents* — This is where you will find the Product Backlog and Iteration Backlog spreadsheets if you are using the agile template.

➤ *Samples and Templates* — This section is where you will find a list of templates for personas, iteration retrospectives, test plans, and so on.

Process Guidance

This link will take you to the process guidance page. The process guidance obviously depends on the process template that you are using. The location could be either the online guidance on MSDN, or the link to the wiki library.

Top Horizontal Menu

Now, let's look at the features available in the top horizontal menu.

New Work Item

This is a shortcut link to create a new work item in your team project. By clicking on the drop-down, you will have the option to pick the type of work item you want to create, as shown in Figure 24-24. After you pick a work item type, that opens a work item form to provide the details.

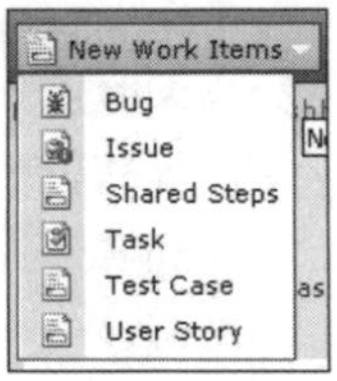

FIGURE 24-24

New Excel Report

Earlier in this chapter, you learned about the steps used to create Microsoft Excel reports. This link automates a couple of the steps in the process by making the necessary data connection. The earlier section in this chapter, "Working with Microsoft Excel Reports," provides more information.

Copy Dashboard

Earlier, you learned that you can add new dashboards. Using Copy Dashboards is a quick way to do that. From the dashboard you are in, click Copy Dashboard. This opens up the form shown in Figure 24-25.

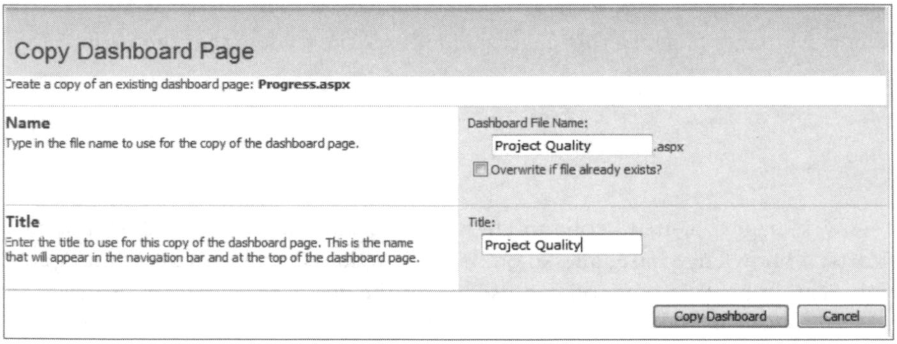

FIGURE 24-25

Fill out the details and click the Copy Dashboard button. This will create the new dashboard and add it to the Dashboard section in the left navigation as well. Now, you can edit this dashboard and include the reports that you want to see in this new dashboard.

SUMMARY

In this chapter, you learned about the various data stores in Team Foundation Server that provide the data for the various reports. You also learned about the tools that are available to create reports. This chapter examined how to create and customize Microsoft Excel reports, and the tools available to create and customize RDL reports (that is, Report Builder and Report Designer), as well as the options available for publishing reports. Lastly, this chapter reviewed the portal and the new dashboards available in Team Foundation Server 2010.

Reporting is a powerful feature in Team Foundation Server. It breaks down the usual barrier within teams caused by a lack of information. Team Foundation Server provides a powerful set of reports out-of-the-box and provides the capability to add additional reports based on your needs. And that is coupled with the capability to quickly share the information using dashboards and portals.

Chapter 25 takes a look at the product planning workbook and the iteration backlog workbook, and how they can be used by agile teams to manage product backlog and iteration backlog.

25

Agile Planning Using Planning Workbooks

WHAT'S IN THIS CHAPTER?

➤ Getting to know product backlog, release planning, and iteration planning

➤ Learning about the new product planning workbook

➤ Learning how to use the product planning workbook for planning the release and iteration, as well as managing the product backlog

➤ Learning about the new iteration planning workbook

➤ Learning how to use it for managing the iteration

➤ Understanding the issues and retrospectives spreadsheet

In Chapter 23, you learned about the process templates included in Visual Studio Team Foundation Server 2010. One of those templates is the Microsoft Solutions Framework (MSF) for Agile Software Development process template. For agile teams, planning is a day-to-day activity, and planning certainly helps the team to stay on track, as well as work toward getting the most important things done on time.

Team Foundation Server 2010 in its MSF for Agile Software Development v5.0 process template includes two new workbooks that are designed specifically to help agile teams with the planning activities. This chapter examines the product planning workbook and the iteration planning workbook. You will learn how these workbooks can be used to manage the product backlog, to plan out iterations and track them, to understand the team capacity and to watch the velocity of the team, which is important to plan future iterations.

It is a common myth that agile teams do less or no planning at all. To the contrary, agile teams require a lot of rigor and discipline when it comes to planning and tracking. It is critical to the success of agile teams that the entire team takes part in the planning process and that team members commit themselves to the plan. That is not to say that the plan is rigid, but rather that every member of the team has skin in the game.

In the book *Planning Extreme Programming* (Boston: Addison-Wesley Professional, 2000), authors Kent Beck and Martin Fowler say, "We plan to ensure that we are always doing the most important thing left to do, to coordinate effectively with other people, and to respond quickly to unexpected events."

Agile teams plan at two different levels — one at the macro level to understand the release schedule and the other at a more granular level to plan and manage each of the iterations.

This chapter delves into how you can use the planning workbooks to help with planning at both levels that are essential for agile teams.

PRODUCT BACKLOG

For agile teams, the *product backlog* serves as the singular representative of the customer requirements in a prioritized (and stack-ranked) order. A product backlog contains a list of user stories as defined by the customer. Hence, it is very important that the team keeps the product backlog up to date. At the beginning of any project, the team will start by adding user stories to this backlog.

As part of the release-planning effort, the stories in the product backlog are prioritized and estimated. Note that the prioritization of the backlog also takes place on an ongoing basis. It is also common for new user stories to show up in the backlog during the course of the project. Typically, it is the responsibility of the product owner to manage the backlog and reprioritize the items in the backlog as appropriate.

By default, in Team Foundation Server, *story points* are used as a unit of measurement to assess the size of the user stories. Story points are based on a relative size, rather than an absolute value. The story point assessment is based on the perceived size and/or complexity of a user story, rather than the time of effort it would take to implement a user story.

Estimates for user stories typically use a non-durational value — for example, a t-shirt size or story point. It is important to note that the goal here is to not get to a level of precision (even if you try, it is really difficult to do this) but to have a relative measurement of each of the user stories. So, a story estimated as a large t-shirt size, or eight story points, should be bigger than a story estimated as a medium t-shirt size, or four story points.

It is helpful (and recommended) that you break down into smaller increments those user stories that are larger and difficult to estimate. These larger user stories sometimes are referred to as *epics* or *novels*. Teams tend to not spend a lot of time in estimating these larger user stories because it is likely that these will be analyzed and split into smaller user stories before this can be assigned to any iteration.

Release Planning

After a set of user stories in the product backlog have been prioritized and estimated, the teams can work to get a release plan in place. A *release plan* is primarily based on the minimal set of features that are required to be implemented for the system/application to have the expected impact. This set of features could be considered a *minimally credible release*. Once this is identified, then, based on the estimates (story points) and the expected (or known) velocity of the team, a release plan that includes a schedule can be derived.

For example, let's say that the total set of user stories to reach a minimal credible release is about 240 story points and the team's known or expected velocity is 30 story points per iteration. In this case, a team will take eight iterations, or about four months, to complete these user stories if the iterations are two weeks long.

Another way to get to a release plan is to use a *time box*. This approach has been effective when targeting a time window to get a project out. When using the time-box approach, a deadline is driven by something such as a marketing ad campaign, a legal requirement, a competitive launch, or some other factor that requires a release by a certain date. In this case, you work back from the release date and figure out how much of the customer requirements or user stories can be fulfilled in the time available, based on the velocity of the team. For example, if a release is required in four months, and the team's expected or measured velocity is about 30 story points per iteration, then a team running two-week iterations could commit to completing user stories totaling 240 story points.

Figure 25-1 shows a representation of a product backlog with a list of user stories and a cut-off line identifying the minimal credible release. The list of user stories above this cut-off line is worked on during one or more iterations. In this example, it takes three iterations to get the first release out.

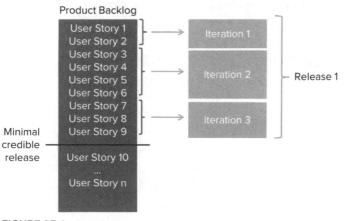

FIGURE 25-1

Note that the customer requirements and the priorities of these requirements could change as the project progresses. It is important that the product backlog is kept up to date with any changes to the backlog in terms of priorities, new user stories to be added, or existing user stories that can removed.

PRODUCT PLANNING WORKBOOK

In its MSF for Agile Software Development process template, Team Foundation Server 2010 includes a Microsoft Office Excel workbook to create and manage the product backlog.

To work with this workbook in Microsoft Office Excel, you should have the Team Foundation Server Office add-in installed.

Locating the Product Planning Workbook

After you create a new team project using the new MSF for Agile Software Development v5.0 template, you will find the planning workbooks (both the product and iteration backlog workbooks) under the My Agile Project ⇨ Documents ⇨ Shared Documents in the Team Explorer, as shown in Figure 25-2. You could also access the workbooks from the SharePoint Team Project Portal under the `Shared Documents` folder.

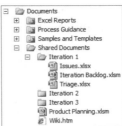

FIGURE 25-2

Setting Up the Product Planning Workbook

The product planning workbook gets the data from a work item query appropriately named Product Planning. This query is created during the team project creation and can be found under My Agile Project ⇨ Work Items ⇨ Team Queries ⇨ Workbook Queries.

Before delving into the details of the product planning workbook, let's take a quick look at the query itself. As you can see in Figure 25-3, this query pulls all work items of type User Story with any state other than closed, and user stories that were closed in the last 90 days.

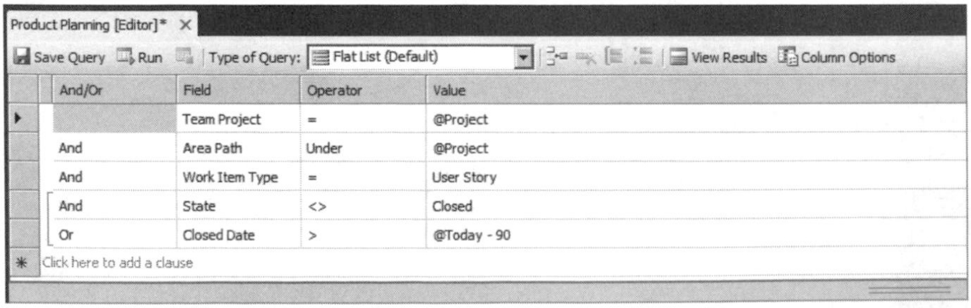

	And/Or	Field	Operator	Value
▶		Team Project	=	@Project
	And	Area Path	Under	@Project
	And	Work Item Type	=	User Story
	And	State	<>	Closed
	Or	Closed Date	>	@Today - 90
✳	Click here to add a clause			

FIGURE 25-3

This query brings a list of user stories that are open and that are recently closed. There is also a Product Backlog query that brings in only open user stories.

Now, let's look at how this query gets wired up to the product planning workbook. To do that, let us switch from Visual Studio to Microsoft Office Excel. From the Excel ribbon, select the Configure ⇨ List option under the Work Items tab group. As shown in Figure 25-4, following this path leads you to the query for the product planning workbook.

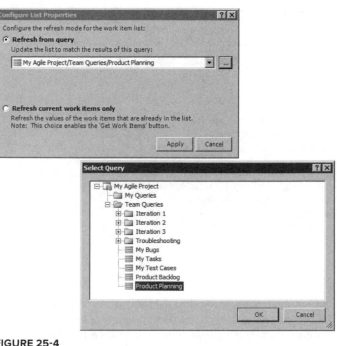

FIGURE 25-4

> *Check that team members have required permissions to modify the workbooks. Team members who would be making changes to the workbooks must be part of the "Contributors" group.*

In the Configure List Properties window, you can see the query that this workbook is attached to.

That concludes this quick overview of the mechanics to get the planning workbook wired up with the corresponding query. With the basics out of the way, let's now focus on the following three worksheets in the product planning workbook:

➤ *Product backlog* — You will use this worksheet to manage the product backlog, including work for various iterations, stack ranking work items, estimation of work items, and more.

➤ *Iterations* — You will use this worksheet to maintain information about iterations, including the duration (start date and end date) and team size.

➤ *Interruptions* — You will use this worksheet to manage interruptions to your schedule (such as holidays).

Using the Product Backlog Worksheet

The *product backlog* worksheet displays a list of user stories, as shown in Figure 25-5. These are the results of the Product Planning query presented in this Excel spreadsheet.

ID	Stack Rank	Story Points	Title	State	Iteration Path	Area Path	Work Item Type
1	1	12	As a user I want to try to login to the website so I can order things.	Active	\Iteration 1	\	User Story
2	2	11	As a user I want to login as guest to the website so I can shop around	Active	\Iteration 1	\	User Story
3	3	17	As a user I want to logout of the site.	Active	\Iteration 1	\	User Story
4	4	5	As a user I want to review the products	Active	\Iteration 1	\	User Story
5	5	4	As a user I want to read product review	Active	\Iteration 1	\	User Story
6	6	8	As an administrator I want be able to update product information	Active	\Iteration 1	\	User Story
7	7	15	As a user I want to sign up for email newsletter	Active	\Iteration 1	\	User Story
8	8	11	As a new user I want a tour of the web site so I can learn about the site	Active	\Iteration 1	\	User Story
36	9	1	As a user I want to automatically log off after 10 minutes of inactivity in the site	Active	\Iteration 1	\	User Story
10	10	8	As a new customer I want to register so that I can use the site.	Active	\Iteration 2	\	User Story
11	11	5	As a new customer I want log in so that I can review the products	Active	\Iteration 2	\	User Story
12	12	3	As a new customer I want to set my profile.	Active	\Iteration 2	\	User Story
13	13	15	As a new customer I want to sign up for alerts.	Active	\Iteration 2	\	User Story
14	14	7	As a customer I want the site to remember my login information.	Active	\Iteration 2	\	User Story
15	15	13	As a user I want to review order information so I can verify.	Active	\Iteration 2	\	User Story
16	16	13	As a user I want to submit product reviews	Active	\Iteration 2	\	User Story
17	17	4	As a user I want to rate the product reviews	Active	\Iteration 2	\	User Story
18	18	6	As an administrator I want to add promotions to the site	Active	\Iteration 2	\	User Story
19	19	5	As an administrator I want to review order history	Active	\Iteration 2	\	User Story
20	20	8	As a user I want to see my order history	Active	\Iteration 2	\	User Story
21	21	7	As a user I want to review reward points	Active	\Backlog	\	User Story
22	22	11	As a user I want to add items to shopping cart	Active	\Backlog	\	User Story
23	23	10	As a user I want to remove items from shopping cart	Active	\Backlog	\	User Story
24	24	12	As a user I want to check out	Active	\Backlog	\	User Story
25	25	7	As a user I want to provide shipping information	Active	\Backlog	\	User Story
26	26	9	As a user I want to enter coupon information	Active	\Backlog	\	User Story
27	27	6	As a user I want to enter gift card information	Active	\Backlog	\	User Story
28	28	10	As a administrartor I want to add special sale items	Active	\Backlog	\	User Story
29	29	11	As a user I want to see the top sellers	Active	\Backlog	\	User Story
30	30	7	As a user I want to see the products by category	Active	\Backlog	\	User Story
9	31	5	As a administrator I want to create product categories	Active	\Iteration 2	\	User Story
31		5	User Story 2	Active	\Iteration 1	\	User Story
32		4	User Story 1	Active	\Iteration 1	\	User Story
35		3	User Story 3	Active	\Iteration 1	\	User Story

FIGURE 25-5

Obviously, you can now use the familiar and powerful capabilities of Microsoft Office Excel to manage the list of user stories in the backlog. This worksheet shows the fields that you require to manage customer requirements using user stories, to prioritize them using stack ranks, to estimate them using story points, and to assign the user stories to iterations using the iteration path.

The list of user stories shown in Figure 25-5 is from a sample team project created to help explain the backlog workbooks. The workbook contains several user stories that are stack-ranked, with the higher-priority ones assigned to either Iteration 1 or 2. There are several user stories in the backlog that are not yet assigned to an iteration.

It is very common to not have all the user stories in the backlog assigned to an iteration. There could be multiple reasons for this. It could be because not all of the user stories in the backlog are going to be worked on by the team for the current release. Or, it could be that the team only wants to commit to work on two iterations at a time, knowing that there will be changes to the backlog as the project progresses, and planning out more than couple of iterations may not be that useful anyway.

The product backlog worksheet is primarily used to do the following:

➤ Create new user stories

➤ Prioritize user stories in the backlog

➤ Estimate user stories

➤ Assign user stories to iterations

Once you have a backlog worksheet, you can add new user stories, stack-rank user stories against the rest of the stories in the backlog, and provide story point estimates.

The changes you make to this worksheet can be published back to Team Foundation Server. Updated data can be pulled from Team Foundation Server to this worksheet using the Publish and Refresh menu items found in the Team tab of the Excel ribbon, as shown in Figure 25-6.

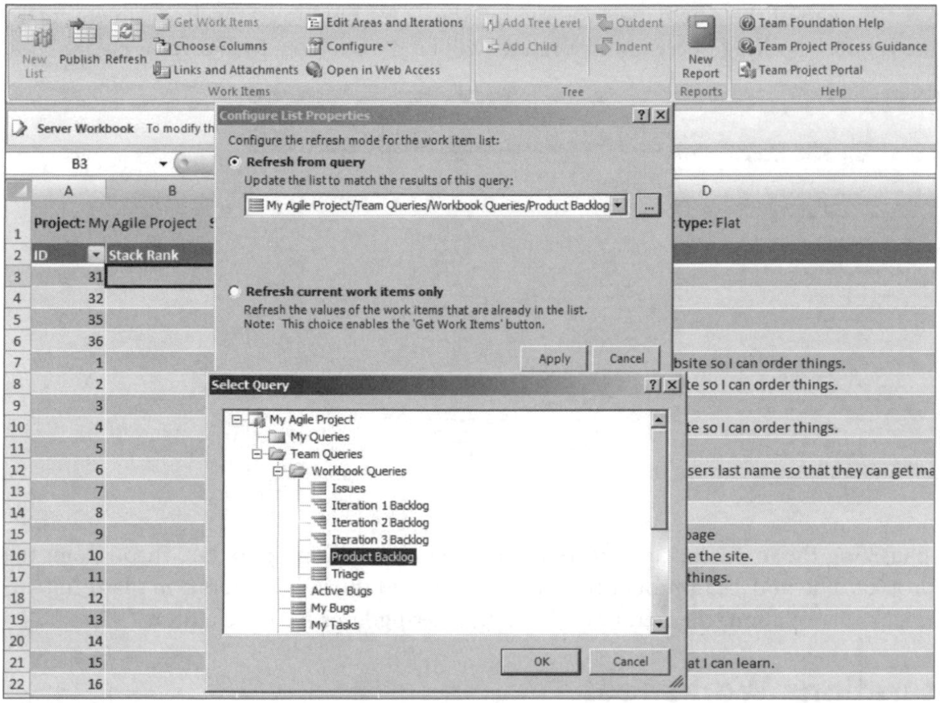

FIGURE 25-6

From within Microsoft Excel you can make bulk edits to the work items. The workbook as part of the publish process will validate the work item entries for any validation errors. Work items that have validation errors will be presented in a dialog, as shown in Figure 25-7, and you will have a chance to fix the errors and republish.

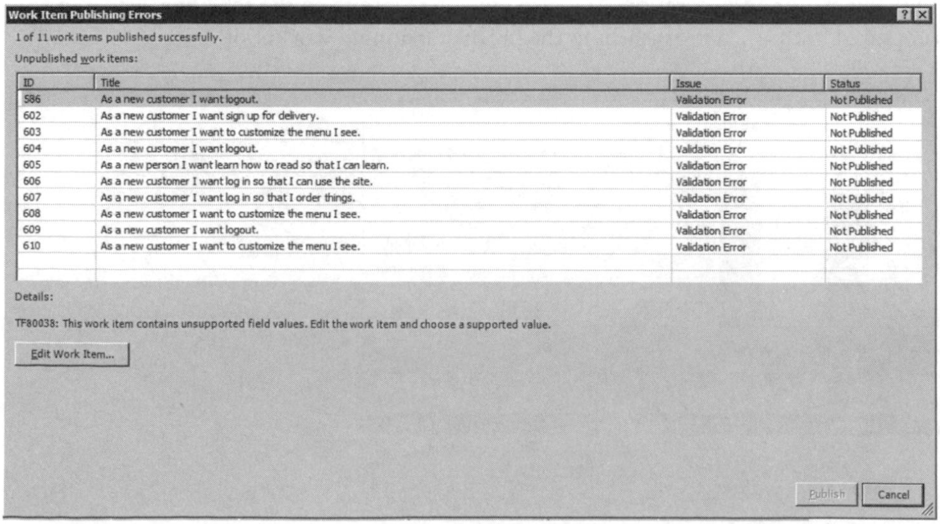

FIGURE 25-7

You could also perform all of these activities from within the Team Explorer as well. From within Team Explorer, run the product backlog query and the results will be the backlog, as shown in Figure 25-8.

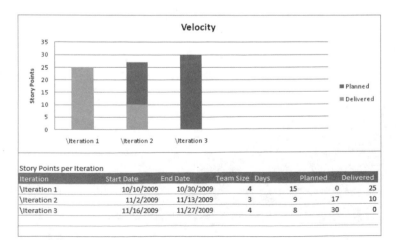

FIGURE 25-8

It is worth emphasizing the importance of keeping the product backlog up to date throughout the course of the project. The updated product backlog will be used during the iteration planning meeting. You'll learn more about the iteration planning meeting later in this chapter.

Using the Iterations Worksheet

The next worksheet in the product planning workbook is the *iterations worksheet*. (Do not confuse this with the *iteration planning workbook*, which will be explored later in this chapter.)

Mostly used by the product owner in the agile team, this worksheet is useful for keeping information about the iteration (such as the start date, end date of iterations, and team size). This worksheet displays a graph of planned and delivered work in each of the iterations, as shown in Figure 25-9. Obviously, the data is based on the status of the work item assigned to the various iterations, duration of the iterations, number of team members for each iteration, and also any interruptions in the schedule. The interruption information is captured in the next worksheet in the product planning workbook.

Story Points per Iteration

Iteration	Start Date	End Date	Team Size	Days	Planned	Delivered
\Iteration 1	10/10/2009	10/30/2009	4	15	0	25
\Iteration 2	11/2/2009	11/13/2009	3	9	17	10
\Iteration 3	11/16/2009	11/27/2009	4	8	30	0

FIGURE 25-9

> *Note that information such as the dates of iterations and team size are not stored in the Team Foundation Server data store. To retain this information, you should save the worksheet and store it in a team SharePoint site or check it in to Team Foundation Server for future reference.*

Using the Interruptions Worksheet

The third worksheet in the product backlog workbook is the *interruptions* worksheet. You use this worksheet to enter time during the iteration that the team member won't be available to work on the project (such as holidays, team off-site meetings, team training, and so on). These days would not be factored in to the total iteration days available in the iteration planning worksheet. Figure 25-10 shows a sample of an interruptions worksheet with holidays and a team offsite meeting marked as days that the team won't be available to work on the project.

Holidays	
Description	Date
Thanskgiving Day	11/25/2009
Thanksgiving Day	11/26/2009
Team Offsite	11/5/2009

FIGURE 25-10

ITERATION PLANNING

As you know, agile teams do their planning on two levels. *Release planning* provides a long-term view (usually 6 to 12 months) of the project, and the estimation of the release planning is usually done using a measure like story points. *Iteration planning* (or *sprint planning*) is more focused on a near-term view (2 to 4 weeks) of the project.

During the iteration planning stage, teams break down user stories into smaller user stories, and identify tasks required to complete each of the user stories. During the release planning, the order and dependencies between user stories are either mostly not known, or, if known, those were not given much attention. But, during the iteration planning, the team knows more about the user stories, as well as any and all dependencies that will impact the order in which the user stories can be worked on during that iteration.

SPRINT OR ITERATION

Agile teams follow a rhythm of execution. The duration of this usually is from two to four weeks. During this period is when agile teams work on the user stories. Extreme Programming refers to this as *iterations,* whereas Scrum refers to this as *sprints.* These two terms are essentially synonymous. So, whether the team is working on an iteration plan or a sprint plan, they are referring to the team having a plan for getting work done in the predefined 2-to-4-week period.

An iteration planning meeting takes place before each iteration starts. During this meeting, the team commits to completing a set of user stories for that iteration. Note that the initial set of user stories identified for a particular iteration during the release planning may change. In addition to the user stories in the backlog, teams would also include bugs, spikes, and any technical debt that must addressed.

Spikes are essentially a time-boxed effort used by teams to explore solutions to tackle a user story, or to make a design decision. Spikes are necessary when further technical exploration is necessary to come up with a plausible solution. Note that spikes are not science projects. So, it is critical that the spikes are time-boxed. The results of the spike effort are reviewed immediately for any impact to the current iteration plan, and, of course, this is factored into the subsequent iteration planning.

The team spends most of its time during the iteration planning meeting identifying tasks and estimating them. Teams use many techniques and tools to aid them in estimation. A good book to serve as a reference for such tools and techniques is *Agile Estimation and Planning* (Upper Saddle River, NJ: Pearson Education, 2006) by Mike Cohn.

> Teams play a game called "planning poker" to help with estimation. This game is very helpful, especially for newly formed teams, and for teams that are just getting started in using agile practices. For more information, check out: `http://www.planningpoker.com/`.

At the end of an iteration planning meeting, the teams have a clear understanding of the work that they have committed to perform.

ITERATION BACKLOG WORKBOOK

In its MSF for Agile Software Development process template, Team Foundation Server 2010 also includes a Microsoft Office Excel workbook called the *iteration backlog workbook* for creating and managing the iteration backlog, which is a workbook similar to the one used for managing product backlogs.

Locating the Iteration Backlog

As part of the setting up the team project, Team Foundation Server creates three iteration backlog workbooks. These will be found under My Agile Project ⇨ Documents ⇨ Shared Documents. As shown in Figure 25-11, there is a folder titled `Iteration #` for each of the iterations. The `Iteration 1` folder contains an iteration backlog workbook named `Iteration Backlog`.

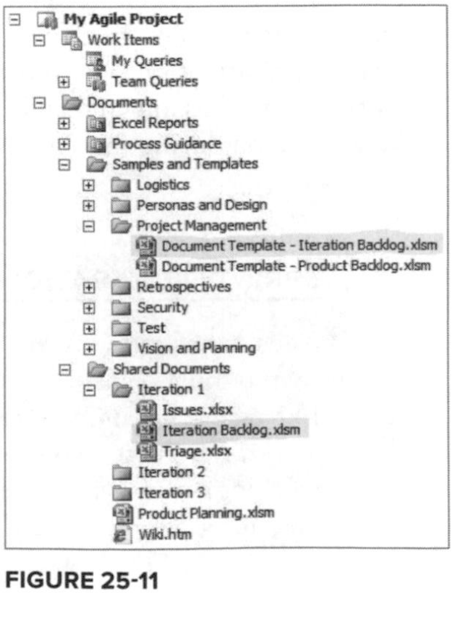

FIGURE 25-11

For further iterations, you want to copy the iteration backlog workbook from either the `Iteration 1` folder, or the template provided in the `Sample and Templates` folder. Once you copy the workbook, configure the workbook with the corresponding iterations backlog query.

As with the product backlog, the iteration backlog is wired up by its own queries. Figure 25-12 shows the iteration backlog query in the query editor.

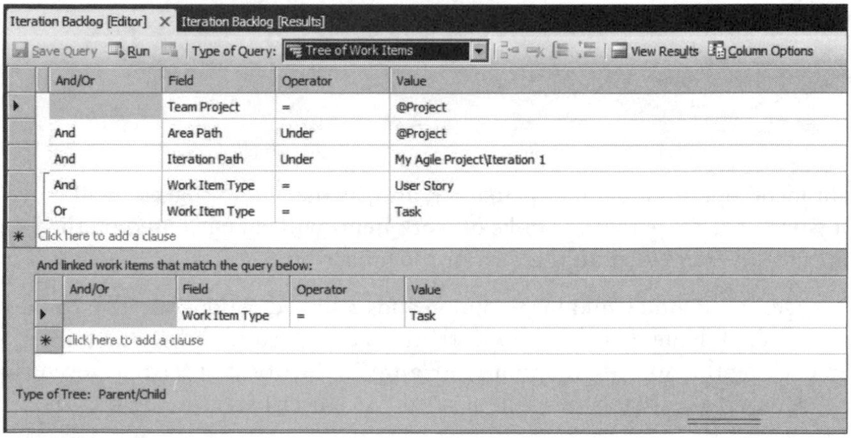

FIGURE 25-12

As you saw in Chapter 22, Team Foundation Server 2010 now supports hierarchical work items. You can now have queries to pull work items in a tree list that will show the linked work items. Iteration backlog uses a query to pull one such tree list. By default, the iteration backlog query retrieves user stories and tasks, as well as any linked task work items.

Note that during the iteration planning meeting, the bugs are prioritized along with the user stories and features. If the bugs get prioritized higher than certain user stories or tasks, then the team works on the bugs.

The iteration backlog workbook contains the following five worksheets:

➤ *Iteration backlog* — Use this worksheet to manage work items in that iteration.

➤ *Settings* — Use this worksheet to specify the iteration start date and end date. Note that these dates are not stored in Team Foundation Server.

➤ *Interruptions* — Use this worksheet to specify any time taken off by the team members during the iteration (such as vacations, training, and so on). You can also specify any interruptions that are team-wide (such as holidays, team-wide meetings, and so on). The interruptions are used when calculating the team capacity for the iteration, as well as individual capacity.

➤ *Capacity* — This worksheet shows the capacity of the team and individuals for the iteration.

➤ *Burn-down* — This worksheet has a chart that shows the trend lines for completed hours, remaining hours, and the ideal trend.

Now, let's take a closer look at the iteration backlog worksheet and the capacity worksheet.

Using the Iteration Backlog Worksheet

Figure 25-13 shows the Team tab in the Excel ribbon. Obviously, you see the familiar Publish, Refresh, and Configure menu options in this tab. However, the menu options that get a lot of use while managing the iteration backlog are Outdent, Indent, and Add Child.

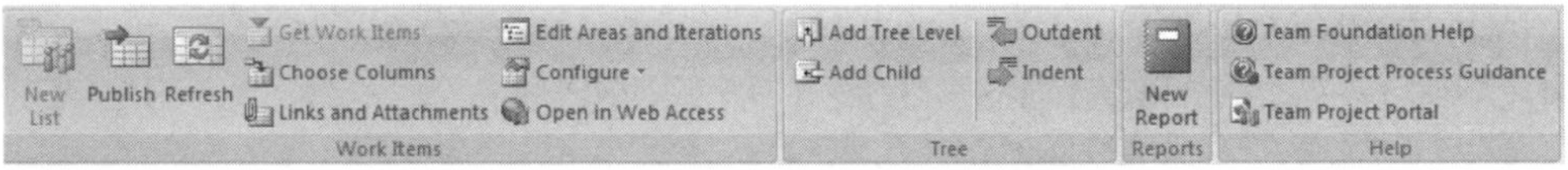

FIGURE 25-13

The Outdent and Indent menu options are self-explanatory, and, as the names suggest, will move up or down the levels of a work item. Note that the links of work items will change based on the level at which the work item ends up after either an Outdent or Indent action.

Similarly, as the name suggests, the Add Child menu option adds a linked child work item to the work item that you have selected. Note that the child work item gets added to the row that is currently selected when clicking the Add Child option. In Figure 25-14, you can see that seven child work items have been added to the user story work item titled "As a user I want to login to the Website so I can order things."

Work Item Type	Title 1	Title 2	Title 3	State
User Story		As a user I want to login to the website so I can order thing:		Active
Task		Task 6		Active
Task		Task 7		Active
Task		Task 5		Active
Task		Task 4		Active
Task		Task 3		Active
Task		Task 2		Active
Task		Task 1		Active

FIGURE 25-14

> *When you add child items in Excel as shown in Figure 25-14, the child work items are not automatically assigned to the same iteration the parent work item is in. You must manually choose the iteration in the Iteration Path column. It is a little annoying, but the Excel bulk edit sure helps. Note that if you add child work items in Team Explorer, the iteration path is automatically set to the iteration of the parent work item. So, this is only an issue in Excel workbooks.*

Iteration worksheets also have several validations built in. When you add child work items and publish the changes to Team Foundation Server, the validation logic runs and looks for any errors. For example, if you did not specify the type of work items for the child work items created, you will see an error and be prompted for those to be fixed before the changes are published to Team Foundation Server.

So, once you have created sub-user stories and tasks, you can do the estimation during the iteration planning meeting.

When it comes to work assignments, you basically have two choices:

➤ Some teams assign the chosen tasks (and bugs) to the individual team members for the iteration.

➤ Other teams identify the work that the team commits to and allow the team members to pick the work during the iteration.

It is common practice not to assign tasks for the entire iteration, but rather identify certain areas where a particular team member has expertise, or has worked on something relatively similar, so you can factor that in to the planning process. However, if you do assign tasks to an individual team member, be aware that these assignments are subject to change during the course of the iteration.

One of the key activities during the iteration planning is the estimation of tasks. The user stories assigned to the iteration from the product backlog have story points. As you learned earlier in this chapter, story points are not a measure of time or actual effort. So, the team spends time estimating the tasks during the iteration planning meeting. You enter the estimations in the Remaining Work column of this worksheet. Once the team finishes the exercise, the backlog worksheet should look similar to Figure 25-15.

	Title 1	Title 2	Title 3	State	Assigned To	Remaining Work	Completed	Story Points	Stack Rank
3	As a user I want to try to login to the website so I can order			Active	John Doe			12	1
4		Task 6		Active	John Doe	8			
5		Task 7		Active	John Doe	8			
6		Task 5		Active	John Doe	8			
7		Task 4		Active	John Doe	4			
8		Task 3		Active	John Doe	4			
9		Task 2		Active	John Doe	8			
10		Task 1		Active	John Doe	4			
11	As a user I want to login as guest to the website so I can sho			Active	John Doe			11	2
12		User Story 2		Active	John Doe			5	
13			Task 2	Active	John Doe	8			
14			Task 1	Active	John Doe	8			
15			User story 2 implemention has a b	Active	John Doe				
16		User Story 1		Active	Sally Smith			4	
17			task 2	Active	Sally Smith	12			
18			task 1	Active	Sally Smith	8			
19		User Story 3		Active	Joe Smith			3	
20	As a user I want to logout of the site.			Active	John Doe			17	3
21		As a user I want to automatically log off after 1		Active	John Doe			1	9
22			task 2	Active	John Doe	4			
23			task 1	Active	John Doe	4			
24	As a user I want to review the products			Active	Joe Smith			5	4
25		task 1		Active	Joe Smith	8			
26		task 2		Active	Joe Smith	4			
27		task 4		Active	Joe Smith	8			
28		task 3		Active	Joe Smith	8			
29	As a user I want to read product review			Active	Joe Smith			4	5
30		task 1		Active	Joe Smith	4			
31		task 2		Active	Joe Smith	4			
32		task 3		Active	Joe Smith				
33	As an administrator I want be able to update product infor			Active	Joe Smith			8	6
34		task 1		Active	Joe Smith	8			
35		task 2		Active	Joe Smith	2			
36		task 3		Active	Joe Smith	8			
37		task 4		Active	Joe Smith	4			
38		task 5		Active	Joe Smith	8			
39		task 6		Active	Joe Smith	2			
40		task 7		Active	Joe Smith	2			
41	As a user I want to sign up for email newsletter			Active	Sally Smith			4	7
42		task 1		Active	Sally Smith	4			
43		task 2		Active	Sally Smith	8			

FIGURE 25-15

As the work gets completed during the iteration, the team members will update the Remaining Work and Completed Work entries for each of the tasks. These will be used in many reports, including a burn-down chart.

It is worth emphasizing that, after the team goes through estimating tasks and, hence, committing to work, it is likely that not all user stories originally assigned for this iteration will be included or committed to in that same iteration.

Once you make these changes (that is, sub-user stories, tasks, estimates, team assignments, if you choose to do so), you save the changes back to Team Foundation Server by using the Publish option in the Excel workbook. Once you publish this workbook, the planning is complete, and the team is set to begin the iteration.

Using the Capacity Planning Worksheet

In the *capacity planning* worksheet, you can specify the availability of team members during the iteration, as well as how many hours each day the team members are available to work on the iteration. This worksheet provides a visual representation of the team capacity as a whole, as well as the workload for the individual team members.

The two sections in this worksheet are for the team capacity and individual team member capacity. Let's look at each of these.

Team Capacity

This worksheet section provides a summary view of the remaining work, team capacity, hours utilized, and whether the remaining work is over or under the capacity.

As you can see in Figure 25-16, this data is also represented in a chart on the top right that provides a color-coded view of the team capacity and the status of allocation. In the example shown, the team's capacity is 162 hours, and the total remaining work for this iteration is 178 hours. That leaves the team with 16 more hours of work than capacity, which is indicated by a red bar at the end of the chart.

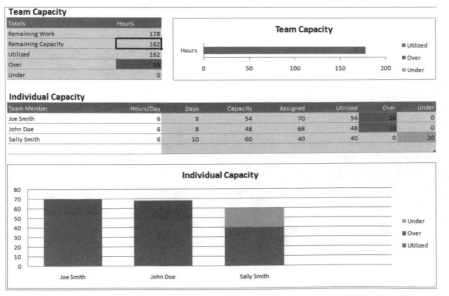

FIGURE 25-16

Team Member Capacity

In the Individual Capacity table in the middle of the Figure 25-16, you see a list of team members with their availability, hours per day, how much work they are assigned to, and what their load looks like.

There is also a chart that shows how the load is distributed among the team members. Anything appearing in red in this chart means a team member is over-allocated, which is never a good sign. In the example shown in Figure 25-16, two members are overloaded (Joe Smith and John Doe).

After looking at the example capacity planning worksheet, there are obviously two issues that must be resolved as a team:

- There is more work planned for than the capacity in this iteration.
- There are team members who are overloaded.

To solve the first issue, the team must get the lowest-priority user story out of this iteration so that the workload can be brought under the capacity. To solve the second issue, work must be reassigned among the team members to get the load balanced.

TRACKING THE ITERATION

During the iteration, it is important that the team watches the progress being made against the plan. It is not uncommon for tasks to take longer or shorter than the estimate derived during the iteration planning meeting. Watching the burn-down chart would give a good sense of the team's progress. It is critical that team members update the Remaining Work and Completed Work entries in the worksheet on a frequent basis. Team members can do this by using the work item form from within Visual Studio, by using a browser with the Web access or by using the Excel backlog.

Dashboards are very handy to get the information you need, regarding the status of the iteration. As you saw in Chapter 24, Team Foundation Server 2010 includes a Project Dashboard that includes the burn-down chart, burn rate of the team (both actual and required), and the backlog, all in one view.

Issues

Stand-up meetings are a great way to get a handle on roadblocks or issues that are being faced by the team that might be impeding the progress. These daily meetings are not the place to analyze and solve the issues, but rather just bring the issues to the surface.

Team Foundation Server 2010 includes an *issues* spreadsheet that can be used to capture and track the issues being identified in the stand-up meetings, or at any time during the project. It is easy to capture them in a spreadsheet and, given that this spreadsheet is wired to Team Foundation Server, issues that are identified can be published to Team Foundation Server and tracked on a regular basis.

Retrospectives

Agile teams run *retrospectives* at the end of every iteration to reflect on the iteration that they just completed. The key areas discussed during the retrospectives enable the team to understand the things that went well, the things that did not go well, and the things that the team can improve during subsequent iterations.

Under My Agile Project ⇨ Documents ⇨ Samples and Templates in Team Foundation Server 2010, you will find a document template titled Iteration Retrospective, as well as a sample document with the same name. In addition, there is also a Team Wiki setup that you can use to capture the findings from retrospectives if you have SharePoint integration enabled.

SUMMARY

In this chapter, you learned about the backlogs included in the MSF for Agile Software Development v5.0 template in Team Foundation Server 2010. You learned how the product backlog works, and how to use this backlog as part of the release planning process.

You also learned about iteration planning and how it is different from release planning. You learned how to use the iteration backlog workbook and how it can help an agile team manage iterations and track the project progress.

You learned how the load-balancing worksheet can be used to manage the workload of the team members, as well as to manage the work planned for iteration against the team capacity.

Lastly, you learned about how the issues worksheet can help in tracking issues identified during the project and during daily stand-up meetings. You also learned about the templates available for capturing information gleaned from retrospectives.

Chapter 26 covers the process customization and the tools available to customize process templates to meet the needs of a project team. Customization also takes place on an ongoing basis, based on learning during the execution of the project. Chapter 26 examines the process template editor and how you can use it to customize the process template of your choice.

26

Process Template Customizations

WHAT'S IN THIS CHAPTER?

➤ Learning about customizing process templates

➤ Understanding the tools available for customization

➤ Learning how to use Process Template Editor

➤ Understanding how to use Process Template Manager

In Chapter 23, you learned about the Microsoft Solutions Framework (MSF) for Agile Software Development process template and MSF for Capability Maturity Model Integration (CMMI) Process Improvement process template. These two templates are available out-of-the box, along with many third-party and community templates. The process template that you choose sets the basic rules of the game for your team project.

As discussed in Chapter 23, process templates (or components of them) show up in many forms throughout the team project, including the following:

➤ Work items (many different types) and work item tracking to define and track the work

➤ Definitions of areas and iterations

➤ Workflow with work item states

➤ Portal to gather information about the project

➤ Reports to drill down into process status

As you can see, templates are a key piece to your team project. So, it is critical that you choose the template and customize it to the state that fits your team environment. It is recommended that you use (and very likely that you will) an existing template as is or as a base for your process template.

This chapter examines the details of the process template components and the customization tools available to modify the template.

 To create and modify process templates, you must have an account within the Team Foundation Administrator group on Team Foundation Server.

CUSTOMIZING PROCESS TEMPLATES

To create a team project, you must first select a process template. Team Foundation Server 2010 ships two process templates (MSF for Agile Software Development and MSF for CMMI Process Improvement).

You can customize a process template on an existing team project, or update the template for all new team projects. Obviously, when you make a change to the template used on an existing team project, those changes don't apply to any new team projects being created. Note that here you are modifying an instance of the process template used to create a team project. Hence, the scope is local to the project to which you are making changes.

In this section, you'll get an end-to-end overview on how to export, design, and import your own process templates.

Process Template Manager is the tool you need to manage the process template. This tool can be used primarily to customize a process template, and you can also use it to create new team projects. To edit a process template on an existing project, you will use the process template editor tool, which will be examined later in this chapter.

To access the Process Template Manager, select Team ⇨ Team Project Collection Settings ⇨ Process Template Manager. You can also access the Process Template Manager by right-clicking your Team Foundation Server icon in the Team Explorer and selecting Team Project Collection Settings ⇨ Process Template Manager.

Downloading a Process Template to Your Desktop

To modify a process template, you must first download it from the Team Foundation Server to a local drive (your desktop, for example). The key tool for all upload/download operations is the Process Template Manager. The Process Template Manager is made available by installing the Team Explorer as a standalone tool or within Visual Studio. The Process Template Manager will download and get all the source files associated with the process template for editing.

Follow these steps to download a process template:

1. Select Team ⇨ Team Project Collection Settings ⇨ Process Template Manager. The Process Template Manager will open with the list of installed templates.

2. Select MSF for Agile Software Development – v5.0.

3. Click the Download button on the right.

4. Navigate to your desktop and click Save. Your process template will download to your desktop, and you will receive a message that says, "Process Template downloaded successfully."

What's in a Process Template?

Once your files have been downloaded, they will appear as shown in Figure 26-1. All these files are part of the Process Template Definition.

As shown in Figure 26-2, `ProcessTemplate.xml` contains four pieces of information about your process: the name, the description, the plug-ins required to create a project, and the XML file associated with each of the plug-ins. Plug-ins are

Build	11/25/2009 3:34...	File Folder
Classification	11/25/2009 3:34...	File Folder
Groups and Permissi...	11/25/2009 3:34...	File Folder
Lab	11/25/2009 3:34...	File Folder
Reports	11/25/2009 3:34...	File Folder
Test Management	11/25/2009 3:34...	File Folder
Version Control	11/25/2009 3:34...	File Folder
Windows SharePoint...	11/25/2009 3:34...	File Folder
WorkItem Tracking	11/25/2009 3:34...	File Folder
ProcessTemplate	10/6/2009 3:04 PM	XML Document	5 KB

FIGURE 26-1

used to extract Work Products (Word, Excel, Project, or Visual Studio documents), directories, and other important files from compressed process templates (stored as binary objects) on Team Foundation Server.

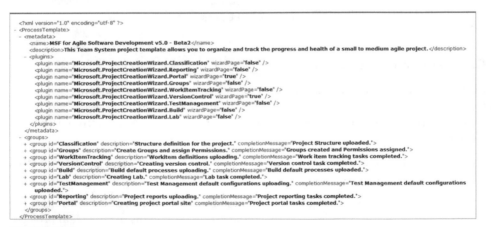

```xml
<?xml version="1.0" encoding="utf-8" ?>
<ProcessTemplate>
  <metadata>
    <name>MSF for Agile Software Development v5.0 - Beta2</name>
    <description>This Team System project template allows you to organize and track the progress and health of a small to medium agile project.</description>
    <plugins>
      <plugin name="Microsoft.ProjectCreationWizard.Classification" wizardPage="false" />
      <plugin name="Microsoft.ProjectCreationWizard.Reporting" wizardPage="false" />
      <plugin name="Microsoft.ProjectCreationWizard.Portal" wizardPage="true" />
      <plugin name="Microsoft.ProjectCreationWizard.Groups" wizardPage="false" />
      <plugin name="Microsoft.ProjectCreationWizard.WorkItemTracking" wizardPage="false" />
      <plugin name="Microsoft.ProjectCreationWizard.VersionControl" wizardPage="true" />
      <plugin name="Microsoft.ProjectCreationWizard.TestManagement" wizardPage="false" />
      <plugin name="Microsoft.ProjectCreationWizard.Build" wizardPage="false" />
      <plugin name="Microsoft.ProjectCreationWizard.Lab" wizardPage="false" />
    </plugins>
  </metadata>
  <groups>
    <group id="Classification" description="Structure definition for the project." completionMessage="Project Structure uploaded.">
    <group id="Groups" description="Create Groups and assign Permissions." completionMessage="Groups created and Permissions assigned.">
    <group id="WorkItemTracking" description="Workitem definitions uploading." completionMessage="Work item tracking tasks completed.">
    <group id="VersionControl" description="Creating version control." completionMessage="Version control task completed.">
    <group id="Build" description="Build default processes uploading." completionMessage="Build default processes uploaded.">
    <group id="Lab" description="Creating Lab." completionMessage="Lab task completed.">
    <group id="TestManagement" description="Test Management default configurations uploading." completionMessage="Test Management default configurations
      uploaded.">
    <group id="Reporting" description="Project reports uploading." completionMessage="Project reporting tasks completed.">
    <group id="Portal" description="Creating project portal site" completionMessage="Project portal tasks completed.">
  </groups>
</ProcessTemplate>
```

FIGURE 26-2

To add a unique name for your new process template, edit `ProcessTemplate.xml`. At the beginning of the file, you'll find two nodes:

➤ `name` — This is a required element.

➤ `description` — The description should explain the process template in a short paragraph and distinguish it from other processes.

Simply edit the nodes as follows:

```xml
<?xml version="1.0" encoding="utf-8" ?>
<ProcessTemplate>
<metadata>

<name>My Custom Template </name>
<description>This is a modified template to meet our team's process requirement
</description>
```

Once you upload this file to the Team Foundation Server, the `name` will appear on the process template list in the Create New Project Wizard. The `description` will appear right below. Figure 26-3 shows how the information appears in the New Project Creation Wizard.

The next part of the XML file contains a list of the required plug-ins in your process template. You can specify whether you want to create a step in the wizard for the plug-ins. If you set the parameter to `true`, then you will see a wizard step as part of the team project creation wizard.

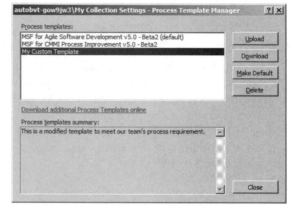

FIGURE 26-3

Process Template Plug-ins

When a new team project is created in Team Foundation Server, process template plug-ins come into play. There are several plug-ins provided within Team Foundation Server that are critical to the setup and configuration of team projects. The following are the plug-ins included in the Team Foundation Server:

➤ *Classification* — This specifies the initial set of areas and iteration setup as part of the team project creation process.

➤ *Work Item Tracking* — This configures the team project with the different work item types, states associated with this, queries, and the initial set of work items for the team project.

➤ *Portal* — This creates project portal and associated process guidance for the team project.

➤ *Version Control* — This sets up the version control access and policies for the team.

➤ *Security* — This configures the team project with the necessary security groups and associated permissions.

➤ *Build* — This sets up the build process templates.

➤ *Lab* — This runs the lab tasks.

➤ *Test Management* — This sets up the default configuration for test management.

➤ *Reports* — As the name suggests, this sets up the initial sets of reports associated with the process template for the team project.

For every process template in Team Foundation Server, the key file is `processtemplate.xml`. Figure 26-4 shows the view of this `.xml` file in Process Template Editor within Visual Studio. You will learn more about the Process Template Editor later in this chapter.

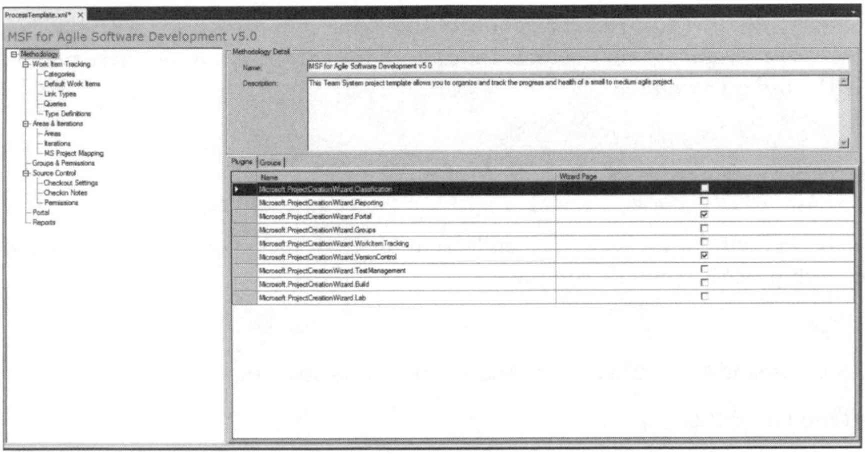

FIGURE 26-4

As you can see, `processtemplate.xml` triggers the various plug-ins associated with the template. The configuration also specifies the plug-ins that should have a page as part of the team project setup wizard. For example, in Figure 26-4, the Portal and Version Control plug-ins have a wizard page, and the rest of them don't.

Each of the plug-ins used by the process template has an XML file associated with it. These XML files specify the set of tasks that are executed as part of team project creation. Figure 26-5 shows the partial view of the `workitems.xml` file that is associated with the Work Item Tracking plug-in.

workitems.xml

```
<?xml version="1.0" encoding="utf-8" ?>
<tasks>
  <task
    id="LinkTypes"
    name="LinkType definitions"
    plugin="Microsoft.ProjectCreationWizard.WorkItemTracking"
    completionMessage="Work item link types created">
    <taskXml>
      <LINKTYPES>
        <LINKTYPE fileName="WorkItem Tracking\LinkTypes\SharedStep.xml"/>
        <LINKTYPE fileName="WorkItem Tracking\LinkTypes\TestedBy.xml"/>
      </LINKTYPES>
    </taskXml>
  </task>
  <task
    id="WITs"
    name="WorkItemType definitions"
    plugin="Microsoft.ProjectCreationWizard.WorkItemTracking"
    completionMessage="Work item types created">
    <dependencies>
      <dependency taskId="LinkTypes" />
    </dependencies>
    <taskXml>
      <WORKITEMTYPES>
        <WORKITEMTYPE fileName="WorkItem Tracking\TypeDefinitions\Bug.xml"/>
        <WORKITEMTYPE fileName="WorkItem Tracking\TypeDefinitions\SharedStep.xml"/>
        <WORKITEMTYPE fileName="WorkItem Tracking\TypeDefinitions\Task.xml" />
        <WORKITEMTYPE fileName="WorkItem Tracking\TypeDefinitions\TestCase.xml" />
        <WORKITEMTYPE fileName="WorkItem Tracking\TypeDefinitions\UserStory.xml" />
        <WORKITEMTYPE fileName="WorkItem Tracking\TypeDefinitions\Issue.xml" />
      </WORKITEMTYPES>
    </taskXml>
  </task>
```

FIGURE 26-5

As you see in Figure 26-5, one of the tasks for this plug-in is to set up the various types of work items associated with this process template — hence, the task named `"WorkItemType definitions"` specifying the XML files for the six different work item types to be created when this process template is used.

It is out of the scope for this chapter to cover the details of the XML files associated with the various plug-ins. Refer to the Visual Studio documentation for more information on these plug-ins and the associated XML configuration files.

TOOLS FOR CUSTOMIZATION

A process template in Team Foundation Server is a collection of XML files. Following are the tools available for working with process template components:

➤   Any XML editor

➤   The `witadmin` command-line utility (for working with work item types and definitions)

➤   The Process Template Editor

XML Editor

You can use your favorite XML editor as a tool whether it is Notepad or Visual Studio or something else. Editing the XML directly is not the ideal choice because it is error-prone, but nevertheless it is an option (and, in some instances, a convenient one) for working with the XML files in the process template.

Let's take a look at an example of how you can add a custom work item type to your process template.

Work item types are quite important because they enable you to define what a work item will contain, as well as the workflow associated with it. For example, you can set fields, transitions, and rules to fit a new bug type or requirement. You can find all of the work item type information in the `TypeDefinitions` folder within the `WorkItem Tracking` directory. The naming conventions are quite simple. For example, a bug schema is located in a file called `Bug.xml`, a task schema is located in a file called `Task.xml`, and so forth.

To create a new work item type, you must first define it within the `workitems.xml` file using your XML editing tool of choice. This file contains the following parts:

➤   Work item type definitions

➤   Link type definitions

➤   Categories

➤   Queries

The work item type portion of the file looks like the following for the MSF for Agile Software Development v5.0 template:

```xml
<task
        id="WITs"
        name="WorkItemType definitions"
        plugin="Microsoft.ProjectCreationWizard.WorkItemTracking"
        completionMessage="Work item types created">
        <dependencies>
            <dependency taskId="LinkTypes" />
        </dependencies>
        <taskXml>
            <WORKITEMTYPES>
                <WORKITEMTYPE fileName="WorkItem
                    Tracking\TypeDefinitions\Bug.xml"/>
                <WORKITEMTYPE fileName="WorkItem
                    Tracking\TypeDefinitions\SharedStep.xml"/>
                <WORKITEMTYPE fileName="WorkItem
                    Tracking\TypeDefinitions\Task.xml" />
                <WORKITEMTYPE fileName="WorkItem
                    Tracking\TypeDefinitions\TestCase.xml" />
                <WORKITEMTYPE fileName="WorkItem
                    Tracking\TypeDefinitions\UserStory.xml" />
                <WORKITEMTYPE fileName="WorkItem
                    Tracking\TypeDefinitions\Issue.xml" />
            </WORKITEMTYPES>
        </taskXml>
    </task>
```

Simply add a new work item type using the WORKITEMTYPE element to point to the specific type definition for your custom type. For example, if you were building a Time Tracking type, then you would insert the following within the WORKITEMTYPES node:

```xml
<WORKITEMTYPE fileName="WorkItem Tracking\TypeDefinitions\TimeTracking.xml"/>
```

You must then create a file called TimeTracking.xml within your TypeDefinitions folder. You have the choice of copying the fields and layout of an existing work item and customizing it to your needs, or, if you are adventurous (not recommended), you can create a work item from scratch.

witadmin Command-Line Utility

In Team Foundation Server 2005 and 2008, there were utilities named witimport, witexport, and witfields to manage work item definitions. In Team Foundation Server 2010, the team has consolidated these into one command-line utility called witadmin that can be used create, delete, import, and export types of work items, work item fields, link types, and categories.

Refer to the MSDN product documentation at http://msdn.microsoft.com/en-us/library/dd236914(VS.100).aspx for more information on this utility, including available commands and parameters.

Process Template Editor

If you have done customization of process templates either in Team Foundation Server 2005 or 2008, you are probably familiar with the Process Template Editor tool. Microsoft provides this tool as part of the power tool offering.

> *Power tools are utilities released by the Visual Studio Team Foundation Server team outside of the product release cycle/timeframe. Check out this Web site for more information:* `http://msdn.microsoft.com/en-us/teamsystem/ bb980963.aspx`.

With Team Foundation Serve 2010, the team is updating the Process Template Editor and will be releasing this as a power tool similar to its prior release.

Installing Process Template Editor

You must download the Team Foundation Server 2010 Power Tool available at `http://msdn .microsoft.com/en-us/teamsystem/bb980963.aspx`. This power tool release includes the Process Template Editor tool.

Once you install the Process Template Editor, you will see a new menu item called Process Editor in the Tools menu, as shown in Figure 26-6.

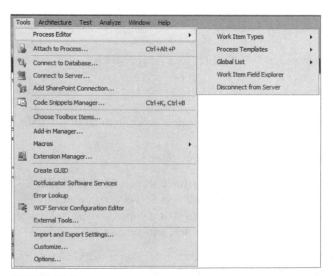

FIGURE 26-6

With the Process Template Editor, you can work both with the template instance on the server (you will do this to make changes to the template on an existing team project) or work with the template offline (you will do this either to verify a change or to make a change and have it available for future team projects use).

Working with a Process Template

To work with a process template, select the Process Templates ⇨ Open Process Template in the Process Editor menu. This will bring up a Windows File Explorer dialog to select the process template XML file. Navigate to the folder where you saved the process template. This is the location to which you downloaded the process template using the Process Template Manager.

When you open the processtemplate.xml file, it will bring up the Process Template Editor window, as shown in Figure 26-7. In this example, the "My Custom Template" process template has been selected for editing.

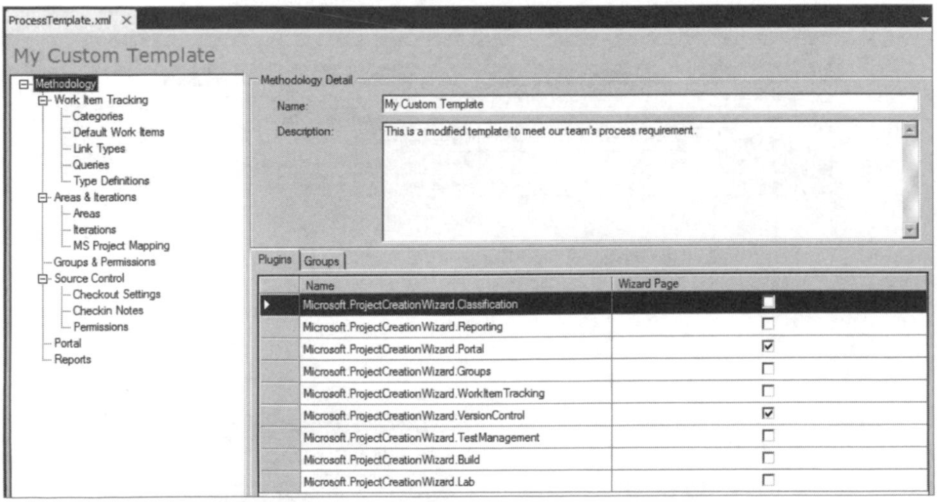

FIGURE 26-7

The editor on the left pane shows a tree control with the various process template components that can be configured using the editor. On the right pane, you see the details of the component chosen on the tree. By default, the right pane shows the name and description of the process template being edited, and the various plug-ins associated with this template.

Let's look at the customization options available for the various process template components from within this editor.

Work Item Tracking

In the Process Template Editor, you can manage the categories in which work items belong, default work items to be created when a team project is set up, link types available as part of this process template, queries, and, most importantly, work item type definitions. Most of the editing capabilities are self-explanatory. One of the common customizations performed by many teams is either updating a work item fields/states, or adding/removing work item types as needed. Let's take a closer look at the capabilities available in Process Template Editor to edit work items.

You start by selecting the Type Definitions node in the tree on the left pane. This brings up the different work item types available in this process template in the right pane, as shown in Figure 26-8.

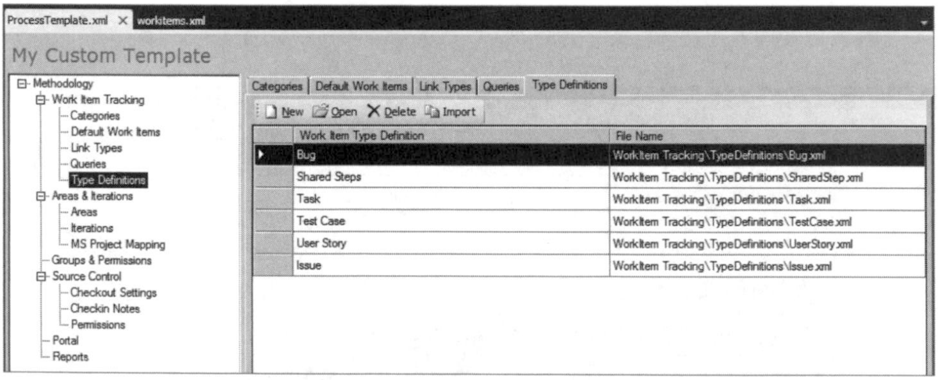

FIGURE 26-8

From this window, you can either create a new work item type, or edit an existing work item type. Clicking New in the menu brings up the dialog to get the process started. As shown in Figure 26-9, specify a name — in this case, "Risk" — and here you will use the Issue work item type as the base for this new work item type. It is easier to start with a copy of an existing work item than starting from scratch.

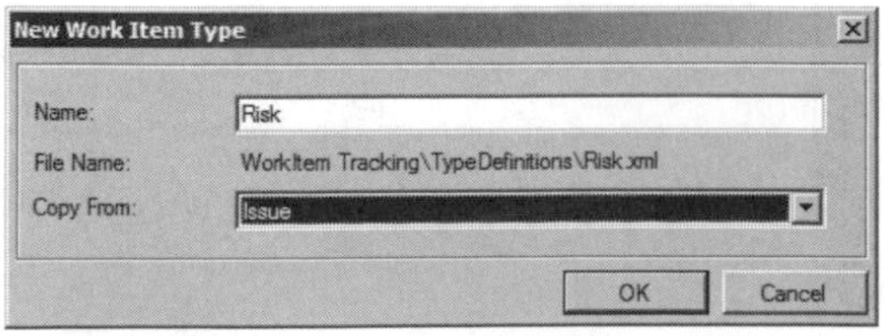

FIGURE 26-9

There you go. Just like that, you have created a new work item type. Now, let's open this work item type and edit the information captured by this work item type, as well as the state associated with this work item. You do that by double-clicking the work item type, which brings up the window shown in Figure 26-10.

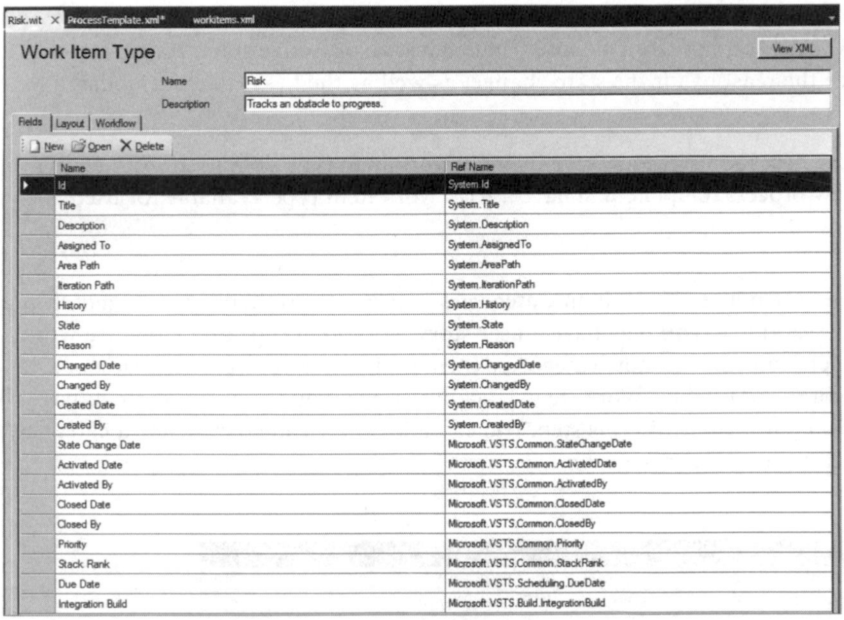

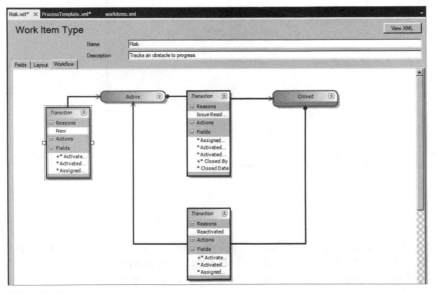

FIGURE 26-10

Here you can modify the fields that are part of the Risk work item, layout of these fields, and the workflow associated with this new work item type. You can add, modify, or remove fields from the work item, update the layout based on these changes, and preview the form before committing these changes.

The workflow for the work item is shown in a visual form in Figure 26-11.

FIGURE 26-11

In this case, the default state for the Risk work item is Active. The work item can transition from that Active state to a Closed state or from a Closed state back to an Active state. As part of the transitions, you can see the reasons for the state change, as well as the fields that are updated based on the state change.

Once you have made the necessary changes, save the new work item type definition. Any team project that is based on this new process template will have a Risk work item type available for use.

Categories

Team Foundation Server introduces Work Item Categories to group work item types together in a common category. For example, you may have a user story work item type and a feature work item type in your project, and you can now categorize them under a "Requirement" category. In the process template editor, under the "Work Item Tracking" node, you have a node to manage the categories. As shown in Figure 26-12, in this step, you can add a new category, delete a category, or add a work item type to a particular category.

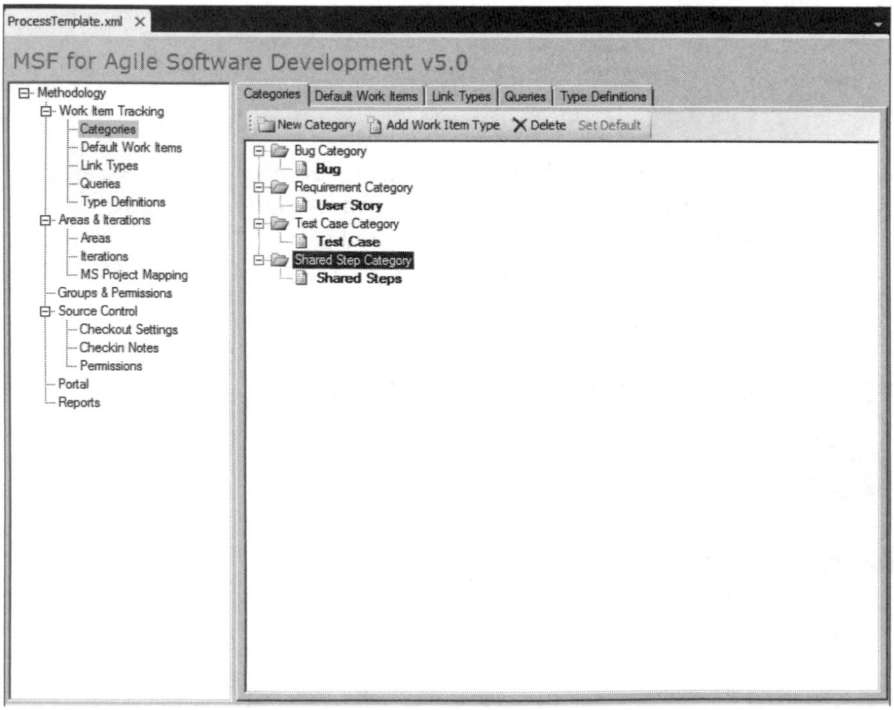

FIGURE 26-12

Link Types

Another new node you will see under work item tracking is the capability to work with link types. You can add, modify, or delete a link type. Figure 26-13 shows the list of link types included in the MSF for CMMI Process Improvement v5.0 template. The Link Type dialog in Figure 26-13 shows the properties you can manage for the link type.

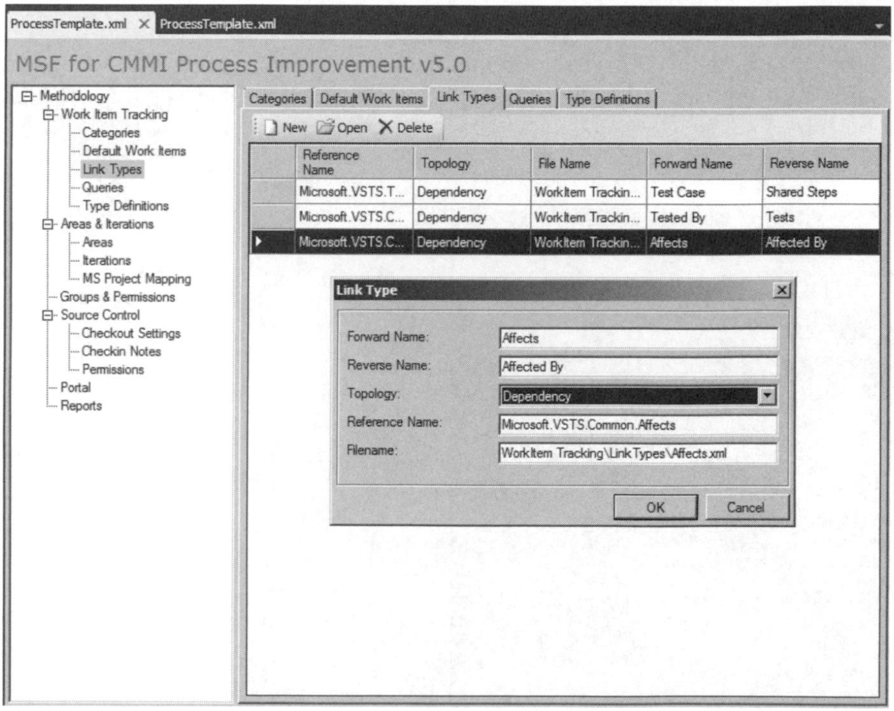

FIGURE 26-13

Areas and Iterations

Use the "Areas and Iterations" section to specify the default set of areas and iterations available to the team project. Team members can add new areas and iterations for their team project by updating the project settings.

You will use this to change the default settings to be used when setting up a new team project. In addition, you can also review and update (as needed) the mappings between the work item fields and Microsoft Office Project fields. Refer to the product documentation on MSDN for more information on the Project field mappings.

Groups and Permissions

As the name suggests, you use this section to work with groups and update the permissions associated with groups.

Source Control

The Process Template Editor enables you to edit the following source control settings:

➤ Enable or disable multiple check-outs

➤ Default check-in notes and the order

➤ Default security permissions

Portal

When a new team project is created, you have the option to get a portal (or a team site) set up for the team project. Figure 26-14 shows the configuration step to create a team site as part of the team project creation.

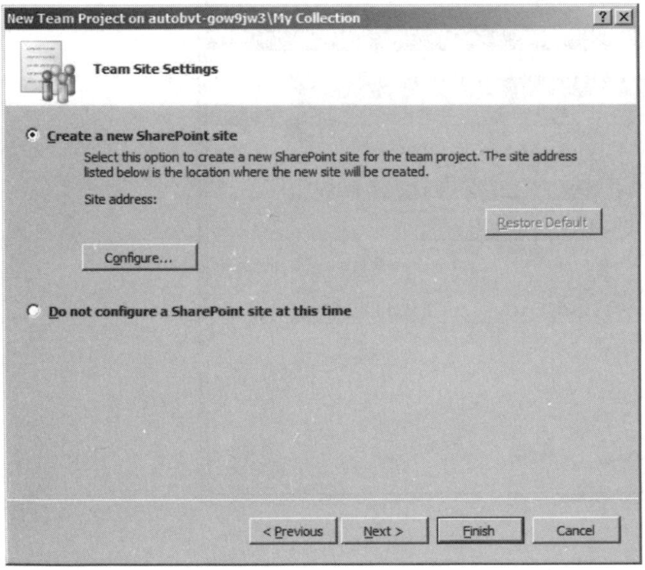

FIGURE 26-14

If you choose to create a team portal site, then Figure 26-15 shows the configuration information that is used to create the various document folders and associated documents.

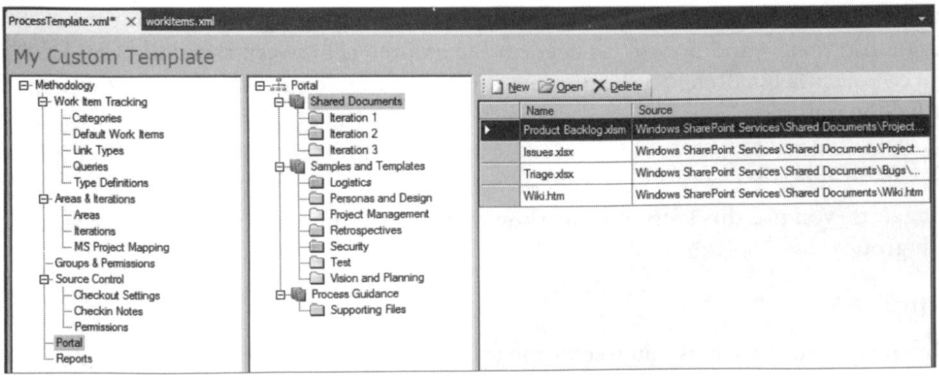

FIGURE 26-15

Figure 26-16 shows the outcome of the configuration as it appears in Team Explorer under the team project.

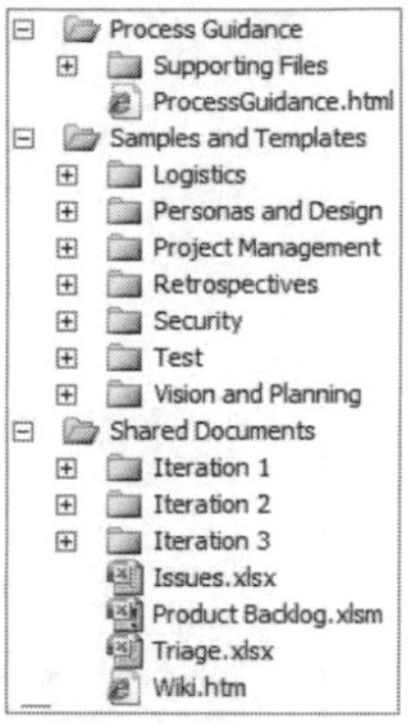

If you would like to add a template for a requirement or risk management document to the team project, then you can add that to the "Samples and Templates" section in the portal configuration. These templates will become available to the team members as part of the team project.

Reports

The last node on the Process Template Editor is the Reports node. Process Template Editor is not the tool to edit the reports themselves. You will do that by using Report Designer. But what you can edit here is the reports included as part of the process template. Figure 26-17 shows the list of reports that are available as part of the MSF for Agile Software Development v5.0 template.

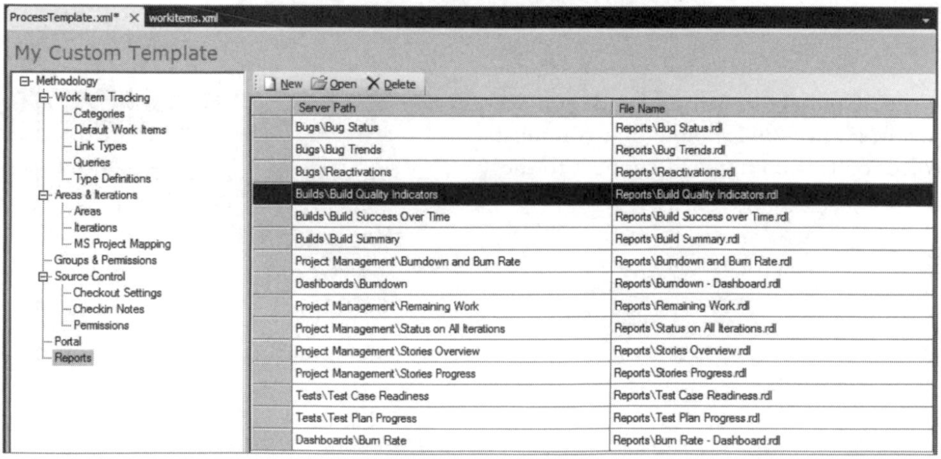

FIGURE 26-16

FIGURE 26-17

You can remove a report from this list for your custom template, or add a new one to the list, provided you have already created or have available to you the .rdl file for the report. Once you add a report to this list, that new report will become part of the default set of reports available with the custom process template.

Editing Work Items on an Existing Team Project

Earlier, you learned how you can use Process Template Editor to customize process templates for use in new team projects. You can also edit work items on an existing team project by connecting to the Team Foundation Server. You do this by selecting "Open WIT from Server," as shown in Figure 26-18.

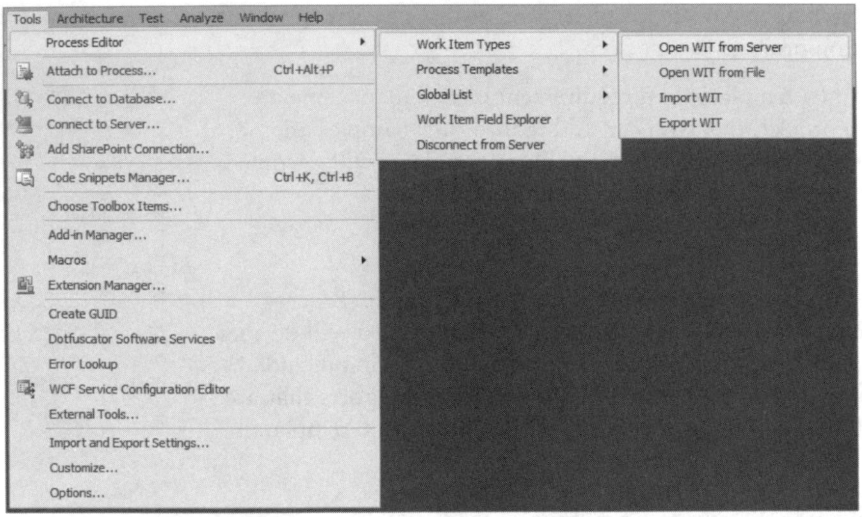

FIGURE 26-18

This brings up the "Connect to Team Foundation Server" dialog, as shown in Figure 26-19. Note that you must provide the project collection name to connect to the corresponding team project.

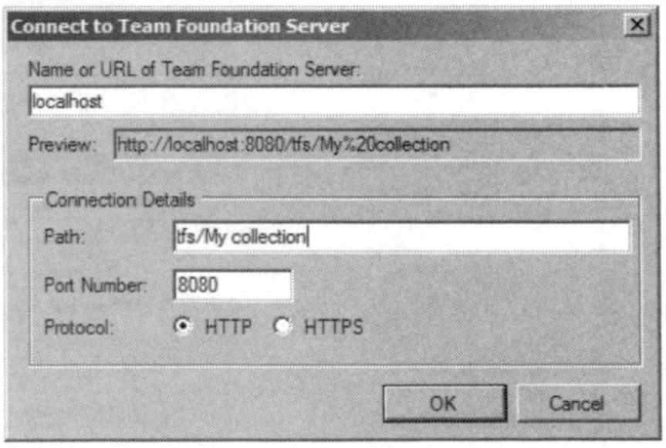

FIGURE 26-19

> If you just provide the Team Foundation Server name, port, and the path without the project collection name, the connection will fail.

Once you connect, you will be prompted to select the work item type that you want work with, as shown in Figure 26-20.

Expand the team project that you want to work with and the corresponding work item type that you want to edit. Once you click OK, the Process Template Editor appears with the work items fields, layout, and workflow information that you can edit.

You can also use Process Template Editor to export and import work item type definitions using the Import WIT and Export WIT options, as shown in Figure 26-18.

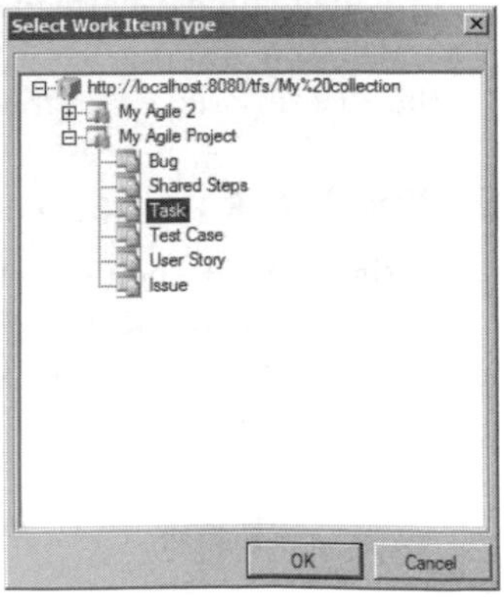

FIGURE 26-20

Note that the changes you make to an existing project takes effect immediately. Though fairly powerful, this type of live customization could also be error-prone. It is common practice for teams to create a separate team project where they try out the customizations before making the change on an existing team project.

Also, there is no support for version control in process templates today. There are obviously workarounds, and one of them is to save the process template files in source control, make the changes in a separate team project, and have the process template files under source control.

UPLOADING PROCESS TEMPLATES IN TEAM FOUNDATION SERVER

Once you have customized the process template to your liking, you must import it into Team Foundation Server to share it with the rest of the project team members. Follow these steps to import a custom process template into Team Foundation Server:

1. Select Process Template Manager by clicking Team Foundation Server Settings within the Team menu. The Process Template Manager will display all the available options.

2. Click the Upload button and select your process template description file (ProcessTemplate.xml) using the Upload Process Template dialog box.

3. As soon as you click the Open button, the process template will import into Team Foundation Server and will appear on the list of available processes. Figure 26-3 earlier in this chapter shows an uploaded process template named "My Custom Template."

4. Close the Process Template Manager.

DELETING PROCESS TEMPLATES

There will be times when process templates are no longer needed because they have been replaced by newer versions, or they have become obsolete.

 You should export a copy of the process template you want to delete as a backup before you take the steps to delete it.

To delete a process template, simply follow these steps:

1. Choose the Process Template Manager by selecting Team Foundation Server Settings from the Team menu. You will then see a list of all the available process templates.

2. Pick a process template to delete and click Delete.

Note that deleting a process template will not affect team projects that were created using the template. This is because a copy of all the artifacts from the process template (documents, source code repository, permissions) has been created on the server, and the project is no longer tied to the template file. Deleting only removes this process template from being available for new team projects.

CUSTOMIZING PROCESS GUIDANCE

In Team Foundation Server 2010, the process guidance is now entirely available online and integrated into MSDN. In the 2008 version, the process guidance files were part of the process template, and the product development team chose to integrate the guidance and make it available online on MSDN. The guidance is also available in an offline version in the form of a wiki library.

Teams should use the wiki library to customize the guidance as needed. You will make the changes to the location of the process guidance (that is, either the wiki library or the MSDN Web site) using the project portal settings.

SUMMARY

One of the key tenets of Team Foundation Server is the capability to adapt the process that works best for your team and use it as part of the team project workflow. Hence, the capability to customize a process template is key to incorporating changes and things that have been learned into the process template, either to an existing team project or to a process template that will serve as a base for new team projects. It is common for teams to update the work item types, fields that are captured in a particular work item, and states associated with work items.

In this chapter, you got an end-to-end look at the process template customization. You learned about the Process Template Manager, and how it can be used to download and upload process templates. You learned about the tools available to work with process templates.

It is not uncommon for teams to use XML editor to work with process template components. Even though it is not an ideal solution or tool, it is often convenient and efficient for making changes to process templates. You learned about the Process Template Editor that is available as a Team Foundation Server power tool. The Process Template Editor provides a visual tool that can be used to manipulate the underlying XML files associated with the various process template components (such as work item definitions, classifications, version control settings, and more).

Finally, you learned how Process Template Manager can be used to upload updated process templates, as well as deleting process templates. You also learned about the options available for customizing process guidance.

INDEX